Bird is the Word

Bird is the Word

An Historical Perspective
on the Names of North American Birds

by

Gary H. Meiter

The McDonald & Woodward Publishing Company
Newark, Ohio

The McDonald & Woodward Publishing Company
Newark, Ohio
www.mwpubco.com

Bird is the Word
An Historical Perspective on the Names of North American Birds

Text copyright © 2020 by Gary H. Meiter

All rights reserved; first printing March 2020

Printed in the United States of America by
Gasch Printing, Odenton, Maryland,
on paper that meets the minimum requirements of permanence
for printed library materials.

10 9 8 7 6 5 4 3 2 1
28 27 26 25 24 23 22 21 20

Library of Congress Cataloging-in-Publication Data

Names: Meiter, Gary H., 1948- author.
Title: Bird is the word : an historical perspective on the names of North American birds / by Gary H. Meiter.
Description: Newark, Ohio : The McDonald & Woodward Publishing Company, [2019] | Includes bibliographical references and index.
Identifiers: LCCN 2019000133 | ISBN 9781935778424 (paperback perfect : alk. paper)
Subjects: LCSH: Birds--North America--Identification.
Classification: LCC QL681 .M486 2019 | DDC 598.097--dc23 LC record available at https://lccn.loc.gov/2019000133

Reproduction or translation of any part of this work, except for short excerpts used in reviews, without the written permission of the copyright owner is unlawful. Requests for permission to reproduce parts of this work, or for additional information, should be addressed to the publisher.

Dedication

This book is dedicated to the memory of
Bill and Margaret Baker
and
Dr. G. William (Bill) Richter,
whose mentoring has greatly expanded and enriched
my birding experience.

Contents

Acknowledgements... ix

Part I
Scope, Structure, and Content

Introduction.. 3

Part II
A Checklist of North American Birds

Anseriformes Waterfowl 19

Galliformes Chicken-like Birds 49

Phoenicopteriformes Flamingos 61

Podicipediformes Grebes 63

Columbiformes Pigeons and Doves 67

Cuculiformes Cuckoos, Roadrunners, and Anis 73

Caprimulgiformes Goatsuckers 77

Apodiformes Swifts and Hummingbirds 83

Gruiformes Cranes, Rails, and Allies... 95

Charadriiformes Shorebirds, Gulls and Terns, and Auks............................... 101

Phaethontiformes Tropicbirds 151

Gaviiformes Loons 153

Procellariiformes Tubenoses.. 157

Ciconiiformes Storks 169

Suliformes Boobies, Gannets Cormorants, and Allies 171

Pelecaniformes Pelicans, Herons, and Allies 177

Cathartiformes New World Vultures 187

Accipitriformes Diurnal Raptors	189
Strigiformes Owls	201
Trogoniformes Trogons	209
Coraciiformes Kingfishers and Allies	211
Piciformes Woodpeckers and Allies	213
Falconiformes Falcons and Caracaras	225
Psittaciformes Parrots and Parakeets	229
Passeriformes Perching Birds	231
Extinct Species and Subspecies	369

Part III
Appendixes

Appendix I: Collective Nouns for Flocks of Birds	377
Appendix II: Glossary	379
Appendix III: An Introduction to the Naturalists Mentioned in the Book	383
Bibliography	419
Index I: Common Names	425
Index II: Scientific Names	431

Acknowledgements

Writing a book and getting it published can be daunting, but it helps immensely to have support of people who believe in your project. I want to recognize them here. First I would like to thank my good friend and birding companion Norma Holzbach, who gave me access to her extensive natural history library. I would also like to thank ornithologist Jim McCormac for his support and inspiration. I am also very grateful to the personnel of the Cleveland Museum of Natural History for their assistance and encouragement — Natural Areas Director Jim Bissell, Curator of Ornithology Andy Jones, Naturalists Larry Rosche and Judy Semroc, and Librarian and Archivist Wendy Wasman.

I particularly want to thank my publisher, Jerry McDonald, who has worked closely with me during the editing process and whose expertise I greatly value.

Finally, I wish to express my deep gratitude to the individuals who granted permission to quote from their publications. Many thanks to Faye Boer of Lone Pine Publishing, Clare Cox and Patricia Zline of Rowman & Littlefield, Thomas Dobrowolski of Trusted Media Brands, Ronald Hussey of Houghton Mifflin Harcourt, Hank Shaw of honest-food.net, William H. Thompson and Dawn Hewitt of *Bird Watcher's Digest*, Stephen Williams of Indiana University Press, the editors of *National Wildlife Magazine*, and to Wallpaper Safari for use of the sky image on the cover (wallpapersafari.com/w/sWpl9C).

Part I

Scope, Structure, and Content

Introduction

It is said the beginning of wisdom is to call things by their right names. With the advent of the modern field guide, outdoor enthusiasts have been doing just that. Growing up as I did on a farm in northeastern Ohio, I developed a great interest in the surrounding wildlife, including birds. I have long had an interest in the names of birds and, as well, in the history of how these species acquired their names — noting, after time, that they all usually had multiple names. My purpose with this book is to present a current, comprehensive compilation of the names of North American birds and perspectives on the history of these names — how, when, and by whom were they named, what were the bases of the names, and when were the species scientifically described.

When we consider the names of birds, or of any organisms for that matter, we might actually be talking about one, two, or three categories of names. First there are the standardized English common names we are all familiar with. Then there are the scientific or Latin names used by scientists around the world. These reflect the binomial system devised by Linnaeus and consist of two essential parts, the generic name and the specific epithet. Scientific names — Linnaean binomials — are universal, so a scientist working in any language or geographic region will know the exact species referred to by such names. The governing body for both the standard English common names and scientific names of North American birds is the American Ornithological Society (AOS), an organization founded in 1883 as the American Ornithologists' Union (AOU).

In the third category are nonstandard colloquial or folk names. These have sprung up — and still do — among groups of local people in different regions. They are usually descriptive or imitative of the sound a bird makes. Some are amusing; some are even profane. A few examples are Skunk-head Coot (Surf Scoter), Cotton-top (Scaled Quail), Call-up-a-storm (Common Loon), Timberdoodle (American Woodcock), Grecian Lady (Anhinga), Thunder Pumper (American Bittern), Rain Crow (Yellow-billed Cuckoo), High-hole (Northern Flicker), Bee Martin (Eastern Kingbird), Butcher Bird (Northern and Loggerhead Shrike), Whiskey Jack (Canada Jay), and Devil Downhead (White-breasted Nuthatch). Thousands of colloquial names have been compiled for inclusion in *Bird is the Word*, perhaps more than are found in any preceding work on the subject.

Early European visitors and settlers in the Americas gave names to many of the birds they encountered. Sometimes they chose names of unrelated Old World species (e.g., robin; redstart) they felt the American birds resembled. During the first half of the 18th Century, Mark Catesby, a naturalist from England, coined many of the common names of birds that we still use today, among them Canada Goose, Blue-winged Teal, Whooping Crane, Laughing Gull, Oystercatcher, Red-headed Woodpecker, Hairy Woodpecker, Blue Jay, Blue Grosbeak, and Purple Finch.

With the transformation of natural philosophy to science in North America in the late 18th and early 19th centuries, a new and sharpening commitment grew in finding and formally describing what to the interests of the time were "new" — or newly recognized — forms of bird life. Most North American birds were new to science, and they were being discovered and reported on by visiting naturalists and others living in the eastern part of the continent and the adjoining waters and islands, by members of various expeditions to the West including the famed Lewis and Clark

William Clark and **Meriwether Lewis**, leaders of the famed Lewis and Clark Expedition, 1804–1806.

John James Audubon, Artistic Father of American Ornithology.

Expedition, by Arctic explorers, and by voyagers to the Pacific, among others.

Late in the 18th and early in the 19th centuries, Alexander Wilson and John James Audubon, for example, described birds scientifically and gave them common names as well. Wilson tended to name birds for the region where he discovered them (e.g., Connecticut Warbler) while Audubon often named birds for friends, colleagues, or patrons of his expeditions (e.g., Baird's Sparrow). Charles Lucien Bonaparte, a French naturalist known as the Father of Systematic Ornithology, updated Wilson's *American Ornithology* while residing near Philadelphia from 1823 to 1826. Elsewhere in North America, from Canada to Central America and the outlying islands, naturalists, explorers, and artists alike were discovering and documenting the bird-life of the region. John Franklin, Johannes Gundlach, Adolphe Neboux, and James Clark Ross were among these important observers and contributors.

Spencer Fullerton Baird, second Secretary of the Smithsonian (1878–1887), brought American ornithology into the modern era. As one important step in this effort, Baird commissioned army surgeons and railroad surveyors stationed on the western frontier to collect specimens for the National Museum. Through Baird's efforts, our knowledge of North American avifauna expanded greatly and many more species were described that make up the continent's rich heritage of bird

Alexander Wilson, Father of American Ornithology.

Charles Lucien Bonaparte, nephew of Napoleon and Father of Systematic Ornithology.

Introduction

Spencer Fullerton Baird, second secretary of the Smithsonian Institution, brought American ornithology into the modern era.

Florence Merriam Bailey, the first female fellow of the American Ornithologists' Union.

life. Other prominent 19th century naturalists who worked with Baird include Elliott Coues and John Cassin, the first American ornithologist to become an authority on birds of the world.

During the 20th Century, Arthur Cleveland Bent contributed immensely to our knowledge of birds as he worked to finish the ambitious *Life Histories of North American Birds*, begun years earlier by Charles Bendire, and published in 26 volumes from 1919 to 1968. During this time work on the tropical southern edge of North America was benefiting from the efforts of regional naturalists such as Charles Barney Cory and James Bond.

Important female contributors to ornithology in the latter 19th and first half of the 20th centuries included Florence Merriam Bailey and Margaret Morse Nice. Mrs. Bailey wrote several books on birds, and along with her husband Vernon conducted field research in the American West. Margaret Morse Nice is considered one of the most important female American ornithologists. Among her work is an eight-year field study of the Song Sparrow which she published as *Studies in the Life History of the Song Sparrow* (1943, in two volumes). Both women were contributors to Bent's *Life Histories of North American Birds*.

Arthur Cleveland Bent consolidated centuries of North American avian natural history.

Margaret Morse Nice at work on Song Sparrows near Columbus, Ohio.

Bird is the Word is an effort to assemble in one volume a record of the rich nomenclature of bird names of the past 500 years, along with insights of the contributions that numerous naturalists have made to North American ornithology. Toward this end, I am providing a detailed introduction to the scientific names, standardized English common names, names used broadly throughout North America in languages other than English, and the many colloquial names of North American birds.

Quotations from notable naturalists that give their own unique perspectives on a bird's name introduce many of the entries. These, along with 42 sidebars of related information and representative pieces of contemporaneous art, afford *Bird is the Word* a rich historical context within which the names themselves are enhanced. Hopefully, readers will enjoyably explore these two sectors of North American avian science and history, and use this book as a frequently consulted companion to their field guides as well.

Bird is the Word is made up of five sections, all as described below.

• **An Introduction to Avian Taxonomy** describes the general taxonomy of bird species with a dual focus on (1) the structure of the general Linnaean taxonomic system and (2) the major subjective categories from which binomial words used in the Linnaean system have been drawn. This segment begins immediately following the current section and makes up the remainder of this introductory chapter, pages 7 to 15.

• **A Checklist of Common and Scientific Names** provides the basic factual details of the common, scientific, and other names for nearly 800 species of birds of North America, and for the nine species and subspecies of North American birds that have become extinct since colonial times. The Checklist is organized first by Order within which species are introduced in taxonomic order, beginning with their common name which is immediately followed by their Linnaean binomial and a guide to the pronunciation of that binomial. The common name is then explained followed by the etymologies of the genus and specific epithet. Next the French and Spanish names are listed, since these are major languages other than English historically spoken in North America. Some North American species are known by a different common name in Britain and where this is so, that name is listed too. Eskimo and Inuit names are listed for many northern species, some with English translations. Finally is a list of "Other Names," mostly colloquial or folk names from various regions of North America. Many of the entries are introduced by a quote from a notable naturalist to give his or her unique perspective on a bird's name, often from observations in the field. Full-color illustrations by eminent artists of the 19th and early 20th centuries — John James Audubon, Louis Agassiz Fuertes, Allan C. Brooks, and Robert Bruce Horsfall, among others — occur throughout this segment, as do brief sidebars that elaborate on the colloquial names, provide insight on name changes, or provide other facts related to the significance of a bird's name. This segment makes up more than 80% of the information in the book and occupies all of "Part II," pages 17 to 373.

• **A List of Collective Nouns for Different Species** provides a lengthy list of species of birds for which species-specific terms have been created that identify aggregations or collections of those birds. This segment is located in Appendix I, pages 377 to 378.

• **A Glossary of Technical Terms** lists and defines taxonomic and ornithological terms that are used throughout the book. This segment is located in Appendix II, pages 379 to 382.

Louis Agassiz Fuertes, a prominent wildlife artist of the late 19th and early 20th centuries.

Allan C. Brooks, a noted Canadian ornithologist and bird artist.

• **An Introduction to the Naturalists** provides short biographical sketches of the nearly 100 naturalists whose names appear throughout the book and who have contributed to the history of North American avian nomenclature and natural history. This segment is located in Appendix III, pages 383 to 417.

An Introduction to Avian Taxonomy

Taxonomy 101

Taxonomy, the process of classifying and naming biological organisms, is one product of the early years of science. When a new species is discovered, a scientist publishes a description and assigns a two-part scientific name now called the Linnaean binomial, made up of a genus and a specific epithet. Scientists base their description on a specimen that was actually collected and preserved. This is called the type specimen, and the place where it was collected is called the type locality.

Scientific names are an enigma to many birders. These names often contain many syllables and seem foreign. After all, they are written in Latin or Latinized Greek. As Shakespeare would have said, "It's all Greek to me." And how the heck do you pronounce them? For most birders, common names work just fine. But scientific names are very important to science and the scientists working in different languages around the world. Each scientific name is unique to a particular species, so there is no confusion as to the species being referenced with any given Linnaean binomial.

Common names are different than scientific names and they have their limitations. Not only do they occur in different languages, but even in the same language a bird may be known by several colloquial or regional names. The Ruddy Duck, for example, has more than 100 colloquial names, and the Northern Flicker more than 160! But scientists in all parts of the world know these species as *Oxyura jamaicensis* and *Colaptes auratus*, respectively. Also, the same common name can apply to more than one species. In America, the name Yellowhammer is a colloquial name for the Northern Flicker. In Europe, the Yellowhammer (*Emberiza citrinella*) is a bunting. Early settlers named many American birds after familiar birds back in the mother countries, which they felt were similar. So the flycatchers, robins, redstarts, warblers, blackbirds, orioles, and buntings in America are very different from those with the same names in Europe. Scientific names can also show relationships. The European Blackbird (*Turdus merula*) is not closely related to the American blackbirds in the family Icteridae. It is a thrush, and as you can see from its genus name is a close relative of the American Robin (*Turdus migratorius*). A male European Blackbird even looks and behaves much like an all-black American Robin.

Before the middle of the 18th Century different forms of naming organisms were created and accepted, but there was no consistency to the scientific names that emerged. A scientist could use any name he wanted for any organism. Latin was used, because that was the language of the learned. The names, while descriptive, were often unwieldy, consisting of many words, not just two or three as they are today. For example, pioneer naturalist Mark Catesby coined the name *Hirundo Marina Minor Capite Albo* (the little white-headed sea swallow) for the Brown Noddy (*Anous stolida*), the current scientific name of which means "the stupid, foolish one." So while it is an improvement in form, it is not so in meaning.

The system of naming living things that emerged during the middle part of the 18th Century and was devised by Swedish botanist

Carolus Linnaeus, Swedish botanist, was the Father of Modern Taxonomy and the binomial system of nomenclature.

Carl von Linné (1707–1778), better known by his Latinized name Carolus Linnaeus, emerged as the preferred version. In 1753, Linnaeus simplified the rules of nomenclature by introducing the binomial system of applying a two-part scientific name to each organism. All scientific botanical names begin with that date of 1753. Those botanical names in use before 1753 have been discarded. Zoological names began in 1758, when the 10th edition of Linnaeus' *Systema Naturae Regnum Animale* was published in Stockholm, Sweden. All zoological names in use before that date have been discarded. In 1844, the binomial system was expanded to a trinomial one that allowed application of a third name as a subspecific epithet, a word denoting a subspecies, also known as a race or variety. A scientific name is written in Latin or Latinized Greek and consists of two parts — a genus or generic name and a species name or specific epithet and both parts of the name are typically italicized. The genus is a noun and is always capitalized. The specific epithet is usually an adjective and is presented in lower case even if derived from a proper name.

You can compare a scientific name to your own, but in reverse. The genus corresponds to your surname and the species to your given name. So when Joe Shwishies fills out a form that asks for last name first, it appears as Shwishies (genus), Joe (species). When the full scientific name of a species is formally given, it is followed by the describer and the year of original publication — for example, "Heermann's Gull *Larus heermanni* Cassin 1852." If the species has been merged into a different genus from the one in which the original describer placed it or created for it, the author's name is enclosed in parenthesis as, for example, "Harris's Sparrow *Zonotrichia querula* (Nuttall) 1840."

Rules of Nomenclature

In order to ensure stability in the naming of organisms, several rules of nomenclature have been introduced. The oldest of these, the principle of priority, dates back to the Strickland Code which British zoologist Hugh E. Strickland presented to the British Association for the Advancement of Science in 1842. The principle of priority states that the earliest name properly published is the valid name. This is important because scientists, unbeknownst to one another, sometimes described the same species. For instance, on Audubon's Missouri River expedition, his friend Edward Harris collected an unusual, large sparrow with a black crown, face, and bib and a pink bill. Audubon described it in the octavo edition of his *Birds of America* (1843) giving it the name *Fringilla harrisii*. But the bird had already been described, not once but twice before — first in 1840 by Thomas Nuttall who named it *Fringilla querula*, then by Alexander Philipp Maximilian II, Prince of Wied-Neuwied, who named it *Fringilla comata* in 1841. Nuttall's description was the first to be published, so his specific epithet *querula* is the valid one. However, Edward Harris is still honored by the common name — Harris's Sparrow.

The principle of priority does not allow for corrections. Once a name is published that is it, even if it is misspelled or there are errors involved. The principle, for example, preserves the Chestnut-sided Warbler's misspelled specific epithet, *pensylvanica*. The erroneous specific epithet *asiatica* for the White-winged Dove is also retained. The White-winged Dove is native to the southwestern United States, Mexico, Central America, and the West Indies, not Asia. Linnaeus made the mistake, because the specimen that came to him was labeled "Indies," which he took to mean India. The specimen had actually been collected in Jamaica. But such errors don't really matter. What is important is that each name is unique to a particular species. See principle of homonymy below. Sometimes the principle of priority can make a situation more complicated than it should be. *Dendroica* (tree-dweller) was formerly the largest genus of American Wood Warblers encompassing more than 20 species. In 2011, it was merged into the monotypic genus *Setophaga* with the American Redstart. It would have been simpler and less confusing to merge the Redstart into the genus *Dendroica.* But since *Setophaga* is the older name, it takes precedence.

A second principle is homonymy. It states that a particular name can be used only once in zoological nomenclature. When William Gambel discovered the Mountain Chickadee in New Mexico in 1843, he gave it the name *Parus montanus*. But that name was already in use for the Willow Tit of Europe, so it couldn't be used for the Mountain Chickadee. Subsequently, Robert Ridgway renamed it *Parus gambeli* in 1886. However, the same specific epithet can be used over and over in different genera as in, for example, Long-tailed Duck (*Clangula hyemalis*), Winter Wren (*Troglodytes hiemalis*), and Dark-eyed Junco (*Junco hyemalis*).

The third principle is the preservation of well-established names. First proposed in 1953, this principle operates by protecting well-established names from being replaced by senior synonyms if one should surface in some long-forgotten publication. Also known as the 50-year rule, it goes by the principle that any scientific name that has been out of use for 50 years or more should not be allowed. This principle is not universally accepted by the scientific community possibly because it violates in part the principle of priority.

Lumping and Splitting

Although we have said the principle of priority preserves the earliest published scientific name, this actually applies only to the specific epithet. Genus names do change. New ones are erected or species are merged into existing ones. The governing body for these name changes in the Nomenclature Committee of the AOS. Through continuous research it is sometimes determined that organisms once considered to be separate species are actually the same species. These are then combined or lumped together as a single species. In 1983, the Myrtle Warbler (*Dendroica coronata*) and Audubon's Warbler (*D. auduboni*) were lumped as the Yellow-rumped Warbler, now scientifically known as *Setophaga coronata*. The Yellow-shafted Flicker (*Colaptes auratus*) and Red-shafted Flicker (*C. cafer*) were combined as the Northern Flicker (*C. auratus*) and the Ipswich Sparrow (*Passerculus princeps*) is now considered to be a subspecies of the Savannah Sparrow (*P. sandwichensis princeps*).

Conversely, a single species may be split into two or more species. In 1995, the AOU split the Scrub Jay (*Aphelocoma coerulescens*) into three species — Florida Scrub-Jay (*A. coerulescens*), Western Scrub-Jay (*A. californica*), and Island Scrub-Jay (*A. insularis*). In 2016, the Western Scrub-Jay was split further into the California Scrub-Jay (*A. californica*) and Woodhouse's Scrub-Jay (*A. woodhouseii*). Occasionally, species that were lumped together are split again. This happened with the Baltimore Oriole (*Icterus galbula*) and Bullock's Oriole (*I. bullockii*), lumped together as the Northern Oriole (*I. galbula*) in 1973. But newer research showed that these were indeed separate species, and so the Northern Oriole was split back to Baltimore Oriole and Bullock's Oriole in 1994.

Scientific names are not generally of much concern to most birders. You certainly wouldn't want to use them in the field. If you did, you might find your fellow birders distancing themselves from you. But discovering the meanings of scientific names can open up a whole new world for you. Some are even poetic when translated into English: *Aix sponsa* (waterfowl in bridal raiment), *Clangula hyemalis* (little babbler of winter), *Nyctanassa violacea* (violet-colored night queen), *Selasphorus calliope* (flame-bearer with a beautiful voice), *Toxostoma rufum* (the reddish brown one with a mouth that curves like an archer's bow), *Bombycilla cedrorum* (silky tail of the cedars), *Mniotilta varia* (variegated moss-plucker), and *Oporornis agilis* (nimble bird of autumn). It is my hope that the information in this book will enrich the totality of your birding experience.

The Basics of Scientific Names

Appearance — Nearly 45% of the genus names and more than 55% of the specific epithets used in Linnaean binomials describe appearance. Examples of descriptive genus names are *Recurvirostra* (bent backwards bill), *Pyrocephalus* (fire head), *Gymnorhinus* (naked nose), and *Dolichonyx* (long claw). Specific epithets frequently describe color, such as *rubra* (red), *caerulea* (sky blue,), or markings as in *macularia* (spotted) and *striatus* (striped). Examples of names that describe plumage include *auritus* (eared), *longicauda* (long tail), and *cristatella* (crested). Or they may describe various other physical characteristics as in *platyrhynchos* (broad or flat bill) and *pusilla* (very small). Many common names describe appearance as well, these including Eared Grebe, Scaled Quail, Ruffed Grouse, Spotted Sandpiper, Hook-billed Kite, Scissor-tailed Flycatcher, and Red-winged Blackbird.

Behavior — Some examples of specific epithets relating to behavior are *sociabilis* (sociable), *pugnax* (combative), *tyrannus* (tyrannical), and *motacilla* (wagtail). Common names describing

Pine Grosbeak, Purple Finch, and Evening Grosbeak, by Louis Agassiz Fuertes

behavior include Shearwater, Skimmer, Limpkin, Roadrunner, Woodpecker, and Wagtail.

Voice — Names related to vocalizations can be descriptive, or in the case of many common names onomatopoetic, names which imitate the sound a bird makes. Specific epithets referring to voice include *vociferous* (noisy), *melodia* (pleasant song), and *tristis* (sad). Common names describing a bird's voice are Mourning Dove, Screech-Owl, Saw-whet Owl, Nightjar, Warbling Vireo, and Song Sparrow. Examples of common names that are onomatopoetic include Chachalaca, Bobwhite, Killdeer, Cuckoo, Whippoorwill, Chickadee, Veery, Dickcissel, and Bobolink.

Food — Specific epithets relating to food include *valisineria* (wild celery), *formicivorus* (ant-eating), *cedrorum* (of the cedars), and *oryzivorus* (rice-eating). Genus names that pertain to food include *Myadestes* (fly eater), *Nucifraga* (nut cracker), *Vermivora* (worm-eating), and *Sporophila* (seed-loving). Food-based common names are more numerous, with examples being Oystercatcher, Herring Gull, Acorn Woodpecker, Sapsucker, Flycatcher, Nutcracker, Gnatcatcher, and Seedeater.

Band-tailed Pigeon, by John James Audubon

Habitat — Examples of specific epithets that allude to habitat are *palustris* (marsh), *montana* (of the mountains), *maritima* (of the sea), and *arvensis* (field). Habitat is less common in genus names, but examples include *Thalasseus* (belonging to the sea), *Limicola* (mud-dweller), and *Riparia* (river bank). Common names frequently refer to habitat, examples of which include Surf Scoter, Mountain Quail, Canyon Wren, Pine Warbler, Swamp Sparrow, and Orchard Oriole.

Toponyms — A toponym is a name derived from a geographical region. It is more commonly used as a specific epithet than a genus name. A toponym often tells where the type specimen was collected and may only represent a portion of the species' range. For example, the Great Horned Owl (*Bubo virginianus*) is named for the Virginia colonies where English settlers first encountered it. But its extensive range covers most of North and South America from Canada and Alaska to Tierra del Fuego and from the Atlantic coast to the Pacific. The specific epithet *ludoviciana* (of Louisiana) can mean the territory rather than the state as with the Western Tanager (*Piranga ludoviciana*) that was collected in present-day Idaho. Other examples of toponyms are *canadensis* (of Canada), *mexicanus* (of Mexico), *hudsonicus* (of Hudson Bay), *lapponica* (of Lapland), *islandica* (of Iceland), and *jamaicensis* (of Jamaica). Places show up in common names, too. Sometimes they refer to where the bird is native, as in Florida Scrub Jay and Gunnison Sage-Grouse. But like the specific epithet, it can also be the place where a species was first collected. Alexander Wilson tended to name birds for where he found them, even if they were only transients in migration. As a result several warblers, Nashville, Cape May, Tennessee, and Connecticut, are stuck with inappropriate place names.

Eponyms — An eponym is a scientific name derived from the name of a person. Authors frequently named birds for the collector, the person who brought a new species to scientific attention. They also named birds for friends, spouses, prominent ornithologists, and wealthy patrons. The specific epithet is placed in the genitive or possessive case, (*-i* or *-ii*) if masculine and (*-ae*) if feminine. These suffixes correspond to the possessive ('s) in English. Examples are Swainson's Hawk (*Buteo swainsoni*), Cassin's Finch (*Haemorhous cassinii*), and Lucy's Warbler (*Leiothlypis luciae*). Note that the eponym often translates into the common name, but not always. There is also a plural form, (*-orum*) masculine and (*-arum*) feminine, as in the specific epithet for Scott's Oriole (*Icterus parisorum*), named for the Paris brothers. Curiously, four birds that commemorate males, Montezuma Quail (*Cyrtonyx montezumae*), Costa's Hummingbird (*Calypte costae*), Fea's Petrel (*Pterodroma feae*), and La Sagra's Flycatcher (*Myiarchus sagrae*), have specific epithets that end in the feminine genitive suffix. The explanation for this is that in Latin, nouns ending in "-*a*" are considered feminine. Genus names can be eponyms, too. The Upland Sandpiper (*Bartramia* longicauda) is named for William Bartram and the former warbler genus *Wilsonia* for Alexander Wilson. A few eponyms are derived from mythology; for example, *Pandion* for a mythical king of Athens, *Athene* for the Greek goddess of wisdom, *Phaëthon* for an ill-fated charioteer, and *Calliope* for the muse of epic poetry. Many believe scientists name new species for themselves, but that is considered a serious breach of etiquette in scientific circles.

Indigo Bunting, Varied Bunting, Lazuli Bunting, and Black-headed Grosbeak, by Allan C. Brooks

Table 1. Sixteen species of North American birds possessing names that are tautonyms.

Harlequin Duck — *Histrionicus histrionicus*
Willow Ptarmigan — *Lagopus lagopus*
Purple Swamphen — *Porphyrio porphyrio*
Northern Lapwing — *Vanellus vanellus*
Black-tailed Godwit — *Limosa limosa*
Dovekie — *Alle alle*
Manx Shearwater — *Puffinus puffinus*
Red-footed Booby — *Sula sula*
Anhinga — *Anhinga anhinga*
Black-crowned Night-Heron — *Nycticorax nycticorax*
Eastern Kingbird — *Tyrannus tyrannus*
Bank Swallow — *Riparia riparia*
Siberian Rubythroat — *Calliope calliope*
Northern Wheatear — *Oenanthe oenanthe*
Yellow-headed Blackbird — *Xanthocephalus xanthocephalus*
Northern Cardinal — *Cardinalis cardinalis*

SeeSidebar 6, Gamble's Faux Pas, page 51, for an elaboration of this point.

Native Names — Although most scientific names come from Latin and classical Greek, some are derived from native names for birds in various languages. *Alle* is the Swedish name for Dovekie and *Alca*, the Swedish name for auk. The Tupi Indians of Brazil have given us *Anhinga, Jacana, ani,* and the tanager genus *Piranga*. *Colibri* is from the Carib Indian word for hummingbird. The specific epithet *sasin* for Allen's Hummingbird is from the language of the Nootka Indians of Canada. *Colinus*, the genus name of the Northern Bobwhite, comes from *zolin*, the Aztec word for "quail," and *pipixcan*, the specific epithet of Franklin's Gull, is also from the Aztec. Anhinga, Jacana, and Ani also serve as the common names for these birds.

Classical Names — Some genus names are derived from the Latin word for a particular kind of bird. Some examples are *Cygnus* (swan), *Anas* (duck), *Grus* (crane), *Aquila* (eagle), *Columba* (dove), *Hirundo* (swallow), *Corvus* (raven), *Turdus* (thrush), and *Passer* (sparrow).

Classification — There are names that show a relationship to another species. The specific epithet of the Lesser Scaup (*Aythya affinis*) means "related to" referring to the similar Greater Scaup (*A. marila*). The Greek suffix (*–oides*) means "resembling" as in the specific epithet of the Mountain Bluebird (*Sialia currucoides*) which implies a similarity to the Lesser Whitethroat (*Sylvia curruca*), an Old World warbler. The genus name of Harris's Hawk, *Parabuteo*, from the Greek *para* (beside or near) and the Latin *buteo* (a buzzard hawk) shows a close relationship between this species and the hawks in the genus *Buteo*.

Tautonyms — A tautonym is a scientific name whose genus is repeated as the specific epithet, e.g., the Northern Cardinal (*Cardinalis cardinalis*). The word derives from the Greek *tauton* (the same) and *onoma* (a name). A tautonym has no particular significance. It does not, as some believe, signify the most typical or common species of its genus. No species is initially given a tautonomous name, and you won't find any among the names of plants, because the use of tautonyms is forbidden for botanical names. Zoologists also debated the merits of tautonyms, and the tautonym faction won out. A tautonym comes about when a species is reclassified and merged into a different genus. Table 1 identifies North American birds that have Linnaean names that are tautonyms.

Colloquial Names

"North American wood warblers comprise an important and conspicuous element in the avifauna of the islands, but only the Black-and-white Warbler and the American Redstart have specific local

names. The *Seiuri* (Ovenbird and waterthrushes) are known by such names as 'Betsey-kick-up,' 'Mary-shake-well,' 'Walk-and-shake,' 'Senorita,' 'Pizpita.' The remainder are called 'Northern Birds,' 'Cold Birds,' 'Christmas Birds,' 'Chip-chips,' 'Bijiritas,' 'Siguitas,' 'Petits Chittes.'"
— James Bond, *Birds of the West Indies* (1937)

The above quote introduces us to some of the colloquial names used for warblers wintering in the West Indies. Colloquial names, also called folk names or nicknames, are nonstandard names, mostly regional, and so are known or used by relatively few people. Importantly though, colloquial names are not a part of formal avian taxonomy, but they are included here because they are widely used for all formally named avian species. Some more examples of names that do not appear in field guides are Cow-frog (Northern Shoveler), Bumblebee Coot (Ruddy Duck), Stake-driver (American Bittern), Timberdoodle (Woodcock), Angel Hawk (White-tailed Kite), Chip-fell-out-of-a-oak (Chuck-wills-widow), Jelly Coat (Red-headed Woodpecker), Whiskey Jack (Canada Jay), and Tarweed Canary (Lesser Goldfinch).

Like the standard common names and scientific names, colloquial names can be placed into categories. Some describe appearance or voice. Some are onomatopoetic or describe a species' preferred food or its habitat. Many are amusing, some are even profane. The following categories provide some examples of colloquial bird names so categorized.

Appearance — Flinthead (Wood Stork); Grecian Lady (Anhinga); Marlinspike (White-tailed Tropicbird); Golden Slippers (Snowy Egret); Calico Jacket (Ruddy Turnstone); Monkey-faced Owl (Barn Owl); Torch Bird (Blacburnian Warbler); Skunk Bird (Bobolink)

Voice — Bogbull and Thunderpumper (American Bittern); Crying Bird (Limpkin); Silver Tongue (Song Sparrow)

Onomatopoeia — Caloo and Kakawi (Long-tailed Duck); Chebec (Least Flycatcher); Harry-wicket (Northern Flicker); Chewink (Eastern Towhee); Old Sam Peabody (White-throated Sparrow)

Nonvocal Sounds — Whistle-wing (American Goldeneye); Drumming Pheasant (Ruffed Grouse)

Food — Mussel Duck (Greater Scaup); Crab-catcher (Yellow-crowned Night-Heron); Orange Borer (Red-bellied Woodpecker); Gut-eater (Canada Jay)

Habitat — Beachbird (Sanderling); Pasture Plover (Upland Sandpiper); Meadow-wink (Bobolink)

Behavior — Poacher (American Wigeon); Hell-diver (Pied-billed Grebe); Lily-trotter (Northern Jacana); Labrador Twister (American Woodcock); Lady Dishwasher (White Wagtail); Betsy Kick-up (Ovenbird); Mope (Pine Grosbeak)

Alleged Stupidity — Booby Coot (Ruddy Duck); Fool Hen (Spruce Grouse); Gooney Bird (Layson Albatross)

Weather Prophets — Rain Goose (Red-throated Loon); Call-up-a-storm (Common Loon); Rain Crow (Yellow-billed Cuckoo); Hurricane Bird (Magnificent Frigatebird)

Various — Shot-pouch (Ruddy Duck); Mother Carey's Chickens (Storm-Petrels); Old Joe (Great Blue Heron); Lady-of-the-waters (Tricolored Heron); Shad Spirit (Wilson's Snipe); Everybody's Darling (Song Sparrow)

American Avocet, by Robert B. Horsfall

Table 2. A primary taxonomic sequence for a North American bird, Harlan's Hawk (*Buteo jamaicensis harlani*).

Kingdom Animalia	All animals
Phylum Chordata	Animals with a notochord
Subphylum Vertebrata	Animals with a backbone[1]
Class Aves	All birds
Order Accipitriformes	Diurnal raptors
Family Accipitridae	Hawks, Eagles, and Kites
Genus *Buteo*	*Buteo* Buzzard Hawks
Specific Epithet	*jamaicensis* Red-tailed Hawk
Subspecific Epithet	*harlani* Harlan's Hawk or Harlan's Red-tailed Hawk

[1] Includes mammals, birds, reptiles, amphibians, bony fish, sharks and rays, and jawless fish.

Table 3. Avian taxonomic orders that are represented in North America.

Anseriformes	Waterfowl
Galliformes	Chicken-like Birds
Phoenicopteriformes	Flamingos
Podicipediformes	Grebes
Columbiformes	Pigeons and Doves
Cuculiforme	Cuckoos, Roadrunners, and Anis
Caprimulgiformes	Goatsuckers
Apodiformes	Swifts and Hummingbirds
Gruiformes	Cranes, Rails, and allies
Charadriiformes	Shorebirds, Gulls and Terns, and Auks
Phaethontiformes	Tropicbirds
Gaviiformes	Loons
Procellariiformes	Tubenoses
Ciconiiformes	Storks
Suliformes	Boobies, Gannets, Cormorants, and allies
Pelecaniformes	Pelicans, Herons, and allies
Cathartiformes	New World Vultures
Accipitriformes	Diurnal Raptors
Strigiformes	Owls
Trogoniformes	Trogons
Coraciiformes	Kingfishers and allies
Piciformes	Woodpeckers and allies
Falconiformes	Falcons and Caracaras
Psittaciformes	Parrots and Parakeets
Passeriformes	Perching Birds

The General Taxonomic Hierarchy

Taxonomists classify organisms in a hierarchy of levels, or groups, called taxa (the singular is taxon), ranging from the most general (kingdom) to the most specific (species). The major taxa are Kingdom, Phylum, Class, Order, Family, Genus, and Species. Sometimes one or more subspecies are recognized within a species. A subspecies is a race that shows some slight physical variations from one or more other groups within the typical species. The scientific name of a subspecies consists of three parts, as in Harlan's Hawk (*Buteo jamaicensis harlani*), a dark race of the Red-tailed Hawk that occurs in Alaska. Audubon described the hawk as a new species in 1830, naming it after his friend Dr. Richard Harlan, a young Quaker surgeon from Philadelphia. The AOU reclassified it as a subspecies in 1983. Table 2 illustrates the taxonomic classification of Harlan's Hawk, showing how that species is classified today through the hierarchy of taxa.

The Bird Orders of North America

An Order is the principal taxon immediately below Class and immediately above Family. Today 25 orders of birds are represented in the avifauna of North America. Some bird orders such as Podicipediformes (grebes) and Gaviiformes (loons) contain only a single family while most encompass several related families. The order Passeriformes (perching birds) is the largest with 138 families worldwide and 37 families in North America. The avian orders represented in North America are presented in Table 3.

This checklist of North American birds is arranged in taxonomic order, beginning with the waterfowl and ending with the perching birds. This sequence of families represents science's current best understanding of the evolutionary sequence and relationships among them. Families at the beginning of the list are believed to have split off earlier from a common ancestor while those toward the end are believed to have diverged more recently. Traditionally taxonomic sequence was based on when a species first appeared in the fossil record and on similarities or dissimilarities in its morphology (physical features) compared to other species. While these factors are still important, advances in DNA research have resulted in many revisions in both the classification of species and the sequential ordering of families. The sequence of families and their species in this book is based on the most recent revision by the AOS — that of 2019 — and therefore will differ in part from the sequences that are presented in earlier checklists.

Part II

A Checklist of North American Birds

Order Anseriformes

Family Anatidae
Waterfowl

Family Anatidae includes the ducks, geese, and swans. The word duck comes from the Anglo-Saxon word *duce* (a diver). Some ducks characteristically dive for food, and others are surface feeders, but most can dive to escape danger. Goose is from the Anglo-Saxon word *gos* (a goose). Swan or *swanne* is the Anglo-Saxon word for these birds.

Black-bellied Whistling-Duck
Dendrocygnus autumnalis
(den-droh-SIG-nus aw-tum-NAY-lis)

Whistling-Ducks are named for their shrill whistling calls given constantly in flight. They are placed in their own subfamily and are more closely allied to geese than to true ducks. Black-bellied refers to the black underparts of both sexes. Formerly known as Black-bellied Tree Duck.

Dendrocygnus — The genus name means "tree swan" from the Greek *dendron* (a tree) and the Latin *cygnus* (a swan). The long neck gives these ducks a swanlike appearance, and they frequently perch in trees and sometimes nest in tree cavities.

autumnalis — The specific epithet is Latin for "autumn" or "belonging to autumn." This may refer to the bird's coloration, warm brown plumage and red bill, the colors of autumn.

French Name: Dendrocygne Ventre Noir
Spanish Names: Pijiji de Ala Blanca; Pijiji Aliblanco; Pijiji Común
Other Names: Autumnal Tree Duck; Red-billed Tree Duck; Red-billed Whistling-Duck; Cornfield Duck; Long-legged Duck; Summer Duck; Chiriria Pinta; Pato Maizal

Fulvous Whistling-Duck
Dendrocygnus bicolor
(den-droh-SIG-nus BY-color)

Fulvous (yellowish-brown) describes the rich tawny color of the plumage. This species utters a high-pitched, shorebird-like double whistle in flight. Formerly known as Fulvous Tree Duck.

Dendrocygnus — This genus name means "tree swan" from the Greek d*endron* (tree) and the Latin *cygnus* (a swan). The long neck gives these ducks a swanlike appearance, but the Fulvous Whistling-Duck does not live up to the meaning of its genus name "tree swan," as it infrequently alights in trees and it doesn't nest in them either.

bicolor — The specific epithet is Latin for "two-colored" and refers to the dark back contrasting with the light underparts.

French Name: Dendrocygne Fauve
Spanish Name: Pijiji Canelo
Other Names: Bicolored Tree Duck; Mexican Duck; Wood Duck; Mexican Wood Duck; Cornfield Duck; Summer Duck; Long-legged Duck; Yankee Duck; Yellow-bellied Fiddler Duck; Redhead; Squealer; Mexican Squealer;

Black-bellied Whistling-Duck, by Louis Agassiz Fuertes

Whistling Teal; Large Whistling Teal; Pato Silvon; Chiriria Dominicana; Vaguasín; Vanguaza Dominicana; Amarillenta; Vingeon Rouge; Tee-kee

Emperor Goose
Anser canagica
(AN-ser can-ADJ-ih-kah)

Emperor pertains to this goose's attractive appearance, white head, black throat, and dark silver-gray plumage. Arthur Cleveland Bent called Emperors "the handsomest and least known American geese." Names of royalty generally either denote striking appearance or large size.

Anser — The genus name is the Latin word for "goose." Formerly *Chen canagica*.

canagica — The specific epithet refers to Kanaga, an island in the Aleutian chain, which includes part of this goose's wintering range.

French Name: Oie Empereur
Spanish Name: Ganso Emperador
Eskimo and Inuit Names: Natchaulik (having hood-like parka); Il-a-ghir-lich; Ka-ghu-mung; Qam-gan; Mik-i-loor-uk; Ness-o-lik
Other Names: White-breasted Goose; White-headed Goose; Beach Goose; Painted Goose

Snow Goose
Anser caerulescens
(AN-ser see-rue-LESS-enz)

This goose is named for the snow-white plumage of the light morph. But it also occurs in a dark morph. See specific epithet below.

Anser — The genus name is the Latin word for "goose." Formerly *Chen caerulescens*.

caerulescens — The specific epithet is Latin for "bluish" and refers to the blue-gray plumage of the dark morph of the Snow Goose. The two color morphs were formerly considered separate species, the white morph, the Snow Goose (*Chen hyperborea*) and the dark morph, the Blue Goose (*Chen caerulescens*). When the two were merged, *Chen* (*Anser*) *caerulescens* became the valid scientific name, because of the law of priority. The Blue Goose had been described and named first.

French Name: Oie des Neiges

Emperor Goose, by Allan C. Brooks

Spanish Name: Ganso Blanco
Eskimo and Inuit Name: Kanguk (white goose)
Other Names — white morph: Common Snow Goose; Greater Snow Goose; Lesser Snow Goose; White Goose; White Jangler; White Devil; Winter Goose; Arctic Goose; Mexican Goose; Wavy Goose; White Brant; Wavy; Common Wavy; White Wavy; Little Wavy; Lesser Wavy; Barking Wavy; White Way-way; Ribeye in the Sky; Flying Rat; Sky Carp; Galoot; Piron; Oie Blanche; Oie Sauvage
Other Names — dark morph: Alaska Goose; Blue Snow Goose; Blue-winged Goose; White-headed Goose; White-headed Wavy; Blue Wavy; Gray Wavy; Black Wavy; Skillet-head; Skillet-head Wavy; Brant; Blue Brant; Bald Brant; Bald-headed Brant; White-headed Brant; White-headed Bald Brant; Eagle-headed Brant; Gray Brant; Silver Brant; Ribeye in the Sky; Flying Rat; Sky Carp; Ganso Prieto; Oie Aigle; Oie Sauvage

Ross's Goose
Anser rossii
(AN-ser ROSS-ih-eye)

Ross's Goose is named for Bernard R. Ross. See specific epithet below.

Anser — The genus name is the Latin word for "goose." Formerly *Chen rossii*.

rossii — The specific epithet honors Bernard Rogan Ross (1817–1874), chief factor of the Hudson's Bay Company.

French Name: Oie de Ross
Spanish Name: Ganso de Ross
Other Names: Little Wavy; Horned Wavy; Wart-nosed Wavy; Scabby-nose; Scabby-

nosed Goose; Scabby-nosed Wavy; Galoot

Greater White-fronted Goose
Anser albifrons
(AN-ser AL-bih-frons)

White-fronted pertains to the white patch that encircles the base of the bill. Greater distinguishes this species from the smaller Lesser White-fronted Goose (*Anser erythropus*) of Eurasia.

Anser — The genus name is the Latin word for "goose."

albifrons — The specific epithet means "white forehead" from the Latin *albus* (white) and Latin *frons* (the forehead).

French Name: Oie Rieuse
Spanish Name: Ganso Careto Mayor
Eskimo and Inuit Names: Nuck-luck; Luk-luk; Nug-lug-rua; Ke-e-ook; Kog-a-la-gich; Niklivik
Other Names: Whitefront; American White-fronted Goose; Tule White-fronted Goose; Tule Goose; Yellow-legged Goose; Grey Goose; China Goose; Field Goose; Laughing Goose; Barred Goose; Mottled Goose; Spotted Goose; Speckle-breast Goose; California Goose; Texas Goose; Specklebreast; Checkerbreast; Checkerbelly; Yellow-legged Brant; Gray Brant; Harlequin Brant; Tiger Brant; Pied Brant; Prairie Brant; Speckled Brant; Speckle-belly Brant; Spotted Brant; Laugher; Laughing Jack; Laughing Wavey; Specklebelly; Speck; Marble-belly; Marbled-breast Mottled Brant; Gray Wavey; Yellowlegs; Ribeye of the Sky; Oie Caille; Oie Nonette

Greater White-fronted Goose, by W. H. Foster

Brant
Branta bernicla
(BRAN-tah BER-nih-clah)

The common name comes from the Anglo-Saxon *brennan* or *bernan* (to burn) and refers to the blackish plumage of this goose as though it were charred. The dark-bellied Pacific coast form was formerly considered a separate species, the Black Brant (*Branta nigricans*).

Branta — The genus name is the Latinized form of brant. See common name above.

bernicla — The specific epithet is the Latinized form of the Middle English *bernekka* (barnacle). It refers to a legend that these geese hatched from barnacles. See Barnacle Goose below.

French Name: Bernache Cravant
Spanish Names: Ganso de Collar; Branta
British Name: Brent Goose
Eskimo and Inuit Names: Nik-ling-a-gak (almost like a goose); Nug-lu-gnu; Nig-lik-nuk; Lik-lik; Luk-hlug-u-nuk
Other Names: Common Brant; American Brant; Eastern Brant; Sea Brant; Light-bellied Brant; White-bellied Brant; Pacific Brant; Brant Goose; Brent Goose; Burnt Goose; Black Goose; Brand Goose; Horrie Goose; Horra Goose; Husky Goose; White-breasted Goose; Little Goose; Chickeny Goose; China Goose; Eskimo Goose; Clatter Goose; Rott Goose; Rat Goose; Road Goose; Rood Goose; Quink; Quink Goose; Ware Goose; Black Wavy; Barnache; Brabt; Barnacle; Cravant; Crocker

Barnacle Goose
Branta leucopsis
(BRAN-tah lew-COP-sis)

The common name comes from medieval folklore, when people believed these geese developed inside the shells of goose barnacles (*Lepas anatifera*). With a little imagination, a goose barnacle's stalk and white, heart-shaped shell decorated with black lines vaguely resembles the head and neck of a Barnacle Goose. This folk tale allowed Roman Catholics to eat goose during Lent, because the Church considered these birds to be fish. Gerald de Barri (Gerald of Wales), a 12th century clergyman and historian, claimed to have witnessed barnacles in the process of turning into geese:

"They are produced from fir timber tossed along the sea and are at first like gum. Afterwards they hang down by their beaks as if they were seaweed attached to the timber, and are surrounded by shells in order to grow more freely. Having thus in process of time been clothed with a strong coat of feathers, they either fall into the water or fly freely away in the air."

Branta — The genus name is the Latinized form of Brant, derived from the Anglo-Saxon *brennan* or *bernan* (to burn) and refers to the blackish plumage of this goose as though it were charred.

leucopsis — The specific epithet means "white appearance" from the Greek *leukos* (white) and Greek *opsis* (appearance). It refers to this goose's white face that contrasts with the black head and neck.

French Name: Bernache Nonnette
Spanish Name: Ganso de Cara Blanca
Other Names: Bar Goose; Rood Goose; Tree Goose; White-faced Barnacle; Norway Barnacle; Routhecock; Clakis

Cackling Goose
Branta hutchinsii
(BRAN-tah HUTCH-in-si-eye)

Resembling a miniature (mallard-sized) Canada Goose, the Cackling Goose is named for the rapid cackle that follows its high pitched *yelk, yelk* or *lik, lik lik* call. Formerly considered a subspecies of the Canada Goose. The AOU made it a full species in 2004.

Branta — The genus name is the Latinized form of Brant, derived from the Anglo-Saxon *brennan* or *bernan* (to burn) and refers to the blackish plumage of this goose as though it were charred.

hutchinsii — In 1831, Sir John Richardson named the Cackling Goose for Dr. Thomas Hutchins, an English naturalist and surgeon of the Hudson's Bay Company.

French Name: Bernache de Hutchins
Spanish Name: Ganso Cascareador
Eskimo and Inuit Names: Tutangaiyak (having white on the cheeks); Luk-hluk-hla-ghuk; Ick-sha-oo-ti-lik; Lig-a-lik; Muh-lar-nuk; Too-tung-ai-uk-chakh
Other Names: Small Goose; Small Canada Goose; Lesser Canada Goose; Little Canada; Little Grey Goose; Little Squeaking Goose; Short-necked Goose; Cackling Canada Goose; Cackler; Hutchin's Goose; Richardson's Goose; Richardson's Canada Goose; Taverner's Canada Goose; Eskimo Goose; Little Honker; Little Wavy; Little Bustard

Canada Goose
Branta canadensis
(BRAN-tah can-ah-DEN-sis)

Once esteemed as "the noblest of our waterfowl," the Canada Goose bred primarily throughout the country of its namesake. It also nested in Alaska and the northern tier of states from Washington east to Michigan. Now the Canada Goose also nests throughout much of the United States, where it never did before. No, it didn't expand its range on its own; it had human help. Beginning in the 1950s, state wildlife agencies introduced Canada Geese to refuges throughout the country to ensure there would be plenty to hunt. These birds had their wings clipped to render them flightless, so they had no choice but to nest wherever they were released. Now there are non-migratory populations of suburban geese that have made themselves unwelcome with their messy habits. People have even coined disparaging nicknames for them like flying pigs, rats with wings, and sky carp:

"As a result of this intensive management, a semi-domesticated resident population has become permanently established. But successful management was achieved with a price.

Canada Goose, Brant, and Tundra Swan, by Louis Agassiz Fuertes

Unlike their warier brethren, our resident geese are accustomed to people and readily adapt to disturbed habitats. No longer restricted to isolated marshes and lakes, they appear anywhere water is available. As this resident population expanded, it developed a reputation as a nuisance, befouling beaches and lawns and damaging corn and winter wheat crops. While this species still looks the same, its behavior is entirely different, and the noble character formerly associated with a skein of migrant geese passing overhead has been tarnished." — Bruce G. Peterjohn (1989)

Branta — The genus name is the Latinized form of Brant, derived from the Anglo-Saxon *brennan* or *bernan* (to burn) and refers to the blackish plumage of this goose as though it were charred.

canadensis — The specific epithet is Modern Latin for "of Canada."

French Name: Bernache du Canada
Spanish Name: Ganso Canadiense
Eskimo and Inuit Names: Longilukfak (same as Cackling Goose, but bigger); Eksrahgotivik (light-colored cheek); Ik-sa-otil-ik
Other Names: Common Canada Goose; Aleutian Canada Goose; Atlantic Canada Goose; Western Canada Goose; Giant Canada Goose; Dusky Canada Goose; Canadian Goose; Big Canada; Big Goose; Labrador Goose; Northern Goose; Southern Goose; West Coast Goose; Gray Goose; Big Gray Goose; Grey; Mud Goose; Grey Mud Goose; Grey-bellied Goose; Winter Goose; Big Mexican Goose; California Goose; China Goose; French Goose; Great Basin Goose; Labrador Goose; Mershon Goose; Chornie Goose; Wild Goose; Common Wild Goose; Black-headed Goose; Black Head; Black-necked Goose; White-cheeked Goose; White-cheek; White-chin; Blackleg; Blackie; Nigger Goose; Ring-neck Goose; Honker Goose; Crow Goose; Husky Goose; Long-necked Goose; Prairie Goose; Reef Goose; Fall Goose; Flight Goose; Cravat Goose; Bay Goose; Calling Goose; Brant; Eastern Brandt; Canada Brant; Black Brandt; Big Gray Brant; Goose Brandt; Bernache; la Barnache; Bomber; Honker; Canada Honker; Big Honker; Old Honker; Gronker; Bullneck; Bustard; Trader; Hunter; Hunker; Greaser; Swamp Donkey; Kennedy; Wavy; Wild Wavy; Hounds; Whistler; Crybaby; Yelper; Brillard; Awicher Yager; Aw-onk; Wilte Gons; Schna Gons; Bisk-a-sish; Outarde; Giadh Fiadh; Piron; Oie Canadienne; Oie Sauvage

Mute Swan
Cygnus olor
(SIG-nus OH-lor)

Swan or swanne is the Anglo-Saxon word for these birds. The Mute Swan isn't truly mute, but it is the least vocal of all the swans. It has no flight calls as the others do, but it can hiss and utter grunting and snorting sounds.

Cygnus — The genus name is the Latin word for "a swan."

olor — The specific epithet is another Latin word for "a swan."

French Name: Cygne Tuberculé
Spanish Name: Cisne Vulgar
Other Names: Common Swan; Wild Swan; Domestic Swan

Trumpeter Swan
Cygnus buccinator
(SIG-nus buck-sih-NAY-tor)

"The voice of the well-named trumpeter resounds with a power equaled only by the French horns blown by red-faced Germans at a Wagner opera." — Neltje Blanchan (1898)

The Trumpeter Swan is named for its vocalizations, which Bent describes as "loud, resonant trumpetings: differing in tone and volume from those of the whistling swan; the windpipe of the larger species has one more convolution, which enables it to produce a louder and more far-reaching note on a lower key, with the musical resonance of a French horn." The calls of the immatures have been compared to the sound of a toy trumpet.

Cygnus — The genus name is the Latin word for "a swan."

buccinator — The specific epithet is Latin for "trumpeter."

French Name: Cygne Trompette
Spanish Name: Cisne Trompetero
Other Names: Wild Swan; American Swan; Bugler

Sidebar 1
Science vs. Historic Tradition

The Tundra Swan was formerly known as the Whistling Swan. While the swan's vocalizations have a musical quality, most observers probably wouldn't perceive any whistle, but Captain Meriwether Lewis did when he coined the name in 1806. A migrating flock sounds a lot like the flying monkeys in *The Wizard of Oz*. The Lewis and Clark Expedition encountered many swans wintering on the Columbia River. There were two species: the larger ones were Trumpeters, the smaller ones Tundra Swans. Captain Lewis also noted a difference in their vocalizations. He entered the following observations in his journal.

"Capt. Lewis, March 9, 1806 — The Large Swan is precisely the same common to the Atlantic States. The small swan differs from the larger one in size and its note. It is about one fourth less and its note is entirely different. the latter cannot be justly imitated by the sound of letters nor do I know any sounds with which a comparison would be pertinent. It begins with a kind of whistling sound and terminates in a round full note which is rather louder than the whistling, or former part; this note is as loud as that of the large swan. From the peculiar whistling of the note of this bird I have called it the *Whistling Swan*."

Now, Tundra Swan is a perfectly good name; it accurately describes this species' nesting habitat in the high Arctic. However, changing long-standing common names does not sit well with many birders, especially when the AOU takes a nice descriptive name like Rufous-sided Towhee and changes it to a colorless one like Eastern Towhee. But, I digress. In this case, it wasn't just birders who were upset, as the National Wildlife Federation editors illustrate:

"Concern over bird-name changes can come from unexpected quarters. One such case occurred in 1983 when the birding world learned that America's most abundant swan, the whistling, was going to be combined with the Old World Bewick's swan because the two interbreed. The duo became the tundra swan, a name chosen in recognition of the three or four months each year that the birds nest in the Far North.

The logic of this change was lost on two history-conscious members of the Lewis and Clark Heritage Trail Association who flew from Portland, Oregon, to New York City so they could corner Monroe [Burt L. Monroe, Jr., chairman of the nomenclature committee] at an AOU meeting and try to persuade him to leave the swan's name unchanged. The whistling swan, they argued, appears in the writings of Lewis and Clark, those stalwart explorers who have won a special place in the hearts of Old West aficionados. For history's sake, the Oregonians asked, couldn't the swan's name remain the same?

Alas, the two met more resistance from AOU than Lewis and Clark did from Native Americans. In brief, the answer was no, and the two men flew back to the West Coast bewildered by the dominance of scientific opinion over historic tradition."

— "The Baltimore Oriole Is Back" from *National Wildlife*, February/March, 1994 issue, Copyright © 1994 *National Wildlife Magazine*. Reproduced with permission of the National Wildlife Federation.

Tundra Swan
Cygnus columbianus
(SIG-nus koh-lum-bih-AY-nus)

The Tundra Swan is named for its breeding habitat on tundra ponds in the high Arctic. Formerly known as Whistling Swan. See sidebar 1.

Cygnus — The genus name is the Latin word for "a swan."

columbianus — The specific epithet is Modern Latin for "of the Columbia River," where Lewis and Clark discovered this species on their expedition to the Pacific Ocean.

French Name: Cygne Siffleur
Spanish Name: Cisne de Tundra
British Name: Bewick's Swan (Old World subspecies)
Eskimo and Inuit Name: Kogruk (white)
Other Names: American Whistling Swan; Common Swan; Wild Swan

Muscovy Duck
Cairina moschata
(KAY-rye-nah mos-KAY-tah)

The common name is believed to be a corruption of musk duck, as the male has a musky odor. By some mistake it was changed to Muscovy (Moscow). While there may indeed be domestic Muscovy Ducks in Russia, the species is native to tropical America from Mexico to Brazil. C. O. Sauer believes Muscovy to be a corruption of Muisca from the Muisca Indians of Colombia, where these birds were first domesticated.

Cairina — In 1822, D. D. Fleming raised this genus from the Italian *Cairino* (a resident of Cairo) in the mistaken belief that this duck comes from Egypt.

moschata — The specific epithet is from the Latin *moschatus* (musky). See common name above.

French Name: Canard Musqué
Spanish Name: Pato Real
Other Names: Musk Duck; Musky Duck

Wood Duck
Aix sponsa
(AIKS SPON-sah)

"Loveliest of all water-fowl, the Wood Duck stands supreme. Deep flooded

Wood Duck, by Louis Agassiz Fuertes

swamps where ancient mossy trees overhang the dark still waters, secluded pools amid the scattered pines where water-lilies lift their snowy heads and turtles bask in the sun, purling brooks flowing through dense woodlands where light and shade fleck the splashing waters, slow flowing creeks and marshy ponds — these are the haunts of the Wood Duck." — Edward Howe Forbush (1925)

The Wood Duck is named after its preferred habitat of wooded swamps as described in the above passage. It also nests in tree cavities and is one of the few species of duck to perch in trees.

Aix — The genus name is from the Greek, a name Aristotle used for some waterfowl or diving bird, not further identified. It is now applied to the Wood Duck and to its Asian counterpart, the Mandarin Duck (*A. galericulata*)

sponsa — The specific epithet is Latin for "betrothed" or "a bride." It refers to the drake's showy color pattern, as though it were dressed for a wedding. A. F. Gotch suggests that the name may have been influenced by the related Mandarin Duck of eastern Asia. In China, a pair of this species was a traditional wedding gift to symbolize marital fidelity:

"The most exquisite of American ducks displays the rainbow in his plumage and a touch of poetry in his scientific name, *Aix sponsa*. A hybrid of Greek and Latin, the phrase signifies "waterfowl in wedding raiment." From crest to tail the male wood duck glows with iridescent hues set off by natty white stripings." — S. Dillon Ripley (1965)

"Few if any more exquisitely beautiful creatures have been fashioned in the workshop of Nature than the Wood Duck of America. Among the Ducks, certainly only the Mandarin (*Aix galericulata*) of China, a near relative, may vie with this species in brilliancy of colouring and delicacy of mould. Linnaeus called the Wood Duck the Bride (Latin, *sponsa*, bride) but, of course, it is the bride*groom* who wears the jewels and inherits the products of Oriental dye-stuffs, bequeathed through a thousand generations; for, males must strut and females must work, is the rule among ducks as among most other birds. Literally all the colors of the rainbow belong to this bird in his nuptial plumage, with black and white thrown in for good measure. And with all this gaudy attire go many accomplishments not attained by any others in the group." — William Leon Dawson (1902)

"The most beautiful of all our ducks, if not all American birds, in the opinion of many, that Linnaeus named the bride (*sponsa*), although it is the groom that is particularly festive in rich apparel and flowing veil-like crest . . ." — Neltje Blanchan (1898)

French Name: Canard Branchu
Spanish Names: Pato Arco Iris; Pato Arcoiris
Other Names: Carolina Duck; Carolina Wood Duck; Crested Wood Duck; Acorn Duck; Tree Duck; Scarlet-eyed Duck; Bush Duck; Swamp Duck; Swamp Guinea; Summer Duck; Bridal Duck; the Bride; Wigeon; Wood Wigeon; Painted Summer Teal; Nuthatch; Plumer; Squealer; Woodrow; Ole Woodrow; Old Wooden Duck; Woody; Block; Canard du Bois; Huyuyo; Branchier; Branchu

Baikal Teal
Siberionetta formosa
(sigh-BEER-ih-oh-NET-ah for-MOW-sah)

This duck is named for Lake Baikal in Siberia, which is within its breeding range.

Siberionetta — The genus name means "Siberian duck" from Siberia plus the Greek *netta* (a duck). The reference is to this species' breeding range in eastern Russia.

formosa — The specific epithet is Latin for "beautiful," which this duck is, particularly the drake's ornately patterned head in green, cream, and black. Ernest Choate believed the specific epithet refers to the island of Formosa (Taiwan), where some of these ducks winter.

French Name: Sarcelle Élégante
Spanish Name: Cerceta del Baikal
Other Names: Formosan Teal; Spectacled Teal; Clucking Teal

Garganey
Spatula querquedula
(SPACH-uh-lah kwer-KWED-you-lah)

Garganey (GAR-gah-nee) is from the Italian *garganello*, which is imitative of the duck's call notes. Swiss naturalist Conrad Gesner first used the name for this duck in his work *Historiae Animalium* (1555).

Spatula — The genus name is Latin for "spoon," and refers to the shape of the Shoveler's bill, narrow at the base, broad towards the tip. The genus was originally erected for the Northern Shoveler. Formerly *Anas querquedula*.

querquedula — The specific name is Latin from the Greek *kerkouris*, a name for some kind of duck, but not necessarily this one. It is probably onomatopoetic.

French Name: Sarcelle d'Été
Spanish Names: Cerceta de Ceja Blanca; Cerceta Cejiblanca
Other Names: Garganey Teal; Summer Teal; Cricket Teal; Crackling Teale; Summer Duck; Pied Wigeon

Blue-winged Teal
Spatula discors
(SPACH-uh-lah DIS-cors)

In hunting circles, this small duck is known as the "panfish of waterfowl hunting."

Teal is a cognate of the Dutch *teling* (a teal) and is believed to be imitative of the ducks' calls. Blue-winged refers to the powder blue patch on the forewing of both sexes. See the specific epithet of the Cinnamon Teal, which has a similar wing pattern.

Spatula — The genus name is Latin for "a

spoon," and refers to the shape of the Shoveler's bill, narrow at the base, broad towards the tip. The genus was originally erected for the Northern Shoveler. Formerly *Anas discors.*

discors — Most authorities say *discors* is Latin for "discordant" or "inharmonious" in reference to this teal's harsh calls. Only the calls of this duck aren't harsh. The male Blue-winged Teal gives a soft peep or whistle and the female utters a soft quack, not the harsh quacks that most people associate with ducks. Another explanation is that *discors* may mean "disc about the mouth" from the Greek *discos* (a disc) and the Latin *os* or *oris* (pertaining to the mouth). The reference would be to the drake's white crescent mark between the eye and the bill.

French Name: Sarcelle à Ailes Bleues

Spanish Names: Cerceta de Ala Azul; Cerceta Aliazul

Other Names: Common Blue-winged Teal; Blue-wing; Blue Teal; Southern Teal; Summer Teal; August Teal; Autumn Teal; Fall Teal; White-faced Teal; Necktie Teal; Teal duck; Duck-and-Teal; White-faced Duck; Breakfast Duck; Fall Duck; Smiler; Blue Rocket; Butterball; Petit Canard; Pato Zarcel; Pato de la Florida; Printanniere; Sarcelle; Sarcelle Printanniere; Sarcelle Autonniere; Sarcelle d'Ete

Cinnamon Teal
Spatula cyanoptera
(SPACH-uh-lah sigh-an-OP-ter-ah)

The Cinnamon Teal is named for the rich cinnamon-brown plumage of the breeding drake.

Spatula — The genus name is Latin for "spoon," and refers to the shape of the Shoveler's bill, narrow at the base, broad towards the tip. The genus was originally erected for the Northern Shoveler. Formerly *Anas cyanoptera.*

cyanoptera — The specific epithet means "blue wing" from the Greek *kuanos* (blue) and *pteron* (the wing). The reference is to the large powder blue patches on the forewings, observable when the ducks are in flight.

French Name: Sarcelle Cannelle

Spanish Names: Cerceta Canela; Cerceta castaña

Other Names: Red Teal; Red-bellied Teal; Red-breasted Teal; Silver Teal; River Teal; South American Teal; Texas Teal; Cinny; Blue-wing; Redhead

Northern Shoveler
Spatula clypeata
(SPACH-uh-lah clip-ee-AY-tah)

"Churning about in tight circles, the little ducks scoop up pond water and ooze with their broad-ended bills. Then, like prospectors panning for gold, the shovelers sift mouthfuls. Water and muck sluice out through comblike "teeth" or lamellae that fringe the mandibles. The 'nuggets' remain — seeds, insects, minnows, mollusks, and tadpoles." — S. Dillon Ripley (1965)

Shoveler refers to the large spatulate bill of this species. The bill is lined with lamellae for straining small plants and animals from the water's surface. The duck feeds with its neck extended and bill submerged, sweeping its head from side to side. Pete Dunne calls the Northern Shoveler "an aquatic vacuum cleaner." Northern distinguishes this northern hemisphere species from shovelers of the southern hemisphere like the Cape Shoveler (*S. smithii*) of South Africa and the Red Shoveler (*S. platalea*) of Patagonia.

Spatula — The genus name is Latin for "a spoon," and refers to the shape of the Shoveler's bill, narrow at the base, broad towards the tip. Formerly *Anas clypeata.*

clypeata — The specific epithet is from the Latin *clypeatus* (shield-bearing), also referring to the shape of the bill, broader towards the tip than at the base.

Northern Shoveler, by C. G. Davis

French Name: Canard Souchet
Spanish Names: Pato Cucharón Norteño; Pato Cuchara
Eskimo and Inuit Name: Chugikpak (big bill)
Other Names: Common Shoveler; Red-breasted Shoveler; Blue-winged Shoveler; Mud Shoveler; Mud Lark; Mud Duck; Mud Mallard; Broad-faced Mallard; Grinning Mallard; Smiling Mallard; Minnesota Mallard; Neighbor's Mallard; Butler Duck; Butter Duck; Chipewyan Duck; Mule Duck; Spoon-bill Duck; Maiden Duck; Till Duck; Trash Duck; Blue-winged Stint; Spoon-billed Teal; French Teal; Spoon-billed Widgeon; Spoon-bill; Spoon Beak; Spoony; Shovel-bill; Shovel-mouth; Shovel-nose; Lips; Boot Lips; Soup Lips; Bologna Snatcher; Bag Beak; Swaddle-bill; Broad-bill; Broady; Scooper; Long-neck; Beck; Cow-frog; Shovelard; Whinyard; Sheldrake; Scopperbill; Scoop de Bill; Hollywood; Kertlutock; Kirk Tullock; Bechleur de Merde; Canard spatule; Caouanne; Mesquin; Moniac; Pato Cuchareta

Gadwall
Mareca strepera
(mar-ECK-ah STREP-eh-rah)

The origin of the name Gadwall is unknown. In an earlier work it was written as Gaddel. One author ventured a guess that it may stem from an Anglo-Saxon word *gad* meaning "a point," the reference being the tooth-like serrations of the mandibles. English ornithologist John Latham presented the possibility that Gadwall stemmed from the Latin *quedul* "quack."

Mareca — The genus name is from Marréco, a Brazilian-Portuguese name for the smaller species of ducks. But compare *Marica*, a water nymph in Roman mythology. Formerly *Anas strepera*.

strepera — The specific epithet is Latin for "noisy" and apparently refers to the loud vocalizations of the female.

French Name: Canard Chapeau
Spanish Names: Pato Friso; Pato Pinto
Other Names: Common Gadwall; Gadwell; Gaddy; Gaddy Daddy; Griswald; Gag; Jagwall; Gray; Gray Duck; Creek Duck; German Duck; Blaten Duck; Bleating Duck; Blarting Duck; Trash Duck; Prairie Mallard; Small Mallard; Louisiana Mallard; Welsh Drake; Wigeon; Gray Wigeon; Sand Wigeon; Cab Driver; Speckle-belly; Chickacock; Minik; Rodge; Red-wing; Canard gris; Courbeaux

Falcated Duck
Mareca falcata
(mar-ECK-ah fal-KAY-tah)

Falcated means "sickle-shaped" and refers to the elongated, curved tertials (the innermost feathers of the upper surface of the wing) that drape over the duck's tail. Formerly known as Falcated Teal.

Mareca — The genus name is from Marréco, a Brazilian-Portuguese name for the smaller species of ducks. But compare *Marica*, a water nymph in Roman mythology. Formerly *Anas falcata*.

falcata — The specific epithet is from the Latin *falx* or *falcis* (a sickle) and means "furnished with sickles" or "sickle-shaped." See common name above.

French Name: Sarcelle à Faucilles
Spanish Name: Cerceta de Alfanjes
Other Name: Bronze-capped Teal

Eurasian Wigeon
Mareca penelope
(mar-ECK-ah pee-NEL-oh-pee)

Wigeon (formerly spelled Widgeon) derives from the French *vigeon* (a whistling duck) and refers either to the bird's call notes or to the whistling sound the wings make in flight. The French word may come from the Latin *vipio*, a name Pliny used for "a small crane." The Eurasian Wigeon occurs across Europe and Asia from Iceland and the British Isles east to Kamchatka. It is casual in North America, but does not breed here. Formerly known as European Wigeon.

Mareca — The genus name is from Marréco, a Brazilian-Portuguese name for the smaller species of ducks. But compare *Marica*, a water nymph in Roman mythology. Formerly *Anas penelope*.

penelope — The specific epithet probably has no relationship with Penelope, the wife of Ulysses in Greek mythology. More likely early ornithologists misspelled *penelops*, a name Aristotle used for a "kind of duck," not further identified.

French Name: Canard Siffleur d'Europe
Spanish Name: Pato Silbón
Other Names: Black Wigeon; Half Duck; Lady Duck; Smee Duck; Whew Duck; Pandle Whew; Grass Whew; Whewer; Whim; Whistler; Winder; Cock Winder; Bald Pate; Golden-head; Yellow Poll; Lady Fowl; Easterling

American Wigeon
Mareca americana
(mar-ECK-ah ah-mer-ih-CANE-ah)

Formerly known as "Baldpate," a name still in wide use, particularly by hunters. Baldpate refers to the drake's shining white crown and forehead that suggests a bald head. In 1957, the AOU changed the name to American Wigeon to show the relationship to its Old World counterpart, the Eurasian Wigeon. The name wigeon from the French for "whistling duck" is particularly appropriate in describing this species' three-note whistling calls, sort of like a rubber squeaky toy. Its wings also make a whistling sound in flight. American distinguishes our species from the Eurasian Wigeon.

Mareca — The genus name is from Marréco, a Brazilian-Portuguese name for the smaller species of ducks. But compare *Marica*, a water nymph in Roman mythology. Formerly *Anas americana*.

americana — The specific epithet is Modern Latin for "of America."

French Name: Canard Siffleur d'Amérique
Spanish Names: Pato Chalcuán; Pato Calvo
Eskimo and Inuit Name: Naskurtulit (white on the head)
Other Names: Green-headed Widgeon; Blue-billed Widgeon; California Wigeon; Cock Widgeon; Southern Wigeon; Bald Wigeon; Bald-faced Wigeon; Ball-pate Widgeon; Bald-crown; Bald-head; Bald-face; Baldy; Whiteface; Wheat Duck; Blue Bill; Blue-bill Duck; Diamond Duck; Gray Duck; Little Grey Duck; Robber Duck; Smoke Duck; Smoking Duck; Smoker; Whistling Duck; Whistling Dick; Whistler; French Teal; Mini Pintail; Swede; Butterball; Canvas-back; Redhead; Speckle-head; White Belly; White Cap; Whiteface; Cottontop; Poacher; Banded Robber; Moñi-blanco; Zan Zan; Pato Cabeciblanco; Pato Lavanco

Mallard
Anas platyrhynchos
(AY-nas plah-tih-RING-koss)

"In domestic or semi-domestic conditions, more than in the wild, Mallards live up to their "male-chauvinist" name. There is no finesse in the pursuit flight of the Mallard; lovemaking drakes will attack female ducks vigorously and if, as is often the case in parks, the females are outnumbered, several males may make repeated assaults, sometimes actually killing the duck. This violent behavior is

---

Sidebar 2
The Poacher

"Rafts of diving ducks — canvasbacks, scaups, and redheads — collect each fall where rivers empty into bays. Here they feast on beds of wild celery. Here too come winged pirates — American widgeon — maneuvering in tight flocks with the grace of swallows. Unadapted for diving, the surface-feeding widgeon wait for divers to bring up the succulent celery, then snatches it away and swims off, chest low and tail high." — S. Dillon Ripley (1965)

The American Wigeon's folkname "poacher" refers to this duck's habit of pirating food from other birds as described above. This behavior, known as kleptoparasitism, is well known in raptors such as the Bald Eagle and such seabirds as jaegers and skuas, frigatebirds, and the larger gulls. Wigeon are dabbling ducks that feed by picking food from the surface or by tipping up in shallow water. Food in deep water is inaccessible to them unless brought to the surface by diving birds like coots and bay ducks. Wigeon like to mingle with such birds. Then when the diver surfaces with a mouthful of food, the wigeon brazenly snatches it right out of the bird's bill.

probably due to over-crowding and seems not to be a modern phenomenon." — Francesca Greenoak (1979)

Mallard, from the Old French *malard*, derives from the Latin *masculus* (male) plus the intensifying suffix *–ard* from the German *–art* (hardy or bold). Earlier this species was known simply as the "Wild Duck," and Mallard referred only to the male. A subspecies *A. p. diazi* (named for Augustin Diaz [1829–1893], a Mexican engineer and geographer) was formerly considered a separate species, the Mexican Duck. The Mallard is the ancestor of every domestic duck breed except the Muscovy. Some examples are: White Pekin; Rouen; Call; Khaki Campbell; Black East India; Cayuga; and Indian Runner.

Anas — The genus name is the Latin word for "a duck."

platyrhynchos — The specific epithet means "broad-billed" or "flat-billed" from the Greek *platus* (broad) and *rhynchos* (the bill) and refers to the typical duck's bill.

French Name: Canard Colvert

Spanish Names: Pato de Collar; Pato Cabeciverde

Eskimo and Inuit Names: Koo-a-ruk-puk (bigger duck); Yukpak (big pintail duck)

Other Names: Mallard Duck; Common Mallard; Northern Mallard; Wild Mallard; Prairie Mallard; Irish Mallard; Green Mallard; Greenhead Mallard; Ice Mallard; Snow Mallard; Red-legged Mallard; Yellow-legged Mallard; Gray Mallard; Mallet; Gray Duck; Black Duck; Ice Duck; Ice Breaker; Stock Duck; Grey Stock Duck; French Stock Duck; Common Duck; Wild Duck; Common Wild Duck; Wild Drake; Flutter Duck; Moss Duck; Mire Duck; Stubble Duck; Yellow-leg Duck; Yellowlegs; Redlegs; Orangelegs; Muir Duck English Duck; French Duck; Duckinmallard; Duck-and-Teal; Green-head; Green-neck; Ringneck; Greentop; Green Bean; Curly-tail; Frosty-beak; Twister; Whistler; Bread Eater; Chuckler; Sookie; Suzie; Canard Ordinaire; Canard Sauvage; Canard Francais; Canard Gris; Gibier Gris; Pato Inglés; Wilte Ent

~

American Black Duck
Anas rubripes
(AY-nas ROO-brih-peez)

"An east wind and a high tide — this is the litany of the hunter on the Atlantic flyway. For when onshore gusts ruffle the estuaries and the surge of the sea whispers through the salt marshes in the gray dawn, the black ducks come. They sweep in, soot-dark shapes flashing their white wing linings, and as they pass over the duck blinds they seem to mock the gunners concealed below: "We are your target — hit us if you can."" — S. Dillon Ripley (1965)

Resembling a dark female Mallard, this duck isn't black at all, but a dark, sooty brown. Hunters probably gave it this name, because the ducks do appear black at a distance, especially against the sky when in flight. Pete Dunne calls it "a Mallard dressed for a funeral." American distinguishes our native species from black ducks in other parts of the world such as the African Black Duck (*A. sparsa*) and the Pacific Black Duck. (*A. superciliosa*).

Anas — The genus name is the Latin word for "a duck."

rubripes — The specific epithet means "red foot" from the Latin *ruber* (red) and *pes* (the foot). It refers to this duck's orange-red feet.

French Name: Canard Noir

Spanish Name: Pato Sombrío

Other Names: Black; Blackie; Black Duck; Florida Black Duck; Florida Duck; Spring Black Duck; Summer Black Duck; Summer Duck; Winter Black Duck; Old Winter Duck; English Black Duck; English Duck; Red-footed Black Duck; Red-leg; Red-legged Black Duck; Red-legged Duck; Blackstock Duck; Blackwood Duck; Common Duck; Wild Duck; Brown Duck; Grey Duck; Velvet Duck; Dusky Duck; Sea Duck; Nigger Duck; Blue-wing; Arctic Blue-wing; Blue-winged Duck; Blue-winged Black Duck; Labrador Duck; Inside Duck; Outside Duck; Outside Black Duck; Ledge Duck; Marsh Duck; Puddle Duck; Beach Duck; Forest Duck; Mallard; Black Mallard; Northern Black Mallard; Brown Mallard; Dusky Mallard; Striped Mallard; Blackjack; Red-paddle; Yellow-pad; Yellow-beak; Fish-eater; Noir;

Canard Noir du Nord; Canard Noir d'Hiver; Pato Oscuro; Shwortsa Ent; Lach Dubh; Tunnag

∽

Mottled Duck
Anas fulvigula
(AY-nas full-VIG-you-lah)

The plumage, streaked and speckled in shades of brown and buff, give this duck its name. Known as Florida Duck until 1957.

Anas — The genus name is the Latin word for "a duck."

fulvigula — The specific epithet means "tawny throat" from the Latin *fulvus* (tawny) and *gula* (throat) and refers to the distinct unmarked buffy throat.

French Name: Canard Brun
Spanish Name: Pato Tejano
Other Names: Florida Duck; Dusky Duck; Black Duck; Summer Duck; Summer Black Duck; Summer French Duck; Mallard Hen; Black Mallard; Florida Mallard; Louisiana Summer Mallard; Mexican Mallard; Canard d'Ete; Canard Noir d'Ete

∽

White-cheeked Pintail
Anas bahamensis
(AY-nas bah-hah-MEN-sis)

This species has an extended, pointed tail, but it is not as long and thin as in the related Northern Pintail. White-cheeked refers to the white sides of the head and throat. Formerly known as Bahama Duck.

Anas — The genus name is the Latin word for "a duck."

bahamensis — The specific epithet is Modern Latin for "of the Bahamas" where the type specimen was collected. The White-cheeked Pintail's normal range includes much of the West Indies as well as parts of South America.

French Name: Canard de Bahamas
Spanish Name: Pato Gargantillo
Other Names: Bahama Pintail; Bahama Duck; Summer Duck; White-head; White-throat; White-jaw; Brass-wing; Pato Quijada Colorado; Pato de la Orilla; Canard Tête-blanche

∽

Northern Pintail
Anas acuta
(AY-nas ah-KEW-tah)

"The pintails carry themselves with a stately elegance that faintly suggests the coming swan. Their necks, which are unusually long and slender for a duck; their well poised heads and trim, long bodies, unlike the squat figure of some of their kindred; their sharp wings and pointed tails, give them both dignity and grace in the air, on land, or in the water, for they appear equally at home in the three elements." — Neltje Blanchan (1898)

Pintail refers to the drake's elongated central tail feathers suggesting a pin. These long tail feathers accentuate the bird's slenderness. Pete Dunne describes the Northern Pintail as a "slim, elegant, even rakish-looking dabbling duck — with the elongated proportions of an El Greco painting." Northern distinguishes this species of the northern hemisphere from more southerly ranging species like the White-cheeked Pintail (see above) of the West Indies and the Yellow-billed Pintail *A. georgica* of South America.

Anas — The genus name is the Latin word for "a duck."

acuta — The specific epithet is from the Latin *acutus* (sharp) and refers to the male's long, pointed tail.

French Name: Canard Pilet
Spanish Names: Pato Golondrino Norteño; Pato Rabudo
Eskimo and Inuit Name: Ukiligask (a fat duck in fall)
Other Names: Common Pintail; American

Northern Pintail, by Archibald Thornburn

Pintail; Gray Duck; Pied Duck; Pied Gray Duck; Fall Duck; Winter Duck; Sharp-ended Duck; Sprig Duck; Spring-tailed Duck; Squaw Duck; Trilby Duck; Water Duck; Wood Duck; Long-neck Duck; Pheasant Duck; Sea-Pheasant; Water Pheasant; Spike; Sprig; Buck Sprig; Bullsprig; Sprig-tail; Sprit-tail; Spring-tail; Kite-tail; Peak-tail; Pike-tail; Spike-tail; Split-tail; Spindle-tail; Spreet-tail; Long-tail; Picket-tail; Pigeon-tail; Sharp-tail; Pile-start; Pile-starter; Pinner; Pinnie; Buck Pinny; Widgeon; Gray Widgeon; Pied Wigeon; Sea Widgeon; Sprig-tailed Widgeon; Kite-tailed Widgeon; Harlan; Coy; Cracker; Long-necked Cracker; Long-neck; Thin Neck; Neck-twister; Lady Bird; Smoker; Canard Gris; Canard Pilier; Courbeaux; Minfolk; Paille-en-Queue; Pato Guineo; Pato Pescuecilargo; Petit Gris; Smee; Smees; Smethe

Green-winged Teal
Anas crecca
(AY-nas CREEK-ah)

"A miniature dabbling duck (the smallest teal, and almost as small as Bufflehead), with a speculum so brilliant green that it challenges a folded wing to hide it and a flight so fast an maneuverable that it borders on reckless." — Pete Dunne (2006)

Green-winged refers to the green speculum, the patch of iridescent color in the secondaries of the wing. Some authorities believe that the fashionable color teal comes from the drake's green eye patch. Others dispute this. Teal is a cognate of the Dutch *teling* (a teal) and is believed to be imitative of the ducks' calls:

"The musical calling of the winter flocks of Teal, the high flutes of the males blending with the rhythmical chirruping of the females, has a wistful soothing quality to it as it echoes over the water." — Francesca Greenoak (1979)

Anas — The genus name is the Latin word for "a duck."

crecca — The specific epithet is a Latinized form of creak or quack representing the call notes of this bird.

French Name: Sarcelle à Ailes Vertes

Green-winged Teal, by Archibald Thornburn

Spanish Names: Cerceta de Ala Verde; Cerceta Aliverde
British Name: Common (Eurasian) Teal
Eskimo and Inuit Name: Tingaskarat (fly quick, jump quick)
Other Names: Green-wing, American Teal; American Green-winged Teal; Least Green-winged Teal; Lake Teal; Mud Teal; Red-headed Teal; Winter Teal; Jay Teal; Throstle Teal; Speckled Teal; Duck-and-Teal; Breakfast Duck; Fall Duck; Green-winged Duck; Teal Duck; Partridge Duck; Little Duck; Water Dove; Water-partridge; Tael Duik; Butterball; Congo; Greased Lightning; Rice Rocket; Mini Rocket; Fast Flyer; Fast Mover; Greenie; Sparrow; Wigeon; Petit Canard; Pato Aliverde; Pato de la Carolina; Pato Serrano; Sarcelle; Sarcelle d'Hiver; Sarcelle du Norde

Canvasback
Aythya valisineria
(AY-thih-ah val-iss-ih-NEAR-ih-ah)

"How handsome these high-fliers are — the females dignified in shades of light gray and a warm rusty brown; the slightly larger males with sleek auburn heads, black chests, white bellies, and backs covered not by canvas but a fine weave of palest gray linen." — Janet Lembke (1992)

The common name refers to the drake's pale gray back and white sides, delicately dotted and lined in a wavelike pattern that suggests the weave of canvas fabric.

Aythya — The genus name is from the Greek *aithuia*, a name Aristotle used for some waterbird, not further identified. It is now applied to this group of diving ducks also called Pochards or Bay Ducks. The genus *Aethia*, to which the auklets belong, also stems from this root.

valisineria — Alexander Wilson gave the Canvasback its specific epithet after one of its staple foods, wild celery (*Vallisneria americana* or *V. spiralis* of early authors), but he misspelled it. However, because of the rule of priority, the mistake stands. Linnaeus named the botanical genus for Antonio Vallisneri (1661–1730), an Italian naturalist and professor of practical medicine at the University of Padua. Wild celery is so important to Canvasbacks that it is said they will change their migration patterns to find it. Wild celery apparently gives this duck the fine flavor that makes it especially prized as a table bird:

"The principal food of the canvasback, or at least the food which has made it most famous as a table delicacy, is the so-called "wild celery" *Vallisneria spiralis*; it is in no way related to our garden celery and is more commonly known as "eelgrass," "tape grass," or "channel weed;" it grows abundantly in the Chesapeake Bay region and is supposed to be the chief attraction for the vast number of canvasbacks and other ducks which resort to these waters in winter . . . The canvasback prefers to feed on the root of the plant only, which is white and delicate in flavor and said to

Redhead and Canvasback, by Louis Agassiz Fuertes

Sidebar 3
"If It Quacks Like a Duck . . ."

A familiar saying goes, "If it looks like a duck, swims like a duck, and quacks like a duck, then it probably is a duck." Only not all ducks quack. Wild species utter a variety of sounds from squeals, peeps, and whistles to moans, coos, squeaks, and growls. So it is not surprising that these vocalizations have prompted a number of colloquial names. The startling alarm notes *oo-EEK! oo-EEK! oo-EEK!* of the female Wood Duck have given this species the nickname Squealer. The Gadwall's series of three to five "burps" have prompted the name Bleating Duck. The Garganey is also called Cricket Teal and Crackling Teale from the high-pitched rattle (like a cricket's chirp) from the courting drake. The nasal squeaks of the Harlequin Duck have given it the names Squeaker and Sea Mouse. Bell-like tones of the White-winged Scoter have coined the names Bell Coot and Bell-tongued Coot, and the Black Scoter is also known as the Sleigh-bell Duck. The Goldeneye's nickname Whistler refers not to its calls, but to the sound the wings make in flight. The sound also prompted the names Whistle-wing and Merry-wing. Amphibian-like calls have given the Hooded Merganser the folk name Frog Duck. The most vocal of all ducks, the Long-tailed Duck is also known by the imitative names Caloo, Cacouy, Coween, Kla-how-ya, Kakawee, Ha-ha-way. South-southerly, Ow-owly, and Jackowly. Newfoundlanders call it Hound because a flock is said to sound like the distant baying of a pack of hounds.

resemble young celery; it is obtained by diving and uprooting the plant; the roots are bitten off and eaten and the leaves or stems are left to float away in tangled masses." — Arthur Cleveland Bent (1925)

See sidebar 4.

French Name: Morillon à Dos Blanc
Spanish Name: Pato Coacoxtle
Other Names: Can; Canny; Bull Can; King Can; King; Canvas; Canvas Duck; Bullneck; Red-headed Bullneck; Canard Cheval; Hickory-Quaker; Gray Duck; Big Gray Duck; Horse-Duck; Black Duck; Redhead; Copper-head; Wedge Head; Goldstandard; Rocket; Sheldrake; Whiteback; Snowball; Pochard; Pato Piquisesgado

~

Sidebar 4
Wild Celery and the Canvasback's Fame as a Table Delicacy

Hunters know the Canvasback as the King of Ducks or King Can, in part due to the large size, partly for the handsome appearance, but most of all for this duck's near-legendary fame as a table delicacy, which has been savored since colonial times. Curiously, this toothsome flavor is present only when the birds have been feeding on their namesake, wild celery (*Vallisneria americana*). Since wild celery is much scarcer today, many Canvasbacks no longer have the distinctive flavor that made them famous. Canvasbacks were especially pursued back in the market hunting days of the late 19th and early 20th centuries, when millions of waterfowl and shorebirds were slaughtered to supply big city markets, upscale restaurants and luxury hotels. The Canvasback was the most prized of all, fetching the highest prices. Here is more on the topic by three writers of the past and one contemporary:

"The Canvas-back, famed by epicures for the flavor of its flesh, is much overrated in this respect. Under ordinary circumstances it is little if any better than the Scaups, and is rather inferior to the Redhead. Only when it has been feeding extensively upon the wild celery (*Vallisneria spiralis*) does its flesh become permeated with the peculiar flavor of that plant, which is supposed to render it unusually palatable." — W. E. Clyde Todd (1940)

""Tell me what you eat and I will tell you what you are" might be resented by a self-respecting human, but it applies pretty accurately to the flavor of ducks. Various writers are wont to extol a bird's flesh as "tender," "juicy," "sapid," "delicious," or to condemn it as "gamy," "rank," "fishy," "unpalatable," according to traditions which prevail locally; so that often the testimony of no two observers will agree as to a duck's fitness or unfitness for the table. The fact is, however, that the flavor of wild meat is pretty much what the feeding of the last week or so has made it, so that it is possible for a single bird to run the whole gamut from "sapid" to "fishy" in a single season. The early Canvas-backs were found feeding on the rank grass, or wild celery, of Chesapeake Bay, and from this circumstance has arisen a most extravagant appreciation of its flesh — or the profession of it — which has pursued the poor duck from Maryland to the Carolinas, and nearly wrought its ruin." — William Leon Dawson (1902)

"There is little reason for squealing in barbaric joy over this over-rated and generally underdone bird," says Dr. Coues, "not one person in ten thousand can tell it from any other duck on the table, and only then under the celery circumstances." Yet it is this darling of the epicures that, with the stewed terrapins of Maryland kitchens, has conferred on Baltimore the title of the "gastronomic capital" of our country. There, where it is brought to market fattened on the wild celery in the Chesapeake, it is in its prime a tender, delicately flavored duck, but not one whit more delicious than the canvasbacks taken in Wisconsin, for example, where the celery beds cover hundreds of miles; or the redheads that feed in the same place; or, indeed, than many of the river and pond ducks unknown to the gourmands of Maryland . . . After all it is the food it lives upon, and not its species, that is responsible for any duck's flavor . . . The wild celery, or *vallisneria spiralis*, which is no celery at all, but an eel grass growing entirely beneath the water, took its name from Antonio Vallisneri, an Italian naturalist, and it was passed on as a specific name to the canvasback. When fattened upon it a brace of these ducks often weigh twelve pounds. To secure its buds and roots, the only parts they eat, they must dive and remain a long time under water, only to be robbed on their return many times by the bold baldpates that snatch the celery from their bills the instant their heads appear above water . . . One would imagine our ornithologists were writing cookbooks, to read their accounts of this duck whose habits have been little studied beyond its feeding grounds in the United States. . . . It is in death that the canvasback is glorified." — Netje Blanchan (1898)

No duck has risen to a higher plane at the table than the canvasback. George Washington prized it, as did the Robber Barons of the Gilded Age and the rough-hewn voyageurs of the Canadian frontier, who traded in beaver pelts and feasted on canvasbacks. It was, for a while, the most prestigious thing anyone could put on a menu.

". . . Every duck species has its own preferred diet. And, given its druthers, a canvasback loves nothing more than the roots of *vallisneria*, the wild celery. Oddly, it does not taste like celery and is not related to the garden plant. But its roots are soft, easily digestible by the ducks, and loaded with carbohydrates. Where *vallisneria* lives, you will find canvasbacks. If they can't find that, canvasbacks switch to *sagittaria*, also known as wapato or duck potato. These are equally loaded with carbs, but they are harder to digest. One step down are sago and wigeongrass. Finally, if pushed, canvasbacks will get all Atkins Diet and switch to a diet almost exclusively of Baltic clams. This is what cans eat when they are in San Francisco Bay, where a quarter of all canvasbacks spend their winters . . . Diet determines flavor, but no matter what they eat, canvasbacks taste different from other ducks. Their meat is a rich crimson, their skin a pinkish buff, their fat a ghostly ivory . . . And no duck — indeed, no other animal save the terrapin or the abalone — has reached the heights of fashion of the canvasback. Imagine the most expensive thing on a menu you can think of, excluding Cognac or rare wine. Caviar, right? A good serving of caviar at a nice restaurant might set you back $50 or more. Canvasback was once like that. A look at the century-old menus of such swanky establishments like the Waldorf Hotel in New York City shows that an order of canvasback duck would cost you $4.50 in 1907. Do a little math and that's the equivalent of about $104 in today's dollars. And that, most likely, is for half a duck. Wow. Even at the market, a canvasback might cost $1.25, or the equivalent of about $32.50 in today's dollars. Consider for a moment that the average worker in the United States earned 19 cents an hour and you realize that it would take nearly three days' pay for that person to earn enough to order canvasback at a restaurant. King of Ducks indeed. So how was that canvasback served at the Waldorf? As it happens, it seems that cans were such a precious item that they were served in only one way: Roasted rare, carved and served with a red currant sauce (or jelly) and a side of "fried hominy." Always. I found nearly 40 recipes or mentions of canvasbacks being served, dating from 1877 to 1907 and they are all done the same way." — Hank Shaw (2011)

Redhead
Aythya americana
(AY-thih-ah ah-mer-ih-CANE-ah)

This duck gets its name from the drake's chestnut-red head.

Aythya — The genus name is from the Greek *aithuia*, a name Aristotle used for some waterbird, not further identified. It is now applied to this group of diving ducks also called Pochards or Bay Ducks. The genus *Aethia*, to which the auklets belong, also stems from this root.

americana — The specific epithet is Modern Latin for "of America." The Redhead is strictly American in distribution and is the North American counterpart of the Common Pochard (*Aythya ferina*) of Eurasia.

French Name: Morillon à Tête Rouge
Spanish Names: Pato de Cabeza Roja; Pato Cabecirrojo
Other Names: Pochard; American Pochard; Raft Duck; Red-headed Raft Duck; Fiddle Duck; Fiddler Duck; Fiddler; Fool Duck; Mule Duck; Muskeg Duck; Red-headed Broadbill; Gray-back; Fall Duck; Washington Canvas-back; Canard Ateterouge; Canard Mullet; Cou-rouge; Violon

Ring-necked Duck
Aythya collaris
(AY-thih-ah coh-LARE-is)

"Ring-necks? Their collars of dark chestnut feathers are well nigh invisible. They should have been called ring-bills for the highly noticeable bands of white that encircle both male and female bills near the tip." — Janet Lembke (1992)

Hunters call them ring-billed ducks, as suggested in the above passage. One would need to have a specimen in the hand to see the chestnut-brown neck-ring, and even then it is barely discernible.

Aythya — The genus name is from the Greek *aithuia*, a name Aristotle used for some waterbird, not further identified. It is now applied to this group of diving ducks also called Pochards or Bay Ducks. The genus *Aethia*, to which the auklets belong, also stems from this root.

collaris — The specific epithet is Latin for "collared" and also pertains to the brownish neck ring that is not visible in the field.

French Name: Morillon à Collier
Spanish Names: Pato de Pico Anillado; Pato Piquianillado; Porrón Collarejo
Other Names: Ring-neck; Ring-necked Scaup; Ring-billed duck; Ringie; Blackhead; Ring-billed Blackhead; Ring-billed Shuffler; Creek Redhead; Moonbill; Tufted-Duck; American Tufted Duck; Black Duck; Bullet Duck; Fall Duck; Muskeg Duck; Marsh Bluebill; Pond Bluebill; Bastard Broadbill; Bastard Redhead; Diver; Blackjack; Buckeye; Bullneck; Bunty; Butterball; Dogy; Golden-eyes; Jet; Greaser; Hummer; Cabezón; Canard Noir; Dos Gris; Pato Negro; Pato del Medio

Tufted Duck
Aythya fuligula
(AY-thih-ah fuh-LIG-you-lah)

The long tuft of feathers hanging from the back of the head give this duck its name.

Aythya — The genus name is from the Greek *aithuia*, a name Aristotle used for some waterbird, not further identified. It is now applied to this group of diving ducks also called Pochards or Bay Ducks. The genus *Aethia*, to which the auklets belong, also stems from this root.

fuligula — The specific epithet means "little sooty one" from the Latin *fuligo* (soot) plus a diminutive suffix and refers to the dark color of the male's upperparts.

French Name: Fuligule Morillon
Spanish Names: Pato Moñudo; Pato-boludo Moñudo
Other Names: White-sided Duck; Black Topping Duck; Gold-eye Duck; Crested Diver; White-sided Diver; Magpie Diver; Doucker; Dovver; Blue Neb; Black Wigeon; Curre Wigeon; Black Curre; Blue-billed Curre; Black Poker

Greater Scaup
Aythya marila
(AY-thih-ah mah-RYE-lah)

This duck's English name comes from a Scottish variant of scalp, which means a rocky ledge that is exposed at low tide. A scaup bank provides a surface on which shellfish can attach, and where sea ducks can feed. Along the seacoasts, the scaup's main food is mollusks, including oysters, mussels, clams, scallops, dog whelks, periwinkles, and limpets. Greater refers to the slightly larger size of this species compared to the Lesser Scaup.

Aythya — The genus name is from the Greek *aithuia*, a name Aristotle used for some waterbird that was not further identified. It is now applied to this group of diving ducks also called Pochards or Bay Ducks. The genus *Aethia*, to which the auklets belong, also stems from this root.

marila — The specific epithet is from the Greek *marile* (charcoal embers), and refers either to the blackish color of the male's head, neck, and breast or his ash-gray back.

French Name: Grand Morillon

Spanish Names: Pato-boludo Mayor; Porrón Mayor

Eskimo and Inuit Name: Kipalik (half white and half black)

Other Names: Bluebill, Big Bluebill; Big Bay Bluebill; Greater Bluebill; Lake Bluebill; Bluebill Duck; Widgeon; Blue-billed Wigeon; Frosty-back Wigeon; Black-headed Wigeon; Broadbill; Greater Broadbill; Broadie; Bay Broadbill; Deep-water Broadbill; Saltwater Broadbill; Winter Broadbill; Silver Pochard; Scaup Pochard; Common Scaup; Scaup Duck; American Scaup Duck; American Scaup; Greater Scaup Duck; Covie Duck; Norway Duck; Norwegian Duck; Holland Duck; Fishing Duck; Raft Duck; Black-headed Raft-Duck; Muskeg Duck; Mussel Duck; Call Duck; Flock Duck; Bridle Duck; Spoonbill Duck; White-faced Duck; Fall Duck; Big Fall Duck; Winter Duck; Black Duck; Wood Duck; Butterball; Butterball Duck; Sea Duck; Troop Duck; Blackhead; Big Blackhead; Bay Blackhead; Black-neck; Blackjack; Large Brownhead; Bullhead; Bullneck; Green-head; Green-headed Diver; Black-headed Diver; Golden-eyed Diver; Black-neck; Gray-back; Grey Backed Curre; Blue Neb; Shoe; Flying Shoe; Old Boot; Bellarge; Coachin; Cold-shin; Coldshins;Dog; Dummy; Dun Bird; Troop-fowl; Floating Fowl; Laker; Shuffler; Bay Shuffler; Whistler; Mule; Nun (female); Plonger; Rook; Canard Cailles; Gros Canard d'Automme; Milouin; Dos-gris de Mer; Sea Dos-gris

Lesser Scaup
Aythya affinis
(AY-thih-ah aff-EYE-niss)

The Lesser Scaup averages about 2 inches shorter than the Greater Scaup.

Aythya — The genus name is from the Greek *aithuia*, a name Aristotle used for some waterbird, not further identified. It is now applied to this group of diving ducks also called Pochards or Bay Ducks. The genus *Aethia*, to which the auklets belong, also stems from this root.

affinis — The specific epithet is Latin for "related to" (*Aythya marila*, the Greater Scaup).

French Name: Petit Morillon

Spanish Names: Pato-boludo Menor; Porrón Menor

Other Names: Lesser Scaup Duck; Common Scaup Duck; Bluebill; Little Bluebill; Marsh Bluebill; Mud Bluebill; River Bluebill; Bay Bluebill; Little Bay Bluebill; Cotton-tail Bluebill; Small Bluebill Duck; Lake Duck; Muskeg Duck; Black Duck; Fall Duck; Summer Duck; Raft Duck; River Duck; Flock Duck; Flocking-fowl; Bluebill Coot; White-winged Teal; Bullhead; Blackhead; Little Blackhead; Creek Blackhead; Brownhead; Small Brownhead; Bullneck; Little Greyback; Blackjack; Broadbill; Broadie; Lesser Broadbill; Freshwater Broadbill; Pond Broadbill; Little Mud Broadbill; River Nun (female); Broadbill; Creek Broadbill; Goshen Broadbill; Shoe; Flying Shoe; Old Boot; Bellarge; Canvasback; Booby; Butterball; Diver; Dummy; Gold-eye; Howden; Milouin' Plongeur; Whistler; She-whistler; Shuffler; River Shuffler; Canard Tête-noire; Canard Caille; Pato del Medio; Pato Morisco; Pato Pechiblanco; Pato Turco

Steller's Eider
Polysticta stelleri
(pol-ih-STICK-tah STEL-er-eye)

Eider stems from *aedhur*, the Icelandic name for the Common Eider. Steller's Eider is named for Georg W. Steller. See specific epithet below.

Polysticta — The genus name is Greek for "many spots" from *poly* (many) and *stiktos* (spotted).

stelleri — The German systematic zoologist

Peter Simon Pallas named this duck in honor of Georg Wilhelm Steller (1709–1746), a German zoologist who collected the type specimen of this species off the coast of Kamchatka in northeast Russia.

French Name: Eider de Steller
Spanish Name: Eider de Steller
Eskimo and Inuit Names: A-noch-a-nee-sak-kuk; Anarnisakak (belly color of face)
Other Names: Lesser Eider Duck; Soldier Duck; Western Duck

Spectacled Eider
Somateria fischeri
(soh-mah-TEER-ih-ah FISH-er-eye)

"An eider that looks like a coal miner who just removed his protective goggles." — Pete Dunne (2006)

The large white eye-patch, rimmed in black, gives this duck its name. The female shows fainter spectacles.

Somateria — The genus name means "wooly body" from the Greek *somatos* (the body) and *erion* (wooly or downy). The reference is to the commercially valuable eiderdown that is gathered from the Common Eiders' nests and used to stuff comforters and pillows.

fischeri — Beginning in 1839, Ilya Vosnesensky spent 10 years collecting birds at various Russian settlements along the coasts of Siberia and Alaska. He took the type specimen of the Spectacled Eider at Saint Michael on the southern shore on Norton Sound, Alaska. Vosnesensky sent his specimens to Johann Friedrich Brandt, Director of the Zoological Museum at the Saint Petersburg Academy. Brandt described the species in 1847, naming it *Fuligula* (*Lampronetta*) *Fischeri* for his colleague at the Moscow Academy, Dr. Johann Gotthelf Fischer von Waldheim (1771–1853).

French Name: Eider à Lunettes
Spanish Name: Eider de Anteojos
Eskimo and Inuit Name: Kaurik (imitative — the way they talk to their young ones)
Other Names: Fischer's Eider; Lesser Eider Duck; Soldier Duck

King Eider
Somateria spectabilis
(soh-mah-TEER-ih-ah speck-TAH-bih-lis)

"The most strikingly beautiful of all the of Arctic birds is undoubtedly the male king eider. His regal plumage warrants fully his royal name." — W. Elmer Ekblaw (1925)

Welsh naturalist Thomas Pennant first described this species under the name King Duck in 1785. In 1828, Fleming introduced the name King Eider which has since replaced Pennant's common name. Ernest Choate wrote that this duck is called the King Eider, because "it has raiment fit for a king." In particular, the male's orange frontal shield suggests a crown. But ornithologist George Miksch Sutton believed the common name was derived from the Inuit word *kingalik* (big nose).

Somateria — The genus name means "wooly body" from the Greek *somatos* (the body) and *erion* (wooly or downy). The reference is to the commercially valuable eiderdown that is gathered from the Common Eiders' nests and used to stuff comforters and pillows.

spectabilis — The specific epithet is Latin for "remarkable, showy, or worth seeing" and refers to the prominent orange knob on the drake's forehead as well as to his colorful plumage. Here is a nice description of the drake:

"Breeding males, with their bold black-and-white upperparts contrasting with their tangerine-blushed breasts and heads whose bulging orange bill and colorful pattern would not seem out of place at a Mardi Gras parade, are unmistakable." — Pete Dunne (2006)

French Names: Eider à Tête Grise; Eider Remarquable
Spanish Name: Eider Real
Inuit Name: King-ahl-ik (big nose)
Other Names: Isle of Shoals Duck; Sea Duck, Eskimo Duck; Mongrel Duck; Passing Duck; King-Duck; King Drake; Bottle-nose Drake; Old King; White-head Coot; Cousin, Wamp's Cousin; Canvasback; Mongrel Drake; King-bird; Kingalik; Warnecootai

Common Eider
Somateria mollissima
(soh-mah-TEER-ih-ah moh-LISS-ih-mah)

Eider stems from *aedhur*, the Icelandic name for this species. The Common Eider is the most abundant sea duck in the world. It also has the most extensive range of the four eider species.

Somateria — The genus name means "wooly body" from the Greek *somatos* (the body) and *erion* (wooly or downy). The reference is to the commercially valuable eiderdown that is gathered from the ducks' nests and used to stuff comforters and pillows.

mollissima — The specific epithet means "very soft" from the Latin *mollis* (soft) plus the superlative suffix *–issima* and refers to the duck's down.

French Name: Eider à Duvet
Spanish Name: Eider Común
British Name: Eider Duck
Eskimo and Inuit Name: Mi't-huk (imitative)
Other Names: American Eider; Canard Eider; Northern Eider; Dresser's Eider; Sea Duck; Sea Ducks and Drakes; Big Sea Duck; Big Saltwater Duck; Husky Duck; Laying Duck; Shoal Duck; Shore Duck; Eskimo Duck; Isle of Shoals Duck; Saint Cuthbert's Duck; Squam Duck; Great Black-and-white Duck; Dusky Duck; Dunter; Dunter Duck; Dunter Goose; Gam Drake; Gambird; Edder; Canvasback; Black and White Coot; Wamp; Pied Wamp; Looby; Canard de Mer; Culverts; Culberduce; Crattick; Colk; Coo-doos; Moiaque Blanche; Moignac; Mooyak; Mojak; Mouniac; Mourriac; Moyac; Moynac; Shoreyer; Siolta

Harlequin Duck
Histrionicus histrionicus
(hiss-trih-OWN-ih-cus)

"Harlequin, well named! Fantastically decorated, but still a thing of beauty. Delightful in color, elegant in form, graceful, in carriage, rightly are its little companies called the "Lords and Ladies" of the waters." — Edward Howe Forbush (1917)

The Harlequin Duck is named for the drake's bizarre color pattern: slate-blue overall with chestnut flanks and odd white splashes outlined in black on the head and body. This showy design suggests the parti-colored tights

Harlequin Duck, Common Eider, and King Eider, by Louis Agassiz Fuertes

and painted face of a harlequin, a theatrical clown, from the Italian *Commedia dell'Arte*. Pete Dunne calls the Harlequin "a duck painted in the pattern and style of Pablo Picasso."

Histrionicus — The genus/species name is from the Latin *histrio* (a stage actor). The striking color pattern of the drake suggests an actor made up to play a part.

French Name: Canard Arlequin
Spanish Name: Pato Arlequín
Eskimo and Inuit Names: Kang-i-auk; Ti-ta-tsik; Aha-lik-nak
Other Names: Rock Duck; Blue Duck; Painted Duck; Circus Duck; Mountain Duck; Glacier Duck; Pie Duck; Surfer Duck; Wood Duck; Old Lord; Lord and Lady Bird; Lords-and-Ladies; Jenny; Imp; Blue-Streak; Hell-diver; Sea Pigeon; Sea Pheasant; Sea Mouse; Harley; Squealer; Squeaker; Canard de Baie; Canard de Roches; Cane de Roche

Surf Scoter
Melanitta perspicillata
(mel-ah-NIT-ah per-spick-ill-AY-tah)

"It was a pretty sight when, under a gray sky, the beautiful long green rolls of surf rose and combed over and the surf scoters came in from the green swells behind to feed in front of the surf and do skillful diving stunts to escape being pounded by the white waterfalls. As the green wall ridged up over their heads they would sit unmoved, but just as the white line of foam began to appear along the crest they would dive, staying under till the surf had broken and the water was level again. When diving through the green rollers near the shore the black bodies of the scoters, paddling feet and all, showed as plainly as beetles in yellow amber." — Florence Merriam Bailey (1916)

Some sources say that scoter is a variation of coot, the name hunters use for these ducks. It may derive from the Old Norse *skoti* (shooter) or *skjota* (to shoot) and refer to their swift flight. Surf refers to the fact that these scoters often feed in or just beyond the breaking waves or ocean surf, as described in the above passage. There the Surf Scoters have little competition from other ducks.

Melanitta — The genus name means "black duck" from the Greek *melas* (black) and *netta* (a duck) and refers to the dark plumage.

perspicillata — The specific epithet is Latin for "conspicuous" or "spectacular," a reference to the drake's multicolored bill that is probably displayed in courtship.

French Name: Macreuse à Front Blanc
Spanish Names: Negreta de Nuca Blanca; Negreta de Marejada
Eskimo and Inuit Names: Ching-ai-yak; Soo-loo-too-ruk
Other Names: Bald-headed Scoter; Surf Scoter; Coot, Bay Coot; Bald Coot; Bald-headed Coot; Bald-pated Coot; Bunk-bill; Blossom-head; Blossom-bill; Blossom-billed Coot; Horse-head Coot; Horse-head; Butter-billed Coot; Butterboat-bill; Butterboat-billed Coot; Button-bill Coot; Hollow-billed Coot; Sea Coot; Patch-head; Patch-head Coot; Patch-poll; Patch-polled Coot; White-head Coot; Rock Coot; River Coot; Surf Coot; Sea Coot; Box Coot; Black Coot; Brown Coot; Gray Coot; Little Gray Coot; King Coot; Spectacled Coot; Speckle-billed Coot; Skunk-bill; Skunk-head Coot; Skunk-head; Skunk-top; Skunk Duck; Niggerhead; Bay Muscovie; Muscle-bill; Picture-bill; Plaster-bill; Baldpate; Basse; Snuff-taker; Diver; Black diver; Bottle-nosed Diver; Sleepy Diver; Whistling Diver; Black Duck; Black Sea-duck; Pied Duck; Indian Duck; Deaf Duck; Sea Duck; Siwash Duck; Spectacled Duck; Squaw-Duck; Surf Duck; Surfer; Booby; Iron Pot; Tar Bucket; Snuff-taker; Google-nose; Morocco Jaw; Pictured-bill; Plaster-bill; Mussel-bill; White-head; Horse-head; Beachcomber; White Scop; Scooter; Surf Scooter; Siwash; Pish-aug; Petit Noir; Gibier Noir; Sac a Plomb; Briseaux de Mer

Velvet Scoter
Melanitta fusca
(mel-ah-NIT-ah FUSS-kah)

This species is named for the drake's matte black plumage suggesting velvet. This scoter is native to Europe, but vagrants probably show up in North America. Formerly considered conspecific with the White-winged Scoter. See next entry.

Melanitta — The genus name means "black duck" from the Greek *melas* (black) and *netta* (a duck) and refers to the dark plumage.

fusca — The specific epithet is from the Latin "dark" or "dusky" and refers to the drake's black plumage. Linnaeus originally described this species in 1758.

French Name: Macreuse Brune
Spanish Name: Negrón Especulado
Other Names: European White-winged Scoter; Double Scoter; Scooter; Scoter Duck; Surf Duck; Great Black Duck; Velvet Duck; Sea Duck; Sea Hen; Surf Duck; Black Diver; Astracannet; Doucker; Whilk

White-winged Scoter
Melanitta deglandi
(mel-ah-NIT-ah deg-LAND-eye)

White-winged refers to the white speculum. In 2019, the AOS split the White-winged Scoter into three species: the Velvet Scoter of Europe, the White-winged Scoter of North America, and Stejneger's Scoter of Siberia. The three were originally described as separate species, but were lumped into a single species in 1920.

Surf Scoter, by Allan C. Brooks

Melanitta — The genus name means "black duck" from the Greek *melas* (black) and *netta* (a duck) and refers to the dark plumage.

deglandi — In 1850, Charles Bonaparte named this species in honor of Dr. Côme Damien Degland (1787–1856), a French ornithologist and author of *Ornithologie Européene* (1849).

French Name: Macreuse à Ailes Blanches

Spanish Names: Negreta de Ala Blanca; Negreta Aliblanca

British Name: Velvet Scoter

Eskimo and Inuit Names: Katklik (chest, good, thick); Tongargakruk (devil)

Other Names: American Velvet Scoter; Lake Huron Scoter; Double Scoter; Scooter; Coot, Bay Coot; Rock Coot; Black Coot; Brown Coot; Gray Coot; Brant Coot; Sea Coot; Bell Coot; Bell-tongue; Bell-tongue Coot; Bull Coot; Pied-winged Coot; White-winged Coot; White-eye Coot; White-eye; Iron-headed Coot; Uncle Sam Coot; White-wing Duck; White-winged Surf Duck; Black Surf Duck; Great Black Duck; Velvet Duck; Squaw Duck; Siwash; Siwash Duck; Channel Duck; Crow Duck; Deaf Duck; Fish Duck; Ice Duck; Sea Duck; Salt-water Duck; Horse-head Duck; Indian Duck; Winter Duck; Bay Muscovie; Black Diver; Brass-winged Diver; White-winged Diver; Big Widgeon; Assemblyman; Half-moon Eye; White-wing; White-winger; Bull White-wing; Black White-wing; Gray White-wing; Great White-wing; May White-wing; Great May White-wing; Eastern White-wing; Booby; Brant; Black Brant; Sea Brant; Black Whistler; Astracannet; Basque; Beachcomber; Niggerhead; Iron Pot; Tar Bucket; Sea Cott; Sea-horse; Canard d'Hiver; Canard Francais; Fausse Moiaque; Fausse Moniac; Gibier Noir

Stejneger's Scoter
Melanitta stejnegeri
(mel-ah-NIT-ah stej-NEG-er-eye)

This species is named for Dr. Leonhard Hess Stejneger, a Norwegian ornithologist and herpetologist. Stejneger's Scoter occurs in Siberia, but it is a regular visitor to Alaska in spring. Formerly considered conspecific with the White-winged Scoter. See previous entry.

Melanitta — The genus name means "black duck" from the Greek *melas* (black) and *netta* (a duck) and refers to the dark plumage.

stejnegeri — Robert Ridgway originally described this species in 1887 and named it in honor of Leonhard Hess Stejneger (1851–1943). See common name above.

French Name: Macreuse de Sibérie

Spanish Name: Negrón Siberiano

Other Name: Siberian Scoter

Black Scoter
Melanitta americana
(mel-ah-NIT-ah ah-mer-ih-CANE-ah)

This scoter is named for the drake's entirely black plumage, showing no white as in the other two species. This is the only all-black duck in North America. Once known as American Scoter, it was formerly considered conspecific with the Common Scoter (*M. nigra*) of Eurasia.

Melanitta — The genus name means "black duck" from the Greek *melas* (black) and *netta* (a duck) and refers to the dark plumage.

americana — The specific epithet is Modern Latin for "of America."

French Name: Macreuse à Bec Jaune

Spanish Name: Negreta Negra

Eskimo and Inuit Name: Kukummyarak (whistling duck)

Other Names: American Black Scoter; American Scoter Duck; Black Duck; Gray Duck; Scoter Duck; Surf Duck; Sea Duck; Deaf Duck; Sleigh-bell Duck; Indian Duck; Siwash; Siwash Duck; Whistling Duck; Sea Hen; Bay Muscovie; Black Diver; Butter-nosed Diver; Sleepy Diver; Whistling Diver; Coot, Black Coot; Black Sea Coot; Sea Coot; Rock Coot; King Coot; Broad-billed Coot; Hollow-billed Coot; Pumpkin-blossom Coot; Courting Coot; Dumb Coot; Whistling Coot; Gray Coot; Smutty Coot; Smutty; Brown Coot; Browny Coot; Butter-billed Coot; Butter-bill; Black Butter-bill; Butter-nose; Butter-nosed Coot; Yellow-billed Coot; Red-billed Coot; Copper-nose; Copper-bill; Yellow-nose; Yellow-bill; Fizzy, Beachcomber; Tar Bucket; Iron Pot; Booby; Willow-legs; Doucker; Gibier Noir; Macreuse; Petit Noir; Siffleur; Whilk; Bec Jaune

Long-tailed Duck
Clangula hyemalis
(KLANG-you-lah high-ah-MAIL-iss)

"Males are showy and elegantly rakish, dressed to go out on the town — a designer duck . . . The male's signature and namesake characteristic is the long flagellum-like tail that often curls up out of the water (or may lie flush). Despite its compact body, the tail makes the male look elegantly long." — Pete Dunne (2006)

The common name refers to the drake's extended central tail feathers, similar to those of the Northern Pintail. These tail streamers may add as much as 9 ½-inches to the duck's overall length. Formerly known as Oldsquaw. See sidebar 5.

Clangula — The genus name means "little shouter" or "little babbler" from the the Latin *clangere* (to resound) plus a diminutive suffix. It derives from the Greek *klagge* (the cries of cranes) and *klangē* (cry or scream). Like many of the folk names, the genus name also refers to this species' vocalizations, as described here.

"Like a crowd of gossiping old women these ducks gabble and scold among themselves all the year round, for in winter when most voices are hushed, they are the noisiest birds that visit us . . . Most of the duck's popular names, as well as its scientific one, allude to its noisy, talkative habit." — Neltje Blanchan (1898)

hyemalis — The specific epithet is from the Latin *hiemalis* (wintry or of winter). This refers to the fact that this breeder of the high Arctic occurs only as a winter visitor in the lower 48 states: Oldsquaws, or long-tailed ducks, as I should prefer to have them called, are lively, restless, happy-go-lucky little ducks, known to most of us as hardy and cheery visitors of our winter seacoasts, associated in our minds with cold, gray skies, snow squalls, and turbulent wintry waves. — Arthur Cleveland Bent (1925)

French Names: Canard Kakawi; Harelde Kakawi

Spanish Names: Pato de Cola Larga; Pato Colilargo; Pato Havelda

Eskimo and Inuit Names: Arangurit (imitative); Sou-sou sally (imitative)

Other Names: Long-tail; Long-tailed Hareld; Northern Hareld; Haveld; Winter Duck; Ice Duck; Noisy Duck; Singing Duck; Organ Duck; Callithumpian Duck; Squeaking Duck; Pheasant-tailed Duck; Sharp-tailed Duck; Swallow-tailed Duck; Injun Duck; Indian Duck; Squaw Duck; Squaw; Long-tailed Squaw; Siwash; Siwash Duck; Butterfly Coot; Swallow-tailed Sheldrake; Pintail; Sea Pintail; Sea Pheasant; Cockertail; Hell's Chicken; Calloo; Calaw; Coween; Cockawee; Kakawi; Cacouy; Kla-how-ya; Hound; John Connolly; Uncle Huldy; My Aunt Huldy; Old Billie; Old Injun; Old Granny; Old Molly; Knockmolly; Mommy; Old Wife; Alewife; Aleck; South-southerly; South-south Southerly; South-southerland; Sou-easterly; Sou' southerland; Souwester; Ow-owly; Jackowly; Hah-ha-way; Scolder; Scoldenore; Darcall; Coldie; Quandy; Pigeon; Coal-and-candlelight; Col-candle Wick; Mealy Bird; Pine Knot; Lightwood Knot; Canard a Longue Queue

Long-tailed Duck, by Archibald Thornburn

Bufflehead
Bucephala albeola
(bue-SEF-ah-lah al-BEE-oh-lah)

"The propriety of applying the name "spirit duck" to this sprightly little duck will be appreciated by anyone who has watched it in its natural surroundings, floating buoyantly, like a beautiful apparition, on the smooth surface of some pond or quiet stream, with its striking contrast of black and white in its body plumage and with the glistening metallic tints in its soft fluffy head, relieved by a broad splash of the purest white; it seems

Sidebar 5
Political Correctness vs. Avian Nomenclature

"If there is one thing for which the old squaw is justly notorious it is for its voice. It certainly is a noisy and garrulous species at all seasons, for which it has received various appropriate names, such as old squaw, old injun, old wife, noisy duck, hound, etc. The names south-southerly, cockawee, quandy, coal and candle light, as well as a variety of Indian and Eskimo names have been applied to it as suggesting its well-known notes; all of which are more or less crude imitations of its notes, which are difficult to describe satisfactorily, but when once heard are afterwards easily recognized, for they are loud, clearly uttered, and very distinctive." — Arthur Cleveland Bent (1925)

The Long-tailed Duck was formerly known as Oldsquaw in North America. As described above, it got its name, because it is a very vocal duck, whose melodious calls, sometimes compared to the baying of distant hounds or the skirling of bagpipes, can carry for a half mile or more across the water. The notes are sometimes rendered as: *owl-omelette* or *ow-owdle-oo* or *ahr-ahr-ahroulit.* In 2000, the AOU changed the evocative American common name to the prosaic British one, Long-tailed Duck. This is perhaps the only bird to have its name changed, because it was deemed to be politically incorrect, although the AOU says it would not consider to change a long-standing common name for that reason. But the nomenclature committee went ahead in this case, because there was an alternate common name already in wide use. The explanation was "to conform with English usage in other parts of the world." But the catalyst for this event was a petition filed by U.S. Fish and Wildlife biologists, because they assumed the name Oldsquaw was offensive to American Indians. The biologists were working on a conservation management strategy for this declining species in Alaska, and they needed the help and cooperation of the local Indians. But it was the Cree Indians who originated the name in the first place.

---

indeed a spirit of the waters, as it plunges, quickly beneath the surface and bursts out again in full flight, disappearing in the distance with a blur of whirring wings." — Arthur Cleveland Bent (1925)

Bufflehead is shortened from "buffalo-head" and refers to the duck's large, puffy head.

Bucephala — The genus name means "ox head" from the Greek *bous* (an ox) and *kephale* (head), and also refers to the duck's large head.

albeola — The specific epithet means "little white one" from the Latin *albus* (white) and –*olus*, a diminutive suffix. The reference is to the drake's mostly white plumage including a white head patch.

French Name: Petit Garrot
Spanish Name: Pato Monja
Eskimo and Inuit Names: Chirr-u-num; Sakh-oi-a; Mith-i-methruh

Other Names: Buffel's Head Duck; Buffle-headed Duck; Buffet-headed Duck; Buffalo-head; Buffalo-headed Duck; Buffle Duck; Black and White; Little Black and White Duck; Pied Duck; Pinto Duck; Little Brown

Bufflehead, by Allan C. Brooks

Duck; Fall Duck; Spring Duck; Spirit; Spirit Duck; Conjuring Duck; Ice Duck; Wood Duck; Butter Duck; Butterball Duck; Bumblebee Duck; Bumblebee Coot; Bumblebee Dipper; Dipper-duck; Dipper; Cock Dipper; Die-dipper; Horsefly Dipper; Pocket Dipper; Robin Dipper, Scotch Dipper; Scotch-duck; Scotch Teal; Scotchman; Fishing Bird; White Rabbit; Shotbag; Shot-eater; Bighead; Dopper; Dapper; Diver; Hell-diver; Sleepy Diver; Butter-bowl; Butter-box; Butterball; Butter-back; Skunkhead; Wool-head; Whistler; Marionette; Pato Pinto

Common Goldeneye
Bucephala clangula
(bue-SEF-ah-lah KLANG-you-lah)

Their bright yellow irises give the goldeneyes their name. The Common Goldeneye has a more extensive range than Barrow's Goldeneye.

Bucephala — The genus name means "ox head" from the Greek *bous* (an ox) and *kephale* (head), and refers to the Bufflehead's large head. The genus was originally erected for that species.

clangula — The specific epithet means "little noise" from the Latin *clangor* (a noise) plus a diminutive suffix. The name is said to refer to the whistling sound the wings make when the ducks are in flight.

French Name: Garrot à Oeil d'Or
Spanish Names: Pato Chillon de Ojos Dorados; Ojodorado Común
Eskimo and Inuit Names: Ya-sikh; Han-ne
Other Names: American Goldeneye; European Goldeneye; Goldeneyed Duck; Spirit Duck; Tree Duck; Black Duck; Pie Duck; Pied Duck; Winter Duck; Ice Duck; Wood Duck; Diving Duck; Butterball Duck; Conjuring Duck; Pork Duck; Fiddler Duck; Gowdy Duck; Oyster Duck; Grey-headed Duck; Brown-headed Duck; Whistle-Duck; Whistle-wing Duck; Whistler Duck; Diver; Whistle Diver; King Diver; Whistler; Pied Whistler; Brass-eyed Whistler; Brass-eye; Whiffler; Rattle-wings; Brass-eye; Whistle-wing; Great-head; Iron-head; Cobhead; Cub-head; Copper-head; Bull-head; Smoky Pie; Pie Bird; Smoky Pie Bird; Pied Wigeon; Popping Wigeon; Freshwater Wigeon; Whiteside; Garrot; Gold-eye; Golden-eyed Garrot; Goldie; Buffle-headed Garrot; Curre; Pied Curre; Jingling Curre; Jingler; Sizzle-britches; Caille; Canard Caille; Canard Canadien; Canard à Grosse Tête; Canard Yankee; Pisque; Pixe; Plongeon; Plongeur; Merry-wing; Morillon; Mussel Cracker; Doucker

Barrow's Goldeneye
Bucephala islandica
(bue-SEF-ah-lah ice-LAND-ih-kah)

In 1832, John Richardson and William Swainson described what they believed to be a new species of duck from a specimen collected by Thomas Drummond in the Rocky Mountains. They gave it the scientific name *Clangula Barrovi* and called it the Rocky Mountain Garrot. Swainson wrote that the "specific appellation [was] intended as a tribute to Mr. Barrow's varied talents, and his unwearied exertions for the promotion of science." However, German naturalist J.F. Gmelin had already described the species in 1789, naming it *Anas islandica*. Gmelin's species name takes priority, but arctic explorer Sir John Barrow (1764–1848) is still commemorated by the common name. Barrow's Goldeneye is

Common Goldeneye, by Louis Agassiz Fuertes

named after Sir John Barrow (1764–1848), arctic explorer and chief founder of the Royal Geographical Society. Point Barrow, Cape Barrow, and the Barrow Straits are also named in his honor.

Bucephala — The genus name means" ox head" from the Greek *bous* (an ox) and *kephale* (head), and refers to the Bufflehead's large head. The genus was originally erected for that species.

islandica — The specific epithet is Modern Latin for "of Iceland," within this duck's breeding range. It also nests in Labrador and in the Rocky Mountains.

French Name: Garrot de Barrow

Spanish Names: Pato Islándico de Ojos Dorados; Ojodorado Islándico

Other Names: Rocky Mountain Goldeneye; Rocky Mountain Garrot; Butterball Duck; Tree Duck; Wood Duck; Pie Duck; Pie-bird; Cockpyeduck; Black and White Diver; Whistle-diver; Whistle-wing; Whistler; Pied Whistler; Pisque; Plongeur; Tete Marteau

Smew
Mergellus albellus
(mur-GEL-lus al-BEL-lus)

The English name is believed to be from a lost word meaning "small." The Smew is the smallest species of merganser, and the name is sometimes written smew merganser. Or, its name could be a contraction of sea mew (gull).

Mergellus — The genus name means "little diver" or "little merganser" from the Latin *mergus*, a name used by Pliny for some diving bird plus the diminutive suffix –*ellus*.

albellus — The specific epithet is Latin for "little white one" from *albus* (white) plus a diminutive suffix. The reference is to the male's mostly white plumage.

French Name: Harle Piette

Spanish Name: Mergo Menor

Other Names: Smee; Smee Duck; Weasel Duck; Weasel Coot; Red-headed Smew; White-headed Goosander; White Merganser; White Wigeon; Vare Wigeon; White Nun; Pied Diver; Magpie Diver; Lough Diver; Small Herring Bar

Hooded Merganser
Lophodytes cucullatus
(low-FOD-ih-teez kuk-ul-LAY-tus)

Merganser means "diving goose" from the Latin *mergus* (a diver) and *anser* (a goose). The showy fan-shaped crest, that can be raised or lowered according to mood, gives this duck its name.

Lophodytes — The genus name means "crested diver" from the Greek *lophos* (crest) and *dytes* (a diver).

cucullatus — The specific epithet is Latin for "hooded."

French Name: Bec-scie Couronné

Spanish Name: Mergo de Caperuza

Other Names: Fan-crested Duck; Round-crested Duck; Tree Duck; Wood Duck; Frog Duck; Beaver Duck; Little Saw-bill Duck; Sawbill Teal; Fish Duck; Little Fish Duck; California Fish Duck; Pied Duck; Shell-Duck; Cock-robin; Cock-robin Duck; Crow Duck; Diving Duck; Pheasant Duck; Pheasant; Water Pheasant; Hooded Sheldrake; Little Sheldrake; Mud Sheldrake; Pied Sheldrake; Pond Sheldrake; Swamp Sheldrake; Summer Sheldrake; Pickaxe; Pickaxe Sheldrake; Wood Sheldrake; Shelhard; Shell-bird; Bastard Teal; Plongeon; Plongeon Diver; Saw-bill; Saw-bill Diver; Hell-diver; Moss-head; Hairyhead; Hairy-crown; Wire-crown; Fanhead; Tow-head; Cottonhead; Cottontop; Sharpy; Spike-bill; Zipper Beak; Smew; Tadpole; Lawn Dart; Indian; Back-warmer; Goosander; Mergansa de Caperuza; Di-dapper; Strawbill; Harle; Hoodie; Hooder; Hoodrat; Snowl; Zin-zin; Hoot-amaganzy; Bec-scie; Bec-scie de Cypriere; Bec-scie du Lac; Whistler; Wilte Ent

Hooded Merganser, by Louis Agassiz Fuertes

Common Merganser
Mergus merganser
(MER-gus mer-GAN-ser)

Merganser means "diving goose." See specific epithet below. Common may or may not be an appropriate name for this species. The Common Merganser has a very extensive range across the Northern Hemisphere, but so does the Red-breasted Merganser. In migration, the Red-breasted Mergansers often greatly outnumber the Common Mergansers. But the numbers may be reversed on their wintering grounds. Formerly known as American Merganser.

Mergus — The genus name is Latin for "a diver," a name Pliny used for some diving bird, not further identified. All of the mergansers are skilled divers, pursuing prey underwater or submerging to escape danger.

merganser — The specific epithet means "diving goose" from the Latin *mergus* (a diver) and *anser* (a goose).

French Name: Grand Bec-scie
Spanish Name: Mergo Mayor
British Name: Goosander
Eskimo and Inuit Names: Chu-vi-ach; Chung-ung-e-koo-loo-ghearch
Other Names: Buff-breasted Merganser; Greater Merganser; Green-headed Goosander; American Goosander; American Sheldrake; Winter Sheldrake; Buff-breasted Sheldrake; Freshwater Sheldrake; Great Lake Sheldrake; River Sheldrake; Swamp Sheldrake; Big Sheldrake; Pond Sheldrake; North Carolina Sheldrake; Bracket Sheldrake; Bracket; Spike; Tweezer; Weaser Sheldrake; Weaser; Shell Bird; Shell-Duck; Winter shell-Duck; Shelhard; Saw-bill; Big Sawbill; Sawn Eb; Sawyer; Jacksaw; Dun Diver; Morocco-head; Fish-duck; Big Fish Duck; Fishing Duck; Big Winter Duck; Fisherman; Spear Duck; Lawn Dart; Gony; Gaspard; Gosset; Gossard; Harle; Dun Diver; Breakhorn; Velvet-breast; Pied Wigeon; Spear Wigeon; Sparkling Fowl; Sparling Fowl; Skunk; Land Cormorant; Pheasant; Water-pheasant; Winter Pheasant; Bec-scie; Big Bec-scie; Rantock; Wilte Ent; Wood Duck

~

Red-breasted Merganser
Mergus serrator
(MER-gus ser-AY-tor)

The male's speckled chestnut-red chest gives this duck its name.

Mergus — The genus name is Latin for "diver", a name Pliny used for some diving bird, not further identified. All of the mergansers are skilled divers, pursuing prey underwater or submerging to escape danger.

serrator — The specific epithet is Latin for "sawer" and refers to the serrated edges of the bill, adapted for gripping slippery prey.

French Name: Bec-scie à Poitrine Rousse
Spanish Name: Mergo Copetón
Eskimo and Inuit Names: Ak-pak-aru-a-yook (runs like a man on top of water); Payit (runs on top of water to take off); Pi-uk (refers to nest shaped like a Pi)
Other Names: Red-breasted Goosander; Shellbird; Shelduck; Shelhard; Red-breasted Sheldrake; Spring Sheldrake; Saltwater Sheldrake; Pied Sheldrake; Pond Sheldrake; Indian Sheldrake; Long Island Sheldrake; Spanish Drake; Sawneb; Sawyer; Saw-bill; Common Saw-bill; Sawbill Wigeon; Saw-bill Duck; Popping Wigeon; Spear Wigeon; Spear Drake; Herald; Herald Duck; Earl Duck; Harle Duck; Diving Duck; Scale Duck; Red-headed Duck; Fish Duck; Little Fish Duck; Red-breasted Fish Duck; Fishing-Duck; Fisherman; Garbill; Sandbill; Hairy-crown; Hairyhead; Fuzzyhead; Robin; Sea Robin; Pheasant; Lesser Toothed Diver; Grey Diver; Hell-diver; Lawn Dart; Harle; Herle; Land Harlan; Whistler; Rodge; Bardrake; Jack; Tuke; Mergansa Pechirroja; Bec-scie; Sea Bec-scie; Bec-scie de Mer; Betsy

~

Masked Duck
Nomonyx dominicus
(no-MON-icks doh-MIN-ih-cus)

The male's black face, contrasting with the chestnut-brown head and neck, give this duck its name.

Nomonyx — The genus name means "orderly nail" from the Greek *nomos* (orderly or regular) and *onux* (a nail or a claw). The nail referred to is at the tip of the upper mandible and is described as small, narrow, and linear.

dominica — The specific epithet is Modern

Latin for "of Santo Domingo" (now Hispaniola), where the type specimen was collected.

French Name: Erismature Routoutou
Spanish Name: Pato Enmascarado
Other Names: White-winged Lake Duck; Quail Duck; Squat Duck; Duck-and-Teal; Canard Routoutou; Canard Zombie; Pato Agostero; Pato Chico; Pato Chorizo; Pato Codorniz; Pato Criollo; Pato Espinoso

Ruddy Duck
Oxyura jamaicensis
(OCKS-ih-YOU-rah jah-may-ih-SEN-sis)

The Ruddy Duck is named for the drake's rich rusty red color in breeding plumage.

Oxyura — The genus name means "sharp tail" from the Greek *oxys* (sharp) and *oura* (tail) and refers to the long, pointed tail which is often cocked upright.

jamaicensis — The specific epithet is Modern Latin for "of Jamaica" where the type specimen was taken.

French Name: Canard Roux
Spanish Name: Pato Tepalcate
Other Names: North American Ruddy Duck; Bumblebee Duck; Bumble-bee Buzzer; Bumblebee Coot; Red-backed Duck; Fall Duck; Chunk Duck; Deaf Duck; Spine-tail Duck; Dumpling Duck; Swamp Duck; Dummy Duck; Fool Duck; Daub Duck; Rubber Duck; Sleepy Duck; Butter Duck; Butterball; Butter Bowl; Spoon-billed Butterball; Spoonbill; Salt-water Teal; Brown Teal; Diving Teal; Brown Diving Teal; Gray Teal; Goose Teal; Goose Widgeon; Pintail; Bristle-tail; Sprig-tail; Stiff-tailed Wigeon; Stiff-tail; Stick-tail; Wire-tail; Cock-tail; Muskrat Chick; Batter-scoot; Blatherskite; Blather-scoot; Bladder-scoot; Blackjack; Bobbler; Booby; Booby Coot; Wigeon-Coot; Creek Coot; Pond Coot; Horse-turd Coot; Quill-tail; Quill-tailed Coot; Heavy-tailed Coot; Sleepy Coot; Broad-billed Coot; Sleepy Brother; Sleepyhead; Sleepy Dick; Diver; Ruddy Diver; Red Diver; Dun-Diver; Dip-tailed Diver; Dip-tail; Dipper; Mud-dipper; Horse-turd Dipper; Broad-billed Buzzer; Broad-billed Dipper; Broadbill; Sleepy Broadbill; Bluebill; Broad-kite; Dicky; Dinky; Dun-Bird; Dumb-Bird; Bullneck; Water Partridge; Spatter; Stub-and-twist; Steel-head; Tough-head, Hickory-head, Hard-tack; Hard-head, Hard-headed Broadbill, Shot-pouch, Sinker; Biddy; Murre; Rook, Rudder Bird, Roody; Noddy; Noddy Paddy; Leather-back; Leather breeches; Paddy; Paddy-whack; Dapper; Dopper; Dickey; Dinkey; God-damn; Flying Rat; Greaser; Little Soldier; Light-wood Knot; Marteau; Coucouraime; Canard Plongeon; Pato Chorizo; Pato Espinoso; Pato Rojo

Order Galliformes

Family Cracidae
Guans

Plain Chachalaca
Ortalis vetula
(OR-tah-liss VET-you-lah)

Chachalaca is the Nahuatl (Mexican) Indian name for this bird and is imitative of its call. Plain describes the overall dull olive-brown color, and the fact that it lacks the ornamental crests and colorful bare facial skin of some of its tropical relatives.

Ortalis — The genus name is Greek for "a young chicken," which this species somewhat looks like. Pete Dunne says it "resembles an emaciated long-tailed turkey.

vetula — The specific epithet is Latin for "a little old woman" referring to the fact that this species is very noisy.

Mountain Quail, by Allan C. Brooks

"To say the bird is noisy sells it short. Raucous is more accurate, and if you are so unfortunate as to be close when a flock erupts, a better description might be ear-splitting." — Pete Dunne (2006)
French Name: Ortalide Chacamel
Spanish Names: Chachalaca Común; Chachalaca Olivácea
Other Names: Common Chachalaca; Mexican Chachalaca

Family Odontophoridae
New World Quail

Quail is from the Old French *quaille* and stems from *quackel*, the Middle Dutch word for quail. *Quackel* in turn comes from the verb *quacken* (to croak) and also gives us the word "quack." Ultimately the name refers to the call notes of the European migratory quail (*Coturnix coturnix*).

Mountain Quail
Oreortyx pictus
(or-ee-OR-ticks PICK-tus)

The Mountain Quail is named for its nesting habitat in montane forests at altitudes from 1500 to 10,000 feet. It is unique among North American quail in that in early fall it migrates on foot to the lower foothills for the winter.

Oreortyx — The genus name means "mountain quail" from Greek *oros* (a mountain) and *ortyx* (a quail).

pictus — The specific epithet is Latin for "painted" and refers to the showy color pattern of chestnut throat and belly, gray breast, and white-barred flanks. Ernest A. Choate wrote, "its plumage appears to be the work of an artist in color."

French Name: Colin des Montagnes
Spanish Name: Codorniz de Montaña
Other Names: Painted Quail; Plumed Quail; San Pedro Quail; Mountain Partridge; Plumed Partridge

Northern Bobwhite
Colinus virginianus
(koh-LINE-us ver-jin-ih-AY-nus)

The call of Bob-white is one of the cheeriest sounds in nature. Nearby, it commands attention; distant, it harmonizes with other sounds of summer, yet never palls upon the ear. It names the bird.

"Northerners call him Quail; Southerners, Partridge; but he has named himself and ornithologists have decided that he is the prior authority." — Edward Howe Forbush (1917)

Bobwhite is onomatopoetic for the male's song, often rendered *bob-white* or *bob-bob-white*. Northern distinguishes this species from several Central American relatives, such as the Black-throated Bobwhite (*C. nigrogulais*) and the Crested Bobwhite (*C. cristatus*). The Masked Bobwhite (*C. v. ridgwayi*), an endangered subspecies named for the male's black face, was formerly considered a full species. Its subspecific epithet honors Robert Ridgway (1850–1929), the Founder President of the AOU.

Colinus — The genus name is the Latinized form of the Spanish word *colin*, derived from the Nahuatl (Mexican) Indian *zolin*, (a quail).

virginianus — The specific epithet is Modern Latin for "of Virginia," the colony where the type specimen was probably obtained.

French Name: Colin de Virginie
Spanish Name: Codorniz-cotui Norteña
Other Names: Quail; American Quail; Maryland Quail; Virginian Quail; Quail-on-Toast; Bob-white Quail; Common Bobwhite; Florida Bobwhite; Texan Bobwhite; Partridge; American Partridge; Common American Partridge; Maryland Partridge; Virginia Partridge; Colin; American Colin; Virginian Colin; Bodreesel; Caille; Codorniz; Feldhinkel; Perdrix; Quail-die

Scaled Quail
Callipepla squamata
(kal-ih-PEP-lah skway-MAY-tah)

The blue-gray contour feathers of the breast and mantle are edged in black, giving the plumage a fish scale pattern.

Callipepla — The genus name means "beautifully adorned" or "beautifully dressed" from Greek *kallos* (beautiful) and *peplos* (a ceremonial robe) referring to the striking color pattern of the plumage.

squamata — The specific epithet is from Latin *squamatus* (scaled).

French Name: Colin Écaillé
Spanish Name: Codorniz Escamosa
Other Names: Cotton-top; Cotton-top Quail; Blue Quail; Blue Racer; Mexican Quail; Top-knot Quail; Scaled Partridge; Scaly; Codorniz Azul; Codorniz Crestiblanca

California Quail
Callipepla californica
(kal-ih-PEP-lah kal-ih-FOR-nih-cah)

The state bird of California, this quail is named for its range along the Pacific coast from southern Oregon to Baja California.

Northern Bobwhite, by Louis Agassiz Fuertes

Callipepla — The genus name means "beautifully adorned" or "beautifully dressed" from Greek *kallos* (beautiful) and *peplos* (a ceremonial robe) referring to the striking color pattern of the plumage.
californica — The specific epithet is Modern Latin for "of California."
French Name: Colin de Californie
Spanish Name: Codorniz Californiana
Other Names: Valley Quail; Catalina Quail; San Lucas Quail; San Quintin Quail; Crested Quail; Helmet Quail; Top-knot Quail; California Partridge; Valley Partridge

Gambel's Quail
Callipepla gambelii
(kal-ih-PEP-lah gam-BELL-ih-eye)

This quail is named for Dr. William Gambel

Gambel's Quail, by Allan C. Brooks

(1823–1849), a Philadelphia physician and protégé of Thomas Nuttall. Actually, Gambel named the bird for himself, which is considered

---

Sidebar 6
Gambel's Faux Pas

Some people believe scientists name organisms for themselves, but that is simply not done in the scientific community. So it is curious that William Gambel would name a quail for himself. But under the circumstances, he can be forgiven as explained here:

"So, the best way to be immortalized is to find a new bird and name it after yourself, right? Actually, no; that violates one of the longstanding prohibitions in the world of nomenclature . . . It's fine if a friend, admirer, or associate names a species for you, but it's considered beyond tacky to do it yourself. Which is why William Gambel may have gone blushing to his early grave." — Scott Weidensaul *Of a Feather* (2007)

In 1841, Gambel headed west for California. Travelling on the Santa Fe Trail through New Mexico, he discovered a chickadee that was new to science. It was eventually named *Parus* (now *Poecile*) *gambeli* in his honor, and is commonly known as the Mountain Chickadee. Then Gambel took the Old Spanish Trail through Nevada, where he collected an attractive quail with plumage strikingly patterned in gray, chestnut, and black and sporting a jaunty topknot that curves forward like a question mark. Gambel wrote the following observation:

We met with small flocks of this handsome species some distance west [*sic*] of California, in the month of November, inhabiting the most barren brushy plains . . .

Here, where a person would suppose it to be impossible for any animal to subsist, they were running about in small flocks of five or six, occasionally uttering a low guttural call of recognition, sometimes of several notes, very different from that of the common species. When flying they utter a loud sharp whistle, and conspicuously display the long crest.

Gambel thought that his mentor Thomas Nuttall had described this species during the Wyeth expedition and had named it for him. So, when Gambel published his description of the bird, he labeled it "Gambel's quail." Only Nuttall hadn't, in fact, collected this quail, nor had he named it for his friend. Gambel's description was the first to be published, and under the rules of priority his name for it became official. Gambel had inadvertently named this new species for himself.

> **Sidebar 7**
> **Harlequin Quail or Fool Quail**
>
> "One of the handsomest and certainly the most oddly marked of the North American quails presents a bizarre appearance when closely examined; one look at its conspicuously marked face would brand it as a clown among birds; its dark-colored breast is contrary to the laws of protective coloration and would make it very conspicuous on open ground. But when one tries to find it in its native haunts, squatting close to the ground among thick underbrush, weeds, and grass, one realizes that its dark belly and spotted flanks are completely concealed, that the grotesquely painted face becomes obliterated among the sharp lights and shadows, and that the prettily marked back matches its surroundings so well that the bird is nearly invisible." — Arthur Cleveland Bent (1932)
>
> This species' former name, as well as the nickname Painted Quail, are quite appropriate for its bold and bizarre color pattern as described above. The names Fool Quail and Fool Hen have been unfairly applied for the bird's seemingly trusting nature. They allow very close approach, refusing to flush until almost stepped on. But the birds don't behave this way, because they are foolishly tame. They are relying on their primary defense of freezing and blending in with their surroundings. Pete Dunne wrote, "Males look like oval rocks dressed for Mardi Gras; females look like oval rocks dressed in fallen oak leaves."

a serious breach of etiquette in scientific circles. See Gambel's Faux Pas. He was the first ornithologist to collect extensively in California.

Callipepla — The genus name means "beautifully adorned" or "beautifully dressed" from Greek *kallos* (beautiful) and *peplos* (a ceremonial robe) referring to the striking color pattern of the plumage.

gambelii — The specific epithet commemorates William Gambel. See common name above.

French Name: Colin de Gambel
Spanish Name: Codorniz de Gambel
Other Names: Arizona Quail; Desert Quail; Gambel's Valley Quail; Olanthe Quail; Codorniz Desertica; Manu-kapapulu

Montezuma Quail
Cyrtonyx montezumae
(SER-toe-nicks mon-teh-ZOO-me)

The Montezuma Quail is named for the Aztec emperor of Mexico, where this species is native. It reaches our area in southern Arizona and New Mexico, and in southwestern Texas. Until 1957, it was known as Mearns's Quail for Dr. Edgar Alexander Mearns, a U.S. Army surgeon, field naturalist, and a founder of the AOU, then Harlequin Quail for the male's bizarre black and white facial pattern suggesting a "harlequin-patterned party mask." The markings on the bird's face reminded nature photographer Leonard Lee Rue III "of a diagram for highway intersections and clover-leaves." The AOU changed the name to Montezuma Quail in 1983.

Cyrtonyx — The specific epithet means "curved claw" from the Greek *kyrtos* (curved) and *onyx* (a claw) and refers to the long, curved claws, adapted for digging down 3 to 4 inches into hard soil to reach their staple food of lily bulbs and tubers.

montezumae — The specific epithet commemorates Montezuma (1480–1520), the emperor of Mexico at the time of the Spanish conquest.

Montezuma Quail, by Louis Agassiz Fuertes

French Name: Colin Arlequin
Spanish Name: Codorniz de Moctezuma
Other Names: Mearns's Harlequin Quail; Fool Quail; Crazy Quail; Fool Hen; Squat Quail; Black Quail; Painted Quail; Cincoreal Quail; Massena Quail; Massena Partridge; Harlequin; Codorniz Pinta; Codorniz Encinara

Family Phasianidae
Upland Gamebirds

Chukar
Alectoris chukar
(ah-LEK-tore-iss choo-KAR)

Chukar is imitative of this partridge's call from the Hindi name for the bird. See specific epithet below.
Alectoris — The genus name is Greek for "a domestic hen."
chukar — The specific epithet is from the Hindi name for the bird, *chukor*, which is imitative of the call.
French Name: Perdrix Choukar
Spanish Name: Periz Chucar
Other Names: Chukor; Gray Partridge; Rock Partridge; Indian Hill Partridge; Red-legged Partridge; Redleg

Himalayan Snowcock
Tetraogallus himalayensis
(tet-rah-oh-GAL-us him-ah-LAY-en-sis)

Snowcock refers to the fact that this is a chicken-like bird whose habitat is snowy alpine meadows at elevations between 8000 and 10,000 feet. Himalayan refers to this species' natural range in the Himalaya Mountains of central Asia, including India, Nepal, Tibet, and Pakistan. It is on the North American checklist, because a small population (fewer than 500 birds) is established in the Ruby Mountains of northeast Nevada. In 1963, the Nevada Division of Wildlife imported birds from Pakistan, releasing nineteen into the wild and initiating a captive breeding program. Annual releases were made from 1970 to 1979, and the species was established by the early 1980s.
Tetraogallus — The genus name means "grouse chicken" from the Greek *tetraon* (a gamebird, particularly a grouse) and the Latin *gallus* (a chicken or a cock).
himalayensis — The specific epithet is Modern Latin for "of the Himalayas" where the species naturally occurs.
French Name: Tetraogalle de l'Himalaya
Spanish Name: Perdigallo Himalayo
Other Name: Snow Partridge

Gray Partridge
Perdix perdix
(PER-dicks)

Partridge is derived from *perdix*, the Latin word for "a partridge." Perdix in turn is a proper name from a character in Greek mythology. See details below. Gray is the dominant color of this bird's plumage.
Perdix — The genus/species name derives from the Latin word for "a partridge" from a proper name. According to Greek legend, Perdix was to apprentice under his uncle, the inventor Daedalus. Perdix became quite a gifted inventor himself, which made his uncle very jealous. The mean old man pushed his nephew off the top of the Acropolis, but the goddess Athena turned Perdix into a partridge before he hit the ground. It is said that the partridge always flies low and nests on the ground, because it remembers the traumatic experience of being thrown off the Acropolis.
French Name: Perdrix Grise
Spanish Name: Perdiz Pardilla
Other Names: Grey Bird; Hun; Hunky; Hungy; Hungarian Partridge; Common Partridge; Brown Partridge; Small Partridge; Mountain Partridge; European Partridge; European Gray Partridge; English Partridge; Bohemian Partridge; Patrick; Redtail; Stumpey

Ring-necked Pheasant
Phasianus colchicus
(fay-sih-AY-nus KOL-kih-kus)

"The oriental splendor of a cock ring-neck in full springtime plumage is beyond belief. Yellow bill, green head with black tufts like little horns, bright red cheeks, a neckband of pure white, and below that a superb and intricate pattern of iridescent browns, gold, bronze, copper, gray, and black clear to the end of an incredibly long-pointed tail — such is a purely factual outline of his color glory. Display it all on a sturdy yet graceful form that may measure three feet from bill tip to tail tip, and you have a magnificence that could make even a peacock look to his laurels." — Robert S. Lemmon (1951)

The Ring-necked Pheasant is so familiar, we think of it as a native species. South Dakota even adopted it as its State Bird. But the pheasant is native to Asia and was introduced to America in the 1880s as a gamebird. Pheasant derives from *phasianos*, the Greek word for "a pheasant." *Phasianos* is named for the Phasis River (now the Rioni River) that flows from the Caucasus Mountains to the Black Sea. The ancients first encountered pheasants along the banks of this river. Ring-necked refers to the white band that encircles the male's neck, although some subspecies lack this field mark.

Phasianus — The genus name is from the Greek *phasianos* (Phasian bird" or pheasant). See common name above.

colchicus — The specific epithet is Modern Latin for "of Colchis," an ancient region (the fabled land of the Golden Fleece) on the eastern shore of the Black Sea. It is said that the Argonauts found many pheasants there. This also refers to part of this species' native range, now the Republic of Georgia.

French Name: Faisan de Colchide
Spanish Names: Faisán Común; Faisán Vulgar
Other Names: Ring-neck; Faisan; Common Pheasant; Black Pheasant; Chinese Pheasant; Mongolian Pheasant; English Pheasant; Cackle-bird; Cock Bird; Cock-up; Fancy Chicken; Road-ditch Chicken; Ditch Parrot; Comet; Kolo-hala

~

Grouse

The origin of grouse is uncertain, but some authorities believe it stems from the old French words *griershe*, *greoche*, or *griais*, meaning "speckled." It was apparently applied to some Old World partridge of uncertain identity.

Ruffed Grouse
Bonasa umbellus
(bon-AY-sah um-BELL-us)

"On a fallen log, a wall, or a broad stump that has been used as a drumming ground perhaps for many years, and well known to the hens as a trysting place, the male puffs out his feathers until, like a turkey cock, he looks twice his natural size, ruffs his neck frills, raises his crest, spreads and elevates his tail, droops his trailing wings beside him, and, with head drawn backward, struts along the surface with the most affected jerking, dandified gait. Suddenly he halts, distends his head and neck, and beats the air with his wings, slowly at first, then faster and faster, until there is simply a blur where the wings should be, so marvelously fast do they go." — Neltje Blanchan (1898)

Known as the "King of Gamebirds," the Ruffed Grouse is named for the black ruffs on the sides of the male's neck. These are erected, framing the head, in courtship display as described above.

Ruffed Grouse, by Louis Agassiz Fuertes

Bonasa — The genus name is from the Latin *bonasum* (a bison). Male Ruffed Grouse perform a territorial display called drumming. Perched on a log, the bird makes a whirring sound by rapidly beating his wings against the air. The sound of the drumming may suggest a thundering bison herd or perhaps the bellowing of a bull. Pete Dunne wrote, "It's a bouncing-ball-accelerating-to-a-stop sound." Neltje Blanchan continues her description of the Ruffed Grouse's courtship:

"The "drumming" of a male ruffed grouse, its most famous characteristic, is surely as remarkable a bird call as is heard in all nature. A thumping, rolling tattoo, like the deep, muffled beating of a drum, sonorous, crepitating, ventriloqual, admirably written down by Ernest Seton Thompson, *thump — — — — thump — — — —thump — — thump, thump; thump, thump-rup, rup, rup, r-r-r-r-r-r-r-r-r*, announces the presence of a cock hopeful of attracting the attention of some shy female hidden in the underbrush."

umbellus — The specific epithet is Latin for "umbrella," referring to the neck ruffs that are spread like an umbrella during courtship. See common name above.

French Name: Gélinotte Hupée
Spanish Name: Gallo de Collar
Eskimo Name: Khu-tuk
Other Names: Partridge; Common Partridge; Brown Partridge; Grey Partridge; Hardwood Partridge; Spruce Partridge; Willow Partridge; Copper-ruffed Partridge; Red-ruffed Partridge; White-fleshed Partridge; White-meat Partridge; Bush Partridge; Brush Partridge; Canadian Partridge; Drumming Partridge; Birch Partridge; Bircher; Moor Fowl; Brown Ruffed Grouse; Gray Ruffed Grouse; Oregon Ruffed Grouse; Canada Ruffed Grouse; Ruffled Grouse; Tippet Grouse; Wood Grouse; Shoulder-knot Grouse; Drumming Grouse; Red Grouse; Brown Grouse; Willow Grouse; Quail; Pheasant; Pine Pheasant; Drumming Pheasant; Mountain Pheasant; Woods Pheasant; Carpenter Bird; Chicken; Pine Hen; Wood Hen; French Hen; Ruffed Heathcock; Fesond; Tippet; Drummer; Spring Drummer; White-flesher; Woodpile Quarker; Cearc-thomain; Perdrix; Perdrix Grise; Perdrix Franche; Perdrix Bois Franc

～

Greater Sage-Grouse
Centrocercus urophasianus
(sen-tro-SER-kus you-row-FAZE-ih-AY-nus)

"The sage and the grouse seem made for each other. The original range of the bird coincided with the range of the sage, and as the sagelands have been reduced, so the populations of grouse have dwindled. The sage is all things to these birds of the plains. The low sage of the foothill ranges shelters their nests and their young; the denser growths are loafing and roosting areas; at all times the sage provides the staple food of the grouse." — Rachel Carson, *Silent Spring* (1962)

The Sage-Grouse is named for the sagebrush (*Artemesia tridentata*), which provides both food and cover for these birds as described in the above passage. Greater

Greater Sage-Grouse, by R. Bruce Horsfall

distinguishes this species from the smaller Gunnison Sage-Grouse.

Centrocercus — The genus name means "pointed tail" from Greek *kentron* (a point) and *kerkos* (a tail) refers to the spiky tail feathers which are fanned out during courtship displays.

urophasianus — The specific epithet means "pheasant tail" from Greek *oura* (the tail) and *phasianos* (a pheasant) and refers to the narrow, pointed pheasant-like tail.

French Name: Tétras des Armoises
Spanish Name: Gallo de las Artemisas
Other Names: Cock of the Plains; Sage Cock; Sage Hen; Sage Chicken; Fool Hen; Spiny-tailed Pheasant

Gunnison Sage-Grouse
Centrocercus minimus
(sen-tro-SER-kus MIN-ih-mus)

The Gunnison Sage-Grouse was only recognized as a separate species in 2000. It is named for the Gunnison Basin in southwest Colorado, where it occurs. Its range does not overlap that of the Greater Sage-Grouse. The two were formerly considered a single species, the Sage Grouse.

Centrocercus — The genus name means "pointed tail" from Greek *kentron* (a point) and *kerkos* (a tail) refers to the spiky tail feathers which are fanned out during courtship displays.

minimus — The specific epithet is Latin for "smallest or least" and refers to this species' smaller size in comparison with the Greater Sage-Grouse.

French Name: Tétras du Gunnison
Spanish Name: Gallo de Gunnison
Other Names: Same as Greater Sage-Grouse

Spruce Grouse
Falcipennis canadensis
(fal-sih-PEN-is can-ah-DEN-sis)

"In the dense spruce, fir, cedar and tamarack swamps of the great Maine woods the Spruce Grouse dwells. Where giant, moss grown logs and stumps of the virgin forest of long ago cumber the ground, where tall, blasted stubs of others still project far above the tree-tops of to-day, where the thick carpet of green sphagnum moss deadens every footfall, where tiny-leaved vinelets radiate over their mossy beds, there we may find this wild bird as tame as a barn-yard fowl." — Edward Howe Forbush (1927)

This grouse is named for its habitat in the northern coniferous forests where spruce, fir, and pine abound. Spruce needles and buds are also an important part of its diet. Known as Franklin's Grouse, for Arctic explorer Sir John Franklin, until 1957.

Falcipennis — The genus name means "sickle-winged" from the Latin *falx* (a sickle) and *pennis* (winged). It refers to the narrow outer tips of the primary feathers.

canadensis — The specific epithet is modern Latin for "of Canada." The greater part of the Spruce Grouse's range is in Canada.

French Name: Tétras du Canada
Spanish Name: Gallo Candiense
Eskimo Name: Napaktom Kadgia (grouse of the trees)
Other Names: Franklin's Spruce Grouse; Black Grouse; Canada Grouse; Crazy Grouse; Mountain Grouse; Pine Grouse; Swamp Grouse; Tyee Grouse; Wood Grouse; Spotted Grouse; Spruce Partridge; Black Partridge; Alaska Spruce Partridge; Hudsonian Spruce Partridge; Spruce Hen; Sprucer; Cedar Partridge; Wood Partridge; Soft-wood Partridge; Swamp Partridge; Fool Partridge; Fool Cock; Fool Hen; Heath-Hen; Black and Spotted Heathcock; Chicken; Spruce Chicken; Yukon Chicken; Hen and Dick; Peurdag; Perdrix; Perdrix d'Epinette; Perdrix de Savane; Perdrix Sapineuse

Willow Ptarmigan
Lagopus lagopus
(LAG-oh-pus or lah-GO-pus)

Ptarmigan (pronounced TAR-mih-gan) is from the Gaelic word *tarmachan*. Some sources say *tarmachan* means "mountaineer" and refers to the grouse's habitat. Or it may be a cognate of *torm* (murmur), perhaps referring to the low growls and croaks of the Rock Ptarmigan. In the 17th century, Robert Siebold, a professor of medicine at Edinburgh, added the initial (p), because he apparently thought the word was of Greek origin as in *pteron* (a wing). Willow refers to the stunted Arctic willows, whose buds and

Willow Ptarmigan, by Allan C. Brooks

twigs are an important food of this grouse.
Lagopus — The genus/species name means "hare foot" from the Greek. *lagos* (a hare) and *pous* (the foot). This refers to the bird's feathered feet suggesting a hare's furry ones. The feathering acts as snowshoes that aid in walking on soft snow. The stiff feathers increase the bearing surface of the foot and reduce the depth the foot sinks in the snow by 50%.
French Name: Lagopède des Saules
Spanish Name: Lagópodo Común
British Name: Willow Grouse; Red Grouse (for the Scottish subspecies that does not turn white in winter)
Eskimo and Inuit Names: Aku-dagin (eye like salmon berry); Kadgivik (having comb on head); A-kuzh-gik (imitative of alarm call)
Other Names: Common Ptarmigan; Alaska Ptarmigan; Alexander's Ptarmigan; Allen's tarmigan; Red Ptarmigan; Brown Ptarmigan; White-shafted Ptarmigan; Browse Partridge; Snow Partridge; Willow Partridge; Snow Grouse; White Grouse; Arctic Grouse; Scottish Grouse; Red Game; Eskimo Chicken; Tundra Chicken; White Bird; Willow Bird; Moss Hen; Moor Game; Moor Fowl; Moor Bird; Moor Poot; Moor Pout; Moor Cock; Moor Hen; Gor Cock; Gor Hen; Snow Hen; Heath Cock; Perdix Blanche

Rock Ptarmigan
Lagopus muta
(LAG-oh-pus or lah-GO-pus MEW-tah)

The Rock Ptarmigan is so named, because of its habitat in rocky alpine tundra. In fact a motionless ptarmigan resembles a small lichen-encrusted rock.
Lagopus — The genus name means "hare foot" from Greek. *lagos* (a hare) and *pous* (foot). This refers to the bird's feathered feet suggesting a hare's furry ones. The feathering acts as snowshoes that aid in walking on soft snow.
muta — The specific epithet is from the Latin *mutus* (silent), because of the bird's soft, low vocalizations.
French Name: Lagopède Alpin
Spanish Name: Lagópodo Alpino
British Name: Ptarmigan
Eskimo and Inuit Names: Niksaktongik (the belcher); Ung-au-wik (imitative of alarm call)
Other Names: Grey Ptarmigan; Chamberlain Ptarmigan; Dixon Ptarmigan; Nelson Ptarmigan; Reinhardt Ptarmigan; Townsend Ptarmigan; Tuirner Ptarmigan; Arctic Grouse; White Grouse; Snow Grouse; Small Grouse; Polar Grouse; Rock Grouse; Barren Partridge; Mountain Partridge; Rock Partridge; White Partridge; Arctic Partridge; White Game; Cairn Bird; Barren-ground Bird; Rocker; Snow Chick; Croaker; Pattermegan; Perdrix Blanche

---

Sidebar 8
Ptarmigan, Alaska?

There is a small town in eastern Alaska that could have been named Ptarmigan. A gold mining community near the South Fork of the 40-Mile River was to be incorporated in 1902, and it needed a name. Many of the locals liked the name Ptarmigan, since Willow Ptarmigan (now Alaska's State Bird) were abundant in the area. However, no one could agree on the correct spelling. Fearing that might set them up for ridicule, the residents opted for the name Chicken, instead. Well, the Willow Ptarmigan is known locally as the Eskimo Chicken.

White-tailed Ptarmigan
Lagopus leucura
(LAG-oh-pus or lah-GO-pus lew-KUR-ah)

The White-tailed Ptarmigan is the only one of the three species of ptarmigan with white tail feathers, and it is pure white in winter plumage. The Willow and Rock Ptarmigans have black tail feathers that they retain even in winter.

Lagopus — The genus name means "hare foot" from Greek. *lagos* (a hare) and *pous* (foot). This refers to the bird's feathered feet suggesting a hare's furry ones. The feathering acts as snowshoes that aid in walking on soft snow.

leucura — The specific epithet means "white tail" from Greek *leukos* (white) and *oura* (the tail).

French Name: Lagopède à Queue Blanche
Spanish Name: Lagópodo de Cola Blanca
Other Names: Rock Ptarmigan; Snow Quail; White Quail; Mountain Quail; Snow Grouse; Rocky Mountain Snow Grouse; Snow Partridge; Rocky Mountain Snow Partridge; Whitetail

Dusky Grouse
Dendragapus obscurus
(den-DRAIG-ah-pus ob-SKUR-us)

Dark gray plumage gives this grouse its name. The Dusky and the Sooty Grouse were formerly considered one species, the Blue Grouse.

Dendragapus — The genus name means "tree loving" from the Greek *dendron* (a tree) and *agape* (to love or be fond of). The reference is to this bird's pine/fir forest habitat.

obscurus — The specific epithet is Latin for "inconspicuous," and refers to the dark gray plumage.

French Name: Tétras Sombre
Spanish Names: Gallo de las Rocasas; Gallo Oscuro
Other Names: Gray Grouse; Pine Grouse; Timber Grouse; Mountain Grouse; Richardson Grouse; Partridge; Black Partridge; Pine Hen; Fool Hen; Hooter

Dusky Grouse, by Louis Agassiz Fuertes

Sooty Grouse
Dendragapus fuliginosus
(den-DRAIG-ah-pus full-IDJ-ih-NO-sus)

Dark sooty-gray plumage gives this grouse its name. This was formerly considered the dark coastal form of the Blue Grouse*Dendragapus* — The genus name means "tree loving" from the Greek *dendron* (a tree) and *agape* (to love or be fond of). The reference is to this bird's pine/fir forest habitat.

fuliginosa — The specific epithet means "sooty or covered with soot" from the Latin *fuligo* (soot).

French Name: Tétras Fuligineux
Spanish Name: Gallo Fuliginoso
Other Names: Same as Dusky Grouse

Sharp-tailed Grouse
Tympanuchus phasianellus
(tim-pan-YOU-kus fay-sih-ay-NELL-us)

Sharp-tailed refers to this species' narrow, pointed tail.

Tympanuchus — The genus name means "neck drum" from the Greek *tympanon* (a kettledrum) and Modern Latin *nucha* (the neck). The reference is to the purple air sacks on either side of the male's neck, that are inflated during courtship. They make pigeon-like cooing notes.

phasianellus — The specific epithet means "little pheasant" from Greek *phasianos* (a pheasant) and a Latin diminutive suffix *ellus* (little). The relatively long, tapered tail suggests that of a pheasant.

French Name: Tétras à Queue Fine
Spanish Name: Gallo de las Praderas Rabudo
Other Names: Grouse; Northern Sharp-tailed Grouse; Columbian Sharp-tailed Grouse;

Prairie Sharp-tailed Grouse; Southern Sharp-tailed Grouse; Sharp-tail; Southern Spike-tailed Grouse; Spike-tail; Pin-tailed Grouse; Pintail; Brush Grouse; Prairie Grouse; Sprig-tailed Grouse; Sprig-tail; Spring-tail; White Grouse; White-breasted Grouse; Willow Grouse; White-belly; Speckle-belly; Blackfoot; Faisan; Prairie Pheasant; Prairie Hen; Prairie Chicken; Prairie-Chicken of the Northwest; Pin-tail Chicken; Spotted Chicken; Poule de Prairies

Greater Prairie-Chicken
Tympanuchus cupido pinnatus
(tim-pan-YOU-kus cue-PIE-doe pin-AY-tus)

"Early in the morning in spring the booming of males assembled on the "scratching-ground" — some slight elevation of the prairie — summons the hens from that territory to witness their extraordinary performances until the whole region re-echoes with the soft though powerful sound, like deep tones from a church organ — harmonious, penetrating, more impressive to the human listener than to the apparently indifferent females. Inflating the loose yellow sacs on the sides of their head, that stand out like two oranges; erecting and throwing forward their Cupid-like feathers at the back of the neck; ruffling the plumage until it stands out straight; drooping the wings and spreading the erect tails, the males present an imposing picture of pompous display and magnificence that melts not the flinty hearts of the coquetting spectators . . . The note of the male bird is closely imitated by many farmers' boys. It may be written, *uck-ah-umb-boo-oo-oo-oo*." — Neltje Blanchan (1898)

Prairie chickens are indeed residents of the prairies, where males display on courtship grounds called leks. Along with quail, pheasants, and partridge, they are classified in the order Galliformes (chicken-like birds), and like their namesake, are ground-dwelling birds that prefer to walk or run rather than fly. Greater distinguishes this species from the smaller Lesser Prairie-Chicken.

Tympanuchus — The genus name means "neck drum" from the Greek *tympanon* (a kettledrum) and Modern Latin *nucha* (the neck). The reference is to the yellow-orange air sacs on either side of the male's neck, that are inflated during courtship. They make a booming sound, sort of like blowing across the mouth of a soda bottle.

cupido — The specific epithet is Latin for the Roman god of love. Cupid is, of course, familiar to anyone who has ever sent a valentine. In art Cupid is usually depicted as a winged infant carrying a bow and quiver of arrows. The reference is to special neck feathers called pinnae that are raised like rabbit ears when the males are displaying. The pinnae are said to resemble Cupid's wings.

pinnatus — The subspecific epithet is Latin for "feathered" or "winged" again referring to the special neck feathers that are erected in courtship displays.

French Name: Tétras des Prairies
Spanish Name: Gallo de las Praderas Mayor
Other Names: Common Prairie Chicken; Louisiana Prairie Chicken; Prairie Hen; Grouse; Prairie Grouse; Pinnated Grouse; Eastern Pinnated Grouse; Square-tailed Grouse; Barren Hen; Heath Hen (eastern subspecies, now extinct); Heath Cock; Pinnated Heath Cock

Lesser Prairie-Chicken
Tympanuchus pallidicinctus
(tim-pam-YOU-kus pal-lih-dih-SINK-tus)

The Lesser Prairie-Chicken is the smaller of the two species.

Tympanuchus — The genus name means "neck drum" from the Greek *tympanon* (a drum) and Modern Latin *nucha* (the neck). The reference is to the orange-red air sacs on either side of the male's neck, that are inflated during courtship. They make a booming sound, higher piched than that of he Greater Prairie-Chicken.

pallidicinctus — The specific epithet means "pale banded" from Latin *pallidus* "pale" and *cinctus* "belted, girdled, encircled, or banded" for the lighter barred pattern compared to that of the Greater Prairie-Chicken.

French Name: Tétras Pâle
Spanish Name: Gallo de las Praderas Menor
Other Names: Prairie Grouse; Prairie Hen; Pinnated Grouse

Wild Turkey
Meleagris gallopavo
(mell-ee-AY-gris gal-low-PAY-voe)

"Before the coming of the white man, a great bird with bronzed feathers and a gobbling call strutted widely through the New World wilderness. From Mexico, where Aztecs domesticated it, to the northern forests, where other Indians hunted it with bow and arrow, the haughty turkey flourished. Europe first learned of it early in the 16th century, when conquistadores brought some back to Spain. By the 1540s the "turkie fowle" graced many English tables, including the royal board of Henry VIII. Apparently this New World bird was confused with the African guinea fowl, which had come to Europe via the Turkish Empire. Both imports were called "turkey." Thus a bird so American that Benjamin Franklin wanted it proclaimed our national symbol took the name of a distant land!" — Alexander Wetmore (1965)

Turkey apparently derives from the Middle Eastern country of that name due to confusion over the origin of this species. When explorers brought domesticated turkeys from Mexico to Spain in 1630, other exotic birds were being brought into Europe as well, often by way of Turkey, including peafowl from India and African guinea fowl. In fact the name turkey was applied to any rare bird imported from a faraway place, but it stuck to the North American bird. Wild distinguishes the species from its barnyard counterpart. Domestic turkeys, which occur in several different breeds, are all descended from the Mexican subspecies of Wild Turkey. The confusion between the turkey and other foreign birds is reflected in its scientific name, too. See below.

Meleagris — The genus name is Greek for "guinea fowl" from a proper name Meleager. According to Greek legend, Meleager was a warrior, who was killed by a wild boar. A goddess then turned his grieving sisters into guinea fowl, their tear stains became the dots on the birds' plumage. As stated above, there was some confusion concerning the various birds being introduced from Asia, Africa, and the Americas. So perhaps Linnaeus, in naming the Wild Turkey, mistook it for a guinea fowl. Both are chicken-like birds with bare heads.

gallopavo — The specific epithet means "chicken-peacock" from the Latin *gallus* (a chicken or cock) and *pavo* (a peacock). It seems Linnaeus covered all bases, when he named the Wild Turkey. Actually the turkey and the peacock share some similar traits. Males of both species display before females by fanning their tails. Turkey gobblers are also quite colorful, although in a more subdued way. The feathers shine in iridescent green, purple, copper, and bronze. Pavo is also the Spanish word for turkey and pavo real (literally royal turkey) means peacock.

French Name: Dindon Sauvage

Spanish Names: Guajalote Norteño; Guajalote Silvestre

Other Names: American Turkey; American Wild Turkey; Common Wild Turkey; Plain Turkey; Eastern Turkey; Northern Turkey; Florida Wild Turkey; Merriam Turkey; Rio Grande Turkey; Wood Turkey; Bronze Turkey; Gobbler; Turkey Gobbler; Torque; Cocono; Cocoano; Coq d'Inde; Poule d'Inde; Peacock; Palahu; Pelehu; Dindon; Dinde sauvage; Ganso; Guajalote; Guijalo; Gallina de la Tierra; Wilte Welshhinkel

Plain Chachalaca and Wild Turkey, by Allan C. Brooks

Order Phoenicopteriformes

Family Phoenicopteridae
Flamingos

American Flamingo
Phoenicopterus ruber
(fee-nih-KOP-ter-us RUBE-er)

Flamingo stems from the Spanish *flamenco* and Portuguese *flamengo*. Most sources say its roots are from the Latin *flamma* "a flame" for the bright pink plumage. Another explanation is the Spanish *flamenco* means Fleming, i.e. an inhabitant of Flanders. This name was first applied to the bird in the first half of the 14th century. The Flemish traders were the best known northern Europeans to the Spaniards of that time. Their fair complexions and rosy cheeks were quite a contrast to the swarthy Mediterranean type, And so the pink wading bird came to be known as flamenco "Fleming." The fiery Andalusian gypsy dance flamenco is said to be so called, because the dancers' movements are like those of courting, marching flamingos. American refers to our species' range in the American tropics. Formerly considered conspecific with the Greater Flamingo (*P. roseus*) of the Old World.

Phoenicopterus — The genus name means "red-winged or red-feathered" from the Greek *phoinix* (crimson red) and *pteron* (a wing or feather). Phoenix is related to Phoenician, the ancient people who traded in a crimson dye. (See Purple Finch). It is also a cognate with phoenix, the mythical bird said to have red plumage that went up in flames after 500 years. The reference is to the birds' pink color, which comes from pigments in their food. Captive birds that don't get the proper diet fade to white.

ruber — The specific epithet is Latin for "red."
French Name: Flamant des Caraibes
Spanish Name: Flamenco Americano
Other Names: West Indian Flamingo; Caribbean Flamingo; Roseate Flamingo; Scarlet Flamingo; Fillymingo; Flamenco; Flamant

American Flamingo, by Allan C. Brooks

Order Podicipediformes

Family Podicipedidae
Grebes

Grebe stems from the Breton word *krib* (a crest). The name was probably first applied to the Great Crested Grebe (*Podiceps cristatus*) of Eurasia. Several other species of grebes sport crests as well.

Least Grebe
Tachybaptus dominicus
(TACK-ee-BAP-tus dom-IN-ih-kus)

At only 9.5 inches long, the Least Grebe is by far the smallest species of grebe. It is only two-thirds the size of a Pied-billed Grebe and half as large as a moorhen. This species was known as San Domingo Grebe before 1910, then Mexican Grebe until 1957.

Tachybaptus — "On the slightest alarm they dive with the quickness of thought, and so vigilant is their eye and so rapid their motion that, ordinarily, the fowling piece is discharged at them in vain." — Philip H. Gosse (1847)

The genus name is Greek for "fast dipped" from *takhus* (fast, quick, or swift) and *baptos* (dipped or to sink under). This refers to the bird's ability to quickly submerge when approached as described above.

dominicus — The specific epithet is Modern Latin for "Santo Domingo" (now the island of Hispaniola in the West Indies) where the type specimen was collected.

French Name: Grèbe Minime
Spanish Names: Zambullidor Menor; Zambullidor Enano
Other Names: San Domingo Grebe; Diver; Hell Diver; Diving Dapper; Chico; Tigua; Duck-and-Teal; Zaramagullón; Zaramagullón Chico; Plongeon; Petit Plongeon

Pied-billed Grebe
Podilymbus podiceps
(pod-ih-LIM-bus POD-ih-seps)

Pied-billed refers to this grebe's black and white bill.

Podilymbus — French naturalist Rene Lesson coined the genus name by combining the first and last parts of two other genera: *Podi(ceps)*, a genus of grebes (see next entry) and *(Co)lymbus*, a genus formerly used for some grebes in North America and for divers (loons) in Britain. The latter, from the Greek *kolumbos* (a diving bird), is no longer a valid genus name.

podiceps — The specific epithet stems from the Latin *podicipes* (rump foot) from *podicis* (rump) and *pes* (foot). This refers to the fact that a grebe's feet are set far back to the rear of the body, an adaptation for swimming and diving. This is also the source of the family name Podicipedidae.

French Name: Grèbe à bec Bigarré
Spanish Names: Zambullidor de Pico Grueso; Zambullidor Piquipinto
Other Names: Thick-billed Grebe; Carolina Grebe; Diver; Gehenna Diver; Hell-diver; Small Hell-diver; Devil-diver; Dive-dapper; Diving-dapper; Di-dapper; Dipper; Dipper Duck; Chicken Duck; Dabchick; Pied-billed Dabchick; American Dabchick; Tad; Dopchick; Sac-a-plomb; Parer-de-plomb; Water Witch; Mud-hen; Water Chicken; Arse-foot; Plongeon; Grand Plongeon; Plongeur; Hades Plunger; Sheol Plunger; Zaramago; Zaramagulon; Moqucuse; Poule d'Eau; Zaramagulón Grande; Zambullidor Piquigrueso; Chien d'Eau; Culotte Drek-shlibber; Wosser Shlibber; Chien d'Eau

Horned Grebe
Podiceps auritis
(POD-ih-seps ar-EE-tus)

"Horned Grebes are commonly known as "Hell-divers" or "Water-witches," because of their facility in disappearing and the mystery as to where they go. This species often mystifies the hunter by sinking slowly backward until nearly out of sight or by diving and disappearing altogether, until the novice is ready to make an oath that the bird has committed suicide for fear of his deadly marksmanship; but the Grebe merely submerges and swims beneath the surface until among the water plants, where it remains secure with its beak just protruding unnoticed above the water, or hidden by some overhanging leaf." — Edward Howe Forbush (1917)

In breeding plumage, the bushy, golden tufts of feathers on the sides of the head suggesting horns give this species its name.

Podiceps — The genus name is Latin for "rump foot" from *podicis* (the rump) and *pes* (the foot). This refers to the fact that a grebe's feet are set far back to the rear of the body, an adaptation for swimming and diving. Like the loons, the feet are set so far back on the body that the birds are nearly helpless on land.

autitus — The specific epithet is Latin for "eared" and refers to the same feathers that give this grebe its common name.

French Name: Grèbe Cornu
Spanish Name: Zambullidor Cornudo
British Name: Slavonian Grebe

Eskimo and Inuit Names: Tulukaruk (when ready to dive one cannot tell); Malikak (little loon)
Other Names: Dusky Grebe; Pink-eyed Diver; Small Diver; Little White Diver; Magpie Diver; Devil-diver; Hell-diver; Big Hell-diver; Didapper; Dipper; Black-and-white Dabchick; Water Witch; Sea Hen; Spirit Duck; Red-eyed Duck; Pipe-neck; Thread-neck; Spraw-foot; Plongeur; Dipper

Red-necked Grebe
Podiceps grisegena
(POD-ih-seps griss-eh-JEE-nah)

The rich chestnut-red neck in breeding plumage gives this grebe its name. Until 1957, known as Holboell's Grebe for Carl Peter Holboell (1795–1856), an officer in the Danish Royal Navy.

Podiceps — The genus name is Latin for "rump foot" from *podicis* (the rump) and *pes* (the foot). This refers to the fact that a grebe's feet are set far back to the rear of the body, an adaptation for swimming and diving. Like the loons, the feet are set so far back on the body that the birds are nearly helpless on land.

grisegena — The specific epithet means "gray cheek" from the Latin *griseus* (gray) and *gena* (the cheek), referring to the pale gray cheeks in breeding plumage.

French Name: Grèbe Jougris
Spanish Names: Zambullidor de Cuello Rojo; Zambullidor Cuellirroja
Eskimo Names: E-ta-ta-tuk; I-u-lee
Other Names: Greve; American Red-necked Grebe; Holboell's Diver; Rolling Pin; Hell-diver; Laughing Diver; Red-eyes; Water-hen; Water-witch; Wagtoe

Eared Grebe
Podiceps nigricollis
(POD-ih-seps nig-rih-COL-liss)

In breeding plumage, this grebe sports wispy yellow tufts of feathers on the sides of its head that suggest its name.

Podiceps — The genus name is Latin for "rump foot" from *podicis* (the rump) and *pes* (the foot). This refers to the fact that a grebe's feet are set far back to the rear of the body, an adaptation for swimming and diving. Like

Red-necked Grebe, by Allan C. Brooks

Eared Grebe, by Allan C. Brooks

the loons, the feet are set so far back on the body that the birds are nearly helpless on land.

nigricollis — The specific epithet means "black neck" from the Latin *niger* (black) and *collum* (the neck). The reference is to the black neck this grebe sports in breeding plumage.
French Name: Grèbe à Cou Noir
Spanish Name: Zambullidor Orejudo; Zambullidor Mediano
British Name: Black-necked Grebe
Other Names: American Eared Grebe; Black Grebe; Lesser Crested Grebe; Eared Diver; Rolling Pin; Hell-diver; Water-hen; Little Water-hen

Western Grebe
Aechmophorus occidentalis
(eek-MOFF-or-us ock-sih-den-TAY-liss)

This grebe's breeding range in the western United States, from the Great Plains to the Pacific coast, gives it its name.

Aechmophorus — The genus name means "spear bearer" from the Greek *aichme* (a spear) and *phoros* (bearing) and refers to the long, thin, sharp pointed bill.
occidentalis — The specific epithet is Latin for "western."
French Name: Grèbe Élégant
Spanish Names: Achichilique de Pico Amarillo; Achichilique Piquiamarillo
Other Names: Swan Grebe; Swan-necked Grebe; Swan-necked Hell-diver; Western Dabchick; Siwash Goose; Hell-diver; Silver Diver; Silver Loon

Clark's Grebe
Aechmophorus clarkii
(eek-MOFF-or-us CLARK-ih-eye)

John Henry Clark collected specimens for the Smithsonian while he was working for the U.S. and Mexican Boundary Survey (1851–1855). He obtained the type specimen of the grebe in the state of Chihuahua in northern Mexico. George Lawrence described the species in 1858, giving it the name *Podiceps clarkii* in honor of the surveyor who had collected it. For many years Clark's Grebe was regarded as only a subspecies of the Western Grebe (*Aechmophorus occidentalis clarkii*), but the AOU reinstated it to full species status in 1985.

Aechmophorus — The genus name means "spear bearer" from the Greek *aichme* (a spear) and *phoros* (bearing) and refers to the long, thin, sharp pointed bill.
clarkii — The specific epithet honors John Henry Clark (ca.1830–ca.1885), a United States surveyor and mathematician. See common name above.
French Name: Grèbe à Face Blanche
Spanish Names: Achichilique de Pico Naranja; Achichilique Piquinaranja
Other Names: Same as Western Grebe

Order Columbiformes

Family Columbidae
Pigeons and Doves

"Pigeon derives from the Old French *pijon* (a young bird) from the Latin *pipio* (to peep) and is thus imitative of the call. Dove is believed to stem from the Anglo-Saxon *dufan* (to dive) and refers to these birds' swift, erratic flight. There is no clear distinction between a pigeon and a dove, except the larger members of the family are generally called pigeons and the smaller ones doves. Here is more on the subject:

"What gosling is to goose and duckling is to duck, pigeon once was to dove. "Dove" has its roots in at least six European languages dating to the late 1100s. "Pigeon" developed a century or two later, probably originating in Latin as pipio, referring to a chirping young bird, then passing into French as pijon then into English as "pejon." Although "pejon" originally meant a young or nestling dove when it came into use in the late 1300s, such application has been entirely lost and forgotten.

"Today, people commonly perceive doves to be either pure white or brightly colored, and somewhat slender of physique, generally "pretty." By contrast, pigeons are larger, more plainly colored, and quite often nuisances or outright pests. Thus, in cultural usage "pigeon" and "dove" differ not by biology or ornithology but by emotional perception only. By quirk of language, one person's dove is another person's pigeon." —Kevin J. Cook, "The Birdwatcher's Question Box," *Bird Watcher's Digest*, September/October 2009

Rock Pigeon
Columba livia
(coh-LUM-bah LYE-vih-ah)

This Old World species is named for its ancestral habitat on the rocky sea cliffs around the Mediterranean and the mountains in the Middle East. Highly adaptive to man-made structures, the Rock Pigeon is now found in cities throughout the world. Formerly known as Rock Dove. The North American birds are termed feral, because they are descended from domestic pigeons that the early colonists brought with them from the Old Country. Domestic breeds, all derived from the Rock Pigeon, fall into several categories. There are the utility breeds (Kings, Giant Runts, and Giant Homers) that are raised for the table as squab. Homing Pigeons are used in the sport of pigeon racing and carried messages during wartime. Fancy fliers like Tumblers and Rollers accomplish acrobatic maneuvers in the air. The ornamental breeds like Fantails, Archangels, Jacobins, and Oriental Frills sport fancy plumage and decorative color patterns. They are raised as pets and for show. Another group of pet and show pigeons includes the curious Pouters and Croppers that can inflate their crops like a balloon.

Columba — The genus name is the Latin word for " a pigeon" or "a dove."

livia — The specific epithet is Modern Latin for "blue, blue-gray, or lead-colored" and refers to the original wild-type coloration. But feral pigeons, descended as they are from domestic birds, come in a variety of additional colors and patterns including white, black, reddish-brown, and black-and-white pied patterns.

French Name: Pigeon Biset
Spanish Name: Paloma Doméstica
Other Names: Common Pigeon; Domestic Pigeon; Feral Pigeon; City Pigeon; Street

Pigeon; Squab Pigeon; Carrier Pigeon; Homing Pigeon; Sea Pigeon; Wild Pigeon; Cliff Pigeon; Blue Rock Pigeon; Blue Dove; Doo; Rock Doo; Sod; Coo; Paloma Casera; Winged Rat

White-crowned Pigeon
Patagioenas leucocephala
(pat-AHJ-ih-ee-nas lew-koh-SEFF-ah-lah)

The brilliant snowy white cap gives this otherwise dark slate-blue pigeon its name.

Patagioenas — The genus name derives from the Greek *patage* (clatter, clap or crash) and *oinas* or *oinados* (a pigeon). Formerly *Columba leucocephala*.

leucocephala — The specific epithet means "white headed" from the Greek *leukos* (white) and *kephale* (the head).

French Name: Pigeon à Couronne Blanche
Spanish Names: Paloma de Corona Blanca; Paloma Coroniblanca
Other Names: Bald-pate; White-head; White-headed Dove; Blue Pigeon; Paloma Cabeciblanca; Paloma Casco Blanco; Paloma Coronita; Torcaza Cabeciblanca; Ramier tête-blanche

White-crowned Pigeon, by John James Audubon

Red-billed Pigeon
Patagioenas flavirostris
(pat-AHJ-ih-ee-nas flay-vih-ROSS-tris)

The base of this pigeon's bill is red, but the tip is yellow as is reflected in the specific epithet. See below. The yellow tip is more visible in the field than the red base.

Patagioenas — The genus name derives from the Greek *patage* (clatter, clap or crash) and *oinas* or *oinados* (a pigeon). Formerly *Columba flavirostris*.

flavirostris — The specific epithet means "yellow beak" from the Latin *flavus* (yellow) and *rostrum* (the beak). Only the tip of this bird's red bill is yellow.

French Name: Pigeon à Bec Rouge
Spanish Names: Paloma Morada; Paloma Piquirroja
Other Name: Blue Pigeon

Band-tailed Pigeon
Patagioenas fasciata
(pat-AHJ-ih-ee-nas fass-ih-AY-tah)

The blackish gray median band of the fan-shaped tail gives this western species its name.

Patagioenas — The genus name derives from the Greek *patage* (clatter, clap or crash) and *oinas* or *oinados* (a pigeon). Formerly *Columba fasciata*.

fasciata — The specific epithet is Latin for "banded" or "striped."

French Name: Pigeon à Queue Barrée
Spanish Names: Paloma de Collar; Paloma Encinera; Paloma Collareja
Other Names: Band-tailed Dove; Band-tail; Wild Pigeon; Wood Pigeon; White-collared Pigeon; White-naped Pigeon; Passenger Pigeon; Blue Pigeon; Blue Rock

Eurasian Collared-Dove
Streptopelia decaocto
(strep-toe-PEEL-ih-ah deck-ah-OCK-toe)

The black half-collar on the back of the neck gives this dove its name. It is native to Eurasia, but was introduced to North America in the 1980s.

Streptopelia — The genus name means "collared dove" from the Greek *streptos* (a collar or necklace) and *peleia* (a dove).

decaocto — The specific epithet means "eighteen" from the Latin *deca-* (ten) and *octo* (eight). It derives from a story of a hardworking servant who cried and complained about her measly pay of 18 pieces/year. The gods taking pity on her turned her into a dove with a mournful cry. *Decaocto* is said to be imitative of this dove's call.
French Name: Tourterelle Turque
Spanish Names: Paloma Turca; Tórtola Turca
Other Names: Common Collared Dove; Collared Turtle Dove; Indian Ring Dove; Eastern Ring Dove; Eurasian Ring Dove

Spotted Dove
Streptopelia chinensis
(strep-toe-PEEL-ih-ah chin-EN-sis)

This dove is named for the white spots that dot the wide black collar on the nape.
Streptopelia — The genus name means "collared dove" from the Greek *streptos* (a collar or necklace) and *peleia* (a dove).
chinensis — The specific epithet is Modern Latin for "of China" where the type specimen was taken near Canton.
French Name: Tourterelle Tigrine
Spanish Names: Paloma de Cuello Moteado; Tórtola Moteada
Other Names: Chinese Dove; Chinese Spotted Dove; Burmese Dove; Burmese Spotted Dove; Indian Dove; Indian Turtle Dove; Chinese Turtle Dove; Malay Turtle Dove; Spotted Turtle Dove; Lace-necked Dove; Spot-necked Dove; Pearl-necked Dove; Tortola Moteada

White-winged Dove
Zenaida asiatica
(zen-AY-ih-dah ay-zhih-AT-ih-kah)

Large, white wing patches give this dove its name.
Zenaida — The genus name honors Princess Zenaide Charlotte Julie Bonaparte (1804–1854), the wife of French ornithologist Charles Lucien Bonaparte.
asiatica — The specific epithet is Modern Latin for "of Asia," a misnomer, as this dove is native to the New World. The information with the specimen that came to Linnaeus said from "Indiis." Linnaeus took this to mean India or the East Indies. The specimen was actually collected in Jamaica in the West Indies. But the rule of priority states the name is valid, even though it is a mistake.
French Name: Tourterelle à Ailes Blanches
Spanish Names: Paloma de Ala Blanca; Paloma Aliblanca
Other Names: Sonora Dove; Sonoran Dove; Singing Dove; Mesquite Dove; Cactus Pigeon; White-wing; Lap-wing; Barbarin; Ali-blanca; Paloma Ali-blanca; Tortola Ali-blanca; Tourterelle de Aile-blanche

Mourning Dove
Zenaida macroura
(zen-AY-ih-dah mah-KROOR-ah)

"The best known characteristic of the Mourning Dove is its call — it can hardly be considered a song — which may suggest hopeless sorrow, or the tenderest love and devotion, according to the mood of the listener." — George Gladden (1917)

This dove's melancholy song gives it its name. Sometimes rendered as *ooAAH coo coo coo*, it sounds as though the bird was inconsolably sad and in mourning. It is sometimes mistaken for the call of an owl.
Zenaida — The genus name honors Princess Zenaide Charlotte Julie Bonaparte (1804–1854), the wife of French ornithologist Charles Lucien Bonaparte.
macroura — The specific epithet means "long tailed" from the Greek *makros* (long) and *ouros* (tailed), referring to the long, narrow, pointed tail.
French Name: Tourterelle Triste
Spanish Names: Paloma Huilota; Paloma Rabuda
Other Names: American Mourning Dove; Carolina Dove; Wild Dove; Moaning Dove; Turtle Dove; Carolina Turtle Dove; Long-tail Pea Dove; Wood Dove; Wood Pigeon; Wild Pigeon; Colombe Sauvage; Pigeon Sauvage; Paloma; Paloma Huilota; Fifi; Dord'l Doub; Rabiche; Tórtola; Tórtola Rabilarga; Tourte; Tourterelle; Tourterelle Queue-fine

Inca Dove
Columbina inca
(col-um-BINE-ah INK-ah)

The common name suggests that this bird's range is in Peru, the land of the Incas. But this dove actually occurs in Mexico and the southwestern United States. Aztec Dove would be a more appropriate name.

Columbina — The genus name means "little dove" from the Latin *columba* (a dove) plus a diminutive suffix.

inca — The specific epithet is a toponym referring to the Inca Empire in Peru. French naturalist René Lesson in naming this species apparently mistook Mexico to be the land of the Incas. See common name above.

French Name: Columbe Inca
Spanish Name: Tórtola de Cola Larga; Tórtola Colilarga; Tórtolita Colilarga
Other Names: Scaled Dove; Scaly Dove; Long-tailed Dove; Tortola Colilarga

Common Ground-Dove
Columbina passerina
(col-um-BINE-ah pass-er-EYE-nah)

Ground-Doves are so-called because they spend much of their time foraging on the ground. This is the Common Ground-Dove, because it has the most extensive range of the Ground-Doves.

Columbina — The genus name means "little dove" from the Latin *columba* (a dove) plus a diminutive suffix.

passerina — The specific epithet is Latin for "little sparrow" referring to this dove's resemblance to a sparrow, particularly its small size, slightly larger than a House Sparrow.

French Name: Columbe à Queue Noire
Spanish Names: Tórtola Común; Tórtolita Común
Other Names: Scaled Ground Dove; Scaly Ground Dove; Rosy Ground Dove; Speckled Ground Dove; Little Dove; Walking Dove; Stone Dove; Moaning Dove; Mourning Dove; Tobacco Dove; Tobacco Bird; Duppy Bird; Ortolan; Rola; Rolita; Tortolita; Tojosa; Palomita de la Virgen

Ruddy Ground-Dove
Columbina talpacoti
(col-um-BINE-ah tal-pah-COAT-ih)

This ground-dove is named for its rufous upperparts.

Columbina — The genus name means "little dove" from the Latin *columba* (a dove) plus a diminutive suffix.

talpacoti — The specific epithet is the Tupi (Brazilian) Indian name for this bird.

French Name: Columbe Rousse
Spanish Names: Tórtola Rojiza; Tórtolita Rojiza
Other Names: Cinnamon Dove; Blue-headed Ground Dove; Talpacoti Dove

White-tipped Dove
Leptotila verreauxi
(lep-TOE-till-ah ver-ROW-eye)

The white corners on the tip of the tail, visible when the bird takes flight, give this dove its name. Formerly known as "White-fronted Dove."

Leptotila — The genus name means "thin feather" from the Greek *leptos* (thin or slender) and *ptilon* (a feather) from the shape of the outermost primary feather. Elliot Coues gave them the nickname "pinwing doves."

verreauxi — In 1855, Charles Bonaparte named this dove in honor of Jules Pierre Verreaux (1807–1873), a French explorer and collector.

Common Ground-Dove, by John James Audubon

French Name: Columbe de Verreaux
Spanish Names: Paloma Arroyera; Paloma Coliblanca
Other Names: Pale-fronted Dove; Wood Pigeon

Key West Quail-Dove
Geotrygon chrysia
(jee-oh-TRY-gon KRIS-ih-ah)

This West Indian species is called a Quail-Dove, because of its rotund body and its habit of walking and foraging on the ground as a quail does. Audubon reported it as nesting in Key West in 1832, but now it is only a rare visitor to Florida.

Geotrygon — The genus name means "earth dove" from the Greek *gaia* (earth) and *trugon* (a turtle dove).

chrysia — The specific epithet means "golden" from the Greek *chrysion* (a piece of gold). All that glitters is not gold. The color of this dove is not actually golden, but a rich chestnut glossed with green and purple.

French Name: Columbe à Joues Blanches
Spanish Name: Paloma Perdiz Barbiqueja
Other Names: Partridge; Perdiz; Perdrix; Torito; Barbiquejo

Key West Quail-Dove, by John James Audubon

Order Cuculiformes

Family Cuculidae Cucukoos, Roadrunners, and Anis

Yellow-billed Cuckoo
Coccyzus americanus
(cock-SIGH-zus ah-mer-ih-CANE-us)

Cuckoo is onomatopoetic, a close rendition of the call of the Common Cuckoo (*Cuculus canorus*) of Eurasia that is well known for its parasitic ways. If you have ever heard a cuckoo clock, you know what one sounds like. American cuckoo's calls are very different. This one's is a rapid staccato *kuk-kuk-kuk-kuk-kuk-kakakowlp-kowlp-kowlp-kowlp*. The last notes sound like a carpenter hammering nails in the distance. To old timers this sound was the call of the "rain crow," which meant a storm was coming. This species' bill is largely bright yellow, although the tip and upper surface of the culmen are dark brown.

Coccyzus — The genus name is from the Greek *kokkuzo* (to cry cuckoo) from *kokkux* (a cuckoo).

americanus — The specific epithet is Modern Latin for "of America," where this species occurs. It breeds in North America and winters in South America.

French Name: Coulicou à Bec Jaune
Spanish Names: Cuco de Pico Amarillo; Cuco Piquiamarillo; Cuclillo Piquigualdo
Other Names: California Cuckoo; Western Cuckoo; Rain Dove; Rain Bird; Rain Crow; Storm Crow; Wild Pigeon; Cow Bird; May Bird; Four O'clock Bird; Coffin Bird; Primavera; Kow-kow; Coucou; Chow-chow; Gukuk; Guluk; Gangan; Guacaira; Coucon Manioe; Mani-coco; Grand Queue; Boba; Carga Agua; Petit Tacot; Primavera; Longue Queue; Raya Fogel; Pajaro Bobo; Pajaro Bobo Piquiamarillo; Arriero Chico; Arrierito

Mangrove Cuckoo
Coccyzus minor
(cock-SIGH-zus MY-nor)

This cuckoo is named for its habitat in coastal tangles of red and black mangroves.

Coccyzus — The genus name is from the Greek *kokkuzo* (to cry cuckoo) from *kokkux* (a cuckoo).

minor — The specific epithet is Latin for "smaller," comparative of *parvus* (small). The Mangrove Cuckoo is actually about the same size as the other cuckoos in this genus.

French Name; Coulicou Manioc
Spanish Names: Cuco Manglero; Cuclillo de Antifaz
Other Names: Bahama Mangrove Cuckoo; Black-eared Cuckoo; Maynard's Cuckoo; Rain Crow; Rain Dove; Rain Bird; Cat Bird; Cowbird; Dumb Bird; May Bird; Four o'clock Bird; Coffin Bird; Guacaira; Gangan; Go-go; Petit Tacot; Mani-coco; Boba; Pájaro Bobo; Pajara Bobo Menor; Arriero Chico; Arrierito; Primavera; Carga-agua; Coucou-manioc

Yellow-billed Cuckoo, by John James Audubon

Bird is the Word

> ### Sidebar 9
> ### Birds As Weather Prophets
>
> When I was a kid, I knew the Yellow-billed Cuckoo as the "Rain Crow" because that is what my grandparents called it. I had no field guide at the time, so there was no way for me to know what this bird really was. In fact, I had never even seen a Yellow-billed Cuckoo. I was only familiar with the rapid notes of this secretive bird resounding from our woodlot, a rapid *kuk-kuk-kuk-kuk-kuk* followed by *kowlp-kowlp-kowlp-kowlp-kowlp*, the final notes sounding like the resonant hammering of a distant roofer. "That's the Rain Crow," my Grandpa would say. "That means it's going to rain." And it did seem the cuckoo was particularly vocal on a hot, sultry summer day, when an afternoon shower was likely. In some regions, it is the Black-billed Cuckoo that is known as Rain Crow, and the name has been applied to the Mourning Dove, as well.
>
> It is said almost every country has a particular "rain-bird," whose call is supposed to foretell wet weather. In the Shetland Islands, the Red-throated Loon is called the "Rain Goose," because the residents believe the birds are especially noisy before a storm. The Nlaka'pamux (Thompson) Indians of British Columbia have given the Common Loon the folk name Call-up-a-storm. They believe the loons' eerie wails not only foretell rain, but cause it, as would a person's imitation of the call.
>
> The common name plover and the genus *Pluvialis* both are derived from the Latin *pluvia* (rain). It is not known for sure what the connection between the birds and rain is, but various explanations have been put forth. It could be the plovers were seen as weather prophets. Perhaps they became more vocal or restless at the approach of a storm. Seafarers noted the little seabirds known as storm-petrels seemed to suddenly appear out of nowhere when the skies darkened and the seas got rough. The birds were seeking shelter on the leeward side of the ship. Here is a collection of weather proverbs that involve birds from *Weather Lore* (1893) by Richard Inward:
>
> > If birds be silent, expect thunder.
> >
> > If fowls roll in the sand,
> > Rain is at hand.
> >
> > If the wild geese gang out to sea,
> > Good weather there surely will be.
> >
> > If larks fly high and sing long,
> > Expect fine weather.
> >
> > When men-of-war hawks fly high,
> > It is a sign of a clear sky,
> > When they fly low,
> > Prepare for a blow.

Black-billed Cuckoo
Coccyzus erythropthalmus
(cock-SIGH-zus er-ih-throf-THALL-mus

This cuckoo's all-black bill gives it its name and distinguishes it from the Yellow-billed Cuckoo.

Coccyzus — The genus name is from the Greek *kokkuzo* (to cry cuckoo) from *kokkux* (a cuckoo).

erythropthalmus — The specific epithet means "red eyed" from the Greek *erythros* (red) and *ophthalmos* (the eye). This species' eye is actually brown, not red. The name refers to the red ring of bare skin that encircles the eye.

French Name: Coulicou à Bec Noir
Spanish Names: Cuco de Pico Negro; Cuco Piquinegro; Cuclillo Piquinegro
Other Names: Rain Crow; Rain Dove; Rain Bird; Cou-cou; Kow-kow; Guluk; Grand Queue; Longue-queue; Poule D'eau; Raya Fogel

Greater Roadrunner
Geococcyx californianus
(jee-oh-COCK-sicks cal-ih-for-nih-AY-nus)

"Comedian of the cuckoo clan, the roadrunner raced stagecoaches in the Old Southwest — and beat them every time. Tiring of the sport, the bird would dart aside, brake with upraised tail, and strike a quizzical stance, seaming to poke fun at

Greater Roadrunner, by Allan C. Brooks

the overmatched horses." — Alexander Wetmore (1965)

Roadrunners really do run along roads at speeds up to 15mph, and are reluctant to fly. Greater distinguishes this species from the smaller Lesser Roadrunner (*G. velox*) of Mexico and Central America.

Geococcyx — The genus name means "earth cuckoo" from the Greek *geo* (earth) and *kokkux* (a cuckoo), referring to the fact that this is a terrestrial species as opposed to most other cuckoos, which are tree-dwelling.

californianus — The specific epithet is Modern Latin for "of California" where the type specimen was collected.

French Name: Grand Geocoucou
Spanish Names: Correcaminos Norteño; Correcaminos Mayor
Other Names: Ground Cuckoo; Chaparral Cock; Cock of the Desert; Snake Killer; Lizard Bird; Churca; Paisano; Correo del Camino; Correcamino; Correcaminos Norteño

Smooth-billed Ani
Crotophaga ani
(crow-TOFF-ah-gah AH-nee)

Ani is the Tupi (Brazilian) Indian name for these birds. This ani's high, puffin-like bill has a smooth surface, which distinguishes it from the next species.

Crotophaga — The genus name means "tick eater" from the Greek *kroton* (a tick) and *phagein* (to eat) from the anis' habit of picking ticks off cattle.

ani — See common name above.

French Name: Ani à Bec Lisse
Spanish Names: Garrapatero de Pico Liso; Garrapatero Piquiliso
Other Names: Savannah Blackbird; Parrot Blackbird; Cuban Parrot; Black Parrot; Black Parakeet; Black Daw; Long-tailed Crow; Chapman Bird; Black Witch; Voodoo Bird; Death-bird; Tick Bird; Old Slut; Old Arnold; Corbeaue; Merle Corbeau; Garrapatero; Bilbitin; Bourse-tabac; Judio; Juif

Groove-billed Ani
Crotophaga sulcirostris
(crow-TOFF-ah-gah sul-sih-ROS-tris)

The furrows in this ani's bill give it its name.

Crotophaga — See Smooth-billed Ani.
sulcirostris — The specific epithet means

Sidebar 10
The Warner Bros Roadrunner and His Many Scientific Names

Unlike the Greater Roadrunner, the star of the animated cartoon has a different Latin name in almost every episode. Although played for humor, they wonderfully show how scientific names are often descriptive. Here are some of the more creative ones:

Acceleratti incredibilus
Hot-Roddicus Supersonicus
Speedipus Rex
Velocitus Delectiblus
Delicius-Delicius
Tastyus Supersonicus
Birdius High-Ballius
Burnius-Roadibus
Digoutius-Unbelieveus
Batoutahelius
Velocitus incalculus
Fastius Tasty-us
Tid-bittius velocitus
Supersonicus Idioticus
disappearialis quickius
Burn-em Upus Asphaltus
Semper Food-Ellus
Ultra-Sonicus Ad Infinitum

"furrow billed" from the Latin *sulcus* (a furrow) and *rostri*s (billed).
French Name: Ani à Bec Cannelé

Spanish Names: Garrapatero Pijui; Garrapatero Asurcado
Other Names: Black Witch; Tick Bird; Jew Bird

Order Caprimulgiformes

Family Caprimulgidae
Goatsuckers or Nightjars

"The odd family name Goatsucker is explained in the following passage: Goatsuckers — the very name springs from superstition. In ancient times these seldom-seen birds with tiny bills and huge mouths were thought to suck at the udders of goats, causing the animals to go blind. Even the family's scientific name — from the Latin *caprimulgus*, milker of goats — reflects the old belief." — Alexander Wetmore (1965)

We can speculate on how such a belief got started. Herders undoubtedly saw nightjars flying around their animals at dusk, perhaps attracted to the insects the goats flushed as they grazed. Ancient people tended to view night creatures with suspicion. Nightjars have very wide mouths that look threatening when they are agape. When the goats went dry, the herders had to have something to blame it on.

The name nightjar refers to these birds' vocalizations, as if to jar the night:

"There is something about nocturnal birds that fascinate one strangely. Doubtless the cloak of darkness that shrouds their movements and activities has a great deal to do with it. One cannot but wonder at their comings and goings; how they pursue their hunting amid the gloom. Their voices too lend much to the fascination, for the notes seem a part of the night itself, just as the bodies of the birds themselves seem more like detached and living particles of darkness than of flesh and feathers." — Alexander Sprunt, Jr. (1940)

Lesser Nighthawk
Chordeiles acutipennis
(core-DIE-leez ah-cute-ih-PEN-iss)

Nighthawks are, of course, not hawks at all, but nightjars. But in flight the birds resemble a hawk or falcon, and that is the source of the name. These birds, however, are not strictly nocturnal, but crepuscular, being active primarily at dusk and dawn.

The Lesser Nighthawk is slightly smaller than the Common Nighthawk.

Chordeiles — The genus name means "dancing in the evening from the Greek *khoreia* (dancing) and *deiles* (evening). The name is descriptive of the nighthawk's erratic flight as it forages for insects at dusk.

acutipinnis — The specific epithet means "pointed wing" from the Latin *acutus* (sharply pointed) and *penna* (a wing or feather), descriptive of the nighthawk's narrow, pointed wings.

French Name: Engoulevent Minime
Spanish Names: Chotacabres Menor; Añapero Menor
Other Names: Texas Nighthawk; Texan Nighthawk; Trilling Nighthawk

Common Nighthawk
Chordeiles minor
(core-DIE-leez MY-nor)

The Common Nighthawk has the widest range of the nighthawks. It occurs in all of the lower 48 states and most of Canada.

Chordeiles — The genus name means "dancing in the evening from the Greek *khoreia* (dancing) and *deiles* (evening). The name is descriptive of the nighthawk's erratic flight as it forages for insects at dusk.

minor — The specific epithet is Latin for "smaller," comparative of *parvus* (small), relative to the European Nightjar (*Caprimulgus europaeus*). When the Common

Common Nighthawk and Eastern Whip-poor-will, by Louis Agassiz Fuertes

Nighthawk was described in 1771, it was placed in the genus *Caprimulgus* with the only other nightjar known at the time.

French Name: Engoulevent d'Amérique

Spanish Names: Chotacabras Zumbón; Chotacabras Mayor; Añapero Zumbón

Other Names: Booming Nighthawk; Bird Hawk; Moth Hawk; Mosquito Hawk; Mosquito Bird; Mosquito Catcher; Booming Swallow; Bull-Bat; Virginia Bat; Moth Hunter; Burnt-land Bird; Long-winged Goatsucker; Virginia Goatsucker; Goatsucker of Carolina; Nightjar; Shad Spirit; Will-o'-the-wisp; Swooper; Pork-and-beans; Besh-que; Engoulevent; Epervier de Nuit; Furze; Furzet; Gie-me-me-bit; Gwen-go-wi-a; Capacho; Chouette; Crapau Volans; Ho-pil-car; Killy-dadick; Mangeur Maringouins; Peut-on-voir; Piramadig; Gaspayo; Pisk; Pik-teis-k Wes; Pick-a-me-dick; Querequeté; Querequesqué; Querequequé Migratorio; Seabhag Oidche; Wib'rwil

Antillean Nighthawk
Chordeiles gundlachii
(core-DIE-leez gund-LOCK-ih-eye)

This nighthawk is named for its breeding range in the Antilles — the islands of the West Indies. In the United States, it only reaches southern Florida. Formerly considered a subspecies of the Common Nighthawk.

Chordeiles — The genus name means "dancing in the evening from the Greek *khoreia* (dancing) and *deiles* (evening). The name is descriptive of the nighthawk's erratic flight as it forages for insects at dusk.

grundlachii — In 1857, George Lawrence named this nighthawk in honor of Cuban ornithologist Juan Cristóbal Gundlach (1810–1896), because of "the zeal with which he is investigating the Ornithology of Cuba."

French Name: Engoulevent Piramidig

Spanish Names: Chotacabras Antillano; Añapero Querequeté

Common Pauraque
Nyctidromus albicollis
(nick-TID-row-mus al-bih-COL-iss)

The common name (pronounced pa-RAW-kee) is a native Mexican name, said to be imitative of the song, although not as apparent as some of the other nightjars. Common refers to this species' wider range when compared to the Least Pauraque (*Siphonorhis brewsteri*) that is restricted to Gonâve Island and Hispaniola in the Caribbean.

Nyctidromus — The genus name means "night runner" from the Greek *nyx* (night) and *dromos* (running). The reference is to the bird's nocturnal habits, and to the fact that, despite its short legs, it has been observed running along the ground while foraging. It can also leap about a foot and a half into the air to catch low-flying insects.

albicollis — The specific epithet means "white necked" from the Latin *albus* (white) and *collis* from *collum* (the neck), referring to the white throat patch.

French Name: Engoulevent Parauqué

Spanish Names: Chotacabras Pauraque; Tapacaminos Picuyo; Tapacaminos Común

Other Names: Merrill's Pauraque; Don Pucuyo; Caballero de la Noche, Cuejo; Culejo

Common Poorwill
Phalaenoptilus nuttallii
(fal-ee-NOP-till-us nut-ALL-ih-eye)

"When the sudden cry of *poor-will, poor-will*, was borne on the air from across the cañon, it was as if a voice from the spirit-land was spoken." — T. Gilbert Pearson (1917)

"When we were camped on the edge of a canyon in the Guadalupe Mountains, at dusk while the bats were flying down in the canyon, up along the edge came the Poor-wills so near that we could hear their syllables distinctly — *poor-will'-uck, poor-will'-uck*.

"Sometimes two would call antiphonally, faster and faster till they fairly tripped over each other. The call as it is often given is a delightfully soft, *poor-will', poor-will', poor-will'-uck*, which like the delicious aromatic smell of the sagebrush clings long to the memory of the lover of the west." — Florence Merriam Bailey (1928)

The common name is onomatopoetic, a close rendition of this bird's two-note song, although at close range a third note can be detected as described above. Common distinguishes this species from three Poorwill species (genus *Nyctiphrynus*) with more restricted ranges in Mexico. Formerly known as Nuttall's Poorwill.

Phalaenoptilus — The genus name means "moth feathered" from the Greek *phalaina* (a moth) and *ptilon* (a feather). The reference is to this bird's velvety, cryptically colored plumage, like that of a moth, and to its manner of flight. Pete Dunne describes the flight as "lofting and moth-like, with deep, silent wingbeats."

nuttallii — Audubon first mentions this species in volume five of the *Ornithological Biography* (1839) from a specimen British botanist Thomas Nuttall (1786–1859) had collected on his trip to the Pacific coast and called it Nuttall's Whip-poor-will. Audubon did not formally describe it as *Capriimulgus Nuttallii* until 1844 in volume seven of the octavo edition of *Birds of America* from a specimen John G. Bell had collected on the Missouri River expedition in September of 1843.

> **Sidebar 11**
> **The Hopi Knew It First**
>
> The Common Poorwill is the only bird known to hibernate for extended periods. In ancient times it was commonly believed that birds hibernated during the winter. Swallows, they thought, spent the cold months buried in the mud in marshlands or at the bottom of the sea. With our knowledge of bird migration, modern science pooh-poohed the idea of any bird hibernating. That is until December of 1946, when biologist Edmund C. Jaeger and two of his students discovered a bird, apparently dead, in a crevice in a canyon wall of the Chuckwalla Mountains of southern California. The bird was cold to the touch and there was no sign of respiration or a heartbeat. But it was actually very much alive. While handling the bird on another visit, it winked, uttered a mouse-like squeak, and yawned. The bird's temperature was 64.4°F, about 42 degrees below normal. What Jaeger had discovered was a hibernating bird. The news astounded everyone. Well, not quite everyone. The Hopi Indians apparently knew it all along. Their name for the Common Poorwill is *holchko* (the sleeping one).

French Name: Engoulevent de Nuttall
Spanish Names: Tapacaminos Tevii; Pachacua Norteña
Other Names: Nuttall's Poorwill; Dusky Poorwill; Desert Poorwill; Frosted Poorwill; Northern Poorwill; Colorado Desert Poorwill; San Ignacio Poorwill; Nuttall's Whip-poor-will; Holchko; Holchoko

Chuck-will's-widow
Antrostomus carolinensis
(an-TROSS-toe-mus car-oh-lin-EN-sis)

"Dusk falls gently over the salt marshes, which reach out from a shoreline where moss-bannered live oaks and stately pines rustle softly in the late March breeze. A faint fragrance of jessamine hangs in the air; the sleepy note of a cardinal echoes from a cassina thicket, while atop a tall palmetto a mockingbird salutes the coming night with a burst of melody. Silence comes and the stars appear, glinting in golden splendor through the purple gloom. Suddenly through the air comes another sound, a sharp, clear-cut, insistent chant. Splitting the silences, it strikes clappingly upon one's ears, ringing with startling emphasis, unmistakable, thrilling and welcome. The first chuck-will's-widow has returned to the Carolina low country, and spring is definitely back again!" — Alexander Sprunt, Jr. (1940)

 The common name is onomatopoetic. Chuck-will's-widow is a close rendition of this bird's nocturnal song, *chuck-will's-WID-ow, chuck-will's-WID-ow.*

Antrostomus — The genus name means "cavern mouth" from the Greek *antron* (a cavern) and *stoma* (the mouth). The reference is to the nightjars' wide gape, adapted to netting flying insects out of the air. Formerly *Caprimulgus carolinensis.*

carolinensis — The specific epithet is Modern Latin for "of Carolina," the English colony where Mark Catesby obtained the type specimen.

French Name: Engoulevent de Caroline
Spanish Names: Tapacamonos de Carolina; Tapacaminos Carolinense; Chotacabras de Paso
Other Names: Dutch Whip-poor-will; Spanish Whip-poor-will; Nightjar; Chuck; Chuckwuts-widow; Chick-a-willa; Chip-fell-out-of-a-oak; Twixt-hell-and-the-white-oak; Hollerin' Boys; Mosquito Hawk; The Great Bat; Guabairo Mayor; Mangeur Maringouins

Buff-collared Nightjar
Antrostomus ridgwayi
(an-TROSS-toe-mus RIDJ-way-eye)

"The family's common European name, nightjar, better suits these shadowy hunters of night-flying insects, for their weird, persistent calls certainly "jar the night."" — Alexander Wetmore (1965)

 Nightjar is the name used primarily for the Old World members of this family. Buff-collared describes the complete, narrow buffy collar that encircles the neck, contrasting with the otherwise grayish plumage. Formerly known as Ridgway's Whip-poor-will.

Antrostomus — The genus name means "cavern mouth" from the Greek *antron* (a cavern) and *stoma* (the mouth). The reference is to the nightjars' wide gape, adapted to netting flying insects out of the air. Formerly *Caprimulgus ridgwayi.*

ridgwayi — In 1897, E. W. Nelson named this species in honor of Robert Ridgway (1850–1929), an American ornithologist, who was curator of birds of the U.S. National Museum from 1880 to 1929.

French Name: Engoulevent de Ridgway
Spanish Names: Tapacaminos Tu-cuchillo; Tapacaminos Préstame-tu-cuchillo
Other Names: Cookacheea; Ridgway's Cookacheea; Preste-me-tu-cuchillo (Please lend me your knife)

Eastern Whip-poor-will
Antrostomus vociferous
(an-TROSS-toe-mus voh-SIFF-er-us)

"To most people a whip-poor-will is simply a mysterious voice somewhere out in the country darkness — mysterious and astoundingly, incredibly, impossibly repetitious. Any bird that can say *whip-poor-will* two hundred or more times in quick succession without a noticeable pause for breath, and always in clear, ringing tones that are audible a quarter mile away, is entitled to be called amazing solely on that score." — Robert S. Lemmon (1952)

 The common name is onomatopoetic. Whip-poor-will is a close approximation of this bird's repetitive nocturnal song, *whip-poor-WILL, whip-poor-WILL, whip-poor-WILL* with the accent on the third note. Eastern refers to this species' range east of the Great Plains.

Antrostomus — The genus name means "cavern mouth" from the Greek *antron* (a cavern) and *stoma* (the mouth). The reference is to the nightjars' wide gape, adapted to netting flying insects out of the air. Formerly *Caprimulgus vociferus.*

vociferous — The specific epithet means "noisy, vociferous or clamorous" from the

Latin *vox* (voice) and *ferre* (to bear or carry). The name is particularly appropriate for this bird's repetitive singing throughout the night. Whip-poor-wills sing so insistently, that you wonder if they ever come up for air. Naturalist John Burroughs once counted 1088 consecutive songs from a single bird. Donald Kroodsma observed a Whip-poor-will that repeated its song an estimated 20,898 times during a nine-hour period. That averages out to 3211 songs an hour or 54 songs a minute.

French Name: Engoulevent Bois-pourri

Spanish Names: Tapacaminos Cuerporruin; Tapacaminos Cuerprihuiu; Chotacabras Gritón

Other Names: Whip-her-well; Wib'rwil; Mimic; Nightjar; Mosquito Hawk; Guabairo; Guabairo Chico; Bois-pourri; Engoulevent; Mangeur Maringouins

Mexican Whip-poor-will
Antrostomus arizonae
(an-TROSS-toe-mus air-ih-ZONE-ee)

Mexican refers to this species' primary range in Mexico. It reaches our area in Arizona, southern New Mexico, and western Texas. The Mexican Whip-poor-will and Eastern Whip-poor-will were formerly considered a single species, the Whip-poor-will.

Antrostomus — The genus name means "cavern mouth" from the Greek *antron* (a cavern) and *stoma* (the mouth). The reference is to the nightjars' wide gape, adapted to netting flying insects out of the air.

arizonae — William Brewster described this as a subspecies of the Whip-poor-will in 1881 from a specimen collected in the Chiricahua Mountains of the Arizona Territory. The specific epithet means "of Arizona," referring to the type locality.

French Name: Engoulevent d'Arizona

Spanish Name: Chotacabras Cuerporruín Mexicano

Other Name: Stephan's Whippoorwill

Order Apodiformes

Family Apodidae
Swifts

Swifts are well named, for they are among the fastest-flying birds. Some have been clocked in excess of 100 mph:

"... the aptly named swifts are built for speed and show it. In normal flight they consistently hit greater speeds than other birds. Their streamlined, cigar-shaped bodies offer minimum resistance to the drag of air, and flat, narrow, swept-back wings provide maximum efficiency for sustained high-speed performance. Though a falcon stooping at prey may exceed a swift's velocity and reach 175 miles per hour, the predator maintains its top speed only during a dive." — Alexander Wetmore (1965)

The family name Apodidae means "without feet" from the Greek prefix *a-* (without) and *pous* or *podos* (the foot). Swifts do have feet, but they are tiny and weak, useless for walking or even perching on twigs or telephone wires. Swifts are only able to cling to vertical surfaces:

"The family's scientific name Apodidae derives from a Greek word meaning "footless." It too is fitting, for though swifts have feet and use them to grip their precipitous perches, the birds do not alight or stand on the ground. Few birds, in fact, are more totally creatures of the air than swifts. They feed and drink on the wing, snapping up insects in midair and scooping water into their gaping mouths as they skim over the surface of a stream. Sometimes they even mate aloft. And when building their nests they gather twigs or other materials in flight and speed with them to the nest site." — Alexander Wetmore (1965)

Black Swift
Cypseloides niger
(sip-seh-LOY-deez NYE-jer)

This swift is named for its all-black plumage.

Cypseloides — The genus name means "swift-like" from the Greek *kypselos* (a swift) and Greek suffix *—oides* (resembling). The reference is to a similarity to the Common Swift (*Apus apus*) of Europe.

niger — The specific epithet is Latin for "black."

French Name: Martinet Sombre
Spanish Name: Vencejo Negro
Other Names: Northern Black swift; Cloud Swift; Black Cloud Swift; Cloud Bird; Rainbird; Black Swallow; Chique-sol; Gros Martinet Noir; Hirondelle de Montagne; Oiseau de la Pluie; Vencejo Negro

Chimney Swift
Chaetura pelagica
(kee-TOUR-ah peh-LADGE-ih-kah)

"One fall they gathered in this way and took refuge for the night in a large chimney-stack near me for more than a month and a half. Several times I went to town to witness the spectacle, and spectacle it was; ten thousand of them, I should think, filling the air above a whole square like a whirling swarm of huge black bees, but saluting the ear with a multitudinous chippering instead of humming... After a great many feints and playful approaches, the whirring ring of the birds would suddenly grow denser above the chimney; then a stream of them, as if drawn down by some power of suction, would pour into the opening. For only a few seconds would this downward rush continue; then, as if the spirit of frolic had again got the upper hand of them, the ring would rise, and the chippering and circling go on. In a minute or two the same maneuver would be repeated, the chimney, as it were, taking its Swallows at intervals to prevent choking. It usually took a half-hour or more for the birds all to disappear down its capacious throat." — John Burroughs (1917)

Roger Tory Peterson, referring to the bird's body shape, said the Chimney Swift is "like a cigar with wings." These swifts are named for the structures where they roost and nest. Chimney Swifts formerly used hollow trees, but now they roost and nest almost exclusively in chimneys and other manmade structures. Chimney Swifts use their saliva to glue their nests of twigs to the inside walls of chimneys. Thousands of migrating swifts will gather above a large chimney at sunset, before dropping in to roost for the night as described above.

Chaetura — The genus name means "bristle tail" from the Greek *chaite* (a bristle or spine) and *oura* (the tail) and refers to the strong protruding shafts at the ends of the tail feathers These are used as props when the bird is clinging to a vertical surface.

Common Nighthawk, Chimney Swift, and Eastern Whip-poor-will, by Louis Agassiz Fuertes

pelagica — The specific epithet means "marine" from the Greek *pelagios* (of the sea), a peculiar name for a small land bird. Pelagic refers to true seabirds like petrels, albatrosses, and auks that spend the greater part of their lives far out at sea and come to land only to nest. Two explanations have been put forth regarding the Chimney Swift's inappropriate specific epithet. It is a misspelling of the word *pelasgica* after the Pelasgi, an ancient nomadic tribe of Greece. The reference is to the swift's migratory habits. They winter in the upper Amazon Basin of eastern Peru, which was discovered as late as 1943. Or the name could refer to an old folktale that swallows hibernated at the bottom of the sea in winter. Swifts superficially resemble swallows, although they are not closely related. In fact, Linnaeus initially placed the Chimney Swift in the genus *Hirundo* with the swallows:

"To early naturalists, the mass disappearance of Swallows in the autumn and their reappearance in the spring were well known but mysterious events. Some ancient Greeks considered the Swallow a bird of passage, flying to an unknown land for the winter, but Aristotle and Pliny considered that they must hide in crevices in rocks, remaining torpid, to escape the winter cold. Other naturalists thought they survived by diving under water and staying on the bottom, again torpid. This version of events seems to have taken root in the sixteenth century, when Olaus Magnus, Bishop of Uppsala in Sweden, reported fishermen pulling up nets full of Swallows, stiff and cold but which revived when taken into a warm room." — Angela K. Turner (1994)

French Name: Martinet Ramoneur

Spanish Names: Vencejo de Chimenea; Vencejo de Paso

Other Names: American Swift; Chimney Sweep; Chimney-sweep Swallow; American Swallow; Chimney Swallow; Chimney Bat; Chimney-bird; Cigar with Wings; Storm Sparrow; Bocanier; Ramono; Hirondelle des Cheminee; Glohlan-gaoith; Martinet des Cheminees; ramoneur; Roos Shwolm; Shornshte Shwolb

~

Vaux's Swift
Chaetura vauxi
(kee-TOUR-ah VAUKS-eye)

John Kirk Townsend discovered this species near Fort Vancouver, Washington. He called it Vaux's Chimney Swallow and described it as *Cypcelus Vauxi* in 1839, in his *The Narrative of a Journey across the Rocky Mountains* with the following dedication:

This species, (which I dedicate to my friend Wm. S. Vaux, Esq., of Philadelphia) is common on the Columbia River; breeds in hollow trees, forming its nest in the same manner as the *pelasgius*, and lays four white eggs.

Chaetura — The genus name means "bristle tail" from the Greek *chaite* (a bristle or spine) and *oura* (a tail) and refers to the strong protruding shafts at the ends of the tail feathers These are used as props when the bird is clinging to a vertical surface.

vauxi — The specific epithet commemorates William Sansom Vaux (1811–1882), a United States archaeologist and mineralogist, and a patron of the Philadelphia Academy of Natural Sciences. See common name above.

French Name: Martinet de Vaux
Spanish Names: Vencejo de Vaux; Vencejo Común
Other Name: Chimney Swallow

White-throated Swift
Aeronautes saxatilis
(air-oh-NAW-teez sacks-AT-ih-lis)

The white of this swift's throat extends as a broad stripe down the breast to the belly.

Aeronautes — The genus name means "air sailor" from the Greek *aeros* (air) and *nautes* (a sailor) The reference is to this bird's remarkable flying abilities. Swifts are among the most aerial of birds, and the White-throated Swift is said to be among the fastest. Swifts not only forage on the wing, but also drink, bathe, and may spend all night on the wing. Even mating occurs in flight. Courtship involves aerial displays with the pair flying toward each other, joining, and then tumbling down together for several hundred feet.

saxatilis — The specific epithet means "rock frequenting," from the Latin *saxum* (a rock or large stone). It refers to this swift's nesting sites in narrow, vertical crevices of mostly inaccessible cliffs.

French Name: Martinet à Gorge Blanche
Spanish Names: Vencejo de Pecho Blanco; Vencejo Gorjiblanco
Other Name: Rock Swift

Family Trochilidae
Hummingbirds

English colonists first applied the name hummingbird (or humbird) to the Ruby-throat, the only species that breeds east of the Great Plains. The incredibly fast-beating wings (50–80 beats/second make a buzzing, droning, or humming sound, like that of an insect, thus the name hummingbird. This characteristic has prompted a number of onomonopoetic names in various languages: *tz'unan* (Mayan), *zumbador* (Spanish), *murmures* (Lesser Antilles), and *zum-zum* (Cuba). Their insect-like flight and tiny size is the origin of the Spanish *pajaro mosca* (fly bird) and the French *oiseau mouche* (fly-sized bird). Their relationship with flowers coined the Spanish *picaflor* (flower piercer) and *chuparosa* (rose sucker), *chupaflor* (flower sucker), *chupamyrta* (sipper of myrtle), the French *suce-fleur* (flower sucker), and Portuguese *beija-flor* (the bird that kisses flowers). Hummingbirds are noted for their dazzling, metallic colors as described in the following passage:

"Brilliant beyond words, the colors of all hummingbirds have long been a source of wonder. The Aztecs of ancient Mexico, for instance, adorned their finery with the skins of hummingbirds. It is easy to understand why, arrayed in feathered robes that shattered sunlight into a rainbow of color, the Aztec leaders were regarded as divine." — *Reader's Digest Birds of North America* (1990)

Association with divinity and the sun is also reflected in a number of aboriginal names: the Arawak *colibre* (bird of the sun god), the Nahuatl *huitzitzil* (shining one with weapon like cactus thorn), the Brazilian Indian *ourissia* (rays of the sun), the Guarani *guanumbi*, the Guichua *quinde*, the Aztec *tozcatl* (the one who brings life), and the Navajo *da-hi-tu-hi* (one who brings new life). The hummingbirds' scintillating colors that seem to glow with their own light and fantastic plumage, crests, whiskers, fans, tufts, puffs, or gracefully trailing tail streamers, have prompted some evocative common names in the South American species, many inspired by gemstones, celestial bodies, or fanciful creatures. A few examples include Purple-crowned Fairy, Festive Coquette, Fiery Topaz, Shining Sunbeam, Tourmaline Sunangel, Crowned Woodnymph, Glowing Puffleg, Red-tailed Comet, Andean Hillstar, Green-tailed Trainbearer, Coppery Metaltail, Rainbow Starfrontler, Violet-tailed Sylph, White-vented Plumeleteer, and Marvelous Spatuletail. Our North American hummingbird fauna bears decidedly less inspired names, but at least they are descriptive. The family name derives from the Greek *trokhilos*, a name Herodotus used for an Egyptian plover and Aristotle used for some small bird, possibly the Eurasian Wren. Linnaeus applied it to the hummingbirds, for no obvious reason.

Mexican Violet-ear
Colibri thalassinus
(KOLE-ih-bree thah-LASS-ih-nus)

This hummingbird is named for the elongated blue-violet ear patch behind the eye. Mexican refers to its range in southern Mexico. It also occurs in Central America, and some stray into Texas. Formerly known as Green Violet-ear.

Colibri — The genus name is derived from the Arawak (Carib) Indian word for "hummingbird," literally meaning "bird of the sun god."

thalassinus — The specific epithet is Latin for "sea-green," which describes the dominant color.

French Name: Colibri Thalassin
Spanish Names: Colibrí de Oreja Violeta; Orejavioleta Verde; Colibrí Orejivioláceo Verde

Green-breasted Mango
Anthracothorax prevostii
(an-thra-so-THOR-acks pre-VOSS ih-eye)

This Mexican hummingbird got the name mango for its fondness for the blossoms of the popular tropical fruit tree. Green-breasted describes the color of the breast, which is actually blue to blue-green. The throat is emerald green and the belly varies from leaf green to golden green.

Anthracothorax — The genus name means "coal chest" from the Greek *anthrakos* (coal) and *thorax* (the chest) and refers to the velvety black stripe that runs from the throat onto the chest.

prevostii — René Primavère Lesson described this species in 1832, naming it in honor of Guillaume Florent Pévost (1794–1870), a French museum artist and author. The type specimen was collected near Veracruz, Mexico.

French Name: Mango de Prévost
Spanish Names: Mango Pechiverde; Manguito Pechiverde

Rivoli's Hummingbird
Eugenes fulgens
(YOU-jen-eez FULL-jenz)

This hummingbird's common name honors Francois Victor Masséna, 2nd Duke of Rivoli (1799–1863), a French ornithologist and owner of an extensive collection of hummingbird specimens. The name derives from the scientific name René Primevère Lesson had given it, *Ornismya Rivoli*. But William Swainson had previously described the species, giving it the specific epithet *fulgens*, so that name takes priority. Rivoli's Hummingbird was known as the Magnificent Hummingbird from 1983 to 2017, an appropriate name, for this hummingbird is magnificent indeed, both for its large size (for a hummer) and its striking color pattern in velvety black with an iridescent green gorget (throat patch) and purple crown.

Eugenes — The genus name means "well-born" or "noble" from the Greek *eu* (good) and *genos* (birth). The reference is to the bird's attractive appearance.

fulgens — The specific epithet is Latin for "glittering" or "resplendent," referring to the metallic green and purple colors in the plumage.

French Name: Colibri de Rivoli
Spanish Name: Colibrí Magnífico
Other Names: Refulgent Hummingbird; Admiral Hummingbird; Costa Rica Hummingbird; Panama Hummingbird

Plain-capped Starthroat
Heliomaster constantii
(HE-lee-oh-MAS-ter kon-STANT-ih-eye)

Starthroat refers to the gorget (throat patch) pattern in the tropical members of this genus. This is the Plain-capped Starthroat, because the crown of the head is dull green, while those of its tropical relatives are more brightly colored.

Heliomaster — The genus name means "sun searcher" from the Greek *helios* (sun) and *master* (searcher or seeker).

constantii — The specific epithet honors Charles Constant (1820–1905), a French physician, taxidermist and collector.

French Name: Colibri de Constant
Spanish Names: Picolargo Coronioscuro; Colibrí Picudo; Colibrí Pochotero

Blue-throated Mountain-gem
Lampornis clemenciae
(lamp-OR-nis clem-EN-sih-ee)

This is the largest species of hummingbird found in North America. Until recently, it was known simply as the Blue-throated Hummingbird. In 2019, the AOS (formerly the AOU) changed its name to Blue-throated Mountain-gem to be consistent with five *Lampornis* species of southern Mexico and Central America. A seventh *Lampornis* species, the Amethyst-throated Hummingbird (*L. amethystinus*) is now the Amethyst-throated Mountain-gem. The name is quite apt for this species, too, although it is fairly drab by hummingbird standards. Its iridescent cobalt to sky-blue gorget qualifies it for the gem part of the name, and its breeding habitat is the edges of mountain forests at altitudes of 3300–12,800 feet.

Lampornis — The genus name means "torch bird" or "radiant bird" from the Greek *lampa* (a torch or lamp) and *ornis* (a bird), and refers to the bright iridescent colors of the Mountain-gems.

clemenciae — French naturalist René Primèvere Lesson (1794–1849) named the Blue-throated Hummingbird *Ornismya clemenciae* in honor of his second wife Marie Clémence Lesson, an artist who specialized in natural history subjects. The type specimen was from the collection of the Duke of Rivoli, who acquired it along with other specimens from Mexico in 1829.

French Names: Colibri a Gorge Bleue; Oiseau-mouche de Clemence
Spanish Names: Colibrí de Garganta Azul; Colibrí Garganta Azul; Colibrí-serrano Gorjiazul; Chupaflor Gorjiazul; Chupamirto Garganta Azul
Other Names: Blue-throated Hummer; Blue-throated Cacique

Lucifer Hummingbird
Calothorax lucifer
(kal-oh-THOR-aks LOO-siff-er)

"Now, who could it be? Could it be . . . . . SATAN?!" — The Church Lady, Saturday Night Live

Actually, this little hummingbird's name has nothing to do with Satan or the devil. Lucifer means "light bearing" from the Latin *lux* (light) and *fer* (bearing). It refers to the male's iridescent plumage, particularly the bright purple gorget that glows in the sunlight.

Calothorax — The genus name means "beautiful breast" from the Greek *kalos* (beautiful) and *thorax* (the breast). The reference is to the male's unusually long gorget that extends to the upper part of the breast.

lucifer — See common name above.

French Name: Colibri Lucifer
Spanish Name: Tijereta Norteña

Ruby-throated Hummingbird
Archilochus colubris
(ar-KILL-uh-kus COL-oo-bris)

"A minute spritelike bird, scarcely bigger than a good-sized insect, it is white below and burnished, sparkling green on the back. The adult male has a gorgeous flaming throat, which, when the sun strikes it, flashes back a deep, glowing orange or red." — Winsor Marrett Tyler

The male's red gorget gives this hummingbird its name. In poor light the throat appears black, but when the sun hits it right, the gorget shines a deep ruby red. This throat patch is used in courtship displays and to intimidate rivals at choice nectar sources.

Archilochus — The genus is named for Archilochus (or Arkhilokhos), a Thracian poet of the 6th century BC, famous for his

Ruby-throated Hummingbird,
by Louis Agassiz Fuertes

satirical wit and a tendency to cut and run in battle. But he lived to fight another day. This is one of eight hummingbird genera that commemorate classical artisans, following the precedent set by Linnaeus and other 18th century authors who took many names from the classics and mythology to express relationships in perplexing genera. It is likely that these names were given without thought of any special significance. Seven genera of South American hummingbirds follow in the tradition of taking names from the classics, *Klais, Damophila, Sappho, Rhodopsis, Doricha, Atthis,* and *Myrtis*.

colubris — As it stands, the specific epithet means "serpent" in Latin, as in the nonvenomous snake family Colubridae. But here it doesn't make much sense. It is likely that Linnaeus misspelled *colibri*, the Arawak Indian word for "hummingbird," literally "bird of the sun god."

French Name: Colibri à Gorge Rubis
Spanish Names: Colibrí Garganta Rubi; Colibrí Gorjirrubi; Garganta de Rubí
Other Names: Ruby-throat; Common

Sidebar 12
Living Gemstones

Audubon called hummingbirds "glittering fragments of the rainbow," but their extraordinary colors are most often compared to precious gems, which are also reflected in many of their names. Only two species in our area, one a summer resident, the Ruby-throated Hummingbird, the other a vagrant from Mexico, the Berylline Hummingbird, are so-named, but gemstones are well represented among the names of tropical species, Horned Sungem, Ruby-topaz Hummingbird, Turquoise-throated Puffleg, Brazilian Ruby, Sapphire-spangled Emerald, Gould's Jewelfront, Lazuline Sabrewing, Garnet-throated Hummingbird, and Amethyst Woodstar to name a few. Ironically, hummingbirds, were once actually used to make jewelry:

So brilliant and gem-like are these tiny birds that at one time they were used for jewelry, and the trade in them was tremendous. During the 19th century millions of hummingbird skins were shipped from northern South America and the West Indies to European markets, where they were fashioned into pins, brooches, and other accessories for feminine adornment. One London dealer imported more than 400,000 skins from the West Indies in one year alone. The center of this trade, which has now fortunately subsided, was Bogotá, Colombia, in the center of the family's abundance and diversity.

""Bogotá trade skins" form the nucleus of many scientific collections of hummingbirds still in existence, and many species were first described by European "cabinet ornithologists" from these commercial skins, which lacked data and were of uncertain source. Some distinctive species are still known only from one or two such native-collected specimens, and have yet to be found in the field by ornithologists." — Oliver L. Austin, Jr. (1961)

Hummingbird; Fly; Hummer; Honey Bird; Honey-sucker; Mange-maringouins; Oiseau Mouche; Suceur de Fleur; Shnaffag'le; Shnarrfagle; Draundeun

Black-chinned Hummingbird
Archilochus alexandri
(ar-KILL-oh-kus al-ig-ZAN-dry)

Unlike most hummingbirds whose gorgets reflect luminous colors, this one's is flat black with just an iridescent purple border along the lower edge.

Archilochus — The genus is named for Archilochus (or Arkhilokhos), a Thracian poet of the 6th century BC, known for his satirical wit and a tendency to cut and run in battle. This is one of eight hummingbird genera that commemorate classical artisans, following the precedent set by Linnaeus and other 18th century authors.

alexandri — The specific epithet honors a physician, Dr. M. M. Alexandre (fl. 1846), who collected birds, including this species, in Mexico and sent specimens to France.

French Name: Colibri à Gorge Noire
Spanish Names: Colibrí Garganta Morada; Colibrí Barbinegro
Other Names: Black-chin; Black-chinned Hummer; Colibri Gorjinegro

Black-chinned Hummingbird, by Allan C. Brooks

Anna's Hummingbird, by Allan C. Brooks

Anna's Hummingbird
Calypte anna
(kal-IP-tee AN-nah)

Italian surgeon Paolo Borta collected the type specimen, possibly near San Francisco, during his three-year (1827–1829) round-the-world voyage on the French trading ship *Le Héros*. Upon returning to France, he gave some of the specimens he had collected to François Victor Masséna, 2nd Duke of Rivoli. Prince Masséna allowed his friend Réne Primevère Lesson to examine the specimens. Lesson described the hummingbird in his *Histoire Naturelle des Oiseaux-Mouches*, naming it *Ornismya Anna* in honor of the prince's wife Anna d' Essling, Duchess of Rivoli. His common name for it was Oiseaux-Mouches Anna.

Calypte — Two explanations have been put forth for this bird's genus name. The first is that it derives from the Greek *kalyptos* (hidden or covered) and could refer to the sea nymph Calypso. Or it may be from the Greek *kaluptre* (a hood or woman's veil) and refer to the combination of the male's glittering crown and gorget suggesting a veil.

anna — The specific epithet commemorates Anna d' Essling, Duchess of Rivoli (1806–1896). Her husband François Victor Masséna, 2nd Duke of Rivoli owned an extensive hummingbird collection that included the type specimen. Rivoli's Hummingbird is named in his honor. See common name above.

French Name: Colibri d'Anna

Spanish Names: Colibrí de Cabeza Roja; Colibrí de Anna

Other Names: Anna's Hummer; Columbian Hummingbird

Costa's Hummingbird
Calypte costae
(kal-IP-tee KOSS-tee)

"This little feathered gem is, to my mind, the prettiest of all the North American hummingbirds. The gorgeous, glowing colors of its brilliant helmet adorn, in the male, the top of the head, the throat, and the elongated feathers on the sides of the gorget; the burnished metallic violet of these feathers changes in certain lights to royal purple, magenta, blue, or even green, a beautiful display of colors at various angles." — Arthur Cleveland Bent (1940)

French naval surgeon Adolphe Simon Neboux collected the type specimen at Magdalena Bay, Baja California in November or December of 1837. When he returned to Paris, he handed over the specimen to naturalist Jules Bourcier who named it Oiseau-Mouche de Costa (*Ornismya costae*) for Savoyard statesman Louis Marie Pantaléon Costa, who owned an extensive hummingbird collection. Wildlife artist and author Scott Weidensaul noted, "This practice of naming new species after powerful and wealthy patrons, was a mixture of sincerity and calculated flattery, for such patrons frequently were a biologist's major source of funding."

Calypte — Two explanations have been put forth for this bird's genus name. The first is that it derives from the Greek *kalyptos* (hidden or covered) and could refer to the sea nymph Calypso. Or it may be from the Greek *kaluptre* (a hood or woman's veil) and refer to the combomation of the male's glittering crown and gorget suggesting a veil.

costae — The specific epithet commemorates Louis Marie Pantaléon Costa, Marquis de Beau-Regard (1806–1864), a Savoyard soldier and naturalist. See common name above.

French Name: Colibri de Costa

Spanish Names: Colibrí de Cabeza Violeta; Colibrí de Costa

Broad-tailed Hummingbird
Selasphorus platycercus
(seh-LASS-for-us plat-ih-SIR-cus)

This hummingbird's long, wide tail gives it its name.

Selasphorus — The genus name means "flame bearing" from the Greek *selas* (a flame) and *phoros* (bearing) and refers to the iridescent

Costa's Hummingbird, by Allan C. Brooks

Rufous Hummingbird, by Louis Agassiz Fuertes

gorgets of these hummingbirds, that glow in the sunlight.

platycercus — The specific epithet means "broad tail" from the Greek *platys* (broad) and *kerkos* (the tail).

French Name: Colibri à Queue Large
Spanish Names: Zumbador de Cola Ancha; Zumbador Coliancho
Other Name: Broad-tailed Hummer

Rufous Hummingbird
Selasphorus rufus
(seh-LASS-for-us ROOF-us)

"Although I have always considered Costa's hummingbird to be the most beautiful of our North American hummingbirds, on account of the charming colors reflected in its crown and gorget, it must yield the palm for brilliancy to the rufous hummingbird and its near relative Allen's. The brilliant scarlet of the rufous hummer's gorget, which often glows like burnished gold, puts it in the front rank as a gleaming gem, a feathered ball of fire. It is not only fiery in appearance, but it has a fiery temper and makes things lively for any rivals near its feeding station or its nest." — Arthur Cleveland Bent (1940)

The fiery rufous upperparts of the male give this hummingbird its name.

Selasphorus — The genus name means "flame bearing" from the Greek *selas* (a flame) and *phoros* (bearing) and refers to the iridescent gorgets of these hummingbirds, that glow in the sunlight.

rufus — The specific epithet is Latin for "reddish."

French Name: Colibri Roux
Spanish Name: Zumbador Rufo

Allen's Hummingbird
Selasphorus sasin
(seh-LASS-for-us SAY-sin)

This hummingbird is named for Charles Andrew Allen (1841–1930), a California collector of birds. In 1877, Henshaw described what he believed to be a new species of hummingbird, from a specimen that Allen had collected, and he named it in his honor. But French naturalist Rene Lesson had already

Allen's Hummingbird, by Allan C. Brooks

given this hummingbird the specific epithet *sasin* in 1830, so Henshaw's name was invalid. However, Allen is still commemorated in the bird's common name.

Selasphorus — The genus name means "flame bearing" from the Greek *selas* (a flame) and *phoros* (bearing) and refers to the iridescent gorgets of these hummingbirds, that glow in the sunlight.

sasin — The specific epithet is the Nootka Indian name for this bird.

French Name: Colibri d'Allen
Spanish Name: Zumbador de Allen

Calliope Hummingbird
Selasphorus calliope
(seh-LASS-for-us cal-EYE-oh-pee)

"Its generic name was well chosen, *Stellula*, little star, for the long, narrow, metallic purple feathers rise and spread, under excitement, above the snow-white background of the gorget, like a scintillating star. The choice of the specific name, *calliope*, was not so fortunate; Calliope was the muse of eloquence, and this is a very silent bird." — Arthur Cleveland Bent (1940)

This hummingbird's former scientific name was *Stellula calliope* (little star with a beautiful voice). It is puzzling why British ornithologist John Gould chose to name this unmusical little bird for the Greek muse of epic poetry. It has been suggested that perhaps he was making a joke to mystify us. Another idea is that the Calliope Hummingbird is named for the musical instrument, because the purple, dagger-shaped throat feathers suggest a calliope's row of steam whistles.

Selasphorus — The genus name means "flame bearing" from the Greek *selas* (a flame) and *phoros* (bearing) and refers to the iridescent gorgets of these hummingbirds, that glow in the sunlight. Formerly *Stellula calliope*.

calliope — The specific epithet means "beautiful voice" from the Greek *kalli* (beautiful) and *ops* (voice). See common name above.

French Name: Colibri Calliope
Spanish Names: Colibrí de Garganta Rayada; Colibrí de Caliop

Calliope Hummingbird, by Allan C. Brooks

Broad-billed Hummingbird
Cynanthus latirostris
(sin-AN-thus lat-ih-ROSS-tris)

It's a pity that such a beautiful hummingbird with its iridescent green and blue plumage and bright red bill is stuck with such a lackluster name. Broad-billed refers to the wide, flattened base of the bill, but you would need to have the bird in your hand to see it.

Cynanthus — There are several explanations for the meaning of the genus name. It appears that the first part is a misspelling of a word meaning "blue." It should be spelled *cyan* from the Greek *kuanos* (dark blue). *Anthus* is said to either mean "brilliant" from the Greek *anthos* or to be the Greek word for "a flower." So the name could refer to the male's shining blue throat, or perhaps refer to this bird's relationship with flowers.

Hummingbird authority Sheri Williamson suggests that *Anthus* is the genus name for pipit. Pipits are songbirds noted for their tail-bobbing habit. The reference is to the fact that the Broad-billed Hummingbird's tail is almost always in motion. Of this behavior, Pete Dunne wrote, "The tail moves like a rippling banner. Opening, closing, fluttering. . . even when the bird lands, the tail seems difficult to tame."

latirostris — The specific epithet means "broad bill" from the Latin *latus* (broad or wide) and *rostrum* (the bill).

French Name: Colibri Circé
Spanish Names: Colibrí de Pico Ancho; Colibrí Piquiancho
Other Name: Circe Hummingbird

Berylline Hummingbird
Amazilia beryllina
(am-ah-ZILL-ih-ah ber-ill-INE-ah)

This hummingbird, with its shining green head, back, and breast, is named for the green gemstone beryl (emerald).

Amazilia — The genus name stems from Amazili, an Inca heroine of an 18th century novel *Les Incas, ou la destruction de l'Empire du Perou* (1777) by Jean Francois Marmontel. The setting of the novel is in Peru, where many of these hummingbirds occur.

beryllina — The specific epithet is Modern

Latin for "emerald green." See common name above.
French Name: Ariane Béryl
Spanish Names: Colibrí Berilo; Colibrí de Berilo

Buff-bellied Hummingbird
Amazilia yucatanensis
(am-ah-ZILL-ih-ah you-kah-tan-EN-sis)

This hummingbird is named for its warm cinnamon-buff belly that contrasts with the metallic green throat and breast.

Amazilia — The genus name stems from Amazili, an Inca heroine of an 18th century novel *Les Incas, ou la destruction de l'Empire du Perou* (1777) by Jean Francois Marmontel. The setting of the novel is in Peru, where many of these hummingbirds occur.

yucatanensis — The specific epithet is Modern Latin for "of the Yucatan Peninsula" in Mexico, where the type specimen was collected, and where the species occurs.

French Name: Ariane du Yucatan
Spanish Names: Colibrí Yucateco; Colibrí Vientre-canelo
Other Names: Fawn-breasted Hummingbird; Yucatan Hummingbird

Violet-crowned Hummingbird
Amazilia violiceps
(am-ah-ZILL-ih-ah vy-OH-lih-seps)

This hummingbird's blue to violet-blue crown gives it its name.

Amazilia — The genus name stems from Amazili, an Inca heroine of an 18th century novel *Les Incas, ou la destruction de l'Empire du Perou* (1777) by Jean Francois Marmontel. The setting of the novel is in Peru, where many of these hummingbirds occur.

violiceps — The specific epithet means "violet headed" from the Latin *viola* (violet-colored) and *ceps* (headed).

French Name: Ariane à Couronne Violette
Spanish Names: Colibrí de Corona Violeta; Colibrí Corona-violeta

Other Names: Salvin's Hummingbird; Azurecrown

White-eared Hummingbird
Hylocharis leucotis
(high-low-CAR-iss lew-COT-iss)

The white ear stripe behind the eye gives this hummingbird its name.

Hylocharis — The genus name means "delight of the woods" from the Greek *hule* (woodland) and *kharis* (delight or beauty). The reference is to the colorful plumage and to this bird's habitat in pine-oak mountain forests at 4500–10,000 feet.

leucotis — The specific epithet means "white eared" from the Greek *leukos* (white) and *otis* (eared).

French Name: Sapphir à Oreilles Blanches
Spanish Names: Zafiro de Oreja Blanca; Colibrí Orejiblanco

Calliope Hummingbird, Broad-billed Hummingbird, White-eared Hummingbird, and Xantus's Hummingbird, by Allan C. Brooks

Order Gruiformes

Family Rallidae
Rails, Gallinules, and Coots

Yellow Rail
Coturnicops noveboracensis
(coh-TURN-ih-kops no-veh-BOR-ah-sen-sis)

Rail stems from the French *rale* (a rail) which comes from the Old French *raale* (to make a scraping noise or a rattle in the throat) and so is imitative of the calls of some of these birds. "Thin as a rail" refers not to a fence, but to the bird. Rails have laterally compressed bodies, an adaptation for moving easily through dense stands of reeds and cattails. This tiny rail's mustard-yellow plumage gives it its name.

Coturnicops — The genus name means "resembling a quail" from Latin *coturnix* (a quail) and the Greek *ops* (appearance). With its plump body, short tail, and streaky plumage, the Yellow Rail does indeed resemble a quail, particularly the Old World migratory quail (*Coturnix coturnix*).

noveboracensis — The specific epithet is Modern Latin for "of New York," where presumably the type specimen was collected.

French Name: Râle Jaune
Spanish Name: Polluela Amarilla
Other Names: Little Yellow Rail; Yellow-breasted Rail; New York Rail; Yellow Crake; Water Sparrow; Clicker

Black Rail
Laterallus jamaicencis
(lat-eh-RAL-us jah-may-ih-SEN-sis)

This sparrow-sized rail is named for its dark plumage, brownish-black with white speckling above, charcoal gray below.

Laterallus — The genus name means "hidden rail" from the Latin *lateo* (to lurk or hide) and *rallus* the Latinized form of rail. The name is very descriptive of this little rail's secretive behavior of staying concealed in marsh grass.

jamaicincis — The specific epithet is Modern Latin for "of Jamaica," where the specimen was first discovered in 1760. German naturalist Johann Friedrich Gmelin described it in 1788 and gave it its specific name. The Black Rail was not discovered in the United States until 1836, when Audubon described and painted it from specimens Titian R. Peale had given him.

French Name: Râle Noir
Spanish Name: Polluela Negra
Other Names: Little Black Rail; Black Crake; Gallito Negro

Clapper Rail
Rallus longirostris
(RAL-us lonj-ih-ROS-tris)

This rail is named for its cackling calls that resemble old-fashioned clappers.

Rallus — The genus name is the Latinized form of rail.

longirostris — The specific epithet means "long bill" from the Latin *longus* (long) and *rostrum* (the bill), which describes this species' long, thin bill.

French Name: Râle Gris
Spanish Name: Rascón Picudo
Other Names: Yuma Clapper Rail; Light-footed Rail; Big Rail; Rattling Rail; Common Clapper; Marsh Clapper; Meadow Clapper; Louisiana Clapper; Mud Hen; Sedge Hen; Prairie Hen; Meadow Hen; Saltwater Meadow Hen; Marsh Hen; Saltwater Marsh Hen; Salt-marsh Hen; Sedge-Hen; Mangrove-Hen; Gallineta; Gallinuela de Agua Salada; Gallinuela de Mangle; Pintade; Pollo de Laguna; Pollo de Mangle; Rateau; Yegua

King Rail
Rallus elegans
(RAL-us EL-ee-ganz)

This rail's large size (it is the largest North American rail) and striking color pattern give it its name.

Rallus — The genus name is the Latinized form of rail.

elegans — The specific epithet is Latin for "elegant" which describes this species' bright, boldly marked plumage.

French Name: Râle Élégant
Spanish Name: Rascón Real
Other Names: Red-breasted Rail; Great Red-breasted Rail; Big Virginia Rail; Bull Rale; Mud Hen; Freshwater Mud Hen; Freshwater Marsh-hen; Fresh-marsh Hen; Fresh-water Hen; Marsh Hen; Meadow Hen; Prairie Chicken; Stage Driver; Grand Rale de Prairie; Martillera; Gallinuela de Agua Dulce

Virginia Rail
Rallus limicola
(RAL-us lye-MICK-oh-lah)

Virginia is not a particularly appropriate name, as this rail only occurs in the extreme eastern part of the state. Its breeding range is primarily in the northern states and southern Canada from New England and the Maritimes west to the Pacific coast. Perhaps like many birds, this rail was named for where it was first discovered.

Rallus — The genus name is the Latinized form of rail.

limicola — The specific epithet means "mud dweller" from the Latin *limus* (mud) and *colo* (to inhabit) and refers to the bird's wetland habitat.

French Name: Râle de Virginie
Spanish Names: Rascón Limícola; Rascón de Virginia
Other Names: Red Rail; Little Red Rail; Little Red-breasted Rail; Long-billed Rail; Lesser Clapper Rail; Bull Rale; Freshwater Marsh Hen; Fresh-water Mud Hen; Small Mud Hen; Water Hen

Virginia Rail, King Rail, and Clapper Rail, by Louis Agassiz Fuertes

Yellow Rail, Black Rail, and Sora, by Louis Agassiz Fuertes

Sora
Porzana carolina
(Por-ZANE-ah car-oh-LINE-ah)

"He is so secretive, so elusive, yet how boldly the Sora proclaims himself upon first arriving on his breeding territory. With rising inflection, the male calls repeatedly, plaintively, *sor-AH . . . sor-AH*, as if asking a mate to join him, calling all day and sometimes all night long until he is successful. Once birds pair, another sound becomes more common, the distinctive horse whinny, *whee-hehehehehehehehe-he-he-he-hee-hee-hee-hee* . . . . It's three or four seconds of the finest sound that ever emerges from a marsh." — Donald Kroodsma (2008)

Sora may be onomatopoetic as suggested in the opening passage. It is believed to be an American Indian name for this bird.

Porzana — The genus name is the Italian word for "crake," a general name for a short-billed rail.

carolina — The specific epithet is Modern Latin for "of Carolina."

French Name: Marouette de Caroline
Spanish Name: Polluela Sora
Other Names: Sora Rail; American Rail; English Rail; Common Rail; Water Rail; Carolina Rail; Chicken-billed Rail; Chicken-bill; Railbird; Little Rice Bird; Carolina Crake; Carolina Crake Gallinule; Sora Crake; Sorus; Soree; Soree Gallinule; Water Partridge; Little American Water Hen; Mud Hen; Meadow Chicken; Tinsmith; Ortolan; Plover; Coot; Widgeon; Rale Musque; Gallito

Purple Gallinule
Porphyrio martinica
(por-FEAR-ih-oh mar-TIN-ih-cah)

"Common, white pond lilies were quite numerous in the open places; and among the "bonnets" they were in full bloom. Water turkeys, wood, and white ibises, and various herons were seen flying over or found nesting in the willows. Least bitterns, sora rails, and boat-tailed grackles were breeding in the saw grass and the loud notes of the grackles and redwings were heard all over the marshes. And in the larger open spaces, where the "bonnets," "lettuce" and pond lilies grew we saw the purple gallinules, together with their more common relatives the Florida gallinules and coots. We were thrilled with the striking beauty of this handsome species, as we saw for the first time its brilliant colors in its native haunts. One can not mistake it as it flies feebly along just over the tops of the "bonnets" with its long yellow legs dangling. And how gracefully and lightly it walks over the lily pads, supported by its long toes, nodding and bowing with a dovelike motion and flirting the white flag of its tail." — Arthur Cleveland Bent (1927)

Gallinule means "little hen." See genus name of Common Gallinule. This species' iridescent bluish-purple head, neck, and underparts give it its name.

Porphyrio — The genus name means "purple water hen" from the Greek *porphyrion* (water hen) from *porphyreos* (purple).

martinica — The specific epithet is Modern Latin for "of Martinique," one of the Windward Islands in the West Indies where the species was first discovered.

French Name: Talève Violacée
Spanish Names: Gallineta Morada; Gallareta Morada
Other Names: Blue Pete; Blue Peter; Blue-pated Coot; Plantain Coot; Hen of Heaven; Marsh Hen; Bonnet-Walker; Marsh Guinea; Pond Guinea; Rale Heae; Sultana; La Poule Sultana; Poule d'Eau à Cachet Bleu; Cascamiol; Gallareta Azul; Gallareta Inglesa; Gallereta Platanera

Purple Swamphen
Porphyrio porphyrio
(por-FEAR-ih-oh)

This Eurasian species is on the American checklist because a small population is established in Florida. The Purple Swamphen resembles a larger, bulkier Purple Gallinule and has similar iridescent bluish-purple plumage. Swamphen refers to this bird's wetland habitat and to its chicken-like movements like those of the gallinules. See next entry.

Porphyrio — The genus/species name means "purple water hen" from the Greek *porphyrion* (water hen) from *porphyreos* (purple).

French Name: Talève Sultane
Spanish Name: Calamón Común
Other Names: Purple Gallinule; Green-backed Gallinule; European Swamphen; Indian Swamphen; Black-headed Swamphen; Black-backed Swamphen

Purple Gallinule and Common Gallinule, by Louis Agassiz Fuertes

Common Gallinule
Gallinula galeata
(gal-IN-you-lah gal-ee-ATE-ah)

"A gallinule, equally with a barnyard chicken, appears ridiculous and out of its element in the air as it labors along a few paces, dragging its legs after it, and drops awkwardly to the ground. The similarity to a chicken does not end with flight. In appearance, as in habits, and particularly in voice, the water hens and hens of the poultry yard have as much in common. A single pair in a swamp keep up clatter enough for a yard full of fowls, "now loud and terror stricken like a hen whose head is just going to be cut off," as a friend of Bradford Torrey's expressed it; "then soft and full of content, as if the aforesaid hen had laid an egg ten minutes before and were felicitating herself upon the achievement."" — Neltje Blanchan (1898)

Gallinule derives from the genus name, meaning "little hen." See genus name below. Common refers to this species' wide range compared to other gallinule species. Known as Florida Gallinule until 1957. The Common Gallinule was formerly considered conspecific with the Common Moorhen (*G. chloropus*) of Eurasia. Despite its name, the Moorhen is not a bird you would find on the heather moorlands of the British Isles. The name is actually a corruption of *merehen*. *Mere* is another word for a small lake, pond, or marsh, which are the Moorhen's true habitats.

Gallinula — The genus name means "little hen" from the Latin *gallina* (a hen or chicken) plus the diminutive suffix *-ula*. The reference is to this species superficial resemblance to a hen both physically and behaviorally. The latter in the bird's foraging method of walking and pecking. These characteristics are also reflected in some of its colloquial names.

galeata — The specific epithet means "helmeted" from the Latin *galea* (a helmet) and refers to the red frontal shield at the base of the bill.

French Name: Gallinule d'Amérique

Spanish Names: Gallineta de Frente Roja; Gallineta Común; Gallareta Frentirroja

Other Names: Florida Gallinule; American Gallinule; Black Gallinule; Scarlet-fronted Gallinule; Moorcock; Bilcock; Bilter; Moor Coot; Kitty Coot; Chicken-foot Coot; Red-seal Coot; Summer Coot; Bonnet-walker; Sedge Peter; Blue Peter; Blue Rail; Water Rail; King-Rail; King Sora; King-Ortolan; Night Bird; Water Fowl; Water Chicken; Water Hen; Marsh Hen; Moat Hen; Pond Hen; Mere Hen; Stank Hen; Mud Hen; Red-billed Mud Hen; Rice-Hen; Rice Bird; Marsh-Pullet; Mud-Pullet; Pond Guinea; Dabchick; Skitty; Stankie; Cuddy; Morant; Gallareta Colorado; Gallareta Pico Colorado; Gallareta Pico Rojo; Gallareta Común; Dagareta; Yagareta; Rale Poule d'Eau; Poule d'Eau à Cachet Rouge; Poule d'Eau de Marquis; Poule de Lac

American Coot
Fulica americana
(FEW-lik-ah ah-mer-ih-CANE-ah)

The origin of coot is not known for certain, but it may be from the Dutch *koet* (short-tailed) or from the Welsh *cwta-iar* (bob-tailed hen). In Europe, the name was originally applied to the Common Murre and may be related to scoot and scout, which were nicknames for this bird. Later the species under discussion was given the name bald coot (bald meaning "white") in reference to the bird's white frontal shield. Duck hunters also call the three North American species of scoters coots. See Black Scoter for details. Cranky old men are sometimes called old coots, presumably after the bird's quarrelsome nature. American distinguishes our native species from the Common Coot (*F. atra*) of Eurasia.

Fulica — The genus name is the Latin word for "coot" possibly from the Latin *fuligo* (soot) for the bird's blackish color.

americana — The specific epithet is Modern Latin for "of America."

French Name: Foulque d'Amerique

Spanish Names: Gallareta Americana; Focha Americana

Other Names: Common Coot; Ivory-billed Coot; White-billed Coot; White-seal Coot; Cinereous Coot; Mud Coot; Freshwater Coot; Baldface; Baldface Coot; Baldface Duck; Crow-Duck; Crowbill Duck; Whiteface Duck; Fish Duck; Black Fish-Duck; Mud Duck; Mud Hen; White-bellied Mud Hen; Blue Hen;

Marsh-Hen; Blue Marsh-Hen; Water Fowl; Water Guinea; Marsh Guinea; Water Hen; Pond-Hen; Sea Hen; Blue Pond Hen; Grey Pond Hen; Meadow Hen; Tule Hen; Indian Hen; Moor-Hen; Fool Hen; Rice Hen; Rail Hen; Water Chicken; Tule Chicken; Prairie Chicken; Mud Chicken; Mud Chick; Blue Pullet; Gull; Barnegat Turkey; Chinese Mallard; Oklahoma Pintail; Poor-man's Goose; Hen-bill; Crow-bill; White-bill; Blue Pete; Blue Peter; Sea-Crow; Pond Crow; Louse Bird; Red-eyed Devil Bird; Republican; Shuffler; Spatterer; Splatterer; Flusterer; Moor-head; Poulet Dean; Poule de Marais; Poule d'Eau; Pull-doo; Pellick; Hell-Diver; Sea-Crow; Pond Crow; Wosserhund; Gallinazo Americano; Judelle; Gallareta Americana; Gallareta Pico Blanco; Dagareta Negra; Gallinazo; Yagareta; Shdink Ent

Family Aramidae
Limpkin

Limpkin
Aramus guarauna
(ARE-ah-mus gwar-OW-nah)

The Limpkin (little limping one) is named for its odd halting gait, seeming to favor one leg.

Aramus — The genus name is from the Greek *aramos* (a kind of heron) mentioned by Hesychius. While not a heron, the Limpkin superficially resembles one.

guarauna — The specific epithet is the Tupi (Brazilian) Indian word for this or some other marsh bird.

French Name: Courlan Brun
Spanish Name: Carrao
Other Names: Crying Bird; Crippled Bird; Clucking Hen; Indian Pullet; Mourning Widow; Screamer; Speckled Curlew; Courlan; Carrao; Scolopaceous Courlan; Colas; Grand Colas; Guareao; Poule de Ajoli

Family Gruidae
Cranes

Crane first appears as a name for these birds as *cran* in Old English. It is said to derive from Indo-European roots such as *gar* (to cry out), a reference to the loud calls of these birds.

Sandhill Crane
Antigone canadensis
(an-TIG-oh-nee can-ah-DEN-sis)

The Sandhill Crane takes its name from the Sandhills region of north central Nebraska, a major staging area for the migrating birds. The rolling prairie of the Sandhills consists of grass-stabilized sand dunes. Much of this region lies within the Platte River watershed. Here, along a 75-mile stretch of the Platte, approximately 500,000 Sandhill Cranes, about 80% of the total population, stop over to rest and refuel for the journey ahead. This is also a Mecca for birders, who contribute millions of dollars to the local economy. In states where it is legally hunted and its flesh prized for the table, the Sandhill

Sandhill Crane, by John James Audubon

Crane has been tagged with the nickname "Ribeye of the Sky."

Antigone — The genus name stems from a Greek mythological character. Antigone of Troy was the daughter of King Laomedon. She boasted that her hair was more beautiful than that of the goddess Hera. Antigone soon learned how foolish it was to compare herself with a being more powerful than she was. Hera, taking offense, changed Antigone's hair into a mass of writhing snakes. Another god, taking pity on Antigone, transformed her into a crane or a stork, birds that eat snakes. Linnaeus confused Antigone with another mythological character, Gerana, princess of the Pygmies. She was changed into a crane under similar circumstances. Formerly *Grus canadensis*.

canadensis — The specific epithet is Modern Latin for "of Canada," where many Sandhill Cranes nest.

French Name: Grue du Canada

Spanish Names: Grulla Gris; Grulla Canadiense

Eskimo and Inuit Name: Kutchilkag (color of body red)

Other Names: Greater Sandhill Crane; Lesser Sandhill Crane; Southern Sandhill Crane; Upland Crane; Field Crane; Blue Crane; Gray Crane; Red Crane; Brown Crane; Little Brown Crane; Florida Crane; Sandhill Whooper; Alaska Turkey; North-west Turkey; Brown Turkey; Baldhead; Garoo; Grulla; Grue Bleue

Whooping Crane
Grus americana
(GROOSE ah-mer-ih-CANE-ah)

"Suddenly the male whooped — a buglelike alarm note that sent a tingle along our spines — *kerloo! ker-lee-oo!* The female's voice echoed his. The birds spread their great satin-white, black-tipped wings, ran several steps, and took off. I knew that they would put at least a mile and perhaps a stretch of deep water between them and us. Then they would land with slow, graceful flaps of their wings, running a few strides with unruffled poise. "What a bird" said Fred, staring in awe. "What a bird!"" — Robert Porter Allen (1965)

This very rare crane is named for its bugling vocalizations, particularly in courtship.

Grus — The genus name is the Latin word for "a crane."

americana — The specific epithet is Modern Latin for "of America."

French Name: Grue Blanche

Spanish Names: Grulla Blanca; Grulla Americana

Other Names: White Crane; Great White Crane; White Turkey; Whooper; Flying Sheep; Garoo; Grus Blanche

Order Charadriiformes

Family Recurvirostridae
Stilts and Avocets

Black-necked Stilt
Himantopus mexicanus
(high-MAN-toe-pus meks-ih-CANE-us)

Fantastically long, orange-red legs give the stilt its name. Pete Dunne calls the Black-necked Stilt, "A stiffly and formally attired shorebird perched on long red circus stilts." Black-necked describes the color on the hind neck, but the crown, back, and wings are black, too.

Himantopus — The genus name means "strap-footed" from the Greek *himantos* (a strap or thong) and *pous* (the foot). The reference is to the long legs.

mexicanus — The specific epithet is Modern Latin for "of Mexico," where the type specimen was collected.

French Name: Echasse d'Amérique

Sidebar 13
Shorebirds

Members of the next five families are known collectively as shorebirds, because many species frequent ocean beaches, tidal mudflats, lakeshores, or rocky seacoasts, particularly outside of the breeding season. The British call them waders. In older literature you may find other terms that refer to the sandpipers and plovers collectively. Wilson used the name strand birds. Hunters in various regions along the east coast called them bay-birds, sand-birds, or marsh-birds. On Long Island, sandpipers were commonly called bay-snipe or shore-snipe. In the late 19th and early 20th centuries, sandpipers and plovers were the victims of market hunting. Gunners slaughtered thousands of shorebirds for restaurants and markets in eastern cities. Populations of many species were decimated. The hunters favored species that occurred in large flocks, because they could shoot into a flock and bring down many birds at once. But they detested the Greater and Lesser Yellowlegs, applying the nicknames tattler and tell-tale to them. This is because the yellowlegs' strident alarm calls alerted the flocks to danger. As explained in the following passage, shorebird does not mean just any bird you might see on the shore:

"The shorebirds, as a group, hold a special place in the affections of many experienced bird watchers. Even to understand the name of the group is to hold membership in a select society, because its meaning is not self-evident. The general public might assume, logically, that a "shorebird" would be any bird normally seen on the shore, like a heron or a gull. But in serious-birder lingo, it's a term of taxonomy, not habitat: "Shorebird" is the word that encompasses all the sandpipers, plovers, and members of a few related families of birds, and nothing else. Mallards or terns or red-winged blackbirds can sit on the shore all week and they still won't be shorebirds.

"Golden-plovers and upland sandpipers are always shorebirds, even when they wander about in grassy fields far from water, as they often do." — Kenn Kaufman, "Fade To Purple," *Bird Watcher's Digest*, September/October 2009

Spanish Names: Candelero Americano; Cigüeñuela Cuellinegro
Other Names: Stilt; Common Stilt; Avocet; Lawyer; Daddy Longlegs; Red Shank; Longshanks; Long-legged Avocett; Yelper; White Snipe; Civil; Cap'n Lewis; Soldat; Soldier; Crackpot Soldier; Telltale; Tilt; Tildilo; Ally-moor; Arcagüete; Becasse de Marais; Becassine de Marais; Becassine de Mer; Cachiporra; Echasse; Ne'o; Péte-péte; Pigeon d'Etang; Religiuse; Viuda; Zancudo

American Avocet
Recurvirostra americana
(re-CURV-ih-ROS-trah ah-mer-ih-CANE-ah)

"Wherever this large, showy bird is found it is always much in evidence. Its large size and conspicuous colors could hardly be overlooked, even if it were shy and retiring; but its bold, aggressive manners force it upon our attention as soon as we approach its haunts." — Arthur Cleveland Bent (1927)

Avocet is from the Italian name for this bird *avosetta*. The name may be derived from the Latin *avis* (a bird) plus a diminutive suffix. Rather than denote "small," the suffix in this case means "graceful" or "elegant." The word "American" distinguishes our species from the Pied Avocet (*R. avosetta*) of the Old World.

Recurvirostra — The genus name is Latin for "bent bill" from *recurvo* (to bend backward) and *rostrum* (the bill) and refers to the fact that the avocet's bill curves upward. This is an adaptation of the bird's peculiar method of feeding:

"The use of the avocet's recurved bill is clearly explained by the manner in which the bird procures its food. In feeding they wade into the water and drop the bill below the surface until the convexity of the maxilla probably touches the bottom. In this position they move forward at a half run and with every step the bill is swung from side to side sweeping through an arc of about 50° in search of shells and other small aquatic animals. The mandibles are slightly opened, and at times the birds pause to swallow their prey. It is evident that birds with a straight or downward curved bill could not adopt this manner of feeding." — Frank Chapman (1891)

americana — The specific epithet is Modern Latin for "of America."
French Name: Avocette d'Amérique
Spanish Name: Avoceta Americana
Other Names: North American Avocet; Avoceta; Irish Snipe; White Snipe; Yellow-necked Snipe; Golden Plover; Blueshanks; Bluestockings; Lawyer; Scooper; Yelper; Becassine de Mer

Family Haematopodidae Oystercatchers

American Oystercatcher
Haematopus palliatus
(he-MAT-oh-pus pal-ih-AY-tus)

"Children brought up on "Alice in Wonderland" might imagine from the name of this bird that oysters are fleet-footed racers along our beaches, overtaken at the end of a breathless chase by the oyster-catcher!" — Neltje Blanchan (1898)

English naturalist Mark Catesby coined the name oystercatcher in his *Natural History of Carolina, Florida, and the Bahama Islands* (1743). Some ornithologists ridicule the name, presumably because it evokes an absurd image of the birds chasing down terrified oysters. As Elliot Coues sarcastically said, "oysters do not run fast." But Ernest Choate points out that catch can also mean "to catch unawares," which the oystercatcher does when it jabs its bill into the open shell of a bivalve. Until the publication

Black-necked Stilt and American Avocet, by Louis Agassiz Fuertes

> **Sidebar 14**
> **Nature's Oyster Knife**
>
> "Every creature with a taste for shellfish faces the same problem: how to breach the shell. Gulls break it by dropping it on rocks. Starfish pull it open with suction-cupped arms. Some snails bore a hole. But the oystercatcher uses nature's oyster knife, a long hard bill, flattened vertically and colored bright red. The ebbing tide signals banquet time for the oystercatchers. Out from the rocks and dunes they fly, dropping in twos and threes on the emerging sandbars . . . At the feet of the assembling birds lies a smorgasbord of oysters and other mollusks, the oysters' valves still parted as they sift the receding water for plankton. Into an open shell goes the red knife, and with a deft snip the bird cuts the adductor muscle before it can slam the door. Then, with vigorous sidewise twists of its head, the "oyster plover" works the half shells apart and gulps the meat inside. Sometimes the bivalve clamps shut on the bird's bill. The oystercatcher then finds a rock, swings its burdened bill like a baseball bat, and shatters its quarry's armor." — Alexander Wetmore (1965)
>
> There are two foraging strategies, stabbing, as described above, and hammering. Individual birds appear to specialize in one or the other. A hammerer simply breaks the shell open with powerful blows of the bill. Ever wonder about the significance of the saying "happy as a clam?" The complete phrase is "happy as a clam at high water," when it would be safe from oystercatchers and other land predators.

of Catesby's book, the Eurasian Oystercatcher (*H. ostralegus*) was known as the sea pie. Although oystercatchers feed on a variety of marine invertebrates, they are especially adapted to dealing with bivalve mollusks such as oysters, clams, and mussels. For more on this bird's foraging strategy, see Sidebar 14. American distinguishes our species from the Eurasian Oystercatcher.

Haematopus — The genus name means "blood-red foot" from the Greek *haimatos* (blood) and *pous* (the foot). The feet of this species are actually flesh-colored.

palliatus — The specific epithet is Latin for "cloaked," referring to the black head, neck, breast, and dark brown back that suggest the bird is wearing a cloak.

French Name: Huîtrier d'Amérique
Spanish Name: Ostrero Americano
Other Names: Common Oystercatcher; Brown-backed Oystercatcher; Sea Crow; Mantled Oystercatcher; Frazer's Oystercatcher; Whelk-cracker; Bank Bird; Ostrero; Caracolero

Black Oystercatcher
Haematopus bachmani
(he-MAT-oh-pus BOCK-man-eye)

This Pacific coast species is named for its all black plumage.

Haematopus — The genus name means "blood-red foot" from the Greek *haimatos* (blood) and *pous* (the foot). The feet of this species are actually flesh-colored.

bachmani — Audubon named this species in honor of his friend the Reverend John Bachman (1790–1874) of Charleston, South Carolina.

French Name: Huîtrier de Bachman
Spanish Name: Ostero Negro de Bachman
Other Names: Bachman's Oystercatcher; Redbill; Sea Parrot

Family Charadriidae
Lapwings and Plovers

For the origin of lapwing, see next entry. Plover is derived from the Latin *pluvia* (rain). Various explanations have been put forth, and it is likely due to some folktale that connects these birds to rain. Perhaps plovers were seen as weather forecasters, becoming more vocal or restless just before a storm. A similar belief involves the Red-throated Loon (rain goose) and the Yellow-billed Cuckoo (rain crow). Other ideas include a reference to a wet habitat, the birds' arrival during the rainy season, being easier to catch in the rain, or speckling on the back that suggest water spots from raindrops.

Northern Lapwing
Vanellus vanellus
(vay-NELL-us)

""For the word Lapwing comes from the Old English *Hleapewince* which has the quite beautiful meaning of 'leap with a waver in it' which conveys so well the tremulous power of the Lapwing's flight. The autumn and winter group flights are particularly "hleapewince," a flock surging and turning, showing first the green-black upperside of the wide wing, then the brilliant white of the underside, moving together like a flickering chequerboard.""
— Francesca Greenoak (1979)

There are two explanations for the origin of lapwing, one pertaining to its manner of flight, as explained above; the other to the bird's curved crest that can be raised or lowered. The alternate explanation claims lapwing derives from an Old English word meaning "movable crest" that was corrupted to *lapwinch, lappinch,* and then to lapwing. Northern distinguishes this Eurasian species names from lapwings of more southerly distribution in South America, Africa, and Australia.

Vanellus — The genus/species name means "little fan" from the Latin *vannus* (a fan) plus a diminutive suffix and refers to the floppy movement of the broad wings in flight.

French Name: Vanneau Huppé
Spanish Name: Avefría Europea
British Name: Lapwing
Other Names: Green Plover; Pewit; Peweep; Peesweep; Peesieweep; Picwipe; Lappie; Lappin; Lappinch; Lipwingle; Lymptwigg; Avefria; Flopwing; Phillipene; Chewit; Tewit; Teuchit; Teufit; Teewheep; Tee Whip; Tee Wup; Tee Whippo; Tieves' Nacket; Hornpie; Old Maid; Wallock; Wallopie Weep; Cornwillen; Scochad

Black-bellied Plover
Pluvialis squatarola
(ploo-vih-AIL-iss skwah-TAR-oh-lah)

"The black-bellied plover is an aristocrat among shore birds, the largest and strongest of the plovers, a leader of its tribe. It is a distinguished-looking bird in its handsome spring livery of black and white; and its attitude, as it stands like a sentinel on the crest of a sand dune or on some distant mud flat, is always dignified and imposing." — Arthur Cleveland Bent (1929)

The Black-bellied Plover is named for the jet black underparts in breeding plumage.

Pluvialis — The genus name is Latin for "pertaining to rain." See introduction to lapwings and plovers.

squatarola — The specific epithet is the Italian word for a plover, possibly but not necessarily this one.

French Name: Pluvier Argenté
Spanish Names: Chorlo Gris; Chorlito Gris
British Name: Grey Plover (for its winter plumage)
Eskimo and Inuit Names: Too-lee-huk; Tu-zhek; Todlivak
Other Names: Black-breast; Black-breast Plover; Black-bellied Killdeer; Mud Plover; Sea Plover; Four-toed Plover; Pigeon Plover; Rock Plover; Sand Plover; Stone Plover; Strand Plover; Grey Field Plover; Silver Plover; Silverback; Whistling Plover;

American Oystercatcher, Killdeer, American Golden-Plover, and Black-bellied Plover (clockwise from top left), by Louis Agassiz Fuertes

Whistling Field Plover; Swiss Plover; Bull-headed Plover; Bullhead; Bull Bird; Beetle; Beetle-head; Bottle-head; Pot-head; Chuckle-head; Chuckly-head; Toad-head; Owl-head; Hollow-head; Grosse-tête; Quebec Curlew; Grump; Sea Pigeon; Sea Cock; May Cock; Pilot; Lapwing; Ox-eye; Pale-belly; Muddy-breast; Ventra Noir; Pigeon de Mer; Playero Cabezon; Corbido; Corbijo; Feadag

European Golden-Plover
Pluvialis apricaria
(ploo-vih-AIL-iss ap-rih-CARE-ih-ah)

Golden-Plovers are named for the golden dappling on their upperparts in breeding plumage. European distinguishes this Old World species from the American Golden-Plover.

Pluvialis — The genus name is Latin for "pertaining to rain." See introduction to lapwings and plovers.

apricaria — The specific epithet is derived from the Latin *apricus* (exposed to the sun or sun-kissed) and refers to the gold-spangled appearance in breeding plumage.

French Name: Pluvier Doré d'Eurasie
Spanish Name: Chorlito Dorado Europeo
British Name: Golden Plover
Other Names: Greater Golden-Plover; Yellow Plover; Grey Plover; Black-breasted Plover; Whistling Plover; Hill Plover; Sheep's Guide

American Golden-Plover
Pluvialis dominica
(ploo-vih-AIL-iss dom-IN-ih-cah)

"Golden grain, golden rod, golden maple leaves, and golden plover all come together; the birds not so yellow, it is true, as they were in the spring, when they gave us only a passing glimpse of their clearer, more intense speckled plumage, but still yellow enough to be in harmony with nature's autumnal color scheme. Indeed, they blend so well with their surroundings as to be all but invisible." — Neltje Blanchan (1898)

This is the American counterpart of the European Golden-Plover. It breeds in Arctic Canada and Alaska, and winters in South America.

Pluvialis — The genus name is Latin for "pertaining to rain." See introduction to lapwings and plovers.

dominica — The specific epithet is Modern Latin for "of Santo Domingo" (now Hispianola), where the type specimen was taken in 1776.

French Name: Pluvier Doré d'Amérique
Spanish Names: Chorlo-dorado Americano; Chorlo-dorado Dominico; Chorlito Dorado Menor
Eskimo and Inuit Names: Too-leek-too-lear; Tuligak
Other Names: Lesser Golden-Plover; Asiatic Golden-Plover; Eastern Golden-Plover; Dark Plover; Bull-head Plover; Common Plover; Whistling Plover; Field Plover; Ground Plover; Lowland Plover; Kankakee Bar Plover; Spotted Plover; Three-toed Plover; Green Plover; Green-head; Greenback; Golden-back; Brass-back; Yellow Back; Field-bird; Frost-bird; Trout-bird; Pasture-bird; Prairie-bird; Prairie Pigeon; Three-toes; Bull-head; Toad-head; Black-breast; Pale-breast; Muddy-breast; Muddy-belly; Pale-belly; Squealer; Hawk's Eye; Little Ox-eye; Corbido; Doré; Grand Chevalier; Grosse-yeux; Kolea; Pigeon de Mer; Playero Dorado; Pluvier doré

Pacific Golden-Plover
Pluvialis fulva
(ploo-vih-AIL-iss FULL-vah)

Until 1993, this and the American Golden-Plover were considered a single species, the Lesser Golden-Plover. But their migration habits are very different. The Pacific Golden-Plover is named for its wintering grounds on South Pacific islands, while the American Golden-Plover migrates to South America.

Pluvialis — The genus name is Latin for "pertaining to rain." See introduction to lapwings and plovers.

fulva — The specific epithet is Latin for "tawny" or "yellowish-brown" and refers to the golden-spangled breeding plumage.

French Name: Pluvier Fauve
Spanish Name: Chorlo-dorado Asiático
Other Names: Same as American Golden-Plover.

Lesser Sand-Plover
Charadrius mongolus
(cah-RAD-rih-us mon-GO-lus)

This plover is named for its sand-colored plumage. Lesser distinguishes this species from the larger Greater Sand-Plover (*C. leschenaultii*). Formerly known as Mongolian Plover.

Charadrius — The genus name is Latin for "a plover" from the Greek *kharadrios*, a name Aristotle and others used for a water bird that nested in ravines. Some believe it was the Stone Curlew (*Burhina oedicnemus*), but now the name is applied to plovers.

mongolus — The specific epithet is Modern Latin for "of Mongolia."

French Name: Pluvier de Mongolie
Spanish Name: Chorlo Mongol Menor
Other Name: Short-billed Sand Plover

Snowy Plover
Charadrius alexandrinus
(cah-RAD-rih-us al-ecks-an-DRY-nus)

"It is a child of the sand, with which its colors blend so well that when crouched in some hollow or against some bleached piece of driftwood or half buried clam shell it seems to be just one more of the numerous, inconspicuous objects which one passes unnoticed on the beach." — Arthur Cleveland Bent (1929)

The Snowy Plover is named for its pale coloration that blends in with white sand beaches and salt flats.

Charadrius — The genus name is Latin for "a plover" from the Greek *kharadrios*, a name Aristotle and others used for a water bird that nested in ravines. Some believe it was the Stone Curlew (*Burhina oedicnemus*), but now the name is applied to plovers.

alexandrinus — The specific epithet is Modern Latin for "of Alexandria," the city in Egypt where the type specimen was collected.

French Name: Gravelot à Collier Interrompu
Spanish Name: Chorlito Nevado; Chorlito Nivéo; Chorlitejo Picudo
British Name: Kentish Plover
Other Names: Western Snowy Plover; Snowy Ringed Plover; Sand Bird; Snipe; Bécassine; Cabezón; Corredor; Frailecito; Playante; Little Ploward; Playero Blanco; Playero Marítimo; Títere de Playa; Putilla; Nit

Wilson's Plover
Charadrius wilsonia
(cah-RAD-rih-us will-SON-ih-ah)

Philadelphia ornithologist George Ord described this plover in 1814, giving it the name *Charadrius wilsonia* for his friend Alexander Wilson who had died the year before. Ord wrote:

"Of this neat and prettily marked species I can find no account, and have concluded that it has hitherto escaped the eye of the naturalist. The bird from which this description was taken, was shot the 13th of May, 1813, on the shore of Cape Island, New Jersey, by my ever-regretted friend; and I have honoured it with his name."

Charadrius — The genus name is Latin for "a plover" from the Greek *kharadrios*, a name Aristotle and others used for a water bird that nested in ravines. Some believe it was the Stone Curlew (*Burhina oedicnemus*), but now the name is applied to plovers.

wilsonia — The specific epithet honors Alexander Wilson (1766–1813), the Father of American Ornithology. See common name above.

French Name: Pluvier de Wilson
Spanish Names: Chorlito de Pico Grueso; Chorlito Piquigrueso; Chorlitejo Picudo
Other Names: Thick-billed Plover; Belding's Plover; Sand Bird; Snipe; Bécassine; Cabezón; Collier; Corredor; Frailecito; Little Ploward; Nit; Playante; Playero Marítimo; Putilla; Títere de Playa

Common Ringed Plover
Charadrius hiaticula
(cah-RAD-rih-us high-ay-TICK-you-lah)

Ringed refers to the dark breast band. This plover is common in northern Europe, but in North America it is a very local nester in Arctic Canada.

Charadrius — The genus name is Latin for "a plover" from the Greek *kharadrios*, a name Aristotle and others used for a water bird that nested in ravines. Some believe it was the Stone Curlew (*Burhina oedicnemus*), but now the name is applied to plovers

hiaticula — The specific epithet means "cleft dweller" from the Latin *hiatus* (a cleft) and *cola* (dweller), perhaps because it nests among rocks on pebbly beaches.

French Name: Grand Gravelot
Spanish Name: Chorlo Anillado Común
Other Names: Stone Plover; Stone Runner; Stonehatch; Ring-neck; Ringed Dotterel; Ringlestone; Sea Lark; Sand Lark; Sand Tripper; Sandy Laverock; Sandy Loo; Shell-turner; Knot; Bull's Eye; Wideawake; Grundling; Dulwilly; Tullet/Tullot

Semipalmated Plover
Charadrius semipalmatus
(cah-RAD-rih us sem-ih-pal-MAY-tus)

Semipalmated refers to the partially webbed toes.

Charadrius — The genus name is Latin for "a plover" from the Greek *kharadrios*, a name Aristotle and others used for a water bird that nested in ravines. Some believe it was the Stone Curlew (*Burhina oedicnemus*), but now the name is applied to plovers.

semipalmatus — The specific epithet means "half-webbed" from the Latin *semi* (half) and *palma* (the hand), and refers to the partially webbed toes.

French Name: Pluvier Semipalmé
Spanish Names: Chorlito Semipalmeado; Chorlito Semipalmado; Chorlitejo Semipalmado
Eskimo and Inuit Names: Wah-huey-yuk; Kodrakoruk
Other Names: Ring Plover; Semipalmated Ring Plover; Ringer; Ring-neck; Black Ringneck; Ring-necked Plover; Beach Bird; Red-eye; Redleg; Alouette cou Blanc; Bodhag; Luatharan; Playero Acollarado; Twillig

Piping Plover
Charadrius melodus
(cah-RAD-rih-us mel-OH-dus)

"Walk along the water's edge and, although the sea may be pounding on the shore and a northerly gale howling about our ears, we shall hear the plover's voice; a soft musical moan, we can not tell from where, but clear and distinct above the sound of the waves and wind. The note has a ventriloquial quality and it is often our first intimation that a piping plover is near, for the soft gray of the bird's plumage matches the sandy background, whereas the note is pervasive and attracts our attention by its strangeness." — Arthur Cleveland Bent (1929)

This little plover is named for its musical piping call.

Charadrius — The genus name is Latin for "a plover" from the Greek *kharadrios*, a name Aristotle and others used for a water bird that nested in ravines. Some believe it was the Stone Curlew (*Burhina oedicnemus*), but now the name is applied to plovers.

melodus — The specific epithet is Latin for "melodious" or "pleasantly singing," which describes the bird's vocalizations.

French Name: Pluvier Siffleur
Spanish Name: Chorlito Chiflador
Other Names: Belted Piping Plover; Western Piping Plover; Sand Plover; Beach Plover; Beach Bird; Mourning Bird; Clam-Bird; Ring-neck; Pale Ring-neck; White Ring-neck; Playero Melodico; Tête de pipe

Killdeer
Charadrius vociferus
(cah-RAD-rih-us voh-SIFF-er-us)

"It may be said of the killdeer that it is probably the most widely distributed and best known of all our shore birds. Unlike most of the group, it is not confined to the borders of lakes and of the sea but is found in meadows, pastures, and dry uplands often many miles from water. Unlike, also, the majority of our shore birds, its sojourn here is not limited to the migration periods, for it breeds and winters throughout a large portion on the United States. It is not of a retiring disposition, and it often makes its presence known by loud calls and cries, to which it owes both its common and scientific names — killdeer and *vociferus*." — Charles Wendell Townsend (1929)

Killdeer is imitative of this plover's loud calls.

Charadrius — The genus name is Latin for "a plover" from the Greek *kharadrios*, a name Aristotle and others used for a water bird that nested in ravines. Some believe it was the Stone Curlew (*Burhina oedicnemus*), but now the name is applied to plovers.

vociferus — The specific epithet is Latin for "clamourous" and refers to this bird's loud

calls. It is particularly noisy when it is disturbed.
French Name: Pluvier Kildir
Spanish Names: Chorlito Tidío; Chorlitejo Tidío
Eskimo and Inuit Name: Talikvak
Other Names: Killdee; Tell-tale Killdeer; Killdeer Plover; Ringneck; Ring-neck Plover; Noisy Plover; Chattering Plover; Field Plover; Meadow Plover; Jack-snipe; Pasture-bird; Marsh-Hawk; Mosquito Hawk; Sand-runner; Soldier Bird; Tip-up; Braillard; Chevalier de Terre; Chewekee; Collier; Cou Collier; Corbijou; Frailecillo; Frailecillo Gritón; Gilderee; Gilleree; Gritón; Playero Sabanero; Títire Sabonero; Ploward; Pouvier Doré; Tilderee

Mountain Plover
Charadrius montanus
(cah-RAD-rih-us mon-TAN-us)

The Mountain Plover is not a bird of the mountains at all, for it nests on open plains, shortgrass prairie, and high desert. It got its inappropriate name, because the type specimen was collected near Sweetwater, Wyoming on the central tableland of the Rockies.

Charadrius — The genus name is Latin for "a plover" from the Greek *kharadrios*, a name Aristotle and others used for a water bird that nested in ravines. Some believe it was the Stone Curlew (*Burhina oedicnemus*), but now the name is applied to plovers.

montanus — The specific epithet is Latin for "of the mountains," a misnomer. See common name above.

French Name: Pluvier Montagnard
Spanish Name: Chorlito Llanero
Other Names: Curlew; Quail; Snipe; Plover; Rocky Mountain Plover; Prairie Plover; Field Plover; Upland Plover; Prairie Turkey; Feldhinkel; Long-baniche Feldhinkel

Eurasian Dotterel
Charadrius morinellus
(cah-RAD-rih-us mor-ih-NEL-us)

The name "little dolt" refers to the species' alleged stupidity. Dotterels were once widely trapped in nets for food in Europe. The trappers believed that the birds imitated any action they made and, thus distracted, were easily caught. The belief was based on the "fact" that when men stretched out their arms, the dotterels followed suit. In reality the trappers were mimicking the broken-wing distraction display typical of many plovers.

"Doubtless, the birds were easy enough to net, since they rely on cryptic coloration and "sitting tight" for protection and are reluctant to leave the vicinity of the nest, once flushed." — Christopher Leahy (1982)

Dotterel means "little dolt" from the Middle English *dote* (to be foolish) plus the diminutive suffix *–erel*. The name refers to a belief that this plover could be distracted with gestures and therefore easily caught. Eurasian refers to this species' normal range in the Old World. It is a rare visitor to North America and a sporadic breeder in western Alaska. Here is another take on this little plover's unfortunate name:

"Perhaps there is in human beings a failure to come to terms with the fact that we are predatory carnivores. Animals who do not resist slaughter we deride, in order to cover up a profound unease about killing a creature which is friendly towards us. This is very clear in our attitude to domestic and farm animals . . . We have made our farm animals trusting and docile. Dotterel are naturally so; in both cases there is an underlying sense that they are not 'fair game' and we transpose our guilt, reviling not ourselves but the animals." — Francesca Greenoak (1979)

Charadrius — The genus name is Latin for "a plover" from the Greek *kharadrios*, a name Aristotle and others used for a water bird that nested in ravines. Some believe it was the Stone Curlew (*Burhina oedicnemus*), but now the name is applied to plovers. Formerly *Eudromias morinellus*.

morinellus — The specific epithet is Modern Latin for "little fool" or "little moron" from the Greek *moros* (stupid) plus the diminutive suffix *–ellus*. See common name above.

French Name: Pluvier Guignard
Spanish Name: Chorlito Carambolo
Other Names: Moor Dotterel; Spring Dotterel; Land Dotterel; Dot Plover; Stone Runner; Wind

Family Jacanidae
Jacanas

Northern Jacana
Jacana spinosa
(jah-KON-ah spin-OH-sah)

"I can almost guarantee you that you will be corrected on the pronunciation of this name, no matter HOW you pronounce it. I don't think I have EVER heard anyone pronounce it "correctly" as the dictionary lists it. Terres gives four pronunciations, two as "many American ornithologists" do it: jah-KON-ah, Yah- sah-NAH; and two dictionary pronunciations: Zha-sah-NAH; JAK-ah-nah. Then he proceeds to pronounce the family jah-CAN-ih dee." — Kevin McGowan, Cornell University

The common name is from the Portuguese jaçanã, their spelling of the Tupi (Brazilian) Indian name for this bird: *jassana*, which means "one that cries out." It refers to the noisy, cackling alarm call the birds utter when they take flight. This is the northernmost member of a tropical family; it just reaches our area in southern Texas. Formerly known as Mexican Jacana. The problem with jacana is that no one can agree on the correct pronunciation, as you can see in the opening passage. Here is more on the subject:

""Jacana" is indisputably derived from a name given this bird by South American indigenes and entered our language via the Portuguese. There all agreement ends. The Tupi-Guarani word was apparently something like jassana, probably with little or no emphasis on any syllable. The "official" Portuguese rendition is close to ZHA-seh-nah. Southwestern birders, presuming it to be a Spanish word, often say hah-CAH-nuh, and eastern elitist bird-tour leaders insist upon jah-CAH-nuh (or jah-KAH-ner, as in CU-ber). The variations are limited only by imagination; jah-KAY-nuh is popular locally, and from some eccentric corner has come the refreshing JACK-a-naw. All of this makes a strong case for "lily trotter."" — Christopher Leahy (1982)

Jacana — See common name above.

spinosa — The specific epithet means "carrying a thorn" from the Latin *spina* (a thorn) and *osus* (carrying). It refers to the spine at the bend in the wing.
French Name: Jacana Mexique
Spanish Names: Jacana Norteña; Jacana Mesoamericana; Jacana Centroamericana
Other Names: American Jacana; North American Jacana; Mexican Jacana; Lily-trotter; Lotus-bird; Jesus Bird; Banana Coot; Brazilian Coot; Spanish Coot; Pond Coot; Queen Coot; Queen Bird; River Chink; Chevalier; Gallito de Agua; Médecin; Poule d'Eau Dorée

~

Family Scolopacidae
Sandpipers and Allies

There is reference to both the bird's habitat and vocalizations in the name sandpiper. Sand refers to the sand beaches where some species forage when not breeding. But many more species prefer mudflats and some occur on rocky shores. Piper describes the piping whistled calls that many utter, particularly when they are disturbed.

Upland Sandpiper
Bartramia longicauda
(bar-TRAM-ih-ah lonj-ih-CAW-dah)

"Let us be thankful that this gentle and lovely bird is no longer called Bartramian sandpiper. It is a sandpiper truly enough, but one that has adopted the haunts and many of the habits of the plovers. To those who love the rolling or hilly pasture lands of the east or the broad flat prairies of the middle west, it will always be known as the upland or "field plover" or "prairie dove," or, more affectionately, as "quailie."" — Arthur Cleveland Bent (1929)

A maverick shorebird that doesn't generally frequent shores, this sandpiper is named for its upland habitat of prairies, fields, and meadows. Formerly known as Upland Plover.

Bartramia — The genus name honors William

Upland Sandpiper, by Louis Agassiz Fuertes

Bartram (1739–1823), known as the "Godfather of American Ornithology," because he was a mentor to Alexander Wilson. Wilson named this bird *Tringa bartramia* in 1813, with the dedication: "I have honored it with the name of my very worthy friend near whose Botanic Gardens on the banks of the river Schuylkill I found it." But German scientist Johann M. Bechstein had already described the species in 1812, giving it the scientific name *Tringa longicauda*, so his specific epithet has priority. When the Upland Sandpiper was removed from the genus *Tringa* in 1831, French naturalist René Primevère Lesson erected *Bartramia* as the new genus.

longicauda — The specific epithet means "long tail" from the Latin *longi* (long) and *cauda* (the tail). Compared to other sandpipers, this species has a long tail that extends beyond the wing tips.

French Name: Maubèche des Champs
Spanish Names: Zarapito Ganga; Pradero
Other Names: Bartram's Plover; Highland Plover; Prairie Plover; Field Plover; Corn-field Plover; Pasture Plover; Grass Plover; Meadow Plover; Gray Plover; Plain Plover; Whistling Plover; the Bartramian; Bartramian Sandpiper; Bartram's Sandpiper; Meadow Sandpiper; Bartramian Tattler; Bartram's Tattler; Bartram's Highland Snipe; Prairie Snipe; Prairie Pigeon; Prairie Dove; Pasture-bird; Hill Bird; Uplander; Humility; Quaily; Papebotte; Ganga

Bristle-thighed Curlew
Numenius tahitiensis
(new-MEAN-ih-us tah-HIT-ih-EN-sis)

Curlew, from the French *corliew*, is imitative of the Eurasian Curlew's call notes, sometimes rendered *cooorweee*. Bristle-thighed refers to the elongated, barbless shafts of the feathers on the flanks.

Numenius — The genus name is derived from *noumenios*, a name used by Hesychius and associated with the curlew. It means "new moon" from the Greek *neos* (new) and *mene* (moon) and refers to the long, curved bill, suggesting a new crescent moon.

tahitiensis — The specific epithet is Modern Latin for "of Tahiti," where the type specimen was collected in 1769. The Bristle-thighed Curlew breeds in Alaska and winters on islands in the South Pacific.

French Name: Courlis de Tahiti
Spanish Name: Zarapito del Pacifíco
Eskimo and Inuit Names: Chiuit (imitative) Ee-kee-kee-kyuk; Mug-u-no-okh-tai-u-li
Other Name: Kioea

Whimbrel, by Allan C. Brooks

Whimbrel
Numenius phaeopus
(new-MEAN-ih-us FEE-oh-pus)

The Whimbrel was named in England for its call notes plus a diminutive suffix. It is said to be derived from whimmer, a lowland Scots term for "whimper." British naturalist Francesca Greenoak wrote, "...Whimbrel could be an allusion to its distinctive rippling call, not unlike the whimpering of hounds." Formerly known as Hudsonian Curlew.

Numenius — The genus name is derived from *noumenios*, a name used by Hesychius and associated with the curlew. It means "new moon" from the Greek *neos* (new) and *mene* (moon) and refers to the long, curved bill, suggesting a new crescent moon.

phaeopus — The specific epithet is Greek for "dusky foot" from *phaios* (dusky) and *pous* (the foot) and refers to the gray feet and legs.

French Name: Courlis Corliue
Spanish Name: Zarapito Trinador
Eskimo and Inuit Names: Ikiikikiat (it will rain); Sigoktovak (long billed)
Other Names: American Whimbrel; Esquimaux Whimbel; Esquimaux Curlew; Great Esquimaux Curlew; Short-billed Curlew; Mountain Curlew; Half Curlew; Small Curlew; Big Curlew; May Curlew; Foolish Curlew; Jack Curlew; Jack; Curlew Jack; Curlew Knot; Curlew Knave; Whimbrel Curlew; Winderal; Chickerel; Titterel; Sickle-bill; Marlin; Crooked-bill Marlin; Hook-billed Marlin; Horse-foot Marlin; Brame; Little Whaup; Tang Whaup; May Whaup; Summer Whaup; Peerie Whaup; Chequer Bird; Doe-bird; May Bird; May Fowl; Blue-legs; Striped-head; Gabriel's Hound; Corpse Hound; Corbigeau; Guilueach; Playero Pico Corvo

Long-billed Curlew
Numenius americanus
(new-MEAN-ih-us ah-mer-ih-CANE-us)

"The extraordinary bill of the curlew, curving in the opposite direction from the avocet's, serves the same purpose, however, and drags small crabs, and other shell fish that have buried themselves in the wet sand, snails, larvae, and worms from their holes, the blades acting like forceps . . . The entire bill so far as the nostrils, nothwithstanding its extreme length, often sinks through the soft sand or mud to probe for some coveted dainty. The curlew, the avocet, the sea parrot, and the skimmer vie with each other in possessing the queerest freak of a bill." — Neltje Blanchan (1898)

This curlew's impressive 9-inch long bill gives it its name.

Numenius — The genus name is derived from *noumenios*, a name used by Hesychius and associated with the curlew. It means "new moon" from the Greek *neos* (new) and *mene* (moon) and refers to the long, curved bill, suggesting a new crescent moon.

americanus — The specific epithet is Modern Latin for "of America," as this is strictly a New World species.

French Name: Courlis à Long Bec
Spanish Names: Zarapito Picolargo; Zarapito Piquilargo
Other Names: Big Curlew; Spanish Curlew; Hen Curlew; Old Hen Curlew; Buzzard Curlew; Turkey Curlew; Sickle-billed Curlew; Sickle-bill; Seckle-bill; Sabre-bill; Smoker; Old Smoker; Mowyer; Snipe; Corpigeon; Guilbueach

Bar-tailed Godwit
Limosa lapponica
(lie-MOE-sah lap-PON-ih-kah)

Fine horizontal barring on the tail give this godwit its name.

Limosa — The genus name means "muddy" from the Latin *limus* (mud) and refers to the fact that these birds feed in muddy habitats such as marshes, estuaries, flooded fields, and tidal mudflats.

lapponica — The specific epithet is Modern Latin for "of Lapland," northern Scandinavia, where this bird breeds in part and the location where the type specimen was collected.

French Name: Barge Rousse
Spanish Names: Picopando de Cola Pinta; Picopando Colibarrado
Eskimo and Inuit Name: Chiuchiuchiak (imitative)
Other Names: Pacific Godwit; Godwin; Half Curlew; Half Whaup; Sea Woodcock; Stone

Plover; Set Hammer; Poor Willie; Shrieker; Yardkeep; Yarwhelp; Yarwhip; Pick; Prine; Scammel; Speethe

Black-tailed Godwit
Limosa limosa
(lie-MOE-sah)

Godwit is believed to stem from the Old English *god* "good" and *wihte* "a creature." Godwits were "good creatures" in that they were good to eat. Shorebirds were traditionally hunted for food, and in fact many species were nearly wiped out by market hunters in the late 19th century. Some sources say that godwit is imitative of the birds' ringing calls. The broad black terminal band on the tail gives this species its name.

Limosa — The genus/species name means "muddy" from the Latin *limus* (mud) and refers to the fact that these birds feed in muddy habitats such as marshes, estuaries, flooded fields, and tidal mudflats.

French Name: Barge à Queue Noire
Spanish Name: Aguja Colinegra
Other Names: Red Godwit; Jadreka Snipe; Small Curlew; Barker; Shrieker; Whelp; Yarwhelp; Whelpmoor

Hudsonian Godwit
Limosa haemastica
(lie-MOE-sah he-MASS-tih-kah)

This godwit is named for Hudson Bay, where the type specimen was collected, and in fact, some nest along the southern shore of Hudson Bay.

Limosa — The genus name means "muddy" from the Latin *limus* (mud) and refers to the fact that these birds feed in muddy habitats such as marshes, estuaries, flooded fields, and tidal mudflats.

haemastica — The specific epithet is Greek for "bloody or blood-red" for the ruddy color of the underparts in breeding plumage, not as brightly colored as the name suggests.

French Name: Barge Hudsonienne
Spanish Names: Picopando Ornemantado; Aguja Lomiblanca
Other Names: American Black-tailed Godwit; Red-breasted Godwit; Bay-breasted Godwit; Rose-breasted Godwit; Foolish Godwit; Straight-billed Curlew; Little Curlew; Carolina Willet; Field Marlin; Ring-tailed Marlin; Blacktail; Spot-rump; White-rump; Goose-bird; Smaller Doe-bird; Smaller Dough-bird; Dotterel; Brant-bird; Barga Aliblanca

Marbled Godwit
Limosa fedoa
(lie-MOE-sah FED-oh-ah)

This godwit is named for its mottled and striped breeding plumage.

Limosa — The genus name means "muddy" from the Latin *limus* (mud) and refers to the fact that these birds feed in muddy habitats such as marshes, estuaries, flooded fields, and tidal mudflats.

fedoa — The specific epithet is believed to be the Latinized form of a lost Old English name for godwit, perhaps from the Italian *vetola* (a godwit).

French Name: Barge Marbrée
Spanish Names: Picopando Canelo; Aguja Canela
Other Names: Great Godwit; Great Marbled Godwit; Greater American Godwit; Curlew; Straight-billed Curlew; Red Curlew; Spike-billed Curlew; Spike-bill; Marlin; Brown Marlin; Common Marlin; Horse-foot Marlin; Red Marlin; Doe-bird; Dough-bird; Dotterel; Badger-bird; Brant-bird; Barga Jaspeada

Ruddy Turnstone
Arenaria interpres
(are-eh-NARE-ih-ah in-TER-pres)

"With a bill curiously like a writing pen, this well named wader turns over pebbles,

Ruddy Turnstone, by John James Audubon

clods of mud, shells, and seaweed on the beaches more commonly about the foot of cliffs and in stony coves than on long, sandy stretches, ever looking for the small marine creatures that satisfy its appetite, particularly for the eggs of the horsefoot or king crab (*Limulus polyphemus*), its favorite dainty. Often not only the head and bill must be used to push over a stone, but the breast assists too; ordinarily, however, the bird simply pokes its bill under a lighter object, and, giving its head a quick jerk, turns over the roof under which some small prey thought itself secure, swallows the morsel, then runs off to the next shell to repeat the operation. Seaweed is simply tossed aside." — Neltje Blanchan (1898)

Turnstone describes this bird's foraging behavior of flipping over pebbles, shells, and other debris with its bill to find the invertebrates hiding beneath as described in the above passage. Ruddy refers to the warm orange-brown breeding plumage.

Arenaria — The genus name means "pertaining to sand" from the Latin *arena* (sand) and refers to the turnstone's seashore habitat outside the breeding season. They also frequent rocky coasts.

interpres — The specific epithet is Latin for "interpreter" or "go-between" and refers to the bird's alarm call that alerts shorebirds of many species of danger. Linnaeus may have made an error in naming this bird. On the island of Gottland, he took the native name *tolk* (= *interpres*) to mean the Ruddy Turnstone when in fact it referred to the Redshank (*Tringa totanus*), which really does have a distinctive alarm call.

French Name: Tournepierre à Collier
Spanish Name: Vuelvepiedras Rojizo
Eskimo Name: Uyaruyat (imitative)
Other Names: Common Turnstone; Chicken-bird Turnstone; Calico-back; Calico Jacket; Calico Bird; Brant-bird; Bead-bird; Brown Bird; Beach Bird; King-crab Bird; Rock-bird; Heart Bird; Whale Bird; Chicken Bird; Chicken; Chicken Plover; Chickling; Bishop Plover; Calico Plover; Pied Plover; Caraquet Plover; Red-legged Plover; Red-legs; Redshank; Rock Plover; Sparked-back Plover; Streaked-backed Plover; Variegated Plover; Hebridal Sandpiper; Checkered Snipe; Horsefoot Snipe; Brant Snipe; Maggot-Snipe; Salt-water Partridge; Sand Runner; Skirl Crake; Sea Dotterel; Sea Lark; Sea Quail; Fat-oxen; Stone Raw; Stanepecker; Stone-pecker; Ebb Pecker; Tangle Picker; Red-legs; Streaked-back; Sparked-back; Jinny; Bracket; Gannet; Creddock; Chuckatuck; Player Turco; Tourne-pierre

Black Turnstone
Arenaria melanocephala
(are-eh-NARE-ih-ah mel-ah-no-SEFF-ah-lah)

The Black Turnstone is named for its largely blackish plumage.

Arenaria — The specific epithet is Latin for "interpreter" or "go-between" and refers to the bird's alarm call that alerts shorebirds of many species of danger.

melanocephala — The specific epithet means "black head" from the Greek *melas* (black) and *kephale* (head).

French Name: Tournepierre Noir
Spanish Name: Vuelvepiedras Negro
Eskimo and Inuit Names: Chilmak (imitative) Chilee-muck (imitative) Tubv-a-ta-tuk; Cho-o-muk
Other Names: Rock Plover; Rock Snipe

Red Knot
Calidris canutus
(cal-ID-ris kay-NEW-tus)

"When King Canute, or Knut, had dined on a dish of strange coast-faring birds, he was gracious enough to express to his blushing chef the royal appreciation of their flavor. Whereupon the eager courtiers dubbed the waders Knuts, or Knots and so they have come down to us — at least so Pennant says; and Linnaeus, not over-curious (he was a busy man with all of Adam's task to finish) accepted the tradition in "*Tringa canutus*." It is certainly fitting that these birds of the farthest north should bear the name of some hardy Norseman." — William Leon Dawson (1902)

Knot is said to be derived from Canute (or Knut), an ancient king of Denmark. Some believe knot is imitative of the bird's call notes. Others think the name stems from gnat, perhaps from the nickname gnat snap. Red describes the robin-red underparts of the birds in breeding plumage. This coloration has prompted the folk names Robin Snipe, Beach Robin, and Red-breast. R. I. Brasher (1917) wrote: "A flock of Knots tripping along the beach in their spring plumage with rufous breasts gives the observer the impression that some Robins have acquired nautical propensities and come down to the ocean for a change of food."

Calidris — The genus name is from the Greek *kalidris*, a name Aristotle used for a "gray speckled waterbird," not further identified, but believed to be a sandpiper.

canutus — "The connection between King Canute and the shorebird can be traced back to the 1607 edition of William Camden's *Brittania*. Camden thought that the word 'knot' alluded to the well-known story concerning Canute, who rebuked his flattering courtiers by physically demonstrating that despite his huge empire he had no power to stop the in-coming tide. Camden was only expressing his opinion that the Red Knot, which often frequents the tide edge, could be connected with Canute, but later authors determinedly repeated the idea and Linnaeus compounded the theory by calling the bird *Tringa Canutus*." — Barbara and Richard Mearns (1992)

Linnaeus named this sandpiper for the Danish King Canute (c.995–1035). They were called King Canute's birds, presumably, because he considered them delicious. There is also a legend concerning the king's attempt to hold back the tide, a reference to these birds foraging in the intertidal zone. See passage above.

French Name: Bécasseau Maubèche
Spanish Names: Playero Canuto; Playero Gordo; Correlimos Grande
British Name: Knot
Other Names: American Knot; Canute's Sandpiper; Freckled Sandpiper; Ash-colored Sandpiper; Griselled Sandpiper; Black Sandpiper; Red Sandpiper; Red-breasted Sandpiper; Robin Sandpiper; Buffbreast; Buff-breasted Plover; Grey Plover; Silver Plover; Blue Plover; Red-breasted Plover; Ebb Cock; Redbreast; Beach Robin; Robin Breast; Robin Snipe; White Robin Snipe; Horsefoot Snipe; Sea Snipe; White-bellied Snipe; Black-cap; Grey-neck; Gray-back; Silver-back; Maybird; Gnat Snap; Dun; Spease; Howster; Male; Alouette; Coochee; Maubeche; Wahquoit

Surfbird
Calidris virgata
(cal-ID-ris ver-GAY-tah)

"Named for its winter haunts, the Surfbird spends the winter (as well as migration seasons) on rocky coastlines pounded by the surf, often clambering about the rocks barely above the reach of the waves. But this stocky little sandpiper leads a double life, abandoning the coast in late spring. Its nesting grounds, high in the mountains in Alaska and the Yukon Territory, were not discovered until the 1920s." — Kenn Kaufman (1996)

The Surfbird is named for its habitat outside of the breeding season as described above.

Calidris — The genus name is from the Greek *kalidris*, a name Aristotle used for a "gray speckled waterbird," not further identified, but believed to be a sandpiper. Formerly *Aphriza virgata*.

virgata — The specific epithet is Latin for "twiggy," meaning "streaked," and refers to the heavily streaked and spotted breeding plumage.

French Name: Bécasseau du Ressac
Spanish Names: Playero de Marea; Playero de Marejada; Chorlito de Rompientes
Other Names: Rock Plover; Rock Snipe; Plover-billed Turnstone; Townsend's Sandpiper

Ruff
Calidris pugnax
(cal-ID-ris PUG-nacks)

"In winter plumage the Ruff and its female, the Reeve, are similar, plain birds that look like large Knots. In springtime, the male develops an extraordinary collar of long varicolored feathers around the neck which he expands when displaying to the female. This collar is of varied combinations of brown, white, black, and buff, and no two males are exactly alike. In courting, males go through a weird little dance in which they posture with their collars expanded, stick their bills into the ground, and quiver all over. They have particular dancing grounds, usually on open hillsides, which the females visit for mating." — Oliver Austin, Jr. (1961)

Male Ruffs are noted for their spectacular courtship in which they erect fancy ruffs of long feathers around their necks on display grounds called leks as described in the opening passage. Logically, we would assume these feather embellishments gave the bird its name. But it may be the other way around. The fancy collars that were fashionable in Elizabethan times may be named for the bird. Ruff and Reeve are both said to be derived from the Old English *gerefa* "commander" or "one in authority." It also gives us the words reeve (the chief officer of a town) and sheriff. The reference is to the males' ritualistic fighting as they compete for females. The Ruff's former genus name *Philomachus* means "loving combat."

Calidris — The genus name is from the Greek *kalidris*, a name Aristotle used for a "gray speckled waterbird," not further identified, but believed to be a sandpiper. Formerly *Philomachus pugnax*.

pugnax — The specific epithet is Latin for "quarrelsome" or "combative."

French Name: Bécasseau Combattant
Spanish Name: Combatiente
Other Names: Fighting Ruff; Gambet; Oxen-and Kine

Sharp-tailed Sandpiper
Calidris acuminata
(cal-ID-ris ah-cew-min-AY-tuh)

This sandpiper's pointed tail gives it its name.

Calidris — The genus name is from the Greek *kalidris*, a name Aristotle used for a "gray speckled waterbird," not further identified, but believed to be a sandpiper.

acuminate — The specific epithet is Latin for "pointed or tapered" and refers to the pointed tail.

French Name: Bécasseau a Queue Pointue
Spanish Names: Playero Acuminado; Correlimos Acuminado
Other Name: Siberian Pectoral Sandpiper

Stilt Sandpiper
Calidris himantopus
(cal-ID-ris high-MAN-toh-pus)

The Stilt Sandpiper is named for its exceptionally long legs that suggest stilts.

Calidris — The genus name is from the Greek *kalidris*, a name Aristotle used for a "gray speckled waterbird," not further identified, but believed to be a sandpiper.

himantopus — The specific epithet is Greek for "strap footed" from *himantos* (a strap or thong) and *pous* (the foot). This refers to the bird's long legs suggesting leather straps or thongs.

French Name: Bécasseau à Échasses
Spanish Names: Playero Zancudo; Correlimos Patilargo
Other Names: Long-legged Sandpiper; Frost Snipe; Bastard Yellowlegs; Mongrel; Playero Patilargo

Curlew Sandpiper
Calidris ferruginea
(cal-ID-ris fer-uh-JIN-ee-ah)

This sandpiper is named for its down-curved bill, suggesting that of a curlew.

Calidris — The genus name is from the Greek *kalidris*, a name Aristotle used for a "gray speckled waterbird," not further identified, but believed to be a sandpiper.

ferruginea — The specific epithet is Latin for "rusty red," the color of the bird in breeding plumage.

French Name: Bécasseau Cocorli
Spanish Names: Playero Zarapito; Correlimos Zarapitín
Other Name: Pigmy Curlew

Red-necked Stint
Calidris ruficollis
(cal-ID-ris rue-fih-CAWL-is)

"The word "Stint" is not often used in everyday speech except in certain idiomatic negative forms . . . The phrase 'doing one's stint' means to do a certain minimum amount of work. There is a sense of limited measure in the word. Applied to birds, it seems to have come into currency during the fifteenth century and then it was applied to a number of little waders, Dunlin and Sanderling especially, no doubt because they seemed scanty little birds alongside the much more substantial Curlews and Redshanks." — Francesca Greenoak (1979)

In Britain, stint is the common name of the smaller members of the genus *Calidris*. In America, these little sandpipers are informally called peeps. Red-necked refers to the rufous color on the throat and upper breast. Formerly known as Rufous-necked Stint.

Calidris — The genus name is from the Greek *kalidris*, a name Aristotle used for a "gray speckled waterbird," not further identified, but believed to be a sandpiper.

ruficollis — The specific epithet means "rusty neck" from the Latin *rufus* (rusty) and *collum* (the neck).

French Name: Bécasseau à Col Roux
Spanish Name: Playerito de Cuello Rojo
Other Names: Rufous-necked Stint; Eastern Little Stint; Red-necked Sandpiper

Sanderling, Semipalmated Sandpiper, and Least Sandpiper, by Louis Agassiz Fuertes

Whitey; Whiting; Sea Lark; Sand Lark; Sand-bird; Sand Runner; Ebb Cock; Ox-eye; White Ox-eye; Tweeky; Curwillet; Towilly; Alouette de Mer; Hunakai; Snent; Stint; Playero Areneo

Sanderling
Calidris alba
(cal-ID-ris AL-bah)

The common name was probably influenced by *sanderla*, the Icelandic word for "a sandpiper." As it stands, with a diminutive suffix, Sanderling translates to "little one of the sand." When not nesting on the tundra, Sanderlings are a familiar sight, running up and down coastal beaches like little wind-up toys, as they forage for marine invertebrates brought in by the waves.

Calidris — The genus name is from the Greek *kalidris*, a name Aristotle used for a "gray speckled waterbird," not further identified, but believed to be a sandpiper.

alba — The specific epithet is Latin for "white" and refers to the bird's largely white winter plumage.

French Name: Bécasseau Sanderling
Spanish Name: Playero Blanco; Playero Arenero
Eskimo and Inuit Names: Kimitkoilyak (having no heel)
Other Names: Ruddy Plover; Beach Plover; Lake Plover; Beach Bird; Bull Peep; Beach Snipe; Sand Snipe; Surf Snipe; Mud Snipe; White Snipe; Sanderling Sandpiper; Snippet;

Dunlin
Calidris alpina
(cal-ID-ris al-PIE-nah)

The common name was originally Dunling, composed of dun (grayish-brown) plus a diminutive suffix. Somewhere along the line the (g) was dropped. Anyway, Dunlin means "little dun-colored one" and refers to the dull winter plumage. In breeding plumage, the Dunlin is quite striking with its rufous upperparts and black patch on the belly. In fact, the Dunlin used to be called the Red-backed Sandpiper.

Calidris — The genus name is from the Greek *kalidris*, a name Aristotle used for a "gray speckled waterbird," not further identified, but believed to be a sandpiper.

alpina — The specific epithet is Latin for "alpine," not particularly appropriate, as the Dunlin is not a bird of alpine regions. It breeds on the Arctic tundra and winters on seacoasts. Perhaps, like the Mountain Plover, the type specimen was collected in a mountainous area.

French Name: Bécasseau Variable
Spanish Names: Playero de Dorso Rojo; Playero Dorsirrojo; Correlimos Pechinegro
Eskimo and Inuit Names: Kayutavak (big dipper); Churumrat (imitative) Charome-ruk;

Cho-gho-mu-ghuk; Cher-oo-me-nok; Me-a-kapin

Other Names: American Dunlin; Red-backed Dunlin; Black-bellied Sandpiper; Jack Plover; Black-heart Plover; Plover's Page; Blackcrop; Black-breast; Little Black-breast; Crooked-billed Snipe; Sea Snipe; Sand Snipe; Jack Snipe; Fall Snipe; Winter Snipe; Brant Snipe; Red-back; Lead-back; Brant-bird; Lead-bird; Ox-bird; Ox-eye; Sea Lark; Stib; Stint; Simpleton; Snippet; Churre; Purre; Peewee; Sea Peek; California Peep; Sandy; Dorbie; Bundie; Sea Mouse; Sand Mouse; Pickerel; Ebb Sleeper; Ebb Cock; Playero Espaldi-colorado

∽

Rock Sandpiper
Calidris ptilocnemis
(cal-ID-ris til-ock-NEE-mis)

When not breeding, the Rock Sandpiper spends its time on rocky shores and rock jetties.

Calidris — The genus name is from the Greek *kalidris*, a name Aristotle used for a "gray speckled waterbird," not further identified, but believed to be a sandpiper.

ptilocnemis — The specific epithet is Greek for "feathered greave" from *ptilon* (a feather) and *cnemis* (greave), the shin armor worn by foot soldiers. The reference is to the leg being feathered to the heel.

French Name: Bécasseau des Aléoutiennes

Spanish Names: Playero Roquero; Correlimos Roquero

Eskimo and Inuit Names: Too-loo-goo-yuch; Chu-lich-tah; Chiu-hauk; Tshai-guk

Other Names: Aleutian Sandpiper; Pribilof Sandpiper

∽

Purple Sandpiper
Calidris maritima
(cal-ID-ris mah-RIT-ih-mah)

"To call them "purple" is a stretch. At best, if we could view the dark slate of their fresh winter plumage at just the right angle, we would see a purplish sheen. So the name is hardly a stellar example of good nomenclature." —Kenn Kaufman, "Fade To Purple," *Bird Watcher's Digest*, September/October 2009

Here is another bird that was named in the hand. The purple gloss on the mantle that gives this sandpiper its name is usually not visible in the field.

Calidris — The genus name is from the Greek *kalidris*, a name Aristotle used for a "gray speckled waterbird," not further identified, but believed to be a sandpiper.

maritima — The specific epithet is Latin for "of the sea." When not nesting on the Arctic tundra, this sandpiper's habitat is rocky seacoasts.

French Name: Béasseau Violet

Spanish Name: Correlimos Oscuro

Other Names: Rock Sandpiper; Rock Snipe; Winter Snipe; Rock Plover; Rock-bird; Winter Rock-bird; Rockweed Bird; Beachy Bird; Sand Peep

∽

Baird's Sandpiper
Calidris bairdii
(cal-ID-ris BAIRD-ih-eye)

In 1861 at the Smithsonian, Elliott Coues was going through bird specimens collected by Robert Kennicott and Bernard R. Ross in the vicinity of Great Slave Lake and the McKenzie River in Canada. He noted an unfamiliar sandpiper clearly related to the Pectoral and White-rumped Sandpipers, but differing from both. Coues named it ACTODROMUS BAIRDII for his mentor Spencer Fullerton Baird with the following dedication:

In presenting to the scientific world this my first new species, I should do violence to my feelings, did I give it any other name than the one chosen. To SPENCER F. BAIRD, I dedicate it, as a slight testimonial of respect for scientific acquirements of the highest order, and in grateful remembrance of the unvarying kindness which has rendered my almost daily intercourse a source of so great pleasure, and of the friendly encouragement to which I shall ever feel indebted for whatever progress I may hereafter make in ornithology.

Calidris — The genus name is from the Greek *kalidris*, a name Aristotle used for a "gray speckled waterbird," not further identified, but believed to be a sandpiper.

bairdii — Elliot Coues named this bird in honor of Spencer Fullerton Baird (1823–1887), an American zoologist and secretary of the Smithsonian Institution. See common name above.

French Name: Bécasseau de Baird

Spanish Names: Playerito de Baird; Correlimos de Baird
Eskimo and Inuit Names: Anakruvuk (sounds like man with a bad cold); Ai-bwukia
Other Names: Grass-bird; Mud Snipe; Sand Snipe; Snippet

Little Stint
Calidris minuta
(cal-ID-ris my-NEW-tah)

The word "Stint" is not often used in everyday speech except in certain idiomatic negative forms . . . The phrase 'doing one's stint' means to do a certain minimum amount of work. There is a sense of limited measure in the word. Applied to birds, it seems to have come into currency during the fifteenth century and then it was applied to a number of little waders, Dunlin and Sanderling especially, no doubt because they seemed scanty little birds alongside the much more substantial Curlews and Redshanks. — Francesca Greenoak (1979)

In Britain, stint is the common name of the smaller members of the genus *Calidris*. In America, these little sandpipers are informally called peeps. At six-inches long, the Little Stint is among the smallest sandpipers.

Calidris — The genus name is from the Greek *kalidris*, a name Aristotle used for a "gray speckled waterbird," not further identified, but believed to be a sandpiper.

minuta — The specific epithet means "very small" from the Latin *minutus* (small or little).

French Name: Bécasseau Minute
Spanish Name: Correlimos minudo
Other Names: Brown Sandpiper; Little Sandpiper; Ox-bird; Purre; Wagtail

Least Sandpiper
Calidris minutilla
(cal-ID-ris min-you-TILL-ah)

This sparrow-sized peep is the smallest species of sandpiper.

Calidris — The genus name is from the Greek *kalidris*, a name Aristotle used for a "gray speckled waterbird," not further identified, but believed to be a sandpiper.

minutilla — The specific epithet is Latin for "very small."

French Name: Bécasseau Minuscule

Spanish Names: Playerito Chichicuilote; Playerito Mínimo; Correlimos Menudo
Eskimo Name: Livalivaurak (small Liva Liva)
Other Names: American Stint; Wilson's Stint; Mud Snipe; Sand Snipe; Peep; Sand-Peep; Little Sand-Peep; Mud-Peep; Mud-picker; Beachy Bird; Ox-eye; Meadow Ox-eye; Snippet; Alouette; Petite Alouette; Maringouin; Playerito Menudo

White-rumped Sandpiper
Calidris fuscicollis
(cal-ID-ris fuss-ih-COL-is)

This is the only small sandpiper with a white rump patch, conspicuous in flight. It is probably a visual signal that helps to keep the flock together.

Calidris — The genus name is from the Greek *kalidris*, a name Aristotle used for a "gray speckled waterbird," not further identified, but believed to be a sandpiper.

fuscicollis — The specific epithet is Latin for "dark neck" from *fuscus* (dark or dusky) and *collum* (the neck). Perhaps it refers to the dark gray neck and head in winter plumage that gives the bird a hooded appearance.

French Name: Bécasseau à Croupion Blanc
Spanish Name: Playerito de Rabadilla Blanca; Correlimos Lomiblanco
Eskimo and Inuit Names: Kai-nialu
Other Names: Bonaparte's Sandpiper; Schinz's Sandpiper; Bull Peep; Mud Snipe; Sand Snipe; Sand-bird; Beachy Bird; Alouette; Snippet; Playero Rabadilla Blanca

Buff-breasted Sandpiper
Calidris subruficollis
(cal-ID-ris sub-ROOF-ih-COL-lis)

The pale, unmarked buffy underparts give this sandpiper its name.

Calidris — The genus name is from the Greek *kalidris*, a name Aristotle used for a "gray speckled waterbird," not further identified, but believed to be a sandpiper. Formerly *Tryngites subruficollis*.

subruficollis — The specific epithet is Latin for "reddish necked" from *subrufus* (reddish) and *collis* (the neck).

French Name: Bécasseau Roussâtre
Spanish Names: Playero Leonado; Playero Pradero; Praderito Pechianteado

Eskimo and Inuit Names: Aklaktak (spotted), Nud-luayu
Other Names: Hill Grass-bird; Robin Snipe

Pectoral Sandpiper
Calidris melanotos
(cal-ID-ris mel-an-OH-tos)

"As my eyelids began to droop and the scene to become indistinct, suddenly a low, hollow, booming note struck my ear and sent my thoughts back to a spring morning in northern Illinois, and to the loud vibrating tones of the prairie chickens ... The note is deep, hollow, and resonant, but at the same time liquid and musical, and may be represented by a repetition of the syllables *too-u, too-u, too-u, too-u, too-u, too-u, too-u*. Before the bird utters these notes it fills its esophagus with air to such an extent that the breast and throat is inflated to twice or more its natural size, and the great air sac thus formed gives the peculiar resonant quality to the note. The skin of the throat and breast becomes very flabby and loose at this season, and its inner surface is covered with small globular masses of fat. When not inflated, the skin loaded with this extra weight and with a slightly serous suffusion which is present hangs down in a pendulous flap or fold exactly like a dewlap, about an inch and a half wide." — Edward W. Nelson (1887)

A pair of air sacs beneath the skin of the male's breast give this sandpiper its name. These are inflated during courtship and resonate the bird's booming calls, as described in the above passage.

Calidris — The genus name is from the Greek *kalidris*, a name Aristotle used for a "gray speckled waterbird," not further identified, but believed to be a sandpiper.

melanotos — The specific epithet is Greek for "black back" from *melas* (black) and *notos* (the back). This sandpiper has a brown back, but perhaps the name refers to the heavy streaking on the back.

French Name: Bécasseau à Poitrine Cendrée
Spanish Names: Playero Pectoral; Playerito Pectoral; Correlimos Pectoral
Eskimo and Inuit Names: Aibwukie (walrus bird); Poviaktook (inflating the chest); Timtimtak (swells chest, makes mumumum sound)
Other Names: Grass-Snipe; Squat Snipe; Meadow Snipe; Jack Snipe; Cow Snipe; Marsh Plover; Grass Plover; Hay-bird; Grass-bird; Crouching Shore-bird; Fat-bird; Beachy Bird; Brown Bird; Brown-back; Brownie; Short-neck; Dowitch; Squatter; Triddler; Chevalier; Creaker; Krieker; Alouette; Alouette de Pres; Playero de Manchado

Semipalmated Sandpiper
Calidris pusilla
(cal-ID-ris pu-SILL-ah)

Semipalmated refers to the partial webbing between the front toes.

Calidris — The genus name is from the Greek *kalidris*, a name Aristotle used for a "gray speckled waterbird," not further identified, but believed to be a sandpiper.

pusilla — The specific epithet is from the Latin *pusillos* (tiny). The Semipalmated is among the smallest sandpipers.

French Name: Bécasseau Semipalmé
Spanish Names: Playerito Semipalmeado; Playerito Semipalmado; Correlimos Semipalmado
Eskimo and Inuit Names: Liva Liva; La-vee-laliber-berg; Nilwiliwiluk
Other Names: Little Peep; Black-legged Peep; Sand-peep; Sand Ox-eye; Snippet; Mud Snipe; Sand Snipe; Alouette de Mer; Playero Gracioso; Beach Bird; Beachy Bird;

Western Sandpiper
Calidris mauri
(cal-ID-ris MORE-eye)

This is the western counterpart of the Semipalmated Sandpiper, breeding along the northwestern Alaskan coast. Many winter along the Pacific coast from Washington to Peru, but they also occur in the east along the Atlantic and Gulf coasts outside of the breeding season.

Calidris — The genus name is from the Greek *kalidris*, a name Aristotle used for a "gray speckled waterbird," not further identified, but believed to be a sandpiper.

mauri — The specific epithet honors Ernesto Mauri (1791–1836), director of the Botanical Gardens in Rome. He assisted his friend Charles Bonaparte when he was writing his *Iconografia della Fauna Italica* (1832–1841). While he was compiling his comparative list of the birds of Philadelphia and Rome in 1838, Bonaparte named this species for his late friend, but did not publish a description. German ornithologist Jean Cabanis shot several Western Sandpipers along the South Carolina coast in May of 1840. Hinrich Lichtenstein, Director of the Berlin Zoological Museum, labeled the specimens *cabanisi*, but he also failed to publish a description. When Bonaparte visited the Berlin Museum, he persuaded Dr. Cabanis to use the name *mauri*, when he wrote the description, which was published in 1857.

French Name: Bécasseau d'Alaska
Spanish Names: Playerito Occidental; Correlimos Occidental
Eskimo and Inuit Names: Libv-i-libv-i-lu-uk; Ee-u-ga-guk; Iyiuarat
Other Names: Mud Snipe; Sand Snipe; Snippet; Peep; Playero Occidental

Short-billed Dowitcher
Limnodromus griseus
(lim-NOD-rah-mus GRISS-ee-us)

There is some dispute on the origin of the name dowitcher. Some say it is an Iroquoian name for a snipe. Other sources say it stems from *Deutcher* (German) or *Duitsch* (Dutch). The name Dutch snipe distinguished the dowitcher from the common (Wilson's) snipe. The name apparently originated in or around the Dutch colony of New Amsterdam (now New York). The Short-billed Dowitcher actually has a very long bill, but it averages just a few millimeters shorter than that of the Long-billed Dowitcher. There is some overlap, however, and bill length is not reliable in distinguishing the two species.

Limnodramus — The genus name is Greek for "marsh runner" from *limne* (a marsh) and *dromos* (running) i.e. "inhabiting." Marshes serve as nesting and feeding habitats.

griseus — The specific epithet is Modern Latin for "gray" from *gris*, the French word for "gray." Gray is the bird's dominant color in winter plumage.

French Name: Bécasseau Roux
Spanish Names: Costurero de Pico Corto; Costurero Piquicorto; Agujeta Común
Other Names: American Dowitcher; Eastern Dowitcher; Brownback Dowitcher; Dowitch; Brown Snipe; Gray Snipe; Robin-Snipe; Quail Snipe; German Snipe; Deutscher Snipe; Red-breasted Snipe; Sand Snipe; Jacksnipe; Spotrump; New York Godwit; Brown-back; Brown Jack; Gray-back; Summer Gray-back; Dormeur; Driver; Sea-pigeon; Becassine de Mer; Becassine Grise; Chorlo Pico Largo

Long-billed Dowitcher
Limnodromus scolopaceus
(lim-NOD-roh-mus skol-ow-PASS-ee-us)

This dowitcher's bill averages just a few millimeters longer than that of the Short-billed Dowitcher.

Limnodromus — The genus name is Greek for "marsh runner" from *limne* (a marsh) and *dromos* (running) i.e. "inhabiting." Marshes serve as nesting and feeding habitats.

scolopaceus — The specific epithet means "resembling a woodcock" from the Greek *scolopax* (a woodcock) and the Latin suffix *–aceus* (resembling). The reference is to this species' similarity in appearance to a woodcock, particularly the long, thin bill.

French Name: Bécasseau à Long Bec
Spanish Names: Costurero de Pico Largo; Costurero Piquilargo; Agujeta Piquilarga
Eskimo and Inuit Names: Kayaryartalik (markings on back look like kayak); Kilyaktalik (like a bundle when seen from behind); Ki-o-kok-ar; Tal-ik; Oo-loo-yahk-na-gak; Kai-a-gwukh-ta-lik
Other Names: Western Dowitcher; White-tail Dowitcher; Long-billed Snipe; Western Red-breasted Snipe; Red-bellied Snipe; Sand Snipe; Jack Snipe; Greater Gray-back; Greater Long-beak

Wilson's Snipe
Gallinago delicata
(gal-ih-NAY-go del-ih-KAH-tah)

"When the first shad run up our rivers to spawn, and the shad bush opens its feathery white blossoms in the roadside thickets in March, the snipe come back from the south to haunt the open wet places of the lowlands, freshwater marshes, soaked fields, and the sheltered sunny spots in a clearing that are the first to thaw. Only in exceptionally dry seasons do these birds go near salt water marshes." — Neltje Blanchan (1898)

Snipe derives from the Old Norse *snipa*, which gave rise to the Old English *snite* and Middle English *snype*, presumably from a Proto-Germanic root *snipon*, meaning "a long, thin object," a reference to the bird's extraordinarily long bill that it probes deep into the mud for its invertebrate prey. Our American species is named for Alexander Wilson, who first pointed out a number of characteristics that distinguish it from the Common Snipe (*G. gallinago*) of Eurasia, although the two were long considered to be conspecific. The folk names Alewife Bird, Shad Bird, and Shad Spirit allude to the time of this bird's spring arrival as explained in the opening passage.

Gallinago — The genus name is derived from the Latin *gallina* (a hen), perhaps referring to the speckled plumage like that of a brown hen.

delicata — The specific epithet is Latin for "dainty" or "nice." It refers to the fact that this species is considered a delicacy in the culinary sense as described here:

"Few birds surpass the snipe in sapid quality of flesh, and many kinds rank high in the estimation of the sportsman and epicure." — Elliot Coues (1898)

"The flesh of this snipe, being tender and well flavored, is much prized by epicures, so that these birds have long been an object of pursuit by sports-men. Indeed, their manner of flight demands great skill to bring them down." — W.E. Clyde Todd (1940)

"Snipe are a real bird. Let's get that straight at the outset. They are a small sandpiper-looking bird that lives on the edges of marshes, sticking its needle of a beak into the mud to fish out yummy wormy things. They are tough to hit with a shotgun — thus the term "sniper" — and they happen to be wonderful eating . . . What, you might ask, does a snipe taste like? It's hard to describe because snipe are not related to any other birds we normally eat. But they are a little ducky, a little grouse-y. Dark, but not red meat like venison. Squirrel comes to mind as something close, but this will not help you if you are not a hunter. The closest I can get you if you are not a hunter is the "oyster" on a good free-range chicken; this is the oval of meat where the thigh connects to the body of the bird." — Hank Shaw (2015), www.honest-food.net

"The food of our Common Snipe consists principally of ground-worms, insects, and the juicy slender roots of different vegetables, all of which tend to give its flesh that richness of flavour and juicy tenderness, for which it is so deservedly renowned, it being equal to that of the Woodcock. Many epicures eat up both Snipe and Woodcock with all their viscera, worms and insects to boot, the intestines in fact being considered the most savoury parts." — web4.audubon.org

French Name: Bécassine des Marais

Spanish Names: Agachona de Wilson; Agachona Común; Becacina Común

Eskimo and Inuit Names: Kukukuak (sound of mating dive); Avikiak (sounds like the walrus); Koo-koo-kwah; Ku-ku-kurik; Goo-lech-arch

Other Names: American Snipe; English Snipe; Bog Snipe; Marsh Snipe; Meadow Snipe; Field Snipe; Little Snipe; Long-bill Snipe; Squatting Snipe; Gutter Snipe; Jacksnipe; Mudsnipe; Snite; Little Woodcock; Bleater; Meadow Hen; Puta-puta Bird; Alewife Bird; Shad Bird; Shad Spirit; Dodger; Drill face;

Wilson's Snipe, by Louis Agassiz Fuertes

Englishe Schneb; Alouette; Bescasina; Becassine; Cache-cache; Cohoon Bird; Croman-loin; Naosg; Twillic

American Woodcock
Scolopax minor
(SKOL-oh-paks MY-nor)

"This mysterious hermit of the alders, this recluse of the boggy thickets, this wood nymph of crepuscular habits is a common bird and well distributed in our Eastern States, widely known, but not intimately known. Its quiet retiring habits do not lead to human intimacy. It may live almost in our midst unnoticed . . . Their haunts are so varied that one may not be surprised to find them almost anywhere, especially on migrations. Flight birds are here to-day and gone to-morrow. Their favorite resorts are alder thickets along the banks of meandering streams or spring-fed boggy runs; rich bottom lands or scrubby hollows, overgrown with willows, maples, alders, and poison sumac; or the scrubby edges of damp, second-growth woods, mixed with birches; any such place will suit them where they can find moist soil, not too wet or too sour, well supplied with earthworms." — Arthur Cleveland Bent (1927)

The wood in woodcock refers to the habitat of moist deciduous or mixed woods, where woodcocks spend the day. At night the birds move into open areas such as pastures to feed. The males also prefer such areas to do their courtship flights. Cock is imitative of the call. American distinguishes our species from the Eurasian Woodcock (*S. rusticola*).

Scolopax — The genus name is Greek for "a woodcock," a name Aristotle used for the Eurasian species. It derives from *skolops*, meaning "anything pointed," which describes the long bill, which the bird uses to probe for earthworms.

minor — The specific epithet is Latin for "smaller" (than the Eurasian Woodcock).

French Name: Bécasse d'Amérique

American Woodcock, by Louis Agassiz Fuertes

Sidebar 15
The Woodcock's Sky Dance

From early to mid-Spring, if you seek out the woodcock's woodland habitat just before dusk, you may witness the male's remarkable courtship flight, or as Aldo Leopold describes it, his sky dance:

"I owned my farm for two years before learning that the sky dance is to be seen over my woods every evening in April and May . . . The stage must be an open amphitheater in the woods or brush, and in the center there must be a mossy spot, a streak of sterile sand, a bare outcrop of rock, or a bare roadway . . . He flies in low from some neighboring thicket, alights on the bare moss, and at once begins the overture: a series of queer throaty *peents* spaced about two seconds apart, and sounding much like the summer call of the nighthawk. Suddenly the peenting ceases and the bird flutters skyward in a series of wide spirals, emitting a musical twitter. Up and up he goes, the spirals steeper and smaller, the twittering louder and louder, until the performer is only a speck in the sky. Then, without warning, he tumbles like a crippled plane, giving voice in a soft liquid warble that a March bluebird might envy. At a few feet from the ground he levels off and returns to his peenting ground, usually to the exact spot where the performance began, and there resumes his peenting." — Aldo Leopold (1949)

Spanish Name: Chocha Americana
Other Names: Lesser Woodcock; Little Woodcock; Great Red Woodcock; Timber-doodle; Labrador Twister; Hookum-pake; Bogsucker; Bog-borer; Bog-bird; Big-eyes; Becasse de nuit; Becasse des bois; Big Snipe; Red-breasted Snipe; Big-headed Snipe; Blind Snipe; Mud Snipe; Big Mud Snipe; Wood Snipe; Whistling Snipe; Whistling Red Snipe; Wall-eyed Snipe; Siphon Snipe; Snipe Owl; Marsh Plover; Wood Hen; Mud Hen; Whistler; Little Whistler; Pewee; Hill Partridge; Mountain Partridge; Night Partridge; Night Peck; Shrups; Cache-cache Rouge; Grosa Brouna Shneb

Spotted Sandpiper
Actitis macularius
(ack-TIE-tis mack-you-LARE-ih-us)

Round, black spots on the breast and belly of the breeding adult give this sandpiper its name.

Actitis — The genus name is Greek for "sea coast dweller or shore dweller." The Spotted Sandpiper is not as strictly coastal as many other nonbreeding sandpipers are. This widespread species often breeds and winters far inland. It does usually nest near water, and so is often a resident of freshwater shores.

macularius — The specific epithet is Latin for "spotted" or "having spots" from *macula* (a spot) and *–arius* (possessing).

French Name: Chevalier Branlequeue
Spanish Names: Playero Alzacolita; Andarríos Maculado
Eskimo Name: Anaktuvuk
Other Names: Gutter Snipe; Bow Snipe; Grey Snipe; River Snipe; Teeter Snipe; Teeterer Snipe; Sand Snipe; Sand Lark; Beachy Bird; Bowing Bird; Crooked-winged Bird; Teeter Bird; Peep; Sand Peep; Teeter Peep; Teeter-tail; Teeter-tip; Teeterer; Tip-up; Tilt-up; Seesaw; Swee-swee; Shneb; Peet-weet; Peeweet; Pewit; Alouette; Branie Queue; Alouette Branie Queue; Chevalier de Batture; Chorook; Curracag; Maubeche; Playero Coleador; Sauté-queue; Wagtail

Solitary Sandpiper
Tringa solitaria
(TRING-ah sol-ih-TARE-ih-ah)

"A lover of wet meadows, and secluded inland ponds, in the lowlands or the mountains rather than the salt water marshes and sand flats of the coast that most of its kin delight in, the wood tattler is a shy recluse, but not a hermit. At least a pair of birds are usually seen together, representatives of small flocks scattered over the neighborhood, but generally hidden in the underbrush. As compared with most other sandpipers that move in compact flocks and are ever inviting other waders to join them, this species is certainly unsocial; but to call it solitary implies that it is a misanthrope like the bittern, which no one knew better than Wilson, who named it, that it is not." — Neltje Blanchan (1898)

The Solitary Sandpiper gets its name from the fact that it is usually seen singly or in pairs, as opposed to large flocks like many other sandpipers.

Tringa — The genus name derives from the Greek *tryngas*, a name Aristotle used for a white-rumped waterbird, not further identified, but taken by later authors to be a sandpiper.

solitaria — The specific epithet is Latin for "solitary."

French Name: Chevalier Solitaire
Spanish Names: Playero Solitario; Andarríos Solitario
Eskimo Name: Kipilugoksioyuk (look for insects)
Other Names: Green Sandpiper; American Green Sandpiper; Wood Sandpiper; American Wood Sandpiper; Wood Tattler; Woodland Tattler; Solitary Tattler; Barnyard Plover; Black Snipe; Beachy Bird; Bullhead; Peet-weet; Swee-sweet; Tie-up; Alouette Grise; Bacassine Gross-tête; Shneb

Wandering Tattler
Tringa incanus
(TRING-ah in-CANE-us)

"Over the entire coast of the Pacific north of the equator its presence has been noted by various naturalists whose

Bohemian tastes have made their lives somewhat akin to that of this gentle wanderer. Across the broad ocean it ranges to those bits of paradise dotting the South Seas, tripping its way daintily on the beaches of the coral-enclosed islands, their feet laved by the warm waters of the tropics, and their eyes familiar with the luxuriant face of nature in its gentlest and most lovely state. The next season may find them thousands of miles to the north, under the shadow of the stupendous cliffs and grand but desolate and repellent scenes of the Aleutian Islands." — Edward W. Nelson (1887)

The name tattler dates back to market hunting days, when thousands of shorebirds were shot to supply the markets of big cities in the east. Hunters were perturbed by this species' shrill alarm calls that alerted the flocks of danger. Tattler is also the nickname of many species of sandpipers, because of their alarm calls. Wandering refers to this sandpiper's long migration travels as described in the opening passage. They breed in Alaska and the Yukon, and migrate along the west coast as far south as Peru and to islands of the South Pacific.

Tringa — The genus name derives from the Greek *tryngas*, a name Aristotle used for a white-rumped waterbird, not further identified, but taken by later authors to be a sandpiper.

incanus — The specific epithet is Latin for "light gray," which is this bird's dominant color.

French Name: Chevalier Errant
Spanish Names: Playero Vagabundo; Correlimos Vagamundo
Eskimo and Inuit Name: Silyirisoktok (like sharpening with a stone)
Other Names: Alaskan Tattler; Rock Snipe; Ulili

Spotted Redshank
Tringa erythropus
(TRING-ah er-ITH-row-pus)

Redshank refers to this sandpiper's dark red legs in summer. They fade to orange in winter. In summer plumage these species sports small white spots on its blackish plumage.

Tringa — The genus name derives from the Greek *tryngas*, a name Aristotle used for a white-rumped waterbird, not further identified, but taken by later authors to be a sandpiper.

erythropus — The specific epithet means "red-footed" from the Greek *eruthros* (red) and *pous* (the foot).

French Name: Chevalier Arlequin
Spanish Name: Achibebe Oscuro

Greater Yellowlegs
Tringa melanoleuca
(TRING-ah mel-an-oh-LEW-kah)

Long, bright yellow legs give this sandpiper its name. Greater distinguishes this species from the smaller Lesser Yellowlegs.

Tringa — The genus name derives from the Greek *tryngas*, a name Aristotle used for a white-rumped waterbird, not further identified, but taken by later authors to be a sandpiper.

melanoleuca — The specific epithet is from the Greek for "black and white" from *melos* (black) and *leukos* (white) and refers to the black and white mottled plumage.

French Name: Grand Chevalier
Spanish Names: Patamarilla Mayor; Patiamarillo Mayor
Eskimo Name: Choo-choo-chak
Other Names: Big Yellowlegs; Horse Yellowlegs; Winter Yellowlegs; Greater Yellow-shanks; Yellow-shins; Big Yellow-legged Plover; Yellow-shanks Plover; Greater Tattler; Long-legged Tattler; Varied Tattler; Telltale Tattler; Greater Tell-tale; Big Tell-tale; Tell-tale Godwit; Cucu; Longlegs; Daddy Longlegs; Big Cucu; Large Cucu; Stone-bird; Stone Curlew; Stone-Snipe; Telltale Snipe; Tell-tale Godwit; Grand Pluvier; Turkey-back; Humility; Yelper; Ansary; Lansary; Nansary; Aunt Sarah; Patte Jaune; Chevalier aux Pattes Jaunes; Pied Jaune; Corbido; Playero Guiniella Grande; Shneb; Klook-klook; Twillick

Willet
Tringa semipalmata
(TRING-ah sem-ih-pal-MAY-tah)

The name Willet comes from this large shorebird's melodic whistled call, *pill-will-willet* or *pill-o-will-o-willet*.

Tringa — The genus name derives from the Greek *tryngas*, a name Aristotle used for a white-rumped waterbird, not further identified, but taken by later authors to be a sandpiper. Formerly *Catoptrophorus semipalmatus*.

semipalmata — The specific epithet is Latin for "half-webbed" from *semi* (half) and *palma* (the hand) and refers to the partially webbed front toes.

French Name: Chevalier Semipalmé
Spanish Names: Playero Pihuihui; Pigüilo
Other Names: Eastern Willet; Western Willet; Pill-willet; Will; Will-willet; Pill-will-willet; Pillo-wee; Pilly-willick; Bill-willie; Tell-bill-willy; Kill-cu; Semipalmated Tattler; Tell-tale; Semipalmated Snipe; Duck Snipe; Goose Bird; Pond Bird; Humility; Old Humility; Spanish Plover; White-wing; White-winged Curlew; Pied-winged Curlew; Stone Curlew; Laughing Jackass; Longlegs; Chevalier; Clewie; Playero Aliblanco; Tinkasheer; Twillick; Virette; Vire-vire; Turn a Vire

Lesser Yellowlegs
Tringa flavipes
(TRING-ah FLAY-vih-peez)

The Lesser Yellowlegs is so called, because it looks like a smaller version of the Greater Yellowlegs. The Lesser is about the size of a Killdeer.

Tringa — The genus name derives from the Greek *tryngas*, a name Aristotle used for a white-rumped waterbird, not further identified, but taken by later authors to be a sandpiper.

flavipes — The specific epithet is Latin for "yellow foot" from *flavus* (yellow) and *pes* (the foot).

French Name: Petit Chevalier
Spanish Names: Patamarilla Menor; Patiamarillo Menor
Eskimo and Inuit Name: Ovingoayook (whistler)
Other Names: Common Yellowlegs; Summer Yellowlegs; Yellow-legged Plover; Small Yellow-legged Plover; Yellow-shanks Plover; Lesser Yellow-shanks; Lesser Yellowshins; Lesser Tell-tale; Little Tell-tale; Lesser Tattler; Lesser Long-legged Tattler; Little Stone-bird; Little Stone Snipe; Small Snipe; Telltale Snipe; Yellow-shanks Snipe; Yellow-shanks Tattler; Yellow-legged Godwit; Aunt Sary; Little Yelper; Small Yelper; Small Cucu; Little Cucu; Petit Pluvier; Playero Guineilla Pequena; Saunder; Shneb; Twillick

> **Sidebar 16**
> **Phalaropes**
> **Genus Phalaropus**
> Phalarope stems from the bird's genus name and means "coot-footed" in reference to the lobed toes like those of a coot rather than the webbed feet of most aquatic birds. See genus name below.

Wilson's Phalarope
Phalaropus tricolor
(fah-LARE-ow-pus TRY-KUL-er)

The common name honors Alexander Wilson (1766–1813), the scientific father of American Ornithology. Joseph Sabine, a great admirer of Wilson, described this species in his zoological appendix to John Franklin's narrative of his first overland expedition to Canada (1823), naming it *Phalaropus Wilsoni*. Sabine was apparently unaware the species had previously been described by Louis Vieillot as *Steganopus tricolor* in 1819, so Vieillot's specific epithet has priority.

Phalaropus — The genus name means "coot-footed" from the Greek *phalaris* (a coot) and *pous* (the foot). The reference is to the lobed toes like those of a coot.

tricolor — The specific epithet is Latin for "three-colored" and refers to the female's

Wilson's Phalarope, by Louis Agassiz Fuertes

showy breeding plumage of white, black, and chestnut.
French Name: Phalarope de Wilson
Spanish Names: Falaropo de Pico Largo; Falárapo de Wilson
Other Names: Summer Phalarope; Swimming Sandpiper; Lobe-footed Holopode Sea Snipe; Sea Goose; Grunter

Red-necked Phalarope
Phalaropus lobatus
(fah-LARE-ow-pus low-BAY-tus)

The rufous patch on the neck of the breeding female gives this phalarope its name. The patch is browner and less extensive in the male. Formerly known as Northern Phalarope.

Phalaropus — The genus name is Greek for "coot-footed" from *phalaris* (a coot) and *pous* (the foot). The reference is to the lobed toes like those of a coot.

lobatus — The specific epithet is Latin for "lobed" and refers to the lobed toes.
French Name: Phalarope Hyperboréen
Spanish Names: Falaropo de Cuello Rojo; Falárapo Cuellirrojo; Falaropo Picofino
Eskimo and Inuit Names: Kaiyorgon (floats like a kayak); Tilikcharak (imitative)
Other Names: Hyperborean Phalarope; Sea-Snipe; Swimming Snipe; Fairy Duck; Sea-goose; Mackerel-goose; Mackerel; Bank-bird; Brown Bank-bird; White Bank-bird; Gale-bird; Ground Bird; Gulf Bird; Whale-bird; Web-footed Peep; Grunter

Red Phalarope
Phalaropus fulicarius
(fah-LARE-ow-pus few-lih-CARE-ih-us)

The Red Phalarope is named for the rich chestnut-red breeding plumage of the breeding female. The male's coloration is duller.

Phalaropus — The genus name is Greek for "coot-footed" from *phalaris* (a coot) and *pous* (the foot). The reference is to the lobed toes like those of a coot.

fulicarius — The specific epithet means "coot-like" from the Latin *fulica* (a coot) and *-arius* (referring to). As with the genus name, this refers to the lobed toes being similar to those of a coot.
French Name: Phalarope Roux
Spanish Names: Falaropo de Pico Grueso; Falárapo Piquigrueso; Falaropo Rojo
British Name: Grey Phalarope (for the winter plumage)
Eskimo and Inuit Names: Augtuarik (red on back); Auksruak (colored like blood)
Other Names: Flat-billed Phalarope; Red-footed Tringa; Red Coot-footed Tringa; Bank-bird; Brown Bank-bird; Gray Bank-bird; Jersey Goose; Mackerel-goose; Sea-goose; Sea-Snipe; Swimming Snipe; Ground Bird; Herring Bird; Gulf Bird; Whale-bird

Family Stercorariidae
Skuas and Jaegers

Skua is from the Faeroese name for the bird, *skuvur*, which is derived from the Old Norse *skúfr*. It is probably imitative, but is also said to mean "brown gull" or "dark gull." Jaeger is derived from the German *jäger* (a hunter). On their Arctic breeding grounds, jaegers are indeed hunters, coursing back and forth over the tundra in search of lemmings, eggs, and young birds. Outside of the breeding season they resort to piracy. See Parasitic Jaeger.

Great Skua
Stercorarius skua
(ster-koh-RARE-ih-us SKEW-ah)

Great refers to this skua's large size, particularly in relation to the somewhat smaller South Polar Skua.

Stercorarius — The genus name is Latin for "having to do with dung" from *stercus* (dung). Early observers watching skuas and jaegers pursue other seabirds until they regurgitated their meal mistook this for excrement, thus the inappropriate genus name.

skua — The specific epithet derives from *skuvur*, the Faeroese name for this species. See common name above.
French Name: Grand Labbe
Spanish Name: Págalo Grande
Other Names: Skua Gull; Black Gull; Brown Gull; Keeask Gull; Sea Hawk; Sea Crow; Sea Hen; Morrel Hen; Gran' Goose; Robber Bird; Nod Bird; Tom Harry; Herdsman; Wease-

alley; Bonxie; Boatswain; Alan; Jager; Pagalo Grande; Tuliac

South Polar Skua
Stercorarius maccormicki
(ster-koh-RARE-ih-us mak-KOR-mik-eye)

The South Polar Skua is named for its breeding range in Antarctica. It occurs off both North American coasts during the southern winter (May-October).

Stercorarius — The genus name is Latin for "having to do with dung" from *stercus* (dung). Early observers watching skuas and jaegers pursue other seabirds until they regurgitated their meal mistook this for excrement, thus the inappropriate genus name.

maccormicki — The specific epithet commemorates Robert M. McCormick (1800–1890), a surgeon with the Royal Navy. Dr. McCormick served as naturalist on John Clark Ross's 4-year Antarctic voyage (1839–1843). In 1841, Ross's party landed on Possession Island, which they claimed for Great Britain. The officers and crew drank a toast to the happiness of Queen Victoria and Prince Albert. During their 25-minute stay, McCormick shot a skua soaring over a penguin rookery. This turned out to be the type specimen of a new species, which British ornithologist Howard Saunders described in 1893.

French Names: Labbe de McCormick; Labbe Antarctique
Spanish Name: Págalo Sureño
Other Names: MacCormick's Skua

Pomarine Jaeger
Stercorarius pomarinus
(ster-koh-RARE-ih-us pom-ah-RINE-us)

Jaeger is from the German jäger "a hunter," an apt name for these predatory birds. Pomarine is derived from the specific epithet. See below.

Stercorarius — The genus name is Latin for "having to do with dung" from *stercus* (dung). Early observers watching skuas and jaegers pursue other seabirds until they regurgitated their meal mistook this for excrement, thus the inappropriate genus name.

pomarinus — The specific epithet means "nose cover" from the Greek *poma* or *pomatos* (a lid or a cover) and *rhinos* (the nose). It refers to a sheath that covers the nostrils during the breeding season.

French Name: Labbe Pomarin
Spanish Name: Salteador Pomarino
Eskimo and Inuit Names: Can-ling-i-tal-luck (fish club tail); Isongngakluk (poorly winged)
Other Names: Pomarine Skua; Pomatorhine Skua; Skuar; Jaeger Gull; Gull-chaser; Gull Hunter; Jiddy Hawk; Sea Robber; Sea Hen; Whip-tail; Marlinspike; Marlingspike; Black *Marling* Spike; Aret; Bo'sn; Bosun Bird; Mason; Pagalo Pomarino

Parasitic Jaeger
Stercorarius parasiticus
(ster-koh-RARE-ih-us par-ah-SIT-ih-cus)

"As one watches a flock of terns whirling like driven snow, now here, now there, and ever and anon plunging for fish, one may sometimes see a dark hawk-like bird

Parasitic Jaeger, Long-tailed Jaeger, Pomarine Jaeger, and Great Skua, by Louis Agassiz Fuertes

suddenly appear on the scene and spread devastation in the ranks. With relentless energy he singles out and pursues some hapless individual until it drops its prey. This is a jaeger, a gull-like bird, with hawk-like characteristics. A more appropriate name for him would be robber rather than jaeger or hunter, for he obtains his food by robbing other birds. He has, however, all the grace and agility of the true hunting birds — the hawks — but his actions rarely end in bloodshed. After all robbery is a less serious crime than murder, but the term robber is opprobrious, while that of hunter is not, so it is perhaps well that the name remains as it is." — Charles Wendell Townsend (1921)

Not a parasite in the sense of a louse or a tapeworm or even a cowbird, the Parasitic Jaeger is so named because it engages in a behavior called kleptoparasitism, in which it harasses another seabird, shadowing its every movement, until it disgorges its meal. Then the jaeger snatches the food right out of the air. Kleptoparasitism can be observed in many other species of seabirds, too, including skuas, gulls, large terns, frigatebirds, even the Bald Eagle.

Stercorarius — The genus name is Latin for "having to do with dung" from *stercus* (dung). Early observers watching skuas and jaegers pursue other seabirds until they regurgitated their meal mistook this for excrement, thus the inappropriate genus name.

parasiticus — The specific epithet is Latin for "parasitic." See common name above.

French Name: Labbe Parasite
Spanish Name: Salteador Parásito
British Name: Arctic Skua
Eskimo and Inuit Names: A-hlukh-ta-yoo-le (thief); Mirgiaksyook (vomit)
Other Names: Richardson's Jaeger; Arctic Bird; Arctic Gull; Black-toed Gull; Robber Gull; Arctic Hawk Gull; Jiddy Hawk; Sea Hawk; Gull-chaser; Dirt Bird; Dirty Allan; Dirty Aulin; Scoutie Aulin; Dung Bird; Dung Hunter; Dung Teaser; Skait Bird; Shite Scouter; Aret; Boatswain; Bosun Bird; Marlinspike; Marlingspike; Man-o'war Bird; Mason; Whiptail; Shooi; Wagel; Trumpie; Labbe; Feaser; Fasceddar

Long-tailed Jaeger
Stercorarius longicaudus
(ster-koh-RARE-ih-us lonj-ih-CAW-dus)

"To watch the long-tailed jaeger in flight is one of the delights of the Arctic summer, for it is one of the swiftest and most graceful of birds on the wing; its light and slender form is propelled by its long, pointed wings with the speed of an arrow, its broad tail serving as an effective rudder, as it twists and turns in pursuit of its fellows or some luckless gull or tern, with its long central tail feathers streaming in the wind." — Arthur Cleveland Bent (1921)

The long central tail streamers, longer than those of the other two jaegers, gives this species its name.

Stercorarius — The genus name is Latin for "having to do with dung" from *stercus* (dung). Early observers watching skuas and jaegers pursue other seabirds until they regurgitated their meal mistook this for excrement, thus the inappropriate genus name.

longicaudus — The specific epithet means "long tail" from the Latin *longus* (long) and *cauda* (the tail), referring to the long central tail streamers.

French Name: Labbe à Longue Queue
Spanish Name: Salteador de Cola Larga
Eskimo and Inuit Names: Yung-uk (little man); Cha-wa-sho-yuk (young or new jaeger); Chungarlugak (color of gall bladder around liver)
Other Names: Aret; Buffon's Jaeger; Bo's'n; Gull-chaser; Gull-teaser; Man of War; Marlinspike; Marlingspike Bird; Mason; Sea Hen; Whip-tail

Dovekie, by John James Audubon

Family Alcidae
Auks, Murres, and Puffins

Ecologically, these are the northern counterparts of the penguins of the Southern Hemisphere, but the two families are not closely related. The common name auk and the family name both derive from the Old Norse *alka*, a name given to several northern seabirds. For the explanation of murre and puffin, see those entries.

Dovekie
Alle alle
(AL-ee AL-ee)

The common name means "little dove," but it does not imply any similarity to a dove. It would be better translated as "little diver," which describes its habit of diving underwater to search for tiny marine crustaceans. This starling-sized seabird is the smallest Atlantic Alcid.

Alle — Most authorities say the genus/species name is the Swedish word for "Dovekie." One source says it is from the Latin *allex* (the big toe). The X in the name is missing to indicate that the Dovekie lacks a hind toe.

French Name: Mergule Nain
Spanish Name: Mérgulo Marino
British Name: Little Auk
Other Names: Alle; Sea Dove; Greenland Dove; Pigeon Diver; Bull; Little Bull; Bull Bird; John Bull; Little Turre; Ice Bird; Little Noddy; Knotty; Pine Knot; Nunchie; Petit Gode; Bonhomme; Petit Bonhomme; Petit Bonhomme de Misere; Rotch

Common Murre
Uria aalge
(YOUR-ih-ah AHL-geh)

Murre is onomatopoetic for the murmuring sound of a nesting colony of these birds. Common is not particularly illuminating, as both murres are abundant, and the Thick-billed Murre actually has the wider breeding range.

Uria — The genus name is from the Greek *ourein* (to dive) or from *ouria* (a dark waterbird).
aalge — The specific epithet is the Danish word for "murre."

French Name: Marmette de Troil
Spanish Name: Arao Común
British Name: Guillemot
Eskimo and Inuit Names: Ahl-pack; Athl-pa
Other Names: Thin-billed Murre; Crow-billed Murre; Atlantic Murre; California Murre; California Guillemot; Foolish Guillemot; Bridled Guillemot; Ringed Guillemot; Guillem; Gwylym; Gwylog; Gode; Gudd; Backaloo Bird; Egg Bird; Farallon Bird; Sea Hen; Sea Pigeon; Tinker; Tinkershire; Tinkershue; Willock; Wil-Duck; Willy; Marrot; Marmette; Marrock; Morrot; Mere; Murse; Muir-cun; Auk; Eligny; Spratter; Quet; Maggie; Tarrock; Turr; Southern Turr; Lavy; Lamy; Loom; Strany; Frowl; Scribe; Kiddaw; Skiddaw; Skuttock; Scout; Ring-eyed Scout; Silvery-eyed Scout

Thick-billed Murre
Uria lomvia
(YOUR-ih-ah LOM-vih-ah)

This species is named for its heavier bill, compared to that of the Common Murre.

Uria — The genus name is from the Greek *ourein* (to dive) or from *ouria* (a dark waterbird).
lomvia — The specific epithet is Faroese for "a small diving bird."

French Name: Marmette de Brünnich
Spanish Name: Arao de Brunnich
British Name: Brünnich's Guillemot, named for M. T. Brünnich (1737–1827), a Danish zoologist and Director of the Natural History Museum, Copenhagen.
Eskimo and Inuit Names: Oo-la-rhook-ta; O-loong-thrah; Atpa
Other Names: Brünnich's Murre; Pallas' Murre; Thick-billed Guillemot; Polar Guillemot; Brunnich's Guillemot; Frank's Guillemot; Baccelieu Bird; Crowbill; Egg Bird; Noddy; Turr; Northern Turr

Razorbill
Alca torda
(AL-kah TOR-dah)

This Alcid's laterally compressed, very sharp bill gives it its name.

Alca — The genus name means "auk" from the Old Norse *alka*, a name given to several northern seabirds.

Razorbill, by John James Audubon

torda — The specific epithet derives from *tordmule*, the Swedish name for the Razorbill.
French Name: Petit Pingoui Araon
Spanish Name: Alca Común
Other Names: Razor-billed Auk; Murre; Hawk-billed Murre; Alk; Bawkie; Sea Blackbird; Baccalew; Backaloo Bird; Sea Crow; Sea Craa; Ice Bird; Little Diver; Tinker; Turre; Scout; Pinwing; Pingouin; Penguin; York Penguin; Puffin; Marrot; Noddy; Gode; Gurfel; Hellejay; Helligog; Falk; Faik

Black Guillemot
Cepphus grille
(SEP-fuss GRILL-ee)

Guillemot means "little William" from the French Guillaume (William) plus a diminutive suffix, an example of a familiar name applied to a bird in the same vein as robin and martin. William Yarrell, author of *British Birds* (1843), says the name is derived from the Breton *gwylon* and may be imitative of the calls of young murres, which are called guillemots in Britain.

The Black Guillemot is black only in summer. Then its plumage is entirely flat black except for a brilliant white wing patch. In winter, its plumage is largely white.

Cepphus — The genus name is from the Greek *kepphos* (a kind of seabird), possibly a petrel or storm-petrel, but now the name is applied to an Alcid.

grille — The specific epithet is the word for this bird in Gothland, an island in the Baltic Sea. But A. F. Gotch believes it is derived from the Latin *gryllus* (a cricket), and says it "can also mean a comic figure; on land, standing upright like a small penguin and its long webbed feet sticking out in front, it is a comical sight; it sits down on the tarso-metatarsus bone giving it a flat-footed appearance."

French Name: Guillemot à Miroir
Spanish Name: Arao de Ala Blanca
Eskimo and Inuit Names: Chee-o-wuk; Su'kubwa
Other Names: Scapular Guillemot; White-winged Guillemot; White Guillemot; Spotted Guillemot; Mandt's Guillemot; Murre; Calman Muir; Rock Dove; Pigeon; Wild Pigeon; Diving Pigeon; Sea Pigeon; Pigeon de Mer; Sea Dovie; Greenland Dove; Spotted Greenland Dove; Turtle Dove; Doveky; Shore Duck; Widgeon; Sea Widgeon; Turtle; Sea Turtle; Greenland Turtle; Geylle; Turr; Turtur; Tystie; Taister; Toyste; Tinkershere; Puffinet; Scraber

Pigeon Guillemot
Cepphus columba
(SEP-fuss coh-LUM-bah)

The association seems to lie in the gentle and affectionate behaviour of Tysties [Black Guillemots]. The Turtle Dove in particular is a symbol of tenderness and fidelity and it lends itself to at least five names for the Tystie. Of all seabirds, Tysties are among the most charming. Not only are mated pairs affectionate and solicitous, the same spirit stretches to larger congregations. — Francesca Greenoak (1979)

The Pigeon Guillemot is so named possibly because it somewhat resembles a pigeon in size and form. One of its nicknames is "sea pigeon." Or it may describe the bird's behavior as suggested in the opening passage.

Cepphus — The genus name is from the Greek *kepphos* (a kind of seabird), possibly a petrel or storm-petrel, but now the name is applied to an Alcid.

columba — The specific epithet is Latin for "a pigeon" or "dove." See common name above.

French Name: Guillemot de Pacifique
Spanish Name: Arao Paloma
Eskimo and Inuit Names: Chig-u-vik; Seev-luch; Ti'-tuk
Other Names: Sea Pigeon; White-winged Diver

Long-billed Murrelet
Brachyramphus perdix
(brack-ih-RAM-fuss PER-diks)

Murrelet means "little murre." These birds are so named, because they resemble miniature murres in the genus *Uria*. This rare visitor from Siberia is named for its relatively long, thin bill, particularly in comparison with the Marbled Murrelet, of which it was formerly considered a subspecies.

Brachyramphus — The genus name means "short beak" from the Greek *brachys* (short) and *ramphos* (the beak). The murrelets in this genus have short bills compared to the murrelets in the genus *Synthliboramphus*.

perdix — The specific epithet is Latin for "partridge" from a proper name in Greek mythology. See Gray Partridge for more details. The reference here is to the murrelet's plump shape.

French Name: Guillemot à Long Bec
Spanish Name: Mérgulo Jaspeado Asiático
Other Names: Dabchick; Sea Chick; Fog Bird

Marbled Murrelet
Brachyramphus marmoratus
(brack-ih-RAM-fuss mar-more-AY-tus)

Marbled describes this species' mottled brown and white summer plumage sporting irregular spots, streaks, and bars.

Brachyramphus — The genus name means 'short beak" from the Greek *brachys* (short) and *ramphos* (the beak). The murrelets in this genus have short bills compared to the murrelets in the genus *Synthliboramphus*.

marmoratus — The specific epithet is Latin for "marbled."

French Name: Alque Marbrée
Spanish Name: Mérgulo Marmoleado
Other Names: Dabchick; Sea Chick; Fog Bird

Kittlitz's Murrelet
Brachyramphus brevirostris
(brack-ih-RAM-fuss brev-ih-ROSS-tris)

Friedrich Brandt, Director of the Zoological Museum in Saint Petersburg, named this alcid *Brachyramphus kittlitzi,* while he was working on a review of the auks in 1837. The name honors Friedrich Heinrich Kittlitz (1779–1874), a German Naval Officer and explorer who collected the type specimen on a Russian expedition to Kamchatka. However, Nicholas Vigors had already described the species in 1829, giving it the name *Uria brevirostris*. Vigors' specific name has priority, but Kittlitz is still commemorated by the common name.

Brachyramphus — The genus name means "short beak" from the Greek *brachys* (short) and *ramphos* (the beak). The murrelets in this genus have short bills compared to the murrelets in the genus *Synthliboramphus*.

brevirostris — The specific epithet means "short bill" from the Latin *brevis* (short) and *rostrum* (the bill).

French Name: Guillemot de Kittlitz
Spanish Name: Mérgulo de Pico Corto
Other Name: Short-billed Murrelet

Scripps's Murrelet
Synthliboramphus scrippsi
(sin-thlih-bo-RAM-fuss SKRIPS-eye)

Scripps's Murrelet is named for U.S. newspaper publisher Robert Paine Scripps. Scripps's Murrelet and the Guadalupe Murrelet were until 2012 considered a single species, Xantus's Murrelet.

Synthliboramphus — The genus name means "pressed beak" from the Greek *synthlibo* (to press) and *ramphos* (beak), referring to the laterally compressed bill.

scrippsi — The specific epithet honors Robert Paine Scripps (1895–1938). See common name above.

French Name: Guillemot de Scripps
Spanish Name: Mérgulo Californiano Aliclaro

Guadalupe Murrelet
Synthliboramphus hypoleucus
(sin-thlih-bo-RAM-fuss high-poe-LEW-kus)

The Guadalupe Murrelet is named for Isla Guadalupe off Baja California, where there is a nesting colony. Louis Jonas Xantus de Vesey, better known as John Xantus, collected the type specimen on July 14, 1859 and described it in the *Proceedings of the Academy of Natural Sciences of Philadelphia* (1860). Until 2012, the Guadalupe Murrelet was considered conspecific with Scripps's Murrelet as Xantus' Murrelet

Synthliboramphus — The genus name means "pressed beak" from the Greek *synthlibo* (to press) and *ramphos* (the beak), referring to the laterally compressed bill.

hypoleucus — The specific epithet means "white beneath" from the Greek *hupo* (beneath) and *leukos (white)*. The reference is to the bird's white underparts.

French Name: Alque à Dos Noir
Spanish Name: Mérgulo de Xantus

Craveri's Murrelet
Synthliboramphus craveri
(sin-thlih-bo-RAM-fuss CRAV-er-eye)

This murrelet is named for Frederico Craveri. See species name below.

Synthliboramphus — The genus name means "pressed beak" from the Greek *synthlibo* (to press) and *ramphos* (beak), referring to the laterally compressed bill.

craveri — The specific epithet honors Frederico Craveri (1815–1890), an Italian scientist who collected the type specimen off the west coast of Baja California.

French Name: Guillemot de Craveri
Spanish Name: Mérgulo de Craveri

Ancient Murrelet
Synthliboramphus antiquus
(sin-thlih-bo-RAM-fuss an-TIE-kwus)

Russian explorers gave the Ancient Murrelet its name, because the white plumes on the head and nape of summer birds reminded them of the graying of hair of old age. The Russian name *starik* means "old man."

Synthliboramphus — The genus name means "pressed beak" from the Greek *synthlibo* (to press) and *ramphos* (beak), referring to the laterally compressed bill.

antiquus — The specific epithet is Latin for "old" or "ancient."

French Name: Alque à Cou Blanc
Spanish Name: Mérgulo Antiguo
Eskimo and Inuit Names: Satrch; Kriz-yung'-a
Other Names: Old Man; Gray-headed Murrelet; Black-throated Murrelet; Black-throated Guillemot; Old Man of the Sea

Cassin's Auklet
Ptychoramphus aleuticus
(tye-koh-RAM-fuss ah-LOO-tih kus)

Auklet is diminutive of auk, i.e. "little auk," as these are among the smallest alcids. William Gambel collected this auklet along the California coast. Believing it to be a new species, he named it *Mergulus Cassinii* in 1845, for John Cassin (1813–1869), Curator of Ornithology at the academy of Natural Sciences of Philadelphia. However, German zoologist Peter Simon Pallas had already described it from specimens collected by a Russian expedition in the North Pacific. Pallas had named it *Uria Aleutica* in 1811, and so his specific epithet takes priority. But Cassin is still commemorated in the common name.

Ptychoramphus — The genus name means "folded beak" from the Greek *ptyk* (a fold) and *ramphos* (the beak). The reference is to the ridges across the bill, but you would need to have the bird in the hand to see them.

aleuticus — The specific epithet is Modern Latin for "of the Aleutian Islands," which include part of this seabird's breeding range.

French Name: Alque de Cassin
Spanish Name: Alcuela Oscura
Eskimo and Inuit Name: Mal-cheeth'-ah
Other Names: Aleutian Auk; Wrinkle-nosed Auk; Sea Quail

Parakeet Auklet
Aethia psittacula
(EE-thee-ah sit-ACK-you-lah)

This little seabird got its name from the thick bright orange bill and rounded head that give it a decidedly parakeet-like appearance.

Aethia — The genus name is from the Greek *aithuia*, a seabird mentioned by Aristotle and other authors not further identified. In

Ancient Murrelet, by Allan C. Brooks

modern times it has been associated with a number of waterbirds, including a loon, a grebe, a skua, and a gull. The genus *Aythya*, to which the bay ducks (pochards) belong, also derives from this root.

psittacula — The specific epithet means "little parrot" from the Latin *psittacus* (a parrot). plus a diminutive suffix.

French Name: Alque Perroquet
Spanish Name: Mérgulo Cotorro
Eskimo and Inuit Names: A-bo-chee-arch; Krech-mo'-ga-tha
Other Names: Paroquet Auklet; Pug-nosed Auklet; Baillie Brushkie

Least Auklet
Aethia pusilla
(EE-thee-ah pew-SILL-ah)

At only 6 inches long, this sparrow-sized auklet is the smallest member of the Alcid family.

Aethia — The genus name is from the Greek aithuia, a seabird mentioned by Aristotle and other authors not further identified. In modern times it has been associated with a number of waterbirds, including a loon, a grebe, a skua, and a gull. The genus *Aythya*, to which the bay ducks (pochards) belong, also derives from this root.

pusilla — The specific epithet derives from the Latin *pusillus*, "very small" or "tiny."

French Name: Alque Minuscule
Spanish Name: Mérgulo Mínimo
Eskimo and Inuit Names: Choo-cheah; A-la-ma-gim
Other Names: Minute Auklet; Knob-billed Auklet; Knob-nosed Auklet; Choochkie

Whiskered Auklet
Aethia pygmaea
(EE-thee-ah pig-MAY-ah)

Wispy, white facial plumes, suggesting whiskers, give this auklet its name.

Aethia — The genus name is from the Greek *aithuia*, a seabird mentioned by Aristotle and other authors not further identified. In modern times it has been associated with a number of waterbirds, including a loon, a grebe, a skua, and a gull. The genus *Aythya*, to which the bay ducks (pochards) belong, also derives from this root.

pygmaea — The specific epithet is Latin for "pygmy" and refers to the bird's small size.

French Name: Starique Pygmée
Spanish Name: Mérgulo Bigotudo
Eskimo and Inuit Names: Choo-chirr'-ech; Tooch'-much
Other Names: Whiskered Auk; Red-nosed Auk; Sea Quail

Crested Auklet
Aethia cristatella
(EE-thee-ah kris-tah-TELL-ah)

The shaggy crest that curves forward over the bill gives this seabird its name. The curved crest is similar to those of the California and Gambel's Quails. In fact, one this bird's nicknames is "sea quail."

Aethia — The genus name is from the Greek aithuia, a seabird mentioned by Aristotle and other authors not further identified. In modern times it has been associated with a number of waterbirds, including a loon, a grebe, a skua, and a gull. The genus *Aythya*, to which the bay ducks (pochards) belong, also derives from this root.

cristatella — The specific epithet means "little crest" from the Latin *cristatus* (crested) plus a diminutive suffix.

Crested Auklet, by Allan C. Brooks

French Name: Alque Panachée
Spanish Name: Alcuela Crestada
Eskimo and Inuit Names: Tu-gi-uk; Tub-e-uk
Other Names: Curled-crested Auklet; Dusky Auklet; Snub-nosed Auklet; Snub-nosed Auk; Sea Quail; Crested Stariki; Kanooska

Rhinoceros Auklet
Cerorhinca monocerata
(ser-oh-RING-kah mon-oh-seh-RAY-tah)

Despite its name, this species is more closely related to the puffins than to the auklets. This alcid is called the Rhinoceros Auklet, because breeding adults sport a short, whitish "horn" at the base of the bill. This is shed in the winter.

Cerorhinca — The genus name means "horn beak" from the Greek *keras* (a horn) and *rhynchos* (the beak).

monocerata — The specific epithet means "one horn" from the Greek *monos* (one) and *keras* (horn).

French Name: Macareux Rhinocéros
Spanish Name: Alca Rinoceronte
Other Names: Unicorn Auk; Horn-bill Auk

Atlantic Puffin
Fratercula arctica
(frah-TER-cue-lah ARK-tik-ah)

Puffin means "little puff" (puff plus a diminutive suffix), derived from the Middle English *poffoun*. The name refers either to the plump appearance of the adult or to the fluffy, downy chicks. Atlantic refers to this species range in the North Atlantic and distinguishes it from the two Pacific species. Formerly known as the Common Puffin.

Fratercula — The genus name is Latin for "little brother," in this case meaning "a friar." The reference is to the black and white plumage suggesting a monastic robe. But R. D. MacLeod suggests that the name refers to the puffin's habit of clasping its feet together as though in prayer when taking off from the water.

arctica — The specific epithet is Modern Latin for "of the arctic" suggesting this bird's northerly breeding range, although it occurs as far south as the Gulf of Maine in North America and the north coast of France in Europe.

French Name: Macareux Moine
Spanish Name: Frailecillo Atlántico
Other Names: Large-billed Puffin; Puffin Auk; Labrador Auk; Bottle-nose; Popey Duck; Pope; Pipe; Scout; Willock; Willy; Bill; Parakeet; Perroquet de Mer; Sea Parrot; Labrador Parrot; Parrot-bill Murr; Parrot-billed Willy; Ailsa Parrot; Ailsa Cock; Bass Cock; Hatchet-bill; Hatchet-face; Coulterneb; Guldenhead; Tinker; Tammy Norie; Tommy; Tommy Noddy; Fachach; Flamborough Head Pilot; Pal; Marrot; Mullet; Baccalieu Bird; Cockandy; Coliaheen; Helegug; Balgan Beiceach; Bouger; Bulker; Lundi; Lunda; Lunda Bouger

Horned Puffin
Fratercula corniculata
(frah-TER-cue-lah corn-ik-you-LAY-tah)

The hornlike protuberance above each eye gives the Horned Puffin its name. Bent takes exception to the relevance of this puffin's name, "This name seems somewhat misleading and not particularly appropriate, for the so-called horn over the eye is not horny at all, but merely a soft epidermal papilla full of living tissue, which the bird can raise and lower at will; moreover a similar but smaller excrescence is found in the Atlantic puffin."

Fratercula — The genus name is Latin for "little brother" in this case meaning "a friar." The reference is to the black and white plumage suggesting a monastic robe. But R. D. MacLeod suggests that the name refers to the puffin's habit of clasping its feet together as though in prayer when taking off from the water.

corniculata — The specific epithet means "horned" from the Latin *corniculum* (little horn).

French Name: Macareux Cornu
Spanish Name: Frailecillo de Cuernitos
Eskimo and Inuit Name: Ka-tukh-puk (big white breast)
Other Names: Large-billed Puffin; Sea Parrot; Old Man of the Sea; Toporkie

Tufted Puffin, by Allan C. Brooks

Tufted Puffin
Fratercula cirrhata
(frah-TER-cue-lah sir-AY-tah)

Wispy, pale yellow head plumes, that these seabirds sport in breeding plumage, give the Tufted Puffin its name. They are similar to the yellow plumes sported by some of the crested penguins such as the Rockhopper and Macaroni Penguins.

Fratercula — The genus name is Latin for "little brother" in this case meaning "a friar." The reference is to the black and white plumage suggesting a monastic robe. But R. D. MacLeod suggests that the name refers to the puffin's habit of clasping its feet together as though in prayer when taking off from the water.

cirrhata — The specific epithet is Latin for "having curled locks" and refers to the breeding plumes that curve back from the eyes and along the back of the neck.

French Name: Macareux Huppé
Spanish Name: Frailecillo Coletudo
Eskimo and Inuit Names: Ke-lang'-uk; Ok-chuch
Other Names: Sea Parrot; Parrot-bill; Jew Duck; Old Man of the Sea; Ikey; Toporkie

Family Laridae
Gulls, Terns, and Allies

The general public calls them seagulls, but there is no bird that officially goes by that name. Seagull isn't particularly apt, either, because many species occur far inland, and only a few are truly pelagic. Gull is of Celtic origin and is related to *gullen* (Cornish), *gwylan* (Welsh), and *gwelan* (Breton), all words for "a gull." The Welsh name also means "throat" and is similar to *gula*, the Latin word for "the throat." The latter has given us the words gulp, gullet, and gullible. Perhaps it is a reference to the gulls' scavenging habits, as they will swallow almost anything. The name could also be imitative as in *goelaff*, the Breton word for "weep." Tern stems from Old Norse *taerne* and Swedish *tarna*, both names for these birds. Ernest Choate suggests that the name was first applied to the Sandwich Tern, and the others were called sea swallows.

Black-legged Kittiwake
Rissa tridactyla
(RISS-ah try-DACK-tih-lah)

"No person who has visited a seabird colony will have any doubt about how the Kittiwake got its name. The high pitched "kitti-kitti-wake" calls with the haunting rise in the last note, echo from the cliffs. It is only during courtship and nesting time that the birds "kittiwake"; for the rest of the year they are mostly silent except for an occasional "kit"." — Francesca Greenoak (1979)

Kittiwake is imitative of this little gull's call as explained in the above passage. Dr. Steve Kress of the National Audubon Society thinks it sounds like the birds are saying *Auntie Em, Auntie Em.*

Black-legged distinguishes this kittiwake, which has black legs and feet, from the Red-legged Kittiwake. Juveniles can have yellow, pink, or orange-red legs, however.

Rissa — The genus name is derived from *rita*, the Icelandic name for this bird.

tridactyla — The specific epithet means "three-toed" from the Greek *tri* (three) and *dactylos* (digit, such as a finger or toe). The Kittiwakes

actually have four toes like other gulls. but the hind one is greatly reduced in size, making the front toes more prominent.
French Name: Mouette Tridactyle
Spanish Names: Gaviota de Patas Negras; Gaviota Patinegra
Eskimo and Inuit Names: Ach-a-leck; Teegle-ga-gha; Nor-o-yow-uk-chok
Other Names: Common Kittiwake; Atlantic Kittiwake; Kittiwake Gull; Jack Gull; Coddy Moddy; Haddock Gull; Mackerel Gull; Fall Gull; Winter Gull; Snow Gull; Frost Gull; Frost Bird; Tickle-arse; Tickle-ass; Tickleace; Tickle-lace; Tickler; Lady; Lady Bird; Mauve; Mouette; Meterick; Coddy-Noddy; Tarrock; Petrel; Pinyole; Pinny Owl; Pick-me-up; Kittick; Kittie; Sea Kittie; Kittiake; Keltie; Kishiefaik; Kittiwaako; Waeg; Cackreen; Craa Maa; Annett

Red-legged Kittiwake
Rissa brevirostris
(RISS-ah brev-ih-ROS-triss)

This kittiwake is named for its coral red legs and feet, which distinguish it from the Black-legged Kittiwake.
Rissa — The genus name is derived from *rita*, the Icelandic name for the Black-legged Kittiwake.
brevirostris — The specific epithet means "short bill" from the Latin *brevis* (short) and *rostrum* (the bill). The Red-legged Kittiwake's bill is noticeably smaller than the Black-legged Kittiwake's.
French Name: Mouette à Pattes Rouges
Spanish Name: Gaviota de Patas Rojas
Eskimo Name: Eg-luk (big throat)

Ivory Gull
Pagophila eburnea
(pag-OFF-ih-lah eh-BURN-ee-ah)

"It was there among the trash that I saw my first living ivory gull — a snow-white creature indeed and a scavenger. Flying, the bird was almost invisible against the whiteness of the ice and fog; as it drew closer I realized that its stubby black legs were easier to see than its head, body, and wings." — George Miksch Sutton (1971)

This gull's pure white plumage gives it its common name.

Pagophila — The genus name means "ice loving" from the Greek *pagos* (ice or frost) and *philos* (loving or fond of). Bent (1921) wrote, ". . . the bird lives almost constantly in the vicinity of ice and snow, where its spotless plumage matches its surroundings. It is largely a bird of the open polar seas, frequenting the edges of the ice floes in company with the fulmars and other Arctic sea birds, and seldom resorting to the land except during the breeding season."
eburnea — The specific epithet is Latin for "ivory-colored."
French Name: Mouette Blanche
Spanish Name: Gaviota Color Marfil
Eskimo Name: Nau'yabwun
Other Names: Snow-white Gull; White-winged Gull; Ice Gull; Winter Gull; Duck Gull; Slob Gull; Snow-bird; Ice Bird; Ice Partridge; Snow Grouse

Sabine's Gull
Xema sabini
(ZEE-mah SAB-in-eye)

In the spring of 1818, Edward Sabine set off with the John Ross expedition in search of the Northwest Passage. On July 15th Sabine, his friend James Clark Ross, and several others were exploring some low, rocky islands near Cape York on the west coast of Greenland. Among the hundreds of Arctic Terns nesting there, were some unusual gulls with dark heads, forked tails, and a bold tricolored wing pattern. Several were collected and these along with the rest of Sabine's collection were transferred to a whaling ship returning to England. The specimens found their way to Edward's older brother Joseph in London, and in mid-December, he displayed the specimens at a meeting of the Linnean Society. Joseph named the gull *Larus Sabini* for his brother "in conformity with the custom of affixing the name of the original discoverer to a new species.
Xema — Dr. William E. Leach gave no explanation for the meaning of the genus he erected for this unique gull. He may have arbitrarily coined it, as Elliot Coues said "a nonsense word." Ernest Choate says it is Modern Latin for "some unknown bird." James Jobling suggests that it may come from

Charadriiformes

Sabine's Gull, by Louis Agassiz Fuertes

the Greek *xene*, the feminine form for "a guest" or "a stranger."

sabini — The specific epithet commemorates General Sir Edward Sabine (1788–1883), an English astronomer and physicist, who accompanied the Ross and Parry expeditions to the Arctic. See common name above.

French Name: Mouette de Sabine
Spanish Names: Gaviota de Cola Hendida; Gaviota de Sabine
Eskimo and Inuit Names: Na-chuthl-nga-uk (refers to the hood); Natchalngrik (having a black cap on his head)
Oher Names: Hawk-tailed Gull; Fork-tailed Gull

Bonaparte's Gull
Chroicocephalus philadelphia
(kroi-koe-SEFF-ah-lus fill-ah-DELL-fee-ah)

Philadelphia scientist George Ord named this gull for Charles Lucien Jules Laurent Bonaparte (1803–1857), the eminent French naturalist and father of avian taxonomy. He was the nephew of Napoleon.

Chroicocephalus — The genus name means "colored head" from the Greek *chroikos*, the adjective form of *chroa* (color) and *kephale* (the head). The reference is to the black heads of the birds in summer plumage. Formerly *Larus philadelphia*.

philadelphia — The specific epithet refers to the city, near which the type specimen was collected.

French Name: Mouette de Bonaparte
Spanish Name: Gaviota de Bonaparte
Eskimo and Inuit Name: A-tung-at
Other Names: Bonaparte's Rosy Gull; Blackhead; Black-headed Gull; Mackerel Gull; Sea Pigeon; Goeland; Mauve

Black-headed Gull
Chroicocephalus ridibundus
(kroi-koe-SEFF-ah-lus rid-ih-BUND-us)

One of the hooded gulls that shows a dark head in breeding plumage. At a distance the head appears black, but it is actually chocolate brown.

Chroicocephalus — The genus name means "colored head" from the Greek *chroikos*, the adjective form of *chroa* (color) and *kephale* (the head). The reference is to the dark brown heads of the birds in summer plumage. Formerly *Larus ridibundus*.

ridibundus — The specific epithet is Latin for "laughing" from *ridere* (to laugh) and refers to this gull's calls that suggest human laughter.

French Name: Mouette Rieuse
Spanish Name: Gaviota Encapuchada
Other Names: Black head; Black Cap; Brown-headed Gull; Masked Gull; Pigeon Gull; Red-legged Gull; Redshank Gull; Puit Gull; Peewit Gull; Tumbling Gull; Collochan

Bonaparte's Gull, by Allan C. Brooks

Gull; Maddrick Gull; Hooded Crow; White Crow; Mire Crow; Sea Crow; Patch; Sprat Mew; Hooded Mew; Red-legged Pigeon Mew; Carr Swallow; Potterton Hen; Scoulton Peewit; Scoulton Pie; Tumbler; Gaviota Cabecinegra; Rittock; Bakie; Cob; Crocker; Pine Maw; Pickie Burnet; Pick Sea; Pictarn; Pickmire

Little Gull
Hydrocoloeus minutus
(HIGH-dro-co-LOW-ee-us mih-NUTE-us)

At only 11–inches long with a 24-inch wingspan, this is the smallest species of gull in the world.

Hydrocoloeus — The genus name means "water daw" from the Greek *hydor* (water) and *koloios* (a jackdaw). Formerly *Larus minutus*.

minutus — The specific epithet is Latin for "minute" or "small."

French Name: Mouette Pygmée
Spanish Name: Gaviota Mínima

Ross's Gull
Rhodostethia rosea
(row-doh-STEE-thih-ah ROW-zee-ah)

Ross's Gull is named for Sir James Clark Ross (1800–1862), a polar explorer from Scotland. Ross collected the first specimen on Melville Peninsula in the Canadian Arctic on William Edward Parry's second voyage in search of the Northwest Passage.

Rhodostethia — The genus name is Greek for "rose breast" from *rhodon* (rose) and *stethos* (the breast). Ross's Gull can develop a distinct blush to its underparts from pigments it gets in certain foods.

rosea — The specific epithet is Latin for "rosy."

French Name: Mouette Rosée
Spanish Name: Gaviota Rosada
Eskimo and Inuit Names: Kakmakloak; Ka'nma-lu
Other Names: Rosy Gull; Ross's Rosy Gull; Wedge-tailed Gull; Cuneate-tailed Gull

Laughing Gull
Leucophaeus atricilla
(lew-KOE-fee-us ay-trih-SILL-ah)

"The strident laughing calls of this well-named gull are among the most characteristic sounds around tidewater along the Atlantic and Gulf coasts, especially in summer." — Kenn Kaufman (1996)

In a seabird colony, the loud, raucous *ha-ha-ha-ha-ha-haah-haah-haah* of the Laughing Gulls invariably dominates the cacophony one hears upon approach. Their calls suggest shrill human laughter.

Leucophaeus — The genus name is from the Greek *leukophaeus* (shining white or gleaming), referring to this gull's largely immaculate white plumage. Formerly *Larus atricilla*.

atricilla — The specific epithet is Latin for "black tail" from *ater* (flat black) and *cilla* (the tail). The reference is to the black terminal band on the tail of the juvenile. Adults have pure white tails.

French Name: Mouette à Tête Noire
Spanish Name: Gaviota Reidora
Other Names: Black-headed Gull; Sea Gull; Laughing Bird; Laugher; Gullie; Booby; Mangui; Galleguito; Gallego Común; Gaviota Boba; Gaviota Cabecinegra; Gaviota Gallega; Goéland Charogne; Mauve à Tête Noire; Pigeon de la Mer; Zo-zo de Mer

Franklin's Gull
Leucophaeus pipixcan
(lew-KOE-fee-us pip-ICKS-can)

Dr. John Richardson described this gull from a specimen collected along the Saskatchewan River in Canada, when he and William Swainson collaborated on the second volume of *The Fauna of Boreali-Americana; or The Zoology of the Northern Parts of British America* (1829–1837). Swainson illustrated the volume with about 50 drawings, and Richardson wrote the descriptions and provided the scientific names. Richardson called the new gull Franklin's Rosy Gull and gave it the scientific name *Larus franklini* in honor of Sir John Franklin (1786–1847), the ill-fated British Arctic explorer. While Franklin was not a naturalist, Richardson felt he should be honored, because of his willingness to promote science for its own sake. But Swainson's other commitments delayed publication, and the volume didn't appear in print until February of 1832. By then, German herpetologist Johann G. Wagler had named this gull *Larus pipixcan* in a publication that appeared in May of 1831. Therefore, Wagler's name has priority, but Franklin is still honored in the gull's common name.

Leucophaeus — The genus name is from the Greek *leukophaeus* (shining white or gleaming), referring to this gull's largely immaculate white plumage. Formerly *Larus pipixcan*.

pipixcan — Wagler's specific epithet derives from *pipizcan*, which according to Francisco Hernandez in *Historia avium Novae Hispaniae* (1615), is an Aztec word for a kind of gull. Wagler apparently chose that name, because the type specimen had been collected in Mexico.

French Name: Mouette de Franklin
Spanish Name: Gaviota de Franklin
Other Names: Sea Gull; Black-headed Gull; Franklin's Rosy Gull; Grasshopper Gull; Prairie Gull; Prairie Dove; Prairie Pigeon; Goeland; Rosette

Black-tailed Gull
Larus crassirostris
(LAR-us krass-ih-ROSS-tris)

The tail is actually mostly white, but the subterminal black band gives this gull its name.

Larus — The genus name is Latin for "a ravenous seabird," possibly a gull, from the Greek *laros* (a seabird).

crassirostris — The specific epithet means "thick beak" from the Latin *crassus* (thick) and *rostrum* (the beak) and refers to this gull's heavy bill.

French Name: Goéland à Queue Noire
Spanish Names: Gaviota Colinegra; Gaviota japanesa
Other Names: Japanese Gull; Temminck's Gull

Heermann's Gull
Larus heermanni
(LAR-us HEER-mann-eye)

On his first expedition to California in 1849, Adolphus Heermann noted distinctive gulls with dark bodies, white heads, and blood-red bills along the coast. They were especially common around San Diego, where Heermann observed their feeding behavior, scavenging along the beaches, catching small fish in the company of Western Gulls, and hunting among

Heerman's Gull, by Allan C. Brooks

the kelp beds well offshore. He also discovered a nesting colony on the Coronados Islands off the Mexican coast, about 20 miles south of San Diego. John Cassin described this species in 1852, from a specimen Heermann had collected at San Diego and named it *Larus heermanni* in his honor.

Larus — The genus name is Latin for "a ravenous seabird," possibly a gull, from the Greek *laros* (a seabird).

heermanni — The specific epithet commemorates Dr. Adolphus Lewis Heermann (1818–1865), a surgeon and collector of birds and their eggs in the western United States. See common name above.

French Name: Goéland de Heermann
Spanish Names: Gaviota Ploma; Gaviota de Heermann
Other Name: White-headed Gull

Mew Gull
Larus canus
(LAR-us CANE-us)

Mew is the Old English name for "a gull" and is imitative of its calls.

Larus — The genus name is Latin for "a ravenous seabird," possibly a gull, from the Greek *laros* (a seabird).

canus — The specific epithet is Latin for "white" or "hoary" and describes the dominant color of the plumage.

French Name: Goéland Cendré
Spanish Names: Gaviota Cana; Gaviota Piquiamarilla
British Name: Common Gull
Eskimo and Inuit Names: Nauyatcheak (beautiful gull); Na-ro-yuk-chuk

Other Names: Short-billed Gull; Green-billed Gull; Winter Gull; Mew; Sea Mew; Winter Mew; Sea Mall; Sea Maw; White Maa; Blue Maa; Small Maa; Mar; Sea Cobb; Coddy Moddy; Annet; Gow; Winter Bonnet; Barley Bird; Seed Bird

Ring-billed Gull
Larus delawarensis
(LAR-us del-ah-war-EN-sis)

The black ring that encircles the adult's yellow bill gives this gull its name.

Larus — The genus name is Latin for "a ravenous seabird," possibly a gull, from the Greek *laros* (a seabird).

delawarensis — The specific epithet is Modern Latin for "of Delaware" and refers to the Delaware River where the type specimen was collected just below Philadelphia.

French Name: Goéland à Bec Cerclé
Spanish Names: Gaviota de Pico Anillado; Gaviota Piquianillada
Other Names: Sea Gull; Common Gull; Common American Gull; Lake Gull; Pond Gull; Squeaky Gull; Squeezy Gull

Western Gull
Larus occidentalis
(LAR-us ock-sih-den-TAY-lis)

The Western Gull is named for its range along the Pacific coast from British Columbia to the Baja Peninsula.

Larus — The genus name is Latin for "a ravenous seabird," possibly a gull, from the Greek *laros* (a seabird).

occidentalis — The specific epithet is Latin for "western."

French Name: Goéland d'Audubon
Spanish Name: Gaviota Occidental

Yellow-footed Gull
Larus livens
(LAR-us LIVE-enz)

This gull is named for its bright yellow feet and legs. It was formerly considered a subspecies of the Western Gull, but the latter has pink feet.

Larus — The genus name is Latin for "a ravenous seabird," possibly a gull, from the Greek *laros* (a seabird).

livens — The specific epithet is Latin for "bluish," pertaining to the dark blue-gray mantle.

French Name: Goéland de Cortez
Spanish Names: Gaviota de Patas Amarillas; Gaviota Patamarilla

California Gull
Larus californicus
(LAR-us cal-ih-FOR-nih-cus)

The California Gull is named for the state where the type specimen was collected near Stockton. This gull winters along the Pacific coast from Washington to Baja, but only a few nest in California. The largest breeding range is inland on the plains of the United States and Canada. Ironically the California Gull was adopted as the State Bird of Utah, because it was credited in saving the Mormons' crops from a Mormon Cricket (*Anabrus simplex*) plague in 1848. The Mormons believed this to be Divine intervention as described in the following passage:

"They [the Mormons] were saved, they believed, by a miracle . . . Just in the midst of the work of destruction great flocks of gulls appeared, filling the air with their white wings and plaintive cries, and settled down on the half-ruined fields . . . all day they gorged themselves, and when full, disgorged and feasted again . . . until the pests were vanquished and the people were saved. The heaven-sent birds then returned to the lake islands whence they came." — Orson F. Whiney (1892)

In 1913, the Mormons erected the Seagull Monument, commemorating the event, at Temple Square in Salt Lake City.

Larus — The genus name is Latin for "a ravenous seabird," possibly a gull, from the Greek *laros* (a seabird).

californicus — The specific epithet is Modern Latin for "of California."

French Name: Goéland de Californie
Spanish Name: Gaviota Californiana
Other Names: Sea Gull; Blue Gull

Herring Gull
Larus argentatus
(LAR-us ar-jen-TAY-tus)

The Herring Gull is named for a family of schooling fish, that undoubtedly forms part of this gull's varied diet. A subspecies Thayer's Gull (*L. a. thayeri*) was formerly considered a separate species. Its name honors John Eliot Thayer (1862–1933), a Boston collector of birds, whose collection is now in Harvard University's Museum of Comparative Zoology.

Larus — The genus name is Latin for "a ravenous seabird," possibly a gull, from the Greek *laros* (a seabird).

argentatus — The specific epithet is Latin for "silvery" and refers to this gull's light gray mantle.

French Name: Goéland Argenté

Spanish Names: Gaviota Plateada; Gaviota Argéntea

Eskimo Name: Na-go-yukh-lik

Other Names: Sea Gull; Common Gull; Common Seagull; Lake Gull; Harbor Gull; Winter Gull; Laughing Gull; Cat Gull; Mackerel Gull; Big White Gull; Grey Gull; Silvery Gull; Blue Gull; Bluey; Silver Back; Sea Mew; Lookabout; Faollin; Farspag; Gaviota Argentus; Goeland; Goeland de fleuve; Mauve; Mouette; Shitehawk; Willie Gow; White Maa

Yellow-legged Gull
Larus michahellis
(LAR-us my-ka-HEL-iss)

The common name is descriptive of this gull's yellow legs and feet.

Larus — The genus name is Latin for "a ravenous seabird," possibly a gull, from the Greek *laros* (a seabird).

michahellis — The specific epithet commemorates Dr. Georg Christian Karl Wilhelm Michahelles, a German zoologist and collector. Formerly *Larus cachinnans*.

French Name: Goéland Leucophée

Spanish Name: Gaviota Patiamarilla

Iceland Gull
Larus glaucoides
(LAR-us glaw-coh-EYE-deez)

The Iceland Gull is named for the site where the type specimen was collected. Although it occurs in Iceland, it does not breed there. The nesting range includes Greenland and Baffin Island, Canada.

Larus — The genus name is Latin for "a ravenous seabird," possibly a gull, from the Greek *laros* (a seabird).

glaucoides — The specific epithet is from the Greek *glaukos* (blue-gray) and *oides*, a suffix meaning "like" or "resembling." In this case it means "like the Glaucous Gull," which once went by the scientific name *Larus glaucus*. The Iceland Gull resembles a smaller version of the Glaucous Gull.

French Name: Goéland Arctique

Spanish Name: Gaviota de Groenlandia

Other Names: White-winged Gull; White-winged Silvery Gull

Lesser Black-backed Gull
Larus fuscus
(LAR-us FUSS-cus)

This gull is named for its dark mantle that varies from charcoal gray to nearly black. Lesser distinguishes this species from the larger Great Black-backed Gull.

Larus — The genus name is Latin for "a ravenous seabird," possibly a gull, from the Greek *laros* (a seabird).

fuscus — The specific epithet is Latin for "dusky" and refers to the color of the mantle.

French Name: Goéland Brun

Spanish Names: Gaviota Sombía; Gaviota Dorsinegra Menor

Other Names: Blackback; Gray Gull; Yellow-legged Gull; Gray Cob; Coddy Moddy; Said Fool; Saith Fowl

Slaty-backed Gull
Larus schistisagus
(LAR-us shis-tih-SAW-gus)

This gull gets its name from its dark slate-gray mantle.

Larus — The genus name is Latin for "a ravenous seabird," possibly a gull, from the Greek *laros* (a seabird).

schistisagus — The specific epithet is Latin for "slate-cloaked" from *schistus* (slate) and *sagus* (a cloak) from the Greek *sagos* (a blanket or mantle).
French Name: Goéland à Manteau Ardoisé
Spanish Name: Gaviota de Kamchatka

Glaucous-winged Gull
Larus glaucescens
(LAR-us glaw-SESS-enz)

Glaucous-winged refers to the light gray of the wings and mantle.
Larus — The genus name is Latin for "a ravenous seabird," possibly a gull, from the Greek *laros* (a seabird).
glaucescens — The specific epithet means "grayish" or "graying" from the Greek *glaukos* (blue-gray).
French Name: Goéland à Ailes Grises
Spanish Names: Gaviota de Ala Glauca; Gaviota Aliglauca
Eskimo and Inuit Names: Na-row-yuk; Ku-kizh-u-wuk; Shlu-ka; Hlu-ka
Other Names: Sea Gull; Sea Mew

Glaucous Gull
Larus hyperboreus
(LAR-us high-per-BORE-ee-us)

"The name burgomaster is a fitting name for this chief magistrate of the feathered tribes of the Arctic seas, where it reigns supreme over all the lesser water fowl, levying its toll of food from their eggs and defenseless young. Well they know its strength and its power, as it sails majestically aloft over the somber, rocky cliffs of the Greenland coast, where, with myriads of sea fowl, it makes its summer home; and useless is it for them to resist the onslaught of its heavy beak when it swoops down to rob them of their callow young. Only the great skua, the fighting airship of the north, dares to give it battle and to drive the tyrant burgomaster from its chosen crag. Its only rival in size and power among the gulls is the great Black-backed gull, and where these two meet on the Labrador coast they treat each other with dignified respect." — Arthur Cleveland Bent (1921)

Glaucous from the Greek *glaukos* (blue-gray) pertains to this large gull's pale gray mantle.
Larus — The genus name is Latin for "a ravenous seabird," possibly a gull, from the Greek *laros* (a seabird).
hyperboreus — The specific epithet is Latin for "northern" and refers to this gull's range in the high Arctic.
French Name: Goéland Bourgmestre
Spanish Name: Gaviota Blanca
Eskimo and Inuit Names: Ko-kezh-vuk (the large one uttering ko-ke); Matuyak (birds that eat together); Nauygavak (large gull)
Other Names: Burgomaster; Burgomaster Gull; Glaucous-winged Gull; White-winged Gull; Blue Gull; Ice Gull; Large Ice Gull; Owl Gull; Harbor Gull; White Winter Gull; Minister Gull; White Minister

Great Black-backed Gull
Larus marins
(LAR-us mah-RYE-nus)

"While cruising along the bleak and barren coasts of southern Labrador I learned to know and admire this magnificent gull, as we saw it sailing on its powerful wings high above the desolate crags and rocky islets of that forbidding shore, its chosen summer home. Its resemblance to the bald eagle was striking, as it soared aloft and wheeled in great circles, showing its broad black back and wings in sharp contrast with its snow-white head and tail, glistening in the sunlight. It surely seemed to be a king among the gulls, a merciless tyrant over its fellows, the largest and strongest of its tribe." — Arthur Cleveland Bent (1921)

The black mantle give this gull its name. Great distinguishes this largest of all gulls from the Lesser Black-backed Gull of the Old World.
Larus — The genus name is Latin for "a ravenous seabird," possibly a gull, from the Greek *laros* (a seabird).
marinus — The specific epithet is Latin for "marine" or "of the sea" and refers to this gull's coastal habitat.
French Name: Goéland à Manteau Noir
Spanish Names: Gaviota Atlántica; Gaviota Dorsinegra Mayor
Other Names: Black Back; Saddleback; Greater

Saddleback; Saddleback Gull; Saddler Gull; Saddler; Old Saddler; Old Settler; Black-backed Gull; Black and White Gull; English Gull; Farmer Gull; Parson Gull; Gray Gull; Great Grey Gull; Goose Gull; Carrion Gull; Wagell Gull; Wagell; Gaviota Major Espaldinegra; Goeland Anglais; Goeland Noir; Black Minister; Coffin-Carrier; Cobb; Black-backed Hannock; Parson Mew; Porte-cercueil; Screecher; Swart Back; Swarbie; Gull Maw; Baagie; Baakie

Kelp Gull
Larus dominicanus
(LAR-us doe-min-ih-CANE-us)

The common name refers to this gull's habit of foraging in intertidal kelp beds.

Larus — The genus name is Latin for "a ravenous seabird," possibly a gull, from the Greek *laros* (a seabird).

dominicanus — The specific epithet is the Latinized form of Dominican, a member of an order of preaching friars established in the Roman Catholic Church by Saint Dominic in 1216. The reference is to the black and white habits of the monks suggesting the color pattern of the gull's plumage.

French Name: Goéland Dominicain
Spanish Name: Gaviota Dorsinegra Sureño
Other Names: Dominican Gull; Southern Black-backed Gull

Brown Noddy
Anous stolidus
(AH-no-us STOL-id-us)

Sailors named this tern noddy (simpleton), because it showed no fear and was easy to catch. It is not unusual for island species to be trusting, because they have little experience with land predators. Brown refers to the bird's overall dark brown plumage, the only other color is the white crown. The Brown Noddy also gets a double dose of "stupid" in two languages in its scientific name. See below.

Anous — The genus name is Greek for "stupid," referring to this bird's trusting nature.

stolidus — The specific epithet is Latin for "stupid."

French Name: Noddi Brun
Spanish Names: Charrán-bobo Café; Golondrina-boba Café; Tiñosa Común

Other Names: Noddy Tern; Black Bird; Booby; Booby Blackbird; Bubi; Egg Bird; Lark; Minime; Moine; Noio Koha; Charles; Gaviota Boba; Cervera; Severo; Zo-zo du Mer

Black Noddy
Anous minutus
(AH-no-us mih-NUTE-us)

The Black Noddy is darker than the Brown Noddy.

Anous — The genus name is Greek for "stupid," referring to this bird's trusting nature.

minutus — The specific epithet is Latin for "minute" or "small." The Black Noddy is smaller than the Brown Noddy.

French Name: Noddi Noir
Spanish Names: Charrán-bobo Negro; Golondrina-boba Negra; Tiñosa Negra
Other Names: Black Noddy Tern; Noio

Sooty Tern
Onychoprion fuscatus
(on-ee-KOH-prih-on fuss-KAY-tus)

The Sooty Tern is named for its jet black upperparts.

Onychoprion — The genus name means "serrated claw" from the Greek *onux* (a claw) and *prion* (a saw), referring to the serrations on claw on the middle toe.

fuscatus — The specific epithet is Latin for "dusky."

French Name: Sterne Fuligineuse
Spanish Names: Golondrina-marina Oscura; Charrán Sombrío
Other Names: Booby; Booby Bird; Bubi; Wide-awake; Egg Bird; Ewa'Ewa; Hurricane Bird; Pigeon de Mer; Gaviota Monja; Gaviota Oscura; Oiseau fou; Touaou

Bridled Tern
Onychoprion anaesthetus
(on-ee-KOH-prih-on ah-NEES-theh-tus)

This tern is named for the black eye line that suggests a bridle.

Onychoprion — The genus name means "serrated claw" from the Greek *onux* (a claw) and *prion* (a saw), referring to the serrations on claw on the middle toe.

anaesthetus — The specific epithet is from the Greek *anaisthetos* (without sense or stupid), as

this tern allows close approach.
French Name: Sterne à Collier
Spanish Name: Golondrina-marina Embridada; Charrán Embridado
Other Names: Booby; Booby Bird; Bubi; Dongue; Egg Bird; Gaviota; Gaviota Monja; Gaviota Oscura; Oiseau Fou; Touaou

Aleutian Tern
Onychoprion aleuticus
(on-ee KOH-prih-on ah-LOO-tih-cus)

This Alaskan specialty nests all along the Alaskan coast including the Aleutian Islands.
Onychoprion — The genus name means "serrated claw" from the Greek *onux* (a claw) and *prion* (a saw), referring to the serrations on claw on the middle toe.
aleuticus — The specific epithet is Modern Latin for "of the Aleutians."
French Name: Sterne des Aléoutiennes
Spanish Name: Charrán Aleutiano
Eskimo and Inuit Names: Eg-lug-na-guk (refers to the white forehead patch); Chuf-chuf-chee-yuk

Least Tern
Sternula antillarum
(STIRN-you-lah an-TILL-ah-rum)

The Least Tern is named for the fact that it is the smallest species of tern.
Sternula — The genus name means "little tern" from the tern genus *Sterna* plus a diminutive suffix. Formerly *Sterna antillarum*.
antillarum — The specific epithet is Modern Latin for "of the Lesser Antilles," a chain of Caribbean islands, which includes part of this species range.
French Name: Petite Sterne
Spanish Names: Golondrina-marina Mínima; Charrán Mínimo; Charrán Chico
Other Names: Little Tern; Minute Tern; Hooded Tern; Silvery Tern; Ternlet; Silver Ternlet; Little Darr; Little Pickie; Little Striker; Dip Ears; Shrimp Catcher; Sea Swallow; Egg Bird; Richel Bird; Fairy Bird; Small Purl; Chit Perl; Kill'-em-Polly; Killing-Peter; Peterman; Oiseau fou; Petite Mauve; Sparling; Gaviotica; Gaviota Chica; Gaviota Pequeña; Golondrina de Mar; Pigeon de la Mer; Skirr; Zo-zo su Mer; Sea Mice (young)

Least Tern, by R. Bruce Horsfall

Gull-billed Tern
Gelochelidon nilotica
(jell-oh-KELL-ih-don nih-LOW-tih-kah)

This tern is named for its stouter bill, suggesting a gull's, as opposed to the thin, dagger-like bill of most terns.
Gelochelidon — The genus name means "laughing swallow" from the Greek *gelos* (laughter) and *chelidon* (a swallow). German zoologist Alfred Edmund Brehm changed the genus from *Hydrochelidon* (water swallow) to *Gelochelidon*, apparently because he felt the bird's call resembled human laughter. Ernest Choate thought this tern's vocalizations sounded more like "the raspberry" or the "Bronx cheer." Formerly *Sterna nilotica*.
nilotica — The specific epithet is Modern Latin for "of the Nile." The type specimen was collected along the Nile River in Egypt.
French Name: Sterne Hansel
Spanish Names: Golondrina-marina Piquigruesa; Charrán Pico de Gaviota; Charrán Piquinegro
Other Names: Egyptian Tern; Nile Tern; Anglican Tern; Nuttall's Tern; Marsh Tern; Egg Bird; Gullie; Gaviota de Pico Corto; Gaviota Piquigorda; Oiseau Fou; Pigeon de la Mer

Caspian Tern
Hydroprogne caspia
(HIGH-droh-PROG-nee CASS-pih-ah)

"Among the vast hordes of sea birds nesting in the great colonies of the southern Atlantic and Gulf coasts, this king of all the terns may be seen climbing into the air on its long, strong wings, its big red bill wide open, yelling out its loud raucous cry of defiance. As the dominant, ruling spirit in the colonies it scorns the companionship of humbler fowl, holds itself aloof, and lives a little apart from the others. The largest, the strongest and the fiercest of the terns, it well deserves the name, imperial tern. It was christened Caspian tern by Pallas, because it was first described from a specimen taken near the Caspian Sea. It is a cosmopolitan species of wide palaearctic and nearctic distribution."
— Arthur Cleveland Bent (1921)

The Caspian Tern is named for the Caspian Sea, where the type specimen was collected. See specific epithet below.

Hydroprogne — The genus name means "water swallow" from the Greek *hydro* (water) and *Progne*, a mythological character who was turned into a swallow. See Purple Martin for details. Terns are commonly called "sea swallows," because of their pointed wings and forked tails. Formerly *Sterna caspia*.

caspia — The specific epithet is Modern Latin for "of the Caspian Sea," where the specimen was collected from which German zoologist Peter Simon Pallas described and named the species in 1770.

French Name: Sterne Caspienne
Spanish Names: Golondrina-marina Caspica; Charrán Caspia; Pagaza Mayor; Pagaza Piquirroja
Other Names: Caspian Sea Tern; Imperial Tern; Redbill; Gannet Striker; Mackerel Gull; Sea Swallow; Gaviota de Caspia; Goeland à Bec Rouge; Goeland Espagnol; Grand Esterlette

Black Tern
Chlidonias niger
(klih-DOAN-ih-us NYE-jer)

This little marsh tern is named for its velvety black breeding plumage; the wings and tail are somewhat lighter, being a silvery gray.

Black Tern, by John James Audubon

Chlidonias — The genus name means "swallow-like" from the Greek *chelidon* (a swallow) plus a Latin suffix *–ias* (like). The reference is to the tern's swallow-like flight and forked tail.

niger — The specific epithet is Latin for "black."
French Name: Guifette Noire
Spanish Names: Golondrina-marina Negro; Fumarel Negro; Gaviotin Negro; Charrán Negro
Other Names: American Black Tern; Marsh Tern; Surinam Tern; Short-tailed Tern; Semipalmated Tern; Black Gannett; Black Gull; Black Sea Swallow; Sea Pigeon; Slough Pigeon; Gaviota Ceniza; Gaviota Negra; Hirondelle de Mer

White-winged Tern
Chlidonias leucopterus
klih-DOAN-ih-us lew-KOP-ter-us)

The white forewings, which this tern shows in breeding plumage, give it its name.

Chlidonias — The genus name means "swallow-like" from the Greek *chelidon* (a swallow) plus a Latin suffix *–ias* (like). The reference is to the tern's swallow-like flight and forked tail.

leucopterus — The specific epithet is Greek for "white-winged" from *leukos* (white) and *pteron* (the wing).

French Name: Guifette Leucoptère
Spanish Name: Charrán de Ala Blanca

Roseate Tern
Sterna dougallii
(STIR-nah dew-GALL-ee-eye)

"I shall never forget the thrill of pleasure I experienced when I held in my hand, for the first time a freshly killed roseate tern and admired with deepest reverence the delicate refinement of one of nature's loveliest productions. The softest colors of the summer sky were reflected on its back and pointed wings, while its breast glowed with the faint blush of some rare seashell. The graceful outlines, the spotless purity of its delicate plumage, and the long tapering tail feathers made it seem like some ethereal spirit of the heavens which it was sacrilege for human hands to touch." — Arthur Cleveland Bent (1921)

"The Roseate Tern is the embodiment of symmetry and grace — its flight the poetry of motion. Its elegant form tapers and swells in lines of beauty. Its lustrous plumage reflects the yellow rays of the sun and the pale refracted light of sea and sands in evanescent pink and rosy tints. These are seen in perfection only in the living bird and fade when the light of life fades from its eyes. The stuffed and distorted specimen on the museum shelf has lost the grace, beauty, and color of the living thing and remains but a sorry travesty of the life that is gone." — Edward Howe Forbush (1917)

The Roseate Tern is named for the pink tinge this bird sometimes shows on the breast.

Sterna — The genus name is the Latinized form of the Old English *stearn* or *starn* (a tern).

dougallii — The specific epithet honors Dr. Peter McDougall (1777–1814), a physician from Glasgow, Scotland. On July 24, 1812, he and two friends were exploring Great Cumbrae, an island in the Firth of Clyde. They found a nesting colony of Common and Arctic Terns on two small islets in Millport Bay. As the alarmed birds flew excitedly overhead, one of his companions shot one which fell near McDougall. He retrieved it and noticed it was different from the other terns. He told his friends to shoot more, while he observed the terns in the sky. McDougall added several specimens to his collection of British and foreign birds, and he mounted three of them in a glass showcase. His friend Captain Laskey arranged for a specimen to be sent to English naturalist George Montagu, who described the species, giving it the name *Sterna Dougallii*, "to make our public acknowledgements to Doctor M'Dougall, for the very liberal and handsome manner in which the history of this interesting bird was communicated to us, and more particularly for the specimen that accompanied it."

French Name: Sterne de Dougall
Spanish Names: Charrán Rosado; Golondrina-marina Rosada
Other Names: McDougall's Tern; Graceful Tern; Mackerel Gull; Sea Gull; Gullie; Carite; Davie; David; Gaviota; Mauve Blanche; Petite Mauve; Oiseau Fou; Palometa; Pigeon de la Mer

Common Tern
Sterna hirundo
(STIR-nah her-UN-doh)

"One of the most charming features of our eastern seacoast is this graceful little "sea swallow." The most attractive combination of summer sea, sky, and sandy beach would be but an empty, lifeless scene without the little "mackerel gull," such a fitting accompaniment of its gentle surroundings and so suggestive of summer sunshine and cooling sea breezes. One cannot help admiring such an elegant and dainty creature, its spotless and delicate plumage and its buoyant, graceful flight, as it flies listlessly up the beach until the discovery of some school of small fry, on which it feeds, causes it to pause, hover for an instant, and plunge headlong into the water for some tiny minnow." — Arthur Cleveland Bent (1921)

The Common Tern may be outnumbered by other tern species in some places, but it has the

Common Tern, by John James Audubon

widest distribution, across North America and Eurasia.

Sterna — The genus name is the Latinized form of the Old English *stearn* or *starn* (a tern).

hirundo — The specific epithet is Latin for "a swallow" and refers to the tern's resemblance to a Barn Swallow, due to the long pointed wings and deeply forked tail. In fact, terns are commonly called "sea swallows."

French Name: Sterne Pierregarin

Spanish Names: Golondrina-marina Común; Charrán Común; Gaviotin Común

Other Names: Wilson's Tern; Great Tern; Greater Tern; Sea Swallow; Mackerel Gull; Bass Gull; Little Gull; Summer Gull; Lake Erie Gull; Gullie; Gull Pigeon; Gull Teaser; Egg Bird; Gannett; Kingfisher; Willie Fisher; High Diver; Striker; Rape; Red-shank; Shear Tail; Skirr; Kip; Clett; Pease Crow; Esterlet; Gaviota; Gaviota Común; Sparling; Rittock; Tarrock; Tarret; Taring; Tarnie; Palometa; Paytrick; Petite Mauve; Pictar; Pictarnie; Picket-a; Pickieterno; Pietrie; Piccatarrie; Pickatiere; Medrick; Miret; Darr; Starn; Stearin; Sparling; Speikintares; Pirre; Skirr; Kirrmew; Great Purl; Dippurl; Scraye; Hirondelle de Mer

Arctic Tern
Sterna paradisaea
(STIR-nah par-ah-DIE-see-ah)

"The world's migration champion is the Arctic Tern. It deserves its title of "Arctic," for it nests as far north as land has been discovered; that is, as far north as the bird can find anything stable on which to construct its nest. Indeed, so arctic are the conditions under which it breeds that the first nest found by man in this region, only 7½° from the pole, contained a downy chick surrounded by a wall of newly fallen snow that had been scooped out of the nest by the parent. When the young are full-grown the entire family leaves the Arctic and several months later they are found skirting the edge of the Antarctic continent." — Wells W. Cooke (1917)

The Arctic Tern is named for its breeding range in the high Arctic of both North America and Eurasia. It also nests as far south as the Gulf of Maine and the British Isles and northern coast of France. As stated above, the Arctic Tern is known as the champion among migrating birds, for it winters in Antarctic waters, and may make a round-trip journey of 31,000 miles in one year.

Sterna — The genus name is the Latinized form of the Old English *stearn* or *starn* (a tern).

paradisaea — Erik Pontoppidan, a Danish scientist and theologian, named the Arctic Tern in 1763, for paradise or heaven, from a specimen collected from Christiansoe Island, Denmark. Ernest Choate wrote, "Possibly his dual career influenced his naming of the bird in the hope he could convey the idea that so beautiful a creature belonged in that perfect home beyond the sky." It has been said that a tern is a gull that died and went to heaven.

French Name: Sterne Arctique

Spanish Names: Golondrina-marina Artica; Charrán Artico; Gaviotin del Artico

Eskimo and Inuit Names: Tu-kuthl-kwi-uk (imitative); Tiruyarak (imitative); Mitkotailyak (drooping feathers)

Other Names: Common Tern; Short-footed Tern; Paradise Tern; Crimson-billed Tern; Long-tailed Tern; Portland Tern; Pike's Tern; Sea Pigeon; Sea Swallow; Greenland Swallow; Mackerel; Steering Gull; Steering;

Stearn; Blackhead; Tarry; Tarrock; Sparling; Skirr; Ritto; Rittock; Rittick; Paytrick; Pictar; Pickieterno; Hirondelle de Mer

Forster's Tern
Sterna forsteri
(STIR-nah FORCE-ter-eye)

"The feet are black; the tail is shorter and much less forked than that described and drawn in the Br. Zool. The outermost tail-feather likewise wants the black, which that in the British Zoology has. In other respects it is the same." — Johann Reinhold Forster (1772)

In 1772, Johann Reinhold Forster wrote the above account in the *Philosophical Transactions of the Royal Society* of birds collected in the Hudson Bay region. He believed the bird he was describing was a variety of the Common Tern. By 1834, Thomas Nuttall had come to realize Forster had described a new species. He gave it the name *Sterna Forsteri* in honor of "the eminent naturalist and voyager who first suggested these distinctions" (from the Common Tern).

Sterna — The genus name is the Latinized form of the Old English *stearn* or *starn* (a tern).

forsteri — The specific epithet commemorates Johann Reinhold Forster (1729–1798), a German naturalist, who accompanied Captain Cook on his voyage around the world in 1772. See common name above.

French Name: Sterne de Forster

Spanish Names: Golondrina-marina de Forster; Charrán de Forster; Gaviote de Forster

Other Names: Marsh Tern; Havell's Tern; Sea Swallow; High Diver; Gullie; Davie; Esterlette; Gaviota de Forster; Pigeon de Mer; Queue-à-ciseau

Royal Tern
Thalasseus maximus
(thal-AS-ee-us MACK-sih-mus)

"Although the royal tern is a splendid bird it seems to me that the name "royal," as well as the specific name *maxima*, should have been applied to its near relative, the Caspian tern, which is both larger and more aggressive, a real king among terns. The two species so closely resemble each other that so good a naturalist as Audubon did not recognize them as distinct, confusing the two under the name Cayenne tern." — Arthur Cleveland Bent (1921)

The Royal Tern got its name from its large size (second only to the Caspian Tern) and impressive appearance, complete with a crest.

Thalasseus — The genus name is from the Greek *thalassa* (of the sea). It refers to the crested terns' maritime habitat of coastal beaches and barrier islands. All sometimes forage well offshore. Formerly *Sterna maximus*.

maximus — The specific epithet is Latin for "largest" or "greatest" from *magnus* (large) plus a superlative suffix. The Royal Tern is one of the largest terns, but the Caspian Tern is larger. See common name above.

French Name: Sterne Royale

Spanish Names: Charrán Real; Golondrina-marina Real; Pagaza Real

Other Names: Cayenne Tern; Redbill; Gabby; Gullie; Gannet; Gannet Striker; Big Striker; Egg Bird; Foquette; Gaviota Real; Goeland a Bec Rouge; Mauve; Oiseau Fou; Sprat; Sprat Bird; Pigeon de la Mar

Sandwich Tern
Thalasseus sandvicensis
thal-AS-ee-us sand-vih-SEN-sis)

The Sandwich Tern is named for the borough of Sandwich in Kent, England, where the type specimen was collected.

Thalasseus — The genus name is from the Greek *thalassa* (of the sea). It refers to the crested terns' maritime habitat of coastal beaches and barrier islands. All sometimes forage well offshore. Formerly *Sterna sandvicensis*.

sandvicensis — The specific epithet is Modern Latin for "of Sandwich."

French Name: Sterne Caugek

Spanish Names: Charrán de Sándwich; Golondrina-marina de Sandwich; Pagaza Puntiamarilla

Other Names: Cabot's Tern; Kentish Tern; Boys' Tern; Ducal Tern; Surf Tern; Gullie; Egg Bird; Sea Swallow; Boatswain; Gaviota de Pico Agudo; Gaviota Piquiaguda; Screecher; Crocker Kip

Elegant Tern, by Allan C. Brooks

Elegant Tern
Thalasseus elegans
(thal-AS-ee-us EL-ee-ganz)

Of the Elegant Tern, Bent wrote, "This beautiful tern well deserves its name, for in color, form, and behavior it is certainly one of the most elegant of our sea birds, the most exquisite member of the charming group of "sea swallows."" — Arthur Cleveland Bent (1921)

Thalasseus — The genus name is from the Greek *thalassa* (of the sea). It refers to the crested terns' maritime habitat of coastal beaches and barrier islands. All sometimes forage well offshore. Formerly *Sterna elegans*.

elegans — The specific epithet is Latin for "elegant."

French Name: Sterne Élégante

Spanish Names: Charrán Elegante: Pagaza Elegante; Golondrina-marina Elegante

Black Skimmer
Rynchops niger
(RING-kops NYE-jer)

"When the rising tide flows in around the island, covering the outer sand bars, driving the birds from their low-tide roosting and feeding places and flooding the shallow estuaries, then the "flood gulls," as they are called, may be seen skimming over the muddy shallows, about the mouths of the creeks, or up into the narrow inlets, gracefully gliding on their long, slender wings close to the surface in search of their finny prey, the tiny minnows, which have followed the advancing tide into the protecting, grassy shallows. It is a pleasure to sit and watch their graceful evolution in their untiring efforts to secure a meal, as they quarter back and forth over the same ground again and again, cutting the smooth surface of the water with their razor-like bills, scaling, wheeling, and turning like giant swallows, silently engrossed in their occupation for which they are so highly specialized." — Arthur Cleveland Bent (1921)

Black Skimmer, by John James Audubon

Skimmers are named for their method of feeding. They are the only birds whose lower mandible is longer than the upper one. Skimmers forage for small fish by skimming over calm water, cutting the surface with the lower mandible. When they detect prey, the bill snaps shut. The Black Skimmer is named for its black upperparts, but it is white underneath.

Rynchops — The genus name means "beak-faced" from the Greek *rhynchas* (the beak) and *ops* (the face). It refers to the very prominent red and black scissor-like bill.

niger — The specific epithet is Latin for "black."

French Name: Bec-en-ciseaux Noir

Spanish Names: Rayador Americano; Rayador Negro; Rayador Arador Pico de Tijera

Other Names: Black Skimmer Gull; Flood Gull; Storm Gull; Cut-water; Shearwater; Black Shearwater; Knifebill; Razor-bill; Scissorbill; Old Wife; Sea-dog; Bec-a-Ciseaux; Bec-a-Lancet-de-Mer; Pico de Tijer

Order Phaethontiformes

Family Phaethontidae
Tropicbirds

"The tropic-birds are well named, for they are always associated with those favored regions, where on the hot, sunny islands they find genial nesting sites and in the warm tropical waters fruitful feeding grounds." — Arthur Cleveland Bent (1922)

These highly pelagic birds are named for their distribution over the warm waters of tropical and subtropical seas.

White-tailed Tropicbird
Phaethon lepturus
(FAY-eh-thon lep-TOUR-us)

"This beautiful white bird with its long streaming tail feathers and its quick pigeon-like flight is one of the familiar sights for visitors to Bermuda. It makes long journeys out across the blue waters of the warm Gulf Stream for its favorite food of small surface fishes." — John Bichard May (1925)

This tropicbird's white tail lacks the black barring of the Red-billed Tropicbird. A third species, the Red-tailed Tropicbird (*P. rubricauda*) of the Indo-Pacific, has a white tail, too, but its streamers are red.

Phaethon — The genus name, meaning "radiant" or "shining," is from a proper name, a character in Greek mythology. Phaëthon, the son of Helios, god of the sun, persuaded his father to let him drive his sun chariot across the sky for one day. However the boy lost control of the immortal steeds, soaring so high that he crashed into stars and burned a gash across the sky that we now know as the Milky Way. Then he plummeted so close to the earth that the fiery chariot set the landscape ablaze. In order to save the earth, Zeus struck the boy dead with a thunderbolt. It is said Linnaeus chose the name for the tropicbirds, because of their habit of soaring to great heights and in allusion to their attempt to follow the path of the sun.

lepturus — The specific epithet means "slender tail" from the Greek *leptos* (slender) and *oura* (the tail). The reference is to a pair of thin central tail feathers that are elongated into wispy streamers, as long or longer than the bird's body.

French Name: Phaéton à Bec Jaune
Spanish Names: Rabijunco de Cola Blanca; Rabijunco Coliblanco
Other Names: Yellow-billed Tropicbird; White Bird; White-tailed Bos'n; Bosun Bird; Boatswain Bird; Marlinespike; Long-tail; Trophic; Truphit; Chitee-churo; Chirre; Chirre de Cola Blanca; Contramaestre; Rabijunco; Flèche-en-cul; Fètu; Ciberou; Gaviota Caracolera; Koae; Koae Kea; Paille-en-queue; Paille-en-cul

White-tailed Tropicbird, by John James Audubon

Red-billed Tropicbird
Phaethon aethereus
(FAY-eh-thon ee-THEER-ih-us)

The blood-red bill gives this tropicbird its name. The bill of the White-tailed Tropicbird is orange-yellow.

Phaethon — The genus name, meaning "radiant" or "shining," is from a proper name, a character in Greek mythology. Phaëthon, the son of Helios, god of the sun, persuaded his father to let him drive his sun chariot across the sky for one day. However the boy lost control of the immortal steeds, soaring so high that he crashed into stars and burned a gash across the sky that we now know as the Milky Way. Then he plummeted so close to the earth that the fiery chariot set the landscape ablaze. In order to save the earth, Zeus struck the boy dead with a thunderbolt. It is said Linnaeus chose the name for the tropicbirds, because of their habit of soaring to great heights and in allusion to their attempt to follow the path of the sun.

aethereus — The specific epithet means "ethereal," "heavenly," "delicate" or "intangible," from the Greek *aitherios* (the upper air). The name probably refers to a combination of the bird's appearance, the bright white plumage and elegant streamers, and its graceful soaring high in the sky.

French Name: Phaéton à Bec Rouge
Spanish Names: Rabijunco de Pico Rojo; Rabijunco Piquirrojo
Other Names: Bosun Bird; Boatswain Bird; White Bird; Marlinespike; Trophic; Truphit; Fétu; Flèche-en-cul; Koae; Koa'e'ula; Rabijunco Piquicolorado; Paille-en-queue; Paille-en-cul

Red-tailed Tropicbird
Phaethon rubricauda
(FAY-eh-thon rube-rih-CAUD-ah)

"To see these birds at their best one must watch them flying around in the bright sunshine when their pale, salmon-pink plumage shines as though burnished, and the satiny feathers stand out like scales. The two long, red tail-feathers are possessed by both sexes, and the female is only a trifle less pink than the male." — Walter Kenrick Fisher (1906)

This species from the tropical Indo-Pacific is a rare visitor off the California coast. The two red tail streamers give this bird its name. Otherwise the tail is white.

Phaethon — The genus name, meaning "radiant" or "shining," is from a proper name, a character in Greek mythology. Phaëthon, the son of Helios, god of the sun, persuaded his father to let him drive his sun chariot across the sky for one day. However the boy lost control of the immortal steeds, soaring so high that he crashed into stars and burned a gash across the sky that we now know as the Milky Way. Then he plummeted so close to the earth that the fiery chariot set the landscape ablaze. In order to save the earth, Zeus struck the boy dead with a thunderbolt. It is said Linnaeus chose the name for the tropicbirds, because of their habit of soaring to great heights and in allusion to their attempt to follow the path of the sun.

rubricauda — The specific epithet means "red tail" from the Latin *ruber* (red) and *cauda* (the tail). See common name above.

French Name: Phaéton à Brins Rouge
Spanish Name: Paiño Colirrojo
Other Names: Bosun Bird; Marlinespike

Order Gaviiformes

Family Gaviidae
Loons

"Crazy as a loon" is a familiar saying. So it would be reasonable to assume that the name refers to the tremolo call of the Common Loon. This call, which is actually uttered when the birds are stressed, has been likened to "the laugh of the deeply insane." In truth, the name stems from the Old Norse word *lamr*, meaning lame. The reference is to the loon's awkwardness on land, due to the fact that the feet are set far back on the body. This is an adaptation for swimming and diving, but makes walking nearly impossible. A loon on land can only push itself along on its belly. Loons come out on land only to nest, which is built at the water's edge. In Britain, loons are called divers, an apt name, since they are skilled at diving to pursue fish underwater or submerge to escape predators.

Red-throated Loon
Gavia stellata
(GAY-vih-ah stel-AY-tah)

Red-throated refers to the brick-red throat patch in breeding adults.

Gavia — The genus name is derived from a Latin word for some seabird, quite possibly a gull. Somehow it was applied to this group of birds, aquatic to be sure, but decidedly ungull-like.

stellata — The specific epithet is Latin for "set with stars" and refers to the white speckling on the backs of birds in winter plumage.

French Name: Huart à Gorge Rousse
Spanish Names: Colimbo de Cuello Rojo; Colimbo Gorjirrojo
British Name: Red-throated Diver
Eskimo and Inuit Names: Kutchunik (lonesome call); Kaksrauk (imitative)

Other Names: Loom; Lune; Little Loon; Peggin'-awl; Pegging-awl Loon; Pegging-owl Loon; Pepper-shinned Loon; Quaker Loon; Sprat Loon; Mag Loon; Speckled Loon; Speckled Diver; Silver Grebe; Rain-goose; Longneck; Scape-grace; Arran Ake; Capederace; Cape Race; Cape Racer; Cape Drake; Cobble; Carbreast; Corbreast; Corbrace; Corbrus; Cou-rouge; Huard; Pegmont; Kashagat; Burrian; Galrush; Spratoon; Waby; Wabby; Whabby; Wobby

Arctic Loon
Gavia arctica
(GAY-vih-ah ARK-tih-kah)

Arctic refers to the breeding habitat of this species, which is on the arctic tundra.

Gavia — The genus name is derived from a Latin word for some seabird, quite possibly a gull. Somehow it was applied to this group of birds, aquatic to be sure, but decidedly ungull-like.

arctica — The specific epithet is from the Greek *arktikos* (northern) from the Greek *arktos* (a bear), referring to the constellation Ursa major (great bear) in the northern sky. This is a reference to this species' breeding range on the Arctic tundra.

French Name: Huart Arctique
Spanish Name: Colimbo Artico
British Name: Black-throated Diver
Other Names: Eurasian Loon; Black-throated Loon; Green-throated Loon; Speckled Loon; Grayback Loon; White-headed Loon; Arctic Diver; Lumme; Lesser Imber; Herring Bar; Northern Doucker

Pacific Loon
Gavia pacifica
(GAY-vih-ah pah-SIF-i-ka)

This is the North American counterpart of the Arctic Loon, with which it was once considered conspecific. It is also an arctic breeder, but it is named for its winter range along the Pacific coast of North America from the Gulf of Alaska to Baja California.

Gavia — The genus name is derived from a Latin word for some seabird, quite possibly a gull. Somehow it was applied to this group of birds, aquatic to be sure, but decidedly ungull-like.

pacifica — The specific epithet is Latin, referring to the Pacific Ocean. See common name above

French Name: Huart du Pacifique
Spanish Name: Colimbo Pacifico
Eskimo Name: Tun-u-chlik (fancy back, light spots)

Common Loon
Gavia immer
(GAY-vih-ah IM-er)

"The woodland lakes would be solitude, indeed, did they lack the finishing touch to make the picture complete, the tinge of wildness which adds color to the scene, the weird and mournful cry of the loon, as he calls to his mate or greets some new arrival. Who has ever paddled a canoe, or cast a fly, or pitched a tent in the north woods and has not stopped to listen to this wail of the wilderness? And what would the wilderness be without it?" — Arthur Cleveland Bent (1919)

The Common Loon, whose haunting calls are a symbol of the northern wilderness, has the most extensive breeding range in North America of the five species. Unfortunately it is declining in many areas due to human disturbance:

"The word *common* in its name is a decidedly qualified adjective; loon populations remain common only in areas away from motors, boaters, and voters — increasingly far north, in other words, though some loons do habituate to the presence of people. Pristine lakes once characterized most of North America above 40 degrees N latitude or so, and even until about 1920, breeding loons remained as far south as central Pennsylvania, northern Indiana, Illinois, and Iowa, plus most of New England. Since then, loons

Red-throated Loon, Common Loon, and Pacific Loon, by Louis Agassiz Fuertes

have been in general decline and withdrawal so that today, in the United States, their distribution is an uneven mosaic — mostly marginal populations, where any exist at all, with rare locales of abundance. Though the species is not on the federal endangered list, many states now label it endangered, threatened, or at risk." — John Eastman (1999)

Fortunately Common Loon populations remain substantial in Canada, where it is a symbol of the north country:

"The loon's image is virtually synonymous with remote lakes and wilderness sunsets. As everybody's favorite bird of the North, the common loon decorates everything from T-shirts and trinkets to coffee mugs. Its icons, always presented in breeding plumage, commercially symbolizes the wild places more often than even the eagle and the wolf." — John Eastman (1999)

Gavia — The genus name is derived from a Latin word for some seabird, quite possibly a gull. Somehow it was applied to this group of birds, aquatic to be sure, but decidedly ungull-like.

immer — There are several explanations for the origin of the specific epithet. One is that it stems from Scandinavian languages, Swedish *immer*, Danish *imber*, and Norwegian *hymber*, meaning "ember goose" and refers to the loon's blackish color as though burnt. Or that it means "diver" from the Latin *immersus* (to plunge into). A final explanation is that it comes from the Icelandic name for the

Common Loon, *himbrimi* (the surf-roarer).
French Name: Huart à Collier
Spanish Names: Colimbo Mayor; Colimbo Común
British Name: Great Northern Diver
Eskimo Name: Tasingik (black bill)
Other Names: Loom; Naak; Big Loon; Black-billed Loon; Ring-necked Loon; Sheep Loon; Salt-water Loon; Inland Loon; Pond Loon; Greater Loon; Lesser Loon; Greatest Speckled Loon; Spotted Loo; Tommy Loo; White-throated Loo; Call-up-a-storm; Rainbird; Weather Signaler; Ember; Ember Goose; Ammer Goose; Emmer-goose; Immer; Immer Goose; German Goose; Ocean Goose; Greenhead; Guinea Duck; Diver; Hell-diver; Big Hell Diver; Imber Diver; Big Diver; Polar Diver; Sea-diver; Greatest Speckled Diver; Big Pullet; Blusterer; Dumpy Herdman; Sea Herdsman; Gunner; Submarine; Wheelbarrow; Walloon; Loo; War-loo; War-loon; Carara; Cobble; Buckalew Bird; Buccalieu; Dipsydoodle; Roarer; Noisy Talker; Surfer; Toadlie; Arran Hawk; Holland Hawk; Great Doucker; Grand Plongeon; Grand Plongeur; Plongeon à Collier; Plongeur à Collier; Hurleur; Huart; Huard; Huard à Collier; Riche-poom; Scaloighter; Buna Chuachaill; Burbhuachaill; Grosa Wosser

Yellow-billed Loon
Gavia adamsii
(GAY-vih-ah AD-am-sih-eye)

This species resembles a large Common Loon with a pale yellow to ivory-white bill.

Gavia — The genus name is derived from a Latin word for some seabird, quite possibly a gull. Somehow it was applied to this group of birds, aquatic to be sure, but decidedly ungull-like.

adamsii — The specific epithet honors Edward Adams (1824–1856), a British surgeon-naturalist.
French Name: Huart a Bec Blanc
Spanish Name: Colimbo de Pico Amarillo
British Name: White-billed Diver
Eskimo Name: Tulik (imitative)
Other Names: Adam's Loon; White-billed Loon; White-billed Northern Diver

Order Procellariiformes

Members of the order Procellariiformes are commonly called "tubenoses," because their nostrils are encased in raised, horny sheaths called naricorns. Scientists believe the naricorns play a role in these birds' well-developed sense of smell. They may also allow the birds to detect subtle differences in barometric pressure and wind direction. These tubes also direct secretions from the birds' salt glands away from the eyes. The salt glands, located above the bill, remove excess salt from the blood, as these birds drink only seawater.

Family Diomediedae
Albatrosses

At length did cross an Albatross,
Through the fog it came;
As if it had been a Christian soul,
We hailed it in God's name.
Samuel Taylor Coleridge

"When 15th-century Portuguese navigators first ventured down the coast of Africa into the windy South Atlantic they encountered large black-and-white sea birds with stout bodies and long pointed wings. They called these strange birds "alcatraz," the Portuguese word for large sea birds, particularly the pelicans familiar to them in Mediterranean waters. English sailors corrupted alcatraz into albatross, the name we have used ever since for these monarchs of the ocean winds." — Oliver Austin, Jr. (1961)

Albatross stems from *alcatraz,* the Portuguese word for "pelican." That in turn comes from the Arabic root *al-qadus* "a bucket on a waterwheel." The reference is to the pelican's pouch, which people once believed the bird used to carry water for its young. Seafarers began using alcatraz in one spelling or another to mean various large seabirds such as gannets, boobies, and cormorants. British seamen also applied alcatraz to the frigatebirds. The modification to albatross may have been influenced by the Latin *albus* (white) in contrast to the frigatebirds, which have black plumage. The family name Diomediedae (as well as the genus *Diomedea* to which the Great Albatrosses of the Southern Ocean belong) comes from a proper name in Greek mythology. Diomedes was a Greek hero of Troy, whose companions were changed into birds.

Laysan Albatross
Phoebastria immutabilis
(fee-BASE-trih-ah im-mew-TAB-il-iss)

The Laysan Albatross is named for Laysan Island in the Hawaiian chain, where the type specimen was collected.

Phoebastria — The genus name is from the Greek *phoibastria* (a prophetess or a soothsayer). It refers to the seafarers' superstition that albatrosses are the reincarnation of drowned sailors and were seen as omens. Formerly *Diomedea immutabilis*.

immutabilis — The specfics epithet is Latin for "unchangeable" or "unchanging" and refers to the juvenile's plumage being similar to that of the adult.

French Name: Albatros de Laysan
Spanish Name: Albatros de Laysan
Other Names: White Albatross; Gooney; White Gooney; Gooney Bird; White Gooney Bird; Moli

Short-tailed Albatross and Black-footed Albatross, by Allan C. Brooks

Black-footed Albatross
Phoebastria nigripes
(fee-BASE-trih-ah NIG-rih-peez)

This dusky colored albatross's black feet give it its name. The feet of most other albatross species are pale, either flesh-pink or bluish-white.

Phoebastia — The genus name is from the Greek *phoibastria* (a prophetess or a soothsayer). It refers to the seafarers' superstition that albatrosses are the reincarnation of drowned sailors and were seen as omens. Formerly *Diomedea nigripes*.

nigripes — The specific epithet means "black foot" from the Latin *niger* (black) and *pes* (the foot).

French Name: Albatros à Pieds Noirs
Spanish Names: Albatros de Patas Negras; Albatros Patinegro
Eskimo and Inuit Names: A-la-gre-gich; A-ga-le-gach
Other Names: Black Albatross; Gony; Gony Bird; Gooney; Gooney Bird; Black Gooney; Brown Gooney

Short-tailed Albatross
Phoebastria albatrus
(fee-BASE-trih-ah AL-bah-trus)

The Short-tailed Albatross has an especially wide tail that makes it appear short.

Phoebastria — The genus name is from the Greek *phoibastria* (a prophetess or a soothsayer). It refers to the seafarers' superstition that albatrosses are the reincarnation of drowned sailors and were seen as omens. Formerly *Diomedea albatrus*.

albatrus — The specific epithet is another spelling of albatross, perhaps related to the German *albatros* (an albatross).

French Name: Albatros à Queue Courte
Spanish Name: Albatros Rabón
Other Name: Steller's Albatross

Family Oceanitidae
Southern Storm-Petrels

These storm-petrels nest mainly in the Southern Hemisphere.

Wilson's Storm-Petrel
Oceanites oceanicus
(oh-see-ah-NIGHT-eez oh-see-AN-ih-kus)

On his return trip from New Orleans to New York, Alexander Wilson observed flocks of petrels that followed the ship as they sailed off the coasts of Florida and the Carolinas. He identified them as the Storm-Petrels (*Hydrobates pelagicus*) of Europe. In 1824, Charles Bonaparte noticed these were different from the European Storm-Petrels and gave them the name *Procellaria wilsonii*. However this species had already been described by German ornithologist Heinrich Kuhl in 1820. Kuhl's specific epithet takes priority, but Alexander Wilson (1766–

Wilson's Storm-Petrel, by John James Audubon

1813), the father of American ornithology, is still commemorated in the common name. Formerly known as Wilson's Petrel.

Oceanites — The genus is named for the Oceanides, sea nymphs, 3000 in number, and daughters of the sea god Oceanus.

oceanicus — The specific epithet is Latin for "belonging to the ocean." Storm-petrels are true pelagic birds that spend the greater part of their lives far out at sea and come to land only to nest.

French Name: Océanite de Wilson
Spanish Name: Paiño de Wilson

Other Names: Long-legged Storm-Petrel; Common Stormy Petrel; Skipjack; Carey; Carey's Chick; Mother Carey's Chicken; Devil's Bird; Witch; Golondrina de Mar; Pamperito; Pamperito Rabo Cundrado

White-faced Storm-Petrel
Pelagodroma marina
(pel-ag-ODD-row-mah mah-RYE-nah)

This pale storm-petrel not only has a white face (with a black mask) but white wing linings and underparts as well.

Sidebar 17
Storm-Petrels

"When the waves are high and the wind fierce, it is pleasant, even amidst the noise of the storm and the heavings of the vessel, to watch the little creatures as they advance against the gale, at the height of scarcely a foot above the surface of the water, which they follow in all its undulations, mounting to the top of the wave, there quivering in the blast, and making good their way by repeated strokes of their long, narrow wings; then sliding down the slope, resting a moment in the shelter of the advancing mass of water, gliding up its side, and again meeting on the summit the force of the rude wind that curls the waves and scatters abroad its foam bells." — William Macgillivray (1852)

Petrels may smell oily, but they are not named for the petrol (gasoline) that fuels your car. Petrel is a diminutive of Peter (little Peter) and refers to Saint Peter, who according to Scripture, walked on the water with Jesus' assistance, Matthew 14: 22–33. The name was first applied to this family in reference to the birds' habit of pattering their feet in the water as they forage for plankton, thus they appear to be walking on the water. Later the name was applied to the larger birds in the family Procellariidae. In 1810, Alexander Wilson wrote the following observation:

". . . The most singular peculiarity of this bird is its faculty of standing, and even running, on the surface of the water, which it performs with apparent facility. When any greasy matter is thrown overboard, these birds instantly collect around it, and, facing to windward, with their long wings expanded, and their webbed feet patting the water, the lightness of their bodies, and the action of the wind on their wings, enable them to do this with ease . . . According to Buffon, it is from this singular habit that the whole genus have obtained the name Petrel, from the apostle Peter, who, as Scripture informs us, also walked on the water."

These birds are called storm-petrels, because they often seek shelter in the lee of a ship when gales arise suddenly. Seamen who saw the birds appear seemingly out of nowhere took them to be weather prophets. Sailors call storm-petrels Mother Carey's Chickens. Some sources say the nickname is a corruption of *mater cara* (dear mother), referring to the Virgin Mary to whom devout sailors might pray during violent weather. Another story tells us that Mother Carey was a sea witch, Davy Jones's aunt, who brought stormy weather and was accompanied by familiars in the form of little black birds. To some, the storm-petrels are the spirits of drowned sailors.

Pelagodroma — The genus name means "sea running" from the Greek *pelagos* (the sea) and *dromos* (running). It refers to the birds' habit of dancing and pattering over the waves as they search for food.

marina — The specific epithet is Latin for "of the sea."

French Name: Océanite Frégate
Spanish Names: Paíño de Cara Blanca; Paíño Pechialbo
Other Name: Frigate Petrel

Family Hydrobatidae
Northern Storm-Petrels

These storm-petrels nest in the Northern Hemisphere.

Fork-tailed Storm-Petrel
Hydrobates furcatus
(high-droe-BAY-teez fur-KAY-tus)

This pearly-gray storm-petrel's deeply notched tail gives it its name, a characteristic not unique to this species, as Leach's, Black, and Ashy Storm-Petrels sport forked tails, too.

Hydrobates — The genus name means "water treader" from The Greek *hydros* (water) and *batein* (to tread). It describes the birds' habit of pattering their feet on the water as they forage. Formerly *Oceanodroma furcata*.

furcatus — The specific epithet is Latin for "forked."

French Name: Oceanite à Queue Fourchue
Spanish Name: Paíño Rabihorcado
Eskimo and Inuit Name: O-ku-ik (oil eater)
Other Name: Fork-tailed Petrel

Leach's Storm-Petrel
Hydrobates leucorhoa
(high-droe-BAY-teez lew-CORE-oh-ah)

In the summer of 1819, William Bullock decided to auction off his vast collection of curios and natural history specimens. The sale attracted dealers from all over Europe, including Franco Bonelli, Hinrich Lichtenstein, Coenraad Temminck, and William Swainson. William Leach, a zoologist with the British Museum, acquired a specimen labeled "an undescribed petrel with a forked tail, taken at Saint Kilda in 1818; the only one known (with egg)." Soon after, Dutch naturalist Coenraad Temminck on a visit to the museum asked to examine the petrel. He described it in his *Manuel d'Ornithologie*, giving it the name *Procellaria Leachii*. This did not sit well with the Reverend John Fleming who felt the species should have been named for Bullock "in order to do an act of common justice to the individual who had energy to undertake a voyage of enquiry, and sagacity to distinguish the bird in question as an undescribed species." As it turned out, this controversy was moot, because Leach's specimen was not the only one known; there were three others, one in the Paris Museum and two in private collections. French ornithologist Louis Jean Pierre Vieillot had already described the species in 1817, from a specimen in L.A.F. Baillon's collection. Vieillot gave it the name *Procellaria leucorhoa*, so his specific epithet takes priority, but the common name still commemorates English naturalist William Elford Leach (1790–1836). Formerly known as Leach's Petrel.

Hydrobates — The genus name means "water treader" from The Greek *hydros* (water) and *batein* (to tread). It describes the birds' habit of pattering their feet on the water as they forage. Formerly *Oceanodroma leucrhoa*.

leucorhoa — The specific epithet means "white rump" from the Greek *leukos* (white) and *orrhos* (the rump), referring to the white rump patch.

French Name: Oceanite Cul-blanc
Spanish Name: Paíño de Leach
Eskimo and Inuit Names: Ki-ki-tich-noch; Ke-kech
Other Names: Leach's Fork-tailed Petrel; Common Fork-tailed Petrel; White-rumped Petrel; Mother Carey's Chicken; Mother Carey's Chick; Carey Chick; Mother Carew's Chicken; Carey; Pall Carey; Kerry Chicken; Lavapiés; Golandrina de Mar; Pamperito; Pamperito Rabo Horquillado

Ashy Storm-Petrel
Hydrobates homochroa
(high-droe-BAY-teez hom-MOK-row-ah)

Ash-gray wing linings give this storm-petrel its name. Formerly known as Ashy Petrel.

Hydrobates — The genus name means "water treader" from The Greek *hydros* (water) and *batein* (to tread). It describes the birds' habit of pattering their feet on the water as they forage. *Oceanodroma homochroa*.

homochroa — The specific epithet stems from the Greek *homokhrous* (of one color), referring to this bird's uniform dark color with no markings.

French Name: Océanite Cendré
Spanish Names: Paiño Ceniciento; Paiño Cenizo
Other Name: Coues' Petrel

Band-rumped Storm-Petrel
Hydrobates castro
(high-droe-BAY-teez CAST-row)

The white band at the base of the tail gives this seabird its name. Formerly known as Harcourt's Petrel for Edwin William Vernon Harcourt (1825–1891), an English naturalist who discovered and described this species in 1851.

Hydrobates — The genus name means "water treader" from The Greek *hydros* (water) and *batein* (to tread). It describes the birds' habit of pattering their feet on the water as they forage. Formerly *Oceanodroma castro*.

castro — Edwin Harcourt discovered this species on the Deserta Islands in Madeira. He described the bird in his *Sketch of Madeira* and wrote:

> "There is another petrel called by the natives "*Roque de Castro*," [Rook of Castro] and pronounced "Roque de Casto," which is likewise an inhabitant of the Dezerta Islands."

Two translations for Roque de Castro have been proposed, rock crow or shrimp crow.

French Name: Océanite de Castro
Spanish Names: Paiño de Madeira; Paiño de Harcourt; Paiño Rabifajeado
Other Names: Harcourt's Petrel; Harcourt's Storm-Petrel; Hawaiian Petrel; Hawaiian Storm-Petrel; Madeiran Storm-Petrel; Madeiran Petrel; Ake'ake; Oweowe

Black Storm-Petrel
Hydrobates melania
(high-droe-BAY-teez meh-LAN-ih-ah)

This darkest storm-petrel is named for its all-black plumage. Formerly known as Black Petrel.

Hydrobates — The genus name means "water treader" from The Greek *hydros* (water) and *batein* (to tread). It describes the birds' habit of pattering their feet on the water as they forage. Formerly *Oceanodroma melania*.

melania — The specific epithet is Greek for "blackness."

French Name: Océanite Noir
Spanish Name: Paiño Negro

Least Storm-Petrel
Hydrobates microsoma
(high-droe-BAY-teez my-crow-SO-mah)

At just under 6 inches long, this sparrow-sized seabird is the smallest storm-petrel. Formerly known as Least Petrel.

Hydrobates — The genus name means "water treader" from The Greek *hydros* (water) and *batein* (to tread). It describes the birds' habit of pattering their feet on the water as they forage. Formerly *Oceanodroma microsoma*.

microsoma — The specific epithet means "small body" from the Greek *mikros* (small) and *soma* (the body).

French Name: Océanite Minute
Spanish Names: Paiño Menor; Paiño Minimo; Paiño Menudo
Other Name: Wedge-tailed Petrel

Family Procellariidae
Shearwaters and Petrels

Northern Fulmar
Fulmarus glacialis
(FULL-mar-us glay-sih-ALE-iss)

Fulmar is Old Norse for "foul mew" or "foul gull." It refers to the bird's defense of ejecting a foul-smelling stomach oil at an intruder to a distance of five feet. While not a gull, the fulmar superficially resembles one. Northern refers to its breeding range on Arctic

Northern Fulmar, by John James Audubon

islands and distinguishes this species from the Southern Fulmar (*F. glacialoides*) of the Southern Hemisphere.

Fulmarus — The genus name is the Latinized form of the common name.

glacialis — The specific epithet is Latin for "icy" and refers to this species' northerly range.

French Name: Fulmar Boréal
Spanish Name: Fulmar Norteño
Eskimo and Inuit Names: Kil-u-ghoo-kin; Ah-ga-luch
Other Names: Fulmar Petrel; White Hagdon; White Puffin; Oil-bird; Sea Horse; John Down; Noddy; Marbleheader; Molly Hawk; Molly-mock; Mollymake; Mollymoke; Mollemawk; Mollemoke; Malmock; Mallemuck; Mallemuke; Mallemoker; Mallimoke; Mallimack; Mallemugge; Malduck

Gadfly Petrels

Petrel means "little Peter" named after Saint Peter. The name was first applied to the storm-petrels in the families Oceanitidae and Hydrobatidae. See Storm-Petrels for the name's significance. The gadfly petrels got their name from their fast, erratic flight as though they were pursued by horse flies.

Herald Petrel
Pterodroma arminjoniana
(ter-ODD-row-mah ar-min-jon-ih-AY-nah)

The Herald Petrel gets its name from a seaman's belief that this bird was an omen. Formerly known as Trinidade Petrel.

Pterodroma — The genus name means "winged runner" from the Greek *pteron* (the wing) and *dromos* (running).

arminjoniana — The specific epithet honors Captain Vittorio Arminjon (1830–1897), commander of the first Italian vessel, the *Magenta*, to sail around the world. The type specimen of the Herald Petrel was taken on this voyage.

French Name: Pétrel de la Trinité du Sud
Spanish Name: Petrel Herááldico

Murphy's Petrel
Pterodroma ultima
(ter-ODD-row-mah ULT-ih-mah)

This petrel is named for Robert Cushman Murphy (1897–1973), the ornithologist who described the species from a specimen collected on Oeno Island in the South Pacific. Dr. Murphy was a notable environmentalist and served as Chairman of the Department of Birds at the American Museum of Natural History from 1942–1955.

Pterodroma — The genus name means "winged runner" from the Greek *pteron* (the wing) and *dromos* (running).

ultima — "For twenty years I have been well aware of the distinctness of this bird, which was obtained in considerable numbers in the central tropical and subtropical Pacific by Mr. Rollo H. Beck and his associates on the Whitney Expedition. Naming has been deferred because of the apparent unlikelihood that such a large, striking, and abundant petrel could fail to turn up in the collections of museums, or at least in the literature of Pacific exploration." — Robert Cushman Murphy (1949)

In 1949, Robert Cushman Murphy, a world authority on oceanic birds, described this petrel, giving it the specific epithet *ultima*, Latin for "last." Dr. Murphy was amazed that such a prominent bird would go so long without being described, and he figured this

would be the last petrel ever to be classified. But he was premature, for yet another species, Barau's Petrel (*Pterodroma baraui*), was described in 1963.
French Name: Pétrel de Murphy
Spanish Name: Petrel de Murphy
Other Names: Petrel Murphy

Mottled Petrel
Pterodroma inexpectata
(ter-ODD-row-mah in-eks-peck-TAY-tah)

Contrasting gray and white mottled markings give this petrel its name. Formerly known as Scaled Petrel.
Pterodroma — The genus name means "winged runner" from the Greek *pteron* (the wing) and *dromos* (running).
inexpectata — The specific epithet is Latin for "unexpected." It probably refers to the fact that this widely wandering species can show up unexpectedly.
French Name: Pétrel Maculé
Spanish Name: Petrel Moteado
Other Name: Peale's Petrel

Bermuda Petrel
Pterodroma cahow
(ter-ODD-row-mah kah-HOO)

This highly endangered species is named for the island where it nests.
Pterodroma — The genus name means "winged runner" from the Greek *pteron* (the wing) and *dromos* (running).
cahow — The specific epithet is from the common name early settlers called this bird and is imitative of its call.
French Name: Pétrel des Bermudes
Spanish Name: Petrel Cahow
Other Names: Cahow; Cowhaw; Cowkoe

Black-capped Petrel
Pterodroma hasitata
(ter-ODD-row-mah hass-ih-TAY-tah)

The brownish-black cap that extends to the eye and the nape gives this petrel its name. The rest of the head including the hindneck is white.
Pterodroma — The genus name means "winged runner" from the Greek *pteron* (the wing) and *dromos* (running).
hasitata — The specific epithet is from the Modern Latin *haesitatus* (hesitant) from the Latin *haesitare* (to stick fast). Apparently the describer of the species was in doubt and therefore hesitated to name it.
French Name: Pétrel Diablotin
Spanish Names: Petrel Antillano; Petrel Gorrinegro
Other Names: West Indian Petrel; Brown Petrel; Dry-land Booby; Blue Mountain Duck; Little Devil; Diablotin; Chathuant

Fea's Petrel
Pterodroma feae
(ter-ODD-row-mah FEE-ee)

This visitor from the eastern Atlantic is named for Leonardo Fea. See specific epithet below.
Pterodroma — The genus name means "winged runner" from the Greek *pteron* (the wing) and *dromos* (running).
feae — In 1899, Tommaso Salvadori named this petrel in honor of Leonardo Fea (1852–1903), an Italian explorer and zoologist, who collected the first specimen while on the Cape Verde Islands.
French Name: Pétrel Gongon
Spanish Name: Petrel Gongón
Other Names: Cape Verde Petrel; Gon-gon

Cook's Petrel
Pterodroma cookii
(ter-ODD-row-mah COOK-ih-eye)

English ornithologist George Robert Gray named this species *Procellaria cookii* in honor of English explorer James Cook, in an ornithological appendix to Ernst Dieffenbach's *Travels in New Zealand* (1843). This was 64 years after Cook's death, and Gray gave no particular reason why he chose to commemorate Captain Cook. Barbara and Richard Mearns feel the name is fitting, however, because when Cook's Petrel is not breeding in New Zealand, it wanders widely over the Pacific, the region Cook explored.
Pterodroma — The genus name means "winged runner" from the Greek *pteron* (the wing) and *dromos* (running).
cookii — The specific epithet honors Captain James Cook (1728–1779), an English naval officer and explorer, who circumnavigated

the world. See common name above.
French Name: Pétrel de Cook
Spanish Name: Petrel de Cook
Other Name: Blue-footed Petrel

Bulwer's Petrel
Bulweria bulwerii
(bull-WER-ih-ah BULL-wer-ih-eye)

We are indebted to the kindness of Mr. "Bulwer, during some years a resident in Madeira, for the subject of this plate which we consider as yet undescribed. It is not to be found in the works of Latham or Shaw, or indeed in any other which we have had the opportunity of consulting; and from its marked characters it is not a species that would be easily overlooked." — Sir William Jardine and John Selby (1828)

The plate in question was of Bulwer's Petrel, published in *Illustrations of Ornithology* along with Jardine's and Selby's description of the species. They named it *Procellaria Bulwerii* in honor of James Bulwer who had collected the type specimen in Madeira. He found this new petrel nesting there in association with Cory's Shearwaters and Band-rumped Storm-Petrels. Aside from his collecting activities and correspondence with Jardine, Bulwer had few connections with ornithology. He was more interested in shells than in birds.

Bulweria — Charles Bonaparte erected the genus *Bulweria* for this petrel in 1843. So James Bulwer is commemorated by all three names, genus, species, and common.

bulwerii — The specific epithet honors James Bulwer (1794–1879), an English clergyman and amateur naturalist who collected the type specimen in Madeira. See common name above.

French Name: Pétrel de Bulwer
Spanish Name: Petrel de Bulwer

Shearwaters

Shearwater refers to these birds' habit of skimming low over the water, seeming to shear the water with their wingtips. Francesca Greenoak explains, "Skimming almost at right angles to the water, the 'shear-water' seems to cut through the waves with its long straight wings, in an action similar to that of a ploughshare on land."

Cory's Shearwater
Calonectris diomedea
(kal-oh-NEK-tris die-oh-me-DEE-ah)

"The flight of this species is much like that of other large shearwaters, swift, strong, and graceful. It glides along smoothly on its stiff, pointed wings, rising easily over the crests of the waves and coasting down into the valleys between them. It usually flies very close to the surface, even in the roughest weather, and I have often admired the skill and confidence with which it rises and skims over the tops of the largest waves in which it seems as if it must be engulfed." — Arthur Cleveland Bent (1922)

Cory's Shearwater is named for Charles Barney Cory (1857–1921), an American naturalist who was with the Chicago Field Museum after 1906.

Calonectrus — The genus name means "beautiful swimmer" from the Greek *calos* (beautiful) and *nectris* (swimmer) The shearwater can alight on the water, but it is usually seen in the air.

diomedea — The specific epithet is also the genus to which the Wandering and Royal Albatrosses belong and suggests a similarity (perhaps the flight pattern) between the shearwater and the albatross. *Diomedea* is from Diomedes, a mythological character whose companions were turned into birds when their ship was lost on their return from the Trojan War.

French Name: Puffin Cendré
Spanish Name: Pardela de Cory
Other Names: Cinereous Shearwater; North Atlantic Shearwater; Mediterranean Shearwater; Cape Verde Shearwater

Buller's Shearwater
Ardenna bulleri
(AR-den-ah BULL-er-eye)

Walter Lawry Buller was an attorney who became New Zealand's first notable ornithologist. He chanced upon a specimen of an undescribed shearwater:

"The only example of this fine Petrel I have had an opportunity of examining in the flesh was picked up by myself on the ocean-beach near the mouth of the Waikanae river on the 1st October, 1884, having been blown ashore . . . It is remarkable for its length of neck and tail. Indeed at first sight it looks more like a small Shag than a Petrel, and several of the Maoris at Waikanae to whom I showed it declared that it really was a Kawau till I pointed out to them its tubular nostrils."

English naturalist Osbert Salvin described this species in the *Ibis* in 1888 and gave it the name *Puffinus bulleri*. Formerly known as New Zealand Shearwater.

Ardenna — The genus name is the Italian dialect name, based on *ardea*, for a shearwater. Formerly *Puffinus bulleri*.

bulleri — The specific epithet commemorates Sir Walter Lawry Buller (1838–1906), an ornithologist and lawyer from New Zealand. See common name above.

French Name: Puffin de Buller
Spanish Name: Pardela de Buller
Other Name: Gray-backed Shearwater

Short-tailed Shearwater
Ardenna tenuirostris
(AR-den-ah ten-you-ih-ROSS-tris)

Short-tailed is an odd name, because this shearwater's tail is not obviously shorter than those of other shearwaters. Formerly called Slender-billed Shearwater.

Ardenna — See Buller's Shearwater. Formerly *Puffinus teuirostris*.

tenuirostris — The specific epithet means "thin beak" from the Latin *tenuis* (thin or slender) and *rostrum* (the beak). This shearwater has a slender bill, but so do other shearwater species.

French Name: Puffin à Bec Grêle
Spanish Names: Pardela de Pico Corto; Pardela Colicorta
Eskimo Name: Muk-luk-ting-u-me-uk
Other Names: Muttonbird; Whalebird

Sooty Shearwater
Ardenna grisea
(AR-den-ah GRISS-ee-ah)

This shearwater's dark sooty-brown plumage gives it its name.

Ardenna — The genus name is the Italian dialect name, based on *ardea*, for a shearwater. Formerly *Puffinus griseus*.

grisea — The specific epithet is Latin for "gray" and refers to the silvery-gray linings of the underwings that contrast with the overall dark plumage.

French Name: Puffin Fuligineux
Spanish Name: Pardela Gris; Pardela Sombría
Other Names: Dark-bodied Shearwater; Black Bauk; Hagdown; Black Hag; Black Hagdon; Black Haddown

Great Shearwater
Ardenna gravis
(AR-den-ah GRAVE-iss)

"The flight of the greater shearwater is extremely graceful and very characteristic. With long sharply pointed, slightly decurved wings they scale along close to the waves, sailing into the teeth of the wind by skillfully taking advantage of the air currents deflected upward from the surges. Now they turn on their side with one wing just grazing the water, the other high in the air. Again they take a few quick wing strokes and launch themselves just above a breaker, but so close that one expects to see them overwhelmed in the foam." — Charles Wendell Townsend (1922)

The Great Shearwater is named for its larger size in comparison with other shearwater species. Formerly known as Greater Shearwater

Ardenna — The genus name is the Italian dialect name, based on *ardea*, for a shearwater. Formerly *Puffinus gavis*.

gravis — The specific epithet is Latin for "heavy" referring to the bird's bulky size.

French Name: Puffin Majeur
Spanish Name: Pardela Mayor
Other Names: Common Atlantic Shearwater; Wandering Shearwater; Cinereous Puffin; Egg Down; Cape Hen; Balk; Bauk; White Bauk; Hag; Hagdon; Haglet; Haglin

Pink-footed Shearwater
Ardenna creatopus
(AR-den-ah kree-AT-oh-pus)

Pink-footed describes the pink to flesh-colored feet of this species.
Ardenna — The genus name is the Italian dialect name, based on *ardea*, for a shearwater. Formerly *Puffinus creatopus*.
creatopus — The specific epithet means "flesh foot" from the Greek *kreatos* (flesh) and *pous* (the foot).
French Name: Puffin à Pieds Roses
Spanish Names: Pardela de Patas Rosadas; Pardela Patirrosada
Other Names: Red-footed Shearwater; Coues' Shearwater; Cooper's Shearwater

Flesh-footed Shearwater
Ardenna carneipes
(AR-den-ah car-NEE-ih-peez)

Flesh-pink feet give this shearwater its name. Formerly known as Pale-footed Shearwater.
Ardenna — The genus name is the Italian dialect name, based on *ardea*, for a shearwater. Formerly *Puffinus carneipes*.
carneipes — The specific epithet means "flesh-colored foot" from the Modern Latin *carneus* (flesh-colored) and *pes* (the foot).
French Name: Puffin à Pieds Pâles
Spanish Names: Pardela de Patas Pálidas; Pardela Patipalida

Manx Shearwater
Puffinus puffinus
(PUFF-in-us)

The Manx Shearwater is name for the Isle of Man (where the tailless cats originated) in the Irish Sea, where it formerly nested in large numbers, but has been absent there since 1800.
Puffinus — The genus/species name is the Latinized form of "puffin." Although puffin now refers to alcids in the genus *Fratercula*, the name was also applied to the shearwaters as well as the Razorbill. Until the end of the 18th century, the name referred to the cured carcasses of nestling shearwaters, which were prized as a delicacy.
French Name: Puffin des Anglais
Spanish Names: Pardela Pichoneta; Pardela Manx
Other Names: Common Shearwater; Manx Petrel; Mackerel Cock; Sea Swift; Night Bird; Booty; Scraber; Skidden; Skinner; Lyre; Yrie; Cocklolly; Cockthrodon; Cuckee; Cuckles; Crew; Baakie Craa

Black-vented Shearwater
Puffinus opisthomelas
(PUFF-in-us oh-pis-THOM-el-as)

This shearwater gets its name from its dark undertail coverts.
Puffinus — The genus name is the Latinized form of "puffin." Although puffin now refers to alcids in the genus *Fratercula*, the name was also applied to the shearwaters as well as the Razorbill. Until the end of the 18th century, the name referred to the cured carcasses of nestling shearwaters, which were prized as a delicacy.
opisthomelas — The species name means "black rear" from the Greek *opisthe* (the rear) and *melas* (black) and refers to the dark undertail coverts.
French Name: Puffin Cul-noir
Spanish Name: Pardela Mexicana

Audubon's Shearwater
Puffinus lherminieri
(PUFF-in-us ler-min-EER-eye)

The common name honors John James Audubon (1785–1851), the artistic father of American ornithology.
Puffinus — The genus name is the Latinized form of "puffin." Although puffin now refers to alcids in the genus *Fratercula*, the name was

Audubon's Shearwater, by John James Audubon

also applied to the shearwaters as well as the Razorbill. Until the end of the 18th century, the name referred to the cured carcasses of nestling shearwaters, which were prized as a delicacy.

lhermineri — In 1839, Renée Lesson named this shearwater in honor of Dr. Felix-Louis l'Herminier (1779–1833) and/or Dr. Ferdinand J. l'Herminier (1802–1866). They were father and son French naturalists.

French Name: Puffin d'Audubon
Spanish Name: Pardela de Audubon
Other Names: Dusky Shearwater; Audubon's Dusky Shearwater; Cahen; Diablotin; Pampero; Pimleco; Rie; Wedrego

Order Ciconiiformes

Family Ciconiidae
Storks

Stork stems from the Old English *storc* and may be a cognate of *stark* (Middle English stiff; strong) and starch, the significance being to the bird's rigid manner. Another idea is that *storc* means "stick" and refers to the stick-like legs. The family name is derived from the Latin *ciconia* (a stork).

Wood Stork
Mycteria americana
(mick-TEER-ih-ah ah-mer-ih-KANE-ah)

The Wood Stork is named for its breeding habitat, stands of huge bald cypress in southern swamps. Known as Wood Ibis until 1983.

Mycteria — The genus name means "resembling a snout" from the Greek *mukter* (a snout) with the Latin suffix *–ius* (resembling) and refers to the stork's long, heavy bill.

americana — The specific epithet is Modern Latin for "of America" where this is the only native stork (north of Mexico).

French Name: Tantale d'Amérique
Spanish Names: Cigueña Americana; Ciguenón

Other Names: American Wood Stork; Wood-Pelican; American Jabiru; Flinthead; Ironhead; Hammerhead; Gourd; Gourdhead; Plumber; Preacher; Gannet; Colorado Turkey; Spanish Buzzard; Blue Charley; Cayama; Coco; Faisán; Flamant

Wood Stork and Roseate Spoonbill, by Allan C. Brooks

Order Suliformes

Family Fregatidae
Frigatebirds

These seabirds are named for light three-mast pirate ships or war vessels. The significance is to these birds' habit of pirating fish from other seabirds, including boobies, pelicans, gulls, and terns, a behavior known scientifically as kleptoparasitism. See Parasitic Jaeger for details. John Terres adds that the "name [was] applied to frigatebirds apparently because of a similarity to a frigate in their light speedy flight, sail-like wings, and marauding habits."

Magnificent Frigatebird
Fregata magnificens
(freh-GAY-tah mag-NIF-ih-senz)

"This well-known buccaneer is widely distributed over the warmer waters and tropical coasts of both hemispheres... Its popular names, man-o'-war-bird, frigate bird, or frigate pelican, reflect its well-known character as a pirate and a tyrannical freebooter. But, with all its faults, it is a picturesque character and one cannot help admiring its wonderful aerial evolutions, for which it is so highly specialized, and which make it such a noticeable and interesting feature in the bird life of tropical seas." — Arthur Cleveland Bent (1922)

The Magnificent Frigatebird is named for its very large, impressive size. With a length of 45 inches and a wingspan up to 96 inches this is the largest of the five frigatebird species. Known as Man-o'war-bird until 1957.

Fregata — The genus name is the Italian word for "frigate."

magnificens — The specific epithet is Latin for "magnificent" or "splendid," referring to the bird's large size.

Magnificent Frigatebird, by John James Audubon

French Name: Frégate Superbe
Spanish Names: Fragata Magnífica; Rabihorcado Magno
Other Names: Man-o-war; Spanish Man-of-war; Frégate; Frigate Pelican; Hurricane Bird; Weather Bird; Cobbler; Gull Hawk; Scissors-tail; Queue en-cisseaux; Tijerilla; Tijereta; Rabijorcado; Rabijunco

Family Sulidae
Boobies and Gannets

"Boobies are so named because some people feel they look stupid or act stupid. They cannot seem to learn that man is their enemy. They earned their name years ago, partly from their appearance, partly from their habit of landing on sailing ships and sitting quietly in the rigging for a hungry sailor to grab." — Oliver L. Austin, Jr. (1961)

Booby stems from the Spanish *bobo* (a dunce) which comes from the Latin *balbus* (stammering). Sailors apparently named the birds, because they were so tame and easily caught. Then the ship's cook could prepare a big pot of booby stew. It is not unusual for birds that nest on isolated islands to be trusting, since they have little experience with land predators. The name could also be influenced by the birds' courtship antics. See comments on the Blue-footed Booby. But the booby's skill and grace in flight belies its awkward reputation. Boobies can even snatch flyingfish right out of the air. Gannet is a cognate with goose. See Northern Gannet.

~

Masked Booby
Sula dactylatra
(SUE-lah dack-tih-LAY-trah)

The slate-blue facial skin around the eyes and bill forms a mask that gives this booby its name. Formerly known as Blue-faced Booby.

Sula — The genus name is the Icelandic word for "gannet." The name is said to be from the Old Norse *sulan* (a cleft stick) which refers to the gannets' crossed wingtips. The boobies are closely related to the gannets. Or *sula* may mean "sharp eye" from the Gaelic *suil* (the eye) and *ghour* (sharp), for the bird's ability to spot fish from high in the air.

dactylatra — The specific epithet means "black fingers" or "black toes" from the Greek *dactyl* (a finger or a toe) and the Latin *atra* (flat black). Since this bird's feet are yellow, the name probably refers to the black flight feathers, suggesting fingers.

French Name: Fou Masqué
Spanish Names: Bobo Enmarscarado; Bobo Blanco

Other Names: White Booby; Whistling Booby; Fou Blanc

~

Blue-footed Booby
Sula nebouxii
(SUE-lah nee-BOO-ih-eye)

This booby's big, bright blue webbed feet, which remind some of scuba diving flippers, give it its name. The birds prominently display their colorful feet during a courting ritual that has been described as "slapstick." Although the name booby stems from these birds' seemingly foolish tameness, it may also be influenced by their courtship antics as described here:

"Whenever a bird alighted, there was a great deal of squawking and bowing and waddling carried on by it and its mate. In latter March during the mating-season at Tagus Cove, Abemarie Island, they were quite demonstrative, the mated birds seeming to talk to each other, and managing to keep up an incessant racket. One of them as a rule did considerable strutting about, lifting its feet very high with each step, and appearing to us very ridiculous. They made a very elaborate bow uttering one or two short notes at the same time. With the breast almost touching the ground, the neck stretched upwards, and the wings outspread but held vertically, the ceremony of bowing would last for about half a minute." — Edward Winslow Gifford (1913)

Sula — The genus name is the Icelandic word for "gannet." The name is said to be from the Old Norse *sulan* (a cleft stick) which refers to the gannets' crossed wingtips. The boobies are closely related to the gannets. Or *sula* may mean "sharp eye" from the Gaelic *suil* (the eye) and *ghour* (sharp), for the bird's ability to spot fish from high in the air.

nebouxii — The specific epithet honors Dr. Adolphe Simon Neboux (fl. 1840), a French surgeon and naturalist. In November 1836, Dr. Neboux was assigned to the frigate *La Vénus* on her thirty-one month voyage around the world. The main interest was the whaling fishery of the north Pacific Ocean. *La Vénus* sailed along the west coasts of both North and South America, visited the Galapagos and Hawaiian Islands, and also journeyed to Kamchatka and the Bering Sea.

In addition to his medical duties, Dr. Neboux collected natural history specimens at sea and at various stopovers. In 1882, forty-three years after the return of *La Vénus*, Alphonse Milne-Edwards was preparing a review of the gannets and boobies for the *Annales des Sciences Naturelles*. In examming specimens from the *La Vénus* expedition, he discovered one that had been overlooked. It was a species new to science, which he named *Sula Nebouxii* in honor of the ship's surgeon.

French Name: Fou à Pieds Bleus
Spanish Names: Bobo de Patas Azules; Bobo Patiazul
Other Name: Camanay

Brown Booby
Sula leucogaster
(SUE-lah lew-koh-GAS-ter)

The Brown Booby is named for its overall dark brown color except for the white belly.

Sula — The genus name is the Icelandic word for "gannet." The name is said to be from the Old Norse *sulan* (a cleft stick) which refers to the gannets' crossed wingtips. The boobies are closely related to the gannets. Or *sula* may mean "sharp eye" from the Gaelic *suil* (the eye) and *ghour* (sharp), for the bird's ability to spot fish from high in the air.

leucogaster — The specific epithet means "white belly" from the Greek *leukos* (white") and *gaster* (the belly).

French Name: Fou Brun
Spanish Names: Bobo Café; Bobo Vientre-blanco; Bobo Moreno
Other Names: Common Booby; White-bellied Booby; Yellow-footed Booby; Catesby's Booby; Booby Gannet; Brown Gannet; Alcatraz; Bubi Chaleco; Fou brun; Fou noir; Pájara Bobo; Pájaro Bobo Prieto

Red-footed Booby
Sula sula
(SUE-lah SUE-lah)

This species gets its name from its bright coral-red feet.

Sula — The genus/species name is the Icelandic word for "gannet." The name is said to be from the Old Norse *sulan* (a cleft stick) which refers to the gannets' crossed wingtips. The boobies are closely related to the gannets. Or *sula* may mean "sharp eye" from the Gaelic *suil* (the eye) and *ghour* (sharp), for the bird's ability to spot fish from high in the air.

French Name: Fou à Pieds Rouges
Spanish Names: Bobo de Patas Rojas; Bobo Patirrojo
Other Names: Red-faced Booby; Tree Booby; White Booby; Pájaro Booby; Pájaro Bobo Blanco; Bubi Blanco; Boba Blanca; Boba Patirroja; Fou blanc

Northern Gannet
Morus bassanus
(MORE-us bass-AY-nus)

Gannet derives from the Old English *gan* meaning "a gander" or "goose-like," perhaps referring to a superficial similarity between a gannet and a goose. Solan Goose is a nickname for gannet. Solan is from a Scandinavian word meaning "the sea." Northern distinguishes this North Atlantic species from two southern relatives, the Cape Gannet (*M. capensis*) of South Africa and the Australasian Gannet (*M. serrator*).

Morus — The genus name is Latin for "foolish" or "silly," probably for the same reasons the boobies got their name.

Brown Booby, by John James Audubon

bassanus — The specific epithet is Modern Latin for "of Bass Rock" at the mouth of the Firth of Forth in Scotland, where there is a nesting colony.
French Name: Fou de Bassan
Spanish Name: Bobo Norteño
Other Names: Common Gannet; White Gannet; Gan; Mackerel Gant; Herring Gant; Soland; Solan Goose; Bass Goose; Channel Goose; Spectacled Goose; Sula; Sulaire; Fou; Gran Fou; Gaunt Grand Fou; Margot; Jan-van-gent

Family Phalacrocoracidae Cormorants

Cormorant means "sea crow" from the Old French *cormoran* derived from the Latin *corvus* (a crow or raven) and *marinus* (of the sea), descriptive of these birds' black plumage and coastal marine habitat.

Brandt's Cormorant
Phalacrocorax penicillatus
(fal-ah-CROW-kor-acks peen-ih-sil-AY-tus)

The common name commemorates Johaan Friedrich Brandt (1802–1879), the German zoologist who described this species as *Carbo penicillatus* in the *Bulletin de l'Académie Impériale des Sciences de St.-Petersbourg* 3 in 1838. He was the Director of the Zoological Museum at the Academy of Sciences in Saint Petersburg.
Phalacrocorax — The genus name stems from the Latin *phalacrorax*, the name Pliny called the Great Cormorant. It means "bald raven" from the Greek *phalakros* (bald) and *korax* (a raven). Raven refers to the black plumage, bald, perhaps to the bare facial skin.
penicillatus — The specific epithet is from the Latin *penicillus* (an artist's brush or a pencil of hairs) and refers to the neck plumes on breeding birds that suggest a brush's bristles.
French Name: Cormoran de Brandt
Spanish Name: Cormorán de Brandt
Other Names: Brown Cormorant; Penciled Cormorant; Tufted Cormorant; Townsend's Cormorant; Shag

Neotropic Cormorant
Phalacrocorax brasilianus
(fal-ah-CROW-kor-acks bra-sil-ih-AY-nus)

This cormorant is named for its range in the American tropics from Mexico through Central and South America. It just reaches our area in southern Texas. Known as Mexican Cormorant before 1957, then Olivaceous Cormorant until 1998.
Phalacrocorax — The genus name stems from the Latin *phalacrorax*, the name Pliny called the Great Cormorant. It means "bald raven" from the Greek *phalakros* (bald) and *korax* (a raven). Raven refers to the dark plumage, bald, perhaps to the bare facial skin.
brasilianus — The specific epithet is Modern Latin for "of Brazil," where this species occurs.
French Name: Cormoran Vigua
Spanish Name: Cormorán Neotropical
Other Names: Brazilian Cormorant; Mexican Cormorant; Nigger Goose; Water Turkey; Cormoril; Corúa; Corúa de Agua Dulce; Cormoran Olivaceo

Double-crested Cormorant
Phalacrocorax auritus
(fal-ah-CROW-kor-acks aw-RYE-tus)

Double-crested refers to the paired tufts of feathers breeding birds display on either side of the head behind the eyes. These are black in eastern birds, white in western ones. This characteristic is also the source of the specific epithet.
Phalacrocorax — The genus name stems from the Latin *phalacrorax*, the name Pliny called the Great Cormorant. It means "bald raven" from the Greek *phalakros* (bald) and *korax* (a raven). Raven refers to the black plumage, bald, perhaps to the bare facial skin.
auritus — The specific epithet is Latin for "eared" referring to the tufts of feathers suggesting ears that the breeding birds acquire.
French Name: Cormoran à Aigrettes
Spanish Names: Cormorán Orejudo; Cormorán Bicrestado
Eskimo and Inuit Names: Uyalit (long neck); Man-uthl-ka-lik (tongue cut off short)
Other Names: Common Cormorant; Farallon Cormorant; Florida Cormorant;

Double-crested Cormorant, Great Cormorant, and Northern Gannet, by Louis Agassiz Fuertes

White-crested Cormorant; White-tufted Cormorant; Cormoran Crestado; Cormoran Ordinaire; Cormoroe; Cormoril; Corúa; Corúa de Mer; Crow-Duck; Fish Duck; African Pintail; Bull Goose; Irish Goose; Mexican Goose; Nigger Goose; Republican Goose; Saint Paul Goose; Yamhill Goose; Taunton Turkey; Water-Turkey; Double Ender; Lawyer; Margot; Old Horse; McCormack; McCormick; Queen Bird; Gooch; Sgarbh; Shaig; Shag; Black Shag; Shillbird; Snakebird; Soldier; Barneche

Great Cormorant
Phalacrocorax carbo
(fal-ah-CROW-kor-acks CARE-boh)

The common name refers to this bird's large size. At 36 inches long and a weight of more than 7 pounds, this is the largest species of cormorant. Known as European Cormorant until 1957.

Phalacrocorax — The genus name stems from the Latin *phalacrorax*, the name Pliny called the Great Cormorant. It means "bald raven" from the Greek *phalakros* (bald) and *korax* (a raven). Raven refers to the black plumage, bald, perhaps to the bare facial skin. Ernest Choate suggests that bald means "white" as it does in the Bald Eagle. The reference is to the appearance of the breeding European subspecies of the Great Cormorant which acquires white nuptial plumes on the head and neck.

carbo — The specific epithet is Latin for "charcoal" and refers to the blackish plumage.

French Name: Grand Cormoran
Spanish Name: Cormorán Grande
Other Names: Common Cormorant; European Cormorant; Black Cormorant; Cormoran; Sea Crow; Coal Goose; Shag; Scart; Scarf; Sgarbh; Hibling; Gorma; Gormer; Locring; Palmer; Margot; Mochrum Elders; Cow'en Elders; Isle of Wight Parsons; Barneche; Brongie (young)

Red-faced Cormorant
Phalacrocorax urile
(fal-ah-CROW-kor-acks YOU-rile)

Bright red facial skin gives this cormorant its name.

Phalacrocorax — The genus name stems from the Latin *phalacrorax*, the name Pliny called the Great Cormorant. It means "bald raven" from the Greek *phalakros* (bald) and *korax* (a raven). Raven refers to the black plumage, bald, perhaps to the bare facial skin.

urile — The specific epithet is believed to be a toponym for the Kurile Island chain (that runs between northern Japan and Kamchatka), where this cormorant formerly occurred. Johann Gmelin named the species in 1789.

French Name: Cormoran à Face Rouge
Spanish Name: Cormorán de Cara Roja
Eskimo Name: Ing-a-tohh

Pelagic Cormorant
Phalacrocorax pelagicus
(fal-ah-CROW-kor-acks peh-LADGE-ih-kus)

Pelagic refers to this bird's marine habitat along the seacoast. The name is a bit misleading, because this is a bird of inshore waters, not the open ocean. It does range out further to sea than most coastal birds.

Phalacrocorax — The genus name stems from the Latin *phalacrorax*, the name Pliny called the Great Cormorant. It means "bald raven" from the Greek *phalakros* (bald) and *korax* (a raven). Raven refers to the black plumage, bald, perhaps, to the bare facial skin.

pelagicus — The specific epithet is Latin for "marine" or "pelagic" from the Greek *pelagos* (the sea.). See common name above.

French Name: Cormoran Pélagique
Spanish Name: Cormorán Pelágico
Eskimo Name: Ug-a-zhuk (cliff dweller)
Other Names: Baird's Cormorant; Violet Cormorant; Violet-green Cormorant

Family Anhingidae
Darters

Darter is the standard common name for birds in this family. It refers to the fast fish-spearing motion of the head and neck.

Anhinga
Anhinga anhinga
(an-HING-ah an-HING-ah)

"In the swamps and marshy lakes of Florida, where the shores are overgrown with rank vegetation and the stately cypress trees are draped with long festoons of Spanish moss, or in the sluggish streams half choked with water hyacinths, "bonnets" and "water lettuce," where the deadly moccasin lurks concealed in the dense vegetation, where the gayly colored purple gallinules patter over the lily pads and where the beautiful snowy herons and many others of their tribe flourish in their native solitudes, there may we look for these curious birds... The anhinga is a water bird surely enough, but I could never see any resemblance to a turkey, and I cannot understand how this name happened to be applied to it. The name "darter" or "snake bird," both of which are descriptive, seem much more appropriate." — Arthur Cleveland Bent (1922)

Anhinga — The only bird whose common, genus, and specific names are identical. Anhingá or anhangá is derived from *ayinga*, which in the folklore of the Tupi (Brazilian) Indians, refers to a malevolent forest spirit. As applied to the bird, it translates to "devil bird," presumably because the Tupi people believed the Anhinga to be an evil spirit. Known as Water Turkey until 1957.

French Name: Anhinga d'Amérique
Spanish Names: Anhinga Americana; Pato Abuja
Other Names: American Anhinga; Snakebird; American Darter; Black Darter; Black-bellied Darter; White-bellied Darter; Water Crow; Grecian Lady; Corúa Real; Bec-a-lancette; Bec-a-lancette-des-bois; Gannet; Marbella

---

Sidebar 18
The Anhinga's Folk Names

The Anhinga's folk names are particularly descriptive. Its former name Water-turkey seems peculiar, because at first glance there is nothing especially turkey-like about an Anhinga. But the name becomes apparent when you see the long tail fanned out like that of a strutting gobbler. Old World members of the genus are called Darters. The name refers to the quick motion of the head when the bird spears a fish with its sharp bill. The Anhinga's black plumage prompted the name Water Crow. The bird's Creole name bec-a-lancette translates to "beak like a lance," for the sharp, thin bill. Snakebird, probably the most widely used of the Anhinga's alternate names, is descriptive of the long, slender, sinuous neck. Anhingas typically swim with the body entirely submerged and only the head and serpentine neck visible above the water. Early European explorers speculated the Anhinga was some bizarre duck x serpent hybrid. Grecian Lady, a name used in parts of Florida, refers to the gracefully curved neck.

Order Pelecaniformes

Family Pelecanidae
Pelicans

Pelican derives from the Greek *pelikas* (a woodpecker), which stems from *pelekus* (an axe) referring to the fact that woodpeckers chisel wood. Over time pelican was applied to other birds noted for their large bills. Pelecanus was even used for a synonym for the spoonbill. Now it applies to these well-known large aquatic birds.

American White Pelican
Pelecanus erythrorhynchos
(pel-ee-KAY-nus er-ith-roh-RING-koss)

"Although ungainly in form and massive in size, weighing from 15 to 20 pounds and stretching from 8 to 10 feet in alar expanse, the white pelican is really a glorious bird, the spotless purity of its snow-white plumage offset by its glossy black wing feathers and enriched by its deep orange bill and feet." — Arthur Cleveland Bent (1922)

Pelecanus — The genus name is the Latinized form of the common name. See above.

erythrorhynchos — The specific epithet means "red beak" from the Greek *erythros* (red) and *rhyncos* (the beak). The White Pelican's bill is yellow to pale orange through most of the year, but it deepens to a vivid orange during the breeding season. At this time the adults develop a vertical horny plate on the upper mandible, which is shed when the eggs are laid. American distinguishes our species from several other species of white pelican elsewhere in the world.

French Name: Pélican d'Amérique
Spanish Name: Pelícano Blanco Americano
Other Names: Common Pelican; Rough-billed Pelican; Pelicano Blanco; Alcatraz Blanco; Grand Gasier

Brown Pelican
Pelecanus occidentalis
(pel-ee-KAY-nus ock-sih-den-TAY-liss)

The gray-brown feathers of the body and the chestnut-brown hind-neck give this pelican its name.

Pelecanus — The genus name is the Latinized form of the common name. See above.

occidentalis — The specific epithet means "western" from the Latin *occidere* (to fall or set, as of the sun in the west). The reference is

Brown Pelican, by John James Audubon

> **Sidebar 19**
> **Thunder Pumper; Sky-gazer**
>
> "Suddenly a succession of snappings and gulpings, to fill its lungs with air, convulses the creature, and then three booming bellowings come forth with gestures that suggest horrible nausea. One who did not see the bird in the act of making these noises would imagine from their quality that they came from below the water, and there are many stories in circulation among people who do not go to the pains to verify them, that water is actually swallowed and ejected by bitterns to assist their voices; but it is not." — Neltje Blanchan (1898)
>
> The American Bittern's booming song has given rise to a number of onomatopoetic folk names. Some examples are: Thunder Pumper, Stake-driver, Belcher-squelcher, Bog-bull, Dunk-a-doo, Punkatunk, and Oomptah. Folklore has it that the large bitterns (*Botaurus* species) make their distinctive sound by piercing a hollow reed with the bill and blowing through it. Another idea was that the sound comes from the bill being thrust deep into the mire and blowing into the saturated soil. The bittern's eerie song has actually creeped out people. It is said that soldiers crossing a marsh in northern Spain were terrorized by the sounds of Eurasian Bitterns, and in 1786, New England Puritans invaded swamps around a Connecticut village to rid themselves of the evil sound. Another group of colloquial names, Sky-gazer, Sun-gazer, Look-up, and Visionnaire, are derived from the bittern's defensive behavior of freezing, neck outstretched, feathers compressed, bill pointing skyward. When among tall reeds, the stripes on the bird's throat and breast help it to blend in perfectly. It will even sway to mimic the movement of the reeds in the breeze. But bitterns have also been known to sky-point when out in the open as on someone's front lawn.

to the Brown Pelican's range in the Western Hemisphere. Five of the seven pelican species of pelicans are Old World birds.
French Name: Pélican Brun
Spanish Names: Pelícano Café; Pelícano Pardo
Other Names: Common Pelican; American Brown Pelican; California Brown Pelican; Pelican of the Wilderness; Joe Bird; Old Joe; Old Tom; Alcatraz; Grand Gosier

~

Family Ardeidae
Bitterns, Herons, and Allies

American Bittern
Botaurus lentiginosus
(boh-TAR-us len-tih-jin-OH-sus)

Bittern stems from the Middle English *bittour/botor* from Old French *butor* which comes from the Latin *butitaurus* (a bird that bellows like an ox). The song is sometimes rendered *oong-ka choonk, oong-ka choonk, oong-ka choonk*. Neltje Blanchan wrote that the bittern "has for its love song the most dismal, hollow bellow, that comes booming from the marshes at evening, a mile away, with a gruesome solemnity." American distinguishes our species from the Eurasian Bittern (*B. stellaris*).

Botaurus — The genus name is derived from the Latin *bos* (an ox) and *taurus* (a bull). The reference is to the bittern's booming song suggesting the bellowing of a bull.

lentiginosus — The specific epithet is Latin for "freckled with lentil-shaped spots" and refers to the small speckles on the bird's upperparts.

French Name: Butor d'Amérique
Spanish Names: Avetoro Norteño; Aviator Americano; Aviator Norteño
Other Names: Booming Bittern; Rice Lake Bittern; Freckled Heron; Pumper; Pump Bird; Thunder Pumper; Pump-thunder; Devil's Pump; Mud Pump; Mud Pumper; Bog Pumper; Slough Pump; Slough Punk;

Slug-toot; Stake-bird; Indian Stake-bird; Stake-driver; Pile-driver; Belcher-squelcher; Water-belcher; Bog-bull; Bull of the Bog; Bull of the Mire; Bog-pumping Hell-driver; Pile-driver; Big Water Hen; Bog Hen; Grass Hen; Heath Hen; Indiana Hen; Marsh Hen; Spotted Marsh Hen; Meadow Hen; Mud Hen; Night Hen; Sedge Hen; Weed Hen; Indian Hen; Indian Pullet; Fool Fowl; Heather Bluiter; Heather Blutter; Full Pot; Caulker; Corker; Fly-up-the-creek; Mire Drum; Bog Drum; Bog Blutter; Bog Bumper; Bog-trotter; Pond Guinea; Barrel-maker; Hit-log; Pine Knot; Bitter Bum; Bumble; Bottle Bump; Butterbump; Butter-bird; Boom Bird; Bill-gudgeon; Plumgudgeon; Dunk-a-doo; Sky-gazer; Sun-gazer; Look-up; Flying Fox; Poke; Shitepoke; Shitipoke; Snake-eater; Punkatunk; Oomptah; Jack Grindle; Scoggin; Sibitron; Jeune Grue; Garde-soleil;

Sidebar 20
The Enigmatic Cory's Least Bittern

In 1885, Boston ornithologist Charles B. Cory described what he believed to be a new species of heron, from a specimen collected on the Caloosahatchee River near Lake Okeechobee, Florida. He gave it the name *Ixobrychus neoxenus*, and it came to be known as Cory's Least Bittern or just Cory's Bittern. Cory wrote that the specimen was "without doubt perfectly distinct from any other known species." His specific epithet *neoxenus* means "new stranger" in Greek. Cory's Least Bittern was initially accepted as a distinct species, but by 1892, its validity was being questioned, and the AOU dropped it from their checklist in 1923. It is now regarded as a very rare erythristic color morph of the Least Bittern. Cory's Least Bittern is a rich chestnut where the typical form is pale yellowish-buff, and its upperparts are black rather than brown. Only thirty-eight specimens are known, twenty-two of these from Ontario, Canada. Other specimens are from Wisconsin, Michigan, Illinois, Ohio, New York, Florida, and Brazil. There have been only six records since the 1950s.

Least Bittern, by R. Bruce Horsfall

Gros-bec-a-gilet; Cou Long; Ave Toro; Biorque; Buncom; Butor; Bittour; Buttal; Bumpy Cors; Bumpy Coss; Clabitter; Quac; Visionnaire; Yaboa Americana; Guanabá Rojo

Least Bittern
Ixobrychus exilis
(icks-OBE-rih-kus ecks-EYE-liss)

Least refers to the small size. Not much larger than a Red-winged Blackbird, the Least Bittern is not only the smallest bittern, but it is also the smallest heron in North America.

Ixobrychus — The genus name means "mistletoe roarer" or "mistletoe boomer" from the Greek *ixos* (mistletoe) and *brukhao* (to roar or to bellow). What the author Gustav Billberg meant was "reed boomer" from the Greek *ixias* (a reed). The reference is to a superstition that the large bitterns (*Botaurus* sp.) make their distinctive booming sounds by piercing a hollow reed with the bill and blowing through it like a musical instrument.

Ernest Choate wrote, "One wonders whether he [Billberg] ever heard the series of soft coos of the Least Bittern."

exilis — The specific epithet is Latin for "little or slender."

French Name: Petit Blongios

Spanish Names: Avetoro Mínimo; Avetorito Americano; Avetorillo Pantanero

Other Names: Dwarf Bittern; Little Bittern; Bittlin; Least Heron; Little Heron; Fly-up-the-creek; Kite; Strike-fire; Crabier; Garcita; Gaulin; Garde soleil; Jean Charlot; Martin García; Martinete; Martinetite; Martinetito; Cop-cop Dore; Veux Clairs

Great Blue Heron
Ardea herodias
(AR-dee-ah her-ODE-ih-us)

"The name says it all." — Pete Dunne (2006)

Heron comes from the Old French *hairon* which stems from the Old High German *heiger* "a heron." The Old English name *hragra* is believed to be imitative of the birds' harsh call. This largest North American heron is named for its large size (standing nearly 4 feet tall with a 6 foot wingspan) and its blue-gray plumage. A white morph found in Florida was formerly considered a full species, the Great White Heron (*A. occidentalis*).

Ardea — The genus name is the Latin word for "heron." This stems from a Roman myth in which Ardea, capital of Rutuli, was burned to the ground. A slender, pale bird, shaking cinders from its wings and calling mournfully, rose from the ashes.

herodias — The specific epithet stems from *erodios* the Greek word for "a heron."

French Name: Grand Héron

Spanish Names: Garzón Cenizo; Garzón Azulado

Other Names: Treganza's Heron; Red-shouldered Heron; Great Heron Blue; Heron Bleu; Heron Brun; California Heron; Espiritu Santo Heron; Florida Heron; Noisy Heron; Northwestern Coast Heron; San Lucas Heron; Ward Heron; hern; Crane; Blue Crane; White Crane; Common Crane; Common Blue Crane; Gray Crane; Fish Crane; Water Crane; Benson's Turkey; Colorado Turkey; Blue Herring; Blue Gaulin; Grey Gaulin; Big Cranky; Poor Joe; Po Joe; Po Job; Blue John; Long John; Long Tom; Gandersnipe; Horse Gannet; Powder Touch; Jackerne; Morgan; Preacher; the Major; Forty Gallons of Soup; Butor; Shit Streaker; Shit-a-stream; San Joie; Arse-nicker; Hamlet-bud Dem; Hamlin; Corr; Corra-ghritheach; Hamlin; Couac; Gironde; Grue; Gum Coat; Guardacosta; Crabier Noir; White Gaulin; Garcilote; Garzón Blanco; Garzón Ceniciento; Lopann

Great Egret
Ardea alba
(AR-dee-ah AL-bah)

Egret stems from the French *aigrette* (an egret or little heron). This in turn comes from the Old High German *heigir* "a heron." Replace the 'ir' with the diminutive suffix *–ette* and you have *heigrette* (little heron). The name was first applied to the Little Egret (*Egretta garzetta*) of the Old World. The Great Egret is the largest of the white egrets. Known as American Egret before 1957; then Common Egret until 1983. Aigrette is also the name of the lacy nuptial plumes the adults sport during the nesting season. These almost doomed the birds, because they became high fashion in the late 19th and early 20th centuries. The plumes were used for decorations on women's hats, and shamefully thousands of birds were killed for vanity. This continued until there was a public outcry, regional Audubon societies were formed, and legislation passed to protect the birds. A Great Egret in flight is the emblem of the National Audubon Society.

Ardea — The genus name is the Latin word for "heron." This stems from a Roman myth in which Ardea, capital of Rutuli, was burned to the ground. A slender, pale bird, shaking cinders from its wings and calling mournfully, rose from the ashes.

alba — The specific epithet is Latin for "white" referring to the pure white plumage.

French Name: Grande Aigrette

Spanish Names: Garza Blanca; Garza Grande; Garceta Grande

Other Names: White Egret; Great White Egret; American Great White Egret; Greater Egret; White Heron; Grand Heron Blanc; Great White Heron; Greater Heron; Florida Heron; White Crane; Angel Bird; Plume Bird; Big

Plume Bird; Long White; White Morgan; White Gaulin; Garza Blanca; Garza Real; Garzón; Garzón Blanco; Crabier Blanc

Snowy Egret
Egretta thula
(ee-GRET-ah THOO-lah)

"This beautiful little heron, one of nature's daintiest and most exquisite creatures, is the most charming of all our marsh birds. The spotless purity of its snowy plumage, adorned with airy, waving plumes, and its gentle, graceful manners, make it the center of attraction wherever it is seen." — Arthur Cleveland Bent (1927)

This small egret is named for its snowy white plumage. Breeding adults also sport the filmy plumes, and like the Great Egret, they were victims of the millinery trade. See sidebar 20.

Egretta — The genus name is the Latinized form of egret. Egret stems from the French *aigrette* (an egret or little heron). This in turn comes from the Old High German *heigir* "a heron." Replace the (*ir*) with the diminutive suffix *–ette* and you have *heigrette* (little heron). The name was first applied to the Little Egret (*Egretta garzetta*) of the Old World.

thula — Most sources say the specific epithet is the Chilean word for Snowy Egret. But James Jobling says *thula* is the Araucano (Chilean) Indian name for the Black-necked Swan (*Cygnus melanocoryphus*) and was applied to the egret by mistake.

French Name: Aigrette Neigeuse
Spanish Names: Garza de Dedos Dorados; Garza Nivea; Garceta Nivosa
Other Names: Brewster's Egret; Common Egret; Lesser Egret; Little Egret; Little White Egret; Little Snowy; Little White Heron; Snowy Heron; Heron Blanc; Small Plume Bird; Poor Job; Bonnet Martyr; Golden Slippers; Yellow-tail; Yaller-tail; Aigrette blanche; Crabier Blanc; Garza Blanca; Garza de Rizos; Garza Real; White Gaulin

Little Blue Heron
Egretta caerulea
(ee-GRET-ah see-RULE-ee-ah)

The Little Blue Heron is considerably smaller than the Great Blue, about the size of a Snowy Egret. Blue describes the overall dark slate-blue color of the plumage, although the head and neck show maroon shadings. Juveniles are white.

Egretta — The genus name is the Latinized form of egret. Egret stems from the French *aigrette* (an egret or little heron). This in turn comes from the Old High German *heigir* "a heron." Replace the (*ir*) with the diminutive suffix *–ette* and you have *heigrette* (little heron). The name was first applied to the Little Egret (*Egretta garzetta*) of the Old World.

caerulea — The specific epithet is Latin for "blue." It can mean either sky blue or dark blue. In this case it is the latter that describes the slaty color of this heron.

French Name: Aigrette Bleue
Spanish Names: Garza Azul; Garceta Azul
Other Names: Calico Heron; Crazy Heron; Blue Heron; Blue Egret; Blue Crane; Little Blue Crane; Little White Crane; White Crane; Spotted Crane; Egrette bleue; Egrette folle; Aligrette blanche; Aligrette bleue; Levee Walker; Crabier Blanc; Crabier Noir; Garza Azul; Garza Blanca; Garza Común; Garza Pinta Blue Gaulin; White Gaulin; Skoggin; Blue Skoggin

Tricolored Heron
Egretta tricolor
(ee-GRET-ah TRI-cull-or)

Tricolored describes this heron's three colors: slate blue above with rusty highlights and a white belly. Known as Louisiana Heron until 1983.

Tricolored Heron, by John James Audubon

Sidebar 21
Long Whites, Short Whites, Little Snowies, and Bonnet Martyrs

The above nicknames for the Great Egret and Snowy Egret come from one of the darkest periods in the history of American ornithology. The late 19th and early 20th centuries saw a fad in which feathers were in high fashion for the millinery trade. The white egrets were hit especially hard. It was estimated that during the 1890s, five million birds were being killed each year. The white egrets sported their elegant plumes only during the nesting season. So when the adults were killed, the eggs and young were left to die in the nest. So it is clear the birds were in danger of extinction. Long White was the plume hunter's name for the Great Egret, referring to its long, lacy plumes called aigrettes in contrast to the shorter but no less elegant ones of the Snowy Egret. The Snowy Egrets were known as Little Snowies or Short Whites. The plumes were worth twice their weight in gold. The Great Egret was the Big Plume Bird, the Snowy the Small Plume Bird. The Snowy's other nickname from the period Bonnet Martyr is particularly apt. Gulls and terns were nearly wiped out as well. This time it was for their wings. And smaller species were used in their entirety, arranged in artistic fashion on milady's chapeau. On two afternoons in 1886, ornithologist Frank Chapman conducted a bird census on 14th Street in Manhattan. He spotted game-birds, grebes, shorebirds, woodpeckers, an owl, and songbirds. Only the birds Chapman was counting weren't living. They were dead ones on the hats of "fashionable" women. He recorded 40 species in all. Here is his tally: 16 Northern Bobwhite, 2 California Quail, 2 Ruffed Grouse, 1 Greater Prairie Chicken, 7 grebes, 1 Green Heron. 1 Virginia Rail, 1 Greater Yellowlegs, 5 Sanderlings, 1 Laughing Gull, 21 Common Terns, 1 Black Tern, 1 Mourning Dove, 1 Northern Saw-whet Owl, 21 Northern Flickers, 2 Red-headed Woodpeckers, 1 Pileated Woodpecker, 1 Eastern Kingbird, 1 Scissor-tailed Flycatcher, 1 Tree Swallow, 5 Blue Jays, 3 Eastern Bluebirds, 4 American Robins, 1 Northern Shrike, 1 Brown Thrasher, 15 Snow Buntings, 1 Bohemian Waxwing, 23 Cedar Waxwings, 1 Blackburnian Warbler, 3 Blackpoll Warblers, 3 Wilson's Warblers, 2 American Tree Sparrows, 1 White-throated Sparrow, 1 Bobolink, 2 Meadowlarks, 5 Common Grackles, 9 Baltimore Orioles, 3 Scarlet Tanagers, and 1 Pine Grosbeak. Eventually all this carnage drew outrage from the general public and began the Audubon movement. George Bird Grinnell, editor of *Forest and Stream* magazine, founded the first Audubon Society in 1886. Although it attained a membership of 48,862 including such prominent citizens as Henry Ward Beecher, Oliver Wendell Holmes, Jr. and John Greenleaf Whittier, the organization folded in just a few years. In 1896, Boston socialite Harriet Hemenway and her cousin Mina Hall founded the Massachusetts Audubon Society. Their goal was to persuade women to avoid feathered hats. In just a couple years there were Audubon Societies in many states. In 1905, the state organizations came together as the National Association of Audubon Societies (now the National Audubon Society). In 1902, the AOU at the bequest of the Florida Audubon Society hired a warden, Guy Bradley, to patrol the Gulf Coast of Florida. Bradley, a reformed plume hunter, became a bonnet martyr himself when he was shot and killed in 1905 by the poachers he was attempting to arrest. In 1908, two more wardens were murdered in the line of duty. But public pressure eventually saw results. Important legislation was passed to protect birds and other wildlife, most notably the Lacey Act of 1900 and the Migratory Bird Treaty Act in 1918. So today we still have the egrets and other birds that were nearly wiped out 100 years ago.

Egretta — The genus name is the Latinized form of egret. Egret stems from the French *aigrette* (an egret or little heron). This in turn comes from the Old High German *heigir* "a heron." Replace the (*ir*) with the diminutive suffix –*ette* and you have *heigrette* (little heron). The name was first applied to the Little Egret (*Egretta garzetta*) of the Old World.

tricolor — The specific epithet is Latin for "of three colors." See common name above.

French Name: Aigrette Tricolore

Spanish Names: Garza Tricolor; Garceta Tricolor

Other Names: Silver-gray Heron; Heron Dos-blanc; Louisiana Egret; Crane; Blue Crane; Lady-of-the-Waters; Switching-neck; Aigrette Caille; Egrette Folle; Demoiselle; Demonoiselle; Crabier; Gaulin; Garza Morada; Garza Perchiblanca; Garza de Vientre Blanco; Skoggin

Reddish Egret
Egretta rufescens
(ee-GRET-ah roof-ESS-enz)

The rusty red head and neck of the dark morph give this egret its name. The body is slate blue. It also occurs in a white morph. Audubon thought the latter to be the immature. Charles Bonaparte described it as a distinct species, naming it Peale's Egret in honor of artist and naturalist Titian Ramsay Peale.

Egretta — The genus name is the Latinized form of egret. Egret stems from the French *aigrette* (an egret or little heron). This in turn comes from the Old High German *heigir* "a heron." Replace the (*ir*) with the diminutive suffix –*ette* and you have *heigrette* (little heron). The name was first applied to the Little Egret (*Egretta garzetta*) of the Old World.

rufescens — The specific epithet is Latin for "reddish."

French Name: Aigrette Roussâtre

Spanish Names: Garza Rojiza; Garceta Rojiza

Other Names: Peale's Egret; Muffle-jawed Egret; Purple Heron; Reddish Heron; Plume Bird; Crabier; Gaulin; Garza; Garza Rojiza

Cattle Egret
Bubulcus ibis
(BUE-bul-kus EYE-bis)

This egret is named for its association with cattle. The birds forage in pastures, feeding on grasshoppers and other insects flushed by the livestock as they graze. They will also follow tractors and mowing machines for the same reason. On the African plains, Cattle Egrets associate with elephants, Cape buffalo, zebras, and other large grazers, sometimes even perching on the animals' backs.

Bubulcus — The genus name is Latin for "herdsman" or "a ploughman that ploughs with oxen," a reference to these birds' associating with cattle. See common name above.

ibis — The specific epithet apparently refers to the Sacred Ibis (*Threskiornis aethiopica*), perhaps for a superficial resemblance between these two wading birds.

French Name: Héron Garde-boeufs

Spanish Names: Garza Ganadera; Garcilla Buyerera

Other Names: Cattle Heron; Buff-backed Heron; Cattle Gaulin; Crabier; Cowbird; Tick Bird; Garde-boeuf; Crabier Garde-boeuf; Garrapatosa; Garza del Ganado; Garza Ganadero; Garza Africana

Green Heron
Butorides virescens
(bew-tor-EYE-deez vie-RES-enz)

The Green Heron is named for the greenish gloss on the back, wings, and crown. Briefly known as Green-backed Heron.

Butorides — The genus name means "resembling a bittern" from the Latin *butor* (a bittern) and the Greek suffix –*ides* (resembling). Perhaps to its similarity to a bittern, especially the juvenile whose neck and breast are streaked like a bittern's.

Reddish Egret, by John James Audubon

Green Heron, by R. Bruce Horsfall

virescens — The specific epithet is Latin for "greenish."
French Name: Héron Vert
Spanish Names: Garceta Verde; Garza Verde; Garcella Verde
Other Names: Anthony Green Heron; Frazar Green Heron; Little Green Heron; Indian Heron; Indian Pullet; Heron Vert; Green Bittern; Blue Bittern; Bitlin; Swamp Squaggin; Poke; Shitepoke; Poor Joe; Chalk-line; Chuckle-head; Fly-up-the-creek; Water Witch; Crab-catcher; Crabier; Caäli; Cagón; Caga-leche; Cop-cop; Cra-cra; Cuaco; Gaulin; Green Gaulin; Least Pond Gaulin; Little Gaulin; Martinete; Petit Butor; Gaulching; Kio; Rac-rac; Skeow; Skow; Aguaita Caimán; Calet de Caïman

Black-crowned Night-Heron
Nycticorax nycticorax
(nick-TICK-or-acks)

Night-Herons are so named, because of their largely, but not strictly, nocturnal habits. They are frequently seen at dusk as they fly off to forage. This species is named for its black cap; the back is black, too.
Nycticorax — The genus/species name means "night raven" from the Greek *nyktos* (night) and *korax* (a raven). The name refers to this bird's harsh raven-like call.
French Name: Bihoreau Gris
Spanish Names: Pedrete de Corona Negra; Garza-nocturna Coroninegra; Martinete Coroninegra
Other Names: American Night Heron; Bancroft's Night-Heron; Night Crane; Gaedenian Heron; Night Gaulin; Night Hawk; Night Scoggins; Big Water Hen; Indian Hen; Indian Pullet; Marsh Hen; Meadow Hen; Mud Hen; Murrell Hen; Night Hen; Swamp Hen; Merle; Fox Bird; Squaw Bird; Red-eye; Crab Catcher; Crabier; Coq d'Eau; Coq de Nuit; Gallinaza; Gros-bec; gros-bec Dos-sole; Velvet-backed Gros-bec; Winter Gros-bec; Gallinaza; Gaulin; Night Gaulin; Guanabá de la Florida; Guanabá Lominegro; Qua-bird; Quac; Quok; Quawk; Rey Congo; Squawk; Yaboa Real

Yellow-crowned Night-Heron
Nyctanassa violacea
(nick-tan-ASS-ah vie-oh-LAY-see-ah)

This heron's pale yellow crown gives it its name.
Nyctanassa — The genus name means "night queen" from the Greek *nyktos* (night) and *anassa* (a queen).
violacea — The specific epithet is Latin for "violet-colored," a little bit of an exaggeration for the pale gray plumage.
French Name: Bihoreau Violacé
Spanish Names: Pedrete de Corona Clara; Garza-nocturna Coroniclara; Martinete Cabecipinto
Other Names: Lesser Ash-colored Heron; Crab-catcher Crab-eater; Fish Crane; Brown Bittern; Crested Bittern; Indian Hen; Indian Pullet; Coq d;Eau; Coq de Nuit; Crabier Gris; Crabier de Bois; Crabier de Montagne; Gallinaza; Gray Gaulin; Night Gaulin; Night Scoggins; Gros-bec; Bald-headed Gros-bec; White-jaw Gros-bec; Guanabá; Guanabá Real; Qua-bird; Quok; Quawk; Squark; Squawk; Yaboa; Yaboa Común

Family Threskiornithidae
Ibises and Spoonbills

Ibis from the Latin and Greek derives from the Egyptian name for the Sacred Ibis (*Threskiornis aethiopicus*), identified with Thoth, the god of wisdom. Spoonbill describes the bird's flat spatula-shaped bill. The family name stems from the Greek *threskos* (religious) and *ornis* (a bird) and refers to the Sacred Ibis' place in ancient Egyptian religion.

White Ibis
Eudocimus albus
(you-DOSS-ih-mus AL-bus)

This ibis is named for the adult's all white plumage, except for the black tips of the primaries. The juveniles are brown.

Eudocimus — The genus name derives from the Greek *eudokimos* (famous, in good standing, or of high repute). The reference is to the Sacred Ibis (*Threskiornis aethiopica*) of Africa. The ancient Egyptians venerated the ibis in their religion, identifying it with the god Thoth, the scribe of the gods. His duty was to record the life story of every individual. Thoth is depicted in art as a man with the head of an ibis.

An alternative explanation has to do with the White Ibis' reclassification. It was originally placed in the genus *Scolopax*. German ornithologist Johann Georg Wagler, quite correctly removed the White Ibis from that genus, where it had been placed in the company of the European Woodcock, and put it into a new genus, *Eudocimus*, which is in an entirely different scientific order. It is said that Wagler could not resist naming the genus after his accomplishment in placing the bird in a scientific classification in good standing.

albus — The specific epithet is Latin for "white."

French Name: Ibis Blanc
Spanish Name: Ibis Blanco
Other Names: White Curlew; Brown Curlew (juvenile); Stone Curlew; Spanish Curlew; Chukoloskee Chicken; Ibis Blanco; Bec-croche; Coco; Coco Blanco; Gant Blanc

Glossy Ibis
Plegadis falcinellus
(PLEG-ah-dis fal-sin-EE-lus)

"Its dark plumage shines in bronzes and purples." — Oliver L. Austin, Jr. (1961)

The green and rose iridescence on blackish wings give this ibis its name.

Plegadis — The genus name is Greek for "a sickle" or "a scythe" and refers to the long, curved bill.

falcinellus — The specific epithet means "little sickle" from the Latin *falx* (a sickle) plus the diminutive suffix *–ellus*.

French Name: Ibis Falcinelle
Spanish Names: Ibis de Cara Oscura; Ibis Lustroso; Ibis Morito
Other Names: Eastern Glossy Ibis; Green Ibis; Bay Ibis; Ord's Ibis; Curlew; Black Curlew; Liver; Black Bec-croche; Ciguena; Coco; Coco Oscuro; Coco Prieto; Ibis Lustroso; Pêcheur

White-faced Ibis
Plegadis chihi
(PLEG-ah-dis CHEE-he)

This ibis gets its name from the line of white border that frames its face during the breeding season.

Plegadis — The genus name is Greek for "a sickle" or "a scythe" and refers to the long, curved bill.

chihi — The specific epithet is possibly a native South American word for this bird. Or it may simply be an imitative name, that French ornithologist Louis Jean Pierre Vieillot (1748–1831) coined when he described this species.

White-faced Ibis, by Louis Agassiz Fuertes

French Name: Ibis à Face Blanche
Spanish Names: Ibis de Cara Blanca; Ibis Cariblanco
Other Names: White-faced Glossy Ibis; Black Curlew

Roseate Spoonbill
Platalea ajaja
(plah-TALE-ee-ah ah-YAH-yah)

"As we started the outboard again, and headed around the shores of the lagoon, a little group of about a dozen pink and white, heron-like birds flew up from some mangroves, circled once or twice, and lit in the trees not far away. Slowly we approached them, our glasses glued to the spot, until we could get every detail of the beautiful birds, their white necks and breasts, their delicately pink wings with the carmine patch at the shoulders, and even their ugly greenish bare heads with the absurd spoon-like bill, that adds a touch of comedy to what otherwise would be an ideal of beauty. Even when at last they flew off into the distance, we almost held our breaths lest the spell be broken."
— John Bichard May (1925)

Spoonbill refers to the spatulate bill, narrow at the base but wide at the tip. The birds feed by wading in the shallows and swinging the spoon-shaped bill from side to side through the water and mud in search of food. Nerve endings inside the mouth are so sensitive that as soon as the bill touches a fish, crustacean, or other food item, the bill snaps shut trapping the prey. Roseate (rose-colored) refers to the vivid rosy pink plumage with a streak of bright carmine across the lesser wing-coverts. This streak of color is called the drip. As with flamingos, the pink color comes from pigment (carotene) in the crustaceans and other food they eat. Captive birds deprived of a proper diet will fade to white.

Roseate Spoonbill, by John James Audubon

Platalea — The genus name is the Latin word for the White Spoonbill (*P. leucorodia*) of the Old World. Formerly *Ajaia ajaja*.
ajaja — The specific epithet is the Tupi (Brazilian) Indian name for this bird.
French Name: Spatule Rosée
Spanish Name: Espátula Rosada
Other Names: Rosy Spoonbill; Pink Curlew; Pink-Bird; Pinkie; Cuchareta; Espatula Rosada; Sebiya; Espátula; Skatule; Spatule

Order Cathartiformes

Family Cathartidae
New World Vultures

The common name is taken directly from the Old World Vultures, to which the New World species are not closely related. In fact, the family has been removed from the order Falconiformes and placed in its own order. Vulture stems from the Latin *vultur* (a vulture) from the infinitive *vellere* (to tear) which describes their feeding by tearing meat off carcasses.

Black Vulture
Coragyps atratus
(KOR-ah-jips ah-TRAY-tus)

"A vulture dressed for a funeral." — Pete Dunne (2006)

This vulture's all black plumage gives it its name. The only other colors are the dark gray head and the white wingtips the bird shows when in flight.

Coragyps — The genus name means "raven vulture" from the Greek *korax* (a raven) for the black plumage and *gyps* (a vulture), a name Homer used for the Griffon Vulture.

atratus — The specific epithet is Latin for "clothed in black" as for mourning.

French Name: Urubu Noir
Spanish Names: Zopilote Común; Zopilote Negro
Other Names: Black Buzzard; Carrion Crow; Jim Crow; John Crow; Black Scavenger; Scavenger; Carencro Noir

Turkey Vulture
Cathartes aura
(kath-AR-teez OR-ah)

With its bare, red head and dark plumage, this vulture is named for its resemblance to a turkey. In fact, it is said that early settlers occasionally shot vultures, mistaking them for turkeys, but were astonished at mealtime by their dinner's disgusting flavor.

Cathartes — The genus name is from the Greek *kathartes* (a cleanser or purifier) and refers to the role of this bird as a scavenger.

aura — The specific epithet derives from *auroura*, the Mexican Indian name for the Turkey Vulture.

French Name: Urubu à Tête Rouge
Spanish Names: Aura Cabecirrojo; Zopilote Aura; Zopilote Cabecirrojo
Other Names: Buzzard; Turkey Buzzard; Red-headed Turkey-Buzzard; Red-headed Turkey Vulture; California Turkey Vulture; Red-necked Buzzard; Crow; Carrion Crow; King Crow; John Crow; John Crow Vulture; John Crow Headman; Jamaica Turkey; Wild

Turkey Vulture, by R. Bruce Horsfall

Turkey; Aura; Aura Común; Aura Tiñosa; Carencro Tête Rouge; Osa; Osfogel; Luder Fogel; Luder Awdler; Luder Krop

California Condor
Gymnogyps californianus
(JIM-no-jips kal-ih-forn-ih-ANE-us)

Condor is Spanish, derived from *cuntur*, the Quechua (Peruvian) Indian name for the Andean Condor (*Vultur gryphus*). California refers to the range of this dwindling species in modern times. A population from a captive breeding program has since been established at the Grand Canyon.

Gymnogyps — The genus name means "naked vulture" from the Greek *gymnos* (naked) and *gyps* (a vulture), the name Homer used for the Griffon Vulture. The reference is to the condor's bare head.

californianus — The specific epithet is Modern Latin for "of California."

French Name: Condor de Californie
Spanish Name: Cóndor Californiano
Other Names: California Vulture; Great Vulture; Queleli

Order Accipitriformes

Family Pandionidae
Osprey

Osprey
Pandion haliaetus
(pan-DIE-on hal-ih-ay-EE-tus)

Osprey stems from *ossifrage* (bone-breaker) from the Latin *os* (a bone) and *frangere* (to break). The *ossifragus* mentioned by Pliny was a name he used for the Lammergeier or Bearded Vulture (*Gypaetus barbatus*), an Old World species known to drop bones from a considerable height onto rocks in order to break them open so it can get to the marrow inside. Apparently the name was mistakenly applied to the Osprey that feeds primarily on fish.

Pandion — The genus is named for Pandion, a mythical king of Athens whose daughters, Philomena and Procne (See Purple Martin) were changed into a nightingale and a swallow respectively, and whose son-in-law Tereus was turned into a hawk. Ernest Choate speculates that Savigny who erected the genus got the characters mixed up and meant to have named the Osprey for Tereus, the one changed into a hawk. Choate also points out that Tereus in hawk form pursued the two birds that were formerly Philomena and Procne, while the Osprey is a fish-eater. It should be understood, though, that mistakes in etymology do not invalidate the scientific name in any way.

haliaetus — The specific epithet is Greek for "sea eagle" from *halos* (the sea) and *aetos* (an eagle). Ospreys occur along the seacoast and also on the shores of lakes and large rivers.

French Name: Balbuzzard Pêcheur
Spanish Names: Gavilán Pescador; Aguila Pescador
Eskimo and Inuit Names: Kalloksioyuk (goes after fish); A-kum-ku-thlayu-li
Other Names: American Osprey; Common Osprey; Fish Hawk; Fishing Hawk; Sea Hawk; Mullet Hawk; Sea Eagle; Fish Eagle; Fishing Eagle; Common Fish Hawk;Common Brown Fishing Eagle; Eagle Fisher; Bald Buzzard; Aiglon; Aguila de Mar Aigle de Mer; Pêcheur; Aigle pêcheur; Awdler; Fish Awdler; Fish-woi; Grepe; Guincho; Halcón Pescador; Malfini de la Mer; Guaraguao de Mar; Lolair; Uisge; Orfraie

Osprey, by Allen C. Brooks

Family Accipitridae Kites, Hawks, Eagles, and Allies

Kite derives from the Old English *cyta*, a name for two Old World raptors in the genus *Milvus*, the Red Kite (*M. milvus*) and the Black Kite (*M. migrans*). The American kites were named for these, because their light, buoyant flight is similar to the Old World kites. Some authors say that *cyta* is derived from the Aryan *skut* (to shoot or to move swiftly), describing the way kites swoop on prey. The man-made paper kite is named for the birds, not vice versa. Hawk derives from the Teutonic root *haf* or *hab*, which means "to seize." Hawks, of course, being raptors seize prey in their talons. Eagle derives from the Middle English *egle*, which comes from the Anglo-Norman *aigla*, ultimately from *aquila*, the Latin word for "an eagle."

White-tailed Kite
Elanus leucurus
(EL-an-us lew-CURE-us)

This kite is named for its largely white tail, although the central feathers are light gray. Formerly considered conspecific with the Black-shouldered Kite (*Elanus caeruleus*) of the Old World.

Elanus — The genus name is the Latin spelling of the Greek *elanos* (a kite).

leucurus — The specific epithet means "white tail" from the Greek *leukos* (white) and *oura* (the tail).

French Name: Élanion à Queue Blanche
Spanish Names: Milano de Cola Blanca; Milano Coliblanco; Elanio Coliblanco
Other Names: White Hawk; Black-winged Hawk; Black-shouldered Elanus; Angelhawk

Hook-billed Kite
Chondrohierax uncinatus
(kon-droh-HIGH-er-acks un-sin-AY-tus)

This kite's large bill with its strongly hooked tip gives it its name. It is uses it to break open the shells of tree snails, its principal food. It forages for the snails by clamoring through tree branches like a parrot.

Chondrohierax — The genus name means

White-tailed Kite, by Allan C. Brooks

"cartilage hawk" from the Greek *chondros* (cartilage) and *hierakos* (a hawk or a falcon). The Hook-billed Kite lacks the supraorbital ridge (bony projections above the eyes) that gives most raptors their fierce expression.

uncinatus — The specific epithet is Latin for "hooked." See common name above.

French Name: Milan Bec-en-croc
Spanish Names: Milano de Pico Ganchudo; Milano Piquiganchudo; Gavilán Piquiganchudo
Other Names: Snail Hawk; Mountain Hawk; Red-collared Hawk; Red-collared Kite; Mexican Hook-billed Kite; Merlion

Swallow-tailed Kite
Elanoides forficatus
(el-ah-no-EYE-deez for-fick-AY-tus)

"Not excepting even the turkey vulture, the tern or the swallow, no bird moves through the sky with more exquisite grace and buoyancy than this beautiful black and white, sharp winged kite, whose motion

Swallow-tailed Kite, by Rex Brasher

combines the special fascinations of each of its three close rivals. Soaring upward, buzzard fashion, until it sometimes fades from sight, or floating like it on motionless pinions; now swooping with the dash of a tern and catching itself suddenly just above the earth to skim along the surface like a swallow; swaying its trim body with a cut of the wing and the lashing of its long forked tail, it pauses neither for rest or food, but apparently spends every waking moment in the air." — Neltje Blanchan (1898)

The deeply forked tail, like that of a Barn Swallow, gives this kite its name. Formerly known as American Swallow-tailed Kite.

Elanoides — The genus name means "kite-like" from the Greek *elanos* (a kite) and *-oides* (resemblence to). It is probably intended to show a relationship or similarity to the White-tailed Kite in the genus *Elanus*.

forficatus — The specific epithet is Latin for "deeply forked," derived from *forfex* (scissors), referring to the tail.

French Name: Milan à Queue Fourchue

Spanish Names: Milano Tijereta; Elanio Tijereta

Other Names: American Swallow-tailed Kite; Fork-tailed Kite; Swallow-tail; Swallow-tailed Hawk; Snake Hawk; Wasp Hawk; Queue Fourchu

Golden Eagle
Aquila chrysaetos
(AK-wil-ah kris-AY-ee-tos)

"This magnificent eagle has long been named the King of Birds, and it well deserves the title. It is majestic in flight, regal in appearance, dignified in manner, and crowned with a shower of golden hackles about its royal head. When falconry flourished in Europe the golden eagle was flown only by kings." — Arthur Cleveland Bent (1937)

The Golden Eagle is named for the metallic golden feathers on the crown and nape.

Aquila — The genus name is the Latin word for "an eagle." As a group, members of this genus are called booted eagles (their legs are feathered to the toes) to distinguish them from the sea eagles in the genus *Haliaeetus*.

chrysaetos — The specific epithet is Greek for "golden eagle" from *chrysos* (golden) and *aetos* (an eagle).

French Name: Aigle Royal

Spanish Name: Aguila Real

Eskimo Name: Tik-mi-ak-puk (largest bird)

Other Names: Black Eagle; Brown Eagle; Dark Eagle; Gray Eagle; Canadian Eagle; White-tailed Eagle; Ring-tailed Eagle; Ringtail; Mountain Eagle; Jackrabbit Eagle; Royal Eagle; Calumet Eagle; Calumet Bird; War Eagle; War Bird; American War Bird; King of Birds; Bird of Jupiter; Awdler; Lolair Dubh; Erne

Golden Eagle, by Louis Agassiz Fuertes

Northern Harrier
Circus hudsonius
(SIR-kus hud-SO-nih-us)

"Close along the ground skims the marsh hawk, since field mice and other small mammals, frogs, and the larger insects that hide among the grass are what it is ever seeking as it swerves this way and that, turns, goes over its course, "quartering" the ground like a well trained dog on the scent of a hare — the peculiarity of flight that has earned it the hare-hound or harrier's name." — Neltje Blanchan (1898)

Formerly considered conspecific with the Hen Harrier (*C. cyaneus*) of Europe. Harrier is derived from the Old English *hergian* (to harass by hostile attacks). Harriers characteristically hunt by flying low over the ground and suddenly pouncing on prey, as described in the above passage. Northern distinguishes this species from harriers in South America, such as the Long-winged Harrier (*C. buffoni*) and Cinereous Harrier (*C. cinereus*). Formerly known as Marsh Hawk.

Circus — The genus name derives from the Greek *kirkos* (a circle), a name Aristotle and other classical authors used for a "type of hawk." The name describes the hawk's habit of circling in the sky as it hunts.

hudsonius — Linnaeus described this species in 1766 and named it for Hudson Bay, where the type specimen was taken. Formerly *Circus cyaneus*.

French Name: Busard des Marais
Spanish Names: Aguilucho de Hudson; Aguilucho Norteño
Eskimo and Inuit Names: Papiktook (long parky tail); Nakh-to-ka-luk
Other Names: Common Harrier; Marsh Harrier; Gorse Harrier; Grey Harrier; Blue Harrier; Brown Harrier; Blue Hawk; White Hawk; White-rumped Hawk; Chicken Hawk; Duck Hawk; Mouse Hawk; Rabbit Hawk; Frog Hawk; Toad Hawk; Mad Hawk; Moor Hawk; Swamp Hawk; Prairie Hawk; Dove Hawk; Seagull Hawk; Grey Buzzard; Blue Kite; White Kite; Brown Kite; Furze Kite; Vuzz Kite; Bog-trotter; Blue Sleeves; Blue Gled; Brown Gled; White Aboon Gled; Ringtail; Hen Driver; Hen Harrow; Miller; Flapper; Boy; Busard; Faller; Katabella; Aquilucho Palido; Chocolatier; Corsage; Cossade; Cossarde; Gavilán de Ciánaga; Gavilán de Sabanero; Woi; Hinkelwoi; Kay-cake; Malfini Savane; Mangepoule

Sharp-shinned Hawk
Accipiter striatus
(ack-SIP-ih-ter strih-AY-tus)

The raised ridge on the inside front of the tarsus gives this species its name. Although we tend to view a bird's tarsus as its "shin," it actually is analogous to the human foot between the ankle and the toes.

Accipiter — The genus name is Latin for "bird of prey," possibly derived from *accipere* (to take), as to seize prey.

striatus — The specific epithet is Latin for "striped" and refers to the blurry streaking on the underparts of the juvenile, from which the species was first described.

French Name: Épervier Brun
Spanish Names: Gavilán de Pecho Rufo; Gavilán Pajarero
Eskimo and Inuit Names: Uv-ing-u-likh-tuk (refers to bars on tail), Chi-kubv-i-uk-shu-guk
Other Names: Little Blue Darter; Sharp-shin; Sharpie; Bird Hawk; Sparrow Hawk; Pigeon Hawk; Chicken Hawk; Little Chicken Hawk; Hen Hawk; Bullet Hawk; Slate-colored Hawk; Falcon de Sierra; Garrapiña; Gavilán Colilargo; Gavilán de Sierra; Guaraguaíto de Sierra; Halcón; Halcón de Sierra; Bon Volee; Épervier; Emouchet; Emerillon; Clairhan Speireag; Shdos Fogel; Shdos Woi; Dauwa Woi; Dauwa Shdosser

Cooper's Hawk
Accipiter cooperii
(ack-SIP-ih-ter COOP-er-ih-eye)

In 1828, when Charles Bonaparte left Philadelphia and returned to Rome, zoologist William Cooper took on the task of editing the second and third volumes of Bonaparte's *American Ornithology; or, The Natural History of Birds Inhabiting the United States Not Given by Wilson*. In gratitude, Bonaparte named a new species of hawk *Falco Cooperii* in the second volume. Bonaparte had examined seven or eight specimens, a male of which he had collected himself while it was feeding on a Ruffed Grouse. He wrote that another specimen had been collected by Cooper, "Mr. Cooper, the friend to

Cooper's Hawk, by Louis Agassiz Fuertes

whom we have dedicated this species, has recently favoured us with an accurate description of a specimen of a somewhat larger size, shot in the early part of November, on the eastern part of Long Island." Audubon, who apparently had little regard for priority, repeatedly named previously described species for his own friends and colleagues. He did so with the Cooper's Hawk, which appeared in Plate 36 of *Birds of America* as *Falco Stanleii* and in his *Ornithological Biography* as *Falco Stanleyii*. Audubon decided to honor Lord Stanley, Earl of Derby as a favor for his subscribing to *Birds of America*. Cooper was not amused. He wrote to Bonaparte that he had no intention of allowing Lord Stanley to "carry off honors" meant for him. He needn't have worried, for Bonaparte's specific epithet had priority. In the fall of 1831, Cooper had the satisfaction of denying Audubon access to the specimens at the Lyceum that he wished to paint.

Accipiter — The genus name is Latin for "bird of prey," possibly derived from *accipere* (to take), as to seize prey.

cooperii — The specific epithet commemorates zoologist William C. Cooper (1798–1864), one of the founders of the New York Lyceum of Natural History (now the New York Academy of Sciences). See common name above.

French Name: Épervier de Cooper
Spanish Name: Gavilán de Cooper
Other Names: Blue Darter; Big Blue Darter; Chicken Hawk; Hen Hawk; Quail Hawk; Swift Hawk; Stanley Hawk; Bluetail; Striker; Coop; Aiglon; Ailerond; Boy; Woi; Hinkelwoi

Northern Goshawk
Accipiter gentilis
(ack-SIP-ih-ter jen-TIE-liss)

Goshawk is derived from the Old English *gos* (a goose) and *hafoc* (a hawk), perhaps referring to the largest prey this hawk is likely to tackle. However, this woodland species is more likely to take grouse and snowshoe hare. Northern distinguishes this hawk from other goshawk species found in Africa, southeast Asia, and Australia.

Accipiter — The genus name is Latin for "bird of prey," possibly derived from *accipere* (to take), as to seize prey.

gentilis — The specific epithet is Latin for "noble." It was named in a time when only nobility could fly this species in the sport of falconry. The Goshawk has been called "the most noble of all falcons." Linnaeus originally named this species *Falco gentilis*, although taxonomically it is not a falcon.

French Name: Autour des Palombes
Spanish Name: Gavilán Azor
Eskimo and Inuit Names: Abv-ung-likh-tuk; Kidgavitch Kiringit
Other Names: American Goshawk; Western Goshawk; Gosh Hawk; Goosehawk; Great Hawk; Grey Hawk; Black Hawk; Winter Hawk; Partridge Hawk; Speckled Partridge Hawk; Dove Hawk; Hen Hawk; Blue Hen Hawk; Chicken Hawk; Blue Darter; Blue Swifter; Tierce; Autour; Boy; Cossard; Gos-sheobhag; Woi; Hinkelwoi; Manageur de Poulets

Northern Goshawk, by Louis Agassiz Fuertes

> **Sidebar 22**
> **Every Hawk Is a Chicken Hawk**
>
> You will notice that "chicken hawk" is an alternate name for many hawk species. This goes back to a time when all raptors were viewed as vermin. Hawks were not only considered a threat to domestic poultry, but sportsmen believed them to be destructive to small game populations as well. Farmers and hunters routinely shot any hawk they encountered, and gunners slaughtered thousands of raptors as they migrated over mountain ridges. One such site, Hawk Mountain in eastern Pennsylvania, is now a sanctuary where birders witness the spectacle of hawk migration every fall. Many state and local governments paid bounties for killing birds of prey. Alaska even had a bounty on the Bald Eagle from 1917 to 1953. By the early 20th century, at least professional biologists were beginning to understand the important role predators play in the natural environment. However, the *Accipiters* (Cooper's Hawk, Sharp-shinned Hawk, and Northern Goshawk), because they prey mainly on small birds, were slow to be granted legal protection. Even such eminent ornithologists as George Miksch Sutton and Arthur A. Allen clung to the old notion that the only good *Accipiter* was a dead one. "This destructive Hawk [Cooper's], together with its two near relatives, should be destroyed by every possible means," wrote Henry W. Henshaw, a former Chief of the U.S. Biological Survey, in 1914. Nature writer Neltje Blanchan was even more over the top in her loathing for the three *Accipiter* species. She wrote that the Cooper's Hawk "lives by devouring birds of so much greater value than itself that the law of the survival of the fittest should be enforced by lead until these villains, from being the commonest of their generally useful tribe, adorn museum cases only." She believed the little Sharp-shinned Hawk took "fiendish satisfaction" in killing its "little prey" and lamented that because it is small and looks inoffensive, "its worse than useless life is spared." But most of all she despised the Northern Goshawk, regarding it as "the most destructive creature on wings." Ms. Blanchan concluded, "Let the guns be turned toward these bloodthirsty, audacious miscreants, and away from the red-tailed and red-shouldered species, beneficent, majestic kings of the air!" Although such outdated notions still persist in some circles, the general public has come to respect raptors in the natural scheme of things. Today, hawks and other raptors are among the most popular birds among birders.

Bald Eagle
Haliaeetus leucocephalus
(hal-ih-ay-EE-tus lew-koh-SEFF-ah-lus)

"Eagles have always been looked upon as emblems of power and valor, so our national bird may still be admired by those who are not familiar with its habits. Its soaring flight, with its pure-white head and tail glistening in the sunlight, is really inspiring; and it adds grandeur to the scene as it sits in a dignified pose on some dead tree, its white head clearly visible against the dark green of the forest background." — Arthur Cleveland Bent (1937)

The Bald Eagle is not bald in the sense that its head is bare like a vulture's. Bald derived from the Old English *balde* meant "white" and this species' name was originally Bald-headed Eagle, meaning "white-headed eagle." The name was eventually shortened to just Bald Eagle. These birds attain their white heads and tails when they mature at four or five years of age. Audubon described the immature as a distinct species, the Washington Eagle.

Haliaeetus — The genus name means "sea eagle" from the Greek *hals* (the sea) and *aetos* (an eagle). Eagles in this genus are associated with water, since fish are a major part of their diet. They occur along lakes and rivers as well as seacoasts.

leucocephalus — The specific epithet means

Bald Eagle, by Louis Agassiz Fuertes

"white head" from the Greek *leukos* (white) and *kephale* (the head).
French Name: Pygargue à Tête Blanche
Spanish Names: Aguila de Cabeza Blanca; Aguila Cabeciblanca
Eskimo and Inuit Names: Mu-tugh-o-wik; Tirrgh-luch
Other Names: American Eagle; Alaska Bald Eagle; Northern Bald Eagle; Bald-headed Eagle; White-headed Eagle; White-headed Sea Eagle; Great American Sea Eagle; Bald Sea Eagle; Fish Eagle; Fishing Eagle; Common Eagle; Washington Eagle; Washington Sea Eagle; Bird of Washington; Black Eagle; Brown Eagle; Gray Eagle; Old Patriarch; Aigle à Tête Blanche; Awdler; Fior-eun; Grepe; Lolair; Nonne

White-tailed Eagle
Haliaeetus albicilla
(hal-ih-ay-EE-tus alb-ih-SILL-ah)

This Eurasian eagle's pure white, wedge-shaped tail gives it its name. Formerly known as Gray Sea Eagle.

Haliaeetus — The genus name means "sea eagle" from the Greek *hals* (the sea) and *aetos* (an eagle). Eagles in this genus are associated with water, since fish are a major part of their diet. They occur along lakes and rivers as well as seacoasts.

albicilla — The specific epithet means "white tail" from the Latin *albus* (white) and *cilla*, actually a diminutive suffix, but taken to mean "the tail" by various authors. See White Wagtail for more on *cilla*.

French Name: Pygargue à Queue Blanche
Spanish Name: Pigargo europeo
Other Names: White-tailed Sea Eagle; European Sea Eagle; Erne

Steller's Sea-Eagle
Haliaeetus pelagicus
(hal-ih-ay-EE-tus peh-LADGE-ih-kus)

Eagles in the genus *Haliaeetus* are collectively known as sea-eagles for their seacoast habitat, although some like the Bald Eagle also occur inland near large bodies of water. This species is named in honor of its discoverer, German zoologist Georg Wilhelm Steller (1709–1746), a member of Vitus Bering's Second Kamchatka Expedition.

Haliaeetus — The genus name means "sea eagle" from the Greek *hals* (the sea) and *aetos* (an eagle). Eagles in this genus are associated with water, since fish are a major part of their diet. They occur along lakes and rivers as well as seacoasts.

pelagicus — The German systematic zoologist Peter Simon Pallas described this species in 1811, from Steller's notes. He gave it the scientific name *Aquila pelagica* (eagle of the sea) for its coastal habitat.

French Name: Pygargue Empereur
Spanish Name: Pigargo gigante
Other Names: Pacific Eagle; White-shouldered Eagle; O-washi

Mississippi Kite
Ictinia mississippiensis
(ick-TIN-ih-ah mis-ih-sip-ih-EN-sis)

This kite is named for the state of Mississippi, where the type specimen was collected.

Ictinia — The genus name is Latin from the Greek *iktinos* (a kite).

mississippiensis — The specific epithet is Modern Latin for "of Mississippi." Alexander Wilson named it for the state where he first collected it.

French Name: Milan du Mississippi
Spanish Names: Milano de Mississippi; Elanio Colinegro
Other Names: Blue Kite; Louisiana Kite; Mosquito Hawk; Locust-eater

Snail Kite
Rostrhamus sociabilis
(rost-RAME-us so-sih-AY-bil-us)

"The everglade kite has been well named "snail hawk," for it feeds exclusively on the meat of a large fresh-water snail (*Ampullaria depressa*), which formerly abounded all over the Everglades and is still abundant in some other fresh-water marshes and sluggish streams in Florida and in many places in South America . . . The kites search for the snails in the open places in the marshes or in shallow ponds, beating slowly back and forth, low over the ground, after the manner of marsh hawks, or hovering over the water like a gull. When the snail is located the kite plunges down to secure it and flies with it in its claws to some favorite perch on a stump, post, low tree, or bush; often an old deserted nest is used as a feeding station. Here the snail is neatly extracted with the aid of the kite's long hooked beak, admirably suited to the purpose, and the shell is dropped unbroken. That the birds use the same perch regularly is shown by the large number of empty shells often found in such places, sometimes as many as 200 or 300. There is no evidence to indicate that this kite ever eats anything but these mollusks." — Arthur Cleveland Bent (1937)

Formerly known as the Everglade Kite, the Snail Kite is particularly well named, as explained in the above passage, for its specialized diet of Apple Snails (*Pomacea paludosa*).

Rostrhamus — The genus name is Latin for "hooked beak" from *rostrum* (the beak) and *hamus* (a hook). This kite's slender, hooked bill is adapted for extracting snails from their shells.

sociabilis — The specific epithet is Latin for "sociable" and refers to this species' habit of nesting in loose colonies.

French Name: Milan des Marais
Spanish Names: Milano Caracolero; Elanio Caracolero
Other Names: Black Kite; Black Hawk; Snail Hawk; Hook-bill Hawk; Sociable Marsh Hawk; Babosero; Gavilán Babosero; Gavilán Caracolero

Common Black-Hawk
Buteogallus anthracinus
(bew-tee-oh-GAL-lus an-thrah-SIGH-nus)

Black-Hawk describes this species coal black plumage. The Common Black-Hawk has the widest range of the black-hawks.

Buteogallus — The genus name means "chicken hawk" or rather "hawk chicken" from the Latin *buteo* (a buzzard hawk) and *gallus* (a barnyard chicken.). But it's not what you think. The name doesn't mean this hawk preys on chickens. The genus was erected for the Rufous Crab Hawk (*B. aequinoctialis*) of South America, because its bare face, small head, and long legs were thought to resemble those of a chicken.

anthracinus — The specific epithet is Latin for "coal black" from the Greek *anthrax* (coal).

French Name: Buse Noire
Spanish Names: Aguililla Negra Menor; Gavilan Cangrejero
Other Names: Lesser Black Hawk; Mexican Black Hawk; Crab Hawk; Gavilán Batista; Halcón Cangrejero

Harris's Hawk
Parabuteo unicinctus
(par-ah-BEW-tee-oh you-nih-SINK-tus)

Audubon illustrated this hawk in *Birds of America* (1837) from a specimen collected in Louisiana. Believing it was an undescribed

Harris's Hawk, by John James Audubon

species, he gave it the name Harris's Buzzard (*Buteo Harrisii*) "after my friend EDWARD HARRIS Esq., a gentleman who, independently of the aid which he has on many occasions afforded me, in processing my examination of our birds, merits this compliment as an enthusiastic Ornithologist." However, Dutch ornithologist Coenraad Jacob Temminck had described this species in 1824, from a specimen collected in Brazil. He named it *Falco unicinctus*, so his specific epithet takes priority. Harris is still commemorated in the common name Audubon gave it.

Parabuteo — The genus name means "beside or near *Buteo*" from the Greek *para* (near or similar to) and the Latin *buteo* (a buzzard hawk). It is intended to show that Harris's Hawk is closely related to hawks in the genus *Buteo*.

unicinctus — The specific epithet means "once girdled" from the Latin *uni* (once) and *cinctus* (girdled). The name refers to the white band at the base of the tail.

French Name: Buse de Harris
Spanish Names: Aguililla de Harris; Gavilán Alicastaño
Other Names: Bay-winged Hawk; Louisiana Hawk; Harris' Buzzard; Chestnut-thighed Buzzard

White-tailed Hawk
Geranoaetus albicaudatus
(jer-an-oh-EE-tus al-bih-cod-AY-tus)

This hawk not only sports a white tail (with a black sub-terminal band), but also a white rump and underparts.

Geranoaetus — The genus name means "crane eagle" from the Greek *geranos* (a crane) and *aetus* (an eagle). Formerly *Buteo albicaudatus*.

albicaudatus — The specific epithet means "white tailed" from the Latin *albus* (white) and *caudatus* (tailed).

French Name: Buse à Queue Blanche
Spanish Names: Aguililla de Cola Blanca; Aguililla Coliblanca; Gavilán Coliblanco
Other Names: White-tail; Sennett's White-tailed Hawk; Prairie Hawk; White-tailed Buzzard

Gray Hawk
Buteo plagiatus
(BEW-tee-oh pla-jih-ATE-us)

The pale gray color of its plumage gives this hawk its name.

Buteo — The genus name is Latin for "a buzzard" or "a type of hawk." In Britain, members of this genus are called buzzards, but in America, buzzard is informally applied to the Turkey and Black Vultures. That is because early settlers called the vultures buzzards, thinking them similar to the dark form of the Common Buzzard (*B. buteo*) they knew back in the Mother Country. Formerly *Asturina nitida.*, The genus name *Asturina* is Latin for "resembling a goshawk." The specific epithet *nitida* is Latin for "shining."

plagiatus — The specific epithet is from the Latin *plaga* (a stripe) and refers to the pattern of fine horizontal bars on the breast and belly.

French Name: Buse Cendrée
Spanish Names: Aguililla Gris; Gavilán Gris
Other Names: Shining Buzzard-Hawk; Gray-lined Hawk; Mexican Goshawk; Nicaraguan Goshawk; Gray Goshawk

Red-shouldered Hawk
Buteo lineatus
(BEW-tee-oh lin-eh-AY-tus)

This species sports rusty red shoulder patches, which give it its name.

Buteo — The genus name is Latin for "a buzzard" or "a type of hawk." In Britain, members of this genus are called buzzards, but in America, buzzard is informally applied to the Turkey and Black Vultures. That is because early settlers called the vultures buzzards, thinking them similar to the dark form of the Common Buzzard (*B. buteo*) they knew back in the Mother Country.

lineatus — The specific epithet is Latin for "striped" and refers to the narrow black and white bands on the flight feathers and tail.

French Name: Buse à Épaulettes

Spanish Names: Aguililla de Pecho Rojo; Aguililla Pechirroja

Other Names: Florida Red-shouldered Hawk; Southern Red-shouldered Hawk; Red-bellied Hawk; Brown Hawk; Winter Hawk; Mouse Hawk; Chicken Hawk; Big Chicken Hawk; Hen Hawk; Red-shouldered Buzzard; Boy; Woi; Hinkelwoi

Broad-winged Hawk
Buteo platypterus
(BEW-tee-oh plah-TIP-teh-rus)

This hawk's short, broad wings give it its name.

Buteo — The genus name is Latin for "a buzzard" or "a type of hawk." In Britain, members of this genus are called buzzards, but in America, buzzard is informally applied to the Turkey and Black Vultures. That is because early settlers called the vultures buzzards, thinking them similar to the dark form of the Common Buzzard (*B. buteo*) they knew back in the Mother Country.

platypterus — The specific epithet means "broad wing" from the Greek *platys* (broad) and *pteron* (the wing).

French Name: Petite Buse

Spanish Names: Aguililla de Ala Ancha; Aguililla Aluda; Gavilán Aludo

Other Names: Marsh Hawk; Chicken Hawk; Chicken-eater; Broad-winged Buzzard; Boy; Woi; Hinkelwoi; Gavilán Bobo; Guaraguao de Bosque; Malfini; Manger-Poulet

Short-tailed Hawk
Buteo brachyurus
(BEW-tee-oh brack-ih-YOUR-us)

This hawk doesn't have a particularly short tail, but it appears so, because the wingtips reach to the tail tip.

Buteo — The genus name is Latin for "a buzzard" or "a type of hawk." In Britain, members of this genus are called buzzards, but in America, buzzard is informally applied to the Turkey and Black Vultures. That is because early settlers called the vultures buzzards, thinking them similar to the dark form of the Common Buzzard (*B. buteo*) they knew back in the Mother Country.

brachyurus — The specific epithet means "short tail" from the Greek *brachys* (short) and *oura* (the *tail*).

French Name: Buse à Queue Courte

Spanish Names: Aguililla de Cola Corta; Aguililla Colicorta; Gavilán Colicorto

Other Names: Little Black Hawk; Short-tailed Buzzard

Swainson's Hawk
Buteo swainsoni
(BEW-tee-oh SWAIN-son-eye)

Audubon named this species *Buteo vulgaris* in 1837. But that name was already in use for the Common Buzzard (now *Buteo buteo*) of Europe. It needed to be given another name, since two different species may not share the same scientific name. Charles Bonaparte renamed it *Buteo Swainsoni* for English zoological illustrator William Swainson. The new name first appeared in Bonaparte's *A Geographical and Comparative List of the Birds of Europe and North America* (1838). Bonaparte gave no particular reason why he chose to honor Swainson.

Buteo — The genus name is Latin for "a buzzard" or "a type of hawk." In Britain, members of this genus are called buzzards, but in America, buzzard is informally applied to the Turkey and Black Vultures. That is because early settlers called the vultures buzzards, thinking them similar to the dark form of the Common Buzzard (*B. buteo*) they knew back in the Mother Country.

swainsoni — This hawk is named in honor of William Swainson (1789–1855), a British

naturalist, artist, and collector. See common name above.
French Name: Buse de Swainson
Spanish Names: Aguililla de Swainson; Gavilán de Swainson
Other Names: Grasshopper Hawk; Gopher Hawk; Telephone-pole Hawk; Brown Hawk; Black Hawk; Brown-throated Hawk; Hen Hawk; Common Hen Hawk; Common Buzzard

Zone-tailed Hawk
Buteo albonotatus
(BEW-tee-oh al-bow-no-TAY-tus)

Zone-tailed refers to the wide and narrow light bands (gray above; white below) that divide the dark tail into distinct zones.

Buteo — The genus name is Latin for "a buzzard" or "a type of hawk." In Britain, members of this genus are called buzzards, but in America, buzzard is informally applied to the Turkey and Black Vultures. That is because early settlers called the vultures buzzards, thinking them similar to the dark form of the Common Buzzard (*B. buteo*) they knew back in the Mother Country.

albonotatus — The specific epithet means "white marked" from the Latin *albus* (white) and *notatus* (marked). It refers to the white bands across the tail.
French Name: Buse à Queue Barrée
Spanish Names: Aguililla Aura; Gavilán Colifajeado
Other Names: Band-tail; Band-tailed Hawk; Zone-tailed Buzzard

Red-tailed Hawk
Buteo jamaicensis
(BEW-tee-oh jah-may-ih-SEN-sis)

The adult's rufous red tail gives this hawk its name, although some subspecies lack this field mark. A dark subspecies *B.j. harlani* was formerly considered a full species, "Harlan's Hawk" (for Dr. Richard Harlan.) A pale color morph that nests in the northern Great Plains is sometimes called "Krider's Hawk" for John Krider, who collected the first specimen in Iowa.

Buteo — The genus name is Latin for "a buzzard" or "a type of hawk." In Britain, members of this genus are called buzzards, but in America, buzzard is informally applied

Red-tailed Hawk and Cooper's Hawk, by Louis Agassiz Fuertes

to the Turkey and Black Vultures. That is because early settlers called the vultures buzzards, thinking them similar to the dark form of the Common Buzzard (*B. buteo*) they knew back in the Mother Country.

jamaicensis — The specific epithet is Modern Latin for "of Jamaica," the island in the West Indies, where the type specimen was collected.
French Name: Buse à Queue Rousse
Spanish Names: Aguililla Cola Roja; Aguililla Colirroja; Gavilán Colirrojo
Other Names: Redtail; Black Redtail; Eastern Redtail; Western Redtail; Alaska Redtail; Red Hawk; Gopher Hawk; Mouse Hawk; Sparrow Hawk; Hen Hawk; Chicken Hawk; White-breasted Chicken Hawk; Buzzard Hawk; Buzzard; Common Buzzard; Red-tailed Buzzard; Harlan's Buzzard; Black Warrior; Squealer; Macaw; Aguililla Colirrufa; Gavilán de Monte; Guaraguao; Guaraguao Colirrojo; Lechuza; Malfini; Pee-ank; Boy; Clamhan; Woi; Hinkelwoi

Rough-legged Hawk
Buteo lagopus
(BEW-tee-oh lag-OH-pus)

The Rough-legged Hawk is so named, because its legs are feathered to the toes.

Buteo — The genus name is Latin for "a buzzard" or "a type of hawk." In Britain, members of this genus are called buzzards, but in America, buzzard is informally applied to the Turkey and Black Vultures. That is because early settlers called the vultures buzzards, thinking them similar to the dark form of the Common Buzzard (*B. buteo*) they knew back in the Mother Country.

lagopus — The specific epithet means "hare footed" from the Greek *lagos* (a hare) and *pous* (the foot) and refers to the feathered shanks suggesting the furry foot of a hare.

French Name: Buse Pattue
Spanish Name: Aguililla Artica
British Name: Rough-legged Buzzard
Eskimo and Inuit Names: Kil-yir-gik (basket sled); Pi-to-ghuk; Kay-u-kye-ule
Other Names: Rough-leg; American Rough-legged Hawk; Rough-legged Falcon; Roughie; Black Hawk; Mouse Hawk; Chicken Hawk; Chap-Hawk; Squalling Hawk; Squealing Hawk; Boy; Woi; Hinkelwoi

Ferruginous Hawk
Buteo regalis
(BEW-tee-oh reg-AY-lis)

Ferruginous means "having the color of iron rust" from the Latin *ferrugo* (iron rust) from *ferrum* (iron). The reference is to this hawk's rusty red back and shoulders in the light morph. The dark morph lacks the reddish color.

Buteo — The genus name is Latin for "a buzzard" or "a type of hawk." In Britain, members of this genus are called buzzards, but in America, buzzard is informally applied to the Turkey and Black Vultures. That is because early settlers called the vultures buzzards, thinking them similar to the dark form of the Common Buzzard (*B. buteo*) they knew back in the Mother Country.

regalis — "This latest name, *regalis*, is a very appropriate one for this splendid hawk, the largest, most powerful, and grandest of our Buteos, a truly regal bird." — Arthur Cleveland Bent (1937)

The specific epithet is Latin for "regal" or "royal," an apt name for this largest North American *Buteo*. But in this case the name is a toponym referring to the Mexican village Real del Monte, where the type specimen was apparently collected.

French Name: Buse Rouilleuse
Spanish Name: Aguililla Real
Other Names: Ferruginous Rough-leg; Ferruginous Rough-legged hawk; Eagle Hawk; Gopher Hawk; Squirrel Hawk; Chap-Hawk; Prairie Eagle

Order Strigiformes

Family Tytonidae
Barn Owls

Barn Owl
Tyto alba
(TIE-toe AL-bah)

This owl is named for its preference for roosting and nesting in barns and silos. Formerly known as Common Barn Owl.

Tyto — The genus name is Greek for "night owl."

alba — The specific epithet is Latin for "white" and describes the pale underparts that make a flying owl look ghostly white against the night sky.

French Name: Effraie des Clochers

Spanish Names: Lechuza de Campanerio; Lechuza Ratonera

Other Names: Common Barn Owl; American Barn Owl; White-breasted Barn Owl; Barnyard Owl; Church Owl; Steeple Owl; Night Owl; Monkey Owl; Monkey-faced Owl; Rat Owl; Sweetheart Owl; Tawny Owl; Yellow Owl; Golden Owl; Orange Owl; Citrus Owl; Silver Owl; White Owl; Delicate Owl; Stone Owl; Straw Owl; Grass Owl; Hobby Owl; Jenny Owl; Screech Owl; Scritch Owl; Screaming Owl; Hissing Owl; Snake Owl; Pudge Owl; Death Owl; Death Bird; Jumbie Bird; Hobgoblin; Roarer; Cherubim; Berthuan; Hoolet; White Hoolet; Jenny Howlet; Madge Howlet; Gillihowlet; Gill Howter; Gil-Hooter; Moggy; Padge; Pudge; Billy Wise; Billy Wix; Hibou Paille; Hullart; Ullat or Ullet; Eil; Sheier Eil; Oolert; Owlerd; Woolert; Chat-huant; Frezaie; Patoo; Lechuza; Lechuza Mono; Queen-of-the-night; *Cailleach-oidhche-Gheal* (white old woman of the night); *L'Effraie* (the frightener)

~

Barn Owl, by Allan C. Brooks

Family Strigidae
Typical Owls

Owl derives from the Latin *ulula* and is imitative suggesting an owl's vocalizations. Howl come from the same root.

Flammulated Owl
Psiloscops flammeolus
(SIGH-low-skops flah-ME-oh-lus)

"How fitting that the flammulated owl, our second smallest owl (after the elf owl), derives its name from *flammeolus*, the Latin word for flame. Although its face and wings are tinged with the orange tones of glowing wood embers, those who first described it were unaware that it depends on fire to renew the brushy, shade-tolerant undergrowth that sustains it in forested mountains from British Columbia to northern Mexico." — *National Audubon Magazine*

Flammulated refers to the orange to reddish markings of the red morph of this owl.

Psiloscops — The genus name means "little bare eared owl" from the Greek *psilos* (bare or naked) and *skops* (a little eared owl). *Psilos* is probably a reference to the unfeathered feet. Formerly *Otus flammeolus*.

flammeolus — The specific epithet is Modern Latin for "flame-red" referring to the rusty markings.

French Name: Petit-duc Nain
Spanish Names: Tecolate de Ojo Oscuro; Tecolote Flameado
Other Names: Flammulated Screech Owl; Flammulated Scops Owl; Dwarf Owl

Western Screech-Owl
Megascops kennicottii
(MEG-ah-skops ken-ih-KOT-ee-eye)

The Western Screech-Owl's typical vocalization is not a screech, but a series of whistled toots that suggests a bouncing ball. See Eastern Screech-Owl for the explanation of the name. Western describes this bird's range west of the Rockies and distinguishes it from the Eastern Screech-Owl, with which it was once considered conspecific.

Megascops — The genus name is Greek for "great little eared owl" from *megas* (great) and *scops* (a little eared owl).

kennicottii — The specific epithet honors Major Robert Kennicott (1835–1866), who collected the type specimen in the 1860s, while on a telegraph survey to Alaska.

French Name: Petit-duc de Montagnes
Spanish Name: Tecolote Occidental
Other Names: Kennicott's Owl; Kennicott's Screech Owl; Washington Screech Owl; Puget Sound Screech Owl; Coastal Screech Owl; Little Horned Owl; Dusk Owl; Ghost Owl; Cat Owl; Little Cat Owl; Mouse Owl

Eastern Screech-Owl
Megascops asio
(MEG-ah-skops AH-sih-oh)

Most sources say screech-owls are misnamed, because they don't really screech. The typical call of the Eastern Screech-Owl is a series of whistled notes either all on one pitch (the tremolo) or in a descending whinny. However it turns out that these owls really do screech under certain circumstances. When defending their nest, the parent owls will dive at the potential threat, screeching loudly and snapping their bills. So if you are ever near a Screech-Owl's nest at night, you may actually hear one screech just before you feel its talons rake your scalp. Eastern describes the range from the Great Plains to the Atlantic coast and distinguishes this owl from the Western Screech-Owl. The Eastern and Western Screech-Owls were formerly considered a single species, known simply as the Screech Owl.

Eastern Screech-Owl, by Louis Agassiz Fuertes

The filename includes the text "Red morph & gray morph Might include in caption as it looks like two different ow

Megascops — The genus name is Greek for "great little eared owl" from *megas* (great) and *scops* (a little eared owl).

asio — The specific epithet is Latin for "a type of eared owl" mentioned by Pliny.

French Name: Petit-duc Maculé

Spanish Name: Tecolote Oriental

Other Names: Common Screech Owl; Texas Screech Owl; Little Owl; Cat Owl; Little Cat Owl; Little Horned Owl; Little Eared Owl; Gray Owl; Little Gray Owl; Red Owl; Mottled Owl; Death Owl; Ghost Owl; Scops Owl; Spirit Owl; Dusk Owl; Mouse Owl; Barn Owl; Hoot Owl; Scritch Owl; Squinch Owl; Shivering Owl; Whinnerying Owl; Whickering Owl; Whistling Owl; Trilling Owl; Little Dukelet; Feathered Wildcat; Le Petit-Duc de l'est; Chat Haut; Chouette; Glana Eil; Nocht Eil; Shta Keitzel

Whiskered Screech-Owl
Megascops trichopsis
(Meg-ah-skops try-COPE-siss)

Especially long facial bristles, modified hair-like feathers about the bill, give the Whiskered Screech-Owl its name. Formerly known as Whiskered Owl.

Megascops — The genus name is Greek for "great little eared owl" from *megas* (great) and *scops* (a little eared owl).

trichopsis — The specific epithet is Greek for "hair appearance" from *trichos* (hair) and *opsis* (appearance). This also refers to the bristles around the bill.

French Name: Petit-duc à Moustaches

Spanish Name: Tecolote Bigotudo

Other Name: Spotted Screech Owl

Great Horned Owl
Bubo virginianus
(BEW-boh ver-jin-ee-AY-nus)

Nicknamed the "Tiger of the Air" for its fierce demeanor, this owl is named for its large size and for the tufts of feathers on the head that suggest horns or ears.

Bubo — The genus name is Latin for "eagle owl."

virginianus — The specific epithet is Modern Latin and refers to the Virginia colonies, where Europeans first encountered this bird, and where the type specimen was likely obtained. The Great Horned Owl actually has one of the most extensive ranges of any North American bird. It occurs over most of Canada, all forty-nine continental states, and south through Mexico and Central America. It is also found in parts of South America. As Ernest Choate wrote, "Considering the extent of its range, *americanus* would be more appropriate."

French Name: Grand-duc d'Amérique

Spanish Names: Búho Cornudo Grande; Búho Cornudo; Búho Grande

Eskimo and Inuit Names: Nukisirgak (powerful); Mu-ga-pai-ukh

Other Names: Horned Owl; Dusty Horned Owl; Dwarf Horned Owl; Pallid Horned Owl; Labrador Horned Owl; Pacific Horned Owl; Western Horned Owl; Saint Michael Horned Owl; Virginia Horned Owl; Virginia Owl; Hoot Owl; Big Hoot Owl; Screech Owl; Meat Owl; Eagle Owl; Eared Owl; Common Owl; Cat Owl; Big Owl; King Owl; Chicken Owl; White Owl; Horn Coot; Tiger of the Air; Winged Tiger; Feathered Tiger; *Cailleach-oidhche* (old woman of the night); Cave-duc; Chaoin; Chat-huant; Grand Duc; Dusty; Hibou Corne; Grand Hibou; Nocht Eil; Grosa Eil; Harn Aowl; Guibou; Bubo Cornado Americano

Snowy Owl
Bubo scandiacus
(BEW-boh skan-dee-AY-kus)

"On one occasion, while traveling south of the Yukon in December, I secured a beautiful specimen of this bird, which was nearly immaculate-milky white, with a rich and extremely beautiful shade of clear lemon-yellow suffusing the entire bird, exactly as the rosy blush clothes the entire plumage of some gulls in spring. The bird was kept until the next morning; an examination then showed that [the] beautiful tinge had vanished and the feathers had become dead white, with barely a trace of coloring seen the previous evening." — Edward W. Nelson (1887)

The Snowy Owl is named for its largely pure white plumage that may show a few dark markings. First year birds show heavy black barring on a white background. Adult males can be pure white.

Snowy Owl, by Louis Agassiz Fuertes

Bubo — The genus name is Latin for "eagle owl." Formerly *Nyctea scandiaca*.

scandiacus — The specific epithet is Modern Latin for "of Scandinavia," where the type specimen was collected.

French Name: Harfang des Neiges
Spanish Name: Búho Nival
Eskimo and Inuit Names: Anipak (white like the snow); Ung-puk (great beard)
Other Names: Snow Owl; White Owl; Great White Owl; Arctic Owl; Northern Owl; Ermine Owl; Ghost Owl; Highland Tundra Owl; Tundra Ghost; Harfang; Hibou Blanc; Wapacuthu; Ookpik; Scandinavian Nightbird; White Terror of the North

~

Northern Hawk-Owl
Surnia ulula
(SIR-nee-ah YOU-loo-lah)

"The hawk owl has been well named, for in appearance and habits it is said to resemble some of our smaller diurnal birds of prey; its flight is swift and graceful, suggesting that of the hawks; and when it is perched on top of some tree or stub, in broad daylight, it has sometimes been mistaken for a hawk. It has also been called the "day-owl," because of its conspicuous diurnal habits; it probably hunts more extensively by day than any of our other owls, except, possibly, the short-eared and pygmy owls." — Arthur Cleveland Bent (1938)

A bird that "appears to be half hawk and half owl," the Northern Hawk-Owl resembles a hawk both in flight and when perched atop a stunted spruce, particularly because of the long tail. The flight is accipiter-like, direct, low and swift with quick, stiff wingbeats, and like a hawk, it is also a diurnal hunter. Northern refers to this owl's northern range across the boreal forests of North America and Eurasia and distinguishes it from hawk-owls in the genus *Ninox* of southeast Asia and Australasia. The genera *Surnia* and *Ninox* are not closely related.

Surnia — French zoologist André Marie Constant Duméril erected the genus in 1806, but gave no explanation as to its meaning. James Jobling suggests that he may have intended a contracted anagram of *Strix funerea*, a former scientific name of the Boreal Owl. Elliot Coues believed the name to be derived from *surnion*, a Greek word meaning "an owl."

ulula — The specific epithet is Latin for "screech owl," mentioned by Pliny and other writers. It is probably imitative of the call.

French Name: Chouette Épervière
Spanish Name: Búho Gavilán
Eskimo and Inuit Names: Tuk-fea-ling-uk (refers to spots on plumage resembling something else); Neakoktoakruk (medium-sized head)
Other Names: American Hawk Owl; Day Owl; Tooting Owl; Toot-aowl; Canadian Owl; Hudsonian Owl; Chouette; Hibou

~

Northern Pygmy-Owl
Glaucidium gnoma
(glaw-SID-ee-um NO-mah)

The pygmy owl well deserves its name, for it is scarcely as big as a bluebird, and not nearly so large as a robin. — Milton Philo Skinner (1938)

This species is called the pygmy-owl, because of its small size as described in the opening passage. Northern distinguishes it from other species of pygmy-owls of more southerly distribution.

Glaucidium — The genus name is Greek for "little glaring owl" and refers to this bird's facial expression.

gnoma — The specific epithet is Latin for "a spirit" or "a sprite," which this tiny owl suggests.

French Names: Chevêchette naine; Chouette Naine

Spanish Names: Tecolote Serrano; Tecolotito Norteño

Other Names: Rocky Mountain Pygmy Owl; California Pygmy Owl; Vancouver Pygmy Owl; Gnome Owl; Dwarf Owl

Ferruginous Pygmy-Owl
Glaucidium brasilianum
(glaw-SID-ee-um brah-sil-ee-AY-num)

Ferruginous means "the color of iron rust" from the Latin *ferrum* (iron) and refers to the orange-brown color of the plumage. Formerly known as Ferruginous Owl.

Glaucidium — The genus name is Greek for "little glaring owl" and refers to this bird's facial expression.

brasilianum — The specific epithet is Modern Latin for "of Brazil," which is part of this species' range.

French Name: Chevêchette Brune

Spanish Names: Tecolotito Común; Mochuelo Común

Elf Owl
Micrathene whitneyi
(mick-rah-THEE-nee WIT-nee-eye)

This tiny sparrow-sized owl reminds one of an elf or a sprite as it peers out of its nesting cavity in a saguaro cactus.

Micrathene — The genus name is Greek for "small Athena" from *mikros* (small) and *Athena,* the Greek goddess of wisdom. The reference is to this owl's tiny size (it is the smallest owl in the world) and to the fact that owls were sacred to Athena.

whitneyi — While working with the Geological Survey of California, headed by Josiah Dwight Whitney (1819–1896), Dr. James G. Cooper discovered this tiny owl in July of 1861 near Fort Mohave in the Colorado River Valley of Arizona: "I found it in a dense thicket, on a very windy morning, where it may perhaps have taken a temporary refuge, after being blown down from some of the caverns in the barren mountains surrounding the valley." Cooper described the owl and Lucy's Warbler in the *Proceedings of the California Academy of Sciences*. He called it Whitney's Owl and gave it the scientific name *Athene whitneyi* in honor of the expedition's director.

French Name: Chevêchette des Saguaros

Spanish Names: Tecolote Enano; Tecolotito Enano

Other Names: Texas Elf Owl; Whitney's Owl; Whitney's Elf Owl; Dwarf Owl

Burrowing Owl
Athene cunicularia
(ah-THEEN-ee kew-nick-you-LAR-ee-ah)

The Burrowing Owl is named for its habit of nesting in the abandoned burrows of small mammals, ground squirrels, woodchucks, badgers, foxes, armadillos, and particularly those of prairie dogs. Burrowing Owls in Florida have earned the nickname Gopher Owl, because they use the burrows of the gopher tortoise. Florida birds have also been known to dig their own burrows in sandy soil.

Athene — The genus name is for Pallas Athena, the Greek goddess of wisdom, to whom the owl was sacred.

cunicularia — The specific epithet is Latin for "a miner" or more precisely "a military engineer" from the Latin *cuniculus* (an underground passage).

French Names: Chevêche des Terriers; Chouette des Terriers

Spanish Names: Tecolote Llanero; Búho Llanero; Lechuza Llanero

Other Names: Burrowing Day-Owl; Ground Owl; Prairie Owl; Prairie Dog Owl; Rattlesnake Owl; Gopher Owl; Cuckoo Owl; Badger-hole Owl; Tunnel Owl; Hill Owl; Long-legged Owl; Billy Owl; Howdy Owl; Howdy Bird; Cuckoo Bird; Cucú; Coucou; Coucouterre

Spotted Owl
Strix occidentalis
(STRICKS ocks-ih-den-TAIL-iss)

This owl is named for the whitish spots on its plumage that help it blend in with the pattern of dappled light filtering through the canopy.

Strix — The genus name is Greek for "a screech owl."

occidentalis — John Xantus discovered this species in the southern Sierra Nevadas near Fort Tejon, California on March 6, 1858. He gave it the specific epithet *occidentalis*, Latin for "western" and refers to this owls' range along the West Coast from British Columbia to southern California, east through Arizona and New Mexico, and south through Mexico. Xantus' specimen was the only one known until 1872, when Major Charles Bendire collected one near Tucson, Arizona. The Spotted Owl is the western counterpart of the Barred Owl.

French Name: Chouette Tachetée
Spanish Name: Búho Manchado
Other Names: Northern Spotted Owl; Western Barred Owl; Brown-eyed Owl; Wood Owl; Hoot Owl; Xantus's Owl

Barred Owl
Strix varia
(STRICKS VARE-ee-ah)

The Barred Owl in named for the horizontal bars on the upper breast.

Strix — The genus name is Greek for "a screech owl."

varia — The specific epithet is Latin for "variegated" and refers to the streaks, spots, and patches of various colors in the plumage.

French Name: Chouette Rayée
Spanish Names: Búho Listado; Búho Barrado
Other Names: Northern Barred Owl; Southern Barred Owl; Striped Owl; Hoot Owl; Laughing Owl; Crazy Owl; Rain Owl; Wood Owl; Grey Owl; Mouse Owl; Swamp Owl; Bottom Owl; Black-eyed Owl; Old-folks Owl; Round-headed Owl; Eight Hooter; Chuckle Head; Chouette du Canada; Combachag; Nocht Eil; Hibou à Grosse Tête

Great Gray Owl, by Louis Agassiz Fuertes

Great Gray Owl
Strix nebulosa
(STRICKS neb-you-LOH-sah)

"With an overall length of up to 32 inches and a wingspan approaching five feet, the great gray owl is considered to be North America's largest owl. But overall dimensions are misleading, for the bird in fact is a fluffy fraud. Cloaked in thick down and insulating feathers that protect it from the numbing cold of its northern haunts, an adult weighs only two to three pounds — barely half the weight of its more formidable cousin the snowy owl."
— *Reader's Digest Book of North American Birds* (2005)

This owl's large size and dark gray plumage give it its name. It is the largest North American owl by length and wingspan, but not by mass as explained in the opening passage.

Strix — The genus name is Greek for "a screech owl."

nebulosa — The specific epithet is Latin for "clouded," "misty," or "foggy," and refers to its color, that of a dark storm cloud, and to the indistinct, blurry-edged spots.

French Name: Chouette Lapone
Spanish Name: Búho Lapón
Eskimo and Inuit Name: Mu-ga-ai-pai-ukh
Other Names: Gray Owl; Spruce Owl; Speckled Owl; Spectral Owl; Cinerous Owl; Great Cinerous Owl; Sooty Owl; Bearded Owl; Lapp Owl; Lapland Owl; Great Gray Ghost; Phantom of the North

Long-eared Owl
Asio otus
(AH-see-oh OH-tus)

Welsh naturalist Thomas Pennant coined the name Long-eared Owl in reference to the tall, closely set ear tufts, which may serve to camouflage the bird. Pete Dunne compares the ear tufts to "licking candle flames."

Asio — The genus name is Latin for "a kind of horned owl," mentioned by Pliny.

otus — The specific epithet is Greek for "an eared owl."

French Name: Hibou Moyen-duc

Spanish Names: Búho Cornudo de Cara Café; Búho-cornudo Caricafé

Other Names: American Long-eared Owl; Horned Owl; Lesser Horned Owl; Little Horned Owl; Cat Owl; Pussy Owl; Brush Owl; Prairie Owl; Cedar Owl; Coulee Owl; Coulier Owl; Tufted Owl; Wilson's Owl; Long Ears; Long-horned Ullat; Hornie Hoolet; Horn Coot; Nocht Eil

Short-eared Owl
Asio flammeus
(AH-see-oh FLAH-me-us)

Pennant also gave this owl its common name for the tiny, inconspicuous ear tufts, not always apparent in the field.

Asio — The genus name is Latin for "a kind of horned owl," mentioned by Pliny.

flammeus — The specific epithet is Latin for "flame-colored" or "fiery," a bit over stated for the tawny cinnamon-buff coloration.

French Name: Hibou des Marais

Spanish Names: Búho de Cuernos Cortos; Búho Orejicorto; Lechuza Campestre

Eskimo and Inuit Names: Muug-ar-ko-jee-wuk (sparkling fire owl); Anipausigak (small owl); Lifliuingauarak (soft flying, makes no noise in flight); Nipailyutak (the screecher)

Other Names: Marsh Owl; Bog Owl; Swamp Owl; Prairie Owl; Meadow Owl; Moor Owl; Grass Owl; Fern Owl; Day Owl; Evening Owl; Hawk Owl; Red Owl; Flat-faced Owl; March Owl; Sea Owl; Woodcock Owl; Pilot Owl; Moss Owl; Mouse Hawk; Cat Ool; Nocht Eil; Brown Yogle; Grey Yogle; Grey Hullet; Carabo; Chat-huant; Lechuza de Sabana; Múcaro de Sabana; Múcaro Real; Pueo

Boreal Owl
Aegolius funereus
(ee-JOLE-ih-us few-NEAR-ee-us)

This little owl is named for its northern range in coniferous forests across North America and Eurasia. Formerly known as Richardson's Owl, named for John Richardson (1787–1865), a Scottish naval surgeon and Arctic explorer.

Aegolius — The genus name is from the Greek *aigolios* (a kind of owl) mentioned by Aristotle but not further identified.

funereus — The specific epithet is Latin for "funereal" or "mournful" and either refers to the owl's reputation as a bird of ill omen or to its melancholy call.

French Names: Nyctale de Tengmalm; Nyctale Boréale

Spanish Name: Tecolote Boreal

British Name: Tengmalm's Owl, named for Peter Gustaf Tengmalm (1754–1803), a Swedish physician and naturalist

Eskimo and Inuit Names: Takpilyakruk (pretty good sighted); Tuk-whe-ling-uk

Other Names: Arctic Saw-whet Owl; Sparrow Owl; American Sparrow Owl; Barn Owl; Little Owl; Pearl Owl; Partridge-haw

Northern Saw-whet Owl
Aegolius acadicus
(ee-JOLE-ih-us ah-KADE-ih-kus)

This tiny owl is named for one of its calls, which has been likened to the sharpening (whetting) of a hand saw. Northern distinguishes this species from the Unspotted Saw-whet Owl (*A. ridgwayi*) of Central America.

Aegolius — The genus name is from the Greek *aigolios* (a kind of owl) mentioned by Aristotle but not further identified.

acadicus — The specific epithet is Modern Latin for "of Acadia" the former name of Nova Scotia, where the type specimen was collected.

French Name: Petite Nyctale

Spanish Names: Tecolote Afilador; Tecolote-abetero Norteño

Other Names: Acadian Owl; Kirtland's Owl; Blind Owl; Sparrow Owl; White-fronted Owl; Barn Owl; Farmland Owl; Cop Owl; Little Owl; Pygmy Owl; Small Owl; Tooting Owl; Queen Charlotte Owl; Little Nightbird; Limard; Whetsaw; Saw-whet; Saw-filer; Sawyer

Order Trogoniformes

Family Trogonidae
Trogons

Trogon is also the genus name. It is a Greek word that means "gnawer," and refers to the fact that these birds enlarge woodpecker holes for nesting by gnawing with their serrated-edged bills.

Elegant Trogon
Trogon elegans
(TROH-gon EL-ee-ganz)

This trogon is elegant indeed, with its sleek lines and bright tropical colors of green and red. Formerly known as Coppery-tailed Trogon.

Trogon — The genus name is Greek for "gnawer." See family introduction above.

elegans — The specific epithet is Latin for "elegant."

French Name: Trogon Élégant
Spanish Name: Trogón Elegante

~

Eared Quetzal
Euptilotis neoxenus
(youp-til-OH-tis nee-oh-ZEE-nus)

Quetzal is American Spanish from the Nahuatl Indian word *quetzal*, which means "large brilliant tail feather." The Resplendent Quetzal (*Pharomachrus mocinno*), the sacred bird of the Mayans and National Bird of Guatamala, is notable for its long, streamer-like tail feathers that were worn by the priests. The Eared Quetzal's tail is not as ornate. It is named for the tufted feathers behind the eyes that resemble ears, but they are so inconspicuous that they are not a reliable field mark. Formerly known as Eared Trogon.

Elegant Trogon, by Louis Agassiz Fuertes

Euptilotis — The genus name means "good ear feather" from the Greek *eu* (good), *ptilon* (a feather), and *otis* (eared).

neoxenus — The specific epithet means "new stranger" from the Greek *neo* (new) and *xenos* (a stranger), perhaps so called, because it was a newly discovered species in an unusual locality, considerably north of most other trogons.

French Name: Quetzal Oreillard
Spanish Name: Quetzal Mexicano

~

Order Coraciiformes

Family Alcedinidae
Kingfishers

"This Izaak Walton of birddom, whom you may see perched as erect as a fish hawk on a snag in the lake, creek, or river, or on a dead limb projecting over the water, on the lookout for minnows, chub, red fins, samlets, or any other small fry that swims past, is as expert as any fisherman you are ever likely to know. Sharp eyes are necessary to see the little fish where sunbeams dance on the ripples and the refracted light plays queer tricks with one's vision. Once a victim is sighted, how swiftly the lone fisherman dives through the air and water after it, and how accurately he strikes its death-blow behind the gills!" — Neltje Blanchan (1917)

Kingfisher refers to the bird's skill in catching fish as described above by plunging headfirst into the water, usually from a perch but sometimes after hovering in midair. Here is another thought on the common name:

"It was 'Kynges' because it was thought to be chief or king of fishers. Possibly its beautiful irridescent plumage enhanced the image of Kingliness in the sense that its garb was fit for a king." — Francesca Greenoak (1979)

Ms. Greenoak is speaking of the colorful Common Kingfisher (*Alcedo atthis*) of the Old World that sports bright blue-green plumage above and orange-chestnut below. The North American species tend to be drabber. Ironically many members of this family don't fish at all. For example, Australia's Laughing Kookubura (*Dacelo novaeguineae*), whose raucous call moviegoers should recognize as Hollywood's all-purpose jungle sound, feeds on lizards, snakes, frogs, and large insects.

Ringed Kingfisher
Ceryle torquata
(SER-ih-lee tor-KWAY-tah)

The wide, white neck-ring gives this large kingfisher its name. Pete Dunne wrote, "The white collar is very conspicuous and is often what draws your eye when birds are perched against a riverbank."

Ceryle — The genus is Latin for "a kingfisher" from the Greek *kerulos*, a seabird mentioned by Aristotle and other authors, but not further identified. It has become associated with the kingfisher.

torquata — The specific epithet is Latin for "collared" from *torquis* (a collar). See common name above.

French Name: Martin-pêcheur à Ventre Roux
Spanish Names: Martin Pescador de Collar; Martin-pescador Collarejo
Other Names: King Kong Fisher; Cra-cra; Pie; Martin Pecheur

Belted Kingfisher
Ceryle alcyon
(SER-ih-lee AL-sih-on)

Like a blue jay with a Bart Simpson haircut.

The common name refers to the slate-blue breast band in both sexes. In addition the female sports a rusty belly band.

Ceryle — The genus is Latin for "a kingfisher" from the Greek *kerulos*, a seabird mentioned by Aristotle and other authors, but not further identified. It has become associated with the kingfisher.

alcyon — The specific epithet is derived from a proper name. Alcyon was the daughter of Aeolus, the god of the wind. When the body of her drowned husband Ceyx washed inshore, she was so grief-stricken that she cast herself into the sea and drowned as well. The gods taking pity changed them both into kingfishers. This is also the root of Halcyon

Belted Kingfisher, by Louis Agassiz Fuertes

Days, a two-week period of calm weather before and after the winter solstice. The Greeks believed that at this time kingfishers built floating nests of fish bones and shells at sea. For the birds' benefit Aeolus kept the seas calm during this period. Halcyon may be influenced by the Greek *hals* (of the sea) and *kuon* (conceiving).
French Name: Martin-pêcheur d'Amérique
Spanish Name: Martin Pescador Norteño
Other Names: Kingfisherman; Fishroyer; Blue Diver; Fly-up-the-creek; Lazy-bird; Ringneck; Halcyon; Cruidein; Sanglode; Martin Pecheur; Martin Pescador Norteno; Plongeur; Martin Pescador; Martin Plongeur; Martin Zambullidor; Martin-Pêcheur; Peche-martin; Pêcheur; Murlach; Pie; Pajaro del Rey; Pitirre de Agua; Pitirre de Mangle; Pitirre de Río

Green Kingfisher
Chloroceryle americana
(klor-oh-SER-ih-lee ah-mer-ih-CANE-ah)

The dark bottle-green upperparts give this kingfisher its name. Formerly known as Texas Kingfisher.
Chloroceryle — The genus name means "green kingfisher" from the Greek *khloros* (yellow green) and *ceryle* (a kingfisher).
americana — The specific epithet is Modern Latin for "of America."
French Name: Martin-pêcheur Vert
Spanish Name: Martin Pescador Verde
Other Name: Texas Green Kingfisher

Order Piciformes

Family Picidae
Woodpeckers

Woodpeckers peck wood for three distinct reasons. They drill into tree trunks to forage for wood-boring insects. They excavate nesting cavities, and they drum by hammering rapidly on a surface to resonate a sound that declares their territory.

Lewis's Woodpecker
Melanerpes lewis
(mel-an-ER-peez LOO-iss)

This woodpecker is named for Meriwether Lewis of the famed Lewis and Clark Expedition. See specific epithet below.

Melanerpes — The genus name means "black creeper" from the Greek *melas* (black) and *herpes* (a creeper). Creeper describes these birds' foraging method of creeping up tree trunks searching bark crevices for insects, although many also hawk flying insects out of the air. Black is a dominant color of some of the species in this genus.

lewis — Alexander Wilson named this species Lewis's Woodpecker – *Picus torquatus* (collared) in honor of Captain Meriwether Lewis (1774–1809), one of the leaders of the Lewis and Clark Expedition (1804–1806), that explored the Louisiana Territory. The type specimen was collected near what is now Helena, Montana, on July 20, 1805.

French Name: Pic de Lewis
Spanish Name: Carpintero de Lewis
Other Names: Black Woodpecker; Crow Woodpecker

~

Red-headed Woodpecker
Melanerpes erythrocephalus
(mel-an-ER-peez eh-rith-row-SEF-ah-lus)

"A splendid red-crimson head is his, one might with good reason call him a

Lewis's Woodpecker, by Allan C. Brooks

miniature Red Riding-hood. His back is a slaty or steely blue in the strong light, the wings and tail are blue-black, on the wing is a broad patch of white, and the under parts and tips of the tail-feathers are white. To a certain degree he suggests the national colors, red, white, and blue." — F. Schuyler Mathews (1921)

Most woodpeckers show some red on the head, particularly in the males, but this is the only eastern species to have an entirely red head. Adults of both sexes sport this field mark, but immatures have brown heads. This woodpecker's colors inspired the colloquial names Flag Bird and Patriotic Bird.

Red-headed Woodpecker and Downy Woodpecker, by Louis Agassiz Fuertes

Melanerpes — The genus name means "black creeper" from the Greek *melas* (black) and *herpes* (a creeper). Creeper describes these birds' foraging method of creeping up tree trunks searching bark crevices for insects, although many also hawk flying insects out of the air. Black is a dominant color of some of the species in this genus.

erythrocephalus — The specific epithet means "red headed" from the Greek *erythros* (red) and *kephalos* (headed).

French Name: Pic à Tête Rouge
Spanish Names: Carpintero de Cabeza Roja; Carpintero Cabecirroja
Other Names: Redhead; Tricolor; Tricolored Woodpecker; Woodpecker; Flag Bird; Patriotic Bird; Shirttail Bird; White-shirt; Half-a-shirt; Jelly Coat; Whitewing; Flying Checkerboard; Rodkup; Rodkuppicher Shbecht; Pique-bois à Tête Rouge

Acorn Woodpecker
Melanerpes formicivorus
(mel-an-ER-peez for-mih-SIV-or-us)

"Some prominent California ornithologists have named this bird the "California acorn-storing woodpecker," a rather long but very appropriate name, for it designates one of its most characteristic habits and names the largest item in its food supply." — Arthur Cleveland Bent (1939)

The Acorn Woodpecker is named for a major food, which makes up more than 50% of this bird's annual diet. Communal groups of these birds cache acorns in granary trees for winter consumption. They spend the summer chiseling small, funnel-shaped holes into the trunks of dead trees, fence posts, or telephone poles. The woodpeckers gather the acorns in late summer and fall and hammer them into the holes one at a time. Since acorns vary in size, the birds must find the right-sized hole so the acorn will fit snugly. Loose ones are easily stolen. As the acorns dry out and shrink from their holes,

Acorn Woodpecker, by Louis Agassiz Fuertes

they may need to be rehoused. The whole group curates their stash and guards it against thieves.

Melanerpes — The genus name means "black creeper" from the Greek *melas* (black) and *herpes* (a creeper). Creeper describes these birds' foraging method of creeping up tree trunks searching bark crevices for insects, although many also hawk flying insects out of the air. Black is a dominant color of some of the species in this genus.

formicivorus — The specific epithet means "ant eating" from the Latin *formica* (an ant) and *vorus* (to devour). Although more than half of this woodpecker's diet consists of acorns and nuts, it does take insects, including grasshoppers, flies, beetles, and ants in spring and summer. Ants make up only a small portion of its insect prey. The Acorn Woodpecker's specific epithet would be more appropriate for the Northern Flicker, which frequently feeds on the ground at ant mounds. It is said the flicker eats more ants than any other species of bird.

French Name: Pic Glandivore

Spanish Names: Carpintero Arlequín; Carpintero Careto

Other Names: Ant-eating Woodpecker; California Woodpecker; California Acorn-storing Woodpecker; Mearns' Woodpecker; San Pedro Woodpecker; Stripe-breasted Woodpecker; Narrow-front Woodpecker; Carpintero; Carpintero Arlequin

Gila Woodpecker
Melanerpes uropygialis
(mel-an-ER-peez your-oh-PIDJ-ih-AY-liss)

The Gila (pronounced HE-lah) Woodpecker is named for the Gila River in Arizona, in the vicinity of which this species was discovered.

Melanerpes — The genus name means "black creeper" from the Greek *melas* (black) and *herpes* (a creeper). Creeper describes these birds' foraging method of creeping up tree trunks searching bark crevices for insects, although many also hawk flying insects out of the air. Black is a dominant color of some of the species in this genus.

uropygialis — The specific epithet means "tail rump" from the Greek *oura* (the tail) and *pyge* (the rump) and refers to the boldly barred rump and central tail feathers, which are field marks.

French Name: Pic des Saguaros

Spanish Names: Carpintero de Desierto; Carpintero de Gila

Other Names: Banded Woodpecker; Brewster's Woodpecker; Saguaro Woodpecker; Cardon Woodpecker; Pechileonado Desertico

Golden-fronted Woodpecker
Melanerpes aurifrons
(mel-an-ER-peez AR-ih-frons)

This woodpecker's bright yellow forehead gives it its name.

Melanerpes — The genus name means "black creeper" from the Greek *melas* (black) and *herpes* (a creeper). Creeper describes these birds' foraging method of creeping up tree trunks searching bark crevices for insects, although many also hawk flying insects out of the air. Black is a dominant color of some of the species in this genus.

aurifrons — The specific epithet means "golden forehead" from the Latin *aurus* (gold) and *frons* (the forehead).

French Name: Pic à Front Doré

Spanish Names: Carpintero de Frente Dorada; Carpintero Frentidorado

Other Name: Golden-front

Red-bellied Wooodpecker
Melanerpes carlinus
(mel-an-ER-peez car-ow-LINE-us)

Whatever possessed the individual who named the Red-bellied Woodpecker? Any normal person would have chosen a prominent feature like the bright red crown and nape. Why not Red-capped Woodpecker? But no, they chose a characteristic that is not at all apparent. The color on the belly is only visible in the field when the bird is hanging upside down from a tree branch, chickadee-fashion. And calling the belly red is a bit of a stretch; at best it just shows a pinkish or slightly orange tinge. Oh well. Probably the same individual named the Ring-necked Duck.

Melanerpes — The genus name means "black creeper" from the Greek *melas* (black) and *herpes* (a creeper). Creeper describes these birds' foraging method of creeping up tree trunks searching bark crevices for insects, although many also hawk flying insects out of the air. Black is a dominant color of some of the species in this genus.

carolinus — The specific epithet is Modern Latin for "of Carolina" and refers to the colonies before statehood, where presumably the type specimen was collected.

French Name: Pic à Ventre Roux

Spanish Names: Carpintero de Carolina; Carpintero Vientrirrojo

Other Names: Sham-shack Woodpecker; Zebra Woodpecker; Zebra; Zebra Bird; Zebra-back; Guinea Sapsucker; Orange Sapsucker; Orange Borer; Chad; Cham-chack; Sham-shack; Ram-shack; Jam-jack; La Petite Pique-bois Barre

~

Sidebar 23
Sapsuckers and Hummingbirds

Sapsuckers have a particularly important relationship with hummingbirds, especially those at the northern limits of their breeding range such as Algonquin Provincial Park in Ontario, Canada:

"Hummingbirds are so tiny and burn up energy at such tremendous rates, they cannot survive without plentiful, daily supplies of high energy food. In the tropics, there are flowers in bloom all year round, and their sugar-rich nectar is always available. Here in Algonquin, however, there are no flowers suitable for hummingbirds before the month of July, and they certainly couldn't delay their return from the tropics that long. In fact, Rubythroats return to the Park in May and for the first two months depend on tree sap (very similar to flower nectar) that oozes from the holes left by sapsuckers . . . So dependent are hummingbirds on Sapsuckers in early summer that they will actually follow them around, and they energetically defend any sapsucker tree they find against other hummers." — Dan Strickland (1995)

Williamson's Sapsucker
Sphyrapicus thyroideus
(sfy-rah-PIE-kus thigh-ROYD-ee-us)

In 1849, New York taxidermist John Graham Bell collected a new woodpecker twelve miles from Sutter's Mill in Eldorado County, California. The bird had a plain brown head, finely barred back, and a black patch on the breast. Bell called it the Brown-headed Woodpecker. John Cassin described the new species in 1852, giving it the name *Picus thyroideus* and called it the Black-breasted Woodpecker. On the Pacific Railway Survey in 1855, the expedition's assistant surgeon Dr. John S. Newberry collected a new woodpecker along the shore of Upper Klamath Lake in Oregon. This one was largely black with white markings, a red throat, and bright yellow belly. He named it *Picus williamsoni* after the expedition's leader Lieutenant Robert Stockton Williamson (1824–1882). What do these two events have in common? Well, in 1873, Henry Henshaw, while stationed at Fort Garland, Colorado, made an amazing discovery. He found a pair of woodpeckers feeding young in a cavity of a live aspen tree. One was a Williamson's Sapsucker, the other a Black-breasted Woodpecker. Turns out these weren't separate species at all, but the male and female of the same species! Williamson's Sapsucker displays striking sexual dimorphism, unusual for a woodpecker. Cassin had described a female specimen, Newberry a male. Cassin's specific epithet has priority, but Williamson is still commemorated by the common name.

Sphyrapicus — The genus name means "hammer woodpecker" from the Greek *sphyra* (a hammer or mallet) and the Latin *picus* (a woodpecker). The reference is to the bird's use of its bill like a hammer, when it drums on tree trunks.

thyroideus — The specific epithet means "shield-like" from the Greek *thyreos* (a shield) and *-oidos* (like) in reference to the female's black breast-band suggesting a breast plate.

French Name: Pic de Williamson

Spanish Names: Chupasavia Oscura; Chupasavia de Williamson

Other Names: Black-crowned Sapsucker; Natalie's Sapsucker; Williamson's

Woodpecker; Black-breasted Woodpecker; Brown-headed Woodpecker; Brown-backed Woodpecker; Round-headed Woodpecker

Yellow-bellied Sapsucker
Sphyrapicus varius
(sfy-rah-PIE-kus VARE-ih-us)

"Over 1000 species of woody plants have been documented as hosts for these sap wells, and the ecological web that results is remarkable. For instance, the Ruby-throated Hummingbird follows sapsuckers and drinks from the wells, and may even time its migration in parts of its range to coincide with peak sapsucker numbers. Several hundred other species use sapsucker wells, including bats, flying squirrels, insects, and other birds such as kinglets and warblers." — Jim McCormac (2004)

Its name sounds like a joke, but there really is such a bird as a Yellow-bellied Sapsucker. Yellow-bellied refers to the pale yellow wash on the lower breast and belly. Sapsucker refers to the fact that these woodpeckers drill horizontal rows of small holes (sap wells) in the trunks and limbs of living trees to feed on the sap. Each hole is inclined slightly downwards, so that it holds a pool of sap. The sapsucker then laps it up with its bristle-tipped tongue. It also takes any insects that have come to feed on the sap. Sapsuckers were once condemned as the enemies of forests, but it turns out they have an important relationship with many other species as described in the opening passage.

Sphyrapicus — The genus name means "hammer woodpecker" from the Greek *sphyra* (a hammer or mallet) and the Latin *picus* (a woodpecker). The reference is to the bird's use of its bill like a hammer, when it drums on tree trunks.

varius — The specific epithet is Latin for "variegated" and refers to the mixed colors of the plumage.

French Name: Pic Maculé

Spanish Names: Chupasavia de Vientre Amarillo; Chupasavia Vientre-amarillo; Carpintero Bebedor

Other Names: Common Sapsucker; Red-throated Sapsucker; Yankee Sapsucker; Sup-sap; Sap-sipper; Yellow-bellied

Yellow-bellied Sapsucker, by Louis Agassiz Fuertes

Woodpecker; Spanish Woodpecker; Pecker-wood; Yellow-belly; Yellow-hammer; Squealer; Bawm Lawffer; Carpintero de Paso; Carpintero Pechiamarillo; Sook; Charpentier; Pic-bois; Pic-bois à Tête Rouge; Pic Maculé; Pie

Red-naped Sapsucker
Sphyrapicus nuchalis
(sfy-rah-PIE-kus new-KAY-lis)

The red patch on the back of the head gives this woodpecker its name. Formerly considered a subspecies of the Yellow-bellied Sapsucker.

Sphyrapicus — The genus name means "hammer woodpecker" from the Greek *sphyra* (a hammer or mallet) and the Latin *picus* (a woodpecker). The reference is to the bird's use of its bill like a hammer, when it drums on tree trunks.

nuchalis — The specific epithet means

"pertaining to the nape" from the Greek *nucha* (the nape or the back of the neck), which is red.
French Name: Pic à Nuque Rouge
Spanish Names: Chupasavia de Nuca Roja; Chupasavia Nuquirroja
Other Names: Same as Yellow-bellied Sapsucker.

Red-breasted Sapsucker
Sphyrapicus ruber
(sfy-rah-PIE-kus RUBE-er)

Not only the breast, but the entire head is bright red in this woodpecker. Formerly considered a subspecies of the Yellow-bellied Sapsucker.

Sphyrapicus — The genus name means "hammer woodpecker" from the Greek *sphyra* (a hammer or mallet) and the Latin *picus* (a woodpecker). The reference is to the bird's use of its bill like a hammer, when it drums on tree trunks.

ruber — The specific epithet is Latin for "red."
French Name: Pic à Poitrine Rouge
Spanish Names: Chupasavia de Cabeza Roja; Chupasavia Pechirroja
Other Names: Red-head; Red-head Woodpecker

American Three-toed Woodpecker
Picoides dorsalis
(pick-oh-EYE-deez dor-SAY-liss)

This and the next species have only three toes on each foot, two facing forward, one backward. American distinguishes our species from the Eurasian Three-toed Woodpecker. They were formerly considered a single species, the Northern Three-toed Woodpecker.

Picoides — The genus name means "woodpecker-like" or "resembling a woodpecker" from the Latin *picus* (a woodpecker) and the Greek suffix *-oides* (like or resembling). The name suggests a similarity or relationship to woodpeckers in the Old World genus *Picus*. *Picus* is from a proper name, a mythological character, whom the sorceress Circe turned into a woodpecker.

dorsalis — The specific epithet is Latin for "of the back," perhaps referring to the distinctive pattern on the back of black horizontal bars on white.

French Name: Pic à Dos Rayé
Spanish Name: Carpintero de Tres Dedos
Eskimo and Inuit Names: Toyukpuk (big borer)
Other Names: Common Three-toed Woodpecker; Alpine Three-toed Woodpecker; Banded Three-toed Woodpecker; White-backed Three-toed Woodpecker; Alaska Three-toed Woodpecker; Ladder-back Woodpecker

Black-backed Woodpecker
Picoides arcticus
(pick-oh-EYE-deez ARK-tih-kus)

The solid, glossy black back, in contrast to the barred pattern on American Three-toed Woodpecker, gives this species its name. Formerly known as Black-backed Three-toed Woodpecker.

Picoides — The genus name means "woodpecker-like" or "resembling a woodpecker" from the Latin *picus* (a woodpecker) and the Greek suffix *-oides* (like or resembling). The name suggests a similarity or relationship to woodpeckers in the Old World genus *Picus*. *Picus* is from a proper name, a mythological character, whom the sorceress Circe turned into a woodpecker.

arcticus — The specific epithet is Latin for "northern," from the Greek *arktikos* (near the Great Bear) referring to the constellation Ursa Major in the northern sky. This species has a range across Canada and the northern United States.

French Name: Pic à Dos Noir
Spanish Name: Carpintero Artico
Other Names: Arctic Three-toed Woodpecker; Little Black Woodpecker; Pique-bois noir

Downy Woodpecker
Dryobates pubescens
(dry-oh-BATE-eez pew-BESS-enz)

The Downy Woodpecker is named for its nasal bristles, modified feathers that cover the nostrils to keep out sawdust. Those of the Downy are fine and fluffy when compared to those of the Hairy Woodpecker.

Dryobates — The genus name means "tree-dweller" from the Greek *drus* (the oak tree or any tree) and *–bates* (inhabitant). Formerly *Picoides pubescens*.

pubescens — The specific epithet is Latin for "downy," referring to the fine bristles that cover the nostrils.
French Name: Pic Mineur
Spanish Names: Carpintero Velloso Menor; Carpintero Plumonado
Eskimo and Inuit Names: Toyuk (the borer); Pu-gukh-tu-yu'-lik
Other Names: Northern Downy Woodpecker; Southern Downy Woodpecker; Little Guinea Woodpecker; Little Woodpecker; Glaner Woodpecker; Tommy Woodpecker; Batchelder's Woodpecker; Gairdner's Woodpecker; Nelson's Woodpecker; Spotted Woodpecker; Willow Woodpecker; Red-headed Woodpecker; Black-and-white Woodpecker; Black-and-white Driller; Little Sapsucker; Pic; Pique-bois

Nuttall's Woodpecker
Dryobates nuttallii
(dry-oh-BATE-eez NUT-all-ih-eye)

William Gambel discovered this woodpecker near Pueblo de los Angeles and found a nest containing young in an oak stump at Santa Barbara. He named it *Picus Nuttallii* in the *Proceedings of the Academy of Natural Sciences of Philadelphia* (1843) in honor of his mentor Thomas Nuttall, to whom he sent the plant specimens he had collected in the West.
Dryobates — The genus name means "tree-dweller" from the Greek *drus* (the oak tree or any tree) and –*bates* (inhabitant). Formerly *Picoides nuttallii*.
nuttallii — The specific epithet commemorates Thomas Nuttall (1786–1859), an English botanist and ornithologist. See common name above.
French Name: Pic de Nuttall
Spanish Names: Carpintero Californiano; Carpintero de Nuttall

Ladder-backed Woodpecker
Dryobates scalaris
(dry-oh-BATE-eez skay-LAIR-iss)

Horizontal black bars on the back, suggesting the rungs of a ladder, give this woodpecker its name.
Dryobates — The genus name means "tree-dweller" from the Greek *drus* (the oak tree or any tree) and –*bates* (inhabitant). Formerly *Picoides scalaris*.
scalaris — The specific epithet is Latin for "ladder' or "a flight of stairs."
French Name: Pic Arlequin
Spanish Names: Carpintero Mexicano; Carpintero Listado
Other Names: Cactus Woodpecker; Texas Woodpecker; Mexican Woodpecker; San Lucas Woodpecker; Texas Downy; Speckle-cheek; Carpinterillo

Red-cockaded Woodpecker
Dryobates borealis
(dry-oh-BATE-eez bor-ee-AH-lis)

A cockade is a rosette or knot of ribbon usually worn as a decoration on a hat. Alexander Wilson named this woodpecker for the tiny tuft of red feathers behind the male's eye. The red cockade is usually not apparent in the field.
Dryobates — The genus name means " tree-dweller" from the Greek *drus* (the oak tree or any tree) and –*bates* (inhabitant). Formerly *Picoides borealis*.
borealis — The specific epithet is Latin for "northern" from the Greek *boreas* (the north wind). French scientist Louis Jean Pierre Viellot was really off the mark when he named this species in 1807. He mistakenly assumed this woodpecker's range was the northern United States, when it actually occurs in the southeastern states from southern Virginia to Florida and west to eastern Texas. *Borealis* would have been more appropriate if this woodpecker occurred in the northern coniferous forests of Canada.
French Name: Pic à Face Blanche
Spanish Name: Carpintero de Florida
Other Names: Sapsucker; Pique-bois

Hairy Woodpecker
Dryobates villosus
(dry-oh-BATE-eez vil-OH-sus)

"Downy and hairy woodpeckers were stupidly misnamed, and the errors remain condoned by a wink of science. Downies have no more underlying down feathers than many other birds, and hairies have no hair. Both birds were saddled with these inappropriate names by a few early observers with questionable visual acuity

who stated that both species looked somewhat hairy. Ornithologists, for some reason, often prefer to maintain long-accepted misnomers than to correct them."
— John Eastman (1997)

With the name hairy, you might expect this bird to have shaggy plumage like a kiwi or a silkie bantam. But the Hairy Woodpecker's plumage is just as sleek as any other woodpecker's. The name may come from the observations of early naturalists as described above, or it may refer to the nasal tufts, modified feathers that cover the nostrils to keep out sawdust. These feathers are distinctly hair-like, especially when compared to those of the Downy Woodpecker.

Dryobates — The genus name means "tree-dweller" from the Greek *drus* (the oak tree or any tree) and *–bates* (inhabitant). Formerly *Picoides villosus*.

villosus — The specific epithet is Latin for "hairy." See common name above.

French Name: Pic Chevelu
Spanish Names: Carpintero Velloso Mayor; Carpintero Serranero
Other Names: Rocky Mountain Hairy Woodpecker; Guinea Woodpecker; Big Guinea Woodpecker; Big Woodpecker; White-breasted Woodpecker; Audubon's Woodpecker; Canadian Woodpecker: Newfoundland Woodpecker; Queen Charlotte Woodpecker; Chihuahua Woodpecker; Modoc Woodpecker; Spanish Woodpecker; Cabanis' Woodpecker; White Woodpecker; Red-headed Woodpecker; Harris' Woodpecker; Harry; Big Sapsucker; Iron-bill; Sook; Pic; Pique-bois

White-headed Woodpecker
Dryobates albolarvatus
(dry-oh-BATE-eez al-bow-lar-VAY- tus)

This unique woodpecker's white head, which contrasts with its black body, gives it its name.

Dryobates — The genus name means "tree-dweller" from the Greek *drus* (the oak tree or any tree) and *–bates* (inhabitant). Formerly *Picoides albolarvatus*.

albolarvatus — The specific epithet means "white masked" from the Latin *albus* (white) and *larvatus* (masked).

French Name: Pic à Tête Blanche
Spanish Name: Carpintero de Cabeza Blanca
Other Names: Northern White-headed Woodpecker; Southern White-headed Woodpecker; White-headed Sapsucker; Little White-headed Sapsucker

Arizona Woodpecker
Dryobates arizonae
(dry-oh-BATE-eez air-ih-ZONE-ee)

This Mexican species, whose range just reaches southern Arizona and New Mexico, is named for the state where the type specimen was collected. Formerly considered conspecific with Strickland's Woodpecker (*P. stricklandi*) of Mexico.

Dryobates — The genus name means "tree-dweller" from the Greek *drus* (the oak tree or any tree) and *–bates* (inhabitant). Formerly *Picoides arizonae*.

arizonae — The specific epithet is Modern Latin for "of Arizona."

French Name: Pic d'Arizona
Spanish Name: Carpintero de Arizona
Other Name: Brown-backed Woodpecker

Northern Flicker, by Louis Agassiz Fuertes

Northern Flicker
Colaptes auratus
(koh-LAP-teez oh-RAY-tus)

There are two possibilities for the origin of Flicker. One is that it is imitative of one of this woodpecker's calls, sometimes rendered as *flicka, flicka, flicka, flicka*. The other is that it refers to the brightly colored wing linings that seem to flicker as the bird flies. Northern distinguishes this species from other flicker species of South America such as the Chilean Flicker (*C. pitius*) and the Andean Flicker (*C. rupicola*). The Northern Flicker was formerly divided into two species, the Yellow-shafted Flicker in the east and the Red-shafted Flicker in the west. Each was named for the color of the undersides of the wing and tail feathers. In addition, the male Yellow-shafted Flicker sports a black moustache mark and the Red-shafted Flicker a red one. These two forms readily interbreed where their ranges overlap, producing intermediate forms. Because of this, they were lumped together as a single species in 1973.

Colaptes — The genus name means "chiseller" from the Greek *kolapto* (to chisel).

auratus — The specific epithet means "gilded" or "ornamented with gold" from the Latin *aurum* (gold) and refers to the yellow linings of the wing and tail shafts of the Northern Flicker's eastern (Yellow-shafted) form.

French Name: Pic Flamboyant

Spanish Names: Carpintero de Pechera Común; Carpintero Collarejo

Other Names: Common Flicker; Golden-winged Flicker; Red-quilled Flicker; Sharp-billed Flicker; Yellow Flicker; Boreal Flicker; Southern Flicker; Northwestern Flicker; California Flicker; Mexican Flicker; Monterey Red-shafted Flicker; Hybrid Flicker; Yellow Woodpecker; Gold Woodpecker; Golden Woodpecker; Gold-winged Woodpecker; Flicker Woodpecker;

Sidebar 24
A Bird of Many Monikers

"The Flicker is the most interesting bird of all the Woodpeckers. The fact that it has been called by so many different names besides that of Flicker shows how very different kinds of people have made very different kinds of observations of the bird. One observer has seen the bird fly into a hole it has chiseled out with its bill near the top of a high dead tree-stub and he has given the bird the name of High-hole or High-holder. Another person has heard the bird calling its *Yarrup-yarrup* while flying about from tree to fence post and to tree again in quest of food; hence the common name of Yarrup. Another person hearing the loud one-syllable call across the fields or swamp lot has named the bird the Clape. Yet another, hear-ing the swish of his friendly *weechem* call as he wings along in a wavy up and down flight from ten to a hundred feet above the ground has named the bird the Flicker." — L. Nelson Nichols (1917)

The Northern Flicker is the champion when it comes to colloquial names. It is said to have at least 160 nicknames, including spelling variations. Not surprisingly, the flicker's folk names can reflect appearance, vocalizations, or behavior. This most terrestrial of woodpeckers frequently feeds on the ground on ants, prompting its nickname Antbird. When flushed, this brown woodpecker suggests a partridge, hence Meadow Partridge and Partridge Woodpecker. As it flies away, the flicker displays its most prominent field mark, its white rump patch. Thus we have Cotton-rump, Cotton-tail, Cotton-backed Yellowhammer, and Silver Dollar Bird. The male's malar stripe is the source of Red-moustashed Woodpecker. The names Black-heart Woodpecker and Crescent-Bird refer to the black mark on the breast. The bird's colorful wing linings have prompted the nicknames Golden-winged Woodpecker, Orange-shafted Woodpecker, Red-quilled Flicker, Yellowhammer, Yellow Jay, Yellow-shafted Woodpecker, Yellow-winged Sapsucker, and Yellow-winged Woodcock.

Yellow-shafted Woodpecker; Red-shafted Woodpecker; Orange-shafted Woodpecker; Gaffer Woodpecker; Gaffle Woodpecker; Black-heart Woodpecker; Spotted Woodpecker; Pigeon Woodpecker; Partridge Woodpecker; Lark Woodpecker; Grasshopper Woodpecker; High-ho Woodpecker; Big Woodpecker; English Woodpecker; French Woodpecker; Red-moustached Woodpecker; Missouri Red-moustached Woodpecker; Woodpeck; Woodpicker; Tree-pecker; Peckerwood; Peckwood; Wood-Lark; Woodpecker Lark; Pigeon; Wood Pigeon; Golden-wing; Yellow-wing; Yellow-hammer; Yeller-hammer; Yallerhammer; Yellow'ammer; Yellowhammer High-hole; Red-hammer; Hammer-head; O-hi-o; Cotton-backed Yellowhammer; Cotton-rump; Cotton-tail; Sucker; Sapsuck; Big Sapsucker; Yellow-winged Sapsucker; Woodcock; Golden-winged Woodcock; Yellow-winged Woodcock; Woodchuck; Little Woodchuck; Ant Woodchuck; Yellow Jay; Winter Robin; Wild Hen; Meadow Partridge; Weather Bird; Weather-Hen; Rain Bird; Rain Fowl; Silver Dollar Bird; Antbird; Crescent-Bird; Taping Bird; Flitter; Fiddler; Gallie; Pink-throat; Shad-spirit; High-hole; High-holer; High-hold; High-holder; He-hi-holder; Heigh-ho; Hairy-wicket; Harry-wicket; Hivel; Hittuck; Hittocks; Hick-wall; Clape; Rampike; Jaune; Pivart; Peerit; Pee-ut; Pi-ute; Pe-up; Pie-bis; Pie-bris; Pic Dove; Pic-a-bois; Pique-a-bois; Pique-bois dore; Le Pic Aux-ailes Dores; Pique-bois-jaune; Poule-de-bois; Wake-up; Wick-up; Wa-wup; Walk-up; Yawker Bird; Yacker; Yecker; Yucker; Yaffle; Yarrup; Yaw-up; Yallow Wheeler; Yallow Whicker; Whittaker; Will Crisson; Cave-duc; Buidheag Bhuachair; Speight; Spright; Specht; Gel Specht; Gelb Specht; Gale Shbecht; Gree-shbecht; Carpintero Escapulario; Carpintero Ribero; Ome-tuc; On-thee-quan-nor-ow; Talpa-na-ni; Mo-ning-qua-na; Paw-paw-say; Paw-paw-say-og; O-zaw-wan-day Paw-paw-say; Wood-wall; Wood-quoi; Zebec

Gilded Flicker
Colaptes chrysoides
(koh-LAP-teez kriss-oh-EYE-deez)

The bright yellow under wings and tail give this flicker its name. For a time it was lumped with the Northern Flicker, but then it was split again.

Colaptes — The genus name means "chiseller" from the Greek *kolapto* (to chisel).

chrysoides — The specific epithet means "resembling gold" from the Greek *chrysos* (gold) and the suffix *-oides* (resembling or like).

French Name: Pic Chrysoïde
Spanish Names: Carpntero de Pechera de Arizona; Carpintero de California
Other Names: Mearns' Gilded Flicker; Wake-up; Wick-up; Yucker

Pileated Woodpecker
Dryocopus pileatus
(dry-OCK-oh-pus pie-leh-AY-tus)

Some pronounce it pie-leh-AY-ted; others pill-eh-AY-ted. Pileated means "capped" and refers to the prominent red crest sported by

Pileated Woodpecker, by Louis Agassiz Fuertes

both sexes. See specific epithet below.

Dryocopus — The genus name means "tree cleaver" or "wood cutter" from the Greek *drys* (an oak tree) and *kopis* (a cleaver).

pileatus — The specific epithet means "capped" from the Latin *pileus* (a felt cap) and refers to the bright red crest.

French Name: Grand Pic

Spanish Names: Carpintero Norteamericano; Carpintero Cabecirroja

Other Names: Northern Pileated Woodpecker; Black Woodpecker; Big Black Woodpecker; Great Black Woodpecker; Giant Woodpecker; Redhead; Large Red-headed Woodpecker; Devil's Woodpecker; Laughing Woodpecker; Good God Woodpecker; Cock of the North; Cock-of-the Woods; Log-cock; Black Logcock; Log-guard; Crow-with-the-hard-face; Good-god; Lord-God; Indian Hen; Carpenter Bird; Pine Duck; Rain Crow; Field Officer; Wood Kate; Laughing Jackass; Woodchuck; Log-cock Woodchuck; Wood Cock; Wood Hen; Coq de Bruyere; Coq des Bois; Pic; Pique; Pic Bois; Pique Bois; Pie; Pie à Tête Escarlate; Pic à Tête Rouge; Grand Pique-bois; Poule de Bois; Gros Pie; Huls Hock

Order Falconiformes

Family Falconidae
Caracaras and Falcons

Falcon derives from the Latin *falx* (a sickle). Depending on the authority, it either refers to the long, pointed scythe-like wings in flight or to the hooked bill and curved talons. Perhaps all three.

Crested Caracara
Caracara cheriway
(KER-ah-CAR-ah [or CAR-ah-CARE-ah] CHAIR-ih-way)

"Often in the morning, or before sundown, it throws back its head until it almost touches its shoulders and gives its high, cackling cry which gave rise to the Brazilian name of Caracara, the Cuban Caraira, and the less apt Argentine name Carancho." — Thomas Barbour (1923)

Caracara is a Tupi (Brazilian) Indian name for this bird, which is imitative of the call.

This species is named for its shaggy, black crest. Pete Dunne calls it "a roadside eagle wearing a badly fitting toupee." Formerly known as Audubon's Caracara.

Caracara — See common name above.

cheriway — The specific epithet is the Carib (Venezuelan) Indian word for this species.

French Name: Caracara du Nord

Spanish Names: Caracara Quebrantahuesos; Caracara Común; Cargahuesos

Other Names: Common Caracara; Northern Caracara; Audubon's Caracara; Caracara Eagle; Brazilian Caracara Eagle; Mexican Eagle; Mexican Buzzard; King Buzzard; King of Vultures; Caraira

American Kestrel
Falco sparverius
(FAL-koh spar-VER-ih-us)

Kestrel comes from the Old French *crecele*, the diminutive of which *crecerelle* means "rattle" and is probably imitative of the call. This species is the American counterpart of the Eurasian Kestrel (*F. tinnunculus*). Formerly known as Sparrow Hawk.

Falco — Like the common name falcon, the genus name stems from the Latin *falx* (a sickle), referring either to the shape of the wings in flight or to the hooked beak and talons.

sparverius — The specific epithet is Latin for "pertaining to sparrows," perhaps alluding to the fact that this little falcon sometimes takes small birds, although its main diet is small mammals and insects. It may have been named for the Eurasian Sparrowhawk (*Accipiter nisus*), which is actually the Old World counterpart of our Sharp-shinned Hawk.

American Kestrel, by Allan C. Brooks

French Name: Crécerelle d'Amérique
Spanish Name: Cernícalo Americano
Other Names: American Sparrow Hawk; Desert Sparrow Hawk; Killy Hawk; Kitty Hawk; Grasshopper Hawk; House Hawk; Mouse Hawk; Cliff Hawk; Short-winged Hawk; Little Brown Hawk; Chicken Hawk; Bastard Hawk; Bullet Hawk; Rusty-crowned Falcon; Falcon Comun; Wood Bird; Cuyaya; Cleek Cleek; Gli-gli; Gri-gri; Killy-killy; Pri-pri; Tilly; Dauwa Shdosser; Dauwa Woi; Emerillon; Halcón; Halcón Cernícalo; Cernícalo; Mangeur de Poule; Mangeur Poulets; Merieleon; Peregreve; Shdos Fogel; Shdos Woi; Speireag; Windhover; Windfucker

~

Merlin
Falco columbarius
(FAL-koh koh-lum-BARE-ih-us)

It would be logical to assume this little falcon was named for the magician of Arthurian legend, particularly since falconry dates back many centuries. But this falcon's name has nothing to do with Arthurian legend. Merlin stems from the Old French *esmerillon*, a name for this species, which in turn comes from the Latin *merula* (a blackbird). The blackbird in this case is the Common Blackbird (*Turdus merula*) of Europe and a possible prey item. Formerly known as Pigeon Hawk, either because it resembled a Rock Pigeon in flight or because it preyed on pigeons.

Falco — Like the common name falcon, the genus name stems from the Latin *falx* (a sickle), referring either to the shape of the wings in flight or to the hooked beak and talons.

columbarius — The specific epithet means "pertaining to pigeons" from the Latin *columba* (a pigeon or a dove) and the suffix *-arius* (pertaining to). See common name above. Nature writer Francesca Greenoak suggests, "Possibly too it might have been thought that the Merlin, a lady's falcon, should catch something fittingly ladylike such as a dove."

French Name: Faucon Émerillon
Spanish Names: Halcón Esmerjón; Esmerejón
Eskimo Name: Kid-ga-viat-chau-rak (smallest hawk)

Other Names: American Merlin; Richardson's Merlin; Black Merlin; Black Hawk; Black Pigeon Hawk; Eastern Pigeon Hawk; Western Pigeon Hawk; Richardson's Pigeon Hawk; Suckley's Pigeon Hawk; Chicken Hawk; Bullet Hawk; Blue Hawk; Small Blue Hawk; Small Bird Hawk; Sparrow Hawk; Stone Hawk; Stone Falcon; Rock Falcon; Pigeon Falcon; Falcon Migratorio; Rock Kestrel; Hawk Kestrel; Hobby; Maalin; Meirneal; Tweedler; Little Blue Corporal; La Petit Caporal; Jack; Emouchet; Gri-gri de Montagne; Esmerejon; Halcón; Halconito;

~

Aplomado Falcon
Falco femoralis
(FAL-koh fem-or-AY-liss)

Aplomado is Spanish for "leaded," referring to the lead gray color of the back and upperwing coverts. Ernest Choate suggests that it refers to a plumb, a lead weight at the end of a line, that a carpenter uses to establish a true vertical. The reference is to the near vertical stoop when this falcon descends on prey.

Falco — Like the common name falcon, the genus name stems from the Latin *falx* (a sickle), referring either to the shape of the wings in flight or to the hooked beak and talons.

femoralis — The specific epithet is Latin for "pertaining to the thighs." The reference is to the rich rufous color of the thighs, which contrast with the bird's gray upperparts.

French Name: Faucon Aplomado
Spanish Name: Halcón Aplomado
Other Names: Femoral Falcon; American Hobby; Orange-chested Hobby

~

Gyrfalcon
Falco rusticolis
(FAL-koh russ-TICK-oh-lus)

"In the days when hawking was at its height in England, the rank of the individual could be told by the particular species of Falcon which he carried on his wrist: the Gyrfalcon was carried by royalty, the Peregrine Falcon was carried by an earl, the Goshawk by a yeoman, the Sparrow Hawk by a priest, and the Kestrel by a servant." — *Birds of America* (1917)

There are several opinions on the origin of

Falconiformes

Gyrfalcon, by Louis Agassiz Fuertes

this falcon's common name. The one that makes the most sense is that it derives from the Latin *gyrfalco* or *girofalco*, a corruption of *hierofalco* meaning "sacred falcon," because the bird was so highly revered in the sport of falconry, particularly the white morph. See opening passage above. Other ideas are that *gyr* stems from the Latin *gyro* (to circle), the Germanic *ger* (a spear), or the High German *giri* (greedy), an arrogant human judgement.

Falco — Like the common name falcon, the genus name stems from the Latin *falx* (a sickle), referring either to the shape of the wings in flight or to the hooked beak and talons.

rusticolus — The specific epithet means "living in the country" from the Latin *rusticulus* (rural or country) and *cola* (inhabitant), referring to this birds remote habitat on the Arctic tundra.

French Name: Faucon Gerfaut

Spanish Name: Halcón Gerifalte

Eskimo and Inuit Names: Okiotak (the one who stays all winter); Atkuaruak (like caribou mittens); Che-kuv-yuk (refers to striping on breast)

Other Names: White Gyrfalcon; Gray Gyrfalcon; Black Gyrfalcon; McFarlane's Gyrfalcon; Asiatic Gyrfalcon; Ice Falcon; Iceland Falcon; Greenland Falcon; Labrador Jer Falcon; Cyrfalcon; Duck Hawk; Killer Hawk; Speckled Hawk; Partridge Hawk; Speckled Partridge Hawk; White Hawk; Winter Hawk

Peregrine Falcon
Falco peregrinus
(FAL-koh per-eh-GRY-nus)

Peregrine means "wandering," and refers to these falcons' long-distance migrations (some go as far as South America) and tendency to disperse widely outside the breeding season. They have even been observed far at sea, capturing birds and eating them on the wing. James Jobling says the Peregrine Falcon is "so called because young birds on their first long distance migration were better suited to falconry than those taken from the nest." Formerly known as Duck Hawk.

Falco — Like the common name falcon, the genus name stems from the Latin *falx* (a sickle), referring either to the shape of the wings in flight or to the hooked beak and talons.

Peregrine Falcon, by Louis Agassiz Fuertes

peregrinus — The specific epithet is Latin for "wandering" or "foreign." Literally it means "across country" from *per* (through) and *ager* (a field). This is also the root of the word pilgrim.
French Name: Faucon Pélerin
Spanish Name: Halcón Peregrino
British Name: Peregrine
Eskimo Name: Kidgavitch Kiriat (small hawk)
Other Names: American Peregrine; Rock Peregrine; Rock Falcon; Mountain Falcon; Wandering Falcon; Blue-backed Falcon; Spotted Falcon; Peale's Falcon; Falcon Peregrino; Great-footed Hawk; Blue Hawk; Bullet Hawk; Stock Hawk; Hunting Hawk; Game Hawk; Eagle Hawk; Peregrine Hawk; Perry Hawk; Pinnacle Hawk; Faakin Hawk; Goshawk; Faucon; Tercel; Aile Pointue; Batarde Aigle; Beau Voleur; Frappe Canard; Mangeur de Canards; Mangeur de Poules; Halcón de Patos; Hinkelwoi; Woi

∼

Prairie Falcon
Falco mexicanus
(FAL-koh meks-ih-CANE-us)

This falcon is named for its open grassland habitat. It also occurs in desert and in mountains above timberline.

Falco — Like the common name falcon, the genus name stems from the Latin *falx* (a sickle), referring either to the shape of the wings in flight or to the hooked beak and talons.

mexicanus — The specific epithet is Modern Latin for "of Mexico," where the type specimen was collected.
French Name: Faucon des Prairies
Spanish Names: Halcón Mexicano; Halcón Pradeño
Other Names: American Lanner (male); American Lanneret (female); Bullet Hawk

∼

Order Psittaciformes

Family Psittacidae
New World Parrots

Our only native parrot the Carolina Parakeet (*Conuropsis carolinensis*) was unfortunately hunted to extinction. The last known living specimen died in the Cincinnati Zoo in 1918. See Extinct Species and Subspecies. A Mexican species, the Thick-billed Parrot (*Rhynchopsitta pachyrhyncha*), used to stray into the mountains of southeastern Arizona and southwestern New Mexico, and may have nested on occasion, but none has been seen there since 1938. The parrots we see now are exotics, escapes from the pet trade, although two species (the Green Parakeet and the Red-crowned Parrot) seen in southern Texas may be wild vagrants from Mexico. Dozens of species may occur in the United States, but the AOS lists only five that have well-established feral breeding populations. Those are the ones covered here. Parrot is derived from the French *perrot*, a nickname for Pierre (Peter) and is thus a pet name for a familiar bird. Parakeet is the Anglicized form of the French *parroquet*, meaning "little Peter."

Monk Parakeet
Myiopsitta monachus
(my-oh-SIT-ah MON-ah-kuss)

This parrot's gray forehead and breast, suggesting a monk's hood, give it its name.

Myiopsitta — The genus name means "fly parrot" from the Greek *myia* (a fly) and the Latin *psitta* from the Greek *psittakos* (a parrot).

monachus — The specific epithet is Greek for "a monk." See common name above.

French Name: Conure veuve
Spanish Name: Perico Monje
Other Names: Green Monk Parakeet; Monk; Quaker Parakeet; Quaker Conure; Gray-headed Parakeet; Gray-breasted Parakeet; Gray-breasted Parrot; Periquito Monje

Green Parakeet
Aratinga holochlora
(ar-ah-TING-ah hoe-low-KLOR-ah)

This parakeet's green plumage gives it its name. The bird is well named for it is green all over, bright green above, and yellowish green below.

Aratinga — The genus name derives from *arucatinga*, the Tupi (Brazilian) Indian name for a parrot. It actually means "colored like a macaw" from the Tupi word *Ara*, a component of several bird names such as *ararauna* (a macaw) and *araracanga* (a parrot).

holochlora — The specific epithet derives from the Greek *holo* (whole) and *khloros* (yellow green).

French Name: Conure Verte
Spanish Names: Perico Mexicano; Perico Verde Mexicano

White-winged Parakeet
Brotogeris versicolurus
(broh-TODGE-er-is ver-sih-COL-oor-us)

Prominent white wing-patches visible in flight, give this parrot its name. Formerly considered conspecific with the Yellow-chevroned Parakeet (*B. chiriri*) under the name Canary-winged Parakeet.

Brotogeris — The genus name means "with a human voice" from the Greek *brotos* (a man) and *gerus* (a voice). The reference is to the parrot's ability to mimic human speech.

versicolurus — The specific epithet means "tail of various colors" from the Latin *versicolor* (parti-colored) and the Greek *ouros* (tailed). The reference is to this parrot's tail sporting two colors, green above and blue below.

French Name: Toui à Ailes Variées
Spanish Name: Perico Versicolor

Red-crowned Parrot
Amazona viridigenalis
(am-ah-ZONE-ah vir-id-ih-gen-ALE-is)

This green parrot sports a bright red crown, which gives it its name.

Amazona — The genus name means "of the Amazon," where many parrots in this genus occur. Spanish explorers are said to have named the region for the female warriors of Greek legend, possibly because they thought the long-haired indigenous people were all women. Another explanation is that Amazon derives from the Tupi (Brazilian) Indian word *amassona* which means "boat destroyer." Birds in this genus are the familiar talking, green parrots associated with pirates.

viridigenalis — The specific epithet means "green cheeked" from the Latin *viridis* (green) and *gena* (the cheek). The reference is to the green cheeks that contrast with the red crown and blue nape.

French Name: Amazone à Joues Vertes
Spanish Name: Loro Tamaulipeco
Other Names: Green-cheeked Amazon; Ootorra Coronirroja

Family Psittaculidae
Old World Parrots

Budgerigar
Melopsittacus undulatus
(mel-oh-SIT-ah-kus un-dul-AY-tus)

This is the familiar "parakeet" sold in pet shops in a variety of artificially-bred colors. The original wild type, native to Australia, is green and yellow. Budgerigar (pronounced BUDGE-er-ih-gar) derives from the Australian aboriginal word *betcherrygah* meaning "good parrot."

Melopsittacus — The genus name means "song parrot" from the Greek *melos* (a song) and *psittakos* (a parrot) and refers to this parakeet's warbling song and pleasant liquid notes.

undulatus — The specific epithet is Latin for "wavy" and refers to the wavy lines on the bird's nape, back, and wings.

French Name: Perruche Ondulée
Spanish Name: Periquito Común
Other Names: Parakeet; Shell Parakeet; Grass Parakeet; Budgie; Budgerygah; Periquito de Australia

Order Passeriformes

Family Tityridae
Becards

Rose-throated Becard
Pachyramphus aglaiae
(pack-ih-RAM-fuss ah-GLAY-ee)

Pronounced BEK-ard. Becard means "big beak" from the French *bec* (the beak) plus the intensifying suffix *–ard* from the German *hart* (bold) and refers to this bird's heavy, slightly crooked bill. Rose-throated refers to the male's rose-colored throat patch.

Pachyramphus — The genus name means "thick bill" from the Greek *pakhus* (thick) and *rhamphos* (the bill).

aglaiae — In 1839, French ornithologist Baron Frédérick de Lafresnaye described this species in the *Revue Zoologique* from a specimen in the collection of M. Charles Brelay. He gave it the scientific name *Platyrhynchus Aglaiae* in honor of Monsieur Brelay's wife, Madame Aglaé Brelay (fl. 1839):

"In dedicating this species to Madame Brelay, our sole aim has been to render homage to the particular zeal with which she busies herself with ornithology and assists Monsieur Brelay in the formation of his large collection, which already numbers several thousand items. We are far from approving of the habit of giving new birds the names of women, who are often strangers to the love of ornithology ... We do not think that personal names are admissible except when they recall that of some naturalist, writer, traveler, artist, or zealous collector who has already rendered or is capable of rendering some service to the science."

French Name: Bécarde à Gorge Rose
Spanish Names: Mosquero Cabezón Degollado; Llorón Degollado; Llorón Plomizo
Other Name: Xantus' Becard

Family Tyrannidae
Tyrant Flycatchers

Flycatchers are named for their foraging behavior called hawking, in which the bird flies out from a perch to snap up a flying insect and then return to the same perch or to a different one nearby. Tyrant refers to the aggressive nature these birds have in defending their territories. See Eastern Kingbird for more on this. These birds are not closely related to the Old World Flycatchers in the family Muscicapidae.

Northern Beardless-Tyrannulet
Camptostoma imberbe
(cam-TOE-stow-mah im-BER-bah)
or (cam-toe-STOW-mah im-BER-bah)

Tyrannulet means "little tyrant" and refers to this bird's tiny size (smaller than most warblers) and its aggressive nature. Beardless refers to the fact that this species lacks the rictal bristles (hair-like feathers at the base of the bill) that are characteristic of most flycatchers. Northern distinguishes this species from the Southern Beardless-Tyrannulet (*C. obsoletum*) of South America. Formerly known as Beardless Flycatcher.

Camptostoma — The genus name is Greek for "bent mouth" from *kamptos* (bent) and *stoma* (the mouth) and refers to the slightly down-curved bill.

imberbe — The specific epithet is Latin for "beardless."

French Name: Tyranneau Imberbe
Spanish Names: Mosquero Lampiño; Mosquerito Lampiño Norteño; Mosquerito Chillón
Other Name: Northern Beardless Flycatcher

Dusky-capped Flycatcher
Myiarchus tuberculifer
(my-ih-ARK-us tew-ber-CUE-lih-fer)

Dusky-capped describes the color of the crown. Formerly known as Olivaceous Flycatcher.

Myiarchus — The genus name means "lord of the flies" from the Greek *muia* (a fly) and *arkhos* (a lord or ruler) and refers to the birds' preying on flying insects.

tuberculifer — The specific epithet means "carrier of little bumps" from the Latin *tuber* (a bump or knob) and *fero* (to bear or carry). The name refers to two small, horny swellings at the bend of each wing.

French Name: Tyran Olivâtre
Spanish Names: Copetón Triste; Copetón Crestioscuro

Ash-throated Flycatcher
Myiarchus cinerascens
(my-ih-ARK-us sin-er-AS-enz)

This flycatcher gets its name from the pale gray throat, suggesting the color of ashes.

Myiarchus — The genus name means "lord of the flies" from the Greek *muia* (a fly) and *arkhos* (a lord or ruler) and refers to the birds' preying on flying insects.

cinerascens — The specific epithet means "ash-gray" or "ashy" from the Latin *cineris* (ashes).

French Name: Tyran à Gorge Cendrée
Spanish Names: Copetón Cenizo; Copetón Gorjicenizo

Great Crested Flycatcher
Myiarchus crinitus
(my-ih-ARK-us crih-NITE-us)

This flycatcher's bushy crest gives it its name. Great describes the relatively large size (8¾ inches) in relation to other flycatcher species.

Myiarchus — The genus name means "lord of the flies" from the Greek *muia* (a fly) and *arkhos* (a lord or ruler) and refers to the birds' preying on flying insects.

crinitus — The specific epithet is Latin for "hairy" and describes the shaggy crest.

French Name: Tyran Huppé
Spanish Name: Copetón Viajero

Other Names: Crested Flycatcher; Great Crested Yellow-bellied Flycatcher; Yellow-bellied Flycatcher; Greatcrest; Crested Phoebe; Snakeskin Bird; May-bird; Wild Irishman of Flycatchers; Frate; Wheep

Brown-crested Flycatcher
Myiarchus tyrannulus
(my-ih-ARK-us tie-RAN-you-lus)

This flycatcher is named for its brownish-olive crest. Formerly known as Wied's Crested Flycatcher for Prince Maximilian zu Wied (1782–1867), a German naturalist and author.

Myiarchus — The genus name means "lord of the flies" from the Greek *muia* (a fly) and *arkhos* (a lord or ruler) and refers to the birds' preying on flying insects.

tyrannulus — The specific epithet means "little tyrant" from the Latin *tyrannus* (a tyrant) plus a diminutive suffix, a reference to this species' aggressive territorial behavior.

French Name: Tyran de Wied
Spanish Names: Copetón Tirano; Copetón Crestipardo
Other Names: Arizona Crested Flycatcher; Mexican Crested Flycatcher; Mexican Flycatcher; Wied's Flycatcher

La Sagra's Flycatcher
Myiarchus sagrae
(my-ih-ARK-us SAG-ree)

This flycatcher is named for Ramón de La Sagra (1801–1871), a Cuban botanist and author. See specific epithet below.

Myiarchus — The genus name means "lord of the flies" from the Greek *muia* (a fly) and *arkhos* (a lord or ruler) and refers to the birds' preying on flying insects.

sagrae — In 1852, Johannes Gundlach pointed out that French naturalist Alcide Dessalines d'Orbigny had incorrectly described this species under the name *Tyrranus Phoebe*. Gundlach gave it "the name *Myiarchus la Sagra*, as he was the first to make it known to the public."

French Name: Tyran de La Sagra
Spanish Name: Copetón de De La Sagra

Great Kiskadee
Pitangus sulphuratus
(pih-TANG-us sul-fur-AY-tus)

Kiskadee is imitative of this bird's call. Great describes its relatively large size, nearly as big as a Belted Kingfisher. Formerly known as Kiskadee Flycatcher.

Pitangus — The genus name is the Latinized form of *pitangua*, the Tupi (Brazilian) Indian name for this bird.

sulphuratus — The specific epithet is Latin for "sulphurous" and refers to the bright yellow underparts.

French Name: Tyran Quiquivi
Spanish Names: Luis Grande; Bienteveo Grande
Other Names: Kiskadee; Greater Kiskadee; Kiskadee Flycatcher; Derby Flycatcher; Big-headed Flycatcher; Bull-headed Flycatcher

Sulphur-bellied Flycatcher
Myiodynastes luteiventris
(my-ih-oh-dih-NAS-teez lew-teh-eye-VEN-triss)

Sulphur-bellied refers to the pale yellow underparts, heavily streaked in black.

Myiodynastes — The genus name means "fly master" or "lord of the flies" from the Greek *muia* (a fly) and *dunastes* (a lord or ruler). The reference is to the bird feeding on flies and other insects.

luteiventris — The specific epithet means "yellow belly" from the Latin *luteus* (saffron yellow) and *venter/ventris* (the belly).

French Name: Tyran Tigré
Spanish Names: Papamoscas Atigrado; Papamoscas Vientre-amarillo; Mosquero Vientriazufrado
Other Name: Arizona Sulphur-bellied Flycatcher

Tropical Kingbird
Tyrannus melancholicus
(tih-RAN-us mel-an-KOH-lih-cus)

Kingbirds are named for their fearlessness in defending their nesting territories. See Eastern Kingbird for more on this. In addition, many species have a hidden patch of colorful feathers that they may erect during aggressive encounters, when it might suggest a king's crown. Tropical describes this species habitat in Mexico.

Tyrannus — The genus name is Latin for "a tyrant," a severe and cruel ruler. Like the common name, it refers to the birds' aggressive territorial behavior. See Eastern Kingbird for more details.

melancholicus — The specific epithet is Latin for "melancholy" from the Greek *melankholikos* and refers to the Tropical Kingbird's irritable disposition.

French Name: Tyran Mélancolique
Spanish Name: Tirano Tropical
Other Names: Olive-backed Kingbird; West Mexican Kingbird; Lichtenstein's Kingbird; Yellow Pipiri; Pipiri Jaune

Couch's Kingbird
Tyrannus couchii
(tih-RAN-us KOUCH-ih-eye)

While associated with the U.S. and Mexican Boundary Survey, Darius Nash Couch collected birds in northern Mexico. He obtained two undescribed flycatchers at Nuevo León and San Diego in March and April of 1853. His notes on the species read, "Very common and noisy; found among the large trees of gardens and luxuriant river bottoms." Spencer Fullerton Baird described this new species from Couch's specimens in *Reports of Explorations and Surveys . . . for a Railroad [Route] from the Mississippi River to the Pacific Ocean* (1858). He gave it the name *Tyrannus couchii* in Couch's honor. Formerly considered a subspecies of the Tropical Kingbird.

Tyrannus — The genus name is Latin for "a tyrant," a severe and cruel ruler. Like the common name, it refers to the birds' aggressive territorial behavior. See Eastern Kingbird for more details.

couchii — The specific epithet commemorates Darius Nash Couch (1822–1897), a Civil War general, who led a zoological expedition to northern Mexico. See common name above.

French Name: Tyran de Couch
Spanish Names: Tirano Silbador; Tirano de Couch
Other Names: Same as Tropical Kingbird.

Cassin's Kingbird
Tyrannus vociferans
(tih-RAN-us voe-SIFFer-anz)

In 1830, ornithologist George Lawrence received a specimen of this flycatcher that was collected in Texas. Believing it to be new to science, he named it *Tyrannus Cassinii* or Cassin's Tyrant Flycatcher in honor of John Cassin (1813–1869), Curator of Ornithology at the Academy of Natural Sciences in Philadelphia. However, William Swainson had already described this species in 1826 from a specimen collected in the state of Temascáltepec, Mexico. Therefore Swainson's scientific name has priority, but the common name still commemorates Cassin.

Tyrannus — The genus name is Latin for "a tyrant," a severe and cruel ruler. Like the common name, it refers to the birds' aggressive territorial behavior. See Eastern Kingbird for more details.
vociferans — The specific epithet is Latin for "clamorous" or "shouting" and refers to the fact that this is our noisiest kingbird.
French Name: Tyran de Cassin
Spanish Names: Tirano Gritón; Tirano de Cassin

Thick-billed Kingbird
Tyrannus crassirostris
(tih-RAN-us kras-ih-ROS-triss)

This kingbird's noticeably heavier bill gives it its name.
Tyrannus — The genus name is Latin for "a tyrant," a severe and cruel ruler. Like the common name, it refers to the birds' aggressive territorial behavior. See Eastern Kingbird for more details.
crassirostris — The specific epithet means "thick beak" from the Latin *crassi* (thick or heavy) and *rostris* (the beak).
French Name: Tyran à Gros Bec
Spanish Names: Tirano de Pico Grueso; Tirano Piquigrueso

Western Kingbird
Tyrannus verticalis
(tih-RAN-us ver-tih-KALE-iss)

This kingbird is named for its range west of the Mississippi. Formerly known as Arkansas Kingbird.

Tyrannus — The genus name is Latin for "a tyrant," a severe and cruel ruler. Like the common name, it refers to the birds' aggressive territorial behavior. See Eastern Kingbird for more details.
verticalis — The specific epithet means "crowned" or "pertaining to the top of the head," from the Latin *vertex* (the crown of the head). The reference is to the concealed red crown patch.
French Name: Tyran de l'Ouest
Spanish Names: Tirano de Bordes Blancos; Tirano Occidental
Other Names: Flycatcher; Arkansas Flycatcher; Bee Bird; Bee Martin; Tirano Palido

Eastern Kingbird
Tyrannus tyrannus
(tih-RAN-us)

"Kingbirds are aptly named, for they are indeed monarchs who brook no intrusion into their nesting territories by birds many times their size . . . From its commanding perch on a fencepost, bush, or telephone

Eastern Kingbird and Red-eyed Vireo,
by Louis Agassiz Fuertes

wire, the Kingbird dashes out fearlessly to harass every passing crow, hawk, or other large bird that dares trespass on its domain. Invariably the trespasser flees ignominiously, but the Kingbird keeps attacking until the interloper is well on his way." — Oliver Austin, Jr. (1961)

Kingbirds are named for their aggressiveness in defending their territories, as described above. Eastern refers to this species' range; it is the common species in the eastern United States and Canada, and distinguishes it from the Western Kingbird and other *Tyrannus* species.

Tyrannus — The genus/species name is Latin for "a tyrant," a severe and cruel ruler. Like the common name, it refers to the birds' aggressive territorial behavior. See above.

French Name: Tyran Tritri

Spanish Names: Tirano de Dorso Negro; Tirano Viajero; Tirano Norteño

Other Names: Tyrant Flycatcher; Pipiry Flycatcher; Killer Bird; Butcher Bird; Bee Bird; Bee Martin; Bee-eater; Field Martin; Black Grasset; Gros Grasset; Barteur de Corbeaux; Fouetteur de Corbeau; Fouetteur de Corville; Mangeur d'Abeilles; Eemafresser; Eema Woi; Tertri; Tritri

Gray Kingbird
Tyrannus dominicensis
(tih-RAN-us dom-in-ih-SEN-sis)

The Gray Kingbird is named for its gray upperparts.

Tyrannus — The genus name is Latin for "a tyrant," a severe and cruel ruler. Like the common name, it refers to the birds' aggressive territorial behavior. See Eastern Kingbird for more details.

dominicensis — The specific epithet is Modern Latin for "of Santo Domingo" (now Hispaniola) in the West Indies where the type specimen was collected.

French Name: Tyran Gris

Spanish Name: Tirano Gris

Other Names: Hard-head; Fighter; Bee Bird; Rain Bird; Chinchary; Christomarie; Petchary; Grey Petchary; Pestigre; Pipiri; Pipirite; Pipiry Flycatcher; Pick-Peter; Pitirre Abejero; Titirre

Scissor-tailed Flycatcher
Tyrannus forficatus
(tih-RAN-us for-fick-AY-tus)

"This is one of the most picturesque and graceful of American birds; and he has individuality, too, which would make him conspicuous without these physical peculiarities. His picturesqueness is due chiefly to his long and strikingly marked tail, which he is likely to open and shut when he is excited about anything. This ornament also serves to accentuate the grace or the erratic character of the bird's aerial gyrations, many of which apparently are indulged in simply for the fun of the thing. One of these is a rapidly executed series of ascents and dives, the bizarre effect of which is heightened by the spreading and closing of the streaming tail-feathers, the performance being accompanied by harsh screams emphasized at each crest of the flight wave. Again and for no apparent reason he will interrupt a slow and decorous straight-line flight by suddenly darting upward, uttering at the same time an ear-piercing shriek. Altogether there is something rather uncanny about much of this bird's conduct; and perhaps its unusual ways are responsible for the Mexican peasants' belief that its food is the brains of other birds, which of course, is a hideous slander." — *Birds of America* (1917)

This elegant flycatcher gets its name from the long, forked tail, suggesting the blades of scissors in appearance and movement as described in the opening passage.

Tyrannus — The genus name is Latin for "a tyrant," a severe and cruel ruler and refers to the birds' aggressive territorial behavior.

forficatus — The specific epithet means "possessing a pair of scissors" from the Latin *forfex/forficis* (scissors) and the suffix –*atus* (possessing).

French Name: Tyran à Longue Queue

Spanish Names: Tirano-tijereta Rosado; Tijereta Rosada

Other Names: Swallow-tailed Flycatcher; Texan Bird of Paradise

Fork-tailed Flycatcher, by John James Audubon

Fork-tailed Flycatcher
Tyrannus savanna
(tih-RAN-us sah-VAN-ah)

The long, deeply forked tail gives this flycatcher its name.

Tyrannus — The genus name is Latin for "a tyrant," a severe and cruel ruler and refers to the birds' aggressive territorial behavior.

savanna — The specific epithet is from the Taino (native people of the Greater Antilles) word *zabana*, meaning "a flat tropical or subtropical grassland" and refers to this flycatcher's habitat.

French Name: Tyran à Queue Fourchue
Spanish Names: Tirano-tijereta Gris; Tirano-tijereta Sabanero; Tijereta Sabanera
Other Name: Swallow-tailed Flycatcher

Olive-sided Flycatcher
Contopus cooperi
(KON-toh-pus COOP-er-eye)

"Mostly dark and somewhat shabby-looking, Olive-sided is a small-town politician in an old dark suit that doesn't fit anymore. Dingy gray upperparts and extremely blurry streaked sides give the bird an open-vested appearance . . . The "white shirt" peeking through the open vest is a standout feature and is usually easier to distinguish at a distance then the vest itself." — Pete Dunne (2006)

Blurry, brownish-olive streaks on its sides, described as a vest in the opening passage, give this flycatcher its name.

Contopus — The genus name means "short foot" from the Greek *kontos* (short) and *pous* (the foot). The reference is to the short tarsus. Formerly *Nuttallornis borealis*.

cooperi — The specific epithet honors zoologist William C. Cooper (1798–1864), a founder of the New York Lyceum of Natural History (now the New York Academy of Sciences).

French Name: Moucherolle à Côtés Olive
Spanish Name: Pibí Boreal
Other Names: Cooper's Flycatcher; Nuttall's Pewee; Boreal Pewee; Whip-poor-will

Greater Pewee
Contopus pertinax
(KON-toh-pus PER-tih-nacks)

Pewee is imitative of the song of the Eastern Wood-Pewee. Greater refers to this species' larger size (8 inches vs. 6 ½ inches) in relation to the Eastern and Western Wood-Pewees. Formerly known as Coues' Flycatcher in honor of Dr. Elliot Coues (1842–1897), an American ornithologist and army surgeon.

Contopus — The genus name means "short foot" from the Greek *kontos* (short) and *pous* (the foot). The reference is to the short tarsus.

pertinax — The specific epithet is Latin for "tenacious."

French Name: Moucherolle de Coues
Spanish Name: Pibí Mayor
Other Names: Coues' Pewee; Greater Pewee; Jose Maria

Western Wood-Pewee
Contopus sordidulus
(KON-toh-pus sore-DID-you-lus)

This is the western counterpart of the Eastern Wood-Pewee. It is named for its range west of the Great Plains.

Contopus — The genus name means "short

foot" from the Greek *kontos* (short) and *pous* (the foot). The reference is to the short tarsus.

sordidulus — The specific epithet means "somewhat dirty" or "the little dirty one" from the Latin *sordidus* (dirty, soiled, or shabby) plus a diminutive suffix. In this case the name refers to the bird's dull color.

French Name: Pioui de l'Ouest
Spanish Name: Pibí Occidental
Other Names: Western Pewee; Large-billed Wood Pewee

Eastern Wood-Pewee
Contopus virens
(KON-toh-pus VIR-enz)

"Tranquil and calming, the plaintive notes of the Eastern Wood-Pewee have been variously described as sweet, pure, peaceful, serene, and sad. The pewee's daytime song is composed of two slurred, whistled phrases — a wavering *pee-a-wee* and a downward *pee-oh*." — Lang Elliot (2006)

Pewee is imitative of this flycatcher's song as described above. The rising and falling inflection of the phrases *pee-a-wee* and *pee-oh* make it sound as though the bird is asking itself questions and then answering them. Wood refers to the species' habitat in deciduous and mixed woodlands. Eastern describes this flycatcher's range east of the Great Plains.

Contopus — The genus name means "short foot" from the Greek *kontos* (short) and *pous* (the foot). The reference is to the short tarsus.

virens — The specific epithet is Latin for "greenish" for the dark grayish-olive upperparts.

French Name: Pioui de l'Est
Spanish Name: Pibí Oriental
Other Names: Eastern Pewee; Pewee Flycatcher; Wood-Pewee Flycatcher; Small Pewee; Pewit; Pewit Flycatcher; Short-legged Pewit Flycatcher; Biwi; Tick Bird

Yellow-bellied Flycatcher
Empidonax flaviventris
(em-PID-oh-nacks flay-vih-VEN-triss)

The yellow wash on the underparts gives this flycatcher its name. Actually most *Empids* show some yellow on the belly, but this one's yellow throat is its most distinctive feature.

Empidonax — The genus name means "king of the gnats" from the Greek *empis/empidos* (a gnat or mosquito) and *anax* (a king or lord). The reference is to the birds' preying on small flying insects that they snatch out of the air.

flaviventris — The specific epithet means "yellow belly" from the Latin *flavus* (yellow) and *venter* (the belly).

French Name: Moucherolle à Ventre Jaune
Spanish Names: Mosquero de Vientre Amarillo; Mosquero Vientre-amarillo; Mosquerito Vientre-amarillo

Acadian Flycatcher
Empidonax virescens
(em-PID-oh-nacks vie-RESS-enz)

This flycatcher is not particularly well named, because it does not occur in Acadia, now Nova Scotia. The Acadian Flycatcher inherited its name from the first in the genus to be described. Here is the story:

"One lingering reminder of that early confusion is the misnamed Acadian flycatcher, a southern member of the clan. Initially ornithologists recognized just one small flycatcher with wing bars and an eye-ring - from a bird collected in Acadia, as Nova Scotia was once called. The specimen was dubbed *Empidonax acadicus*, and for years the subtle differences between it and other birds within this genus went unnoticed. Over time, it was realized that several different species do exist, distinguished by their songs, nesting practices, and habitats, rather than by appearance. But it was a southern flycatcher, which ranges no closer to Nova Scotia than Connecticut, that inherited the name from the original bird from far-off Acadia. Its scientific name was changed to *Empidonax virescens*, but the common name, Acadian flycatcher, stubbornly persists to this day."— *Reader's Digest Book of North American Birds* (2005)

Empidonax — The genus name means "king of the gnats" from the Greek *empis/empidos* (a gnat or mosquito) and *anax* (a king or lord). The reference is to the birds' preying on small flying insects that they snatch out of the air.

virescens — The specific epithet means "greenish" from the Latin *virescere* (to become green). It refers to the olive-green plumage. Peterson says this is "the greenest of all the *Empidonaces.*"

French Name: Moucherolle Vert
Spanish Names: Mosquerito Verdoso; Mosquero Verdoso
Other Names: Green Flycatcher; Green-crested Flycatcher; Small Green-crested Flycatcher; Small Pewee

Alder Flycatcher
Empidonax alnorum
(em-PID-oh-nacks all-NOR-um)

The Alder Flycatcher is named for one of its favored habitats, alder swamps. Until the early 1970s, this and the Willow Flycatcher were considered a single species, Traill's Flycatcher. See Willow Flycatcher below.

Empidonax — The genus name means "king of the gnats" from the Greek *empis/empidos* (a gnat or mosquito) and *anax* (a king or lord). The reference is to the birds' preying on small flying insects that they snatch out of the air.

alnorum — The specific epithet means "of the alders" from the Latin *alnus* (an alder tree).

French Name: Moucherolle des Aulnes
Spanish Names: Mosquero Ailero; Mosquerito de Charral
Other Name: Short-legged Pewit Flycatcher

Willow Flycatcher
Empidonax traillii
(em-PID-oh-nacks TRAIL-ih-eye)

This flycatcher is named for a favored habitat, willow thickets near water, but it also nests in dry, brushy fields. This species was formerly lumped with the Alder Flycatcher as Traill's Flycatcher. Although the AOU split the species in 1973, scientists had long suspected there were two species involved. As early as 1939, Roger Tory Peterson noted that the birds in Ohio sounded different from the ones in New York. The New York birds sang a three-note song *fee-BEE-o* and the ones in Ohio sang a two-note, sneezy *fitz-bew*. Also their breeding habitats were different. The birds in New York favored wet habitats such as alder thickets, while the Ohio birds preferred drier habitats. So Traill's Flycatcher was indeed two different species.

Empidonax — The genus name means "king of the gnats" from the Greek *empis/empidos* (a gnat or mosquito) and *anax* (a king or lord). The reference is to the birds' preying on small flying insects that they snatch out of the air.

traillii — In 1831, Audubon named this species in honor of his friend Dr. Thomas Stewart Traill (1781–1862), a physician of Edinburgh, Scotland.

French Name: Moucherolle des Saules
Spanish Names: Mosquerito de Traill: Mosquero Saucero

Least Flycatcher
Empidonax minimus
(em-PID-oh-nacks MIN-ih-mus)

"As its name indicates, the Least Flycatcher is the smallest of our common Flycatchers, but it makes up in energy of manner and emphasis of utterance what it lacks in size. As one observer remarked, the little fellow announces his name, *Che-bec*, with such a fervid jerk of both head and tail that he seems to be in real danger of snapping his head off. And this *che-becing* sometimes continues at a rate and with a persistency which almost make one wish that something of the kind might happen." — *Bird of America* (1917)

This flycatcher is named for its small size. It is the smallest eastern flycatcher. Chebec is a colloquial name, an imitation of its song.

Empidonax — The genus name means "king of the gnats" from the Greek *empis/empidos* (a gnat or mosquito) and *anax* (a king or lord). The reference is to the birds' preying on small flying insects that they snatch out of the air.

minimus — The specific epithet is Latin for "smallest" or "least." It is the superlative of the Latin *parvus* (small). The Least Flycatcher is the smallest flycatcher in the east, but the Buff-breasted Flycatcher and Northern Beardless Tyrannulet of southern Arizona are even smaller.

French Name: Moucherolle Tchébec
Spanish Names: Mosquero Mínimo; Mosquerito Chebec
Other Names: Chebec; Little Chebec; Sewick; Pewee

Hammond's Flycatcher
Empidonax hammondii
(em-PID-oh-nacks ha-MOND-ih-eye)

John Xantus discovered this species at Fort Tejon, California while he was serving there with the U.S. Army. He described it in the *Proceedings of the Academy of Natural Sciences of Philadelphia* (1858) and named it *Tyrannula hammondii* for his friend and mentor William A. Hammond, an Army surgeon who taught Xantus how to collect and prepare specimens for the Smithsonian, while they were both stationed at Fort Riley, Kansas.

Empidonax — The genus name means "king of the gnats" from the Greek *empis/empidos* (a gnat or mosquito) and *anax* (a king or lord). The reference is to the birds' preying on small flying insects that they snatch out of the air.

hammondii — The specific epithet commemorates Dr. William Alexander Hammond (1828–1900), a surgeon in the U.S. Army. See common name above.

French Name: Moucherolle de Hammond
Spanish Name: Mosquero de Hammond

Gray Flycatcher
Empidonax wrightii
(em-PID-oh-nacks RIGHT-ih-eye)

The Gray Flycatcher is named for its gray color in summer, showing no green or yellow as in most other *Empids*. But in fresh fall plumage, it shows a distinct olive wash above and yellowish below. This and the Dusky Flycatcher were formerly considered to be a single species, Wright's Flycatcher.

Empidonax — The genus name means "king of the gnats" from the Greek *empis/empidos* (a gnat or mosquito) and *anax* (a king or lord). The reference is to the birds' preying on small flying insects that they snatch out of the air.

wrightii — In 1858, Spencer F. Baird named this species in honor of Charles Wright (1811–1855), a plant hunter who collected for American botanist Asa Gray. Wright sent Baird notes on the birds he observed, but only collected a few. These included at least two specimens of the Gray Flycatcher he obtained near El Paso during his work with the Exploratory Team for the Pacific Railroad.

French Name: Moucherolle Gris
Spanish Name: Mosquero Gris

Dusky Flycatcher
Empidonax oberholseri
(em-PID-oh-nacks oh-ber-HOLE-ser-eye)

The Dusky Flycatcher is probably named for its overall darker color in comparison with the paler Gray Flycatcher. The two were formerly considered to be a single species, Wright's Flycatcher.

Empidonax — The genus name means "king of the gnats" from the Greek *empis/empidos* (a gnat or mosquito) and *anax* (a king or lord). The reference is to the birds' preying on small flying insects that they snatch out of the air.

oberholseri — In November of 1937, Allan R. Phillips of Flagstaff, Arizona paid a visit to the National Museum to study *Empidonax* flycatcher specimens. In 1939, he published a paper in *The Auk*, separating the Dusky Flycatcher from Wright's Flycatcher. He named the new species *Empidonax oberholseri* in honor of Harry Church Oberholser (1870–1963), a leading American taxonomist and later curator of ornithology at the Cleveland Museum of Natural History. Phillips wrote: "It gives me great pleasure to dedicate this species to Dr. Oberholser, whose unfailing assistance has made possible the preparation of this note."

French Name: Moucherolle Sombre
Spanish Name: Mosquero Oscuro

Pacific-slope Flycatcher
Empidonax difficilis
(em-PID-oh-nacks diff-ISS-ih-liss)

"As a bird watcher's identification skills grow, there are formidable challenges to be confronted and conquered. Learning the sparrows requires patience; mastering the profusion of fall warblers is an anguishing rite of passage; and sorting out small sandpipers is an enduring trial. But for pure consternation, all other groups pale next to the scientific genus *Empidonax*. These small, enigmatic, gray-green flycatchers can bring tears of frustration to the most skilled birder's eyes." — *Reader's Digest Book of North American Birds* (2005)

This flycatcher is named for its range along the Pacific coast from the Alaska panhandle to Baja California. Until 1989, this and the Cordilleran Flycatcher were considered to be a single species, the Western Flycatcher.

Empidonax — The genus name means "king of the gnats" from the Greek *empis/empidos* (a gnat or mosquito) and *anax* (a king or lord). The reference is to the birds' preying on small flying insects that they snatch out of the air.

difficilis — The specific epithet is Latin for "difficult" as in difficult to distinguish from other *Empids*, they are so similar in appearance:

"This remarkable group of smallish *Empidonax* flycatchers looks so much alike that they're essentially impossible to identify one from another visually. Nature's wicked trick, most birders might say, but how fascinating that, although their plumages have not changed since the ancestral Empid, their songs have, so it is by their songs that we can know them." — Donald Kroodsma (2008)

French Name: Moucherolle Côtier
Spanish Names: Mosquero Californiano; Mosquero Occidental
Other Name: Santa Barbara Flycatcher

Cordilleran Flycatcher
Empidonax occidentalis
(em-PID-oh-nacks ock-sih-den-TAIL-iss)

Cordilleran (pronounced kor-dil-YARE-an) is from the Spanish *cordilla*, a diminutive of *cuerda* (a cord). It refers to an extensive chain of mountains, in particular the principal mountain range of a continent. In this case it pertains to this flycatcher's range in the Rockies. This and the Pacific-slope Flycatcher were formerly considered the same species, the Western Flycatcher.

Empidonax — The genus name means "king of the gnats" from the Greek *empis/empidos* (a gnat or mosquito) and *anax* (a king or lord). The reference is to the birds' preying on small flying insects that they snatch out of the air.

occidentalis — The specific epithet is Latin for "western" and refers to this flycatcher's range in the western states.

French Name: Moucherolle des Ravins
Spanish Name: Mosquero Barranqueño

Buff-breasted Flycatcher
Empidonax fulvifrons
(em-PID-oh-nacks FULL-vih-fronz)

This flycatcher is named for the warm cinnamon-buff on the breast.

Empidonax — The genus name means "king of the gnats" from the Greek *empis/empidos* (a gnat or mosquito) and *anax* (a king or lord). The reference is to the birds' preying on small flying insects that they snatch out of the air.

fulvifrons — The specific epithet means "tawny forehead" from the Latin *fulvus* (tawny) and *frons* (the forehead). In this case *frons* is taken to mean "front" referring to the buffy chest.

French Name: Moucherolle Beige
Spanish Names: Mosquero de Pecho Leonado; Mosquero Pechicanelo
Other Names: Fulvous Flycatcher; Ruddy Flycatcher

Black Phoebe
Sayornis nigricans
(say-ORN-iss NIG-rih-kanz)

For phoebe, see next entry. This species is named for its largely flat black plumage. Only the belly and undertail coverts are white.

Sayornis — British naturalist William Swainson described this species in 1827 and gave it the name *Tyrannula nigricans*. In 1854, Charles Bonaparte erected the genus *Sayornis* (Say's bird) for the Black Phoebe. The name commemorates American entomologist Thomas Say. *Sayornis* now encompasses the Eastern Phoebe and Say's Phoebe as well. See Say's Phoebe.

nigricans — The specific epithet is Latin for "blackish."

French Name: Moucherolle Noir
Spanish Names: Papamoscas Negro; Mosquero Negro; Mosquero de Agua
Other Names: Black-headed Flycatcher; Western Black Phoebe; Western Black Pewee

Eastern Phoebe
Sayornis phoebe
(say-ORN-iss FEE-bee)

This flycatcher's common name is imitative of its song, the spelling influenced by the name Phoebe, Artemis the Greek goddess of the moon. Eastern refers to this species' range from the plains states east to the Atlantic coast, although in Canada it occurs as far west as Alberta and northeast British Columbia.

Sayornis — British naturalist William Swainson described the Black Phoebe in 1827 and gave it the name *Tyrannula nigricans*. In 1854, Charles Bonaparte erected the genus *Sayornis* (Say's bird) for the Black Phoebe. The name commemorates American entomologist Thomas Say. The genus *Sayornis* now encompasses the Eastern Phoebe and Say's Phoebe as well. See Say's Phoebe.

phoebe — See common name above.

French Name: Moucherolle Phébi

Spanish Names: Papamoscas Fibi; Mosquero Fibí

Other Names: Dusky Flycatcher; Black Cap Flycatcher; Pewit Flycatcher; Pewit; Wagtail; Phoebe Bird; Bridge Phoebe; Bean Bird; Tick Bird; Pewee; Bridge Pewee; Water Pewee; Barn Pewee; Pevrette; Fauvette; Biwi

Say's Phoebe
Sayornis saya
(say-ORN-iss SAY-yah)

In 1819–1820, Thomas Say accompanied Major Stephen H. Long and naturalist Titian Ramsay Peale on an expedition to the Rocky Mountains. Say discovered this bird on the Arkansas River near Pueblo, Colorado, but it was actually Peale who collected the first specimen on July 17, 1820. Charles Bonaparte named it *Muscicapa saya* in 1825. Bonaparte wrote the dedication in his *American Ornithology*; or *The Natural History of Birds Inhabiting the United States Not Given by Wilson*:

"I dedicate it to my friend THOMAS SAY, a naturalist, of whom America may justly be proud, and whose talents and knowledge are only equaled by his modesty."

Sayornis — British naturalist William Swainson described the Black Phoebe in 1827 and gave it the name *Tyrannula nigricans*. In 1854, Charles Bonaparte erected the genus *Sayornis* (Say's bird) for the Black Phoebe. The name commemorates American entomologist Thomas Say. *Sayornis* now encompasses the Eastern Phoebe and Say's Phoebe as well.

saya — The specific epithet commemorates Thomas Say (1787–1843), the Father of American Entomology. See common name above.

French Name: Moucherolle à Ventre Roux

Spanish Names: Papamoscas Llanero; Mosquero Llanero

Other Names: Say's Pewee; Flycatcher; Say's Flycatcher

Vermilion Flycatcher
Pyrocephalus rubinus
(pier-oh-SEFF-ah-lus rube-EYE-nus)

In a family whose members are mostly dressed in drab browns, grays, and olive-greens, here is a flamboyant exception. This spectacular flycatcher is named for the brilliant red of the male's crown and underparts. Vermilion is a vivid orange-red pigment made from the mineral cinnabar, ground to a fine powder. Chemically cinnabar is mercury sulfide (HgS). The word vermilion stems from the Old French *vermeillon* from the Latin *vermiculus*, a diminutive of the Latin *vermis* (a worm). Vermilion was so named, because its hue is similar to that of a red dye made from the scale insect (*Kermis vermilio*). In Mexico, the Vermilion Flycatcher is referred to as *sangre de toro* (blood of the bull) or *la brasita de fuego* (little coal of fire).

Pyrocephalus — The genus name means "fire head" from the Greek *pyros* (fire) and *kephale* (the head), in reference to the red crown of the male.

rubinus — The specific epithet is Latin for "ruby red."

French Name: Moucherolle Vermillon

Spanish Name: Mosquero Cardenal

Other Name: Mosquero Cardenalito

Vermilion Flycatcher, by Louis Agassiz Fuertes

Family Laniidae
Shrikes

Shrike is a cognate of "shriek" and refers to the harsh, shrill calls of many species. Some shrikes do have pleasant, musical songs, however.

Loggerhead Shrike
Lanius ludovicianus
(LANE-ih-us lewd-oh-VISS-ih-ANE-us)

Loggerhead means a disproportionately large head. The shrike's head is noticeably larger in proportion to its body than in most other Passerine birds.

Lanius — The genus name is Latin for "a butcher" and in fact one of this bird's nicknames is butcher bird. This comes from the habit of impaling their prey on thorns or barbwire.

Although shrikes are songbirds, they behave like little raptors, taking not only large insects but also small vertebrates including mammals, birds, and herptiles.

ludovicianus — The specific epithet is Modern Latin for "of Louisiana" and refers to the Louisiana Territory, the type locality.

French Name: Pie-grièche Migratrice
Spanish Names: Alcaudón Verdugo; Lanio Americano
Other Names: Southern Loggerhead Shrike; Migrant Shrike; White-rumped Shrike; Nelson's Shrike; California Shrike; Island Shrike; Migrant Loggerhead; Southern Butcher Bird; Summer Butcher Bird; Mouse-bird; French Mockingbird; Cotton-picker; Nine-killer; Ecorcheur; Verdugo Americano

Northern Shrike
Lanius borealis
(LANE-ih-us bore-eh-AY-liss)

"The great northern shrike, or butcherbird, is known to most of us only as a rather uncommon winter visitor throughout the northern half of the United States, where we see it as a solitary sentinel perched on the top of a tree, looking for some luckless small bird, or hovering over

Northern Shrike and Loggerhead Shrike, by Louis Agassiz Fuertes

an open field, ready to pounce on the timid little mouse as it threads his winter runway. Either bird or mouse is to be added to his larder, impaled on a nearby thorn or crotch, as the butcher hangs his meat; hence the appropriate name of butcherbird." — Arthur Cleveland Bent (1950)

The Northern Shrike is named for its more northerly breeding range compared to that of the Loggerhead Shrike. It breeds in Canada and Alaska. The Loggerhead's range is mainly in the Lower 48 States, but extends into southern Canada. Formerly considered conspecific with the Great Grey Shrike (*L. excubitor*) of Eurasia.

Lanius — The genus name is Latin for "a butcher" and in fact one of this bird's nicknames is butcher bird. This comes from the habit of impaling their prey on thorns or barbwire.

Although shrikes are songbirds, they behave like little raptors, taking not only large insects but also small vertebrates including mammals, birds, and herptiles.

borealis — The specific epithet is Latin for "northern" from the the Greek *Boreas*, a personification of the north wind. Formerly *Lanius excubitor*. The specific epithet *excubitor* is Latin for "sentinel."

French Name: Pie-grièche Boreale

Spanish Names: Alcaudón boreal; Alcaudón Norteño; Lanio Norteño
Eskimo and Inuit Names: Irirgik (eye extractor); Ti-ki-chiu-wuk
Other Names: Skrike; Shreek; Great Shrike; Great Northern Shrike; Northwestern Shrike; Winter Shrike; Sentinel Shrike; Butcher Bird; Northern Butcher Bird; Winter Butcher Bird; Mockingbird; Nine-killer; Joy-killer; Devil's Bird; Whiskey Jack; Devil's Whiskey-jack; White Whiskijohn; White Jay; Silky Jay; Murdering Bird; Murdering Pie; Pie Boreale; Ecorcheur; Wierangle

Family Vireonidae
Vireos

"The vireo is the only bird who has a verb for a name — "vireo" literally is Latin for "I am green." So he is, but not brilliantly so and that is one of the reasons why the layman who is not even a bird watcher hardly notices him despite the fact that some members of the genus are among the most abundant of our birds. Nearly everyone who has ever been in the country has heard a vireo sing but not one in ten has seen or at least noticed him." — Joseph Wood Krutch (1962)

Vireo doubles as both the common and genus name for this family. It is derived from the Latin *virere* (to be green), as olive-green is a dominant color in this family. Vireo is a name Aristotle used for an Old World bird, thought by some to be the European Greenfinch (*Carduelis chloris*), but vireos are not closely related to finches. Greenlet and Greeny are colloquial names for the Vireos.

Black-capped Vireo
Vireo atricapilla
(VEER-ee-oh ay-trih-cap-ILL-ah)

The male's black hood gives this species its name.
Vireo — The genus name is derived from the Latin *virere* (to be green), as olive-green is a dominant color in this family.
atricapilla — The specific epithet means "black haired," i.e. "black capped" or "black headed" from the Latin *ater* (flat black) and *capilla* (the hair).
French Name: Viréo à Tête Noire
Spanish Names: Vireo de Gorra Negra; Vireo Gorrinegro
Other Name: Black-capped Greenlet

White-eyed Vireo
Vireo griseus
(VEER-ee-oh GRISS-ee-us)

The adults of this species have white eyes.
Vireo — The genus name is derived from the Latin *virere* (to be green), as olive-green is a dominant color in this family.
griseus — The specific epithet is Latin for "gray" and refers to the olive-gray upperparts.
French Name: Viréo aux Yeux Blancs
Spanish Names: Vireo de Ojo Blanco; Vireo Ojiblanco
Other Names: Small White-eyed Vireo; Bermuda Vireo; Rio Grande Vireo; Key West Vireo; Maynard's Vireo; White-eyed Greenlet; Politician; Basket-bird; Hanging Bird; Julian Chivi Ojiblanco

Bell's Vireo
Vireo bellii
(VEER-ee-oh BELL-ih-eye)

Audubon named many birds for individuals, particularly those who supported his work. But he named this vireo in honor of John G. Bell out of gratitude for saving his life. The incident occurred near Fort Union, North Dakota in June of 1843 when one of the fort's hunters shot a bison bull. Audubon and Bell, thinking the animal was dead, ran down to join the hunter. But when they got close to the bison they discovered it wasn't dead after all. It got up and charged. When their pistols failed to stop it, Bell snatched the hunter's rifle and killed the bison when it was just a few feet from Audubon.
Vireo — The genus name is derived from the Latin *virere* (to be green), as olive-green is a dominant color in this family.
bellii — In 1844, Audubon named this bird in honor of John Graham Bell (1812–1889), a taxidermist from New York who accompanied him on his Missouri River trip in 1843. See

common name above.
French Name: Viréo de Bell
Spanish Name: Vireo de Bell
Other Names: Least Vireo; Texas Vireo; Arizona Vireo; Arizona Least Vireo; California Least Vireo; Bell's Greenlet

Gray Vireo
Vireo vicinior
(VEER-ee-oh vih-SIN-ih-or)

This species is named for its overall pale gray color without the olive wash of many other vireos.

Vireo — The genus name is derived from the Latin *virere* (to be green), as olive-green is a dominant color in this family.

vicinior — The specific epithet derives from the Latin *vicinus* (neighboring) and suggests that it means "similar to" (other species of vireos).

French Name: Viréo Gris
Spanish Name: Vireo Gris

Hutton's Vireo
Vireo huttoni
(VEER-ee-oh HUT-ton-eye)

In 1851, John Cassin named this bird for William Hutton at Spencer Fullerton Baird's request. Cassin initially objected:

"Calling that Vireo after your friend Hutton is one of the severest things. I don't want to do it — when he gets better known I will call something after him. This kind of thing is bad enough at best, but to name a bird after a person utterly unknown is worse than that. I do not doubt his entire capability but I don't like to thrust honors upon him."

Eventually Cassin complied with Baird's wishes and named the bird *Vireo Huttoni*, writing that the vireo was "presented with many other birds, by Mr. William Hutton, a zealous and talented young naturalist now resident at San Diego, in California, in honor of whom I have taken the liberty of naming it."

Vireo — The genus name is derived from the Latin *virere* (to be green), as olive-green is a dominant color in this family.

huttoni — The specific epithet commemorates William Hutton (fl.1851), a collector who had obtained the type specimen near Monterey, California. See common name above.

French Name: Viréo de Hutton
Spanish Names: Vireo Reyezuelo; Vireo de Hutton
Other Names: Anthony Vireo; Stephan's Vireo

Yellow-throated Vireo
Vireo flavifrons
(VEER-ee-oh FLAY-vih-frons)

"In a family not conspicuous for its fine feathers, this is certainly the beauty. The clear lemon-yellow worn at its throat spreads over its vest; its coat is a richer and more yellowish green than the other vireos wear, and its two wing-bars are as conspicuous as the white-eyed vireo's." — Neltje Blanchan (1917)

This vireo's bright yellow throat and breast, as described above, give it its name.

Vireo — The genus name is derived from the Latin *virere* (to be green), as olive-green is a dominant color in this family.

flavifrons — The specific epithet is Latin for "yellow forehead" from *flavus* (yellow) and *frons* (the forehead). In this case *frons* is taken

Yellow-throated Vireo, by John James Audubon

to mean "front," referring to the yellow throat and breast.
French Name: Viréo à Gorge Jaune
Spanish Names: Vireo de Garganta Amarilla; Vireo Gorjimarillo; Vireo Pechiamarillo
Other Names: Yellow-throated Greenlet; Julian Chivi Gargantiamarillo

Cassin's Vireo
Vireo cassinii
(VEER-ee-oh cass-IN-ih-eye)

This vireo is named for John Cassin. See specific epithet below. Formerly considered conspecific with Plumbeous and Blue-headed Vireos.
Vireo — The genus name is derived from the Latin *virere* (to be green), as olive-green is a dominant color in this family.
cassinii — The specific epithet honors John Cassin (1813–1869), Curator of Ornithology at the Academy of Natural Sciences of Philadelphia.
French Name: Viréo de Cassin
Spanish Name: Vireo de Cassin
Other Names: Western Blue-headed Vireo; Mountain Vireo

Blue-headed Vireo
Vireo solitarius
(VEER-ee-oh sol-ih-TARE-ih-us)

"The yellow-throated vireo may be more brilliantly colored, with its bright yellow throat, but, to my mind, the subject of this sketch is the handsomest of the vireos. His gray-blue head is accented by a pair of pure-white spectacles, eye rings, and loral stripes; in marked contrast are his olive-green back, his pure-white throat and breast, and his yellow sides. The soft color tones combine to make a most charming picture of pleasing loveliness."
— Arthur Cleveland Bent (1950)

This vireo is named for its dark blue-gray head, which along with its white spectacles gives it a helmeted appearance. The Blue-headed, Plumbeous, and Cassin's Vireos were previously considered to be a single species, the Solitary Vireo.
Vireo — The genus name is derived from the Latin *virere* (to be green), as olive-green is a dominant color in this family.

Blue-headed Vireo, by John James Audubon

solitarius — The specific epithet is Latin for "solitary" or "alone." Alexander Wilson possibly chose this name, because this vireo is usually seen singly in migration.
French Name: Viréo à Tête Bleue
Spanish Name: Vireo Solitario
Other Names: Mountain Vireo; Blue-headed Greenlet

Plumbeous Vireo
Vireo plumbeus
(VEER-ee-oh PLUM-bee-us)

Plumbeous derives from *plumbum*, the Latin word for "lead" and describes the lead-gray color of the plumage. The Plumbeous, Blue-headed, and Cassin's Vireos were previously considered conspecific.
Vireo — The genus name is derived from the Latin *virere* (to be green), as olive-green is a dominant color in this family.
plumbeus — The specific epithet is Latin for "leaden" or "lead-gray."
French Name: Viréo Plombé
Spanish Name: Vireo Plomizo
Other Name: Western Blue-headed Vireo

Philadelphia Vireo
Vireo philadelphicus
(VEER-ee-oh fill-ah-DEL-fih-kus)

This vireo is named for Philadelphia, Pennsylvania where the type specimen was collected during fall migration. Eastern Pennsylvania is outside this species' normal breeding and wintering range.

Vireo — The genus name is derived from the Latin *virere* (to be green), as olive-green is a dominant color in this family.

philadelphicus — The specific epithet is Modern Latin for "of Philadelphia." In 1851, John Cassin named and described this species from a specimen collected in woods near Philadelphia in September of 1842.

French Name: Viréo de Philadelphie
Spanish Names: Vireo de Filadelfia; Vireo Amarillento
Other Names: Brotherly-love Vireo; Brotherly-love Greenlet; Philadelphia Greenlet; Philly

Warbling Vireo
Vireo gilvus
(VEER-ee-oh JILL-vus)

"Whenever we turn in the literature of the warbling vireo we find that the author, after commenting on the bird's inconspicuousness, speaks enthusiastically of its song, pointing out the difference from the songs of the other vireos, the length of the song period, and the charm of the smoothly flowing warble . . . The song, as it goes on hour after hour, suggests a spirit of happiness, a contrast to the flaunting, martial bugling of the Baltimore oriole, another of the vireos' neighbors, and to the slow, sweet notes of the wood pewee with their hint of pathos. In the vireo's song there is an air of unhurried calm, a leisureliness we seldom hear in the voice of a bird. Spring brings us greater artists, more proficient technicians, birds of more exuberant joyousness, but no such comfortable and welcome 'guest of summer' as the warbling vireo." — Winsor Marrett Tyler (1950)

This vireo's pleasant warbling song, that rapidly runs up and down the scale, gives it its name, Here are a couple of mnemonic devices to help you learn the Warbling Vireo's song. First, imagine that the vireo is threatening a caterpillar, *When I see you, I will seize you, and squeeze you till you squirt!* Or try, *Iggledy piggledy, wiggledy piggledy, iggledy piggledy, weep!* Here are two more. *Can't you see it's best to work and sing like me?* or *I'll clear this tree of every wriggling worm I see.* Sure, they sound kind of silly. That's why we also call them moronic devices. But they do suggest the general cadence, if not the beauty, of the song.

Vireo — The genus name is derived from the Latin *virere* (to be green), as olive-green is a dominant color in this family.

gilvus — The specific epithet is Latin for "yellowish" or "pale yellow." This grayish species has white underparts that sometimes show a yellow wash.

Sidebar 25
The Long-wided Preacher

"The red-eye's eloquence was never very persuasive to my ear. Its short sentences, its tiresome upward inflections, its everlasting repetitiousness, and its sharp, querulous tone long since became to me an old story; and I have always thought that whoever dubbed this vireo the "preacher" could have had no very exalted opinion of the clergy." — Bradford Torrey (1889)

"No other of our birds sings so persistently all day long," wrote Winsor Marrett Tyler (1950), "and because his long-continued series of utterances, given in short, emphatic phrases, going on for hours, calls to mind a lengthy sermon, he has won the title "Preacher." Also known as preacher bird, the Red-eyed Vireo's short phrases heard all day long have been rendered *You see it, - you know it, - do you hear me? — do you believe it?* or *look up, way up, tree top, see it.* This vireo probably sings more songs in a day than any other species. In fact, in 1954, Canadian ornithologist Louise de Kiriline Lawrence counted 22,197 songs from a single bird in a fourteen-hour period. Now that is some long-winded preacher.

French Name: Viréo Mélodieux
Spanish Names: Vireo Gorjeador; Vireo Canoro
Other Names: Eastern Warbling Vireo; Western Warbling Vireo; Warbling Greenlet; Warbling Flycatcher

Red-eyed Vireo
Vireo olivaceus
(VEER-ee-oh awl-ih-VAY-see-us)

This vireo is named for the adults' bright red eyes.

Vireo — The genus name is derived from the Latin *virere* (to be green), as olive-green is a dominant color in this family.

olivaceus — The specific epithet is Latin for "olive-colored" and refers to the olive-green upperparts.

French Name: Viréo aux Yeux Rouges
Spanish Names: Vireo de Ojo Rojo; Vireo Ojirrojo
Other Names: Bartram's Vireo; Red-eye; Red-eyed Greenlet; Preacher; Preacher Bird; Teacher; Hang-nest; Little Hang-nest; Julian Chivi Ojirojo

Yellow-green Vireo
Vireo flavoviridis
(VEER-ee-oh flay-voh-VEER-ih-dus)

This vireo looks much like a more vividly colored Red-eyed Vireo. Where the latter is olive-green, this one is a brighter yellow-green, and it has bright yellow sides and undertail coverts.

Vireo — The genus name is derived from the Latin *virere* (to be green), as olive-green is a dominant color in this family.

flavoviridis — The specific epithet is Latin for "yellow-green" from *flavus* (yellow) and *viridis* (green).

French Name: Viréo Jaune-verdâtre
Spanish Names: Vireo Amarillo Verdoso; Vireo Cabecigrís

Black-whiskered Vireo
Vireo altiloquus
(VEER-ee-oh al-tih-LOW-kwus)

This vireo is named for the dark whisker stripe between the cheek and the throat.

Vireo — The genus name is derived from the Latin *virere* (to be green), as olive-green is a dominant color in this family.

altiloquus — The specific epithet means "high speaker" from the Latin *altus* (high) and *loqui* (to speak) and refers to this species' habit of singing high in the treetops.

French Name: Viréo a Moustaches
Spanish Name: Vireo Bigotudo
Other Names: John Philip; John-chew-it; John-to-whit; Tom Kelly; Whip-Tom-Kelly; Cheap-John-Stirrup; Lady Bird; Predicator; Bastard Grive; Greenlet; Juan Chivi; Julián Chivi; Julián Chivi Bigotinegro; Petit Panache; Bien-te-veo; Pere Gris; Chavos-por-el; Piad; Chouèque; Oiseau Canne

Family Corvididae
Jays, Magpies, and Crows

Jay is believed to stem from *Gaius*, a Roman personal name. In Britain, common dooryard birds were often given familiar names like robin, martin, and jackdaw. It may also be imitative of the harsh calls of some of these birds, in particular Blue Jays and Steller's Jays. Magpie is a contraction of Magot Pie. See Black-billed Magpie. Crow is imitative.

Canada Jay
Perisoreus canadensis
(per-ih-SOAR-ih-us can-ah-DEN-sis)

Until recently, this bird was known as the Gray Jay, named for its fluffy plumage in shades of gray, varying from light to dark. In 2018, the AOS (a merger of the AOU and the Cooper Society in 2016) restored the previous historical common name Canada Jay, which dates back at least to 1831. It is an appropriate name, too, for the larger portion on this bird's range is in the boreal forests of Canada from the Maritimes to the Pacific coast and from Labrador and the Yukon south through the Rockies to New Mexico. The AOU had changed the common name to Gray Jay in 1957. Why? Perhaps they liked a descriptive name that was in line with other jay species such as Blue Jay, Green Jay, and Brown Jay. Another possible

Canada Jay, Pinyon Jay, and Clark's Nutcracker,
by Louis Agassiz Fuertes

explanation was to avoid geographically awkward subspecies names such as Idaho Canada Jay or Oregon Canada Jay. But this explanation doesn't hold up, because in 1954, the AOU elected to not use common names for subspecies anymore. In any case the common name for this bird has been Gray Jay for sixty years. The move to restore the original name was spurred by Canadian biologist Dan Strickland and six other ornithologists. They argued that both Canada Jay and Gray Jay were used concurrently for different subspecies, that the change to Gray Jay violated an AOU principle of retaining traditional vernacular names whenever possible, and there was precedent involving another species, the Mexican Jay which the AOU changed to Gray-breasted Jay in 1983 and then reversed its decision in 1995. Another matter they considered was the possibility of designating the species as Canada's National Bird.

Perisoreus — "The genus name means "hoarder" from the Greek *perisoreuo* (to heap up) and refers to the Canada Jay's food-caching behavior as explained here:

Unlike the vast majority of northern birds, the Gray Jay is a permanent resident, performing the seemingly impossible task of surviving the long season of cold and snow when there is no obvious food supply. The Gray Jay manages this trick by storing insects, berries, and pieces of meat or mushrooms all over its territory during summer and fall. It is these thousands of hidden food stores, tucked away in the trees behind flakes of bark or tufts of lichen, that comfortably sustain Gray Jays through the winter. Food storage is so central to the survival of the Gray Jays that it affects almost every aspect of their lives. For example they have special, enlarged salivary glands so that they can cover the food they hide with a sticky coating and fasten it more securely in their hiding places. They even nest in March when the snow is still deep so that the young will fledge that much earlier and have a head start on amassing food stores they will need to get through their first winter." — Dan Strickland (1995)

canadensis — The specific epithet is Modern Latin for "of Canada" where this species has an extensive range.

French Names: Geai du Canada; Mésangeai du Canada

Spanish Name: Chara Gris

Eskimo and Inuit Names: Kirik (imitative) Ku-pa-nu-ukh-puk; Kobarno

Other Names: Alaska Jay; Rocky Mountain Jay; Oregon Jay; Oregon Gray Jay; Coastal Gray Jay; Cat Jay; Dumb Jay; Venison Jay; Jay-bird; Jay-jack; Lumberjack; Camp Robber; Thief; Camp Bird; Whiskey Jack; Whiskey John; Mohawk; Meat Hawk; Meat Bird; Venison Bird; Venison Heron; Grease Bird; Tallow Bird; Carrion Bird; Caribou Bird; Moose Bird; Potato Bird; Moon Bird; Snow Bird; Molly Bird; Cat Bird; Hudson Bay Bird; Butcher Bird; Butcher's Boy; Gut-eater; Deer Hunter; Geal Bleu; Pie; Magpie; Pigheid; Gorby; Eun Gorm; Screuch Ancoille

Sidebar 26
The Trickster of the North Woods

"The name Canada jay, accepted by ornithologists, is seldom used by the backwoodsman, the hunter, the trapper, and the wanderer in the north woods, who know this familiar bird by a variety of other common names. The name most commonly applied to the bird is "whisky jack," with no reference, however, to any fondness for hard liquor; the old Indian name "wiss-ka-chon," or "wiska-tjon," has been corrupted to "whisky john," and then to "whisky jack." It is also often called "camp robber," "meat bird," "grease bird," meat hawk," "moose bird," "lumber jack," "venison hawk," and "Hudson Bay bird," all of which are quite appropriate and expressive of the bird's character and behavior." — Arthur Cleveland Bent (1947)

One of the Canada Jay's colloquial names Whiskey Jack is the anglicization of the Cree Indian word *Wisakedjak*, a trickster character of their legends. Unlike the tricksters of the Plains Indians, Wisakedjak is portrayed as a benevolent culture hero. He is neither god nor man, good nor evil. As a teacher, he exposes the dangerous and the absurd. His name means flatterer. Somewhat resembling a fluffy, oversized chickadee and said to be "deceptively cute," the Canada Jay is indeed a trickster well known for its habit of making off with food from picnic tables, which it then caches. It will even enter a tent or a cabin in search of food, prying into any box, can, jar, or open container. The jay may take inedible objects as well. This behavior originated the colloquial names Camp Robber, Camp Bird, and Thief. The Canada Jay can be unusually tame if it feels a handout is imminent. A visitor to the North Woods may experience a magical Disney moment, if he offers trail mix on an extended hand. Here is what to expect when you camp in the north country:

"When "Whiskey Jack" calls, loggers and trappers look to their stores. This bird seizes bacon from the frying pan, pecks at fresh meat hung up to cool, and shows special fondness for baked beans. He filches chunks from fresh-caught fish and steals the bait from traplines. He invades a tent to snatch a cracker from an open box, and makes off with matches, pencils, cigarettes, and chewing tobacco. He pecks to pieces candles and bars of soap. A gunshot brings *canadensis* winging, for he knows great feasting is in store when a moose or deer is killed." — Olin Sewall Pettingill (1964)

But there are some positive aspects to the Canada Jay's behavior, too:

"Although cordially disliked by the trapper and the hunter, because it interferes with their interests, this much maligned bird has its redeeming traits; it greets the camper, when he first pitches camp, with demonstrations of welcome, and shares his meals with him; it follows the trapper on his long trails through the dark and lonesome woods, where any companionship must be welcome; it may be a thief, and at times a nuisance, but its jovial company is worth more than the price of its board." — Arthur Cleveland Bent (1947)

Brown Jay
Psilorhinus morio
(sigh-low-RYE-nus MORE-ee-oh)

This very large tropical jay is overall a dull, smoky brown in color.

Psilorhinus — The genus name means "bare nose" from the Greek *psilos* (bare or smooth) and *rhinos* (the nose). It refers to the Brown Jay's lack of the nasal tufts that cover the nostrils of most Corvids.

morio — The specific epithet is from *morion*, a contraction of the Latin *mormorion* (smoky quartz), a brownish-gray crystal. The reference is to this jay's sooty brown plumage.

French Name: Geai Enfumé
Spanish Names: Chara Papán; Urraca Parda
Other Names: Plain-tailed Brown Jay; White-tipped Brown Jay

Green Jay
Cyanocorax yncas
(sigh-an-oh-KOR-acks INK-as)

"This brilliantly colored jay brings to that favored region of the lower Rio Grande Valley in Texas a touch of tropical color that adds much to the many thrills one feels as he meets for the first time the many new forms of Mexican bird life to be found only in that unique region. As I sat on a log near the edge of a stream in a dense forest along one of the resacas near Brownsville, I caught my first glimpse of a green jay, a flash of green, yellow, and blue, as it flitted through the thick underbrush and the trees above me. In spite of its brilliant colors it was surprisingly inconspicuous among the lights and shades of the thick foliage . . . The curious chachalaca and the red-billed pigeon had their nests in the vicinity, and there were a host of other interesting birds all about me, but the green jay was the gem of the forest." — Arthur Cleveland Bent (1947)

"Like buoyant jewels catching the light, green jays bounce and dash through the willows, flashing colors of blue, yellow, and green." — Tony Angell (1978)

This colorful, tropical jay is named for its bright green plumage, olive above, paler below. Pete Dunne calls it "a visual knockout."

Cyanocorax — The genus name means "blue raven" from the Greek *kyanos* (dark blue) and *korax* (a raven). Only the head of the Green Jay is blue, but several of its tropical congeners have largely blue plumage. Although it is related to the raven, it doesn't resemble one.

yncas — The specific epithet is from the Incas, the native people of Peru, where the type specimen was collected.

French Name: Geai Vert
Spanish Name: Chara Verde
Other Names: Rio Grande Jay; Pajaro Verde

Pinyon Jay
Gymnorhinus cyanocephalus
(jim-no-RYE-nus sigh-an-oh-SEFF-ah-lus)

The Pinyon Jay is named for the Pinyon Pine (*Pinus edulis*), whose seeds (pine nuts) are an important food of this bird.

Gymnorhinus — The genus name means "naked nose" from the Greek *gymnos* (naked) and *rhinos* (the nose). It refers to the exposed nostrils, which are not covered by the nasal bristles that are characteristic of most Corvids.

cyanocephalus — The specific epithet means "blue head" from the Greek *kyanos* (dark blue) and *kephale* (the head). Not just the head, but the entire bird is dull blue.

French Name: Geai des Pinèdes
Spanish Name: Chara Piñonera
Other Names: Cassin's Jay; Maximilian's Jay; Maximilian's Crow; Blue Crow; Pinyon Crow; Pine Jay; Pinyonero

Steller's Jay
Cyanocitta stelleri
(sigh-an-oh-SIT-ah STELL-er-eye)

This jay is named for George W. Steller, who in July of 1741, collected the first specimen on Kayak Island off the southeast coast of Alaska. Steller's Jay was the first bird ever recorded for Alaska. See specific epithet below.

Cyanocitta — The genus name means "blue jay" from the Greek *kyanos* (dark blue) and *kitta* (a jay or a chattering bird). It describes the overall color of this and the next species.

stelleri — In 1781, English naturalist John Latham described this species, based on Steller's journals and on a skin collected by the Cook expedition on Vancouver Island.

In 1788, Johann Gmelin named this jay in honor of George Wilhelm Steller (1709–1746), a German naturalist, who accompanied Vitus Bering on the Russian expedition that discovered Alaska.

French Name: Geai de Steller
Spanish Names: Chara Crestada; Chara de Steller
Other Names: Long-crested Jay; Black-headed Jay; Blue-fronted Jay; Mountain Jay; Blue-crested Jay; Blue Jay; Blue-grey Jay; Coast Jay; Pine Jay; Conifer Jay; Silk Jay; Silken Jay; Aztec Jay; Sierra Nevada Jay; Grinnell's Jay;

Queen Charlotte Jay; Jay-bird; Bluebird; Rain Bird; Screech Bird; Screuch Ancoille; Charra Copetona; Geai Bleu; Eun Gorm; Pigheid

Blue Jay
Cyanocitta cristata
(sigh-an-oh-SIT-ah kris-TAY-tah)

"Blue is an insufficient title for him. See how bright he appears in the sunshine; the simple word blue does not fit those lustrous colors at all. His wings alone display, besides the white bars, four distinctly different hues, turquoise, cerulean, cadet, and ultramarine blue all graded one into the other yet quite separated by bars of black. The tail is like the wings, but the back is entirely different, a soft metallic lilac; the crest, or 'top-knot,' is a sheeny lilac-blue, the neck is white-gray bordered all about with black, and the breast is a warm, light quaker drab. What a showy fellow he is!" — F. Schuyler Mathews (1921)

Blue Jay, Steller's Jay, and Green Jay, by Louis Agassiz Fuertes

Mark Catesby gave the Blue Jay its common name, but he spelled it blew jay. The upperparts are various shades of blue as described in the above passage. Sexes are alike.

Cyanocitta — The genus name means "blue jay" from the Greek *kyanos* (dark blue) and *kitta* (a jay or a chattering bird). It describes the overall color of this and the previous species.

cristata — The specific epithet is Latin for "crested" and refers to the bird's prominent crest.

French Name: Geai Bleu
Spanish Names: Chara Azul; Chara Crestada
Other Names: Common Jay; Northern Jay; Southern Jay; Jay-bird; Blue Coat; Corn Thief; Nest Robber; Gudhaar; Heckert; Herrafogel

Florida Scrub-Jay
Aphelocoma coerulescens
(ah-fel-OCK-oh-mah see-rue-LESS-enz)

"Some birds are so thoroughly typical of certain habitats that one looks for them almost automatically when passing through such places. Perhaps of no species is this more true than the Florida jay. Indeed, so true is it that the local term for the *habitat* is applied to the bird itself, and thus we have the "scrub jay," the universal name of this species in Florida." — Alexander Sprunt, Jr. (1947)

This species, endemic to central Florida, is named for its fire-dependent habitat, consisting of thickets of evergreen scrub oaks, interspersed with sand pine and a groundcover of saw palmetto and Florida rosemary. This and the next three species were formerly considered a single species, the Scrub Jay.

Aphelocoma — The genus name means "smooth hair" from the Greek *apheles* (smooth) and *komē* (the hair). It refers to the fact that the scrub-jays lack a crest.

coerulescens — The specific epithet means "bluish" or "to become blue" from the Latin *caeruleus* (sky blue or dark blue). The reference is to the blue head, wings, and tail.

French Name: Geai à Gorge Blanche
Spanish Name: Chara de Pecho Rayado
Other Name: Florida Jay

Island Scrub-Jay
Aphelocoma insularis
(ah-fel-OCK-oh-mah in-soo-LARE-iss)

The Island Scrub-Jay is named for the fact that it is endemic to Santa Cruz Island (one of California's Channel Islands), twenty-five miles off Santa Barbara. Formerly considered conspecific with the Florida Scrub-Jay and the next two species.

Aphelocoma — The genus name means "smooth hair" from the Greek *apheles* (smooth) and *komē* (the hair). It refers to the fact that the scrub-jays lack a crest.

insularis — The specific epithet is Latin for "belonging to an island."

French Name: Geai de Santa Cruz
Spanish Name: Chara Insular
Other Names: Island Jay; Santa Cruz Jay; Santa Cruz Island Jay

Woodhouse's Scrub-Jay, California Scrub-Jay, Island Scrub-Jay, and Florida Scrub-Jay, by Louis Agassiz Fuertes

California Scrub-Jay
Aphelocoma californica
(ah-fel-OCK-oh-mah cal-ih-FOR-nic-ah)

This scrub-jay is named for its range throughout California west of the Sierra Nevada. The California Scrub-Jay and Woodhouse's Scrub-Jay were formerly considered a single species, the Western Scrub-Jay.

Aphelocoma — The genus name means "smooth hair" from the Greek *apheles* (smooth) and *komē* (the hair). It refers to the fact that the scrub-jays lack a crest.

californica — The specific epithet is Modern Latin for "of California," which forms most of its range.

French Name: Geai Buissonnier
Spanish Names: Chara Californiana; Chara Azuleja
Other Names: Long-tailed Jay; Smooth-headed Jay; California Jay; Grinnell's California Jay; Belding's Jay; Swarth's California Jay; Texan Jay; Texas Jay; Nicasio Jay; Woodhouse's Jay; Xantus' Jay; Blue-eared Jay; Blue Jay; Blue-grey Jay; Chara Pechirrayada

Woodhouse's Scrub-Jay
Aphelocoma woodhouseii
(ah-fel-OCK-oh-mah WOOD-hous-ih-eye)

Woodhouse's Scrub-Jay is named for Samuel Woodhouse. See specific epithet below. Woodhouse's Scrub-Jay and the California Scrub-Jay were formerly considered a single species, the Western Scrub-Jay.

Aphelocoma — The genus name means "smooth hair" from the Greek *apheles* (smooth) and *komē* (the hair). It refers to the fact that the scrub-jays lack a crest.

woodhouseii — In 1858, Spencer Fullerton Baird named this species in honor of physician and naturalist Samuel Washington Woodhouse (1821–1904). Baird based this on the bird referred to as *Cyanocitta californica* in Woodhouse's official report (1853) of the Sitgreave's Expedition.

French Name: Geai de Woodhouse
Spanish Name: Chara de Woodhouse
Other Name: Woodhouse's Jay

Mexican Jay
Aphelocoma wollweberi
(ah-fel-OCK-oh-mah woll-WEB-er-eye)

This jay is named for its range in Mexico. It reaches the United States in southern Arizona, New Mexico, and western Texas. The Mexican Jay and Transvolcanic Jay (*A. ultramarina*) of central Mexico were formerly considered conspecific. Known as the Gray-breasted Jay from 1983 to 1998.

Aphelocoma — The genus name means "smooth hair" from the Greek *apheles* (smooth) and *komē* (the hair). It refers to the fact that the Mexican Jay as well as the scrub-jays lack a crest.

wollweberi — The specific epithet honors German naturalist Wollweber (fl.1859) who collected specimens in Mexico.

French Name: Geai du Mexique
Spanish Names: Chara de Pecho Gris; Chara Pechigrís
Other Names: Ultramarine Jay; Arizona Jay; Couch's Jay

Clark's Nutcracker
Nucifraga columbiana
(new-SIFF-rah-gah co-lum-bih-AY-nah)

"Lewis's woodpecker and Clark's nutcracker were named for the two famous explorers who made that historic trip to the sources of the Missouri River and down the Columbia River to the Pacific coast, as they were responsible for the discovery of these two unique and interesting birds. Capt. William Clark, who was the first one to mention the nutcracker, referred to it as "a new species of woodpecker;" and Wilson described it as a crow, Clark's crow, *Corvus columbianus*. These impressions are not to be wondered at, for its flight and some of its actions are much like those of woodpeckers, and it resembles the crows in much of its behavior . . . Its names, both scientific and common, are all well chosen, indicating its feeding habits, its discoverer, and the place of its discovery." — Arthur Cleveland Bent (1947)

Nutcracker describes this bird's feeding on the nutlike seeds of White-barked Pine (*Pinus albicaulis*). The chisel-like bill is used to pry open the cones with pickax strokes and extract the seeds. The nutcrackers carry the pine nuts in a pouch under the tongue and stash them (as many as 35,000/year) in underground caches, for retrieval during the winter. In so doing, the birds are important seed dispersers. Alexander Wilson named this species in honor of Captain William Clark (1770–1838), who discovered the bird on the famed Lewis and Clark Expedition (1803–1806).

Nucifraga — The genus name means "nut breaker" from the Latin *nux* (a nut) and *frangere* (to break or to shatter). See common name above.

columbiana — The specific epithet is Modern Latin for "of the Columbia River." William Clark first discovered it along the Clearwater River, a tributary of the Columbia.

French Name: Cassenoix d'Amérique
Spanish Name: Cascanueces Americano
Other Names: Clark's Crow, Woodpecker Crow; Grey Crow; Pine Crow; Meat Bird; Meat Hawk; Camp Robber; Whiskey Jack

Black-billed Magpie
Pica hudsonia
(PIE-kah hud-SO-nih-ah)

Magpie is a contraction of Magot Pie. The first part is from the familiar name Margot, a diminutive of the French name Marguerite. The second part derives from pied, referring to the bird's black and white color pattern. Dating from the late Middle Ages, it was customary in Europe to give human names to familiar birds and animals. Magpie, first recorded in 1605, gradually replaced the French *pie* and the English *piannet*. The latter is a contraction of pie and Annet, a pet name for Agnes. Some believe the choice of female pet names equates the bird's noisy chattering to that of a talkative woman. Magpie became standard with the publication of *British Zoology* (*Birds*) by Thomas Pennant in 1768. Black-billed distinguishes this species from the Yellow-billed Magpie. Formerly considered the same species as the Magpie (*P. pica*) of Eurasia.

Pica — The genus name is the Latin word for "a magpie" and is believed to be imitative.

hudsonia — The specific epithet refers to Hudson Bay. While this species' range does not actually reach the shores of the bay, the

Black-billed Magpie and Yellow-billed Magpie, by Louis Agassiz Fuertes

name may refer to the region in Canada controlled by the Hudson's Bay Company.
French Names: Pie d'Amerique; Pie Bavarde
Spanish Name: Urraca de Pico Negro
Other Names: American Magpie; Common Magpie; Pie; Rudder-bird; Heart-bird; A'dn; Aiarat; Atat; Atce'tc; Otccotc; Pyet

Yellow-billed Magpie
Pica nuttalli
(PIE-kah NUT-all-eye)

The yellow bill, which distinguishes this species from the Black-billed Magpie, gives this endemic of California its name.
Pica — See Black-billed Magpie.
nuttalli — Audubon named this magpie in honor of English botanist Thomas Nuttall (1786–1859), who collected the type specimen near Santa Barbara in 1836. Audubon wrote: "I have conferred on this beautiful bird the name of a most zealous, learned and enterprising naturalist, my friend Thomas Nuttall."
French Name: Pie à Bec Jaune
Spanish Name: Urraca de Pico Amarillo
Other Name: California Magpie

American Crow
Corvus brachyrhynchos
(CORE-vus brack-ih-RING-koss)

Crow is imitative of the bird's cawing calls. American refers to the fact that this is the most widespread species across North America and distinguishes it from other species of crows here and around the world. Formerly known as Common Crow.
Corvus — The genus name is the Latin word for "a raven" or "a crow" and is believed to be imitative of the bird's call.
brachyrhynchos — The specific epithet means "short beak" (compared to the Common Raven's) from the Greek *brachys* (short) and *rhynchos* (the beak).
French Name: Corneille d'Amérique
Spanish Name: Cuervo Americano
Other Names: Eastern Crow; Carrion Crow; Jim Crow; Otter Crow; Southern Crow; Western Crow; Florida Crow; Crow Bird; Corn-thief; Caw; Rook; Corbeau; Creamhach; Fitheach; Grob; Kraa; Krop; Rocais

Northwestern Crow
Corvus caurinus
(CORE-vus caw-RYE-nus)

Northwestern describes the range of this species along the coast of the Pacific Northwest, from southern Alaska to Puget Sound.
Corvus — The genus name is the Latin word for "a raven" or "a crow" and is believed to be imitative of the bird's call.
caurinus — The specific epithet is Latin for "of the northwest wind."
French Name: Corneille d'Alaska
Spanish Name: Cuervo del Noroeste

Tamaulipas Crow
Corvus imparatus
(CORE-vus im-par-AY-tus)

This small tropical crow gets its name from the Mexican state of Tamaulipas, where the type specimen was collected. In the United States the Tamaulipas Crow occurs in the vicinity of Brownsville, Texas.
Corvus — The genus name is the Latin word for "a raven" or "a crow" and is believed to be imitative of the bird's call.
imparatus — The specific epithet is Latin for "unprepared." Early authors incorrectly used the scientific name *Corvus mexicanus* for the Tamaulipas Crow. German naturalist Johann Gmelin erected the name in 1788, but he had applied it to the Great-tailed Grackle (*Quiscalis mexicanus*), not to the crow. In 1929, James Lee Peters, Curator of Birds at the Museum of Comparative Zoology, Harvard,

discovered the error and gave this corvid the specific epithet *imparatus*. The implication is that the naturalists who were applying Gmelin's name to the Tamaulipas Crow were unprepared.

French Name: Corneille du Mexique
Spanish Name: Cuervo Tamaulipeco
Other Names: Mexican Crow; Sinaloa Crow

Fish Crow
Corvus ossifragus
(CORE-vus oss-IFF-rih-gus)

"Like other crows the fish crow is largely omnivorous, with a long list of acceptable material available. As it spends most of its time along the seashore, the banks of streams, and the shores of inland bodies of water, its food consists largely of various kinds of marine or aquatic life, or other material washed up on such shores. It may often be seen hovering over the water, like a gull, looking for floating objects that it can pick up. On the beaches and salt marshes these crows feed on small crabs, especially fiddlers, shrimps, crawfish, dead fish, and perhaps some live fish, and any kind of carrion or offal they can find. They steal the eggs from the nests of terns, willets, Wilson's plovers, and clapper rails." — Arthur Cleveland Bent (1947)

As stated above, this crow feeds on a variety of marine life including dead fish it finds washed up on the beach.

Corvus — The genus name is the Latin word for "a raven" or "a crow" and is believed to be imitative of the bird's call.

ossifragus — The specific epithet means "bone breaker" from the Latin *os* (a bone) and *frangere* (to break). This may refer to the habit of dropping clams and other mollusks on rocks to break the shells.

French Name: Corneille de Rivage
Spanish Name: Cuervo Pescador

Chihuahuan Raven
Corvus cryptoleucus
(CORE-vus krip-toe-LEW-kus)

Raven is from the Anglo-Saxon *hrafn*, the name for the Common Raven and imitative of the bird's calls. This species is named for the Mexican state of Chihuahua, which is part of its range. Formerly known as White-necked Raven.

Corvus — The genus name is the Latin word for "a raven" or "a crow" and is believed to be imitative of the bird's call.

cryptoleucus — The specific epithet means "hidden white" from the Greek *kryptos* (hidden) and *leukos* (white). The reference is to the neck feathers, which are white at the base. The white band is usually hidden. This was the source of the former common name. Bent (1947) wrote, "The name *cryptoleucus* is well chosen, for the white bases are well hidden; they can be seen, with the specimen in hand, by lifting the feathers; but in life they are seldom seen, except when the wind ruffles the plumage or when the bird bends its neck far downward in feeding."

French Name: Corbeau à Cou Blanc
Spanish Name: Cuervo Llanero
Other Names: Chihuahuan Crow; American White-necked Raven; White-necked Crow; Cuervo Llanero

Common Raven, by John James Audubon

Common Raven
Corvus corax
(CORE-vus COR-acks)

Raven is from the Anglo-Saxon *hrafn*, the name for this bird and imitative of the bird's croaking calls. This is the Common Raven in that it has the widest range in the Northern Hemisphere, across Eurasia and the wilder parts of North America. It plays an important part in the folklore of many diverse cultures. Formerly known as Northern Raven.

Corvus — The genus name is the Latin word for "a raven" or "a crow" and is believed to be imitative of the bird's call.

corax — The specific epithet is the Greek word for "a raven" and is imitative of its call. *Corax* is a cognate of the Greek *krazo* (to croak).

French Name: Grand Corbeau
Spanish Names: Cuervo Común; Cuervo Grande
Eskimo and Inuit Names: Tulugak (imitative) Tulukaruk (bird that plays bashful when it pretends it wants something it does not)
Other Names: Western Raven; Holarctic Raven; American Raven; Mexican Raven; Giant Crow; Sheeps Crow; Black Bird; Corbie; Corbie Caw; Coir-bidh; Corbeau de Mer; Cuervo Grande Ronco; Croupy Caw; Fang; Fiach; Marburan; Ralph; Rook

~

Family Alaudidae
Larks

Lark stems from the Middle English *laverock* from Old English *lawerce* (treason worker). This may refer to the bird's habit of landing some distance from its nest and then walking to it under the concealment of vegetation; or to its feigning injury to lead an intruder away from the nest. Paul F. Donald wrote: "The word 'lark' is also intriguingly close to the Middle English word *laik*, meaning to play or fool around, and there is a possibility that the two words are connected. The expression 'larking about' may derive from the behavior of fighting Skylarks."

Eurasian Sky Lark
Alauda arvensis
(ah-LAW-dah ar-VEN-sis)

Celebrated by English poets and the subject of Shelley's *Blithe Spirit*, the Sky Lark is famous for singing its sweet song while ascending high in the sky. Those who witness the Sky Lark's song flight find it to be spiritually uplifting. It is said that "this behavior has raised it in public consciousness, and the poetic canon, as no other small, brown bird, with the possible exception of its musical rival, the Nightingale." Eurasian refers to its native range.

Alauda — The genus name is believed to be a Latin corruption of the Celtic for "great singer" from *al* (great) and *awd* (song). This was the word Pliny used for lark.

arvensis — The specific epithet is Latin for "of the cultivated field," one of this species' habitats.

French Name: Alouette des Champs
Spanish Name: Alondra Euopea
Other Names: European Skylark; Rising Lark; Field Lark; Ground Lark; Short-heeled Lark; Clod Lark; Clodhopper; Sky-flapper; Ladyhen; Our Lady's Hen; Ehidit; Ehedydd; Uchedydd; Fuiseog; Melhuez; Pelhuez; Lintwhite; Laverock; Lavrock; Sky Laverock; Learock; Lerruck; Lievling; Lavro; Leeuwerik; Lewerik;

~

Horned Lark
Eremophila alpestris
(er-ee-MOE-fill-ah al-PES-tris)

Two tiny tufts of black feathers that look like horns give the Horned Lark its name.

Eremophila — The genus name means "desert loving" from the Greek *eremos* (a desert or a desolate place) and *philos* (loving). The Horned Lark is a barren ground specialist, favoring such places as desert, tundra, dry prairies, beaches, and cultivated fields.

alpestris — The specific epithet is Latin for "alpine" and refers to another habitat, rocky alpine slopes.

French Name: Alouette Cornue
Spanish Name: Alondra Cornuda
British Name: Shore Lark
Eskimo Name: Nakrulik (horned)
Other Names: Northern Horned Lark; Prairie Horned Lark; Winter Horned Lark; California Horned Lark; Desert Horned Lark; Dusty

Passeriformes

Horned Lark, by Louis Agassiz Fuertes

Horned Lark; Hoyt Horned Lark; Island Horned Lark; Montezuma Horned Lark; Pallid Horned Lark; Ruddy Horned Lark; Scorched Horned Lark; Streaked Horned Lark; Texan Horned Lark; Mud Lark; Sea Lark; Western Shore Lark; Skylark; Road Lark; Road Chippie; Road Trotter; Grey Bird; Life Bird; Low Bird; Spring Bird; Wheat Bird; Prairie Bird; Snowbird; Snowflake; Luatharan; Ortolan; Quaker

Family Hirundinidae
Swallows

Swallow may stem from the Old Norse *svala* meaning a "cleft stick." The reference is to the deeply forked tail of some species, such as the Barn Swallow. Another possibility is that swallow comes from the Old English root verb *swel* (to swirl) and refers to the bird's swooping flight.

Bank Swallow
Riparia riparia
(rip-AIR-ih-ah)

"Perhaps you have seen a sand bank somewhere, probably near a river or pond, where the side of the bank was filled with holes as if a small cannon had been trained against it as a target. In and out of the holes fly the smallest of the swallows, that are sometimes, with good reason, called sand martins." — Neltje Blanchan (1917)

Bank Swallows are named for their nesting sites, steep, sandy riverbanks, where colonies of birds dig long, horizontal tunnels. They also accept sand and gravel piles at excavation sites.

Riparia — The genus/species name is Latin for "of or relating to the banks of a natural watercourse."
French Name: Hirondelle de Rivage
Spanish Name: Golondrina Ribereña
British Name: Sand Martin
Eskimo Name: Tuluganek (like a raven)
Other Names: River Swallow; Sand Swallow; Sandy Swallow; Bank Martin; Pit Martin; Shore Bird; Sand Backie; Ainleag; Bitter Bank; Bitterie; Golondrina Parda; Stairneal; Witchuk

Tree Swallow
Tachycineta bicolor
(tack-ih-sin-EE-tah BYE-color)

This swallow gets its name from its nesting in natural cavities and abandoned woodpecker holes in snags and dead trees. It also accepts bird boxes.

Tachycineta — The genus name means "swift mover" from the Greek *tachys* (swift) and *kineo* (to move) and refers to the birds' flight as they forage for flying insects. Pete Dunne describes the Tree Swallow's flight as "active, energetic, somewhat playful..."

Tree Swallow and Barn Swallow,
by Louis Agassiz Fuertes

257

bicolor — The specific epithet is Latin for "two colored" and describes the color pattern of bluish-green upperparts contrasting with the brilliant white underparts.
French Name: Hirondelle Bicolore
Spanish Names: Golondrina Arbolera; Golondrina Bicolor
Eskimo and Inuit Names: Igkarlik (lives in a hole); Tulugaknek (like a raven); Kau-tagh-i-ya-ghuk
Other Names: Blue-backed Swallow; Green-blue Swallow; White-breasted Swallow; White-bellied Swallow; Stump Swallow; Eave Swallow; French Swallow; Singing Swallow; Water Swallow; Wood Swallow; Blue Martin; White-bellied Martin; Flycatcher; Golondrina Vientriblanca

Bahama Swallow
Tachycineta cyaneoviridis
(tack-ih-sin-EE-tah sigh-AN-eh-oh-VER-ih-dis)

This rare vagrant to Florida is named for its breeding range in the northern pine-forested islands of the Bahamas.
Tachycineta — The genus name means "swift mover" from the Greek *tachys* (swift) and *kineo* (to move) and refers to the birds' flight as they forage for flying insects.
cyaneoviridis — The specific epithet means "blue and green" from the Latin *cyaneus* (dark blue) derived from the Greek *kuanos* (dark blue) and the Latin *viridis* (green) and refers to the blue and green iridescence in the plumage.
French Name: Hirondelle des Bahamas
Spanish Name: Golondrina de las Bahamas
Other Names: Summer Swallow; Golondrina

Violet-green Swallow
Tachycineta thalassina
(tack-ih-sin-EE-tah thal-AS-in-ah)

The purple and green iridescence on the back and wings gives this swallow its name.
Tachycineta — The genus name means "swift mover" from the Greek *tachys* (swift) and *kineo* (to move) and refers to the birds' flight as they forage for flying insects. Pete Dunne says of the Violet-green Swallow's flight, "Combines the maneuverability of a swallow with the speed and erratic stiffness of a swift . . ."
thalassina — The specific epithet is from the Greek *thalassinos* (sea green) and refers to the green gloss on the bird's upperparts.
French Name: Hirondelle à Face Blanche
Spanish Names: Golondrina Verde Tornasol; Golondrina Cariblanca; Golondrina Verde Violácea
Other Names: Northern Violet-green Swallow; Martin

Violet-green Swallow, by John James Audubon

Northern Rough-winged Swallow
Stelgidopteryx serripennis
(stel-jih-DOP-ter-icks seh-RIP-en-iss)

The Rough-winged Swallow gets its name from the recurved hooks along the leading edge of the primary feathers. The function of these hooks is not known, but some scientists speculate that they make a whistling sound during courtship flights. Northern distinguishes this species from the Southern Rough-winged Swallow (*S. ruficollis*) of Central and South America.
Stelgidopteryx — The genus name means "scraper wing" from the Greek *stelgidos* (scraper) and *pteryx* (the wing).
serripennis — The specific epithet means "saw winged" from the Latin *serra* (a saw) and *pennis* (winged).
French Name: Hirondelle à Ailes Hérissées
Spanish Names: Golondrina de Ala Aserrada; Golondrina-aliserrada Norteña
Other Names: Rough-wing; Bridge Swallow; Gully Martin

Purple Martin
Progne subis
(PROG-nee SUE-biss)

Martin is a French pet name, a diminutive of Mars. In Britain, pet names were often given to familiar dooryard birds. Other examples are robin and jackdaw. In North America, martin is used for the larger species of swallows in the genus *Progne*. In Britain, swallows with square tails are called martins.

Progne — The genus name is from Prokne, the daughter of Pandion (See Osprey) a mythical king of Athens, and according to legend was turned into a swallow by the gods.

subis — The specific epithet is from a word the Roman naturalist Pliny used for "a bird that breaks eagles' eggs." The name appears to have been used randomly here.

French Name: Hirondelle Noire

Spanish Names: Golondrina Azul-negra; Martín Azul; Martín Purpúrea

Other Names: Black Martin; Large Black Martin; House Martin; Gourd Martin; Western Martin; Martinet; Great Blue Swallow; Purple Swallow; Barn Swallow; Blue Bird; Golondrina Azul; Golondrina de Iglesias; Golondrina Grande; Golondrina Purpura; Hirondelle; Hirondelle Bleue; Hirondelle Pourpree

Barn Swallow
Hirundo rustica
(hir-UN-doh RUSS-tih-kah)

"We associate the Swallow with comfortable old-fashioned barns, which had open rafters, doors that could not be shut tight, and windows with many panes lacking. Within such buildings, almost as easy to get into and out of as were the caves and broken crags to which they resorted before barns were built, the Barn Swallows used to nest sometimes in large colonies, while their cousins, the Cliff Swallows, had quarters beneath the outside eaves in a line of gourd-shaped tenements." — Mabel Osgood Wright (1917)

The Barn Swallow is named for its habit of plastering its mud nest to beams and rafters inside barns and sheds.

Hirundo — The genus name is the Latin word for "a swallow."

rustica — The specific epithet is Latin for "rustic" or "rural" and refers to this swallow's association with farmland, typically foraging for insects over pastures and cultivated fields. Ernest Choate says the name compares this species with the House Martin (*Delichon urbica*), an Old World swallow typical of urban areas, where it nests under the eaves of houses. Its specific epithet *urbica* is Latin for "urban" or "frequenting a town or city."

French Name: Hirondelle des Granges

Spanish Names: Golondrina Ranchera; Golondrina Tijereta

British Name: Swallow

Eskimo and Inuit Names: Tuluganek (like a raven); Tu-lu'-kugh-u-na-guk; Jo-lu-kar-nar'-uk; Po-yok-o-che-ach

Other Names: American Barn Swallow; Inside Barn Swallow; European Swallow; Common Swallow; House Swallow; Chimney Swallow; Eave Swallow; Mud Swallow; Fork-tailed Swallow; Barn-loft Swallow; Red-fronted Swallow; Gobhlan-gaoith; Golondrina de Horquilla; Hirondelle Rousse; Swallie; Tsi-kuk

Cliff Swallow
Petrochelidon pyrrhonota
(pet-row-KEL-ih-don pih-row-NO-tah)

The swallow that returns to Capistrano, this species is named for its traditional breeding sites on the faces of cliffs, where they plastered their jug-shaped mud nests. Now they accept manmade structures such as the sides of buildings and the supports of bridges.

Petrochelidon — The genus name means "rock swallow" from the Greek *petros* (a rock) and *chelidon* (a swallow). The reference is to the birds' nesting sites on the sides of rocky cliffs.

pyrrhonota — The specific epithet means "fire back" from the Greek *purrhos* (flame-colored) and *notos* (the back) and refers to the orange rump.

French Name: Hirondelle à Front Blanc

Spanish Name: Golondrina Risquera

Other Names: Northern Cliff Swallow; Eave Swallow; Eaves Swallow; Jug Swallow; Mud Swallow; Barn Swallow; House Swallow; Republican Swallow; Crescent Swallow; Moon-fronted Swallow; Rain Bird;

Hirondelle; Martin; Golondrina de Cuevas; Golondrina de Penasco

Cave Swallow
Petrochelidon fulva
(pet-row-KEL-ih-don FULL-vah)

This swallow is named for the fact that it once nested only in the dimly lit interiors of limestone caves in the American southwest. Now it also nests under bridges and culverts.

Petrochelidon — The genus name means "rock swallow" from the Greek *petros* (a rock) and *chelidon* (a swallow). The reference is to the birds' traditional nesting sites on the walls of caves.

fulva — The specific epithet is Latin for "tawny" or "reddish yellow" and refers to the buffy underparts.

French Name: Hirondelle à Front Brun
Spanish Name: Golondrina Pueblera
Other Names: Buff-throated Swallow; Cuban Cliff Swallow; Coahuila Cliff Swallow; Hirondelle; Golondrina de Cuevas; Rain Bird

Cliff Swallow, by John James Audubon

Family Paridae
Chickadees and Titmice

"The chickadee is perhaps the best-known bird in its range and appears so trustful of man that we look on it with real affection. And no wonder — for chickadees are such cheerful little birds. When we watch a flock of them in winter they remind us of a group of happy, innocent little children playing in the snow. Thinking back to the early days of New England's history, we can imagine that the Pilgrim Fathers, when the chickadees came about the settlement at Plymouth in 1620, watched them as we do now. They were, perhaps, the first friends to welcome the travelers to the New World." — Winsor Marrett Tyler (1947)

Chickadee is imitative of the alarm notes of some species, often rendered as *chick-a-dee-dee-dee*. Researchers have discovered that chickadees use one of the most sophisticated signaling systems observed among animals. The chickadee call can indicate whether the predator is moving or stationary as well as the degree of the threat. It also rallies other birds to mob the predator. Titmouse is derived from the Icelandic *tittr* (any small object) and *mase*, an Anglo-Saxon word for "various small birds." The family name stems from the Latin *parus* "a titmouse." The North American chickadees and titmice were formerly placed in the genus *Parus*, but now that genus is restricted to the Old World tits.

Carolina Chickadee
Poecile carolinensis
(PEE-sil-ee kar-oe-lin-EN-sis)

This chickadee is named for South Carolina, where Audubon discovered it along the seacoast. Carolina also suggests this species more southerly range compared to the Black-capped Chickadee.

Poecile — The genus name derives from the Greek *poikilos*, which can mean "variegated," "spotted," "dappled" or "pied." In the case of the chickadees, pied is descriptive of these birds' black and white color pattern.

carolinensis — The specific epithet is Modern

Latin for "of South Carolina." See common name above.
French Name: Mésange Minime
Spanish Name: Carbonero de Carolina
Other Names: Plumbeous Chickadee; Florida Chickadee; Texan Chickadee; Carolina Titmouse

Black-capped Chickadee
Poecile atricapillus
(PEE-sil-ee ay-trih-cap-ILL-us)

This chickadee's black crown gives it its name, but other species of chickadees also sport black caps.

Poecile — The genus name derives from the Greek *poikilos*, which can mean "variegated," "spotted," "dappled" or "pied." In the case of the chickadees, pied is descriptive of these birds' black and white color pattern.

atricapillus — The specific epithet means "black hair" from the Latin *ater* (flat black) and *capillus* (the hair of the head), in other words the "crown."

French Name: Mésange à Tête Noire
Spanish Name: Carbonero de Gorra Oscura
Eskimo and Inuit Names: Misikakak (the jumper); Chi-ku-pi-pi-a-uk
Other Names: Common Chickadee; Eastern Chickadee; Western Black-capped Chickadee; Blackhead Chickadee; Long-tailed Chickadee; Oregon Chickadee; Yukon Chickadee; Phoebe; Black-capped Tit; Black-capped Titmouse; Tom-tee; Tom-tit; Sow-the-wheat; Sweet Weather Bird; Tiny Mite; Mesange; Pig-a-pee; P'tit; Pin-pin; Qui-es Tu; Tchicadee; Tchick-a-didi; Thick-a-di-di

Mountain Chickadee
Poecile gambeli
(PEE-sil-ee GAM-bell-eye)

The Mountain Chickadee is named for its breeding habitat in the coniferous forests of western mountain ranges at elevations of 6000 to 11,000 feet.

Poecile — The genus name derives from the Greek *poikilos*, which can mean "variegated," "spotted," "dappled" or "pied." In the case of the chickadees, pied is descriptive of these birds' black and white color pattern.

gambeli — The specific epithet honors its collector William Gambel (1819–1849), a

Mountain Chickadee and Black-capped Chickadee, by Louis Agassiz Fuertes

Philadelphia physician and ornithologist who collected extensively in California. He first discovered the Mountain Chickadee in 1841, about a day's journey west of Santa Fe, and later he observed large flocks of this species on high wooded ridges in the Rockies. Gambel published his description of this new species in the *Proceedings of the Academy of Natural Sciences of Philadelphia* in 1843, giving it the name *Parus montanus*. But that name was already in use for the Willow Tit of Europe. Robert Ridgway changed the name to *Parus gambeli* in 1886.

French Name: Mésange de Gambel
Spanish Names: Carbonero de Ceja Blanca; Paro Cejiblanco
Other Names: Short-tailed Chickadee; Inyo Chickadee; Inyo Mountain Chickadee; Bailey's Chickadee; Mrs. Bailey's Chickadee; Grinnell's Chickadee

Mexican Chickadee
Poecile sclateri
(PEE-sil-ee SKLAY-ter-eye)

The Mexican Chickadee is named for its range in the mountain forests of Mexico. It barely enters the United States, crossing the border to the Chiricahua Mountains in Arizona and the Animas Mountains in New Mexico.

Poecile — The genus name derives from the Greek *poikilos*, which can mean "variegated," "spotted," "dappled" or "pied." In the case of the chickadees, pied is descriptive of these birds' black and white color pattern.

sclateri — The specific epithet honors Dr. P. L. Sclater (1829–1913), a British ornithologist and a founder of the British Ornithologists' Union.

French Name: Mésange Grise
Spanish Names: Carbonero Mexicano; Paro Mexicano
Other Names: Sclater's Chickadee; Gray-sided Chickadee

Chestnut-backed Chickadee
Poecile rufescens
(PEE-sil-ee roof-ESS-enz)

This most colorful chickadee is named for its rich chestnut brown back.

Poecile — The genus name derives from the Greek *poikilos*, which can mean "variegated," "spotted," "dappled," or "pied." In the case of the chickadees, pied is descriptive of the black and white color pattern of most species of chickadees.

rufescens — The specific epithet is Latin for "reddish" and refers to the chestnut back and sides.

French Name: Mésange à Dos Marron
Spanish Name: Carbonero de Espalda Castaña
Other Names: Chestnut-sided Chickadee; California Chickadee; Marin Chickadee; Nicasio Chickadee; Barlow's Chickadee; Santa Cruz Chickadee; Chestnut-backed Titmouse

Boreal Chickadee
Poecile hudsonica
(PEE-sil-ee hud-SOAN-ih-kah)

The Boreal Chickadee is named for its habitat in the boreal forests of Canada and Alaska.

Poecile — The genus name derives from the Greek *poikilos*, which can mean "variegated," "spotted," "dappled," or "pied." In the case of the chickadees, pied is descriptive of these birds' black and white color pattern.

hudsonica — The specific epithet is Modern Latin for "of Hudson Bay." The type specimens were collected on the west shore of Hudson Bay at the mouth of the Severn River.

French Name: Mésange à Tête Brune
Spanish Name: Carbonero Boreal
Other Names: Blackcap; Brown-cap; Brown-capped Chickadee; Brownie; Hudsonian Chickadee; Acadian Chickadee; Tom-tit

Gray-headed Chickadee
Poecile cinctus
(PEE-sil-ee SINK-tus)

This chickadee is named for its grayish-brown cap. Briefly known as Siberian Tit.

Poecile — The genus name derives from the Greek *poikilos*, which can mean "variegated," "spotted," "dappled," or "pied." In the case of the chickadees, pied is descriptive of these birds' black and white color pattern.

cincta — The specific epithet is Latin for "girdled," "encircled," or "wreathed" from *cingere* (to encircle). Not particularly apt, as this species is not banded. Joel Holloway speculates that the author meant "crowned" for this chickadee's grayish-brown cap.

French Name: Mésange Lapone
Spanish Name: Carbonero de Cabeza Gris
Other Names: Alaska Chickadee; Siberian Chickadee

Bridled Titmouse
Baeolophus wollweberi
(bee-OLE-oh-fuss woll-WEB-er-eye)

Bridled refers to the black stripes on the cheeks, suggesting a horse's bridle.

Baeolophus — The genus name means "short crest" from the Greek *baios* (short or small) and *lophos* (a crest). The reference is to the small crest that distinguishes the titmice from the chickadees.

wollweberi — Charles Bonaparte named this species in honor of Herr Wollweber (fl. 1850), a German naturalist who collected the type specimen in Zacatecas, Mexico.

French Name: Mésange Arlequin
Spanish Names: Carbonero Embridado; Paro Embridado
Other Names: Wollweber's Titmouse

Oak Titmouse
Baeolophus inornatus
(bee-OLE-oh-fuss in-or-NAY-tus)

The Oak Titmouse is named for its habitat of dry oak and pine-oak woodlands. This and the Juniper Titmouse were formerly considered a single species, the Plain Titmouse.

Baeolophus — The genus name means "short crest" from the Greek *baios* (short or small) and *lophos* (a crest). The reference is to the small crest that distinguishes the titmice from the chickadees.

inornatus — The specific epithet is Latin for "unadorned" or "plain," which accurately describes this plain gray bird.

French Name: Mésange Unicolore
Spanish Names: Carbonero Sencillo; Paro Sencillo
Other Names: Gray Titmouse; Oregon Titmouse; San Diego Titmouse

Juniper Titmouse
Baeolophus ridgwayi
(bee-OLE-oh-fuss RIDJ-way-eye)

This titmouse is named for its habitat in pinyon-juniper woodlands. This and the Oak Titmouse were formerly considered a single species, the Plain Titmouse.

Baeolophus — The genus name means "short crest" from the Greek *baios* (short or small) and *lophos* (a crest). The reference is to the small crest that distinguishes the titmice from the chickadees.

ridgwayi — The specific epithet honors Robert Ridgway (1850–1929), Curator of Birds at the National Museum, Washington D C.

French Name: Mésange des Genévriers
Spanish Name: Carbonero Piñsonero
Other Name: Gray Titmouse

Tufted Titmouse
Baeolophus bicolor
(bee-OLE-oh-fuss BY-color)

This titmouse is named for the small crest, which is characteristic of all titmice.

Baeolophus — The genus name means "short crest" from the Greek *baios* (short or small) and *lophos* (a crest). The reference is to the small crest that distinguishes the titmice from the chickadees.

bicolor — The specific epithet means "two colors" from the Latin *bi* (two) and *color* (color), referring to the gray upperparts and white underparts. But there is a third color, the rusty wash on the flanks.

French Name: Mésange Bicolore
Spanish Name: Carbonero Copetósn
Other Names: Tufted Tit; Crested Titmouse; Crested Tom-tit; Tufted Chickadee; Pete Bird; Peter Bird; Peto Bird

Black-crested Titmouse
Baeolophus atricristatus
(bee-OLE-oh-fuss ay-trih-kris-TAY-tus)

The black crown and tuft give this titmouse its name. Formerly considered a subspecies of the Tufted Titmouse.

Baeolophus — The genus name means "short crest" from the Greek *baios* (short or small) and *lophos* (a crest). The reference is to the small crest that distinguishes the titmice from the chickadees.

atricristatus — The specific epithet means "black crested" from the Latin *ater* (flat black) and *cristatus* (crested).

French Name: Mésange à Plumet Noir
Spanish Names: Carbonero de Cresta Negra; Paro Crestinegro
Other Names: Sennett's Titmouse

Family Remizidae
Penduline Tits

Penduline Tits are an Old World family with only one representative in North America. They are named for their hanging nests, suspended from twigs often over water. The Verdin's nest is not typical of the family; it is a spherical structure of thorny twigs with a side entrance. The family name is derived from the Polish word *remiz*, their name for the Penduline Tit (*Remiz pendulinus*) of Eurasia.

Verdin
Auriparus flaviceps
(ah-RIP-ar-us FLAY-vih-seps)

Verdin, from the Latin *viridis* (green) is a French nickname for the Yellowhammer

Verdin, by Allan C. Brooks

(*Emberiza citrinella*), an Old World bunting with a yellow head. Presumably our species was so named, because of the similarity in coloration to the bunting.

Auriparus — The genus name means "golden tit" from the Latin *aurum* (gold) and *parus* (a tit). The name refers to the bird's yellow head and titmouse-like behavior. It was formerly placed with the chickadees and titmice in the family Paridae.

flaviceps — The specific epithet means "yellow headed" from the Latin *flavus* (golden yellow) and *ceps* (headed).

French Name: Auripare Verdin
Spanish Name: Baloncillo
Other Names: Eastern Verdin; Goldtit; Bushtit

~

Family Aegithalidae
Long-Tailed Tits

Long-tailed Tits are named for their relatively long tails, particularly in comparison with the true tits in the family Paridae. The family name is from the Greek *aigithalos* (a tit or titmouse).

Bushtit
Psaltriparus minimus
(sal-TRIP-ar-us MIN-ih-mus)

"At times, especially towards evening, the flocks become more restless and move along from bush to bush and tree to tree much more rapidly than when feeding, the birds straggling hurriedly after each other in irregular succession. During these hurried cross-country excursions, the simple location-notes are pronounced louder and are interlarded at frequent intervals with a shrill quavering note. The faster the band travels, the louder and more oft-repeated becomes these all-imprtant location-notes; for the greater becomes the danger of individuals becoming separated from the main flock. Bush-tits are usually hidden from each other in dense foliage. They have no directive color-marks; therefore, being gregarious birds, the great value of their location-notes becomes apparent." — Dr. Joseph Grinnell (1903)

The Bushtit was formerly classified in the family Paridae with the chickadees and titmice,

Bushtit, by Louis Agassiz Fuertes

which it resembles in behavior. Flocks of these little birds actively forage for insects in trees and bushes. Formerly split into two species, the Common Bushtit and the Black-eared Bushtit.

Psaltriparus — The genus name is a combination of the Greek *psaltris* (a harp player) and the Latin *parus* (a titmouse). The Bushtit is named for its similarity to the Pygmy Tit *(Psaltria exilis)* of Java. *Psaltria* is the root of psaltery, an ancient stringed instrument played wih a bow or a plectrum. It refers to the bird's high-pitched calls that presumably resemble the notes of a psaltery.

minimus — The specific epithet is Latin for "least" or "smallest." Smaller than a chickadee, the Bushtit is one of the smallest of all North American birds.

French Name: Mésange Buissonnière
Spanish Name: Sastrecillo
Other Names: Coast Bushtit; California Bushtit; Black-tailed Bushtit; Lead-colored Bushtit; Plumbeous Bushtit; Lloyd's Bushtit

Family Sittidae
Nuthatches

No, nuthatches don't try to hatch nuts. Nuthatch is a corruption of "nuthack" and refers to a behavior seen in several Old World species, but not often observed in North American ones. That is to wedge an acorn or hazelnut in a bark crevice and hack it open with violent strikes of the bill.

Red-breasted Nuthatch
Sitta canadensis
(SIT-ah can-ah-DEN-sis)

This species is named for its rusty red underparts.

Sitta — The genus name comes from the Greek *sitte*, a name Aristotle used for a bird of undetermined species that pecks tree bark, possibly a woodpecker. Now it is identified with the nuthatches.

canadensis — The specific epithet is Modern Latin for "of Canada," where much of the breeding range occurs.

French Name: Sittelle à Poitrine Rousse

Red-breasted Nuthatch, Pygmy Nuthatch, and White-breasted Nuthatch, by Louis Agassiz Fuertes

Spanish Names: Sita Canadiense; Saltapalos Canadiense
Other Names: Canada Nuthatch; Canadian Nuthatch; Red-bellied Nuthatch; Devil Downhead; Tip-up; Cardy Bird; Topsy-turvy-bird; Upside-down Bird; Tomtit; Little Quank; Sapsucker

White-breasted Nuthatch
Sitta carolinensis
(SIT-ah cah-row-lin-EN-sis)

This species is named for its largely white underparts, which includes the breast.

Sitta — The genus name comes from the Greek *sitte*, a name Aristotle used for a bird of undetermined species that pecks tree bark, possibly a woodpecker. Now it is identified with the nuthatches.

carolinensis — The specific epithet is Modern Latin for "of Carolina." The White-breasted Nuthatch has a more southerly range than the Red-breasted.

French Name: Sittelle à Poitrine Blanche
Spanish Names: Sita de Pecho Blanco; Saltapalos Pechiblanco

Other Names: Common Nuthatch; White-bellied Nuthatch; Carolina Nuthatch; Florida Nuthatch, Rocky Mountain Nuthatch; Inyo Nuthatch; Inyo Slender-billed Nuthatch; Slender-billed Nuthatch; Nutcracker; Nuthack; Nut Topper; Nut Jobber; Woodhacker; Woodpecker; Glaner Bloer Woodpicker; Woodjar; Sapsucker; Devil Downhead; Yank; Big Quank; Jobbin; Mud Dabber; Mud Stopper; Jar Bird; Sapsucker; Tree Mouse; Tip-up; Tom-tit; Topsy-turvy-bird; Sita Pechiblanca

Pygmy Nuthatch
Sitta pygmaea
(SIT-ah pig-ME-ah)

This species is so-named because it is the smallest nuthatch.

Sitta — The genus name comes from the Greek *sitte*, a name Aristotle used for a bird of undetermined species that pecks tree bark, possibly a woodpecker. Now it is identified with the nuthatches.

pygmaea — The specific epithet is from the Latin *pygmaeus* (pygmy) denoting this bird's small size

French Name: Petite Sittelle
Spanish Names: Sita Enano; Saltapalos Enano
Other Names: Black-eared Nuthatch; Pine Nuthatch; White-naped Nuthatch; California Nuthatch; Nevada Nuthatch; Nevada Pigmy Nuthatch

Brown-headed Nuthatch
Sitta pusilla
(SIT-ah pew-SILL-ah)

Brown-headed refers to the brown cap that contrasts with the bluish-gray back and wings.

Sitta — The genus name comes from the Greek *sitte*, a name Aristotle used for a bird of undetermined species that pecks tree bark, possibly a woodpecker. Now it is identified with the nuthatches.

pusilla — The specific epithet is Latin for "very small." Next to the Pygmy Nuthatch, this is the smallest species.

French Name: Sittelle à Tête Brune
Spanish Name: Sita de Cabeza Café
Other Names: Gray-headed Nuthatch

Family Certhiidae Treecreepers

Brown Creeper
Certhia americana
(SER-thih-ah ah-mer-ih-CANE-ah)

"Instantly the little creature flattened himself against the trunk, spreading his wings to their very utmost and ducking his head until, though I had been all the while eying his motions through a glass at the distance of only a few rods, it was almost impossible to believe that yonder tiny brown fleck upon the bark was really a bird and not a lichen." — Bradford Torrey (1917)

Creeper refers to this species' foraging behavior. Starting at the base of a tree, the bird creeps up the trunk in a spiral, as it searches bark crevices for insects. When the creeper is near the top, it flies to the base of another tree and repeats its search. Brown refers to the streaky brown upperparts that give this bird excellent camouflage, blending in with the bark of a tree trunk. This is the bird's main defense as described in the opening passage.

Certhia — The genus name is Latin for "a creeper." It is derived from the Greek *kerthios*, a name Aristotle used for some tree-creeping bird.

americana — The specific epithet is Latin for "of America" and distinguishes our species from the Eurasian Treecreeper (*C. familiaris*) with which it was formerly considered conspecific.

French Name: Grimpereau Brun
Spanish Name: Trepador Americano
Other Names: American Creeper; American Brown Creeper; Little Brown Creeper; Common Creeper; Tree Creeper; California Creeper; Nevada Creeper; Sierra Creeper; Rocky Mountain Creeper; Mexican Creeper; Tree Climber; Tree Climmer; Tree Crawler; Tree Clipper; Creep Tree; Climb Tree; Creepy Tree; Tree Speiler; Bark Speiler; Bark Creeper; Ox-eye Creeper; Bark Runner; Brown Tree-creeper; Woodpecker; Brown Woodpecker; Little Woodpecker; Tree Mouse; Daddy-ike; Cuddy; Tomtit

Family Troglodytidae
Wrens

Wren stems from the Middle English *wrenne* and Old English *wraene* or *wraenna*. Ultimately these may derive from the Anglo-Saxon *wroene* (lascivious) and refer to the wrens' polygamous breeding system.

Rock Wren
Salpinctes obsoletus
(sal-PINK-teez ob-so-LEE-tus)

The Rock Wren is named for its habitat in rocky desert washes, canyons, rocky outcroppings, and rockslides.

Salpinctes — The genus name is Greek for "trumpeter" referring to this wren's call note, a loud, ringing *tk-keeer*.

obsoletus — The specific epithet is Latin for "shabby," "plain," or "indistinct" and describes the bird's dull, cryptic coloration.

French Name: Troglodyte des Rochers
Spanish Names: Saltapared Roquero; Soterrey Roquero
Other Names: Common Rock Wren

Canyon Wren
Catherpes mexicanus
(kath-ER-peez meks-ih-KANE-us)

The Canyon Wren is named for its preferred habitat of steep-walled canyons and around the bases of cliffs.

Catherpes — The genus name is Greek for "a creeper" which is descriptive of its movements as described here:

"An active animate wren that moves jerkily but nimbly up, down, over, and into cliffs — often disappearing into one crevice and appearing somewhere else. Moves in short and long hops (sometimes with wings fanned for balance) and in short and lengthy fluttering sallies. Climbs up, down, and across rock faces with nuthatchlike hops." — Pete Dunne (2006)

mexicanus — The specific epithet is Modern Latin for "of Mexico" where the type specimen was collected.

French Name: Troglodyte des Canyons
Spanish Names: Saltapared Barranqueño;

Canyon Wren, by Allan C. Brooks

Saltapared Barranquero
Other Names: Auburn Wren; White-throated Wren; Dotted Wren; Nevada Wren

House Wren
Troglodytes aedon
(trog-low-DIE-teez ay-EE-don)

"No native bird so quickly accepts an invitation to make our home his than the House Wren. Offer him a bird-box at the right time and place and the chances are in favor of his investigating it before the sun has set. When the opening to this dwelling is small enough to prevent the entrance of competing species, he is provided with quarters in which he is exempt from many of the dangers that beset nesting birds." — Frank Chapman (1923)

The House Wren got its name, because it is a common dooryard bird that will nest in crevices in or around human dwellings or perhaps because it accepts bird houses.

Troglodytes — The genus name means "cave dweller" or "one who creeps into holes" from the Greek *trogle* (a hole) and *dytes* (a diver). Oliver Austin, Jr. wrote, "This derives partly from the large covered nest the wren makes, partly from its habitual skulking and roosting in rock crevices and root tangles."

House Wren, by Louis Agassiz Fuertes

aedon — In 1807, amateur French ornithologist Louis Jean Pierre Viellot named this species for Aedon, a mythical queen of Thebes, whom Zeus turned into a nightingale, possibly alluding to the wren's bubbling song, which some compare to that of a nightingale:

"No song could be more spontaneous and rollicking than that of the House Wren, though it lacks a distinct and full tone, that defect is more than atoned for by irrepressible spirit . . . Aside from musical form of the song it possesses a rapturous abandon which at once captures the heart of the listener just as his eyes would be entranced by the sight of a beautiful cascade in a mountain glen. The jubilant music drops like silvery spray; the songster should have been name Minnehaha — Laughing Water!" — F. Schuyler Mathews (1904)

French Name: Troglodyte Familier
Spanish Names: Saltapared Continental Norteño; Soterrey Cucarachero

Other Names: Common Wren; Brown Wren; Stump Wren; Wood Wren; Short-tailed Wren; Short-tailed House Wren; Jenny Wren; Apache Wren; Parkman's Wren; Pacific House wren; Western Wren; Western House Wren; God Bird; Rock Bird; Wall Bird; Mangeur de Gadelles; Mouskanich; Oiseau bon Dieu; Roitelet; Roitelet de Maison; Rossignol; Zaw Shlibber; Zounshlibber

Pacific Wren
Troglodytes pacifica
(trog-low-DIE-teez pa-SIFF-ih-kuh)

Formerly considered conspecific with the Winter Wren, the Pacific Wren is named for its range in western North America from California to Alaska.

Troglodytes — The genus name means "cave dweller" or "one who creeps into holes" from the Greek *trogle* (a hole) and *dytes* (a diver). Oliver Austin, Jr. wrote, "This derives partly from the large covered nest the wren makes, partly from its habitual skulking and roosting in rock crevices and root tangles."

pacifica — The specific name is Latin for "of the Pacific." See common name above.

French Name: Troglodyte de Baird
Spanish Name: Chochin del Pacífico
Other Names: Western Wren; Western Winter Wren; Alaska Wren; Aleutian Wren; Attu Wren; Kodiak Wren; Kodiak Winter Wren; KiskaWren; Unalaska Wren

Winter Wren
Troglodytes hiemalis
(trog-low-DIE-teez high-eh-MAIL-iss)

"The inch-long bird with the mile-long song."

This wren got its name, because in winter this breeder of the North Woods replaces the similar House Wren in much of that species' summer range. The House Wren in turn retreats to the southern states. The Winter Wren, Pacific Wren, and Eurasian Wren (*T. troglodytes*) were formerly considered a single species. The nickname that opens this entry alludes to this bird's complex, melodious song that goes on and on:

"This energetic midget is best known for its song, an unmistakable, remarkable, prolonged melody of tiny tonal notes. He begins softly, launching into a jumble of ultra-brief whistled notes, and after a second or two he perhaps hits a high, rapid, half-second trill, then jumbles tiny notes for another second or two, then maybe hits a low trill of slow, sweet, whistled notes, two more seconds of jumble, another high trill, perhaps ending there or adding a little more jumble on the end. It's a wild ride from beginning to end, the sweetest of tiny notes rising and falling in an undulating pattern. Stick with him, and after as many as thirty or forty songs of the same pattern you'll hear a different song, this one with high and low trills in different places." — Donald Kroodsma (2008)

Troglodytes — The genus name means "cave dweller" or "one who creeps into holes" from the Greek *trogle* (a hole) and *dytes* (a diver). Oliver Austin, Jr. wrote, "This derives partly from the large covered nest the wren makes, partly from its habitual skulking and roosting in rock crevices and root tangles."

hiemalis — The specific epithet means "wintry" or "of winter" from the Latin *hiemis* (winter). See common name above.

French Name: Troglodyte des Forêts

Sedge Wren, by John James Audubon

Spanish Names: Chochin hiemal; Saltapared Invernal

Eskimo and Inuit Names: Kach-tai-ach; Kat-chrai-uh

Other Names: Mouse Wren; Short-tailed Wren; Spruce Wren; Wood Wren; Semidi Wren; Tanaga Wren; Stephenson's Wren; Cutteley Wren; Tiddy Wren; Titty Wren; Tidley Wren; Jenny Wren; Kitty Wren; Bobby Wren; Chitty Wren; Juggy Wren; Gilliver Wren; Puggie Wren; Puffy Wren; Kitty-me-Wren; Our Lady's Hen; Tom Tit; House Bird; Sally; Jenny; Jitty; Crackil; Cracket; Crackeys; Crackadee; Wran; Wranny; Wrannock; Cut; Cutty; Cuddy; Poulette de bois; scutty; Skiddy; Stumpy Toddy; Stumpit; Titty Todger; Titmeg; Tintie; Guradnan; Stag; Tope

Sedge Wren
Cistothorus platensis
(sis-TOTH-or-us plah-TEN-siss)

The Sedge Wren is named for its preferred habitat of wet meadows where sedges and tall grasses abound. Formerly known as Short-billed Marsh Wren.

Cistothorus — The genus name means "shrub leaper" from the Greek *kistos* (a shrub or rockrose) and *thouros* (leaping or rushing). Presumably this refers to the wren's taking cover in shrubs.

platensis — The specific epithet is Modern Latin for "Rio de la Plata" near Buenos Aires, Argentina, where the type specimen was collected.

French Name: Troglodyte à Bec Court

Spanish Names: Saltapared Sabanero; Soterrey Sabanero

Other Names: Freshwater Marsh Wren; Meadow Wren; Grass Wren

Marsh Wren
Cistothorus palustris
(sis-TOTH-or-us pal-US-triss)

The Marsh Wren is named for its preferred habitat in freshwater and salt marshes, favoring tall rank vegetation such as cattails, bulrushes, reeds or cordgrass. Formerly known as Long-billed Marsh Wren.

Cistothorus — The genus name means "shrub leaper" from the Greek *kistos* (a shrub or rockrose) and *thouros* (leaping or rushing).

Presumably this refers to the wren's taking cover in shrubs.

palustris — The specific epithet is Latin for "marshy."

French Name: Troglodyte des Marais
Spanish Name: Saltapared Pantanero
Other Names: Cattail Wren; Reed Wren; Tule Wren; Prairie Marsh Wren; Saltwater Marsh Wren; Western Marsh Wren; Alberta Marsh Wren; California Marsh Wren; Louisiana Marsh Wren; Marian's Marsh Wren; Pacific Marsh Wren; Suisan Marsh Wren; Wayne's Marsh Wren; Worthington's Marsh Wren

Carolina Wren
Thryothorus ludovicianus
(thry-OTH-or-us lewd-oh-VISS-ih-ANE-us)

Carolina suggests a portion of this wren's range. It is essentially a southern species, although young birds will move into the northern states and establish breeding populations until a severe winter wipes them out.

Thryothorus — The genus name means "reed rushing" from the Greek *thryon* (a reed) and *thouros* (rushing), perhaps suggesting where this wren might take cover, as it is frequently found near water.

ludovicianus — The specific epithet is Modern Latin for "of Louisiana," the state where the type specimen was collected.

French Name: Troglodyte de Caroline
Spanish Name: Saltapared de Carolina
Other Names: Great Carolina Wren; Louisiana Wren; Florida Wren; Lomita Wren; Mocking Wren; Teakettle Bird

Bewick's Wren
Thryomanes bewickii
(thrih-OM-ah-neez bue-WICK-ih-eye)

Audubon collected the type specimen near Saint Francisville, Louisiana, in October of 1821. He named it *Troglodytes Bewickii* for English artist Thomas Bewick:

"I honoured this species with the name of BEWICK, a person too well known for his admirable talents as an engraver on wood, and for his beautiful work on the Birds of Great Britain, to need any eulogy of mine. I enjoyed the pleasure of a personal acquaintance with him, and found him at all times a most agreeable, kind, and benevolent friend."

Thryomanes — The genus name means "reed cup" from the Greek *thryon* (a reed) and *manes* (a cup) and describes the deep cup nest that is placed in a natural cavity, woodpecker hole, or brush pile.

bewickii — The specific epithet commemorates Thomas Bewick (1754–1828), an English artist known for his woodcut illustrations. See common name above.

French Name: Troglodyte de Bewick
Spanish Name: Saltapared de Bewick
Other Names: Desert Wren; Long-tailed Wren; Long-tailed House Wren; Song Wren; Sooty Wren; Baird's Wren; Nicasio Wren; Texas Wren; Catalina Island Wren; San Clemente wren; San Diego Wren; San Joaquin Wren; Santa Cruz Wren; Seattle Wren; Vigors' Wren

Cactus Wren
Campylorhynchus brunneicapillus
(kam-pih-low-RING-kus broon-ih-CAP-ill-us)

The Cactus Wren is named for its nesting sites among the wicked thorns of cactus, particularly cholla.

Cactus Wren, by Allan C. Brooks

Campylorhynchus — The genus name means "curved beak" from the Greek *campylos* (curved) and *rhynchos* (the beak) and describes this wren's long, de-curved bill.

brunneicapillus — The specific epithet means "brown-capped" from the Latin *brunneus* (brown) and *capillus* (capped) and refers to this bird's brown cap.

French Name: Troglodyte des Cactus
Spanish Names: Matraca del Desierto; Matraca Desértica
Other Names: Brown-headed Cactus Wren; Coues' Cactus Wren; Bryant's Cactus Wren

Family Polioptilidae
Gnatcatchers

Blue-gray Gnatcatcher
Polioptila caerulea
(pol-ih-OP-tih-lah see-RUE-lee-ah)

"It is adept as a catcher of flying insects (many other kinds besides gnats!) and even in winter is often seen to secure food in this way. Its darts after flying insects differ markedly from the long swings of the true flycatchers, for its forays are seldom more than five or six feet in extent and are usually vertically upward with a quick drop back to the starting point." — Arthur Cleveland Bent (1949)

Gnatcatcher refers to these birds' habit of darting out to catch tiny insects they flush from the foliage as described above. Blue-gray describes the color of the upperparts.

Polioptila — The genus name means "gray feather" from the Greek *polios* (gray) and *ptilon* (a feather).

caerulea — The specific epithet is Latin for "sky blue."

French Name: Gobemoucheron Gris-bleu
Spanish Names: Perlita Azul Gris; Perlita Grisilla
Other Names: Common Gnatcatcher; Western Gnatcatcher; Blue-gray Flycatcher; Small Blue-gray Flycatcher; Sylvan Flycatcher; Little Blue-gray Wren; Little Bluish-gray Wren; Catbird; Chew Bird; Cotton Bird; Rabuita; Chay-chay; Spain-spain

Blue-gray Gnatcatcher, by John James Audubon

California Gnatcatcher
Polioptila californica
(pol-ih-OP-tih-lah cal-ih-FORN-ih-kah)

This endangered species is named for its range in coastal southern California. It also occurs in the Mexican state of Baja California. Until the late 1980s, it was considered a form of the Black-tailed Gnatcatcher.

Polioptila — The genus name means "gray feather" from the Greek *polios* (gray) and *ptilon* (a feather).

californica — The species name is Modern Latin for "of California."

French Name: Gobemoucheron de Californie
Spanish Name: Perlita Californiana

Black-tailed Gnatcatcher
Polioptila melanura
(pol-ih-OP-tih-lah mel-an-OOR-ah)

This gnatcatcher's black tail, with a narrow white outer edge, gives it its name.

Polioptila — The genus name means "gray

feather" from the Greek *polios* (gray) and *ptilon* (a feather).

melanura — The specific epithet means "black tail" from the Greek *melas* (black) and *oura* (the tail).

French Name: Gobemoucheron à Queu Noire
Spanish Names: Perlita Desierto; Perlita Colinegra
Other Name: Plumbeous Gnatcatcher

Black-capped Gnatcatcher
Polioptila nigriceps
(po-ih-OP-tih-lah NIG-rih-seps)

The male's black crown gives this gnatcatcher its name.

Polioptila — The genus name means "gray feather" from the Greek *polios* (gray) and *ptilon* (a feather).

nigriceps — The specific epithet means "black-crowned" from the Latin *niger* (black) and *ceps* (crowned).

French Name: Gobemoucheron à Coiffe Noire
Spanish Names: Perlita Sinaloense; Perlita Gorrinegra
Other Name: Black-headed Gnatcatcher

Family Cinclidae
Dippers

American Dipper
Cinclus mexicanus
(SINK-lus meks-ih-CANE-us)

Dippers are unusual aquatic songbirds that are named for their habit of dipping their whole body up and down , as though they are doing deep knee bends. When agitated, they dip more frequently. American distinguishes our species from dippers in the Old World.

Cinclus — The genus name is from the Greek *kinklos*, a name Aristotle and other authors called a waterside bird, possibly a wagtail or sandpiper, but now applied to the dippers.

mexicanus — The specific epithet is Modern Latin for "of Mexico" which includes part of this species' wide range in western North America.

French Name: Cincle d'Amérique
Spanish Names: Mirlo Acuático Americano; Mirlo-acuático Plomizo

Eskimo Name: Anaruk Kiviruk (old woman sunk)
Other Names: Water Ouzel; American Water Ouzel; Grey Singing Wren; Hell-diver; Slate Bobber; Water Witch

Family Pycnonotidae
Bulbuls

Red-whiskered Bulbul
Pycnonotus jocosus
(pick-no-NO-tus joe-KOE-sus)

Bulbul is an ancient Persian name for a small bird, possibly a species of nightingale (*Luscinia* sp.), and is probably onomatopoetic. Anyway bulbul is usually translated as "nightingale" when it appears in the writings of the medieval poets Omar Khayyam and Hafiz. It is believed that later Muslim poets in India and Pakistan, where no nightingales occur, applied the name to this family of birds. Red-whiskered refers to the red whisker-stripe on the cheek.

Pycnonotus — The genus name means "thick back" from the Greek *puknos* (thick or compact) and *noton* (the back). It refers to the plumage on the back, which is thick when compared to the sparse, hair-like feathers on the nape.

jocosus — The specific epithet is Latin for "merry" or "humorous" and refers either to the red cheek or the birds' liveliness and cheerful demeanor.

French Name: Bulbul Orphée
Spanish Name: Bulbul de Barbas Rojas

Family Regulidae
Kinglets

Golden-crowned Kinglet
Regulus satrapa
(REG-you-lus SAT-rah-pah)

"Many years ago, a boy found on the doorstep the body of a tiny feathered gem ... He picked it up and was entranced with the delicate beauty of its soft olive colors and with its crown of brilliant orange and

Golden-crowned Kinglet, Brown Creeper, and
Ruby-crowned Kinglet, by Louis Agassiz Fuertes

gold, which glowed like a ball of fire." —
Arthur Cleveland Bent (1949)

Kinglet means "little king" from the Anglo-Saxon *cyning* (a king) plus the diminutive suffix *-let*. Kinglets are tiny birds named for the patch of colorful feathers on top of the head, suggesting a king's crown. In this species the crown patch, bordered with black, is orange in the male, yellow in the female.

Regulus — The genus name means "little king" from the Latin *rex* (a king) plus a diminutive suffix. The reference is to the colorful crown patch in both sexes.

satrapa — The specific epithet means "a ruler" i.e. "one who wears a crown" from the Greek *satrapēs* (satrap, a governor or viceroy of a province in ancient Persia).

French Name: Roitelet à Couronne Dorée
Spanish Name: Reyezuelo Corona Dorada
Other Names: Golden-crested Kinglet; Fire-crested Kinglet; Fire-crowned Kinglet; Golden-crested Wren; Fiery-crowned Wren; Fire-crested Wren; Golden-crowned Wren; Golden Wren; Golden Cutty; Marigold Finch; Tidley Goldfinch; Wood Titmouse; Gold-crest; Golden-crested Goldcrest; Fire-crest; Flame-crest; Moon; Moonie; Miller's Thumb; Kingbird; Thumb Bird

Ruby-crowned Kinglet
Regulus calendula
(REG-you-lus kah-LEND-you-lah)

"How does the Ruby-crowned Kinglet know he has a bit of color on his crown which he can uncover at will, and has great charms for the female? During the rivalries of the males in the mating season, and in autumn also, they flash this brilliant ruby at each other . . . They behaved exactly as if they were comparing crowns, and each extolling his own. Their heads were bent forward, the red crown patch uncovered and showing as a large, brilliant cap, their tails were spread, and the side feathers below the wings were fluffed out. They did not come to blows, but followed each other about amid the branches, uttering their thin, shrill notes and displaying their ruby crowns to the utmost. Evidently it was some sort of strife or dispute or rivalry that centered about this brilliant patch." — John Burroughs (1904)

"The Ruby-crowned Kinglet is a similarly small green-gray character with a tiny scarlet-red crest which you do not often see unless the bird is in an excited state of mind, then it rises like a flame of ruby from his perky little crown and you may be sure trouble is brewing for somebody in his vicinity. Two of these Kinglets together in the branches of a white birch usually mean a display of red feathers and acrobatic feats on the wing which it would be difficult for even your sharp eyes to follow." — F. Schuyler Mathews (1921)

The ruby crown that gives this kinglet its name is usually hidden but can be displayed as described in the above passages.

Regulus — The genus name means "little king" from the Latin *rex* (a king) plus a diminutive suffix. The reference is to the male's ruby-red crown feathers.

calendula — There are two explanations for the specific epithet. One is that it derives from the Latin *calendus* (glowing) and refers to the male's ruby crown patch. The other is that it stems from the Greek *kalandros* (the Calandra Lark). It refers to this kinglet's remarkably loud, musical song that has been compared to that of the Eurasian Sky Lark (*Alauda arvensis*). The song is sometimes rendered as *See. See. See. Where? Where? Where? Look at me! Look at me! Look at me!* Here is one naturalist's observation of the Ruby-crowned Kinglet's song:

"The longer and more eagerly I followed the unseen singer, the greater the mystery became. It seemed impossible that a bird which I supposed was at least as large as a Bluebird could escape observation in the partly leaved trees. The song was mellow and flute-like, and loud enough to be heard several hundred yards; an intricate warble past imitation or description, and rendered so admirably that I never hear it now without feeling an impulse to applaud. The bird is so small, the song so rich and full, that one is reminded of a chorister with the voice of an adult soprano." — Frank Chapman (1917)

French Name: Roitelet à Couronne Rubis
Spanish Names: Reyezuelo de Corona Roja; Reyezuelo Sencillo
Other Names: Ruby-crown; Ruby-crowned Wren; Ruby-crowned Warbler; Foxy Chub; Kingbird

Family Phylloscopidae
Leaf Warblers

Arctic Warbler
Phylloscopus borealis
(fill-OSS-koh-pus bore-eh-AY-lis)

Not a close relative of our Wood Warblers, this Old World species is not particularly well named, as its song is a slow, unmusical, buzzy trill. Arctic refers to its range in arctic and subarctic willow thickets in western Alaska and across northern Eurasia.

Phylloscopas — The genus name means "leaf watcher" from the Greek *phullon* (a leaf) and *skopos* (watcher or one who looks about). The reference is to this bird's foraging method of peering under leaves in search of insects.

borealis — The specific epithet is Latin for "northern" from the Greek *Boreas*, a personification of the north wind.

French Name: Pouillot Boréal
Spanish Name: Curruca Ártica
Eskimo and Inuit Names: Songakpalutunygik (small bird the color of bile); Chung-ukh-tai-uk
Other Names: Arctic Willow Warbler; Kennicott's Willow Warbler; Evermann's Warbler

Family Sylviidae
Old World Warblers

Wrentit
Chamaea fasciata
(kah-ME-ah fass-ih-AY-tah)

The Wrentit is so named, because it was once believed to be intermediate between the wrens and the titmice, but actually it is not closely related to either. It does have characteristics that are reminiscent of birds in both families. The Wrentit sometimes hangs upside down while foraging like a chickadee or titmouse. Its brown color and often vertically cocked tail suggest a wren.

Chamaea — The genus name is derived from the Greek *khamai*, which means "on the ground." It apparently refers to this species foraging low in dense brush, but it usually doesn't feed on the ground.

fasciata — The specific epithet is Latin for "striped" referring to the blurry stripes on the breast.

French Name: Cama Brune
Spanish Name: Camea
Other Names: Coast Wren-tit; Gambel's Wren-tit; Pallid Wren-tit

Family Muscicapidae Old World Flycatchers and Chats

Bluethroat
Cyanecula svecica
(sigh-an-EE-coo-lah SWEE-sih-kah)

"A Janus-plumaged passerine — bland on one side, stunning on the other — that shows plain gray-brown upperparts and paler underparts, emblazoned with a bright blue-rust-black-and-white bib." — Pete Dunne (2006)

Bluethroat refers to the male's color pattern as described above.

Cyanecula — The genus name is Modern Latin for "little blue one" from the Greek *kuaneos* (dark blue) plus a diminutive suffix. Formerly *Luscinia svecica*.

svecica — The specific epithet stems from the Modern Latin *Suecicus* (Swedish). Olof Rudbeck, a Swedish explorer and scientist, collected the type specimen in Lapland in 1695. Impressed with the bird's beauty and noting it sported the colors of the Swedish flag, he called it *Avis Carolina* for Carl XI, the king of Sweden. Linnaeus described and named it in 1758, giving it the specific epithet *svecica* for the bird's range, but it may also link the Bluethroat's colors with the Swedish flag.

French Name: Gorgebleue à Miroir
Spanish Name: Garganta Azul
Eskimo Name: Soo-kuk
Other Name: Red-spotted Bluethroat

Siberian Rubythroat
Calliope calliope
(cal-EYE-oh-pee)

"This charming little thrush, with the ruby-jewelled throat, and the song that is said to be of the angels, was quite common and nesting in the woods surrounding Petropavlovsk. It was also found high on the hilltops where it could be called out of every alder tangle." — Hamilton M. Laing (1925)

Rubythroat is descriptive of the male's ruby-red throat. Siberian refers to its natural range in eastern Russia.

Calliope — The genus/species name is a proper name from Greek mythology. Calliope was the muse of epic poetry. Her name literally means "beautiful voice" and is quite apt for a bird that has been praised for its "angelic song." Formerly *Luscinia calliope*. Here is more on the Rubythroat's song:

"Impressions of the song vary somewhat. Dybowski says that the rubythroat is one of the pleasantest songsters in Dauria, but describes the song as soft, quiet and somewhat unvaried. Others are less sparing in their praise: Clark (1910), for example, speaks of its fine, clear song and (1945) calls it "the finest and most persistent songster in Kamchatka;" David and Oustalet (1877) describe it as equally remarkable for the vivacity and grace of its movements as for the beauty of its song. Seebohm (1879), again, speaks of a wonderfully fine song, richer and more melodious than that of the bluethroat and scarcely inferior to that of the nightingale." — Bernard William Tucker (1949)

French Names: Rossignol Calliope; Calliope de Sibérie
Spanish Name: Ruiseñor calíope
Other Names: Kamchatka Nightingale; Red-necked Nightingale

Northern Wheatear
Oenanthe oenanthe
(ee-NAN-thee ee-NAN-thee)

In 1654, John Taylor explained in a poem that this bird is called wheatear "because they come when wheat is yearly reaped." And twenty-four years later, Francis Willughby wrote that the bird got its name because "at the time of Wheat harvest they wax very fat." This implies that wheatears eat wheat, which they don't. The truth is the common name has nothing to do with wheat or ears at all. Wheatear is a euphemism for "white arse" from the Anglo-Saxon *hwit* (white) and *aers* (the rump). It refers to the bird's bright white rump patch, which it uses as a visual signal in a variety of displays from courtship to confronting a rival:

"One of the actions which has prime significance in a wide range of displays is the exposure of the rump by fanning the tail out sideways and drooping the wings a fraction ... The white rump and black and white tail pattern are exposed in self-advertisement display, in aggressive situations, and when fleeing an enemy (when it may act as an alarm to neighbors)." — Peter Conder (1989)

Northern refers to its North American range in Alaska and northern Canada. It is much more widespread in the Old World, where it occurs over all of Europe from the Arctic Ocean south to the Mediterranean. Northern is appropriate here, too, because other wheatear species range primarily in the arid regions of Africa and the Middle East.

Oenanthe — The genus/species name is from the name Aristotle gave this bird. It means "wine blossom" from the Greek *oinos* (wine) and *anthos* (a blossom or flower). Some speculate that the name refers to the wheatears' arriving in Greece at the time when grapevines are sprouting.

French Name: Traquet Motteux
Spanish Name: Collalba Norteña
Eskimo Name: Tikmiapaurut (little eagle)
Other Names: Wheatears; European Wheatear; Greenland Wheatear; White Tail; White Rump; White Arse; White Ase; White Ass; Whitestart; Wittol; Whittol; Whishie; Ortolan; English Ortolan; Steinkle; Stinkle; Stinklin; Arlyng; Arling; Utick; Bigh Utick; Bog-an-lochan; Bogachan; Bru-gheal; Clocharet; Caislincloch; Cooper; Cracker; Stanechacker; Jobbler; Underground Jobbler; Jocktibeet; Jocktie; Snorter; Clot Bird; Clod Bird; Clodhopper; Dyke Hopper; Straw Mouse; Smatch; Horse Smatch; Horse Musher; Horse Masher; Passage-bird; Shepherd Bird; Singing Skyrocket; Burrow Bird; Moor Warbler; Fallow Finch; Fallow Lunch; Fallow Smith; Fallow-smich; Fallow Smirch; Fallow Smiters; Fallow Chat; Bushchat; White-rumped Stonechat; Furze Chat; Fuzz Chat ; Chat; Chickell; Hedge-chicken; Hedge Chicker; Chickstane Chickin; Chickwell; Check; Check Bird; Checkle; Chick-chack; Steincheck; Stanechack; Stane-pecker; Barley-bird; Barley-ear; Ear-bird; Chack; Chacker; Chackeret; Chocharet; Chacks; Chack Bird; Chattie; Chatterer; Chock; Chat-chock; Chuck; Clacharan; Clackaran; Clocharet; Crineachan; Coney; Coney Chuck; Coney Sucker; Snorter; Stone-chat; Stonechard; Stone-breaker; Stone-check; Stone-chacker; Stanechacker; Stone-chucker; Stone-clatter; Stone Cracker

~

Family Turdidae
Thrushes

Thrush stems from Middle English *thrusche* and Anglo Saxon *thrysce* (a thrush). Some authorities believe these to be related to the Latin *turdus* (a thrush) or the German *trizo* (to twitter).

Eastern Bluebird
Sialia sialis
(sigh-AY-lih-ah SIGH-al-iss)

"The bluebird is well named, for he wears a coat of the purest, richest, and most gorgeous blue on back, wings, and tail; no North American bird better deserves the name, for no other flashes before our admiring eyes so much brilliant blue. It has been said that he carries on his back the blue of heaven and the rich brown of the freshly turned earth on his breast; but who has ever seen the bluest sky as blue as the bluebird's back." — Arthur Cleveland Bent (1949)

The Bluebird is named for the male's bright blue upperparts. The grayish females also show some blue in the wings and tail. Eastern refers to the range from the Great Plains east to the Atlantic coast and distinguishes this species from the Western Bluebird.

Sialia — The genus name is from a kind of a bird mentioned by Athenaeus, Hesychius, and other ancient Greek writers, but not otherwise identified. It is now applied to the bluebirds. Some authors have suggested that the name stems from the Greek *sialon* (spittle) or *sializein* (to slather) and implies a sibilant sound.

sialis — The specific epithet is a variation of the genus name.

French Name: Merle-bleu de l'Est

Spanish Names: Azulejo de Garganta Canela; Azulejo Gorjicanelo
Other Names: Common Buebird; American Bluebird; Azure Bluebird; Wilson's Bluebird; Red-breasted Bluebird; Blue Robin; Blue Redbreast; Blofogel; Grive Bleu; Oiseau Bleu; Rouge-gorge; Rouge-gorge Bleu; Eun Gorm

Western Bluebird
Sialia mexicana
(sigh-AY-lih-ah meks-ih-CANE-ah)

This species is named for the male's deep ultramarine blue upperparts. Western refers to its range in the western United States, which extends from the Rockies to the Pacific coast.
Sialia — The genus name is from a kind of a bird mentioned by Athenaeus, Hesychius, and other ancient Greek writers, but not otherwise identified. It is now applied to the bluebirds. Some authors have suggested that the name stems from the Greek *sialon* (spittle) or *sializein* (to slather) and implies a sibilant sound.
mexicana — The specific epithet is Modern Latin for "of Mexico" where the type specimen was collected.
French Name: Merle-bleu de l'Ouest
Spanish Names: Azulejo de Garganta Azul; Azulejo Gorjiazul
Other Names: Mexican Bluebird; Chestnut-backed Bluebird; California Bluebird; San Pedro Bluebird;

Mountain Bluebird
Sialia currucoides
(sigh-AY-lih-ah cure-you-co-EYE-deez)

"The mountain bluebird is not so gaudily or so richly colored as the western bluebird, but it is no less pleasing in its coat of exquisite turquoise-blue. As it flies from some low perch to hover like a big blue butterfly over an open field, it seems to carry on its wings the heavenly blue of the clearest sky, and one stands entranced with the purity of its beauty." — Arthur Cleveland Bent (1949)

"No words can describe his brilliancy in the breeding season, as he flies through the sunny clearings of the high Sierra Nevada, or sits like a bright blue flower against the dark green of the pines." — Irene Grosvenor Wheelock (1904)

This bluebird is turquoise blue, paler underneath. Mountain describes one of its habitats in alpine zones above tree line, but it occurs in lowland areas as well.
Sialia — The genus name is from a kind of a bird mentioned by Athenaeus, Hesychius, and other ancient Greek writers, but not otherwise identified. It is now applied to the bluebirds. Some authors have suggested that the name stems from the Greek *sialon* (spittle) or *sializein* (to slather) and implies a sibilant sound.
currucoides — The specific epithet means "like a hedge sparrow" from the Latin *curruca* (a hedge sparrow) and the Greek suffix *–oides* (similar to or resembling). German naturalist Johann Matthäus Bechstein described this species in 1798, and apparently saw a similarity between the Mountain Bluebird and birds classified in the genus *Curruca*, which once encompassed more than 400 species including ones now classified as finches and warblers. The name could also refer to the specific epithet of the Lesser Whitethroat (*Sylvia curruca*). Perhaps Bechstein saw some similarity between the

Mountain Bluebird, by Allan C. Brooks

Mountain Bluebird and this drab Old World warbler.
French Name: Merle-bleu Azuré
Spanish Name: Azulejo Pálido
Other Names: Rocky Mountain Bluebird; Arctic Bluebird; Ultramarine Blue-Bird

Townsnd's Solitaire
Myadestes townsendi
(my-ah-DESS-teez TOWN-send-eye)

"Audubon (1840) named and figured this rather puzzling bird from a single female obtained by that pioneer naturalist J. K. Townsend near the Columbia River; this one specimen remained for a long time unique . . . Its status has at last been fixed as a member of the thrush family, though at first glance it would hardly seem to belong there. It looks and acts much like a flycatcher, with its somber colors and flycatching habits. In flight the light patches in its wings and the white in the tail suggest the mockingbird. Its feeding habits remind one of the bluebirds. But its song is decidedly thrushlike, though not equal to the songs of the star performers in this gifted group, and its spotted young proclaim its close relationship to the thrushes . . . It is generally regarded as a solitary, quiet, retiring bird, often being seen singly, in pairs, or in family groups, but at times, mainly on the fall migration, it is some- times seen in larger groups." — Arthur Cleveland Bent (1949)

Solitaire refers to the fact that this species is essentially a loner. It is even territorial in winter, when a bird will defend its patch of junipers from all other solitaires. Its name honors John K. Townsend. See specific epithet below.

Myadestes — The genus name means "fly eater" from the Greek *myia* (a fly) and *edestes* (an eater). In summer, it preys mainly on flying insects, which it snatches out of the air. In winter its principal food is juniper berries.

townsendi — In 1838, Audubon named this species in honor of John Kirk Townsend (1809–1851), a Philadelphia ornithologist and collector of the type specimen.

French Name: Solitaire de Townsend
Spanish Name: Clarín Norteño

Other Names: Fly-catching Thrush; Townsend's Fly-catching Thrush

Veery
Catharus fuscescens
(KATH-ah-rus fuss-KESS-enz)

"One of the strangest songs among birds, the Veery's song is unmistakable and unforgettable. Some have called it enchanting, tranquilizing, exquisite, magical; it's unanimously ethereal. It's a loud, breezy, rolling, wheeling, downward spiral of three to five fluty phrases, all with a nasal quality that echoes as if he sings into a metal pipe. Captured in a mnemonic, perhaps the sound would be something like *da-veeyur, veeyr, veeer, veer* . . ." — Donald Kroodsma (2008)

The Veery is named for its call note, an emphatic *veer!* and for the phrases of its downward spiraling song as described above. The song has an other worldly quality. Some think it sounds as though the bird is singing from the bottom of a barrel, thus the folk name Barrel Bird.

Catharus — The genus name is from the Greek *katharos* (pure or clear) and refers to the clear, musical notes of the thrush's songs. James Jobling suggests the name refers to "the immaculate brown and white plumage of the Orange-billed Nightingale Thrush (*C. aurantiirostris*) of Central America, the first species described in this genus.

fuscescens — The specific epithet is from the Greek for "slightly dark" from *fuscus* (dark or dusky) and the suffix *–escens* (slightly). The Veery's plumage is a warm cinnamon brown, not particularly dark or dusky. Its French name *Grive fauve* (deer-colored thrush) is more appropriate.

French Name: Grive Fauve
Spanish Names: Zorzal Rojizo; Zorzalito Rojizo; Zorzal Dorsirrojizo
Other Names: Tawny Thrush; Willow Thrush; Ground Thrush; Wilson's Thrush, Swamp Robin; Flute; Barrel Bird; Cathedral Bird; Merle; Piou-piou; Nightingale

Gray-cheeked Thrush
Catharus minimus
(KATH-ah-rus MIN-ih-mus)

The common name comes from this thrush's gray face, a decidedly colder tone than the warm buff of the similar Swainson's Thrush.

Catharus — The genus name is from the Greek *katharos* (pure or clear) and refers to the clear, musical notes of the thrush's songs. James Jobling suggests the name refers to "the immaculate brown and white plumage of the Orange-billed Nightingale Thrush (*C. aurantiirostris*) of Central America, the first species described in this genus.

minimus — The specific epithet is Latin for "least" or "smallest," a curious choice, since this is one of the largest members in the genus.

French Name: Grive à Joues Grises
Spanish Names: Zorzalito Carigrís; Zorzal de Cara Gris; Zorzal Carigrís
Eskimo and Inuit Names: Niviolruksioyuk (goes after flies)
Other Names: Alice's Thrush; Merle

Bicknell's Thrush
Catharus bicknelli
(KATH-ah-rus BICK-nell-eye)

"On June 15, 1881, a 21-year-old amateur ornithologist named Eugene P. Bicknell hired a local guide and climbed his way toward the summit of Slide Mountain in the Catskills not far from New York City. After a difficult hike through rain, cold and fog he arrived near the summit to parting skies. In a small opening in the fir forest Mr. Bicknell heard Swainson's Thrushes singing and calling. Then he heard an unfamiliar song that was more reminiscent of a Veery. A thrush-sized bird flew across the opening enabling him a clean shot to collect it. Upon close inspection he believed it to be a Gray-cheeked Thrush. Confused about its identity, Mr. Bicknell sent the specimen to Dr. Robert Ridgway at the American Museum of Natural History. Based on its morphological features he placed it as a new subspecies of the Gray-cheeked Thrush and gave it the name Bicknell's Thrush. Eugene Bicknell surprised the ornithological community with this startling discovery of an unknown thrush just outside of America's largest metropolitan area in the backyard of many great ornithologists." — www.ns.ec.gc.ca

This thrush is named for New York banker Eugene P. Bicknell, who collected the type specimen as presented in the opening passage. At first, it was considered just a subspecies of the Gray-cheeked Thrush (*Catharus minimus*). In the 1930s, George J. Wallace, a doctoral student at the University of Michigan, chose Bicknell's Thrush for his dissertation work. He found that there were differences in size and color between Bicknell's and the Gray-cheeked Thrush, but he apparently felt that Bicknell's should remain a subspecies. It was not until 1993, that Canadian researcher Dr. Henri Ouellet published a paper that convinced scientists that Bicknell's was indeed a separate species. He found differences in the color of the plumage of Bicknell's and Gray-cheeked Thrushes. He also showed that the breeding and wintering ranges of the two birds did not overlap, nor was there any evidence of interbreeding. The songs were different, and Bicknell's Thrush did not respond to recordings of the Gray-cheeked Thrush's song. Dr. Gilles Seutin completed the mtDNA analysis and found significant divergence between the two birds. Based on this new evidence, the AOU gave Bicknell's Thrush full species status in 1995.

Catharus — The genus name is from the Greek *katharos* (pure or clear) and refers to the clear, musical notes of the thrush's songs. James Jobling suggests the name refers to "the immaculate brown and white plumage of the Orange-billed Nightingale Thrush (*C. aurantiirostris*) of Central America, the first species described in this genus.

bicknelli — Robert Ridgway initially described this bird in 1882 as a subspecies of the Gray-cheeked Thrush and named it *Hylocichla aliciae bicknelli* in honor of Eugene Pintard Bicknell (1859–1925), a founder of the AOU and collector of the type specimen. See common name above.

French Name: Grive de Bicknell
Spanish Name: Zorzal de Bicknell

Swainson's Thrush
Catharus ustulatus
(KATH-ah-rus yewst-you-LAY-tus)

Swainson's Thrush is named for William Swainson (1789–1855), a notable English naturalist, collector, and writer. Known as Olive-backed Thrush until 1957.

Catharus — The genus name is from the Greek *katharos* (pure or clear) and refers to the clear, musical notes of the thrush's songs. James Jobling suggests the name refers to "the immaculate brown and white plumage of the Orange-billed Nightingale Thrush (*C. aurantiirostris*) of Central America, the first species described in this genus.

ustulatus — The specific epithet is Latin for "burnt" and refers to the bird's brownish color.

French Name: Grive à Dos Olive
Spanish Names: Zorzalito de Swainson; Zorzal de Swainson
Other Names: Russet-back; Russet-backed Thrush; Little Tawny Thrush; Alma's Thrush; Swamp Robin; Ciarsach; Merle; Smeorach

Hermit Thrush
Catharus guttatus
(KATH-ah-rus gut-AY-tus)

"Mounting toward the upland again, I pause reverently at the hush and stillness of twilight come upon the woods. It is the sweetest, ripest hour of the day. And as the hermit's evening hymn goes up from the deep solitude below me, I experience that serene exaltation of sentiment of which music, literature, and religion are but the faint types and symbols." — John Burroughs (1880)

"The hermit thrush ranks high in the list of our favorite North American birds. The exquisite song of this modest bird of the northern woodlands has captivated the affections of a host of bird lovers. Those who have been privileged to hear its song possess delightful memories of association with the hermit; perhaps the wooded border of some mirrored lake or some fern-carpeted woodland; or again they may have heard the fluted notes ringing across some brilliant sunset scene." — Alfred Otto Gross (1949)

Wood Thrush and Hermit Thrush,
by Louis Agassiz Fuertes

The Hermit Thrush is named for its reclusive nature, occurring in northern spruce-fir forests. There is an Indian legend, that is suspiciously similar to a European folktale, that seeks to explain the retiring nature and beautiful song of this bird. It seems that the Great Spirit was to grant each bird its own unique song, and the one that flew the highest would get the most beautiful song of all. The Hermit Thrush knew it had no chance of winning, but then it got an idea, it would hide in the eagle's feathers. So when the eagle got as high as it could, the little stowaway launched itself into the air and flew even higher, actually entering into heaven. So that is why the Hermit Thrush sings such an otherworldly beautiful song, arguably the most exquisite of any North American bird. But because it cheated, the thrush is so ashamed, that it only sings hidden away like a hermit in the densest evergreen forests. The similar European folktale explains how the Eurasian Wren became "the King of the Birds."

Catharus — The genus name is from the Greek *katharos* (pure or clear) and refers to the clear, musical notes of the thrush's songs. James Jobling suggests the name refers to "the immaculate brown and white plumage of the Orange-billed Nightingale Thrush (*C. aurantiirostris*) of Central America, the first species described in this genus.

guttatus — The specific epithet is Latin for "spotted" and refers to the spotted breast.

French Name: Grive Solitaire

Spanish Names: Zorzal de Cola Rufa; Zorzalito Colirrufo

Other Names: Solitary Thrush; Rufous-tailed Thrush; Little Thrush; American Nightingale; Swamp Angel; Swamp Robin; Cathedral Bird; Evening Bird; Night Bird; Rain Bird; Flute; Hautbois; Merle; Rossignol

Wood Thrush
Hylocichla mustelina
(high-low-SICK-lah mus-teh-LIN-ah)

"The nature lover who has missed hearing the musical bell-like notes of the wood thrush, in the quiet woods of early morning or in the twilight, has missed a rare treat. The woods seems to have been transformed into a cathedral where peace and serenity abide. One's spirit seems truly to have been lifted by this experience." — Florence Grow Weaver (1949)

The Wood Thrush is named for its breeding habitat in moist eastern deciduous and mixed forests.

Hylocichla — The genus name means "wood thrush" from the Greek *hule* (a woodland) and *kikhle* (a thrush).

mustelina — The specific epithet is Latin for "weasel." This thrush's warm, reddish brown plumage is similar in color to the summer pelage of a weasel.

French Name: Grive des Bois

Spanish Names: Zorzal Maculado; Zorzalito Maculado; Zorzal del Bosque

Other Names: Song Thrush; Wood Robin; Swamp Robin; Swamp Angel; Bellbird; Brown Linnet; Flute; Merle; Frush; Hulsfrush; Hautbois; Drush'l

Eyebrowed Thrush
Turdus obscurus
(TUR-dus ob-SKURE-us)

This vagrant from Siberia is named for its prominent white eyebrow stripe (supercilium).

Turdus — The genus name is Latin for "a thrush."

obscurus — The specific epithet is Latin for "dark" or "dusky" and refers to this thrush's dull-colored plumage.

French Name: Merle Obscur

Spanish Name: Mirlo Cejudo

Dusky Thrush
Turdus naumanni
(TUR-dus NOW-man-eye)

This Siberian thrush's dark brown plumage gives it its name.

Turdus — The genus name is Latin for "a thrush."

naumanni — In 1820, Dutch ornithologist Coenraad Jacob Temminck named this Eurasian thrush in honor of Johann Andreas Naumann (1744–1826), a German farmer and amateur naturalist.

French Name: Grive de Naumann

Spanish Name: Mirlo de Ala Roja

Other Name: Naumann's Thrush

Fieldfare
Turdus pilaris
(TUR-dus pill-AIR-iss)

Fieldfare means "the traveler over the fields" from the Anglo-Saxon *feld* (a field) and *faran* (to fare or to travel). Each fall, large flocks of Fieldfares migrate to Great Britain from Scandinavia to search the fields for food, mostly berries such as hawthorn, rosehips, and rowan. This Eurasian thrush is a rare visitor to North America, usually seen here in the company of American Robins.

Turdus — The genus name is Latin for "a thrush."

pilaris — The specific epithet means "hairless," i.e. "crestless," from the Latin *pilus* (the hair). It was actually supposed to mean "thrush." The name was coined in error, confusing the Greek *trikhos* (the hair) for *trikhas* (a type of thrush).

French Name: Grive Litorne

Spanish Name: Zorzal Real
Other Names: Blue Back; Blue Bird; Blue Tail; Felt; Blue Felt; Big Felt; Pigeon Felt; Cock Felt; Grey Thrush; Jack Bird; Snow Bird; Hill Bird; Storm Bird; Storm Cock; Screech Bird; Screech Thrush; Velverd; Feltyfare; Feldefare; Fellfare; Feltiflier; Felfer; Felfaw; Felfit

Redwing
Turdus iliacus
(TUR-dus eye-lih-AY-kus)

Rusty red underwing coverts, visible in flight, give this Eurasian thrush its name.
Turdus — The genus name is Latin for "a thrush."
iliacus — The specific epithet is Latin for "of the flanks," referring to the reddish-chestnut wash on the flanks.
French Name: Grive Mauvis
Spanish Name: Zorzal alirrojo
Other Name: Red-winged Thrush; Redwing Mavis; Redwing Throlly; Red Thrush; Wind Thrush; Windle; Windle Thrush; Winnard; Felt; Little Feltyfare; Pop; Swine Pipe

Clay-colored Thrush
Turdus grayi
(TUR-dus GRAY-eye)

Like a dull brown (clay colored) American Robin. The upperparts are a unique buffy-olive; the underparts an even, cinnamon-buff. Formerly known as Clay-colored Robin.
Turdus — The genus name is Latin for "a thrush."
grayi — Colonel Valasquez de Leon collected the type specimen near Alta Vera Paz, Guatemala. The specimen was taken to Europe, where Charles Bonaparte published his description in *Proceedings of the Zoological Society of London* (1837). He named it in honor of George Robert Gray (1808–1872) with the dedication, "A typical species; which I have much pleasure in dedicating to Mr. G. R. Gray, a young ornithologist." George Gray was then twenty-nine and had not yet published any scientific papers. He published his first paper in 1840 and later worked at the British Museum of Natural History for more than forty years.
French Name: Merle Fauve
Spanish Names: Zorzal Pardo; Mirlo Pardo
Other Names: Tamaulipas Thrush; Gray's Robin

Rufous-backed Robin
Turdus rufopalliatus
(TUR-dus RUE-foe-pal-ih-AY-tus)

The reddish brown back and upperwing coverts, which contrast with the bird's gray nape and rump, give this Mexican thrush its name. The reddish color extends to the breast and flanks as well.
Turdus — The genus name is Latin for "a thrush."
rufopalliatus — The specific epithet means "red mantled" fron the Latin *rufus* (red) and *pallium* (a mantle or pallium, a cloak worn by ancient Greeks and Romans).
French Name: Merle à Dos Roux
Spanish Names: Zorzal Dorsirrufo; Mirlo de Dorso Rufo
Other Name: Rufous-backed Thrush

American Robin
Turdus migratorius
(TUR-dus my-grah-TOR-ih-us)

"Robin is a nickname, the affectionate diminutive of Robert. It is a name associated with at least three particular favourites: Robin Hood, Robin Goodfellow, and Robin Redbreast. It carries with it connotations not just of fond familiarity but also of certain spirited contrariness; thus, a generous hearted outlaw, the mischief-making Puck and a distinctive bird who sings all through the winter. — Francesca Greenoak (1979)"

The name Robert originated centuries ago in Normandy. It was a term used for a love-struck youth, and it means "gleaming fame." The Normans introduced the name along with its diminutive form Robin to the British Isles when they invaded in 1066. In Britain there was a small bird with an orange-red face and breast called the ruddock. This is the bird referred to in the opening passage. The ruddock was known to fiercely defend its breeding territory like a passionate young swain. And so, by the mid-16th century, robin was replacing ruddock as the name for the little bird with the red breast. Not surprising, since the English tended to give pet names like martin, jackdaw, jay, and jenny wren

American Robin and Eastern Bluebird,
by Louis Agassiz Fuertes

to familiar dooryard birds. Homesick English colonists named the American Robin for their beloved Robin Redbreast, they left behind in the Mother Country. The colonists saw a similarity between the American Robin and the European Robin (*Erithacus rubecula*), not only in their coloration, but in the friendly demeanor and fiery spirit of the two birds, although they are not closely related. The European Robin is not a thrush, but belongs to the Old World Flycatcher family (Muscicapidae). Wherever they settled, the English named birds showing any red or rufous in their plumage robins. So now there are more than seventy species of birds all over the world called robins. Even some North American birds have robin as a nickname: Red-breasted Merganser (sea robin), Short-billed Dowitcher (robin snipe), Red Knot (beach robin), Eastern Bluebird (blue robin), Hermit Thrush (swamp robin), Wood Thrush (wood robin), Varied Thrush (Marsh Robin), Cedar Waxwing (Canada robin; cherry robin), Eastern Towhee (ground robin; brush robin; bush robin), and Baltimore Oriole (golden robin). However the colonists failed to see the close relationship between the American Robin and the European Blackbird (*Turdus merula*), whose genus name clearly shows that the two are closely related. The European Blackbird looks and behaves much like an all-black American Robin, even their songs are similar! American distinguishes our robin from all the other robins in the world, in particular its Old World namesake.

Turdus — The genus name is Latin for "a thrush."

migratorius — The specific epithet is from the Latin *migrator* (wanderer), and said to refer to this thrush's rare visits to western Europe in fall and winter.

French Name: Merle d'Amérique

Spanish Names: Mirlo Primavera; Zorzal Petirrojo

Eskimo and Inuit Names: Kayapigakturuk (imitative); Kre-ku-ak'tu-yok; Shab'wak

Other Names: Common Robin; Northern Robin; SouthernRrobin; Western Robin; Canada Robin; San Lucas Robin; Carolian Robin; Redbird; Redbreast; Robin Redbreast; Red-breasted Thrush; Red-breasted Mockingbird; Red-breasted Thrush; Migratory Thrush; Fieldfare; Brown Back; Grive Rouge; Merle; Mirlo Norteamericano; Omshel; Roi; Rouge-gorge; Smeorach; Zoral Pechirrojo

Varied Thrush
Ixoreus naevius
(icks-OAR-ih-us NEE-vih-us)

Varied describes the striking color pattern of this thrush, as Pete Dunne describes it, "a bold mosaic of black, blue-gray, and orange makes Varied Thrush look like a robin that's been decorated for Halloween."

Ixoreus — The genus name means "mistletoe mountain" from the Greek *ixos* (mistletoe) and *oreos* (a mountain). Although the Varied Thrush does feed on berries, it isn't particularly partial to those of mistletoe. It is likely that it was named for a superficial resemblance to the Mistle Thrush (*Turdus viscivorus*) of Eurasia. In Mediterranean countries, The Mistle Thrush is known to feed on the berries of a red-fruited species of mistletoe that grows on olive trees.

Varied Thrush, by Allan C. Brooks

naevius — The specific epithet is Latin for "spotted" or "varied."
French Name: Grive à Collier
Spanish Names: Mirlo de Pecho Cinchado; Zorzal Pechicinchado
Other Names: Northern Varied Thrush; Pacific Varied Thrush; Pale Varied Thrush; Alaska Robin; Oregon Robin; Golden Robin; Marsh Robin; Hudson Bay Robin; Swamp Robin; Wood Robin

Aztec Thrush
Ridgwayia pinicola
(RIDJ-way-ih-ah pin-ICK-oh-lah)

This Mexican species is named for its range, the former Aztec Empire.

Ridgwayia — Philip Lutley Sclater described this species in 1859 in *Proceedings of the Zoological Society of London* from a specimen collected from the pine forests above Jalapa, Mexico. He gave it the name *Turdus pinicola*. In 1883, Leonhard Hess Stejneger, the Smithsonian's first full-time curator of herpetology, erected the genus *Ridgwayia* for the Aztec Thrush in honor of his colleague Robert Ridgway (1850–1929), the Curator of Birds at the Institution.

pinicola — The specific epithet means "an inhabitant of a pine tree" from the Latin *pinus* (a pine tree) and –*cola* (inhabitant). The reference is to this species' habitat in montane coniferous forests.
French Name: Grive Aztèque
Spanish Name: Mirlo Pinto

Family Mimidae
Mimic Thrushes

Gray Catbird
Dumetella carolinensis
(due-meh-TELL-ah care-oh-lin-EN-sis)

This familiar bird is named for its alarm call, which sounds remarkably like the mewing of a cat. Its overall color is slate gray except for the black cap and rusty undertail coverts.

Dumetella — The genus name means "little one of the bramble thicket" from the Latin *dumetum* (a thicket) plus a diminutive suffix –*ella*. The reference is to the catbird's habitat in woodland thickets, brambles, and garden shrubbery.

carolinensis — The specific epithet is Modern Latin for "of Carolina" referring to the Carolina colonies where the type specimen was collected.
French Name: Moqueur Chat
Spanish Names: Maullador gris; Pájaro-gato Gris
Other Names: Mockingbird; Black Mockingbird; Slate-colored Mockingbird; Black Thrush; Black-capped Thrush; Cat Flycatcher; Chicken Bird; Lazy Bird; Mary Bird; Taylor-made Bird; Chat; Kotsafogel; Merle Chat; Oiseau-chat; Zorzal Gato

Curve-billed Thrasher
Toxostoma curvirostre
(tocks-OSS-toh-mah cur-vih-ROSS-trih)

This thrasher's moderately curved black bill gives it its name, but some of the desert thrashers have a sharper bend in their bills.

Toxostoma — The genus name means "bow mouth" from the Greek *toxon* (a bow) and *stoma* (the mouth). The reference is to the thrashers' curved bills suggesting an archer's bow.

curvirostre — The specific epithet means curved bill from the Latin *curvus* (curved) and *rostrum* (the bill).
French Name: Moqueur à Bec Courbe
Spanish Names: Cuitlacoche de Pico Curvo; Cuitlacoche Piquicurvo
Other Names: Palmer's Thrasher; Cuitlacoche Común

Brown Thrasher
Toxostoma rufum
(tocks-OSS-toh-mah ROOF-um)

Some authorities say thrasher is derived from thrush. Birds in this family are known as mimic thrushes, and some are thrush-like in coloration. Others say thrasher refers to these birds' foraging behavior of thrashing the ground for insects. The thrashers sweep their long bills briskly from side to side to move leaf litter and other debris to uncover hidden prey. Brown describes this species' rich reddish-brown plumage.

Toxostoma — The genus name means "bow mouth" from the Greek *toxon* (a bow) and *stoma* (the mouth). The reference is to the thrashers' curved bills suggesting an archer's bow.

rufum — The specific epithet is Latin for "reddish" and refers to the bird's reddish brown color.
French Name: Moqueur Roux
Spanish Name: Cuitlacoche rojizo

Sidebar 27
Advisement for the Farmer

Planter Bird is a folk name derived from a mnemonic for the Brown Thrasher's song. The phrases are delivered in couplets, and it seems, according to F. Schuyler Mathews (1904), "that the Thrasher advises the farmer about his various duties in emphatic insistence:"

Shuck it, shuck it; sow it, sow it;
Plough it, plough it; hoe it, hoe it;
Harrow it, harrow it; scatter it, scatter it;
Seed it, seed it; cover it, cover it;
Rake it, rake it; push it in, push it in;
Weed it, weed it; pull it up, pull it up.

Brown Thrasher, by Louis Agassiz Fuertes

Other Names: Thrasher; Brown Mocker; Brown Mockingbird; Ferruginous Mockingbird; Sandy Mocker; Sandy Mockingbird; Ground Mocking-Bird; French Mockingbird; Song Thrush; Brown Thrush; Red Thrush; Ferruginous Thrush; Fox-colored Thrush; Ground Thrush; Long Thrush; Cane-bird; Death Bird; Planter Bird; Planting Bird; Robin; Mavis; Red Mavis; Drush'l; Drushdel; Grive Rousse; Shpottfogel

Long-billed Thrasher
Toxostoma longirostre
(tocks-OSS-toh-mah lonj-ih-ROSS-trih)

This thrasher's bill is slightly longer than that of the Brown Thrasher. But some of the western species have even longer bills.

Toxostoma — The genus name means "bow mouth" from the Greek *toxon* (a bow) and *stoma* (the mouth). The reference is to the thrashers' curved bills suggesting an archer's bow.

longirostre — The specific epithet means "long bill" from the Latin *longus* (long) and *rostrum* (the bill).
French Name: Moqueur à Long Bec
Spanish Names: Cuitlacoche de Pico Largo; Cuitlacoche Piquilargo
Other Names: Sennett's Thrasher

Bendire's Thrasher
Toxostoma bendirei
(tocks-OSS-toh-mah ben-DIRE-eh-eye)

In July, 1871, Major Charles Emil Bendire collected a female thrasher near Fort Lowell, Arizona. He sent the skin to Elliot Coues, who sent it on to Robert Ridgway. Ridgway identified it as the westernmost subspecies of the Curve-billed Thrasher (*Toxostoma curvirostre palmeri*). Coues was unconvinced and requested additional information from Bendire, who sent him the skin of a male specimen along with notes on the bird's behavior. He also wrote that the eggs of his specimen were different from those of the Curve-billed Thrasher. Coues described the specimen as a new species in 1873, naming it *Harporhynchus Bendirei*, and referred to it as Bendire's Thrush.

Toxostoma — The genus name means "bow mouth" from the Greek *toxon* (a bow) and *stoma* (the mouth). The reference is to the thrashers' curved bills suggesting an archer's bow.

bendirei — This thrasher is named in honor of Charles Emil Bendire (1836–1897), who collected the first specimen near Fort Lowell, Arizona. See common name above.
French Name: Moqueur à Bec Droit
Spanish Names: Cuitlacoche de Pico Corto; Cuitlacoche de Bendire

California Thrasher
Toxostoma redivivum
(tocks-OSS-toh-mah red-ih-VIE-vum)

This thrasher is named for its range in California and Baja California.

Toxostoma — The genus name means "bow mouth" from the Greek *toxon* (a bow) and *stoma* (the mouth). The reference is to the thrashers' curved bills suggesting an archer's bow.

redivivum — The specific epithet means "revived" or in this case "rediscovered." Naturalists on the La Pérouse Expedition (1785–1787) to find the Northwest Passage described this species, placing it in the genus *Promerops* (similar to a bee-eater). The significance was to the thrasher's curved bill being similar to the curved bills of the colorful bee-eaters of the Old World. This species was not seen again until 1845, when William Gambel described it and placed in the genus *Toxostoma*. He gave it the specific epithet *redivivum*, because this bird had been rediscovered sixty years later.
French Name: Moqueur de Californie
Spanish Name: Cuitlacoche Californiano
Other Names: Sonoma Thrasher; Pasadena Thrasher

LeConte's Thrasher
Toxostoma lecontei
(tocks-OSS-toh-mah leh-KONT-eh-eye)

This species is named for Dr. John L. LeConte. See specific epithet below.

Toxostoma — The genus name means "bow mouth" from the Greek *toxon* (a bow) and

Crissal Thrasher and LeConte's Thrasher, by Allan C. Brooks

stoma (the mouth). The reference is to the thrashers' curved bills suggesting an archer's bow.

lecontei — In 1851, George N. Lawrence named this species in honor of Dr. John Lawrence LeConte (1825–1883), a Philadelphia physician and entomologist.

French Name: Moqueur de Le Conte
Spanish Name: Cuitlacoche Pálido
Other Names: Desert Thrasher; LeConte's Mocking Bird

Crissal Thrasher
Toxostoma crissale
(tocks-OSS-toh-mah kris-AIL-ee)

Crissal refers to this species chestnut crissum (undertail coverts), which contrasts with its otherwise grayish plumage.

Toxostoma — The genus name means "bow mouth" from the Greek *toxon* (a bow) and *stoma* (the mouth). The reference is to the thrashers' curved bills suggesting an archer's bow.

crissale — The specific epithet is from the Latin *crissalis* and refers to the crissum, the undertail coverts. See common name above.

French Name: Moqueur Cul-roux
Spanish Name: Cuitlacoche Crisal
Other Name: Red-vented Thrasher

Sage Thrasher
Oreoscoptes montanus
(or-eh-oh-SKOP-teez mon-TAN-us)

The Sage Thrasher is named for its breeding habitat on open sagebrush flats.

Oreoscoptes The genus name means "mountain mimic" from the Greek *oros* (a mountain) and *scoptes* (a mimic). An older name for this species is mountain mockingbird. The mimic part of the name is apt, but mountain is not. This a bird of high desert, not alpine regions.

montanus The specific epithet is Latin for "a mountain," a misnomer. See genus name above.

French Name: Moqueur des Armoises
Spanish Name: Cuitlacoche de Artemesia
Other Names: Sage Thrush; Sage Mockingbird; Mountain Mockingbird

Bahama Mockingbird
Mimus gundlachii
(MY-mus gund-LOCK-ih-eye)

This rare visitor to Florida is named for its range in the Bahama Islands.

Mimus — The genus name is Latin for "a mimic" or "imitator."

gundlachii — The specific epithet honors Cuba's greatest naturalist Johannes Christopher Gundlach (1810–1896), author of *Ornitologia Cubana* (1893).

French Name: Moqueur des Bahamas
Spanish Name: Cenzontle de las Bahamas
Other Names: Spanish Mockingbird; Spanish Thrasher; Spanish Nightingale' Salt Island Nightingale; Sinsonte Prieto; Sinsonte Carbonero

Northern Mockingbird
Mimus polyglottos
(MY-mus pol-ih-GLOT-os)

"There is no possibility of doubt that the vocal attainments of the mockingbird are its primary characteristics. Its voice overshadows its every other trait, habit, and

Northern Mockingbird, by Louis Agassiz Fuertes

even appearance. Recognition of it is evident in both the common and the scientific name of the species, and neither could be more appropriate. Though its amazing powers of imitation were not known to Linnaeus except second-hand, his designation *Mimus polyglottos* as its name was well chosen, for as "many-tongued mimic" the mockingbird stands alone. Catesby's name of "Mock-bird" is practically the same as its present-day appellation. Some years ago Herbert R. Sass, of Charleston, S.C., referred to the mockingbird in one of his inimitable nature articles as "Mimus the Matchless," and it has always seemed to this writer that no more descriptive adjective could be used in connection with it. Truly, that is the word for the mocker — matchless!" — Arthur Cleveland Bent (1948)

One of our best known songbirds, the mockingbird is famous for its ability to mimic the songs of other birds. Pioneer naturalist Mark Catesby, the first European to scientifically chronicle the "mock-bird of Carolina," wrote, "The Indians, by way of eminence or admiration, call it *Centcontlatolly* or 400 tongues." This is not much of an exaggeration, for individual mockers have been known to mimic the songs of between 100 and 200 different species of birds. A mockingbird may imitate more than 30 bird songs in rapid succession, and throw in some other sounds, too, an automobile horn, a barking dog, a rooster's crow, a squeaky wheelbarrow, the chirp of a cricket, a treefrog's trill, a truck's backup beeps, even a chain saw. At an outdoor concert, a mockingbird even imitated the flute's rendition of Sasha the bird in *Peter and the Wolf*. Scientists believe that female mockingbirds are attracted to males with complex, varied songs. It shows that he is older and experienced and

---

Sidebar 28
Mockingbird vs. Nightingale

"When the moonlight sheds a silvery radiance about every sleeping reature, the mockingbird sings to his mate such delicious music as only the European nightingale can rival. Perhaps the stillness of the hour, the beauty and fragrance of the place where the singer is hidden among the orange blossoms or magnolia, increase the magic of his almost pathetically sweet voice; but surely there is no lovelier sound in nature on this side of the sea." — Neltje Blanchan (1917)

Gifted American songsters such as the Hermit Thrush and Mockingbird are invariably compared to the most celebrated of Old World songbirds, the Common Nightingale (*Luscinia megarhynchos*). John Burroughs called the Mockingbird "the lark and the nightingale in one," and birders have argued back and forth across the Pond as to which is the superior singer. Here is a story in which it appears that the Mockingbird can beat the Nightingale at its own game:

"In connection with the reference to the nightingale, probably the most famous Old World songsters, an amusing story is even related in Florida connected with this species and the mocker. It seems that Edward Bok, who created the well-known Singing Tower near Lake Wales, had several nightingales imported and confined there in cages. When the strangers had settled down and had begun to voice their famous song abroad across the orange groves, great satisfaction was felt, of course. Before long, however, nightingale songs were heard all over the surrounding territory! Here, there, and yonder the foreign strains were echoing, but all the captives remained in their cages. The mockingbirds of the area had taken charge and were broadcasting nightingale melodies over the countryside! It is said that the European performers were put to silence and soon refused to sing at all." — Arthur Cleveland Bent (1948)

will make a good father for her young. Northern distinguishes our species from relatives of more southerly distribution such as the Bahama Mockingbird (*M. gundlachii*) and the Tropical Mockingbird (*M. gilvus*) of Central America.

Mimus — The genus name is Latin for "a mimic" or "imitator."

polyglottos — The specific epithet means "many tongued" from the Greek *poly* (many) and *glottos* (the tongue).

French Name: Moqueur Polyglotte
Spanish Name: Cenzontle Norteño
Other Names: Common Mockingbird; Mocker; Mock Bird; Mocking Thrush; Mimic Thrush; the Singing Bird; English Thrasher; Nightingale; Jamaica Nightingale; Centzontle Aliblanco; Sinsonte; Sinsonte Norteño; Rossignol; Ruiseñor

Family Sturnidae
Starlings and Allies

European Starling
Sturnus vulgaris
(STIR-nus vul-GARE-is)

*Nay, I'll have a starling shall be taught to speak
Nothing but "Mortimer," and give it him
To keep his anger still in motion.*

Starling means "little star" and refers to the spangled appearance of the birds in fresh fall plumage; by spring the buff-colored, starry spots have worn away, leaving the starling in its greasy-appearing summer plumage. The line above from *Henry IV* is the reason we have European Starlings in North America. An outfit called the American Acclimatization Society, chaired by Eugene Scheiffelin, a wealthy drug manufacturer from the Bronx, wanted to establish in America every kind of bird mentioned in the works of Shakespeare. Fortunately, their attempts to establish bullfinches, chaffinches, skylarks, and nightingales failed, but the European Starling thrived in its new home. Here is the story:

The fateful day was March 16, 1890. The place, Central Park in New York City. Overhead circled 60 European starlings

European Starling, by Louis Agassiz Fuertes

(*Sturnus vulgaris*) released by a zealous group that planned to introduce into the United States all the birds mentioned by Shakespeare. Anxious eyes followed the birds' every flit and hop. Would they survive? Previous attempts to establish them in this country had failed. Within weeks came the answer. A pair were nesting under the eaves of the American Museum of Natural History. The eggs hatched. The next year 40 more immigrant starlings were freed in Central Park. A Pandora's box had been opened. From these 100 starlings sprang the unnumbered millions that now inhabit North America. Hardy, prolific, aggressive, they have pushed far northward into Canada, southward to southern Mexico, westward to California, Vancouver Island, and even Alaska. In many areas they assemble each fall and winter in mighty flocks — sometimes miles long — that blot out the sun ... A plague to other birds as well as to people, starlings evict bluebirds and swallows from nest boxes and tree holes, often destroying eggs and young in the process. — Alexander Wetmore (1964)

Sturnus — is the Latin word for "a starling."

vulgaris — The specific epithet means "common" which it is, both in its native Europe and most especially here in North America.

French Name: Étourneau Sansonnet
Spanish Name: Estornino Europeo
British Name: Common Starling
Other Names: English Starling; Black Starling; Shepstarling; Shepster; Sheppie; Sheeprack; Shepstare; Sheep Stare; Jacob; Fstornino; Etourneau; Gyp; Gyp Starnil; Staynil; Stare; Starn; Starnel; Black Steer; Black Felt; Church-Martin

Common Myna
Acridotheres tristis
(ack-rid-OTH-er-eez TRIST-iss)

Myna derives from *maina* (a starling), the Hindi word for these birds. This species is common in its native Asia.

Acridotheres — The genus name means "locust hunter" from the Greek *acris/acridos* (a locust) and *theres* (a hunter).

tristis — The specific epithet is Latin for "sad," "gloomy," or "dull-colored" referring to the blackish plumage.

French Name: Martin Triste
Spanish Name: Myna Común
Other Names: Indian Myna; House Myna; Piha 'e-kelo

Family Bombycillidae
Waxwings

Waxwings are named for the bright red droplets on the tips of the secondary wing feathers, that resemble sealing wax. These droplets are prolongations of the feather shafts. They are acquired after the birds are fourteen months old and may play a role in mate selection. Older, experienced birds, showing more color on the wingtips than younger ones, tend to have a higher breeding success:

"By their bloodlines, waxwings are songbirds, but one would never know that by what emerges from the bill of these gregarious birds. Waxwings are by all accounts, songbirds without a song. But if we consider a "song" more broadly as a device to impress members of the opposite sex, perhaps the Cedar Waxwing's waxy wing tips, though silent, function as a song - perhaps you could think of these birds as "Cedar Waxsings."" — Donald Kroodsma (2005)

Bohemian Waxwing
Bombycilla garrulous
(bom-bih-SILL-ah GAR-you-lus)

"To most of us, these Bohemians are birds of mystery; we never know when or where we may see these roving bands of gypsies. They come and they go, we know not whence or whither, in the never-ending search for a bounteous food supply on which to gorge themselves." — Arthur Cleveland Bent (1950)

The common name does not refer to the region in Europe, although this species does occur in the Old World as well as the New. Bohemian in this case is a synonym for "gypsy" in the sense that these birds are highly nomadic in their search for berry crops, as described in the above passage.

Bombycilla — The genus name means "silk tail," a translation of the German name for this bird, *seidenschwanz*. It derives from the Greek *bombyx* (silk) and Modern Latin *cilla*, actually a diminutive suffix, but taken by some early naturalists to mean "tail." See *Motacilla*, the genus of the wagtails. The reference is to the smooth, silky plumage or to the yellow terminal band on the tail.

garrulous — The specific epithet is Latin for "chattering," which does not accurately describe these birds' vocalizations. Waxwings utter very thin, high-pitched calls. The Bohemian Waxwing is actually named for the Eurasian Jay (*Garrulus glandarius*), because of a slight physical resemblance, both species sport crests.

French Name: Jaseur Boréal
Spanish Name: Ampelis Europeo
British Name: Waxwing
Eskimo Name: Tik-e-che-u-wuk (killer of small birds as shown by clotted blood on wings)
Other Names: Northern Waxwing; Black-throated Waxwing; Greater Waxwing; Lapland Waxwing; Cherry Bird; Silktail; Bohemian Chatterer; Bohemian Wax-chatterer; Northern Chatterer; Waxen Chatterer; Recollet

Cedar Waxwing
Bombycilla cedrorum
(bom-bih-SILL-ah see-DROR-um)

"When the cedar ripens its glaucous-blue berries, these same birds are sure to be found there, gorging themselves on this fruit till they are literally choke-full — the last few berries sticking in their capacious throats for want of room below. These gourmands grow extremely fat at times; they are commonly called Cedar-birds, and their flesh is accounted a delicacy. They are also named Cherry-birds, from their fondness for cherries; and might with equal propriety be known as Gum-birds, or Huckleberry-birds, or by any other set of names indicating that they feed on a great variety of edible small-fruits." — Elliott Coues

The Cedar Waxwing is named for the Eastern Redcedar (*Juniperus virginiana*), whose berry-like cones are a staple food of this bird. Cedar berries can make up 50% of the waxwing's winter diet.

Bombycilla — The genus name means "silk tail," a translation of the German name for the Bohemian Waxwing, *seidenschwanz*. It derives from the Greek *bombyx* (silk) and Modern Latin *cilla*, actually a diminutive suffix, but taken by some early naturalists to mean "tail." (See *Motacilla*, the genus of the wagtails) The reference is to the smooth, silky plumage or to the yellow terminal band on the tail.

cedrorum — The specific epithet is Latin for "of the cedars." See common name above.

French Name: Jaseur des Cèdres

Cedar Waxwing and Red-eyed Vireo, by Louis Agassiz Fuertes

Spanish Names: Ampelis Chinito; Ampelis Americano
Other Names: Southern Waxwing; Carolina Waxwing; Lesser Waxwing; Cherry Waxwing; Cherry-bird; Cherry Robin; Canada Robin; Canadian Robin; Cedar Bird; Apple Bird; Blossom Bird; Bonnet Bird; Cankerbird; Spider Bird; Comb-wing Bird; Blockhead; Mangeur de Cerises; Basque; Huppe; Recollet; Recellet; Picotera

Family Ptilogonatidae
Silky-Flycatchers

Phainopepla
Phainopepla nitens
(fay-noh-PEP-lah NIGH-tenz)

"What I call the Phainopepla's elegance comes partly from its form, which is the very perfection of its shapeliness, having in

Phainopepla, by Allan C. Brooks

the highest degree that elusive quality which in semi-slang phrase is designated as "style;" partly from its motions, all prettily conscious and in a pleasing sense affected, like the movements of a dancing-master; and partly from its color, which is black with the most exquisite bluish sheen, set off in the finest manner by broad wing-patches of white." — Bradford Torrey (1904)

"The outstanding attributes of this bird, in the eyes of those who named it, are revealed by a translation of its scientific name: *Phainopepla*, from two Greek words meaning "shining robe;" *nitens*, a Latin word also meaning "shining;" *lepida* from the Latin and meaning "charming."" — Arthur Cleveland Bent (1950)

This bird's glossy plumage gives it its common and genus name. See genus name below.

Phainopepla — The genus name means "shining robe" from the Greek *phainos* (shining) and Greek *peplos* (a robe) and refers to the glossy black plumage. See opening passages above.

nitens — The specific epithet is Latin for "shining."
French Name: Phénopèple
Spanish Name: Capulinero Negro
Other Names: Silky Flycatcher; Black Flycatcher; Black-crested Flycatcher; Shining Crested Flycatcher; Shining Fly-snapper; Silky Fly-snapper

Family Peucedramidae
Olive Warbler

Olive Warbler
Peucedramus taeniatus
(pew-SED-rah-mus tee-nih-AY-tus)

The Olive Warbler was formerly classified as a Wood-Warbler in the family *Parulidae*. But recent DNA studies have shown that it warranted a family of its own. It may actually be more closely related to the Old World Warblers. It still retains the name warbler from its former classification. Olive would suggest an overall dull greenish color to the plumage, but the only olive this bird displays is a patch on the nape. The name more accurately describes the color of the immature birds. Bent refers to the juvenile's upperparts as dull olive or brownish olive.

Peucedramus — The genus name means "pine-runner" (but here taken to mean pine-dweller) from the Greek *peuke* (a pine) and *dramein* (to run). This refers to this species breeding habitat of montane coniferous forests above elevations of 7000 feet.

taeniatus — The specific epithet is Modern Latin for "striped" and is a reference to the black eye-line of the male.
French Name: Fauvine des Pins
Spanish Names: Ocotero Enmascarado; Chipe Ocotero
Other Name: Northern Olive Warbler

Sidebar 29
The Great Sparrow War

"Without question the most deplorable event in the history of American ornithology was the introduction of the English Sparrow. The extinction of the Great Auk, the passing of the Wild Pigeon and the Turkey — sad as these are, they are trifles compared to the wholesale reduction of our smaller birds, which is due to the invasion of that wretched foreigner, the English Sparrow." — William Leon Dawson (1902)

The House Sparrow used to be called the English Sparrow, a name still in wide use. In 1850, Nicholas Pike, a director of the the Brooklyn Institute, imported eight pairs of House Sparrows from England. He released them in Brooklyn in the spring of 1851. These birds did not survive, so Pike imported more in 1852. Fifty were released at the Narrows; the remainder were kept in captivity until the following spring, then liberated in Greenwood Cemetery. From 1854 to 1881, crates of sparrows were released all over the country from Boston to San Francisco. The alleged reason behind the introductions was to control cankerworms that were defoliating orchards and shade trees. The House Sparrow was an odd choice for biological pest control, since it is chiefly a ground-feeding seed eater. Insects comprise only about 10% of the bird's diet. It is unlikely a House Sparrow would even find many cankerworms, because it does not glean foliage for caterpillars as a warbler does. But many welcomed the new species anyway. The city of Boston erected nesting boxes on the Boston Common, and the city fathers hired a forester to kill predators that were a threat to the sparrows. During the winter of 1876–1877, he shot eighty-nine Northern Shrikes. By the 1870s the House Sparrow had taken hold with a vengeance. Ornithologists were aghast when they saw the aggressive sparrows displace such beloved cavity nesters as Purple Martins, Tree Swallows, and Eastern Bluebirds. An 1889 study found that House Sparrows attacked seventy different species of native birds. This sparked what was to become known as the Sparrow War, not an actual war but a war of words between two factions of professional ornithologists. Boston ornithologist Thomas Mayo Brewer was the chief advocate for the sparrow, and Elliot Coues represented the anti-sparrow faction. Bitter attacks from both sides appeared in the editorials of many eastern newspapers, and even nonprofessionals got into the act. Henry Bergh, founder of the ASPCA, called Coues "a murderer," and Henry Ward Beecher condemned him, paraphrasing Scripture, 1 Kings 17:6, "No raven shall ever bring him meat." Brewer in a scathing rebuke of the members of the Nuttall Club who sided with Coues, called them "overmodest young gentlemen." Coues continued to take digs at Brewer, even after Brewer's death in 1880. Of course the antis were right, as the House Sparrow proved to be an invasive species, particularly in its competition with native songbirds. But the House Sparrow is here to stay, although its numbers have been declining in recent decades.

Thomas Mayo Brewer, chief proponent for the House Sparrow

Elliott Coues was staunchly anti-House Sparrow.

Family Passeridae
Old-World Sparrows

House Sparrow
Passer domesticus
(PASS-er dom-ESS-tih-kus)

Sparrow derives from Middle English *sparowe* and Old English *spearwa*, which means "flutterer." The name was originally applied to any small bird. House refers to the fact that this species almost always occurs in habitats modified for humans, particularly towns and cities. In rural areas, House Sparrows congregate around barns, pole buildings and other outbuildings as well as in hedges and windbreaks. It likes to forage around feedlots. In urban areas, House Sparrows can be found in city parks, zoos, boardwalks at coastal resorts, and outdoor cafes. House Sparrows have associated with man since the Neolithic Age nine thousand years ago, and they have been introduced to every continent except Antarctica. Now they even occur on the Hawaiian Islands. The introduction of foreign species by "acclimatization societies" became a controversial issue among professional ornithologists, sparking the so-called Sparrow War. See sidebar 29.

Passer — The genus name is the Latin word for "sparrow."

domesticus — The specific epithet means "belonging to a household" from the Latin *domus* (a house). See common name above.

French Name: Moineau Domestique

Spanish Names: Gorrión Domestico; Gorrión Común

Other Names: English Sparrow; European House Sparrow; Domestic Sparrow; Town Sparrow; Hedge Sparrow; Thatch Sparrow; Thack Sparrow; Easing Sparrow; Bull Sparrow; House Bird; Grey Bird; Spadger; Grey Spadger; Spurdie; Spurgie; Spuggie; Spatzie; Sputzie; Speug; Sproug; Sprug; Craff; Cuddy; Lum Lintie; Roo-doo; Row-dow; Hoodlum; Gamin; Glaiseun; Gorrión; Gorrión Ingles; Manu Liilii; Moineau Anglais; Moineau Pierrot; Pinson Anglais; Tramp

House Sparrow, by Louis Agassiz Fuertes

Eurasian Tree Sparrow
Passer montanus
(PASS-er mon-TAN-us)

This bird is called a tree sparrow, because it nests in tree cavities. Eurasian refers to its natural range from the British Isles through the Middle East to Siberia and Southeast Asia. It also distinguishes this species from the American Tree Sparrow in the family Passerellidae. The Eurasian Tree Sparrow was introduced to North America from Germany in 1870, when twelve birds were released in Saint Louis, Missouri. There is now a small resident population around Saint Louis and across the river in western Illinois.

Passer — *The genus* name is the Latin word for "sparrow."

montanus — The specific epithet is Latin for "of the mountains." This is not a particularly appropriate name, since this species is not associated with mountainous areas.

French Name: Moineau Friquet

Spanish Name: Gorrión Molinero

Other Names: European Tree Sparrow; Rock Sparrow; Red-headed Sparrow; Tree Finch; Copper Head

Family Motacillidae
Wagtails and Pipits

Wagtails are named for the habit of most species of constantly pumping their long, narrow tails up and down as they forage on the ground. Pipit is imitative of the call notes. It derives from the Latin *pipio* (to chirp or peep).

Eastern Yellow Wagtail
Motacilla tchutschensis
(moe-tah-SILL-ah tchut-CHEN-sis)

"Early June in western Alaska finds the yellow wagtails arriving from Asia for the brief summer. The slim, restless birds are a common sight, but usually at long range ... Seemingly always on the move, the birds scuttle briskly across the meadows and coastal mud flats. At every abrupt, momentary pause they flirt their tails up and down or back and forth. Their heads bob in accompaniment." — Alexander Wetmore (1964)

Motacilla — The genus name is usually translated as "moving tail" from the Latin *motus* (moving) and the Modern Latin *cilla*, incorrectly taken to mean "the tail." The Roman scholar Varro, who coined the name for wagtail wrote, "The bird owes its name to the fact that it is always moving its tail." Actually, *-illa* is a diminutive suffix, so the literal translation of *Motacilla* is "little mover." Later authors have also used *cilla* to mean "tail" as in such names as a*tricilla* (black tail), *ruticilla* (red tail), and *Bombycilla* (silk tail). The Eastern Yellow Wagtail was split from the Yellow Wagtail (*Motacilla flava*) of Eurasia.

tchutschensis — The specific epithet means "of Chukotskiy," a peninsula in Siberia where presumably the type specimen was collected.

French Name: Bergeronnette Printanière
Spanish Name: Lavandera Amarilla
Eskimo and Inuit Names: Pshu-kuk (imitative); Piorgak (imitative)
Other Names: Alaska Yellow Wagtail; Spring Wagtail; Summer Wagtail; Yellow Waggie; Yellow Molly; Dishwasher; Golden Dishwasher; Quaketail; Ladybird; Barley Bird; Barley-seed Bird; Oatseed Bird; Oat-ear; Potato Dropper; Potato Setter; Cow-bird; Cow-klit; Maw-daw

White Wagtail
Motacilla alba
(moe-tah-SILL-ah AL-bah)

The White Wagtail is named for its immaculate white underparts in contrast to wagtail species that are yellow underneath. The White Wagtail also sports a white face, but its upperparts are mostly gray and black.

Motacilla — The genus name is usually translated as "moving tail" from the Latin *motus* (moving) and the Modern Latin *cilla*, incorrectly taken to mean "the tail." The Roman scholar Varro, who coined the name for wagtail wrote, "The bird owes its name to the fact that it is always moving its tail." Actually, *-illa* is a diminutive suffix, so the literal translation of *Motacilla* is "little mover." Later authors have also used *cilla* to mean "tail" as in such names as a*tricilla* (black tail), *ruticilla* (red tail), and *Bombycilla* (silk tail).

alba — The specific epithet is Latin for "white" which refers to the dominant color of this bird's plumage.

French Name: Bergeronnette Grise
Spanish Name: Lavandera Blanca
Other Names: Pied Wagtail; Nannie Wagtail; Willie Wagtail; Lady Wagtail; Piedie Wagtail; Water Wagtail; Wattertiwagtail; Wattie Wagtail; Wattie; Watitty; Seed Bird; Seed Lady; Devil Bird; Deviling; Dishwasher; Lady Dishwasher; Dishwipe; Dishlick; Washdish; Molly Washdish; Polly Washdish; Dish-dasher; Ditchwatcher; Nanny Washtail; Quaketail; Scullery Maids

Red-throated Pipit
Anthus cervinus
(AN-thus sir-VINE-us)

The spring male's salmon pink throat gives this pipit its name. The color also extends to the face and breast.

Anthus — The genus name is Latin for a small bird of the grasslands mentioned by Pliny from the Greek *Anthos*, a small, colorful bird mentioned by Aristotle but not further identified. Some believe it to be the Yellow Wagtail (*Motacilla flava*), but now the genus encompasses the Pipits. The name is from the mythological character

Anthus, a young man who was killed an eaten by his father's hungry horses. Zeus, taking pity on the grieving family, changed its members into birds. Anthus was turned into a bird that uttered a horse-like whinny, but always fled from horses.

cervinus — The specific epithet is Latin for "stag-like" pertaining to the color of a deer. It refers particularly to the pipit's salmon pink face, throat, and breast.

French Name: Pipit à Gorge Rousse
Spanish Names: Bisbita de Garganta Roja; Bisbita Gorjirrufa

American Pipit
Anthus rubescens
(AN-thus rue-BESS-enz)

American distinguishes this North American species from the many Eurasian pipits. Formerly known as Water Pipit. It was considered conspecific with the Rock Pipit (*A. spinoletta*) of Eurasia.

Anthus — The genus name is Latin for a small bird of the grasslands mentioned by Pliny from the Greek *Anthos*, a small, colorful bird mentioned by Aristotle but not further identified. Some believe it to be the Yellow Wagtail (*Motacilla flava*), but now the genus encompasses the Pipits. The name is from the mythological character Anthus, a young man who was killed an eaten by his father's hungry horses. Zeus, taking pity on the grieving family, changed its members into birds. Anthus was turned into a bird that uttered a horse-like whinny, but always fled from horses.

rubescens — The specific epithet is Latin for "reddish" or "blushed" from *rubescere* (to become red) and refers to the pinkish buff underparts.

French Name: Pipit d'Amérique
Spanish Name: Bisbita Americana
Eskimo and Inuit Names: Piorgavik (imitative); Assu Ka-vij; Chi-ching-uk
Other Names: Rock Pipit; Rock Lintie; Wagtail; Titlark; American Titlark; Brown Lark; Red Lark; Rock Lark; Dusky Lark; Hudsonian Lark; Louisiana Lark; Sea Lark; Sea Lintie; Sea Titling; Tangle Sparrow; Alouette Pipi; Teetan; Gutter Teetan; Shore Teetan; Teetuck; Sea Mouse

Sprague's Pipit
Anthus spragueii
(AN-thus SPRAIG-ih-eye)

In 1843, Isaac Sprague accompanied Audubon on his Missouri River expedition along with John Graham Bell, Edward Harris, and Lewis Squires. In the afternoon of June 19th, Bell and Harris shot at the same small brown bird near Fort Union, North Dakota. It turned out to be a new species, and Audubon named it Sprague's Missouri Lark in honor of his assistant artist. On June 24th, Sprague himself went out into the field and found a nest containing five eggs in a hollow in the ground, concealed by a tuft of prairie grass. He also collected a second specimen. See specific epithet below.

Anthus — The genus name is Latin for a small bird of the grasslands mentioned by Pliny from the Greek *Anthos*, a small, colorful bird mentioned by Aristotle but not further identified. Some believe it to be the Yellow Wagtail (*Motacilla flava*), but now the genus encompasses the Pipits. The name is from the mythological character Anthus, a young man who was killed an eaten by his father's hungry horses. Zeus, taking pity on the grieving family, changed its members into birds. Anthus was turned into a bird that uttered a horse-like whinny, but always fled from horses.

spragueii — In 1844, Audubon described this new species in volume seven of the octavo edition of *Birds of America*, naming it for Isaac Sprague (1811–1895), a botanical illustrator who accompanied him on his Missouri River trip the previous year.

French Name: Pipit des Prairies
Spanish Names: Bisbita Llanero; Bisbita de Sprague
Other Names: Skylark; Prairie Skylark; Missouri Skylark; S-jingler; Titlark

Family Fringillidae
Fringillid Finches

Finch derives from the Anglo-Saxon *finc* and is thought to be onomonopoetic. The family name is from the Latin *fringilla*, a name

Terentius Varro and other authors used for some small bird, possibly the Chaffinch (*Fringilla coelebs*) of Europe.

Evening Grosbeak
Coccothraustes vespertinus
(cock-oh-THROUSE-teez ves-per-TINE-us)

"At twilight, the bird which I had before heard to cry in a singular strain, and only at this hour, made its appearance close by my tent, and a flock of about half a dozen perched in the bushes in my encampment . . . I recognized this bird as similar to one in possession of Mr. Schoolcraft at the Sault Ste. Marie. Its mournful cry about the hour of my encamping (which was at sunset) had before attracted my attention, but I could never get sight of the bird but on this occasion. There is an extensive plain and swamp through which flows the Savannah river, covered with a thick growth of sapin trees. My inference was then, and is now, that this bird dwells in such dark retreats, and leaves them at the approach of night." — Major Joseph Delafield (1823)

Grosbeak stems from the French *gros* "large" and French *bec* "beak," and refers to the over-sized, conical bill adapted for cracking seeds such as wild cherry pits. This species is called the Evening Grosbeak, because of the mistaken belief that it sings primarily at dusk. William Cooper, who described and named this species from a specimen sent to him by Henry R. Schoolcraft, read the report of the first recorded sighting by Major Joseph Delafield in 1823 near Thunder Bay, Ontario. See opening passage above. Below is a commentary on this bird's misleading name:

"Major Delafield's inference is the source of the species' vernacular name — manifestly a misnomer. I do not doubt that the good major's birds cried out at sunset "in singular strain" because he and his party disturbed them as they made camp. Ordinarily the species is not crepuscular, and in fact it might better be called "morning grosbeak," for it is most active early in the day. Yet its scientific name, *Hesperiphona vespertina*, is romantic, beautiful, and imaginative." — Doris Huestes Speirs (1968)

Sidebar 30
Daughters of the Night

The Evening Grosbeak was originally placed in the genus *Hesperiphona*, the name Mrs. Speirs describes as "romantic, beautiful, and imaginative." In the 1990s, the AOU merged it into the genus *Coccothraustes* with the Hawfinch of Eurasia. The former name moved two prominent ornithologists of the past to wax poetic:

"Its generic name is derived from the Greek, referring to the Hesperides, "Daughters of the Night," who dwelt on the western verge of the world where the sun goes down." — Edward Howe Forbush (1929)

"A BIRD of the most distinguished appearance, indeed, is the Evening Grosbeak, whose very name of "Vesper-voiced" suggests at once the far-away land of the dipping sun, and the tuneful romance which the wild bird throws around the fading light of day. Clothed in the most striking color-contrasts of black, white, and gold, he seems to represent the allegory of diurnal transmutations; for his sable pinions close around the brightness of his vesture, just as the night encompasses the golden hues of the sunset; while the clear white space enfolded in these tints foretells the dawn of the morrow." — Elliot Coues (1879)

Coccothraustes — The genus name means "kernal breaker" from the Greek *kokkos* (kernel) and *thrauo* (to break or to shatter) and refers to this bird's ability to crack fruit pits. The Ojibwa name for the Evening Grosbeak is *Paushkundamo* (berry breaker). The Evening Grosbeak was originally placed in the genus *Hesperiphona*, which is Greek for "voice of the evening." See sidebar 30.

vespertinus — The specific epithet is Latin for "of the evening" also referring to the belief that this bird sings only at dusk.

Evening Grosbeak, by Allan C. Brooks

French Name: Gros-bec Errant
Spanish Names: Picogordo Norteño; Pepitero Norteño
Other Names: Eastern Evening Grosbeak; Western Evening Grosbeak; Mexican Evening Grosbeak; Columbian evening grosbeak; American Hawfinch; English Parrot; Winter Canary; Sugar Bird; Pashcundamo

Pine Grosbeak
Pinicola enucleator
(pie-NICK-oh-lah ee-new-klee-AY-tore)

As in other grosbeaks the name refers to the thick bill adapted for cracking seeds. Pine refers to its habitat in northern evergreen forests.

Pinicola — The genus name is Latin for "pine dweller" from *pinus* (a pine) and *colere* (to inhabit).

enucleator — The specific epithet is from the Latin enucleare and means "to take out kernels" or "one who shells out." This refers to the grosbeaks ability to extract seeds from their hulls.

French Name: Dur-bec des Pins
Spanish Name: Picogordo Pinero
Eskimo and Inuit Names: Ni-kubv-u-ghakh-tukh-tuk; Kayatavak
Other Names: American Pine Grosbeak; Alaska Pine Grosbeak; Kodiak Pine Grosbeak; California Pine Grosbeak; Queen Charlotte Pine Grosbeak; Rocky Mountain Pine Grosbeak; Canadian Pine Grosbeak; Canadian Grosbeak; Pine Bullfinch; Common Pine Finch; Mope

Gray-crowned Rosy-Finch
Leucosticte tephrocotis
(lew-koe-STICK-tee tef-ROCK-oh-tiss)

The pinkish wash on the wings, rump, and underparts give the rosy-finches their name. This species shows gray on the nape and crown. In coastal populations, the gray extends to the cheek.

Leucosticte — The genus name means white-dotted from the Greek *leukos* (white) and Greek *stiktos* (dotted, dappled, or punctured).

tephrocotis — The specific epithet is from the Greek *tephros* (ash-colored) and *kotis* (eared) for the gray about the head.

French Name: Roselin à Tête Grise
Spanish Name: Pinzón Rosa de Corona Gris
Eskimo and Inuit Names: Kaviksruak (refers to red color); Kohl-grha-ghuch; Cha-nuh

Gray-crowned Rosy-Finch, by Allan C. Brooks

Other Names: Gray-crowned Purple Finch; Gray-crowned Leucosticte; Brown Snow-bird; Pink Snow-bird; Aleutian Rosy Finch; Hepburn's Rosy Finch; Pribilof Rosy Finch; Sierra Nevada Rosy Finch

Black Rosy-Finch
Leucosticte atrata
(lew-koe-STICK-tee ay-TRAY-tah)

This species takes its name from the overall blackish-brown color of the male.

Leucosticte — The genus name means white-dotted from the Greek *leukos* (white) and Greek *stiktos* (dotted, dappled, or punctured).

atrata — The specific epithet is Larin for "blackened" or "clothed in black" and refers to the male's dominant color.

French Name: Roselin Noir
Spanish Name: Pinzón Rosa Negra

Brown-capped Rosy-Finch
Leucosticte australis
(lew-koe-STICK-tee aus-TRAIL-us)

This species has a dark brown crown and lacks the gray headband of the other rosy-finches.

Leucosticte — The genus name means white-dotted from the Greek *leukos* (white) and Greek *stiktos* (dotted, dappled, or punctured).

australis — The specific epithet is Latin for "southern" and refers to this species' more southerly range, in the mountains of Colorado and Wyoming compared to the other rosy-finches.

French Name: Roselin à Tête Brune
Spanish Name: Pinzón Rosa de Gorra Café

House Finch
Haemorhous mexicanus
(he-MOR-us meks-ih-CANE-us)

"The pretty little House Finch of the Far West is among the most domestic of American birds, and exhibits a predilection for the neighborhood of houses almost as strong as that of the English Sparrow. It carols its sprightly lay from the tops of buildings in villages and even in cities, and from the shrubbery of lawn and park. So confiding has the bird become that it places its nest in any crack or cranny of house or outbuilding that is large enough for its housekeeping operations." — Henry W. Henshaw (1968)

The House Finch is so named, because it is common around human dwellings, particularly in the suburbs as described in the above passage.

Haemorhous — The genus name means "washed with blood" from the Greek *haima* (blood) and *rhous* (a stream or current). It refers to the reddish color of the plumage, which is especially intense on the head, breast, and rump. Formerly *Carpodacus mexicanus*.

mexicanus — The specific epithet is Modern Latin for "of Mexico," where the type specimen was collected.

French Name: Roselin Familier
Spanish Names: Pinzón Mexicano; Fringílido Mexicano
Other Names: Linnet; Red-headed Linnet; California Linnet; Hollywood Linnet; Red-head; Burion; Mexican House Finch; Mexican Rose Finch; Guadalupe House Finch; McGregor's House Finch; Crimson-fronted Finch; Crimson-fronted Bullfinch; Papayabird; Carpodaco Domestic

---

Sidebar 31
The Hollywood Finch

The original range of the House Finch was from the Rockies west to the Pacific coast and from southern British Columbia down through northern Mexico. Now they occur from coast to coast. This expansion began in the early 1940s, when cage bird dealers in southern California were trapping House Finches illegally in the wild and shipping them to pet shop merchants in New York. The birds were sold under the trade name "Hollywood Finch." Agents of the Fish and Wildlife Service were alerted to this violation of the Migratory Bird Treaty (1918) and quickly put an end to the trafficking. To avoid prosecution, pet shop merchants released their birds, which soon began to nest on Long Island. Since then, the House Finch has spread clear across the country.

House Finch and Purple Finch,
by Allan C. Brooks

Purple Finch
Haemorhous purpureus
(he-MOR-us pur-PUR-ee-us)

"The above name may be misleading to the novice, for it is no more purple, as we understand the term today, than it is blue or yellow. Crimson finch would be a more appropriate name. (However, the "purple" of the Bible and of classical writers was not very different from the red of the male purple finch.)" — Arthur Cleveland Bent (1953)

""Purple" didn't seem right for the feathers that covered the bird's head, chest, back, and rump. Raspberry, I thought, or wine, or the plush red velvet that covers antique chairs." — Gale Lawrence, *Bird Watcher's Digest* (1983)

Roger Tory Peterson described the male Purple Finch as "a sparrow dipped in raspberry juice." Other sources describe the color as wine red, old rose, pale geranium-red, carmine; brick red, madder pink, burgundy, rose red, rich scarlet-lake, plum red, dull crimson, or sober Venetian red, but not purple, at least not in the current sense of the word. So, what was Mark Catesby thinking when he christened this bird "Purple Finch?" Was he colorblind? He apparently had "the purple of the Bible and of classical writers" in mind, as mentioned in the above passage. The root of the word purple can be traced back to the Greek *porphyra*, a name for a marine snail, the Spiny Dye-murex (*Bolinus brandaris*), that yielded an expensive crimson dyestuff. The dye, known as Tyrian purple after an ancient Phoenician seaport, was used to color the robes of royalty. It was also used to dye the vestments of the cardinals of the Roman Catholic Church, which is a clue that the hue was more red than purple. So the Purple Finch's name refers to a specific shade, that of the Tyrian purple dye of ancient commerce.

Haemorhous — The genus name means "washed with blood" from the Greek *haima* (blood) and *rhous* (a stream or current). It refers to the reddish color of the plumage, which is especially intense on the head, breast, and rump. Formerly *Carpodacus purpureus*.

purpureus — The specific epithet is the Latin spelling of the Greek *porphyra* (purple).

See common name above.

French Name: Roselin Pourpré
Spanish Names: Pinzón Morado; Fringílido Purpureo
Other Names: Crested Purple Finch; Crimson-fronted Purple Finch; Eastern Purple Finch; California Purple Finch; Purple Linnet; Red Linnet; Gray Linnet; California Linnet; Purple Grosbeak

Cassin's Finch
Haemorhous cassinii
(he-MOR-us cass-IN-ih-eye)

Dr. Caleb Kennerly and H. B. Möllhausen, naturalists with the Pacific Railroad Survey, collected the type specimen near Pueblo Creek, New Mexico during the winter of 1853–1854. Spencer Fullerton Baird of the Smithsonian Institution described the new species giving it the name *Carpodacus cassinii* in honor of his friend John Cassin.

Haemorhous — The genus name means "washed with blood" from the Greek *haima* (blood) and *rhous* (a stream or current). It refers to the reddish color of the plumage, which is especially intense on the head, breast, and rump. Formerly *Carpodacus cassinii*.

cassinii — The specific epithet honors John Cassin (1813–1869), Curator of Ornithology at the Acadamy of Natural Sciences of Philadelphia. See common name above.

French Name: Roselin de Cassin
Spanish Names: Pinzón de Cassin; Fringílido de Cassin
Other Name: Cassin's Purple Finch

Common Redpoll
Acanthis flammea
(ah-KAN-thiss FLAH-me-ah)

Redpoll refers to the bird's red cap. This is the Common Redpoll, because it is the more widespread of the two species.

Acanthis — The genus name is from the Greek *akanthis*, a small bird mentioned by Aristotle and other authors, but not further identified. The name has been associated with the Linnet and the European Goldfinch. Ultimately the name may derive from *akantha* (a thistle), a favored food plant of redpolls and goldfinches. Formerly *Carduelis flammea*.

flammea — The specific epithet is Latin for "flame colored" and refers to the pinkish wash on the breast.

French Name: Sizerin Flammé
Spanish Names: Dominico Común; Pardillo sizerin
Eskimo and Inuit Names: Puyitarat (smoke bird); O-kwikh-ta-ghuk; Suksangik
Other Names: Greater Redpoll; Lesser Redpoll; Little Redpoll; Holboell's Redpoll; Holbrook's Redpoll; Mealy Redpoll; Linnet; Red Linnet; Red-polled Linnet; Little Redpole Linnet; Chevy Linnet; Chivey Linnet; Chippet Linnet; French Linnet; Lintie; Rose Lintie; Linaria; Little Meadowlark; Passenger Bird; Chaddy; Chitty; Redcap; Red-crown

Hoary Redpoll
Acanthis hornemanni
(ah-KAN-thiss HOR-neh-man-eye)

"I'd been wondering about the differences, supposed to be far from distinct, between the common redpoll and the hoary, both of which species are found here at Churchill. But with that beautifully-marked male, it was plain. The white rump patch above the tail, unlike that of the common redpoll, is unstreaked. The lovely breast, all suffused with deep rose, instead of plain white or pale pink as in the female, and the coloring of his whole body, was noticeably and exquisitely all sort of frosted over with white." — Theodora C. Stanwell-Fletcher (1952)

The Hoary Redpoll is named for its whitish plumage, much paler than that of the Common Redpoll.

Acanthis — The genus name is from the Greek *akanthis*, a small bird mentioned by Aristotle and other authors, but not further identified. The name has been associated with the Linnet and the European Goldfinch. Ultimately the name may derive from *akantha* (a thistle), a favored food plant of redpolls and goldfinches. Formerly *Carduelis hornemanni*.

hornemanni — Carl Peter Holboell named the Hoary Redpoll in honor of his friend Jens Wilken Hornemann (1770–1841), a Danish scientist and professor at the University of Copenhagen. In return, Hornemann paid tribute to Holboell by naming a plant Holboell's Rock Cress (*Arabis holboelli*) after him.

French Name: Sizerin Blanchâtre
Spanish Names: Dominico Cano; Pardillo ártico
British Name: Arctic Redpoll
Eskimo Name: Ok-fek-ta-gak (dweller among the alder patches)
Other Names: Greenland Redpoll; Hornemann's Redpoll; Coues' Redpoll; Mealy Redpoll Linnet

Red Crossbill
Loxia curvirostra
(LOCK-si-ah cur-vih-ROS-trah)

Red refers to the male's overall brick red coloration. According to a Christian legend, the Red Crossbill bent its bill in attempting to remove the nails that held Jesus to the cross. In the process it got spattered with blood, thus the red color.

Loxia — The genus name is from the Greek *loxos* (crosswise) referring to the crossed mandibles.

curvirostra — The specific epithet is Latin for "curved billed" from *curvus* (curved) and *rostrum* (the bill). The Red Crossbill occurs in ten different forms. Some of these forms may eventually be split into distinct species. One already has. See next entry.
French Name: Bec-croisé Rouge
Spanish Name: Picotuerto Rojo
British Name: Common Crossbill
Other Names: American Crossbill; Robin Hawk; Shell Apple

~

Cassia Crossbill
Loxia sinesciurus
(LOCK-si-ah sin-eh-SIGH-your-us)

Ornithologists recognize at least ten types of Red Crossbill that differ slightly in overall size, the size and structure of the bill, and vocalizations. They have long suspected that some of these may represent separate species. Dr. Craig Benkman and his student from the University of Wyoming conducted research on one type including detailed genetic work. From this research, Type 9 was the first to be split off as a full species in 2017. It was given the name Cassia Crossbill after the county in southern Idaho where it is resident. There, it occurs in lodgepole pine forests in the South Hills and Albion Mountains in the Sawtooth National Forest.

Loxia — The genus name is from the Greek *loxos* (crosswise) referring to the crossed mandibles.

sinesciuris — The specific epithet means "without squirrels" derived from the Latin *sine* (without) and *sciūrus* (a squirrel), a curious meaning indeed. The significance is explained in the following passage:

"*Sinesciuris* means "without squirrels." The South Hills area is surrounded by sage habitat, a natural barrier preventing emigration of pine squirrels. The absence of red squirrels enables Rocky Mountain lodgepole pines [*Pinus contorta*] and crossbills to engage in a "coevolutionary arms race" with the pines developing larger and thicker scales and crossbills evolving larger and deeper-based bills. A result is lodgepole pines' serotinous cones remain un-opened until a fire sweeps through melting the cone scales. Without fire or squirrels, tightly closed scales surrounding lodgepole pine seeds are only opened by the seed predator, red crossbills." — www.birding.typepad.com
French Name: Bec-croisé de l'Idaho
Spanish Name: Piquituerto de Cassia
Other Name: South Hills Crossbill

~

White-winged Crossbill
Loxia leucoptera
(LOCK-si-ah lew-COP-teh-rah)

Two broad white wing bars give this crossbill its name.

Loxia — The genus name is from the Greek *loxos* (crosswise) referring to the crossed mandibles.

leucoptera — The specific epithet means "white wing" from the Greek *leukos* (white) and *pteron* (the wing).

Sidebar 32
Genus Loxia
Crossbills

"The Crossbill owes its peculiar mandibles to an age-long hankering for pine-seeds — a desire fully satisfied according to the fashion of that Providence which works so variously through nature, and whose method we are pleased to call evolution. The bill of the bird was not meant for an organ of the finest precision, and Buffon, the deist, once won a cheap applause by railing at the Almighty for a supposed oversight in this direction; but as a matter of fact its wonderful crossed mandibles enable the crossbill to do what no other bird can, viz., pry open the scales of a pine cone and extract the tiny seed with its tongue. Besides this the bird is not so awkward in the use of its bill as was formerly supposed, since it frequently alights on the ground and picks up the fallen seeds, together with other food."
— William Leon Dawson (1902)

Crossbill refers to the specialized beak whose curved tips cross. This is an adaptation to extracting seeds from the cones of pine, spruce, fir, and other conifers as described above.

White-winged Crossbill, by John James Audubon

French Name: Bec-croisé à Ailes Blanches
Spanish Name: Picotuerto de Ala Blanca
British Name: Two-barred Crossbill
Eskimo and Inuit Names: Pakagik
Other Names: Periquito; Turquesa

Pine Siskin
Spinus pinus
(SPINE-us PINE-us)

Our Pine Siskin was named after the Eurasian Siskin (*Carduelis spinus*). Siskin derives from the Danish *sidsken* or Swedish *siska* meaning "chirper" and thus is imitative. Pine refers to the breeding habitat in evergreen forests.

Spinus — The genus name is from the Greek *spinos*, a name used by Aristotle, Dionysius, and other authors for "a small finch-like bird," not further identified, but thought by some to refer to the Chaffinch (*Fringilla coelebs*). Formerly *Carduelis pinus*.

pinus — The specific epithet is Latin for "a pine."
French Name: Chardonneret des Pins
Spanish Name: Dominico Pinero
Other Names: American Siskin; Gray Linnet; Pine Linnet; Pine Finch; Northern Canary Bird

Lesser Goldfinch
Spinus psaltria
(SPINE-us SALL-trih-ah)

Male goldfinches show much yellow in the plumage. The Lesser Goldfinch is so named, because it is the smallest of the three North American goldfinches at 3¾ to 4¼ inches long.

Spinus — The genus name is from the Greek *spinos*, a name used by Aristotle, Dionysius, and other authors for "a small finch-like bird," not further identified, but thought by some to refer to the Chaffinch (*Fringilla coelebs*). Formerly *Carduelis psaltria*.

psaltria — The specific epithet is Greek for "a harpist" and refers to this species' musical song.
French Name: Chardonneret Mineur
Spanish Names: Dominico de Dorso Oscuro; Dominico Dorsioscuro; Jilguero Menor
Other Names: Dark-eyed Goldfinch; Dark-backed Goldfinch; Green-backed Goldfinch; Black-headed Goldfinch; Yarrell's Goldfinch; Arkansas Goldfinch; Arkansas Greenback; Mexican Goldfinch; Tarweed Canary; Shiner

Lesser Goldfinch, by Louis Agassiz Fuertes

Lawrence's Goldfinch, by Allan C. Brooks

Lawrence's Goldfinch
Spinus lawrencei
(SPINE-us LAW-rence-eye)

The yellow of the male's plumage gives the goldfinches their name. In 1850, John Cassin described a new species of goldfinch in *Proceedings of the Academy of Natural Sciences of Philadelphia* from specimens John Graham Bell had collected near Sonoma, California. He named it *Carduelis Lawrencei* with the dedication:

"I have named this bird in honor of Mr. George N. Lawrence, of the city of New York, a gentleman whose acquirements, especially in American Ornithology, entitle him to a high rank amongst naturalists, and for whom I have a particular respect, because, like myself, in the limited leisure allowed by the vexations and discouragements of commercial life, he is devoted to the more grateful pursuits of natural history."

Spinus — The genus name is from the Greek *spinos*, a name used by Aristotle, Dionysius, and other authors for "a small finch-like bird," not further identified, but thought by some to refer to the Chaffinch (*Fringilla coelebs*). Formerly *Carduelis lawrencei*.

lawrencei — The specific epithet commemorates George Newbold Lawrence (1806–1895), an American businessman and collector. He assisted John Cassin and Spencer F. Baird in describing the birds collected on the Pacific Railroad Surveys. See common name above.

French Name: Chardonneret Gris
Spanish Name: Dominico de Lawrence

American Goldfinch
Spinus tristis
(SPINE-us TRIS-tis)

"The yellow warbler is sometimes called a wild canary because he looks like a canary; the goldfinch has the same misleading name applied to him because he sings like one . . . An old field, overgrown with thistles and tall, stalky wild flowers, is the paradise of the goldfinches, summer or winter. Here they congregate in happy companies while the sunshine and goldenrod are bright as their feathers, and cling to the swaying slender stems that furnish an abundant harvest, daintily lunching upon the fluffy seeds of thistle blossoms, pecking at the mullein-stalks, and swinging airily among the asters and Michaelmas daisies; or, when snow covers the same field with a glistening crust, above which the brown stalks offer only a meagre dinner, the same birds, now somberly clad in winter

American Goldfinch, by Louis Agassiz Fuertes

feathers, cling to the swaying stems with cheerful fortitude." — Neltje Blanchan (1897)

Goldfinch refers to the yellow color of the male in breeding plumage. American distinguishes this widespread species from other goldfinches, in particular the European Goldfinch (*Carduelis carduelis*) of the Old World.

Spinus — The genus name is from the Greek *spinos*, a name used by Aristotle, Dionysius, and other authors for "a small finch-like bird," not further identified, but thought by some to refer to the Chaffinch (*Fringilla coelebs*). In 1983, the goldfinches and redpolls were merged into the Old World genus *Carduelis*, an appropriate name that stems from the Latin *carduus* meaning "a thistle." Goldfinches are partial to thistles both for food (the seeds) and for nesting material (the thistledown). In fact goldfinches delay nesting until the thistles have gone to seed. The commercial thistle seed, also called niger (or nyjer), is not from a true thistle, but it is favored by finches. The European Goldfinch is sometimes depicted in religious paintings, presumably because of its association with thorns as in the crown of thorns. In 2008, the AOU returned the goldfinches and redpolls to their former genera *Spinus* and *Acanthis* respectively. Formerly *Carduelis tristis*.

tristis — "What tone of sadness in his music the man found who applied the adjective *tristis* to his scientific name it is difficult to imagine when listening to the notes that come bubbling up from the bird's happy heart." — Neltje Blanchan (1897)

The specific epithet is Latin for "sad," and refers to one of the goldfinch's call notes that has a melancholy quality. Ornithologist Arthur A. Allen wrote, "One of the goldfinch's calls, repeated over and over again in the autumn from a tree limb, sounds like weeping."

French Name: Chardonneret Jaune
Spanish Name: Dominico Americano
Other Names: Common Goldfinch; Eastern Goldfinch; Western Goldfinch; Pale Goldfinch; Willow Goldfinch; California Goldfinch; Wild Canary; Yellowbird; Black-winged Yellowbird; Thistle-bird; Catnip-bird; Beet-bird; Hemp-bird; Lettuce-bird; Salad-bird; Shiner; Guldfink; Gale Fogel; Zolawd Fogel; Zolawd Shbeds'l

Family Calcariidae Longspurs and Snow Buntings

The extremely long, curved claw on the hallux (hind toe) gives the longspurs their name. Several other ground-dwelling passerines, including larks, pipits, wagtails, and snow buntings, also have this characteristic.

Lapland Longspur
Calcarius lapponicus
(cal-CARE-ih-us lap-ON-ih-cus)

The Lapland Longspur is circumpolar in distribution, and so it does occur in Lapland (northern Scandinavia), where the type specimen was collected.

Calcarius — The genus name means "spurred" from the Latin *calcar* (a cock's spur). The reference is to the long claw on the hind toe.

lapponicus — The specific epithet is Modern Latin for "of Lapland."

French Name: Bruant lapon
Spanish Name: Escribano Artico
British Name: Lapland Bunting
Eskimo and Inuit Names: Natchakuparuk (hood-like marking on head); Tik-i-chi-ling-uk; Pig-git-tig-wuk; Chi-loch
Other Names: Common Longspur; Labrador

Lapland Longspur, by R. Bruce Horsfall

Bunting; Alaska Longspur; Alaska Lark Bunting; Common Lark Bunting; Lapland Lark Bunting; Lapland Snowbird; Chiddick Bird; Stubble Sparrow; Dirty-face

Chestnut-collared Longspur
Calcarius ornatus
(cal-CARE-ih-us or-NAY-tus)

The rich chestnut nape of the male in breeding plumage gives this longspur its name.
Calcarius — The genus name means "spurred" from the Latin *calcar* (a cock's spur). The reference is to the long claw on the hind toe.
ornatus — The specific epithet is Latin for "ornate" or "adorned" and refers to the male's striking breeding plumage.
French Name: Bruant à Ventre Noir
Spanish Names: Escribano de Collar Castaño; Escribano Cuellicastaño
Other Names: Chestnut-collared Lark Bunting; Butterfly Bird

Smith's Longspur
Calcarius pictus
(cal-CARE-ih-us PICK-tus)

Edward Harris and John G. Bell collected this species on Audubon's expedition up the Missouri River in 1843. The birds were best viewed from horseback, because they hunkered down in the ankle-high prairie grass and were reluctant to flush. The longspurs were found to be particularly abundant near Edwardsville, Illinois. Audubon named the "new" species Smith's Lark Finch and dedicated it to his "good friend GIDEON B. SMITH, Esq., M.D. of Baltimore, Maryland, who has done much for science in several of its departments." Dr. Smith (1793–1867) was a subscriber to *Birds of America* and served as Audubon's agent in Baltimore. Only the species wasn't new. Dr. John Richardson had collected the type specimen during John Franklin's second overland expedition in 1827. Franklin shot the bird on the banks of the Saskatchewan River in Canada in April of that year. British naturalist William Swainson described it in the second volume of *Fauna Boreali-Americana*, published in 1832. He gave it the scientific name *Emberiza picta*. Together Swainson and Richardson proposed Painted Buntling as the common name.

Calcarius — The genus name means "spurred" from the Latin *calcar* (a cock's spur). The reference is to the long claw on the hind toe.
pictus — The specific epithet is Latin for "painted," referring to the breeding male's striking black and white head pattern and yellowish-buff underparts.
French Name: Bruant de Smith
Spanish Name: Escribano de Smith
Eskimo Name: Kallorgosiksook (sings with the voice of many birds)
Other Names: Painted Longspur; Smith's Painted Longspur; Smith's Lark Finch; Smith's Lark Bunting; Painted Lark Bunting; Painted Buntling

McCown's Longspur
Rhynchophanes mccownii
(rink-OFF-ah-neez mack-COWN-ih-eye)

The discovery of McCown's Longspur has been described as "a tale of two captains." In June of 1805, members of the Lewis and Clark Expedition first encountered this bird along the Marias River near present-day Loma, Montana. Captain Meriwether Lewis entered the following account in his journal:

"Also a small bird which in action resembles the lark, it is about the size of a large sparrow of a dark brown colour with some white feathers in the tail; this bird or that which I take to be the male rises into the air about 60 feet and supporting itself in the air with a brisk motion of the wings sings very sweetly, has several shrill soft notes rather of the plaintive order which it frequently repeats and varies, after remaining stationary about a minute in this aerial station he descends obliquely occasionally pausing and accompanying his descension with a note something like *twit twit twit*; on the ground he is silent. Thirty or forty of these birds will be stationed in the air at a time in view. These larks as I shall call them add much to the gayety and cheerfulness of the scene."

It might have been named "Lewis's Longspur" if a specimen had been secured. However none were, and the species went undescribed. Nearly fifty years later in the spring of 1851, John P. McCown, a U.S. Army captain, came upon this species again, wintering on the prairies of western Texas. He fired into a flock of Horned Larks and found an unfamiliar small, brown bird with white outer tail feathers among the casualties. Captain McCown sent the specimen to ornithologist George Newbold Lawrence, who named it in his honor. See specific epithet below.

Rhynchophanes — The genus name means "showing a beak" from the Greek *rhynchos* (the beak) and *phaino* (to show). Perhaps this alludes to the McCown's Longspur's somewhat larger, thicker bill, in comparison to those of the other longspur species. Formerly *Calcarius mccownii*.

mccownii — In 1851, George Newbold Lawrence named this bird in honor of its collector, John Porter McCown (1815–1879), with the dedication: "It gives me pleasure to bestow upon this species the name of my friend Capt. J. P. McCown, U.S.A. Two specimens were obtained on the high prairies of Western Texas. When killed, they were feeding in company with Shore Larks. Although procured late in the spring, they still appear to be in their winter dress."

French Name: Bruant à Collier Gris
Spanish Name: Escribano de McCown
Other Names: Black-breasted Longspur; McCown's Bunting; Black-breasted Lark-Bunting; Rufous-winged Lark Bunting; Ground Lark

Snow Bunting
Plectrophenax nivalis
(pleck-TROF-eh-nacks nih-VAY-liss)

"His name is 'snowflake,' and when he migrates south in late fall, this reason is clear. For he travels in flocks, every bird swooping and veering in unison, and as they pass overhead only the white undersides of the wings and the white bellies can be seen. They look like giant snowflakes blown before the autumn gust and are indeed harbingers of the winter to come." — Arthur A. Allen (1964)

"Snow buntings are aptly named, for snow is most certainly their element. Their summer nests are at the very edge of the icy Arctic frontier, and they winter no farther south than the limits of the snow. Fluffy drifts are for them friendly insu-

Lapland Longspur and Snow Bunting, by Louis Agassiz Fuertes

lation in which to sleep snugly through the cold of winter nights. So long as winds or weak Arctic sunshine expose patches of bare earth and the seeds of hardy plants, the snow bunting is content." — *Reader's Digest Book of North American Birds* (1990)

The common name is appropriate both for this bird's largely white plumage and with its association with snowy fields in winter, often in the company of Horned Larks as described above.

Plectrophenax — The genus name means "a false spur or claw" from the Greek *plektron* (a cock's spur or a claw-like tool for striking the strings of a lyre) and *phenax* (false, an imposter, or a cheat). The genus name was originally *Plectrophanes* from the Greek *plektron* (a spur or claw) and *phanein* (to appear or display). So the original meaning was "showing a spur," referring to the long claw on the hind toe. Norwegian ornithologist Leonhard Hess Stejneger for reasons unknown, changed it to the present genus name.

nivalis — The specific epithet is Latin for "snowy."

French Name: Bruant des Neiges
Spanish Name: Escribano Nival
Eskimo and Inuit Names: Kanguruarak (bird of the snow); Amauligak (variegated black and white); A-mou-o-thlif-uk (refers to white plumage as contrasted to black); Ko-ka-noch; Math-a wach
Other Names: Common Snow Bunting; Snowbird; White Snowbird; Whitebird; Little

Whitebird; Snowdrift; Snowflake; Snow Lark; Snow Lark Bunting; Arctic Sparrow; Ortolan; Oiseau Blanc; Oiseau de Misere; Oiseau de Neige; Waddlin

McKay's Bunting
Plectrophenax hyperboreus
(pleck-TROF-eh-nacks high-per-BORE-ee-us)

Robert Ridgway described this species in 1884 and named it "in memory of Mr. Charles L. McKay, who sacrificed his life in prosecution of natural history investigations in Alaska, and in whose collection the new species was first noticed." Charles Leslie McKay (1855–1883), while serving with the U.S. Army Signal Corps in Alaska, collected natural history specimens and native artifacts for the U.S. National Museum. Ridgway discovered a pair of undescribed buntings in winter plumage in McKay's collection of 340 specimens. McKay had collected them at Nushagak in November and December of 1882. Ridgway compared them to two specimens in summer plumage that Edward W. Nelson, also a Signal Officer, had collected at Nulato and Saint Michael on Norton Sound in April, 1879. Although McKay is commemorated by the common name, Ridgway chose not to honor him in the scientific name as well.

Plectrophenax — The genus name means "false spur or claw" from the Greek *plektron* (a cock's spur or a claw-like tool for striking the strings of a lyre) and *phenax* (false, an imposter, or a cheat). The genus name was originally *Plectrophanes* (showing a claw) from the Greek *plektron* (*a spur or claw*) and *phanein* (to appear or display). The name refers to the long claw on the bird's hind toe.

hyberboreas — The specific epithet is Latin for "beyond the north wind" referring to its range in the Arctic.

French Name: Bruant Blanc
Spanish Name: Escribano de Mckay
Eskimo Name: Con-go-way
Other Names: McKay's Snow Bunting; Snowflake; Hyperborean Snowflake

Family Passerellidae
New World Sparrows and Allies

Sparrow stems from the Anglo-Saxon (Old English?) word *spearwa* meaning "flutterer." The name originally meant any small bird and then was applied to members of the family Passeridae, to which the introduced House Sparrow and Eurasian Tree Sparrow belong. English colonists named the superficially similar but unrelated American birds after them. The New World sparrows were formerly classified in the family Emberizidae with the Old World Buntings.

Rufous-winged Sparrow
Peucaea carpalis
(PEW-sih-ah car-PAY-liss)

This sparrow is named for its reddish wing patch, but it is not a good field mark, because it is difficult to see.

Peucaea — The genus name, first erected for Bachman's Sparrow, is from the Greek *peukaeis* (of the fir) referring to Bachman's Sparrow's breeding habitat in southern pine woods.

carpalis — The specific epithet means "having to do with the wrist" from the Latin *carpus* (the wrist). The reference is to the reddish wing patch.

French Name: Bruant à Épaulettes
Spanish Names: Zacatonero de Ala Rufa; Zacatonero Alirrufo

Botteri's Sparrow
Peucaea botterii
(PEW-sih-ah BOT-er-ih-eye)

In 1854, botanist Matteo Botteri set up a base at Orizaba, Mexico, to collect plants for the Royal Horticultural Society of London. He also collected natural history specimens for the Academy of Sciences of Paris. Botteri sent his surplus specimens to his agent Samuel Stevens, a natural history dealer in London. Stevens invited ornithologist Philip Sclater to evaluate the bird collection representing more than 120 species. Sclater published notes on thirty-eight species in the *Proceedings of the Zoological Society* including two that were new to science, a vireo and a sparrow. He named the sparrow *Zonotrichia botterii*, now known as Botteri's Sparrow. This Mexican species occurs in our area only in southeastern Arizona, southwestern New Mexico, and the southern tip of Texas. Henry W. Henshaw, with the Wheeler Survey, collected the first United States specimens around Camp Grant, Camp Crittenden, and Cienaga, Arizona during the 1870s.

Peucaea — The genus name, first erected for Bachman's Sparrow, is from the Greek *peukaeis* (of the fir) referring to Bachman's Sparrow's breeding habitat in southern pine woods.

botterii — In 1857, Sclater named this sparrow in honor of its collector Matteo Botteri (1808–1877), a botanist from Yugoslavia, who discovered this species near Orizaba, Mexico. See common name above.

French Name: Bruant de Botteri

Spanish Names: Zacatonero de Botteri; Sabanero Pechianteado

Cassin's Sparrow
Peucaea cassinii
(PEW-sih-ah kass-IN-ih-eye)

Dr. Samuel Woodhouse discovered this sparrow near San Antonio, Texas when he travelled to the Zuni and Colorado Rivers with Lieutenant Sitgreaves in 1851–1852. At first he identified it as a Savannah Sparrow, but on closer examination he discovered it was distinct. Woodhouse described the new species with the following dedication: "I have named this in honor of my friend Mr. John Cassin, the Corresponding Secretary of the Society, to whose indefatigable labor in the department of Ornithology we are so much indebted."

Peucaea — The genus name, first erected for Bachman's Sparrow, is from the Greek *peukaeis* (of the fir) referring to Bachman's Sparrow's breeding habitat in southern pine woods.

cassinii — The specific epithet commemorates John Cassin (1813–1869), a leading 19th century taxonomist and Curator of Birds at the Academy of Natural Sciences in Philadelphia. See common name above.

French Name: Bruant de Cassin

Spanish Name: Zacatonero de Cassin

Bachman's Sparrow
Peucaea aestivalis
(PEW-sih-ah es-tih-VAY-liss)

Until 1957, this bird was known as the Pinewoods Sparrow for its habitat in southern pine forests. Audubon named it *Fringilla Bachmani* or Bachman's Pinewood-Finch in honor of his close friend Dr. John Bachman (1790–1874), a Lutheran minister from Charleston, South Carolina, who discovered this species on the Edisto River at Parker's Ferry, South Carolina in 1832. In his description Audubon wrote: "In honoring so humble an object as this Finch with the name of Bachman, my aim is to testify the high regard in which I hold that learned and most estimable individual." But it turned out not to be a new species. German ornithologist Hinrich Lichtenstein had previously described it in 1823 from a specimen collected in Georgia. He gave it the scientific name *Fringilla aestivalis*, so his specific name has priority.

Peucaea — The genus name is from the Greek *peukaeis* (of the fir) referring to this sparrow's breeding habitat in southern pine woods. See common name above.

aestivalis — The specific epithet means "summer-like" from the Latin *aestus* (summer).

French Name: Bruant des Pinèdes

Spanish Name: Zacatonero de Bachman

Other Names: Bachman's Pinewood Finch; Southern Pine Finch

Grasshopper Sparrow
Ammodramus savannarum
(am-ODD-rah-mus sah-van-AY-rum)

"In any fair-minded compilation of attractive birdsongs and calls, the grasshopper sparrow's efforts deserve to be about as far down on the list as a peacock's, which is very far down indeed. Some birders, in fact, do not even consider this sparrow's grasshopperlike buzzing to be any kind of song at all. But the female of the species clearly has a better opinion of her prospective mate's musicianship as he pursues her in flight, even while emitting sounds that are too high-pitched for most human ears to hear." — *Readers Digest Book of North American Birds* (1990)

The Grasshopper Sparrow's buzzy, insect-like song gives this bird its name. It reminds one of the stridulation of a long-horned grasshopper (meadow katydid) and is sometimes rendered as *tsik tsik zeeeeeeeee* or *chip chip scheeeeeeeeee*.

Ammodramus — The genus name means "sand runner" from the Greek *ammos* (sand) and *dramein* (to run).

savannarum — The specific epithet means "of the meadows" and is the Latinized form of the English savanna (from Spanish *zavana*), an open, treeless plain. Unlike the Savannah Sparrow, this species is named for its grassland habitat and not for the city.

French Name: Bruant Sauterelle
Spanish Names: Gorrión Saltamontes; Gorrión Chapulín; Sabanero Colicorto
Other Names: Cricket Sparrow; Yellow-winged Sparrow; Quail Sparrow; Savanna Bird; Grass-dodger; Grass Pink; Tichicro; Chamberguito; Chingolo Chicharra; Tumbarrocio; Gorrion de Chicharra; Oiseau Canne

Olive Sparrow
Arremonops rufivirgatus
(ah-REE-mon-ops rue-fih-ver-GAY-tus)

The dull greenish wash to the upperparts gives this sparrow its name. Known as the Texas Sparrow until 1957.

Arremonops — The genus name means "like Arremon" from the Greek *arrhemon* (silent or speechless) and *ops* (appearance). The reference is to a similarity between this species and the Brushfinches of South America in the genus *Arremon*.

rufivirgatus — The specific epithet is Latin for "reddish striped" and refers to the two dull brown stripes on the crown.

French Name: Tohi Olive
Spanish Names: Gorrión Olivác̃eo; Saltón Aceitunado
Other Names: Texas Sparrow; Green Finch

Five-striped Sparrow
Amphispiza quinquestriata
(am-fih-SPY-zah kwin-kweh-stry-AY-tah)

Five white facial stripes give this sparrow its name.

Amphispiza — The genus name is often translated as "a finch on both sides" from the Greek *amphi* (around or near) and *spiza* (a finch). It was coined to show relationships with other genera in the family.

quinquestriata — The specific epithet means "five striped" from the Latin *quinque* (five) and *striatus* (striped or streaked).

French Name: Bruant Pentaligne
Spanish Name: Zacatonero de Cinco Rayas

Black-throated Sparrow
Amphispiza bilineata
(am-fih-SPY-zah by-lin-ee-AY-tah

"This attractive sparrow is a common dweller of the arid southwest. As much as the currently accepted name refers to its most prominent field mark, the often used alternate "desert sparrow" refers to its most characteristic habitat. Herbert Brandt (1951) combined these two features quite well when he referred to this species as a "handsome, black-bibbed obligate of the hot, little-watered areas.'" — Richard C. Banks (1968)

The triangular black patch on the throat and breast gives this sparrow its name.

Amphispiza — The genus name is often translated as "a finch on both sides" from the Greek *amphi* (around or near) and *spiza* (a finch). It was coined to show relationships with other genera in the family.

bilineata — The specific epithet means "two-striped" or "two-lined" from the Modern Latin *bi* (two) and *linea* (a line) and refers to the two white stripes on either side of the face.

French Name: Bruant à Gorge Noire
Spanish Names: Gorrión de Garganta Negra; Gorrión Gorjinegro
Other Names: Desert Sparrow; Desert Black-throated Sparrow; Black-throat

Lark Sparrow
Chondestes grammacus
(kon-DESS-teez GRAM-ah-cus)

This sparrow is so-named, because it sings its musical song in flight like a skylark.

Chondestes — The genus name means "seed eater" from the Greek *chondros* (seed or grain) and *edestes* (eater). About 75% of this sparrow's diet is weed and grass seeds.

grammacus — The specific epithet derives from

the Greek *grammikos* (striped or linear) and refers to the boldly striped black, white, and chestnut head pattern.
French Name: Bruant à Joues Marron
Spanish Name: Gorrión Arlequín
Other Names: Western Lark Sparrow; Lark Finch; Little Meadowlark; Quail-head; Road-bird

Lark Bunting
Calamospiza melanocorys
(kal-ah-moh-SPY-zah mel-ah-NOCK-or-us)

" . . . In some ways it is like a Lark, has the bill of a Grosbeak, the seasonal plumage changes of the Bobolink, notes and manner of singing like the Yellow-breasted Chat, gregarious habits of the Blackbirds, and a nest and eggs almost indistinguishable from those of Dickcissel, with which bird it is somewhat akin in its nomadic habits." — Thomas Sadler Roberts (1936)

John Kirk Townsend, travelling with the Wyeth Expedition, discovered the Lark Bunting in central Nebraska on May 24, 1837. His companion Thomas Nuttall believed it to be a close relative of the Bobolink and classified it in the same genus. In some regions it is still referred to as a bobolink. Like the Lark Sparrow, the Lark Bunting is named for the fact that the males sing in flight like the skylark as described here:

"In every direction, first here and then there, often in a dozen places at once, Lark Buntings shot into the air, usually from the ground, as though propelled by guns, pouring out the most infectious and passionate song, perhaps sung by any bird in the United States." — Mr. Whittle (1922)

Calamospiza — The genus name means "reed finch" from the Greek *kalamos* (a reed) and *spiza* (a finch). This is an inappropriate name, because the Lark Bunting is a bird of dry short-grass prairie and agricultural lands, not reed beds.

melanocorys — The specific epithet means "black lark" from the Greek *melas* (black) and *corys* (a lark) and refers to the male's all-black plumage (except for the white wing patch) and his lark-like habit of singing in flight.
French Name: Bruant Noir et Blanc
Spanish Names: Gorrión de Ala Blanca; Gorrión Alipálido
Other Names: White-winged Bunting; White-winged Blackbird; Buffalo Bird; White-winged Prairie Bird; Prairie Bobolink; Prairie Lark Finch

Chipping Sparrow
Spizella passerina
(spy-ZELL-ah pass-er-EYE-nah)

"The Chipping Sparrow is the little brown-capped pensioner of the dooryard and lawn, that comes about farmhouse doors to glean crumbs shaken from the tablecloth by thrifty housewives. It is the most domestic of all the sparrows. It approaches the dwellings of man with quiet confidence and frequently builds its nest and rears its young in the clustering vines of porch and veranda under the noses of the human tenants." — Edward Howe Forbush (1929)

The Chipping Sparrow is named for chipping call notes and for its song, a dry chipping, insect-like trill. Its colloquial names Social Sparrow and Door-step Sparrow allude to its being a familiar bird around yards and gardens as illustrated in the opening passage.

Lark Sparrow, by Allan C. Brooks

Spizella — The genus name means "little finch" from the Greek *spiza* (a finch) plus a Latin diminutive suffix.

passerina — The specific epithet is Latin for "sparrow-like" from *passer* (a sparrow) and *ina* (like).

French Name: Bruant Familier

Spanish Names: Gorrión de Ceja Blanca; Gorrión Cejiblanco; Chimbito Común

Other Names: Western Chipping Sparrow; Chip Sparrow; Chipping Bunting; Chippy; Chipper; Chip-bird; Field Sparrow; Social Sparrow; Door-step Sparrow; Little House Sparrow; Hair Sparrow; Hair-bird; Hay Bird; Grey Bird; Little Grey Bird; Red-headed Grass Bird; Moineau; Serin du Pays; Titit; Tsitcha

Clay-colored Sparrow
Spizella pallida
(spy-ZELL-ah PAL-ih-dah)

"The clay-color is a trim little fellow, neat of form, clothed mostly in shades of brown and gray, with clay-colored trimmings and a three-cornered ear patch of darker brown. A gray and buffy streaked crown helps to distinguish him from his city cousin, the chipping sparrow." — Oscar M. Root (1968)

Dressed in browns, buffs, and pale gray, the pale colors of this sparrow's plumage suggest those of dried clay.

Spizella — The genus name means "little finch" from the Greek *spiza* (a finch) plus a Latin diminutive suffix.

pallida — The specific epithet is Latin for "pale" or "pallid" and refers to the light gray and brown plumage. Dr. John Richardson, surgeon-naturalist, and Thomas Drummond, assistant naturalist and botanist, on Sir John Franklin's second Arctic Land Exploring Expedition, collected the type specimen at Carlton House on the North Saskatchewan River in Canada on May 14, 1827. They transported it, along with hundreds of other plant and animal specimens, thousands of miles by canoe and portage. The specimen eventually found its way to England, where zoologist William Swainson described it giving it the name *Emberiza pallida* (pale bunting), and called it the Clay-coloured Buntling. The specimen is now in the collection of the University Museum, Cambridge, England.

French Name: Bruant des Plaines

Spanish Name: Gorrión Pálido

Other Name: Clay-colored Bunting

Black-chinned Sparrow
Spizella atrogularis
(spy-ZELL-ah ay-tro-gew-LARE-iss)

The black chin patch of the summer male gives this sparrow its name.

Spizella — The genus name means "little finch" from the Greek *spiza* (a finch) plus a Latin diminutive suffix.

atrogularis — The specific epithet means "black throat" from the Latin *ater* (flat black) and *gula* (the throat).

French Name: Bruant à Menton Noir

Spanish Name: Gorrión de Barba Negra; Gorrión Barbinegro

Other Names: California Black-chinned Sparrow; Arizona Black-chinned Sparrow

Field Sparrow
Spizella pusilla
(spy-ZELL-ah pew-SIL-lah)

"While the neighborly song sparrow and the swamp sparrow delight to be near water, the field sparrow chooses to live in dry uplands where stunted bushes and cedars cover the hills and overgrown old fields, and towhees, meadowlarks, and brown thrashers keep him company." — Neltje Blanchan (1917)

This sparrow is named for its habitat, successional old fields with tall weeds and scattered shrubs.

Spizella — The genus name means "little finch" from the Greek *spiza* (a finch) plus a Latin diminutive suffix.

pusilla — The specific epithet is Latin for "very small." It is one of the smaller sparrows, but it is larger than a Chipping Sparrow.

French Name: Bruant des Champs

Spanish Name: Gorrión Llanero

Other Names: Field Chippy; Field Bunting; Bush Sparrow; Rush Sparrow; Wood Sparrow; Ground Sparrow; Ground-bird; Huckleberry-bird

Brewer's Sparrow
Spizella breweri
(spy-ZELL-ah BREW-er-eye)

In 1856, while examining specimens in the Philadelphia Academy's collection, John Cassin described this species which he split from the similar Clay-colored Sparrow. He wrote that he took "much pleasure in embracing the present opportunity to dedicate a bird of the United States to my esteemed friend Thomas M. Brewer, M.D., of Boston, one who to the highest abilities and social qualities adds an ardor of devotion to Ornithological science rarely paralleled."

Spizella — The genus name means "little finch" from the Greek *spiza* (a finch) plus a Latin diminutive suffix.

breweri — The specific epithet commemorates Thomas Mayo Brewer (1814–1880), a Boston physician and friend of Audubon. See common name above.

French Name: Bruant de Brewer
Spanish Name: Gorrión de Brewer
Other Name: Roadrunner

Fox Sparrow
Passerella iliaca
(pass-er-EL-ah eye-lih-AY-kah)

This bird was originally named the Fox-colored Sparrow for the tawny red color of the eastern population. Three western subspecies are colored differently in dark browns and grays. In the future the Fox Sparrow may be split into four species, the Red Fox Sparrow (*P. iliaca*), Thick-billed Fox Sparrow (*P. megarhyncha*), Slate-colored Fox Sparrow (*P. schistacea*), and Sooty Fox Sparrow (*P. unalaschensis*).

Passerella — German zoologist Blasius Merrem originally described this species as *Fringilla iliaca* in 1786. In 1837, William Swainson erected the genus *Passerella* for this unique sparrow. The genus name means "little sparrow" from the Latin *passer* (a sparrow) and the diminutive suffix *-ella* (little). The Fox Sparrow is actually one of the larger members of the family, about the size of a Hermit Thrush.

iliaca — The specific epithet is Latin for "of the flanks." Merrem named the Fox Sparrow for its superficial resemblance to the Redwing (*Turdus iliacus*) a European thrush. The specific epithet is a reference to the Redwing's chestnut flanks and to the Fox Sparrow's heavily streaked sides.

French Name: Bruant Fauve
Spanish Name: Gorrión Rascador
Eskimo and Inuit Names: Iklikvik (tool container); Cha-pang-uk
Other Names: Townsend's Fox Sparrow; Shumagin Fox Sparrow; Stephen's Fox Sparrow; Kodiak Fox Sparrow; Yakutat Fox Sparrow; Great Sparrow; Wilderness Sparrow; Swamp Sparrow; Hedge Sparrow; Ferruginous Finch; Foxy Finch; Fox-coloured Finch; Foxy Tom; Tom Fox; Fox-tail; Fox Bird; Partridge Bird; Red Thrush; Red Singer; Bobby-rooter; Brown Bobber; Gratteur; Rossignol Francais

American Tree Sparrow
Spizelloides arborea
(spy-zell-LOY-deez ar-BOR-ee-ah)

"The tree sparrow is another example of a misnomer by our pioneer forefathers, for few birds spend less time in trees, either in winter or summer. The early Settlers saw in it a superficial resemblance to the chestnut-capped tree sparrow (*Passer montanus*) of Europe and, either in ignorance of the specific differences or in nostalgic recollection, called this little American sparrow by the same name. Actually our tree sparrow might more accurately be called brush sparrow, for its haunts include the scrubby edges of our fields and marshes, hedgerows, and fallow fields." — A. Marguerite Baumgartner (1968)

This sparrow is not well named, as it has no particular affinity for trees, except to occasionally feed on catkins in birch trees. It winters in weedy fields and breeds on the arctic tundra, which is virtually treeless except for a few stunted willows and spruces. This bird was actually named for an Old World species it was said to resemble as explained in the opening passage. American distinguishes this New World bird from the Eurasian Tree Sparrow in the family Passeridae.

Spizelloides — The genus name means "like a little finch" from the Greek *spiza* (a finch) and

American Tree Sparrow and Snow Bunting,
by Louis Agassiz Fuertes

a Latin diminutive suffix plus the Greek suffix *–oides* (like or resembling). The reference is to this species relationship to sparrows in the genus *Spizella*.

arborea — The specific epithet means "arboreal" i.e. "relating to trees" from the Latin *arbor* (a tree). See common name above.

French Name: Bruant Hudsonien
Spanish Name: Gorrión Arbóreo
Eskimo and Inuit Names: Misapsak; Mut-chuk-ut
Other Names: Winter Chippy; Snow Chippy; Arctic Chipper; Winter Chip-bird; Winter Sparrow; Canada Sparrow; Canada Bunting; Tree Bunting

Dark-eyed Junco
Junco hyemalis
(JUNG-koh high-eh-MAIL-iss)

Junco, which is also the genus name, derives from a Latin word that means "a rush." But juncos are birds of open coniferous and mixed forests, not wetlands. Perhaps Linnaeus confused it with an Old World species, such as the Reed Bunting (*Emberiza schoeniclus*) that really does nest where reeds and rushes grow. Dark-eyed pertains to the black eyes and distinguishes this species from the Yellow-eyed Junco. The Dark-eyed Junco was formerly divided into four different species: Slate-colored Junco (*J. hyemalis*), Oregon Junco (*J. oreganos*), White-winged Junco (*J. aiken*), and Gray-headed Junco (*J. caniceps*).

Junco — The genus name derives from the Latin *juncus* (a rush). See common name above.

hyemalis — The specific epithet is from the Latin *hiemalis* (winter). The Dark-eyed Junco is known in much of the lower forty-eight states only as a winter visitor and one of the most familiar species at feeders. Many people call them snowbirds.

French Name: Junco Ardoisé
Spanish Names: Junco de Ojo Oscuro; Junco Ojioscuro
Eskimo and Inuit Names: Kaytavaurak (small grosbeak); Su'ksaxia
Other Names: (Slate-colored Junco): Eastern Junco; Carolina Junco; Cassiar Junco; Bad-weather Bird; Common Snowbird; Black Snowbird; Blue Snowbird; Gray Snowbird;

Dark-eyed (Oregon) Junco, by Allan C. Brooks

Slate-colored Snowbird; Blue Bird; Ivory-billed Bluebird; Grey Bird; Goose Bird; Hen Bird; Male Bird; Chip Bird; Chipping Bird; Black Chipping Bird; Chippy; White-bill; White-tail; Blue Sparrow; Nonne; Nonnette; Tip; Titoc; Tomtit; (Oregon Junco): Pink-sided Junco; Mountain Junco; Sierra Junco; Thurber's Junco; Shufeldt's Junco; Oregon Snowbird; (Gray-headed Junco) : Red-backed Junco

Yellow-eyed Junco
Junco phaeonotus
(JUNG-koh fee-oh-NO-tus)

This junco gets its name from its yellow eyes. Formerly known as "Mexican Junco."
Junco — The genus name derives from the Latin *juncus* (a rush).
phaeonotus — The specific epithet means "dun-colored back" from the Greek *phaios* (dun-colored or dusky) and *notan* (the back) and refers to the brown back, which is more of a warm reddish brown than dun (gray-brown).
French Name: Junco aux Yeux Jaunes
Spanish Names: Junco Ojo de Lumbre; Junco Ojilumbre
Other Names: Arizona Junco; Red-backed Junco; Baird's Junco; Townsend's Junco

White-crowned Sparrow
Zonotrichia leucophrys
(zoe-no-TRICK-ih-ah lew-KOFF-riss)

This showy sparrow has a bright white crown with contrasting black stripes.
Zonotrichia — The genus name means "banded hair" from the Greek *zone* (a girdle, belt, or band) and *trichos* (the hair). The reference is to the striped crowns of the sparrows in this genus.
leucophrys — The specific epithet means "white eyebrow" from the Greek *leukos* (white) and *ophrys* (the eyebrow), referring to the broad white supercillium (eyebrow stripe).
French Name: Bruant à Courrone Blanche
Spanish Names: Gorrión de Corona Blanca; Gorrión Coroniblanco
Eskimo and Inuit Names: Cha-pang-akh-tu-le-a-gak (small fox sparrow); Nungaktuakruk; Me-chok-chok-pi-e-nuk
Other Names: White-crowned Finch; White-crown; White-cap; Jockey-cap; Gambel's Sparrow; Nuttall's Sparrow; Hedge Sparrow; Scratch Sparrow; Chip-bird; Grey Bird; Rain Bird; Striped-head; Muee

Golden-crowned Sparrow
Zonotrichia atricapilla
(zoe-no-TRICK-ih-ah ay-trih-CAP-ih-lah)

This sparrow is named for its yellow forecrown.
Zonotrichia — See White-throated Sparrow.
atricapilla — The specific epithet means "black haired" from the Latin *atrus* (flat black) and *capilla* (the hair). The reference is to the broad, black band just below the yellow crown.
French Name: Bruant à Couronne Dorée
Spanish Names: Gorrión de Corona Dorada; Gorrión Coronidorado
Eskimo and Inuit Name: Wee-pen-ee-pahk
Other Names: Black and Yellow-crowned Finch; Golden-crown; Rain Bird

Harris's Sparrow
Zonotrichia querula
(zoe-no-TRICK-ih-ah KWER-you-lah)

"The Harris's Sparrow is a handsome member of the finch tribe. It is considerably larger than an English Sparrow. It has a pink bill, black crown, face, and throat; streaked back and sides; and white underparts ... It was discovered, in 1837, by a young naturalist named Thomas Nuttall, who described it three years later, naming it *Fringilla querula*, the Mourning Finch. A few years later the famous ornithologist-artist, John James Audubon, rediscovered the bird, bestowing upon it, in honor of his excellent and constant friend Edward Harris, Esq., the common name it now bears." — George Miksch Sutton (1936)

On May 4, 1843, Edward Harris shot a large sparrow with a black face and bib, and pink bill, near the Blacksnake Hills trading post (now Saint Joseph, Missouri). Audubon was sure it was a new species and dedicated it, "I am truly proud to name it *Fringilla Harrisii*, in honor of one of the best friends I have in this world." Of course, as the above passage relates, ornithologist Thomas Nuttall had described and named this species three years earlier. He collected the type specimen near Independence, Missouri while travelling with John Kirk Townsend on the Wyeth expedition to the Pacific coast.

Zonotrichia — The genus name means "banded hair" from the Greek *zone* (a girdle, belt, or band) and *trichos* (the hair). The reference is to the striped crowns of the sparrows in this genus.

querula — The specific epithet is Latin for "plaintive" or "lamenting" and refers to the melancholy quality of this sparrow's whistled song.

French Name: Bruant à Face Noire
Spanish Name: Gorrión de Harris
Other Names: Mourning Sparrow; Hooded Sparrow; Hooded-crowned Sparrow; Black-hood

White-throated Sparrow
Zonotrichia albicollis
(zoe-no-TRICK-ih-ah al-bih-CALL-is)

"To hear the white-throat at its best, go to the evergreen country of the North in June. There, around the old clearings and open windfalls, the stillness will be broken at intervals by one of the loveliest of all bird songs, a series of fine, pensive, almost tremulous whistles, leisurely, dying away slightly toward the close. "Old, old Sam Peabody, Peabody, Peabody, Peabody" the singer seems to say, and the purity of his voice passes all belief." — Robert S. Lemmon (1951)

White-throated Sparrow and White-crowned Sparrow, by Louis Agassiz Fuertes

This sparrow's white throat patch gives it its name. In New England the White-throated Sparrow is known as the Peabody-bird for the mnemonic mentioned in the opening passage. See sidebar 33.

Sidebar 33
Old Sam Peabody of New England

New Englanders know the White-throated Sparrow as the Peabody-bird. The name comes from a mnemonic for this species' sweet, plaintive song, as the following passage illustrates:

"There is the White-throated Sparrow, or so-called Peabody bird, in the maple over there, you can see his white throat and black-striped crown quite distinctly. How clear and soft his perfect whistle is! No one can quite imitate its charm and dainty sweetness. Always the rhythm is the same: *Old Sam Peabody, Peabody, Peabody,* or, *Sow wheat Peaverly, Peaverly, Peaverly,* or — and naturally you ought to be in Canada to hear this — *O sweet Canada, Canada, Canada,* or, if you are the right girl with the right name he will call to you, *O hear me Theresa, Theresa, Theresa,* or if you are an idle, lounging, whittling, country fellow he will chide you with, *All day long whittlin', whittlin', whittlin'.* Yes, there are lots of ways of translating the song, but the words always seem to refer to oneself and not to the bird — who and where you are, what you are doing, and what you ought to do! There, if you listen a moment and stop giggling you will hear what that Peabody bird over yonder has to say about yourself: *All noontime fiddlin', fiddlin', fiddlin'.* Evidently he heard you practicing on your violin yesterday, and took note of the hour that got on the family's nerves! But musically speaking, you see, he always sticks to triplets, and you can fit any syllables you like to these; they are the gist of his song." — F. Schuyler Mathews (1921)

Zonotrichia — The genus name means "banded hair" from the Greek *zone* (a girdle, belt, or band) and *trichos* (the hair). The reference is to the striped crowns of the sparrows in this genus.

albicollis — The specific epithet means "white necked" from the Latin *albus* (white) and *collum* (the neck).

French Name: Bruant à Gorge Blanche

Spanish Names: Gorrión de Garganta Blanca; Gorrión Gorjiblanco

Other Names: White-throat; White-throated Crown Sparrow; White-throated Finch; Canada Whitethroat; Canada Sparrow; Canadian Song Sparrow; Whistling Sparrow; Whistle Bird; Canada Bird; Hard-times Canada Bird; Sweet Sweet Canada Bird; Sweet Pinkey; Peabody; Peabody-bird; Peabiddy Bird; Old Sam Peabody; Poor Sam Peabody; Tom Peabody; Old Tom Peabody; Paddy-whack; Peverly-bird; Cherry-bird; Kennedy Bird; Poor Kennedy Bird; Widow Bird; Widow Woman; Nightingale; Night-singer; Striped-head; Chingolo Gargantiblanco; Siffleur; Linnotte; Rossignol; Frédéric; Petit Frédéric; Pison à Gorge Blanche

Sagebrush Sparrow
Artemisiospiza nevadensis
(art-eh-MISS-ih-oh-SPY-zah neh-vah-DENS-iss

The Sagebrush Sparrow is named for one of its habitats, stands of Big Sagebrush (*Atremisia tridentata*).

Artemisiopiza — The genus name means "sage finch" from the Greek *Artemisia*, the genus to which sagebrush belongs and *spiza* (a finch) identified by some authors as the Chaffinch (*Fringilla coelebs*) of Europe. The plant genus *Artemisia* encompasses some 300 species. Besides sagebrush, it includes mugwort, sweet Annie, the culinary herb tarragon, dusty miller, old woman, sagewort, and wormwood which flavors the liqueur absinthe. The genus is named either directly or indirectly for Artemis, the Greek goddess of the hunt and the moon, and twin sister of Apollo. Wormwood, a medicinal herb, is said to be sacred to her. Some sources say the genus commemorates Artemisia ll, Queen of Caria (now Turkey), who was a noted botanist and medical researcher. She was named for the goddess. The Sagebrush Sparrow and Bell's Sparrow were formerly considered conspecific, the Sage Sparrow.

nevadensis — The specific epithet means "of Nevada" part of the species' range and probably where the type specimen was collected.

French Name: Bruant des Armoises

Spanish Names: Zacatonero de Artemisa; Gorrión de Artemesia

Other Names: Northern Sage Sparrow; Gray Sage Sparrow

Bell's Sparrow
Artemisiospiza belli
(art-eh-MISS-ih-oh-SPY-zah BELL-eye)

Bell's Sparrow commemorates John Graham Bell. See specific epithet below. Formerly considered conspecific with the Sagebrush Sparrow.

Artemisiopiza — The genus name means "sage finch" from the Greek *Artemisia*, the genus to which sagebrush belongs and *spiza* (a finch) identified by some authors as the Chaffinch (*Fringilla coelebs*) of Europe. The Sagebrush Sparrow and Bell's Sparrow were formerly considered conspecific, the Sage Sparrow.

belli — In 1850, John Cassin named this sparrow in honor of John Graham Bell (1812–1889), a taxidermist from New York, who accompanied Audubon on his trip up the Missouri River in 1843.

French Name: Bruant de Bell

Spanish Name: Gorrión de Bell

Other Names: Same as Sagebrush Sparrow

Vesper Sparrow
Pooecetes gramineus
(poe-ee-SEE-teez gray-MIN-ee-us)

"In the hush of the evening, as shadows lengthen over meadows and woods, a sweet, clear bird song echoes — two long, low notes, two higher ones, then a rippling trill. From a distant fence post or telephone wire the vesper sparrow sings, and his music seems to complement the peacefulness of the sunset . . . He sings off and on all day, sometimes even in the middle of the night. But his vesper song earned him his present name." — Arthur A. Allen (1964)

Pioneer naturalists Audubon and Wilson knew this species as the Bay-winged Bunting for the small patch of chestnut-brown at the bend of the wing, but nature writer John Burroughs renamed it the Vesper Sparrow, for the whimsical notion that it sings its sweetest song in the evening. He wrote:

His song is most noticeable after sundown, when other birds are silent, for which reason he has been aptly called the vesper sparrow. The farmer following his team from the field at dusk catches his sweetest strain. His song is not so brisk and varied as is that of song sparrow, being softer and wilder, sweeter and more plaintive. Add the best parts of the lay of the latter to the sweet vibrating chant of the wood [field] sparrow, and you have the evening hymn of the vesper-bird — the poet of the plain, unadorned pastures . . . It is one of the most characteristic sounds in Nature. The grass, the stones, the stubble, the furrow, the quiet herds, and the warm twilight among the hills, are all subtly expressed in this song.

Pooecetes — The genus name means "grass dweller" from the Greek *poe* (grass) and *oiketes* (an inhabitant). This sparrow nests in open fields and grasslands.

gramineus — The specific epithet is Latin for "grassy," referring to the habitat.

French Name: Bruant Vespéral

Spanish Names: Gorrión de Cola Blanca; Gorrión Coliblanco

Other Names: Eastern Vesper Sparrow; Western Vesper Sparrow; Oregon Vesper Sparrow; Grass Sparrow; Grass Finch; Bay-winged Finch; Bay-winged Bunting; Pasture-bird; Grass-bird; Gray-bird; Ground-bird

LeConte's Sparrow
Ammospiza leconteii
(am-oh-SPY-za lee-KONT-ih-eye)

John G. Bell collected this sparrow near Fort Union, North Dakota on May 24, 1843, during Audubon's expedition up the Missouri River. They apparently didn't initially recognize it as a new species, for Audubon made no mention of it in his journal. The following year, back at his home at *Minnie's Land*, Audubon described the new species in volume seven of the octavo edition of *Birds of America*. He called it LeConte's Sharp-tailed Bunting and gave it the scientific name *Emberiza le conteii* in honor of John Lawrence LeConte:

"I have named this interesting species after my young friend Doctor LE CONTE, son of Major LE CONTE, so well known among naturalists, and who is, like his father, much attached to the study of natural history."

Ammospiza — The genus name means "sand finch" from the Greek *ammos* (sand) and *spiza* (a finch). Formerly *Ammodramus leconteii*.

leconteii — The specific epithet commemorates Dr. John Lawrence LeConte (1825–1883), the leading entomologist of the 19th century with "an inordinate fondness for beetles." He served as a physician during the Civil War. See common name above.

Sidebar 34
The Other John LeConte

Many sources say LeConte's Thrasher was named for John Lawrence LeConte, but that LeConte's Sparrow was named for another man, John Lawrence's first cousin Dr. John LeConte (1818–1891), the son of a wealthy Georgia plantation owner. Dr. LeConte practiced medicine briefly, but soon gave it up to teach chemistry and physics at several southern universities. During the Civil War, he worked as superintendent of a Confederate niter works, which manufactured explosives. In 1869, when he joined the faculty of the University of California at Berkeley, he was appointed acting president until Henry Durant assumed the position in 1870. Then from 1875 to 1881, he again served as president of the university. Dr. John LeConte was elected to membership in the National Academy of Sciences in 1878. Although Audubon did not state Dr. LeConte's full name in his dedication, he did say "son of Major LeConte." John Lawrence's father John Eatton LeConte served in the military, but his cousin's did not. So it is most likely that both the thrasher and the sparrow are named for John Lawrence LeConte.

French Name: Bruant de Le Conte
Spanish Name: Gorrión de Le Conte
Other Names: LeConte's Bunting; LeConte's Sharp-tailed Bunting; Yellow Sparrow

Seaside Sparrow
Ammospiza maritimus
(am-oh-SPY-za mah-RIT-ih-mus)

"Of this bird I can find no description. It inhabits the low rush-covered sea islands along our Atlantic coast, where I first found it; keeping almost continually within the boundaries of tidewater, except when long and violent east and northeasterly storms, with high tides, compel it to seek the shore. On these occasions it courses along the margin, and among the holes and interstices of the weeds and sea-wrack, with a rapidity equaled only by the nimblest of our sandpipers, and very much in their manner. At these times also it roosts on the ground, and runs about after dusk. Amidst the recesses of these wet sea marshes, it seeks the rankest growth of grass and sea weed, and climbs along the stalks of the rushes with as much dexterity as it runs along the ground, which is rather a singular circumstance, most of our climbers being rather awkward at running." — Alexander Wilson (1811)

Alexander Wilson discovered this bird on the Jersey Shore in 1810. He called it the Sea-side Finch. See Wilson's description of it above.

The Seaside Sparrow is named for its habitat in coastal saltmarshes, above the high tide line. Dominant vegetation there includes rushes, spartina, and saltgrass. Two subspecies, the Cape Sable Seaside Sparrow (*A.m. mirabilis*) and the Dusky Seaside Sparrow (*A.m. nigrescens*), were formerly considered full species. The Dusky Seaside Sparrow is now extinct. See Extinct Species and Subspecies.

Ammospiza — The genus name means "sand finch" from the Greek *ammos* (sand) and *spiza* (a finch). Formerly *Ammodramus maritimus*.
maritimus — The specific epithet is Latin for "maritime" or "of the sea."
French Name: Bruant Maritime
Spanish Name: Gorrión Marino
Other Names: Seaside Finch; MacGillivray's Shore Finch; Meadow Chippy

Nelson's Sparrow
Ammospiza nelsoni
(am-oh-SPY-za NEL-son-eye)

This sparrow is named for Edward W. Nelson. See specific epithet below. This and the Saltmarsh Sparrow were formerly considered a single species, the Sharp-tailed Sparrow. The name was changed to Nelson's Sharp-tailed Sparrow, then shortened to the present one.

Ammospiza — The genus name means "sand finch" from the Greek *ammos* (sand) and *spiza* (a finch). Formerly *Ammodramus nelsoni*.
nelsoni — In 1875, Joel Asaph Allen named this species in honor of Edward William Nelson (1855–1934), an American ornithologist and founding president of the AOU. In 1874, at age 18, he collected the first specimen of this sparrow at Calumet Lake in south Chicago.
French Name: Bruant de Nelson
Spanish Name: Gorrión de Nelson
Other Name: Sharp-tailed Finch

Saltmarsh Sparrow
Ammospiza caudacutus
(am-oh-SPY-za caud-ah-CUE-tus)

This sparrow is named for its habitat in coastal saltmarshes. Formerly considered conspecific with Nelson's Sparrow as the Sharp-tailed Sparrow. The name was changed to Saltmarsh Sharp-tailed Sparrow, then shortened to the present one. The AOU committee felt that the names Nelson's Sharp-tailed Sparrow and Saltmarsh Sharp-tailed Sparrow were too cumbersome. But no more so than Northern Beardless Tyrannulet.

Ammospiza — The genus name means "sand finch" from the Greek *ammos* (sand) and *spiza* (a finch). Formerly *Ammodramus caudacutus*.
caudacutus — The specific epithet means "sharp tail" from the Latin *cauda* (the tail) and *acutus* (sharp) and refers to the pointed tail feathers.
French Name: Bruant à Queue Aiguë
Spanish Names: Gorrión de Cola Aguda; Gorrión Coliagudo
Other Name: Sharp-tailed Finch

Baird's Sparrow
Centronyx bairdii
(sen-TRON-icks BAIRD-ih-eye)

When he was just a teenager, Spencer Fullerton Baird began to correspond with Audubon, even sending him specimens he and his brother had collected. Two of these, the Yellow-bellied Flycatcher and the Least Flycatcher, proved to be new to science. Audubon was so impressed with the young naturalist, he invited the twenty year-old on his expedition up the Missouri River in 1843. Audubon would even pay for Baird's expenses. But alas, Baird's family, concerned over the young man's health and safety on such a long and arduous journey, persuaded him to turn down the trip of a lifetime. With both men disappointed, Audubon set out on his expedition with companions John Graham Bell, Edward Harris, Isaac Sprague, and Lewis Squires. At the confluence of the Missouri and Yellowstone Rivers, near Fort Union, North Dakota, Bell collected a pair of sparrows with an ochre-wash on the face and a necklace of sparse, dark streaks on the breast. Audubon named the new species Baird's Bunting "after my young friend Spencer F. Baird, of Carlisle, Pennsylvania." This was the last species Audubon described, named, and painted, the 500th plate in volume seven of the octavo edition of *Birds of America*.

Centronyx — The genus name means "pointed claw" from the Greek *kentron* (point) and *onux* (a claw or spur). Formerly *Ammodramus bairdii*.

bairdii — Audubon described this species in 1844, giving it the name *Emberiza Bairdii* for his friend Spencer Fullerton Baird (1823–1887), who would become secretary of the Smithsonian Institution (1878–1887). See common name above.

French Name: Bruant de Baird
Spanish Name: Gorrión de Baird
Other Names: Scrub Sparrow; Baird's Bunting

Henslow's Sparrow
Centronyx henslowii
(sen-TRON-icks HEN-slow-ih-eye)

Audubon discovered this secretive sparrow in Kentucky across the river from Cincinatti. He described it in his *Ornithological Biography* (1831), giving it the name *Emberiza Henslowii* for his friend, English theologian and naturalist John Stevens Henslow:

"In naming it after the Rev. Professor HENSLOW of Cambridge, a gentleman so well known to the scientific world, my object has been to manifest my gratitude for the many kind attentions which he has shown towards me."

Centronyx — The genus name means "pointed claw" from the Greek *kentron* (point) and *onux* (a claw or spur). Formerly *Ammodramus henslowii*.

henslowii — The specific epithet commemorates John Stevens Henslow (1796–1861), a clergyman and professor of botany at Cambridge University. See common name above.

French Name: Bruant de Henslow
Spanish Name: Gorrión de Henslow
Other Names: Henslow's Bunting

Savannah Sparrow
Passerculus sandwichensis
(pass-ER-cue-lus sand-wich-EN-sis)

"In view of its extensive distribution, it is interesting to note that while the common name, Savannah sparrow, truly indicates its preferred habitat, it was actually named by Wilson for the town of Savannah, Ga., where the type specimen was collected. It is also something of a paradox that the species should acquire its familiar name from a town in the only section (southeastern United States) of the continent in which it does not breed." — James Baird (1968)

As stated above, Alexander Wilson discovered this species near Savannah, Georgia in 1811. He gave it the name *Fringilla savanna*. However the species had already been described, so Wilson's specific epithet now designates a subspecies, the Eastern Savannah Sparrow (*Passerculus sandwichensis savanna*). See specific epithet below. Formerly known as Sandwich Sparrow and Aleutian Savannah Sparrow. A large, pallid subspecies, *P. s. princeps*, was formerly considered a full species, the Ipswich Sparrow. It was discovered wintering in sand dunes near the coastal town of Ipswich, Massachusetts.

Passerculus — The genus name is Latin for "little sparrow."

sandwichensis — German naturalist Johann

Gmelin described this species in the 13th edition of *Linnaeus Systemae naturae* (1789). He named it *Emberiza sandwichensis* for the type locality, Sandwich Bay on Unalaska Island in the Aleutians. The type specimen had been collected on James Cook's voyage to the west coast of North America (1778). In 1790, British naturalist John Latham described it in his *General Synopsis of Birds* and gave it the common name Sandwich Bunting.

French Name: Bruant des Prés

Spanish Names: Gorrión Sabanero; Sabanero Zanjero

Eskimo and Inuit Names: Okpisio-yuk (staying mostly in willows); Mi-ju-kuk; Chit-tah

Other Names: Western Savannah Sparrow; Aleutian Savannah Sparrow; Field Sparrow; Grass Sparrow; Belding's Sparrow; Large-billed Sparrow; Ipswich Savannah Sparrow; Maynard's Sparrow; Sable Island Sparrow; Pallid Sparrow; Marsh Sparrow; Ground Sparrow; Ground-bird; Gray Bird; Meadow Bird; Savannah Bunting; Sandwich Bunting

---

Sidebar 35
Subspecies of the Savannah Sparrow

"Ask ornithologists to think about Savannah sparrows and there is no telling what mental imagery will be conjured up. One will think immediately of a lush, spring-green meadow visited on a misty May morning; there the thin song of the Savannah could barely be heard over the more robust songs of the redwing, meadowlark, and bobolink. Then he will remember, with a certain lingering discomfort that same field during the heat of a hot July day. Another will think of sand in his shoes, the roar of the nearby surf, and see once again a Savannah's nest hidden under some flotsam at the base of a Cape Cod sand dune. Still another bird man will remember cussing out a persistent yellowlegs that yodeled his alarm from atop a black spruce while he was trying to observe, unseen, a pair of Savannahs on a Labrador sphagnum bog. To the next, to think of Savannah sparrows will recall a bleak Alaskan tundra, longspurs, jaegers, godwits, lemmings and ice in the coffee pot on a midsummer morning. That the Savannah sparrow should be able to evoke such a variety of climatic, geographic, and ecological memories is primarily due to its extensive breeding range, which covers nearly the whole of the North American continent from the arctic circle to the tropics." — James Baird (1968)

With such a wide range, it is not surprising that the Savannah Sparrow has evolved into seventeen recognized subspecies. Three of these are so distinct, they were formerly considered full species. The Ipswich Sparrow (*Passerculus sandwichensis princeps*) is a large, ghostly pale race, 10% larger than a typical Savannah Sparrow. It breeds only on Sable Island, about 140 miles south of Cape Breton Island, Nova Scotia, the only land bird to occur there. It winters along the Atlantic coast from Massachusetts to Cumberland Island, Georgia. Its common name is for Ipswich, Massachusetts, where naturalist Charles Johnson Maynard discovered it wintering in nearby sand dunes in 1868. He initially misidentified it as a Baird's Sparrow, but later described it as a new species, giving it the specific epithet *princeps*, Latin for "chief,'" "leader," or "most distinguished," referring to the large size. Belding's Sparrow (*P.s. beldingi*) is a dark race, resident in Pacific coast saltmarshes from Santa Barbara south through Baja California. In 1885, Robert Ridgway named it for naturalist Lyman Belding (1829–1917), who collected the type specimen at San Quentin Bay, Baja California. The Large-billed Sparrow (*P.s. rostratus*) is named for its distinct bill, 30% larger than that of a typical Savannah Sparrow. It breeds in northern Baja California and at the Salton Sea. Its specific epithet *rostratus* is Latin for "large-billed."

Song Sparrow, by Allan C. Brooks

Song Sparrow
Melospiza melodia
(mel-oh-SPY-zah mel-ODE-ih-ah)

"What bird lives up to his name more faithfully than *melodia*? Day or night, in any season, you may hear his delightful little jingle — a few long, bright notes and trills. Thoreau rendered the ditty as *Maids! Maids! Maids! Hang up your teakettle — ettle — ettle*. When winter has scarcely relaxed its icy grip, this heavily streaked little bird with a dark breast spot may repeat his cheerful melody as many as 300 times an hour, for this is the time to warn off territorial intruders and attract a mate." — Arthur A. Allen (1964)

The Song Sparrow has a particularly musical song that it sings throughout the year. Margaret Morse Nice, who did an intensive study of the Song Sparrow from 1929 to 1936, in Columbus Ohio, wrote of the song's character:

"The songs of each male are entirely distinct; as a rule they sound pleasant and "cheerful" to human ears, yet a few are disagreeable, while others are of great beauty. Many individuals have no specially distinctive songs, while some have one or two songs which are unforgettable to an attentive observer. The same individual may have songs of all degrees of quality; harsh, typical and especially musical."

Melospiza — The genus name means "song finch" from the Greek *melos* (song) and *spiza* (a finch). New World Sparrows were formerly classified in the finch family Fringillidae. For a description of the Song Sparrow's song, see common name above.

melodia — The specific epithet is Latin for "a pleasant song."

French Name: Bruant Chanteur
Spanish Name: Gorrión Cantor
Other Names: Brown Song Sparrow; Mountain Song Sparrow; Sooty Song Sparrow; Ground Sparrow; Hedge Sparrow; Bush Sparrow; Marsh Sparrow; Song Finch; Swamp Finch; March Sparrow; Spring Bird; Grey Bird; Ground-bird; Grassbird; Red Grassbird; Everybody's Darling; Silver Tongue; Rossignol; Gealbhonn; Glaiseun; Shbeds'l

Lincoln's Sparrow
Melospiza lincolnii
(mel-oh-SPY-zah ling-CONE-ih-eye)

In 1833, Audubon and his son John made an expedition to the Labrador coast. With them were four other young men, George Shattuck, Joseph Coolidge, William Ingalls, and Thomas Lincoln. One morning, near the mouth of the Natashquan River in Quebec, Audubon heard an unfamiliar song and called to the others to come over:

"They came, and we all followed the songster as it flitted from one bush to another to evade our pursuit. No sooner would it alight than it renewed its song; but we found more wildness in this species than in any other inhabiting the same country, and it was with difficulty that we at last procured it. Chance placed my young companion, THOMAS LINCOLN, in a situation where he saw it alight within shot, and with his usual unerring aim, he cut short its career. On seizing it, I found it to be a species which I had not previously seen; and, supposing it to be new, I named it *Tom's Finch*, in honour of our friend LINCOLN, who was a great favourite among us. Three cheers were given him, when proud of the prize, I returned to the vessel to draw it, while my son and his companions continued to search for other specimens." — John James Audubon (1833)

Melospiza — The genus name means "song finch" from the Greek *melos* (song) and *spiza* (a finch). New World Sparrows were formerly classified in the finch family Fringillidae. The Lincoln Sparrow'a song is a loud, bubbling trill, similar to a House Wren's song.

lincolnii — In 1834, John James Audubon named this species in honor of Thomas Lincoln (1812–1883), who at age 21, traveled with him to the Maritimes of Canada the previous year. See common name above.

French Name: Bruant de Lincoln
Spanish Names: Gorrión de Lincoln; Sabanero de Lincoln
Other Names: Lincoln's Song Sparrow; Lincoln's Finch; Tom's Finch

Swamp Sparrow
Melospiza georgiana
(mel-oh-SPY-zah jorj-ih-AY-nah)

This sparrow is named for its habitat in freshwater marshes and open wooded swamps. It is often found nesting in cattails.

Melospiza — The genus name means "song finch" from the Greek *melos* (song) and *spiza* (a finch). New World Sparrows were formerly classified in the finch family Fringillidae. The Swamp Sparrow's song is a slow, musical trill on one pitch and has been likened to the sound of a sewing machine.

georgiana — The specific epithet is Modern Latin for "of Georgia," the state where the type specimen was collected.

French Name: Bruant des Marais
Spanish Name: Gorrión Pantanero
Other Names: Marsh Sparrow; Reed Sparrow; Swamp Song Sparrow; Swamp Finch; Red Grass-bird; Grey Bird

Canyon Towhee
Melozone fuscus
(mel-OZE-oh-nee FUSS-cus)

Towhee is imitative of the Eastern Towhee's two-note alarm call, rendered *tow-hee*. The Canyon Towhee takes its name from some of its habitat, dry, brushy foothills and canyons in the arid Southwest. This and the California Towhee were previously considered to be one species, the Brown Towhee.

Melozone — The genus name means "banded cheek: from the Greek *melon* (the cheek) and *zone* (a band or a girdle) and refers to the crescent-shaped black and chestnut earpatch of Prevost's Ground-Sparrow (*M. biarcuatum*) of Central America, the first species assigned to this genus.

fuscus — The specific epithet is Latin for "dusky" and refers to this bird's overall dull gray-brown color.

French Name: Tohi des Canyons
Spanish Names: Rascador Pardo; Rascador Arroyero
Other Names: Fuscous Towhee; Canyon Bunting; Catbird; Ground Robin; Swamp Robin; Brown Chippy; La Viejita (the little old woman); Rascador Pardo

Abert's Towhee, by Allan C. Brooks

Abert's Towhee
Melozone aberti
(mel-OZE-oh-nee AY-bert-eye)

In 1852, after examining "a small but exceedingly interesting collection of birds and mammals" collected in New Mexico, Spencer F. Baird described this species in *Exploration and Survey of the Valley of the Great Salt Lake of Utah* by S. F. Baird and H. Stansbury. He named it *Pipilo aberti* and dedicated it "to its accomplished discoverer, Lieutenant Jas. W. Abert."

Melozone — The genus name means "banded cheek: from the Greek *melon* (the cheek) and *zone* (a band or a girdle) and refers to the crescent-shaped black and chestnut earpatch of Prevost's Ground-Sparrow (*M. biarcuatum*) of Central America, the first species assigned to this genus.

aberti — The specific epithet commemorates Major James William Abert (1820–1897), a topographical engineer who collected the type specimen in New Mexico. See common name above.

French Name: Tohi d'Abert
Spanish Name: Rascador de Abert
Other Names: Gray Towhee

Green-tailed Towhee, by Allan C. Brooks

California Towhee
Melozone crissalis
(mel-OZE-oh-nee kris-SAY-liss)

The California Towhee is named for its range from northern California and Oregon south through Baja California. Formerly considered conspecific with the Canyon Towhee as the Brown Towhee.

Melozone — The genus name means "banded cheek: from the Greek *melon* (the cheek) and *zone* (a band or a girdle) and refers to the crescent-shaped black and chestnut earpatch of Prevost's Ground-Sparrow (*M. biarcuatum*) of Central America, the first species assigned to this genus.

crissalis — The specific epithet is Modern Latin and refers to the crissum or undertail coverts, which are rusty or cinnamon, contrasting with the bird's overall gray-brown color.

French Name: Tohi de Californie
Spanish Name: Rascador Californiano
Other Names: Crissal Bunting; Sacramento Brown Towhee Otherwise same as Canyon Towhee. See above.

Rufous-crowned Sparrow
Aimophila ruficeps
(ay-MOFF-ih-lah ROOF-ih-seps)

This sparrow's rusty crown gives it its name.

Aimophila — The genus name means "thicket-loving" or "thorn-loving" from the Greek *aimos* (a thorn) and *philos* (loving or fond of). William Swainson erected this genus for Bachman's Sparrow (which has since been merged into the genus *Peucaea*) in 1837. Presumably this refers to some of the vegetation Bachman's Sparrow might take cover in, such as brambles in its southern pinewoods habitat.

ruficeps — The specific epithet means "reddish headed" from the Latin *rufus* (reddish) and *ceps* (the head).

French Name: Tohi à Calotte Fauve
Spanish Names: Zacatonero de Corona Rufa; Zacatonero Coronirrufo
Other Names: Ashy Rufous-crowned Sparrow; California Rufous-crowned Sparrow; Scott's Rufous-crowned Sparrow; Rock Rufous-crowned Sparrow; Rock Sparrow; Western Swamp Sparrow

Green-tailed Towhee
Pipilo chlorurus
(PIP-ih-low klor-OOR-us)

Towhee is imitative of the Eastern Towhee's two-note alarm call, rendered *tow-hee* or *chewink*. Green-tailed describes the olive-green tail. Actually the bird's entire upperparts, except for the rufous crown, are a yellowish olive-green.

Pipilo — The genus name is Latin for "to chirp" or "twitter" and refers to the call notes.

chlorurus — The specific epithet means "green tail" from the Greek *khloros* (yellow-green) and *oura* (the tail).

French Name: Tohi à Queu Verte
Spanish Names: Racador de Cola Verde; Rascador Coliverde
Other Names: Chestnut-crowned Towhee; Green-tailed Bunting; Blanding's Finch

Spotted Towhee
Pipilo maculatus
(PIP-ih-low mack-you-LAY-tus)

White spots on this towhee's back and wings give this bird its name. Previously considered conspecific with the Eastern Towhee as Rufous-sided Towhee.

Pipilo — The genus name is Latin for "to chirp" or "twitter" and refers to the call notes.

maculatus — The specific epithet is Latin for "spotted."

French Name: Tohi Tacheté
Spanish Name: Rascador Manchado
Other Names: Oregon Towhee; San Clemente Towhee; San Diego Towhee

Eastern Towhee
Pipilo erythrophthalmus
(PIP-ih-low er-ih-throf-THALL-mus)

"One of the worst name changes ever made by the AOU was changing the rufous-sided towhee to the eastern towhee. — Norma Siebenheller." *Bird Watcher's Digest* (2007)

Towhee is imitative of this species' two-note alarm call, rendered *tow-hee* or *chewink*, a nickname for this bird. Eastern refers to the range east of the Great Plains. This and the Spotted Towhee were formerly considered a single species, the Rufous-sided Towhee.

Eastern Towhee, by Louis Agassiz Fuertes

Pipilo — The genus name is Latin for "to chirp" or "twitter" and refers to the call notes.

erythropthalmus — The specific epithet means "red eye" from the Greek *erythros* (red) and *opthalmos* (the eye) and refers to this species' bright red eyes, although the Florida population has white eyes.

French Name: Tohi à Flancs Roux
Spanish Names: Rascador de Ojo Rojo; Rascador Ojirrojo
Other Names: Arctic Towhee; Florida Towhee; Red-eyed Towhee; White-eyed Towhee; Spurred Towhee; Mountain Towhee; Towhee Bird; Towhee Bunting; Ground Bunting; Arctic Ground Finch; Towhee Ground Finch; Ground Robin; Brush Robin; Bush Robin; Swamp Robin; Marsh Robin; Rood Robin; Bush-bird; Catbird; Chewink; Bullfinch; Turkey Sparrow; Low-ground Stephen; Joreetz; Joree or Joe-Ree; To-whitt To-whee

Family Spindalidae
Spindalises

Western Spindalis
Spindalis zena
(spin-DAY-lis ZEE-nah)

Formerly known as the Stripe-headed Tanager. In 1997, the AOU split this species into four allospecies, the Puerto Rico Spindalis (*S. portoricensis*), the Hispaniolan Spindalis (*S. dominicensis*), the Jamaican Spindalis (*S. nigricephala*), and the Western Spindalis (*S. zena*). The latter is a rare visitor to southern Florida, and there is a nesting record for Everglades National Park (1997). Western pertains to its range in the West Indies relative to the other three species. The Western Spindalis occurs in Cuba, the Cayman Islands, Turks and Caicos Islands, and as far west as Cozumel off the coast of the Yucatan Peninsula. Spindalis is also the genus name. See below.

Spindalis — The genus name means "firebrand siskin" from the Greek *spinos* (a siskin or a linnet) and *dalos* (a firebrand or shining brightness). The first part of the name refers to this bird's finch-like appearance particularly its conical bill, and the second part to the male's striking color pattern. An alternate explanation is that the name stems from the Greek *spindalos* (an unidentified bird of India). It could be akin to the Greek *attagis* or *attagas* (Black Francolin), an Asian bird in the pheasant family.

zena — The specific epithet is from the Greek *zene* (a type of finch possibly a goldfinch).

French Name: Zena a Tête Rayee
Spanish Names: Tangara de Cabeza Rayada; Tángara Cabecirrayada
Other Names: Orange Bird; Gold Bird; Goldfinch; Cashew Bird; Tom James' Bird; Spanish Quail; Markhead; Silver-head; Robin; Red Robin; Rooster Robin; Hen Robin; Bastard Cock; Cabrero; Moundele; Reina Mora; Sigua Amarilla

Family Icteriidae
Yellow-Breasted Chat

Yellow-breasted Chat
Icteria virens
(ick-TEER-ih-ah VER-enz)

The Yellow-breasted Chat was formerly classified in the Wood-Warbler family Parulidae. In 2017, the AOU merged it into its own family Icteriidae, not to be confused with Icteridae, the Blackbird family. It is possible that English colonists named the Yellow-breasted Chat after an unrelated European bird, the Stonechat (*Sexicola torquata*), because they heard a similarity in the two species' harsh calls. It is more likely that the American bird was named independently. Chat is from "chatterer," which Ernest Choate wrote, " . . . the bird surely is, with its unique and amazing conglomerations of whistles, squeaks, squeals, musical single notes and phrases, and harsh chattering in varied sequence and timing, poured out in unpremeditated artlessness." Here is another description of the Chat's song:

Yellow-breasted Chat, by Ernest T. Seton

"Repertoire includes mellow whistles, high squeaks, slurping gurgles, raspy admonitions, liquid burps, and a sprinkling of other bird calls (American Crow is a favorite); for example: "*cha-cha-cha-cha-cha* (pause) *whirt*! (pause) *Wok Wok Wok Wok* (pause) *Ur* (pause) *Ur* (pause) *Cah Cah Cah Cah Cah* (pause) *toot*! (pause) *chachacha*." Calls include low growl, "*chowl*"; a soft hollow "*tok*" (sometimes doubled) that sounds like a soft tapping on wood; and a loud, buzzy, descending "*bzeert*" — a contagious call to which other chats within earshot respond." — Pete Dunne (2006)

Yellow-breasted refers to the bright orange-yellow underparts.

Icteria — The genus name is from the Greek *ikteros* (jaundice), "yellow," and refers to the yellow throat and breast.

virens — The specific epithet is Latin for "greenish" and refers to the olive-green upperparts.

French Name: Paruline Polyglotte

Spanish Names: Chipe de Pecho Amarillo; Gritón Pechiamarillo; Reinita Grande

Other Names: Chat; Common Chat; Yellow Chat; Long-tailed Chat; Polyglot Chat; Yellow Mockingbird

Family Icteridae
Blackbirds and Allies

Yellow-headed Blackbird
Xanthocephalus xanthocephalus
(zan-thoh-SEFF-ah-lus)

"By far the most abundant birds in the slough were the Yellow-headed Blackbirds, the the characteristic bird of every North Dakota slough; they fairly swarmed everywhere, and the constant din of their voices became almost tiresome. The old males are strikingly handsome with their bright yellow heads and jet black plumage, offset by the pure white patches in their wings, the duller colors of the females and young males making a pleasing variety." — Arthur Cleveland Bent (1958)

Yellow-headed Blackbird, by Allan C. Brooks

"Apparently Nature started out with the intention of making an Oriole, but decided to make a Blackbird instead — and behold the Yellowhead." — Henry W. Henshaw

The common name describes the male's color pattern, a bright yellow head, throat, and breast that, as nature columnist Sheryl De Vore (1992) put it, "Looks as if they had been dipped in gold paint and sealed with a shiny finish . . . in striking contrast to a sooty black body and wings that appear to have been splashed with white paint."

Xanthocephalus — The genus/species name means "yellow head" from the Greek *xanthos* (yellow) and *kephale* (the head).

French Name: Carouge à Tête Jaune

Spanish Names: Tordo de Cabeza Amarilla; Tordo Cabeciamarillo; Tordo Cabecidorado

Other Names: Yellow-headed Troupial; Yellowhead; Copperhead; Yellowhammer; California Blackbird; Saffron-headed Marsh Blackbird

Sidebar 36
Describing the Bobolink's Unique Song

Although the Bobolink's name is onomatopoetic, its bubbling song is quite a challenge to describe, much less put into words. Various authors have tried over the years. Here are some of their wonderful descriptions of the Bobolink's song:

"This flashing, tinkling meteor bursts through the expectant meadow air, leaving a train of tinkling notes behind." — Henry David Thoreau

"Next after Bluebird, the coming of Bobolink marks the broadest step in that golden stair of springtime, by which we yearly attain the height of ornithological joy . . . Without waiting for their more modest mates, the males press northward, hot-winged, to riot for a while over the dank meadows in bachelor companies, and to perfect that marvel of tumultuous song. Oh how they sing! those Bacchanals of springtime. From fence-post or tree-top, or quivering in mid-air, they pour forth such an ecstasy of liquid gurgling notes as must thrill the very clods. Such exuberance of spirit, such reckless abandon of mirth-compelling joy would cure a sick preacher on blue Monday. As the bird sings he bows and scrapes and pirouettes till, as Wheaton says, "he resembles a French dancing master in uniform, singing, fiddling, dancing, and calling off at the same time."" — William Leon Dawson (1902)

"Robert is likely to become suddenly a sort of hysterical music-box, and to produce a burst of sound pyrotechnics which make one fear that the next second he is going to explode outright and vanish in a cloud of feathers." — George Gladden (1917)

"On a May morning, when buttercups spangle the fresh grasses in the meadows, this rollicking jolly fellow rises from their midst into the air with the merriest frolic of a song you ever heard. Loud, clear, strong, full of queer kinks and twists that could not be possibly written down in our musical scale, the rippling, reckless music seems to keep his wings in motion as well as his throat; for when it suddenly bursts forth, up he shoots into the air like a skylark, and paddles himself along with just the tips of his wings while it is the "mad music" that seemingly propels him — then he drops with his song into the grass again." — Neltje Blanchan (1917)

"It is one of the wildest of jingles, beginning in moderate waltz time, with four or five well-sustained notes, then rapidly increasing in energy and tempo, and finally breaking loose in a rollicking, 'tumble-down-dick' scattering of high-pitched tones which remind one of a music-box gone wild by reason of a broken escapement. He promises well in the beginning but goes all to pieces before he reaches the end of his tune." — F. Schuyler Mathews (1921)

"In June our fields and meadows echo with the Bobolink's 'mad music' as, on quivering wings, he sings in ecstasy to his mate on her nest in the grasses below. What a wonderful song it is! An impressible outburst; a flood of melody from a heart overflowing with the joy of early summer." — Frank Chapman (1923)

"The Bobolink is the harlequin of the spring meadows. He is a happy-go-lucky fellow, with his suit on the wrong side up, the black below and the white above; a reckless, rollicking, sort of a fowl, throwing care to the winds, and always bent on a lark. His spirits are of the effervescent kind, and his music bubbles irrepressibly forth at such a rate that half a dozen notes seem to be crowding upon the heels of every one uttered. Indeed, this is about the only bird that completely baffles the latter-day "interpreters" of bird music. His notes tumble out with such headlong rapidity, in an apparent effort to jump over each other, that it is next to impossible for the scribe to set them down in the proper sequence of musical notation. Nevertheless, this harum-scarum expression of irrepressible joy is of the most pleasing character, and ranks among the finest music of the fields." — Edward Howe Forbush (1925)

"On a morning in early May, in one of their favored haunts, a tinkle of fairy music, like the strains of an old Greek harp, seems to come from the sky and may be traced to a company of male bobolinks, circling on fluttering wings high above. While you watch, the tinkling notes descend earthward, and an exuberant male sinks to a swaying weed stalk; with tail spread, wings partly opened, and the feathers of his nape ruffled, he concludes his song with a few enchanting notes addressed to the mate he is wooing." — W. E. Clyde Todd (1940)

"No description of the song of the bobolink is adequate to convey to the reader who has not heard it any appreciation of its beauty and vivacity. It is unique among bird songs, the despair of the recorder or the imitator; even the famed mockingbird cannot reproduce it. It is a bubbling delirium of ecstatic music that flows from the gifted throat of the bird like sparkling champagne."
— Arthur Cleveland Bent (1953)

"The exuberant notes produced by the male seem otherworldly in quality and to my mind, resemble the silly sounds produced by R2-D2 in the *Star Wars* movies." — Lang Elliot (2006)

"Song of male is lively, bubbling, comical, and complex. Begins with a few pinging or metallic-sounding notes or two-note phrases that accelerate in tempo and volume into a binking, gurgling frenzy. One bird can sound like a whole pet shop full of caged birds in full chorus." — Pete Dunne (2006)

And William Leon Dawson was even so bold as to put the song into words, offering this mnemonic:

Oh, geezeler, geezeler, gilipity, onkeler. oozeler, oo.

George Gladden wrote of Dawson's mnemonic: "[It] really is a clever rendition in that it suggests clearly the essentially liquid and vowel character of the opening notes." If you say so.

Bobolink
Dolichonyx oryzivorus
(doll-ih-KOH-nicks aw-rih-ZIH-vor-us)

Merrily swinging on brier and weed,
Near to the nest of his little dame,
Over the mountain-side or mead,
Robert of Lincoln is telling his name,
Bob-o'-link, bob-o'-link,
Spink, spank, spink;

American poet William Cullen Bryant is credited in coining the name Bobolink, onomatopoetic for the bird's bubbling song, in his poem *Robert of Lincoln*, which describes the breeding cycle of the Bobolink. The poem's first stanza is printed above. Putting the song into words, or even describing it, is quite a challenge, although many ornithologists and nature writers have tried over the years. See *Describing the Bobolink's Unique Song*. George Gladden (1917) referred to the Bobolink "as the handsome and rollicking minstrel of the meadows."

Dolichonyx — The genus name means "long claw" from the Greek *dolichos* (long) and *onus* (a claw). The Bobolink has exceptionally long claws, especially the one on the hind toe, an adaptation to grasp wispy weed stalks and grass stems on which it typically perches.

oryzivorus — The specific epithet means "rice eater" from the Latin *oryza* (rice) and *voro* (to devour). The reference is to the Bobolink's fondness for rice to the extent that it was once

Bobolink, by Louis Agassiz Fuertes

a problem for farmers, as described here:

"When rice was a major crop in the Carolinas in the 19th and early 20th centuries migrating Bobolinks were a serious pest to the sprouting seeds in spring and to the maturing grain in fall. They were killed by the thousands to protect the crops, and marketed as "reed birds" or "rice birds." The fall migrants are very fat, and they were brought to market skewered a dozen to a stick." — Oliver Austin, Jr. (1961)

George Gladden (1917) wrote, "Once upon a time somebody called the Bobolink the 'Dr. Jekyll and Mr. Hyde of the bird-world.' The Jekyll comparison doubtless originated with the Southern planters, who hated the bird for the damage it did to their rice fields." Actually, the Bobolink was Mr. Hyde in the South and Dr. Jekyll in the North. The northerners appreciated it for its bright breeding plumage, its rollicking song, and the fact that it ate many insect pests. The migrating birds that descended on the southern rice fields in the fall looked totally different in their dull, sparrow-like winter plumage.

French Name: Goglu
Spanish Name: Tordo Arrocero
Other Names: American Bobolink; Boblink; Bob; Bob-Lincoln; Robert, Towhee; Roberti Towhee; Skunkbird; Skunk Blackbird; Skunk-head Blackbird; White-winged Blackbird; Reed Bird; Rice Bird; Sharp-tailed Rice-bird; Wandering Ricebird; Rice Bunting; Butter-bird; May-bird; October Bird; Pink; October Pink; Chatter Bird; Meadow-bird; Meadow-wink; Ortolan; American Ortolan; Reedfogel; Chambergo

Eastern Meadowlark
Sturnella magna
(stir-NELL-ah MAG-nah)

"The meadowlark is the outstanding and the most characteristic bird of the American farm. It is revered by the farmer not only because of its charming simplicity and its cheerful, spirited song, but also for its usefulness as a destroyer of harmful insects and the seeds of obnoxious weeds. The coming of the meadowlark in the early spring, while the fields are still brown, is a thrilling event. His arrival is made known by his plaintive but not complaining or melancholy song as he stands mounted atop some tall tree in a grassy meadow, with his bright yellow breast surmounted by a black crescent gleaming in the morning sun." — Alfred O. Gross (1958)

Meadowlarks are not larks at all, but blackbirds. But they were given the name, because of their musical song and the fact they sometimes sing in flight. They reminded English colonists of the Sky Larks back home. Meadow describes these birds' habitat of open grasslands including pastures, prairies, and hayfields. Eastern refers to this species' range from the Great Plains east to the Atlantic coast.

Sturnella — The genus name means "little starling" from the Latin *sturnus* (a starling) plus the diminutive suffix *–ella* (little). While not a starling, the profile of a meadowlark remarkably resembles that of the European Starling.

magna — The specific epithet is Latin for "large," so the entire scientific name translates to "big little starling." This meadowlark is large in comparison with other *Sturnella* species.

French Name: Sturnelle des Prés

Spanish Names: Pradero Tortilla con Chile; Pradero Común; Zacatero Común

Other Names: Common Meadowlark; Southern Meadowlark; Rio Grande Meadowlark; Texas Meadowlark; Arizona Meadowlark; Florida Meadowlark; Common Lark; Field Lark; Old Field Lark; Marsh Lark; Swamp Lark; Sedge Lark; Mudlark; Medlark; Medlar; Meadow Starling; Alouette de Prairie; Grive; Larrich; Ortolan; Riabhag; Uiseag; Sabanero; Marsh Quail; Crescent Stare

Western Meadowlark
Sturnella neglecta
(stir-NELL-ah nee-GLECK-tah)

"I shall never forget the day I first heard the glorious song of the western meadowlark; the impression of it is still clear in my mind, though it was May 30, 1901! It was my first day in North Dakota, and we were driving from Lakota to Stump Lake when we heard the song. I could hardly believe it was a meadowlark singing, so different were the notes from those we were accustomed to in the east, until I saw the plump bird perched on a telegraph pole, facing the sun, his yellow breast and black cravat gleaming in the clear prairie sunlight. His clear voice fairly thrilled us and seemed to combine the flutelike quality of the wood thrush with the rich melody of the Baltimore oriole. I have heard it many times since but have never ceased to marvel at it. It seems to be the very spirit of the boundless prairie." — Arthur Cleveland Bent (1958)

The Western Meadowlark is named for its range from the Great Plains west to the Pacific coast. Meadowlark refers to its musical song sometimes given in flight like the Sky Lark.

Sturnella — The genus name means "little starling" from the Latin *sturnus* (a starling) plus the diminutive suffix *–ella* (little). While not a starling, the profile of a meadowlark remarkably resembles that of the European Starling.

neglecta — In 1844, Audubon gave this bird its specific epithet, which is Latin for "neglected," because it was nearly 100 years before ornithologists recognized that it was a separate species from the Eastern Meadowlark, which was described in 1758. Audubon wrote, "Although the existence of this species was known to the celebrated explorers of the west, Lewis and Clark, during their memorable journey across the Rocky Mountains and to the Pacific; no one has since taken the least notice of it."

French Name: Sturnelle de l'Ouest

Spanish Name: Pradero Occidental

Other Names: Common Meadowlark; Missouri Meadowlark; Lark of the West; Field Lark of the West; Prairie Lark; King Syble-a-bon; Pradero Gorjeador

Western Meadowlark, by Louis Agassiz Fuertes

> **Sidebar 37**
> **Genus Icterus**
> **Orioles**
>
> European colonists named the American orioles after the unrelated Golden Oriole (*Oriolus oriolus*) of the Old World. All of these sport a striking color pattern of yellow and black or orange and black. Oriole stems from the Latin *aureolus*, a diminutive of *aureus* (gold) and refers to the bright yellow or orange plumage.

Orchard Oriole
Icterus spurious
(ICK-ter-us SPYOOR-ih-us)

"As its name implies, the orchard oriole shows a decided preference for orchards in rural districts near human dwellings, where apples, pears, or peaches are cultivated; and when these colorful trees are in bloom in spring, we are likely to find these orioles gleaning among the opening foliage or preparing to build their basket nests." — Arthur Cleveland Bent (1958)

This oriole is named for the fact that it frequently nests in orchards, favoring open areas with scattered trees.

Icterus — The genus name is from the Greek *ikteros* (jaundice) and a name given to a small yellowish bird, possibly the Golden Oriole (*Oriolus oriolus*) of Europe. The ancients believed the sight of this yellow bird would cure jaundice, at which the poor bird died.

spurious — This oriole's unfortunate specific epithet is Latin for "illegitimate" and stems from Mark Catesby's original name for this bird, Bastard Baltimore. The name suggests an inferior relationship, or perhaps he believed the bird was a hybrid. Alexander Wilson pointed out that Catesby had misidentified a female Baltimore Oriole for the male of this species.

French Name: Oriole des Vergers
Spanish Name: Bolsero Castaño
Other Names: Brown Oriole; Orchard Starling; Orchard Hang-nest; Basket-bird; Bastard Baltimore; Fig-eater; Swinger; Sanguillah

Hooded Oriole
Icterus cucullatus
(ICK-ter-us cue-cue-LAY-tus)

This oriole is named for its orange crown and nape, forming a hood that contrasts with its black face and throat.

Icterus — The genus name is from the Greek *ikteros* (jaundice) and a name given to a small yellowish bird, possibly the Golden Oriole (*Oriolus oriolus*) of Europe.

cucullatus — The specific epithet means "hooded" from the Latin *cucullus* (a hood or cowl).

French Name: Oriole Masqué
Spanish Names: Bolsero Enmascarado; Bolsero Cuculado
Other Names: Arizona Hooded Oriole; Palm-leaf Oriole; Nelson's Oriole; Sennett's Oriole

Streak-backed Oriole
Icterus pustulatus
(ICK-ter-us pus-tue-LAY-tus)

Broken black streaks on this bird's back give it its name. Formerly called "Scarlet-headed Oriole."

Hooded Oriole, by Allan C. Brooks

Icterus — The genus name is from the Greek *ikteros* (jaundice) and a name given to a small yellowish bird, possibly the Golden Oriole (*Oriolus oriolus*) of Europe.
pustulatus — The specific epithet is Latin for "blistered" and refers to the rows of black spots that form the streaks on the back.
French Name: Oriole à Dos Rayé
Spanish Names: Bolsero de Dorso Rayado; Bolsero Dorsirrayado; Bolsero Dorsilistado
Other Names: Western Streak-backed Oriole; Flame-headed Oriole

Bullock's Oriole
Icterus bullockii
(ICK-ter-us bull-OCK-ih-eye)

This oriole is named for William Bullock. See specific epithet below. Formerly considered conspecific with the Baltimore Oriole under the name Northern Oriole. See Baltimore Oriole for more details.
Icterus — The genus name is from the Greek *ikteros* (jaundice) and a name given to a small yellowish bird, possibly the Golden Oriole (*Oriolus oriolus*) of Europe.
bullockii — In 1827, William Swainson named this species in honor of William Bullock (1775–1840), a British antiquarian, naturalist, and showman. Swainson wrote, "This, the most beautiful of the group yet discovered in Mexico, will record the name of those ornithologists [William Bullock and his son] who have thrown so much light on the birds of that country." Bullock had collected the type specimen near Mexico City.
French Name: Oriole de Bullock
Spanish Names: Bolsero de Bullock; Bolsero Colipinto
Other Name: Bullock's Troupial

Spot-breasted Oriole
Icterus pectoralis
(ICK-ter-us peck-tor-AL-iss)

Heavy black spotting on the upper breast gives this oriole its name.
Icterus — The genus name is from the Greek *ikteros* (jaundice) and a name given to a small yellowish bird, possibly the Golden Oriole (*Oriolus oriolus*) of Europe.
pectoralis — The specific epithet is Latin for "pertaining to the breast" and refers to the black spots on the sides of the breast.
French Name: Oriole Maculé
Spanish Names: Bolsero de Pecho Manchado; Bolsero Pechimanchado

Altamira Oriole
Icterus gularis
(ICK-ter-us gew-LAIR-us)

Formerly known as "Lichtenstein's Oriole" for A. A. H. Lichtenstein (1753–1816), a German theologian and natural historian.
Icterus — The genus name is from the Greek *ikteros* (jaundice) and a name given to a small yellowish bird, possibly the Golden Oriole (*Oriolus oriolus*) of Europe.
gularis — The specific epithet means "of the throat" from the Modern Latin *gula* (the throat) and refers to this species' black throat patch.
French Name: Oriole à Gros Bec
Spanish Name: Bolsero de Altamira
Other Name: Black-throated Oriole

Audubon's Oriole
Icterus graduacauda
(ICK-ter-us grad-you-ah-COD-ah)

This striking black and yellow Mexican species is named for John James Audubon (1785–1851), the Artistic Father of American Ornithology. Formerly known as Black-headed Oriole.
Icterus — The genus name is from the Greek *ikteros* (jaundice) and a name given to a small yellowish bird, possibly the Golden Oriole (*Oriolus oriolus*) of Europe.
graduacauda — The specific epithet means "graduated tail" from the Latin *gradus* (a step) and *cauda* (the tail). This characteristic is not obvious in the field.
French Name: Oriole d'Audubon
Spanish Names: Bolsero de Cabeza Negra; Bolsero de Audubon

Baltimore Oriole
Icterus galbula
(ICK-ter-us GAL-bew-lah)

"The brilliancy of the Oriole's feathers has given him two significant names, Golden Robin and Firebird, also the pendent character of his nest has added

> **Sidebar 38**
> **Baltimore Oriole + Bullock's Oriole = Northern Oriole?**
>
> In the late 1960s, scientists noted that Baltimore Orioles and Bullock's Orioles interbred where their ranges overlapped on the Great Plains. What's more, the offspring were fertile. The scientists hypothesized that over time the two orioles would blend into just one type. The Baltimore and Bullock's Orioles must only be varieties of a single species. Here is more on the story:
>
> "And so in 1973, ornithologists officially lumped the two birds into a single species, the northern oriole. Angry objections followed. Baltimore's city fathers felt bereft and betrayed, an American League baseball team found itself named for a bird that did not exist, and birders were forced to scratch two popular species off their life lists. Too bad. Science had decreed that the birds were a single species. The Baltimore and Bullock's orioles would be no more, and that was that." — "The Baltimore Oriole Is Back" from *National Wildlife*, February/March, 1994 issue, Copyright © 1994 *National Wildlife Magazine*. Reproduced with permission of the National Wildlife Federation.
>
> But wait. There's more! Scientists revisiting the zone of hybridization in the 1990s, found there was no blending of the two types. There were still hybrids, but there were pure Baltimore and Bullock's Oriole types, too. Apparently hybridization was not as extensive as previously thought. Additional data support the view that the Baltimore and Bullock's Orioles are indeed separate species. One is time of molt. The Baltimore Oriole typically molts in summer after nesting, but before migration. Bullock's Orioles molt during migration and on their wintering grounds. Studies of mitochondrial DNA show that the Baltimore and Bullock's Orioles are not even each others closest relatives. The Baltimore Oriole is more closely related to the Altimira Oriole and Black-backed Oriole, while Bullock's shows more affinity to the Streak-backed Oriole. Based on this new evidence, the AOU split the Northern Oriole back into the Baltimore Oriole and Bullock's Oriole in 1994.

another, Hangnest. But the name Baltimore Oriole has prevailed above the others, and it is to be hoped will eventually displace them, for the bird is no relation whatever to either the American or English Robin, and in appearance it does not suggest a fire nor a nest. It does, however, deserve the historic name of the first Lord Baltimore, as his Lordship's arms were blazoned orange and black, and the bird's colors are the same." — F. Schuyler Mathews (1904)

"A flash of fire through the air; a rich, high whistled song floating in the wake of the feathered meteor: the Baltimore oriole cannot be mistaken. When the orchards are in blossom he arrives in full plumage and song, and awaits the coming of the female birds, that travel northward more leisurely in flocks . . . There is a popular tradition about the naming of this gorgeous bird: When George Calvert, the first Lord Baltimore, worn out and discouraged by various hardships in his Newfoundland colony, decided to visit Virginia in 1628, he wrote that nothing in the Chesapeake country so impressed him as the myriads of birds in its woods. But the song and color of the oriole particularly cheered and delighted him, and orange and black became the heraldic colors of the first lords proprietors of Maryland." — Neltje Blanchan (1917)

The 18th century English naturalist Mark Catesby named this the Baltimore-bird for Sir George Calvert, 1st Baron of Baltimore and an

Pea-bird; Bolsero Colipinto; Calandria del Norte; Guldt Omshel; Loriot

Scott's Oriole
Icterus parisorum
(ICK-ter-us par-eye-SOAR-um)

The common name commemorates General Winfield Scott (1786–1866), who commanded the United States forces in the Mexican-American war. While collecting in northern Mexico in 1853, Lieutenant Darius Nash Couch found this striking black and yellow oriole to be common in the states of Coahuila and Nuevo León. Thinking it was a new species, he named it *Icterus Scottii* in the *Proceedings of the Academy of Natural Sciences of Philadelphia* (1854) with the dedication: "I have named this handsome bird as a slight token of my high regard for Major General Winfield Scott, Commander in Chief of the U.S. Army." However, Charles Bonaparte had already described this species seventeen years earlier, giving it the scientific name *Icterus Parisorum*, so Couch's name was invalid. However, General Scott is still honored in the common name.

Icterus — The genus name is from the Greek *ikteros* (jaundice) and a name given to a small yellowish bird, possibly the Golden Oriole (*Oriolus oriolus*) of Europe.

Baltimore Oriole and Blue Jay, by Louis Agassiz Fuertes

early colonizer of Maryland. The oriole's brilliant cadmium orange and jet black colors match those of the Baron's coat of arms, as mentioned in the opening passages. The Baltimore Oriole is, of course, the State Bird of Maryland. In 1973, the AOU lumped the Baltimore and Bullock's Orioles together as the Northern Oriole. See sidebar 38.

Icterus — The genus name is from the Greek *ikteros* (jaundice) and a name given to a small yellowish bird, possibly the Golden Oriole (*Oriolus oriolus*) of Europe.

galbula — The specific epithet is Latin, referring to a "small yellow bird" identified by some authors as the Golden Oriole (*Oriolus oriolus*) of the Old World.

French Name: Oriole de Baltimore
Spanish Names: Bolsero de Baltimore; Bolsero Norteño
Other Names: Golden Oriole; Baltimore-bird; Golden Robin; English Robin; Golden Bird; Orange Bird; Firebird; Fire Hang-bird; Hang-bird; Hammock-bird; Hang-nest;

Scott's Oriole, by Allan C. Brooks

parisorum — In 1838, Charles Bonaparte named this oriole in honor of the Paris brothers (fl. 1837), natural history dealers who collected specimens in Mexico. Bonaparte's dedication read, "I have much pleasure in naming this bird after the brothers Paris, who not withstanding the arduous nature of their professional engagements in Mexico, allowed no opportunity of furthering the interests of science to pass unimproved."
French Name: Oriole Jaune-verdâtre
Spanish Name: Bolsero Tunero
Other Names: Common Troupial; Bolsero Parisino

Red-winged Blackbird
Agelaius phoeniceus
(ah-jeh-LAY-us fee-NIH-seh-us)

"Vital to behavioral interactions of the red-winged blackbird is its most distinctive feature, the red epaulets (lesser wing coverts) of the male. Males fully expose and display them during their so-called "song-spread," in which the perched bird leans forward, partially spreads his wings, flaunting the red shoulder patches, spreads his tail, and utters his liquid "konk-kee-ree" song. Song-spread is mainly a threat and advertising action aimed at other males and at arriving females. Aggressiveness in redwings, the ability to establish and hold a territory or successfully challenge a territory holder, is also a function of badge display and apparently is proportional to epaulet size and conspicuousness — the bigger and gaudier the epaulets, the more belligerent and successful the bird. Yet actual combat and fighting are rare; most boundary disputes are settled by threat displays alone." — John Eastman (1999)

The red epaulets, or shoulder patches edged in yellow, give this blackbird its name. These are used in territorial and courtship display as described above. A population in central California sport epaulettes that lack the yellow border. These are sometimes called Bicolored Red-wings.

Agelaius — The genus name is from the Greek *ageleios* meaning "of or belonging to a flock." When not breeding, these blackbirds travel in

Red-winged Blackbird, by Louis Agassiz Fuertes

huge flocks that can contain thousands of birds. Sometimes the flocks are mixed, with several species of blackbirds (including grackles and cowbirds) present.

phoeniceus — The specific epithet is Latin for "deep red" or "purple-red" from the Greek *phoinikos* (Phoenicians), the Mediterranean people who traded in an expensive crimson dye they produced from marine mollusks. The reference is to the red epaulets.
French Name: Carouge à Épaulettes
Spanish Name: Tordo Sargento
Other Names: Redwing; Red-shouldered Blackbird; Marsh Blackbird; Swamp Blackbird; Thick-bill Red-wing; Northwestern Red-wing; San Diego Red-wing; Red-winged Starling; Red-shouldered Starling; Red-winged Oriole; Red-winged Grackle; Harper; Caporal; Rice Bird; Field Officer; Field Officer Bird; Soldier Bird; Soldier Blackbird; Chirriador; Rtourneau; Geai à Aile Rouge; Mayito de la

Ciénaga; Totí de la Ciénaga; Rodfleeg'lter Shdawr; Tordo Sargento

Tricolored Blackbird
Agelaius tricolor
(ah-jeh-LAY-us TRY-kul-er)

This blackbird is named for the three colors present in its plumage. It is black overall with red epaulets that are bordered with white.

Agelaius — The genus name is from the Greek *ageleios* meaning "of or belonging to a flock." When not breeding, these blackbirds travel in huge flocks that can contain thousands of birds. Sometimes the flocks are mixed, with several species of blackbirds (including grackles and cowbirds) present.

tricolor — The specific epithet is Latin for "three-colored."

French Name: Carouge de Californie
Spanish Name: Tordo Tricolor
Other Names: Tricolored Redwing; Tricolored Oriole; Red & white-shouldered Marsh Blackbird

Shiny Cowbird
Molothrus bonariensis
(moll-OTH-rus bon-ar-ih-EN-siss)

Cowbirds are named for their association with cattle. The shiny purple gloss of the male's plumage gives this cowbird its name.

Molothrus — The genus name is a misspelling of the Greek *molobros* (a parasite or a greedy person). The reference is to the fact that cowbirds are brood parasites that lay their eggs in the nests of other species of birds. The foster parents then raise the young cowbird, often to the detriment of their own young, particularly if they are of a smaller species than the cowbird.

bonariensis — The specific epithet is Modern Latin for "of Buenos Aires." This species has a wide range throughout South America.

French Name: Vacher Luisant
Spanish Names: Vaquero Brillante; Vaquero Brilloso

Bronzed Cowbird
Molothrus aeneus
(moll-OTH-rus EE-nee-us)

The green-bronze metallic sheen on the male's head, back, and underparts gives this cowbird its name.

Molothrus — The genus name is a misspelling of the Greek *molobros* (a parasite or greedy person). The reference is to the fact that cowbirds are brood parasites that lay their eggs in the nests of other species of birds. The foster parents then raise the young cowbird, often to the detriment of their own young, particularly if they are of a smaller species than the cowbird.

aeneus — The specific epithet is Latin for "of a bronze color."

French Name: Vacher Bronzé
Spanish Names: Vaquero de Ojo Rojo; Vaquero Ojirrojo
Other Names: Glossy Cowbird; Red-eyed Cowbird; Red-eye

Brown-headed Cowbird
Molothrus ater
(moll-OTH-rus AY-ter)

Naturalist Mark Catesby called this species the "cow-pen bird," because "They delight much to feed in the pens of cattle, which have given them their name." The name was later shortened to cowbird. In pre-Columbian times, Brown-headed Cowbirds followed bison herds on the Great Plains, feeding on the insects flushed by the bison.

Brown-headed refers to the male's coffee-brown head that contrasts with his otherwise glossy black plumage.

Molothrus — The genus name is a misspelling of the Greek *molobros* (a parasite or greedy person). The reference is to the fact that cowbirds are brood parasites that lay their eggs in the nests of other species of birds. The foster parents then raise the young cowbird, often to the detriment of their own young, particularly if they are of a smaller species than the cowbird. Some species have evolved defenses. Robins and catbirds will remove the foreign egg from their nest, and Yellow Warblers will build a new nest on top of the old one, burying the cowbird egg along with its own.

ater — The specific epithet is Latin for "flat black," but in the case of this cowbird the plumage is glossy.

French Name: Vacher à Tête Brune

Spanish Names: Vaquero de Cabeza Café; Vaquero Cabecicafé
Other Names: Common Cowbird; Eastern Cowbird; Dwarf Cowbird; Grey Cowbird; Nevada Cowbird; Brown-headed Oriole; Brown-headed Blackbird; Little Blackbird; Cow Blackbird; Cow Bunting; Black Robin; Black Sparrow; Cow-pen Bird; Buffalo Bird; Herd Bird; Lazy Bird; Cuckold; Etourneau; Geai; Kee Shdawr; Tordo Cabecicafe; Vacher

Rusty Blackbird
Euphagus carolinus
(YOU-fah-gus car-oh-LIN-us)

Rusty refers to the rusty appearance of the birds in fresh fall plumage due to the brown-edged feathers. By coincidence their calls have been compared to the squeaky sound of a rusty gate.

Euphagus — The genus name means "good to eat" from the Greek *eu* (good) and *phago* (to eat.). In the 19th century many songbirds were shot and sent to market in large eastern cities.

carolinus — The specific epithet is Modern Latin for "of Carolina," where the type specimen was taken, far from the breeding grounds across Canada and Alaska.

French Name: Quiscale Rouilleux
Spanish Names: Tordo Rojizo; Tordo Canadiense
Eskimo and Inuit Names: Tikchugpak (big longspur); Talungiksyaurak (little raven); Kath-ka-ga-yuk
Other Names: Cattle Blackbird; Little Blackbird; Marsh Blackbird; Swamp Blackbird; Thrush Blackbird; Rusty Oriole; Rusty Grackle; Crow; Rusty Crow; Rusty Crow Blackbird; Black Robin; Cowbird; Etourneau

Brewer's Blackbird
Euphagus cyanocephalus
(YOU-fah-gus sigh-an-oh-SEFF-ah-lus)

On the 20th of June, 1843, at Fort Union, North Dakota, John Bell and Edward Harris went out to collect specimens, in particular Sprague's Pipits, which they had discovered the day before. They returned with several small birds including one similar to the Rusty Blackbird, but obviously a different species. In the octavo edition of his *Birds of America* (1844),

---

Sidebar 39
The Importance of Scientific Names

Melanie (on phone): "Crows I think. Well, I don't know, Daddy. Is there a difference between crows and blackbirds?"
Mrs: Bundy: "There is very definitely a difference, Miss."
Melanie: "Thank you. They're different, Daddy . . ."
Mrs. Bundy: "They're both perching birds, of course, but quite different species. The crow is *Corvus brachyrhynchos* and the blackbird is *Euphagus cyanocephalus*."
Melanie: "Thank you."

The above dialog is from Alfred Hitchcock's famous movie *The Birds*.

Melanie, at the Tides Restaurant, is speaking on the phone to her father, the editor of a San Francisco newspaper. She is telling him about an attack by birds on the children at the Bodega Bay School, but she doesn't know whether they were crows or blackbirds.

Mrs. Bundy, the local amateur ornithologist, enters the restaurant to buy a pack of cigarettes and overhears the conversation. She chimes in and informs them that there is a difference and states the scientific name of each. Although there are several species of both crows and blackbirds, we now know from the scientific names stated by Mrs. Bundy that the species in question are the American Crow and Brewer's Blackbird.

Audubon named the new species *Quiscalus breweri* for his Bostonian friend Dr. Thomas Mayo Brewer. Only it wasn't a new species. German naturalist Johannes Wagler had already described it in 1829, from a specimen that had been collected in Mexico. He named it *Psarocolius cyanocephalus*, so his specific epithet has priority, but the bird retains the common name Audubon had given it.

Euphagus — The genus name means "good to eat" from the Greek *eu* (good) and *phago* (to eat). In the 19th century many songbirds were shot and sent to market in large eastern cities.

cyanocephalus — The specific epithet means "blue head" from the Greek *kyanos* (dark blue) and *kephale* (the head), referring to the purplish gloss on the male's head.

French Name: Quiscale de Brewer
Spanish Name: Tordo de Brewer
Other Names: Glossy Blackbird; Satin Bird; Starling; Tordo Ojiclaro

Common Grackle
Quiscalus quiscula
(KWIS-kah-lus KWIS-cue-lah)

Grackle is from the Modern Latin *gracula* (a jackdaw). The Jackdaw (*Corvus monendula*) is an Old World crow, not closely related to grackles. *Gracula* was the former genus name, and was applied to black birds as diverse as jackdaws and cormorants. It is now the genus to which the familiar talking Indian Hill Mynah (*Gracula religiosa*) belongs. So the significance is apparently to the grackle's black plumage. The Common Grackle has the widest range of the three North American species.

Quiscalus — There are three explanations for the etymology of the genus name. The first is that it is Modern Latin for "a quail." Janet Lembke wrote, "How peculiar! What connection can possibly exist between a plump, hen-like creature and a lean, mean blackbird?" The second idea is that the Latin roots *quis* (what) and *qualis* (of what kind). Linnaeus had conflicting reports from various naturalists working in North America. Catesby called the grackle a jackdaw. Another naturalist called it a bee-eater. Linnaeus wasn't sure if this was a crow, a starling, or a blackbird, hence the odd scientific name. Newton believed it to stem from the Spanish *quisquilla* (a trifling dispute), referring to the birds' loud, noisy calls.

quiscula — The specific epithet is a variant spelling of the genus name.

French Name: Quiscale Bronzé
Spanish Names: Zanate Norteño; Tordo Común
Other Names: Bronzed grackle; Purple Grackle; Keel-tailed Grackle; Florida Grackle; Blackbird; Big Blackbird; Fan-tailed Blackbird; China-eyed Blackbird; Rudder-tail; Rudder-tail Blackbird; Crow Blackbird; Purple Crow Blackbird; Crow Grackle; Small Crow Bird; Purple Jackdaw; White-eyed Jackdaw; New England Jackdaw; Starling; Swamp Robin; Maize Thief; Etourneau; Eun Dubh; Geai; Merle Noir; Oiseau Bleu; Shdawr; Shwortsa Fogel

Boat-tailed Grackle
Quiscalus major
(KWIS-kah-lus MAY-jer)

This grackle's long tail, creased down the middle, reminds one of the keel of a boat.

Quiscalus — There are three explanations for the etymology of the genus name. The first is that it is Modern Latin for "a quail." Janet Lembke wrote, "How peculiar! What connection can possibly exist between a plump, hen-like creature and a lean, mean blackbird?" The second idea is that the Latin roots *quis* (what) and *qualis* (of what kind). Linnaeus had conflicting reports from various naturalists working in North America. Catesby called the grackle a jackdaw. Another naturalist called it a bee-eater. Linnaeus wasn't sure if this was a crow, a starling, or a blackbird, hence the odd scientific name. Newton believed it to stem from the Spanish *quisquilla* (a trifling dispute), referring to the birds' loud, noisy calls.

major — The specific epithet is from the Latin *maior* (greater), a comparative of *magnus* (great). The Boat-tailed Grackle is larger than the Common Grackle.

French Name: Quiscale des Marais
Spanish Names: Zanate Mayor; Tordo del Costa
Other Names: Crow Blackbird; Saltwater Blackbird; Mexican Blackbird; Jackdaw; Daw

Great-tailed Grackle
Quiscalus mexicanus
(KWIS-kah-lus meks-ih-CANE-us)

The male's exceptionally long tail gives this grackle its name.

Quiscalus — There are three explanations for the etymology of the genus name. The first is that it is Modern Latin for "a quail." Janet Lembke wrote, "How peculiar! What connection can possibly exist between a plump, hen-like creature and a lean, mean blackbird?" The second idea is that the Latin roots *quis* (what) and *qualis* (of what kind). Linnaeus had conflicting reports from various naturalists working in North America. Catesby called the grackle a jackdaw. Another naturalist called it a bee-eater. Linnaeus wasn't sure if this was a crow, a starling, or a blackbird, hence the odd scientific name. Newton believed it to stem from the Spanish *quisquilla* (a trifling dispute), referring to the birds' loud, noisy calls.

mexicanus — The specific epithet is Modern Latin for "of Mexico" where this species occurs.

French Name: Grand Quiscale
Spanish Name: Zanate Mexicano
Other Names: Mexican Blackbird; Crow Blackbird; Zanate Mayor; Zanate Mexicano; Clarinero Grande

Family Parulidae
Wood-Warblers

"With a few exceptions . . . the warblers are not outstanding singers. Their voices are weak, high, and insect-like, often with hissing, buzzing, or lisping qualities. Yet the warblers are persistent singers in spring, and each species has a distinctive song of its own." — Oliver L. Austin, Jr. (1961)

The definition of warble is "to sing in trills, quavers, runs, or other melodic embellishments." However, as described above, relatively few members of the Wood-Warbler family can be said to be gifted singers. The Wood-Warblers got their name, because pioneer ornithologists like Alexander Wilson incorrectly placed them in the family Sylviidae, the Old World Warblers. Wood describes the breeding habitat in various woodlands of most species and distinguishes the American family from the Old World Warblers. Roger Tory Peterson called the colorful Wood-Warblers "the butterflies of the bird world."

Ovenbird
Seiurus aurocapilla
(sigh-YOU-rus aw-row-kah-PILL-ah)

This ground-nesting warbler is named for the appearance of its nest, domed with a side-entrance, like a tiny, old-fashioned Dutch oven. Here is a good example of why scientific names are important. There is an unrelated family (Furnariidae) of South American birds called ovenbirds. They were also named for their clay nests that look even more like Dutch ovens.

Seiurus — The genus name means "wagtail" from the Greek *seio* (to shake or wag to and fro) and *oura* (the tail) for the way the Ovenbird cocks its tail up and slowly lowers it as it walks on the forest floor.

aurocapilla — The specific epithet means "gold crown" from the Greek *aurum* (gold) and *capillus* (the hair or crown) and refers to the orange patch on top of the head.

French Name: Paruline Couronnée
Spanish Names: Chipe-suelero Coronado; Reinita Hornera
Other Names: Teacher; Teacher-bird; Wagtail, Wood Wagtail; Golden-crowned Wagtail; Thrush; Golden-crowned Thrush; Golden-crowned Accentor; Ground Bird; Wood bird; Night-walker

Ovenbird, by Louis Agassiz Fuertes

Worm-eating Warbler
Helmitheros vermivorum
(hel-mih-THEE-roze ver-MIH-vor-um)

"Hillside warbler would not have been a bad name for this bird, which shows a decided preference for wooded hillsides covered with medium-sized deciduous tree and an undergrowth of saplings and small shrubbery. Often a running stream with numerous swampy places, overgrown with brier tangles and alders, bounds the base of the hill as an additional attraction."
— Arthur Cleveland Bent (1953)

Frankin Lorenzo Burns (1905) suggested another appropriate name, Laurel Warbler, because in the Appalachians this species favors thickets of mountain laurel. No, the Worm-eating Warbler doesn't hop on lawns, searching for earthworms as a robin does. The worms in this case are moth larvae, caterpillars (some of which go by names like armyworm, cankerworm, cutworm, spanworm, etc.) which are important in the diets of many woodland birds, particularly ones feeding young. Actually this species eats many different kinds of insects, grasshoppers, walkingsticks, weevils, beetles, sawfly larvae, also spiders, not just caterpillars.

Helmitheros — The genus name means "worm hunter" from Greek *helminthos* (a worm) and *theran* (to hunt). See common name above.

vermovorum — The specific epithet means "worm-eating" from the Latin *vermis* (a worm) and *voro* (to eat).

French Name: Paruline Vermovore

Spanish Names: Chipe Gusanero; Reinita Gusenera

Other Names: Worm-eater; Worm-eating Swamp Warbler

Louisiana Waterthrush
Parkesia motacilla
(PARKS-ih-ah moh-tah-SILL-ah)

"Only the most picturesque and unfrequented glens are tenanted by this poet-bird from the South. Where cool waters trickle down from mossy ledges and pause in shallow pools to mirror the foliage of many trees, here, and here alone, you will find the Water Thrush at home."
— William Leon Dawson (1902)

The waterthrushes are Wood-Warblers disguised as tiny thrushes with their brown upperparts and spotted breasts. Both choose nesting sites along waterside habitats. Waterthrushes also feed along the water's edge, taking aquatic insects, snails, crustaceans, and even minnows and small amphibians. The Louisiana Waterthrush prefers to nest near running water, such as wooded streams and brooks as described above. Louisiana implies a more southern range compared to the Northern Waterthrush, which nests in Canada and the northeastern states. The Louisiana nests in most of the eastern states, and its range just overlaps the southern edge of the Northern Waterthrush's. Louisiana may be the state where early ornithologists first saw this species.

Parkesia — The genus name honors Kenneth C. Parkes (1922–2007), a former Curator of Birds at Carnegie Museum of Natural History. The waterthrushes were formerly assigned to the genus *Seiurus* with the Ovenbird. Dr. Parkes had long argued that the waterthrushes should be placed in their own genus apart from the Ovenbird, despite their similarities. Formerly *Seiurus motacilla*.

motacilla — The specific epithet means "wagtail" from the Latin *motus* (moving) and *cilla*, a word taken to mean "tail" but actually a diminutive Latin suffix. (See White Wagtail for more details). The reference is to the waterthrush's habit of constantly bobbing the tail like a miniature Spotted Sandpiper.

French Name: Paruline Hochequeue

Spanish Names: Chipe Arroyero; Chipe-suelero Arroyero; Reinita Acuatica Piquigrande

Other Names: Southern Waterthrush; Large-billed Waterthrush; Wagtail; Water Wagtail; Wagtail Warbler; Pizpita de Rio

Northern Waterthrush
Parkesia noveboracensis
(PARKS-ih-ah no-veh-bore-ah-SEN-sis)

The Northern Waterthrush is usually associated with still-water habitats like wooded swamps, bogs, and lakeshores. Northern refers to the breeding range across Canada and the northern United States, particularly in relation to the Louisiana's more southerly distribution.

Bird is the Word

Parkesia — The genus name honors Kenneth C. Parkes (1922–2007), a former Curator of Birds at Carnegie Museum of Natural History. The waterthrushes were formerly assigned to the genus *Seiurus* with the Ovenbird. Dr. Parkes had long argued that the waterthrushes should be placed in their own genus apart from the Ovenbird, despite their similarities. Formerly *Seiurus noveboracensis*

noveboracensis — The specific epithet is Modern Latin for "of New York" where this species was first discovered.

French Name: Paruline des Ruisseaux

Spanish Names: Chipe Charquero; Chipesuelero Charquero; Reinita Acuática Norteña

Eskimo and Inuit Names: Che-ching-uk (imitative); Chif-chi-wok-guk

Other Names: New York Waterthrush; Grinnell's Waterthrush; Northern Small-billed Waterthrush; Aquatic Thrush; Aquatic Wood Thrush; Wagtail, Aquatic Wood Wagtail; Water Wagtail; Wagtail Warbler; New York Warbler

Golden-winged Warbler
Vermivora chrysoptera
(ver-MIV-or-ah kris-OP-ter-ah)

The Golden-winged Warbler is named for its yellow wing patch. The Golden-winged Warbler readily hybridizes with the Blue-winged Warbler. See sidebar 40.

Vermivora — The genus name means "worm-eating from the Latin *vermis* (a worm) and *voro* (to eat). The name refers not to earthworms, but to caterpillars, an important food of these warblers, particularly when they are feeding young.

chrysoptera — The specific epithet means "golden wing" from the Greek *chrysos* (gold) and *pteron* (the wing).

French Name: Paruline à Ailes Dorées

Sidebar 40
Hybrid Warblers

A few warblers described as species turned out to be hybrids, instead. The Blue-winged Warbler readily hybridizes with the Golden-winged Warbler. The offspring were originally thought to be true species and given scientific names. The result of a first generation cross is Brewster's Warbler. William Brewster described it as a new species and named it *Vermivora leucobronchialis* (white-throated.). This name is, of course, invalid, since Brewster's is a hybrid, not a true species. Brewster's Warbler looks very much like the Blue-winged Warbler, except that it has whitish underparts, rather than yellow. Two Brewster's Warblers rarely mate, because they are so rare. So a Brewster's is more likely to backcross to one of the parent species. When a Brewster's mates with a Golden-winged Warbler, the recessive hybrid can appear, Lawrence's Warbler. This hybrid has the black facial markings of the Golden-winged Warbler and the yellow underparts of the Blue-winged Warbler. In the 1870s, Harold H. Herrick, an amateur ornithologist, collected a warbler new to him near Chatham, New Jersey. He named it *Vermivora lawrencei* in honor of his former classmate Newbold Trotter Lawrence, who was also an amateur ornithologist. In 1910, Brewster's and Lawrence's Warblers were no longer recognized officially as species and were dropped from the AOU Check-list. In 1880, F.W. Langdon described a new warbler species, collected in Madisonville, Ohio (near Cincinnati). He named it *Helminthophaga cincinnatiensis*, and its common name was Cincinnati Warbler. It is now regarded as a hybrid between a Blue-winged Warbler and a Kentucky Warbler. Two specimens (a male and a female) of another warbler were collected eighteen miles apart south of Martinsburg, West Virginia and were described as a new species. Known as the Potomac Warbler or Sutton's Warbler (for ornithologist George Miksch Sutton), the bird is now believed to be a cross between a Northern Parula and a Yellow-throated Warbler.

Spanish Names: Chipe de Ala Dorada; Chipe Alidorado; Reinita Alidorada
Other Names: Golden-winged Swamp Warbler; Blue Golden-winged Warbler; Golden-winged Flycatcher

Blue-winged Warbler
Vermivora cyanoptera
(ver-MIV-or-ah sigh-an-OP-ter-ah)

This warbler's blue-gray wings give it its name. The Blue-winged Warbler readily hybridizes with the Golden-winged Warbler. See sidebar 39.

Vermivora — The genus name means "worm-eating from the Latin *vermis* (a worm) and *voro* (to eat). The name refers not to earthworms, but to caterpillars, an important food of these warblers, particularly when they are feeding young.

cyanoptera — The specific epithet means "blue-winged" from the Greek *kuanos* (dark blue) and *pteron* (the wing). Formerly *Vermivora pinus*.

French Name: Paruline à Ailes Bleues
Spanish Names: Chipe de Ala Azul; Chipe Aliazul; Reinita Aliazul
Other Names: Blue-winged Yellow Warbler; Blue-winged Swamp Warbler

Black-and-white Warbler, by Louis Agassiz Fuertes

Black-and-white Warbler
Mniotilta varia
(nye-oh-TILL-tah VARE-ih-ah)

"The bird is admirably marked; he is a symphony in black and white; Nature has rung all the changes possible with those colors." — F. Schuyler Mathews (1904)

Wilson called this dapper warbler the Black-and-white Creeper for its foraging behavior. See genus name below. It is named for the striking black and white striped pattern in both sexes.

Mniotilta — The genus name means "moss plucker" from Greek *mnion* (moss) and *tillein* (to pull out). The Black-and-white Warbler forages nuthatch-like, creeping along tree trunks and large limbs in search of prey. The significance of the name is that the bird sometimes probes into moss and lichen-covered bark for the insects hidden there.

varia — The specific epithet is Latin for "variegated" and refers to the contrasting color pattern of the plumage.

French Name: Paruline Noir et Blanc
Spanish Names: Chipe Trepador; Reinita Trepadora
Other Names: Creeping Warbler; Black-and-white Creeping Warbler; Varied Creeping Warbler; Striped Warbler; Whitepoll Warbler; Creeper; Tree Creeper; Pied Creeper; Blue-and-white Pied Creeper; Black-and-white Creeper; Striped Creeper; Blue-and-white Creeper; Blue-and-white Striped Creeper; Black-and-white Nuthatch; Christmas Bird; Japanese Canary; Anse Bird; Ant Bird; Ants Bird; Ants Picker; Ant-eater; Bijirita Trepadora; Reinita Trepadora; Madras; Mi-deuil

Prothonotary Warbler
Protonotaria citrea
(pro-tow-no-TARE-ih-ah SIT-ree-ah)

"What a name to saddle on the Golden Swamp-bird! Wrongly compounded in the first place, wrongly spelled, wrongly pronounced! We understand that Protonotarius is the title of papal officials whose robes are bright yellow, but why say "First Notary" in mixed Greek and Latin, instead of Primonotarius? Proto is Greek for first, as in prototype. Why and when did it come to be misspelled Protho? Both Wilson and Audubon wrote Protonotary Warbler, a name seemingly first given to the bird by Louisiana Creoles. Both etymology and sense call for stress on the third syllable, yet one most often hears the stress laid on the second. Here, certainly, is a bothersome name fit only to be eschewed!" — Aaron Clark Bagg and Samuel Atkins Elliot, Jr. (1937)

Some purists show scorn for this warbler's unusual name, as in the above passage. Arthur Cleveland Bent didn't like it, either, preferring Golden Swamp Warbler instead. But the name is unique with an interesting etymology. It comes from *protonotary*, meaning "first scribe." The prothonotaries were twelve ecclesiastics in the Roman Catholic Church, who kept records of important pontifical proceedings. The connection is to the yellow robes they wore and to the bright saffron yellow color of this warbler's plumage.

Protonotaria — The genus epithet is from the Greek *protos* (first) and the Latin *notarius* (a scribe or note taker). See common name above.

citrea — The specific epithet is from the Latin *citreus* (a citrus tree) or in this case lemon-colored and refers to this warbler's bright yellow plumage.

French Name: Paruline Orangée

Spanish Names: Chipe Dorado; Chipe Protonotario; Reinita Cabecidorada

Other Names: Golden Warbler; Golden Swamp Warbler; Prothonotary Swamp Warbler; Blue-winged Yellow Swamp Warbler; Willow Warbler; Flame Bird; Reinita Anaranjada

~

Swainson's Warbler
Limnothlypis swainsonii
(lim-no-THLIP-iss swain-SON-ih-eye)

Audubon's good friend John Bachman discovered this warbler along the Edisto River near Charleston, South Carolina in 1832. Audubon named three species of birds for Bachman, but he chose to name this one *Sylvia Swainsonii* for English artist-naturalist William Swainson:

"To none of my ornithological friends could I assuredly with more propriety have dedicated this species than to him, the excellent and learned author, whose name you have seen connected with it — to him, who has himself traversed large portions of America, who has added so considerably to the list of known species of birds, and has enriched the science of ornithology by so many valuable works."
— John James Audubon (1834)

Actually, Swainson never visited North America, but he did go on a two-year collecting trip to Brazil. He also described many new species from America, as well as other parts of the world.

Limnothlypis — The genus name means "marsh finch" from the Greek *limne* (a marsh) and *thlypis* (a kind of finch), a name Aristotle used for a small seed-eating bird of undetermined identity, but now applied to a wood-warbler. Marsh refers to this warbler's breeding habitat, in part, because it also nests in montane forests in the Appalachians. Along the coastal plain in the southeast, Swainson's Warbler favors canebrakes and palmetto thickets.

swainsonii — The specific epithet commemorates William Swainson (1789–1855), an English ornithologist and artist. See common name above.

French Name: Paruline de Swainson

Spanish Names: Chipe de Corona Café; Chipe de Swainson

Other Name: Swainson's Swamp Warbler

~

Tennessee Warbler
Leiothlypis peregrina
(lye-OTH-lip-iss per-eh-GRIN-ah)

Alexander Wilson discovered this warbler along the Cumberland River in Tennessee and named it for that state. The Tennessee Warbler only occurs in Tennessee when it is traveling through on migration.

Leiothlypis — The genus name means "plain finch" from the Greek *leios* (plain) and *thlypis*, a name Aristotle used for some small bird, not further identified. In a family of largely colorful birds, the species in this genus are relatively drab. Formerly *Vermivora peregrina*. In 2010, it was merged into the genus *Oreothlypis* (mountain finch). In 2019, the genus was changed yet again to the present name.

peregrina — The specific epithet is Latin for "wanderer." Wilson considered this species very rare, having only seen two in his lifetime. He figured the bird he found in Tennessee had wandered far from its normal range. Actually Tennessee is far from both this warbler's breeding grounds in Canada and New England, and its wintering grounds in Central and northern South America.

French Name: Paruline Obscure
Spanish Names: Chipe Peregrino; Reinita Verdilla
Other Names: Swamp Warbler; Tennessee Swamp Warbler

~

Orange-crowned Warbler
Leiothlypis celata
(lye-OTH-lip-iss see-LAH-tah)

:
"The plainly colored and unobtrusive Orange-crowned Warbler has a very misleading name, for the feathers on the top of the head, which give it its name, are not a true orange but are tawny, and at their base only, so that the 'crown' is hidden from view unless the greenish tips of the feathers are separated. Possibly this concealed patch of color is displayed by the males during their courtship or perhaps when disputing nesting territory with other males, like the similarly hidden but much more brilliant crest of the Ruby-crowned Kinglet, but ordinarily it is invisible in the field." — John Bichard May (1925)

The brownish-orange patch that gives this warbler its name is difficult to see in the field and may be concealed altogether. See opening passage above.

Leiothlypis — The genus name means "plain finch" from the Greek *leios* (plain) and *thlypis*, a name Aristotle used for some small bird, not further identified. In a family of largely colorful birds, the species in this genus are relatively drab. Formerly *Vermivora celata*. In 2010, it was merged into the genus *Oreothlypis* (mountain finch). In 2019, the genus was changed yet again to the present name

celata — The specific epithet is Latin for "concealed" and refers to the orange patch on the crown that is often hidden by adjacent feathers.

French Name: Paruline Verdâtre
Spanish Names: Chipe Oliváceo; Chipe Corona-naranja; Reinita Olivada
Eskimo Name: Chung-ukh-tai-uk
Other Names: Eastern Orange-crowned Warbler; Dusky Warbler; Dusky Orange-crowned Warbler; Orange-crowned Swamp Warbler; Rocky Mountain Orange-crowned Warbler; Lutescent Warbler; Lutescent Orange-crowned Warbler; Orange-crown

~

Colima Warbler
Leiothlypis crissalis
(lye-OTH-lip-iss kris-ALE-iss)

The Colima Warbler is named for the state in southwest Mexico, where W.B. Richardson first collected it in 1889.

Leiothlypis — The genus name means "plain finch" from the Greek *leios* (plain) and *thlypis*, a name Aristotle used for some small bird, not further identified. In a family of largely colorful birds, the species in this genus are relatively drab. Formerly *Vermivora crissalis*. In 2010, it was merged into the genus *Oreothlypis* (mountain finch). In 2019, the genus was changed yet again to the present name

crissalis — The specific epithet is Modern Latin for "pertaining to the crissum" and refers to this warbler's bright yellow crissum (undertail coverts).

French Name: Paruline de Colima
Spanish Name: Chipe Colimense

~

Lucy's Warbler
Leiothlypis luciae
(lye-OTH-lip-iss LEW-sih-ee)

Dr. James G. Cooper discovered this pale gray warbler with a chestnut crown and rump in 1861, while working with the Geological Survey of California based at Fort Mohave in the Colorado River Valley of Arizona. He described the new warbler and the Elf Owl in the *Proceedings of the California Academy of Sciences*. He named the warbler *Helminthophaga luciae* for Lucy Hunter Baird and dedicated it "to the interesting little daughter of my kind friend, Prof. S.F. Baird." Lucy was just 13 years old at the time, perhaps the youngest individual to be commemorated in a scientific name.

Leiothlypis — he genus name means "plain finch" from the Greek *leios* (plain) and *thlypis*, a name Aristotle used for some small bird, not further identified. In a family of largely colorful birds, the species in this genus are relatively drab. Formerly *Vermivora luciae*. In 2010, it was merged into the genus *Oreothlypis* (mountain finch). In 2019, the genus was changed yet again to the present name.

luciae — The specific epithet honors Spencer Fullerton Baird's daughter Lucy Hunter Baird (1848–1913). See common name above.

French Name: Paruline de Lucy
Spanish Names: Chipe de Rabadilla Rufa; Chipe de Lucy
Other Name: Desert Warbler

Nashville Warbler
Leiothlypis ruficapilla
(lye-OTH-lip-iss rue-fih-cap-ILL-ah)

"This beautiful, bright and sprightly little bird was named the Nashville Warbler by Alexander Wilson, who first discovered it in 1808 near Nashville, Tennessee. How inappropriate is the name when we realize that the bird in not known to breed in Tennessee. Its specific name *ruficapilla* or 'red-haired' is much more fitting." — Edward Howe Forbush (1925)

Alexander Wilson tended to name birds for where he found them, but he could not have known where this species breeds or winters. The Nashville Warbler nests in the boreal forests of eastern Canada and the northern United States and winters in Mexico, Central America, and the West Indies. It only occurs as a transient in Tennessee during spring and fall migration. See opening passage above.

Leiothlypis — The genus name means "plain finch" from the Greek *leios* (plain) and *thlypis*, a name Aristotle used for some small bird, not further identified. In a family of largely colorful birds, the species in this genus are relatively drab. Formerly *Vermivora ruficapilla*. In 2010, it was merged into the genus *Oreothlypis* (mountain finch). In 2019, the genus was changed yet again to the present name.

ruficapilla — The specific epithet means "reddish hair" from the Latin *rufus* (reddish) and *capillus* (the hair) and refers to the chestnut patch on the crown.

French Name: Paruline à Joues Grises
Spanish Names: Chipe de Nashville; Reinita Cachetigrís
Other Names: Nashville Ground Warbler; Nashville Swamp Warbler; Red-crowned Warbler; Birch Warbler; Calaveras Warbler

Virginia's Warbler
Leiothlypis virginiae
(lye-OTH-lip-iss ver-JIN-ih-ee)

Dr. William Wallace Anderson, a U.S. Army surgeon, discovered this warbler near Fort Burgwyn, New Mexico. He sent specimens to Spencer F. Baird and asked that the new species be named in honor of his wife Mary Virginia Childs Anderson.

Leiothlypis — The genus name means "plain finch" from the Greek *leios* (plain) and *thlypis*, a name Aristotle used for some small bird, not further identified. In a family of largely colorful birds, the species in this genus are relatively drab. Formerly *Vermivora virginiae*. In 2010, it was merged into the genus *Oreothlypis* (mountain finch). In 2019, the genus was changed yet again to the present name.

virginiae — The specific epithet honors Mary Virginia Childs Anderson (1833–1912), the wife of a U.S. Army surgeon. See common name above.

French Name: Paruline de Virginia
Spanish Name: Chipe de Virginia

Connecticut Warbler
Oporornis agilis
(op-or-OR-nis AH-jil-is)

Alexander Wilson named this warbler for the state where he discovered it in 1812, far from its breeding grounds in the north woods of Canada, Michigan, Wisconsin, and Minnesota. The Connecticut Warbler occurs in Connecticut only as a transient during fall migration.

Oporornis — The genus name means "autumn bird" from the Greek *opora* (autumnal) and *ornis* (a bird) The Connecticut Warbler is seen in New England, where it was discovered, only in the fall, because it follows a different migration route in the spring. In spring, the birds take a northwesterly route west of the Alleghenies, through the Mississippi Valley to their breeding grounds in Canada. The

Connecticut Warbler, by Louis Agassiz Fuertes

Connecticut Warbler is rarely seen east of the Alleghenies during spring migration. In fall, the birds move east or southeast to New England before heading south along the Atlantic coast to their wintering grounds in South America.

agilis — The specific epithet is Latin for "agile," "active," "nimble," or "busy." Alexander Wilson gave the bird this name, because it "seemed more than commonly active, not remaining for a moment in the same position."

French Name: Paruline à Gorge Grise

Spanish Names: Chipe de Connecticut; Reinita Ojianillada

Other Names: Tamarack Warbler; Swamp Warbler; Bog Black-throat; Reinita de Connecticut

MacGillivray's Warbler
Geothlipis tolmiei
(jee-OTH-lip-is toll-MIH-eye)

"J. K. Townsend discovered the bird and really published it first, saying, "I dedicate the species to my friend, W.T. Tolmie, Esq., of Fort Vancouver." Audubon, being entrusted with Townsend's specimens, but disregarding the owner's prior rights, published the bird independently, and tardily, as it happened, as *Sylvia macgillivrayi*, by which specific name it was long known to ornithologists. MacGillivray was a Scotch naturalist who never saw America, but Tolmie was at that time a surgeon and later a factor of "the Honorable the Hudson's Bay Company," and he clearly deserves remembrance at our hands for friendly hospitality and cooperation which he invariably extended to men of science." — William Leon Dawson (1923)

John James Audubon scientifically described this species, naming it for Scottish ornithologist William MacGillivray (1796–1852) in gratitude for editing his *Ornithological Biography*. However this warbler had already been described in 1839 by Philadelphia ornithologist John K. Townsend, who discovered it near Vancouver, Washington. He gave it the name *Sylvia tolmiei*, and for a time it was known as Tolmie's Warbler, particularly in the West. Eventually, Audubon's proposal replaced it as the common name, but Townsend's specific epithet has priority and remains the valid scientific one. See specific epithet below.

Geothlypis — The genus name means "earth finch" from the Greek *geo* (the earth) and *thlypis*, a name Aristotle used for some Old World seed-eating bird of undetermined identity. Linnaeus sometimes applied ancient names of birds to unrelated species. The significance of "earth" is that these warblers typically stay in low vegetation, and nests on or near the ground. Formerly *Oporonis tolmiei*.

tolmei — John Kirk Townsend named this species for Dr. William Fraser Tolmie (1812–1886), a Scottish medical officer with the Hudson's Bay Company.

French Name: Paruline des Buissons

Spanish Names: Chipe de Tolmie; Reinita de Tupidero

Other Names: Tolmie's Warbler; Northern MacGillivray's Warbler

Mourning Warbler
Geothlypis philadelphia
(jee-OTH-lip-is fill-ah-DEL-fih-ah)

"Mourning is scarcely a justly chosen adjective and consequently not a fair name for so lively and attractive a bird as this, the hood he wears is not black and the song he sings is not sad!" — F. Schuyler Mathews (1904)

"This crêpe-like marking about the breast is the only thing about the bird that would suggest mourning, for it seems as happy and active as most birds, and its song is a paean of joy." — Edward Howe Forbush (1929)

Alexander Wilson named the Mourning Warbler for the black patch on the male's breast, black being the symbol for mourning.

Geothlypis — The genus name means "earth finch" from the Greek *geo* (the earth) and *thlypis*, a name Aristotle used for some Old World seed-eating bird of undetermined identity. Linnaeus sometimes applied ancient names of birds to unrelated species. The significance of "earth" is that these warblers typically stay in low vegetation, and nests on or near the ground. Formerly *Oporornis philadelphia*.

philadelphia — Alexander Wilson discovered this warbler "on the border of a marsh, within a few miles of Philadelphia," hence the specific epithet.

French Name: Paruline Triste
Spanish Names: Chipe Llorón; Reinita Enlutada
Other Names: Philadelphia Warbler; Mourning Ground Warbler; Black-throated Ground Warbler; Crape Warbler

Kentucky Warbler, by Louis Agassiz Fuertes

Kentucky Warbler
Geothlypis formosus
(jee-OTH-lip-is for-MOE-sus)

Like several other warblers, Alexander Wilson named this one for the place where he discovered it. Finally he chose a state where the bird actually nests. The Kentucky Warbler's breeding range extends well beyond Kentucky, though, through much of the eastern United States.

Geothlypis — The genus name means "earth finch" from the Greek *geo* (the earth) and *thlypis*, a name Aristotle used for some Old World seed-eating bird of undetermined identity. Linnaeus sometimes applied ancient names of birds to unrelated species. The significance of "earth" is that these warblers typically stay in low vegetation, and nests on or near the ground. Formerly *Oporornis formosus*.

formosus — The specific epithet is Latin for "beautiful," which this bird is with its bright yellow underparts and striking black face markings that suggest Elvis's sideburns.

French Name: Paruline du Kentucky
Spanish Names: Chipe Patilludo; Chipe de Kentucky; Reinita Cachetinegra
Other Names: Kentucky Wagtail; Reinita de Kentucky

Common Yellowthroat
Geothlypis trichas
(jee-OTH-lip-is TRY-kas)

This little warbler is named for its bright yellow throat and breast that contrasts with its distinctive "Lone Ranger" mask. The Common Yellowthroat has the widest range of all the species in its genus, breeding in all 49 continental states and every Canadian province and territory except Nunavut. Other yellowthroats such as the Bahama and Gray-crowned have more restricted ranges. The Common Yellowthroat may indeed be the most common warbler in North America.

Geothlypis — The genus name means "earth finch" from the Greek *geo* (the earth) and *thlypis*, a name Aristotle used for some Old World seed-eating bird of undetermined identity. Linnaeus sometimes applied ancient names of birds to unrelated species. The significance of "earth" is that these warblers typically stay in low vegetation, and nests on or near the ground.

trichas — The specific epithet is Greek for "a thrush," a name Aristotle used for a bird whose identity is lost to history. As with the genus name, Linnaeus apparently felt the name was just as good for an American warbler as it was for an Old World thrush.

French Name: Paruline Masquée

Spanish Names: Mascarita Común; Antifacito Norteño

Other Names: Maryland Yellowthroat; Northern Maryland Yellowthroat; Florida Yellowthroat; Northern Yellowthroat; Western Yellowthroat; Black-cheeked Yellow-throat; Ground Warbler; Black-masked Ground Warbler; Delafield's Ground Warbler; Maryland Ground Warbler; Olive-colored Yellow-throated Wren; Bandit Bird

Hooded Warbler
Setophaga citrina
(see-TOFF-ah-gah sit-RYE-nah)

"Take a lump of molten gold fashioned like a bird, impress upon it a hood of steel, oxidized, as black as jet, overlay this in turn with a half-mask of the gold, tool out each shining scale and shaft and filament with exquisite care, and you may have the equal of one of those ten thousand dollar vases of encrusted steel and gold, which the Spanish are so clever at making, an heirloom to be handed down from father to son. But let Nature breathe upon it; let the Author of Life give it motion and song; and you will have a Hooded Warbler, not less beautiful that you cannot handle it, but infinitely more so in that its beauty takes a thousand forms, a fresh one for every turn of fancy that may stir an avian breast." — William Leon Dawson (1902)

This warbler is named for the black hood or cowl that frames the male's bright yellow face as poetically described in the above passage. The female may show a partial hood.

Setophaga — The genus name means "moth eater" from the Greek *setos* (a moth) and *phago* (to eat). The warblers in this genus eat many kinds of insects including moths. *Setophaga* was formerly a monotypic genus encompassing only the American Redstart. In 2011, based on DNA analysis, warblers in the genera *Dendroica* and *Parula,* and the Hooded Warbler (formerly in the genus *Wilsonia*) were merged into *Setophaga*.

citrina — The specific epithet means "lemon-colored" in Latin and refers to the bright yellow face and underparts.

French Name: Paruline à Capuchon

Spanish Names: Chipe Encapuchado; Reinita Encapuchada

Other Names: Black-headed Warbler; Hooded Flycatching Warbler; Mitered Warbler; Hooded Titmouse; Selby's Flycatcher

American Redstart
Setophaga ruticilla
(see-TOFF-ah-gah root-ih-SILL-ah)

"The bright flashes of orange-red which it proudly displays in its frequently spread tail and fluttering wings has suggested to the imaginative Cubans the beautiful name Candelita, the "little torch," which in such unusual numbers brightens the dark shadows of their tropical forests. In the Provence of Quebec, the Canadian French know it as "La Fauvette a Queue Rousse," another allusion to the bright red patches in the male's tail." — Alfred Otto Gross (1953)

American Redstart, by Louis Agassiz Fuertes

Early settlers named this American warbler for the Common Redstart (*Phoenicurus phoenicurus*) of Europe, an unrelated species in the Old World Flycatcher family (Muscicapidae). The name redstart derives from the German *rothsteort,* which means "red tail." The European bird has a rust-red tail. The American Redstart sports orange-red patches in its tail as well as its wings. When foraging, this hyperactive warbler fans its tail and droops its wings to display the bright colors, apparently to flush insects which it then darts out to capture in midair like a flycatcher. This behavior has prompted Pete Dunne to nickname the redstart "flash dancer" and Ohio ornithologist Jim McCormac to refer to it as "a little feathered bull in a botanical china shop."

Setophaga — The genus name means "moth eater" from the Greek *setos* (a moth) and *phago* (to eat). The warblers in this genus eat many kinds of insects including moths. *Setophaga* was formerly a monotypic genus encompassing only the American Redstart. In 2011, based on DNA analysis, warblers in the genera *Dendroica* and *Parula,* and the Hooded Warbler (formerly in the genus *Wilsonia*) were merged into *Setophaga.*

ruticilla — The specific epithet means "reddish tail" from the Latin *rutillus* (reddish) and *cilla,* a diminutive suffix taken by later authors to mean "tail." See White Wagtail.

French Name: Paruline Flamboyante
Spanish Names: Chipe Flameante; Pavito Migratorio; Candelita Norteña
Other Names: Common Redstart; Redstart Warbler; Yellow-tailed Warbler; Halloween Warbler; Butterfly Warbler; Butterfly Bird; Christmas Bird; Firetail; Candelita; Redstart Flycatcher; Alder Bird; Bean Bird; Goldfinch; Carougette; Carte; Mariposera; Officier; Gabriel du Feu; Petit du Feu; La Fauvette à Queue Rousseà

Kirtland's Warbler
Setophaga kirtlandii
(see-TOFF-ah-gah kurt-LAND-ih-eye)

On May 13, 1851, Charles Pease presented his father-in-law Dr. Jared Kirtland with a warbler he had shot along the Lake Erie shore just west of Cleveland. Dr. Kirtland compared the specimen with other warblers in his collection and found that it matched none of them. Spencer Fullerton Baird, the Secretary of the Smithsonian, returning home to Washington from a meeting he had attended in Cincinnati, paid Dr. Kirtland a visit on his farm in Rockport Township (now Lakewood), Ohio. Kirtland gave him the specimen, and the following year, Baird published the first description of this new species, naming it *Sylvicola kirtlandii,* and dedicated it, "This species, which was shot near Cleveland, Ohio, by Mr. Charles Pease, May 13, 1851, is appropriately dedicated to Dr. Jared P. Kirtland, of Cleveland, a gentleman to whom, more than anyone living, we are indebted for a knowledge of the Natural History of the Mississippi Valley." The natural range of Kirtland's Warbler remained a mystery until after Kirtland's death. See sidebar 41.

Setophaga — The genus name means "moth eater" from the Greek *setos* (a moth) and *phago* (to eat). The warblers in this genus eat many kinds of insects including moths. Formerly *Dendroica kirtlandii.*

kirtlandii — The specific epithet honors Dr. Jared Potter Kirtland (1793–1877), a prominent physician and naturalist. See common name above.

French Name: Paruline de Kirtland
Spanish Name: Chipe de Kirtland
Other Names: Jack-Pine Warbler; Jack-Pine Bird

Cape May Warbler
Setophaga tigrina
(see-TOFF-ah-gah tig-RYE-nah)

"This is the bird that made Cape May famous." — Arthur Cleveland Bent (1953)

Alexander Wilson named this species the Cape May Warbler, because his friend George Ord collected the first specimen in a maple swamp in Cape May County, New Jersey in May, 1811. But the Cape May Warbler only occurs as an uncommon transient in New Jersey. Its breeding grounds are in New England and eastern Canada and it winters in Mexico, Central America, and the West Indies. In fact, another specimen was not seen in Cape May again until 1920!

Setophaga — The genus name means "moth eater" from the Greek *setos* (a moth) and *phago* (to eat). The warblers in this genus eat many kinds of insects including moths. Formerly *Dendroica tigrina*.

tigrina — The specific epithet is Latin for "striped like a tiger" and refers to the black stripes on the bird's yellow breast. Tiger is also descriptive of the bird's behavior. Richard C. Harlow wrote that "the male Cape May is the tiger of the north woods in defending his territory. He attacks all birds that come close to the nest, up to the size of the olive-backed thrush, and is absolutely fearless."

French Name: Paruline Tigrée
Spanish Names: Chipe Atigrado; Reinita Tigrina
Other Names: Spotted Creeper; Reinita Tigre

Sidebar 41
Bird of Fire

Charles Pease was not the first person to collect a Kirtland's Warbler. Ten years earlier, in October of 1841, Boston ornithologist Samuel Cabot, Jr. was on an expedition to the Yucatan Peninsula. He shot a male specimen near Abaca Island in the Bahamas and added it to his collection. It is said Cabot became so captivated by the colorful tropical birds of the Yucatan, he completely forgot about the unidentified bird that was to languish in his collection for more than 20 years.

Jared Potter Kirtland, physician, legislator, and naturalist. He was a founder of the Cleveland Medical College and the Cleveland Museum of Natural History.

Neither the breeding grounds nor the wintering area of Kirtland's Warbler were known during Dr. Kirtland's lifetime. Ornithologist Charles B. Cory, also from Boston, discovered the wintering grounds in the Bahamas when he collected a specimen on Andros Island in January of 1879. The breeding grounds were not discovered until 1903. That June, Earl H. Frothingham, a graduate student of the University of Michigan, and his friend T. G. Gale were trout fishing on the Au Sable River in the north central portion of Michigan's lower peninsula. Frothingham heard an unfamiliar song coming from the stand of Jack Pines on the north side of the river. Gale collected a specimen, and they took it back to the University Museum at Ann Arbor, where Norman F. Wood identified it as Kirtland's Warbler. Wood immediately set out for the Au Sable region to search for a nest. On July 8th, he found one containing two nestlings and an egg, and the next day found another with five partially grown young.

The alternate name Jack-Pine Warbler is a particularly apt one for this species. It refers to this bird's specialized breeding habitat in dense stands of young Jack Pines (*Pinus banksiana*) on loose, sandy soil. Another requirement is a fairly thick ground cover of grasses, sedges, ferns, wintergreen, and bearberry, interspersed with blueberry, sheep laurel, and sweet fern. The habitat is literally born of fire, which burns mature growth and stimulates germination of seeds. The warblers first occupy the stands when the trees are five or six years old and three to six feet in height. They abandon the area after about fifteen years, when the Jack Pines reach ten to fifteen feet or more tall. Then the trees shade out the ground cover making the habitat unsuitable for the birds. Today Kirtland's Warbler is a conservation reliant species, dependent on human management through controlled burns and control of the parasitic Brown-headed Cowbird.

Cerulean Warbler
Setophaga cerulea
(see-TOFF-ah-gah see-RULE-ee-ah)

Cerulean describes the lovely cerulean or sky blue upperparts of both sexes, although the color is brighter in the male. Unfortunately for most birders, this species usually stays high in the canopy, so the only view you get is of the white underparts and the black necklace across the breast.

Setophaga — The genus name means "moth eater" from the Greek *setos* (a moth) and *phago* (to eat). The warblers in this genus eat many kinds of insects including moths. Formerly *Dendroica cerulea*.

cerulea — The specific epithet is Latin for "sky blue."

French Name: Paruline Azurée
Spanish Names: Chipe Cerúleo; Reinita Cerúlea
Other Names: Blue Warbler; Azure Warbler

Northern Parula
Setophaga americana
(see-TOFF-ah-gah ah-mer-ih-CAY-nah)

"A snowy spray of apple blossoms makes a an exquisite setting for this dainty bird of blue and gold. And you can see the little insect hunter from all angles as he hangs from a blossom cluster like a chickadee or titmouse. Indeed, Parula means "little titmouse." And since this is considered the typical genus, the whole family is known as the Parulidae." — John W. Aldrich (1964)

The preferred pronunciation of this little warbler's common name (which was formerly also its genus name) is PAR-you-lah. Most birders, however pronounce it pa-ROO-lah. So, take your pick. Mark Catesby called this Wood-Warbler the Finch Creeper, and Bartram called it the Various Coloured Little Finch Creeper. To Audubon and Wilson it was the Blue Yellow-backed Warbler. Until recently, Parula was also the genus name, but now this and the next species have been merged into the genus *Setophaga*. *Parula* means "little titmouse" from the Latin *parus* (a titmouse) plus a diminutive suffix. It refers to the bird's foraging behavior, often hanging upside down like a chickadee as described above. Until recently, North American titmice and chickadees were placed in the genus *Parus*, but they have now been merged into separate genera. *Parus* now encompasses only the Old World tits. Northern distinguishes this species, which nests in most of the eastern states and southern Canada, from the Tropical Parula, a Mexican species, whose northern limit just reaches southern Texas. Formerly known as Parula Warbler.

Setophaga — The genus name means "moth eater" from the Greek *setos* (a moth) and *phago* (to eat). The warblers in this genus eat many kinds of insects including moths. Formerly *Parula americana*.

americana — The specific epithet is Modern Latin for "American" and refers to the species' range in the New World.

French Name: Paruline à Collier
Spanish Name: Parula Norteña
Other Names: Bonaparte's Flycatching Warbler; Blue Yellow-backed Warbler; Blue Yellowback; Finch Creeper; Various-colored Little Finch Creeper; Reinita Pechidorada

Northern Parula, by Louis Agassiz Fuertes

Tropical Parula
Setophaga pitiayumi
(see-TOFF-ah-gah pit-ih-ah-YOU-me)

This species is named for its habitat in subtropical forests of Mexico. Formerly known as Olive-backed Warbler.

Setophaga — The genus name means "moth eater" from the Greek *setos* (a moth) and *phago* (to eat). The warblers in this genus eat many kinds of insects including moths. Formerly *Parula pitiayumi*.

pitiayumi — The specific epithet is the Guarani Indian name for this bird. It means "little yellow chest" and refers to this warbler's bright yellow and orange throat and breast.

French Name: Paruline à Joues Noires
Spanish Name: Parula Tropical
Other Names: Pitiayumi Warbler; Sennet's Warbler; Sennet's Olive-backed Warbler

Magnolia Warbler
Setophaga magnolia
(see-TOFF-ah-gah mag-NO-lih-ah)

Spruce Warbler would be a more apt name for this lovely black and yellow bird, because it nests in the spruce-fir forests of Canada and northeastern United States. So how did this denizen of the North Woods come to be named for a symbol of the Deep South? Alexander Wilson tended to name birds for where he found them, even if they were only passing through on migration. In the spring of 1810, he collected the first specimen in a magnolia tree along the Mississippi River, near Fort Adams, Mississippi. He gave it the scientific name *Sylvia magnolia*, from which its common name is derived, although Wilson used Black-and-yellow Warbler for the common name. The botanical genus *Magnolia* honors Pierre Magnol (1638–1715), a French botanist.

Setophaga — The genus name means "moth eater" from the Greek *setos* (a moth) and *phago* (to eat). The warblers in this genus eat many kinds of insects including moths. Formerly *Dendroica magnolia*.

magnolia — The specific epithet is from the species of tree where the type specimen was collected. See common name above.

French Name: Paruline à Tête Cendrée
Spanish Names: Chipe de Magnolia; Reinita Colifajeada

Other Names: Black-and-yellow Warbler; Blue-headed Yellow-rumped Warbler; Spotted Warbler; Maggie

Bay-breasted Warbler
Setophaga castanea
(see-TOFF-ah-gah cas-TAY-nee-ah)

Wilson collected the first specimen of this understated, yet handsome warbler in eastern Pennsylvania in 1832. He called it the Little Chocolate-breasted Titmouse. The common name refers to the rich reddish-brown color of the breast and sides. Bay derives from the Latin *badius* (chestnut-colored).

Setophaga — The genus name means "moth eater" from the Greek *setos* (a moth) and *phago* (to eat). The warblers in this genus eat many kinds of insects including moths. Formerly *Dendroica castanea*.

castanea — The specific epithet is Latin for "chestnut" and also refers to the color of the crown, throat, and breast.

French Name: Paruline à Poitrine Baie
Spanish Names: Chipe de Pecho Castaño; Chipe Pechicastaño; Reinita Castaña
Other Names: Bay-breast; Autumnal Warbler; Little Chocolate-breast Titmouse

Blackburnian Warbler
Setophaga fusca
(see-TOFF-ah-gah FOOS-kah)

"Blackburnian seems to be a doubly appropriate name, for its upper parts are largely black and its throat burns like a brilliant orange flame amid the dark foliage of the hemlocks and spruces. A glimpse of such a brilliant gem flashing out from its somber surroundings is fairly startling." — Arthur Cleveland Bent (1953)

In his *Arctic Zoology* (1785), Welsh naturalist Thomas Pennant named this bird in honor of Anna Blackburn (1740–1793), an English botanist and patron of ornithology, who maintained a private museum of natural history specimens. Mrs. Blackburn made her specimens accessible to many prominent naturalists of her time including Pennant. Thomas Pennant expressed his gratitude to her:

"To the rich museum of American Birds, preserved by Mrs. Anna Blackburn, of Orford, near Warrington, I am indebted for the opportunity of describing almost every one known in the provinces of Jersey, New York, and Connecticut. They were sent over to that lady by her brother the late Ashton Blackburn; who added to the skill and zeal of a sportsman, the most pertinent remarks on the specimens he collected for his worthy and philosophical sister."

Setophaga — The genus name means "moth eater" from the Greek *setos* (a moth) and *phago* (to eat). The warblers in this genus eat many kinds of insects including moths. Formerly *Dendroica fusca*.

fusca — The specific epithet derives from the Latin *fuscus* (dark) and refers to the bird's blackish upper parts. In 1788, Johann Gmelin named this warbler *Motacilla blackburniae*, a latinization of the common name Pennant had given it. The specimen had been collected in New York presumably by Anna's brother Ashton. However, this species had already been described in 1776 by Philipp Ludwig Statius Müller from a specimen collected in French Guiana. He gave it the specific epithet *fusca*, and since the rule of priority dictates that the first published name is the official one, Gmelin's name was invalid.

French Name: Paruline à Gorge Orangée
Spanish Names: Chipe de Garganta Naranja; Chipe Gorjinaranja; Reinita Gorjinaranja
Other Names: Hemlock Warbler; Orange-throated Warbler; Promethean Warbler; Prometheus; Firebrand, Torch Bird; Reinita Fuego

~

Yellow Warbler
Setophaga petechia
(see-TOFF-ah-gah (peh-TEACH-ih-ah)

"By living in perpetual sunshine his feathers seemed to have absorbed some of it, so that he looks like a stray sunbeam playing among the shrubbery on the lawn, the trees in the orchard, the bushes in the roadside thicket, the willows and alders beside the stream." — Neltje Blanchan (1917)

Yellow is a dominant color in this family, but no other warbler is as extensively yellow as this one. Both the male and female are entirely yellow, but the female's color has a greenish tinge.

Setophaga — The genus name means "moth eater" from the Greek *setos* (a moth) and *phago* (to eat). The warblers in this genus eat many kinds of insects including moths. Formerly *Dendroica petechia*.

petechia — The specific epithet is Modern Latin for "purplish spot." It is a medical term for a purplish or reddish rash on the skin. The reference is to the rusty streaks on the male's breast and sides, suggesting a skin ailment.

French Name: Paruline Jaune
Spanish Names: Chipe Amarillo; Reinita Amarilla
Eskimo Name: Chung-uk-chu-ug-u-nuk
Other Names: Golden Warbler; Summer Warbler; Blue-eyed Yellow Warbler; Willow Warbler; Mangrove Warbler; Rathbone Warbler; Yellowbird; Summer Yellowbird; Yellow Titmouse; Yellow Poll; Canary; Wild Canary; Bastard Canary; Seaside Canary; Mangrove Canary; Canary Bird; Spider Bird; Thumb Bird; Chippin' Chick; Serin Sauvage; Canario; Canario de Manglar; Canario de Mangle; Didine; Rossignol; Fauvette Jaune; Petit-jaune; Oiseau Jaune; Toute Jaune; Sucrier Barbade; Sucrier Mangle

~

Chestnut-sided Warbler
Setophaga pensylvanica
(see-TOFF-ah-gah pen-sill-VAY-nih-kah)

A broad chestnut-brown stripe on the sides of both sexes gives this warbler its name.

Setophaga — The genus name means "moth eater" from the Greek *setos* (a moth) and *phago* (to eat). The warblers in this genus eat many kinds of insects including moths. Formerly *Dendroica pensylvanica*

pensylvanica — The specific epithet (note the misspelling) is Modern Latin for "of Pennsylvania." It is named for the state where Audubon had collected the type specimen near Philadelphia.

French Name: Paruline à Flancs Marron
Spanish Names: Chipe de Flanco Castaño; Chipe Flanquicastaño; Reinita de Costillas Castañas
Other Names: Bloody-sided Warbler; Yellow-crowned Warbler; Quebec Warbler; Golden-crowned Flycatcher; Reinita Costadicastaña

~

Blackpoll Warbler
Setophaga striata
(see-TOFF-ah-gah stry-AY-tah)

Blackpoll refers to the black cap on the spring male. That and the white cheeks make this warbler look somewhat like a chickadee.

Setophaga — The genus name means "moth eater" from the Greek *setos* (a moth) and *phago* (to eat). The warblers in this genus eat many kinds of insects including moths. Formerly *Dendroica striata*.

striata — The specific epithet is Latin for "striped" and refers to the black streaks on the bird's back and sides.

French Name: Paruline Rayée
Spanish Names: Chipe de Gorra Negra; Chipe Gorrinegro; Reinita Rayada
Other Names: Blackpoll; Black-polled Warbler; Black-poll Wood Warbler; Autumnal Warbler

Black-throated Blue Warbler
Setophaga caerulescens
(see-TOFF-ah-gah see-roo-LES-enz)

The name describes the field marks of the spring male, black throat (the black also extends to the face and down the sides) and cadet blue upperparts.

Setophaga — The genus name means "moth eater" from the Greek *setos* (a moth) and *phago* (to eat). The warblers in this genus eat many kinds of insects including moths. Formerly *Dendroica caerulescens*.

caerulescens — The specific epithet means "bluish" from the Latin *caeuleus* (sky-blue).

French Name: Paruline Bleue à Gorge Noire
Spanish Names: Chipe Azul Negro; Chipe Azuloso; Reinita Azul y Negro
Other Names: Black-throat; Blue Flycatcher; Reinita Azul

Palm Warbler
Setophaga palmarum
(see-TOFF-ah-gah palm-AIR-um)

The Palm Warbler has no particular affinity for palm trees. It got its name because Johann Gmelin discovered the bird in palm groves on its wintering grounds on the island of Hispaniola.

Setophaga — The genus name means "moth eater" from the Greek *setos* (a moth) and *phago* (to eat). The warblers in this genus eat many kinds of insects including moths. Formerly *Dendroica palmarum*.

palmarum — The specific epithet is Latin for "of the palms."

French Name: Paruline à Couronne Rousse
Spanish Names: Chipe Playero; Reinita Coronicastaña
Other Names: Yellow Palm Warbler; Redpoll Warbler; Yellow-bellied Red-poll Warbler; Yellow Redpoll Warbler; Yellow Redpoll; Wagtail Warbler; Tip-up Warbler; Yellow Tip-up; Yellow Tip-up Warbler; Reinita Palmera

Pine Warbler
Setophaga pinus
(see-TOFF-ah-gah PIE-nus)

"Never was a bird more aptly named than the Pine Warbler. Except when migrating, it sticks to pine woods as a cockle-bur sticks to a dog's tail." — Gerald Thayer

"Few of our birds are so aptly named as the Pine Warbler, which first, last, and all the time, except in migration, resorts to pine woods. It summers in them in the north and it winters in them in the south. Even its feathers often bear conclusive evidence of its predilection for pines, being besmeared with their gum." — Henry W. Henshaw (1914)

The Pine Warbler prefers open woods and associates with different species of pine in various parts of its range, white and red pines in the North, pitch pine along the Atlantic coast, Virginia pine in the southern Midwest, and shortleaf, longleaf, and loblolly pines in the South.

Setophaga — The genus name means "moth eater" from the Greek *setos* (a moth) and *phago* (to eat). The warblers in this genus eat many kinds of insects including moths. Formerly *Dendroica pinus*.

pinus — The specific epithet is Latin for "a pine tree" and refers to this warbler's affinity for pines as described above.

French Name: Paruline des Pins
Spanish Names: Chipe Pinero; Reinita de Pinos
Other Names: Pine Creeper; Pine-creeping Warbler; Chip-chip; Petit-chitte de Bois Pin; Siguita del Pinar

Yellow-rumped Warbler
Setophaga coronata
(see-TOFF-ah-gah core-oh-NAY-tah)

Birders affectionately call them "butter-butts." The name refers to the yellow rump-patch in both sexes. The western and eastern populations of Yellow-rumped Warbler were formerly considered separate species. The western birds with yellow throats were called Audubon's Warbler (*Dendroica auduboni*) They were, of course, named for the famous artist and ornithologist John James Audubon. The eastern population (with white throats) were known as Myrtle Warbler (*D. coronata*), named after a shrub, the wax myrtle or bayberry (*Myrica cerifera*), whose fragrant, gray berries are an important winter food of this warbler. The berries are coated with a wax that the Yellow-rumped Warbler can digest because of a special enzyme. Because they can utilize this fat-rich food, Yellow-rumps can winter farther north than most other warblers that depend on insects.

Audubon's and Myrtle are names that can still be properly applied to the subspecies of the Yellow-rumped Warbler.

Setophaga — The genus name means "moth eater" from the Greek *setos* (a moth) and *phago* (to eat). The warblers in this genus eat many kinds of insects including moths. Formerly *Dendroica coronata*.

coronata — The specific epithet is Latin for "crowned" and refers to the yellow patch on the top of the head, suggesting a crown.

French Name: Paruline à Croupion Jaune

Spanish Names: Chipe Rabadilla Amarilla; Reinita Lomiamarilla

Other Names: Yellow-rump; Golden-crowned Warbler; Yellow-crowned Warbler; Yellow-crowned Wood Warbler; Audubon's Wood Warbler; Black-fronted Warbler; Hoover's Warbler; Golden-crowned Flycatcher; Myrtle-bird; Spider Bird; Reinita Coronada

Yellow-throated Warbler
Setophaga dominica
(see-TOFF-ah-gah dom-IN-ih-kah)

Formerly known as the Sycamore Warbler, an apt name because this species does have an affinity for sycamore trees growing in the bottomlands of streams. Yellow-throated is descriptive for the rich yellow throat that contrasts dramatically with its gray, black, and white plumage. However, the name is sometimes confused with the Common Yellowthroat, also a warbler.

Yellow-throated Warbler, by Louis Agassiz Fuertes

Setophaga — The genus name means "moth eater" from the Greek *setos* (a moth) and *phago* (to eat). The warblers in this genus eat many kinds of insects including moths. Formerly *Dendroica dominica*.

dominica — The specific epithet is Modern Latin for "of Santo Domingo," the former name of the island of Hispaniola in the West Indies where the type specimen was collected.

French Name: Paruline à Gorge Jaune

Spanish Names: Chipe de Garganta Amarilla; Chipe Gorjiamarillo; Reinita Gorjiamarilla

Other Names: Sycamore Warbler; Sycamore Yellow-throated Warbler; Eastern Yellow-throated Warbler; Yellow-throated Gray Warbler; White-browed Warbler; White-browed Yellow-throated Warbler; Dominican Yellowthroat; Domino Bird; Yellow-throated Creeper; Chip-chip; Reinita Gargantiamailla

Prairie Warbler
Setophaga discolor
(see-TOFF-ah-gah DISS-color)

Not a resident of the lone prairie, but of second growth woodlands and overgrown fields. Ludlow Griscom has suggested that Scrub Warbler would be a more appropriate name. Perhaps, but it would be a decidedly less aesthetic one. Actually this species received its common name, because resident Florida birds frequent grassy clearings in pine woods locally known as prairies.

Setophaga — The genus name means "moth eater" from the Greek *setos* (a moth) and *phago* (to eat). The warblers in this genus eat many kinds of insects including moths. Formerly *Dendroica discolor*.

discolor — The specific epithet is Latin for "of different colors," olive green above, bright yellow below wth black and chestnut markings.

French Name: Paruline des Prés

Spanish Names: Chipe de Pradera; Chipe Pradeño; Reinita Galana

Grace's Warbler
Setophaga graciae
(see-TOFF-ah-gah GRACE-ih-ee)

On his way to his post, Army surgeon Dr. Elliot Coues obtained an undescribed gray and white warbler with a yellow throat and yellow eyebrow stripe at Whipple Pass on July 2, 1864. At his post at Fort Whipple near Prescott, Arizona, he collected nine more specimens. Coues wrote in his notes that he wanted to name the new species in honor of his sister Grace Darling Coues in hope "that my affection and respect keep pace with my appreciation of true loveliness of character." When Spencer Fullerton Baird described the species in 1865, he gave it the name *Dendroica graciae* in accordance with Dr. Coues' wish.

Setophaga — The genus name means "moth eater" from the Greek *setos* (a moth) and *phago* (to eat). The warblers in this genus eat many kinds of insects including moths. Formerly *Dendroica graciae*.

graciae — The specific epithet commemorates Grace Darling Coues (1847–1939), the sister of Army surgeon and ornithologist Elliot Coues. See common name above.

French Name: Paruline de Grace

Spanish Names: Chipe de Ceja Amarilla; Chipe de Grace

Other Names: Northern Grace's Warbler; Grace Warbler

Black-throated Gray Warbler
Setophaga nigrescens
(see-TOFF-ah-gah nih-GRES-enz)

The common name is descriptive of this warbler's plumage, largely gray with a black throat.

Setophaga — The genus name means "moth eater" from the Greek *setos* (a moth) and *phago* (to eat). The warblers in this genus eat many kinds of insects including moths. Formerly *Dendroica nigrescens*.

nigrescens — The specific epithet means "blackish" from the Latin *niger* (black). It refers to the bird's black markings, black stripes on the sides and black crown and cheek patches as well as a black throat.

French Name: Paruline Grise à Gorge Noire

Spanish Name: Chipe Negrogrís

Townsend's Warbler
Setophaga townsendi
(see-TOFF-ah-gah TOWN-send-eye)

This warbler is named for John Kirk Townsend (1809–1851), an ornithologist and collector, best known for his *Narrative Of A Journey Across The Rocky Mountains*.

Setophaga — The genus name means "moth eater" from the Greek *setos* (a moth) and *phago* (to eat). The warblers in this genus eat many kinds of insects including moths. Formerly *Dendroica townsendi*.

townsendi — The specific epithet honors John Townsend. See common name above.

French Name: Paruline de Townsend

Spanish Names: Chipe de Townsend; Reinita de Townsend

Hermit Warbler
Setophaga occidentalis
(see-TOFF-ah-gah ocks-ih-den-TAY-liss)

This warbler earned its name for its reclusive habit of staying out of sight high in the tops of dense evergreen stands.

Setophaga — The genus name means "moth eater" from the Greek *setos* (a moth) and *phago* (to eat). The warblers in this genus eat many kinds of insects including moths. Formerly *Dendroica occidentalis*.

occidentalis — The specific epithet means "western" from the Latin *occidere* (to fall or

set, as of the sun in the west). The name refers to this warbler's range along the Pacific coast from Washington to central California.
French Name: Paruline à Tête Jaune
Spanish Names: Chipe de CabezaAmarilla; Chipe Cabeciamarillo; Reinita Cabecigualda

Golden-cheeked Warbler
Setophaga chrysoparia
(see-TOFF-ah-gah kris-op-AIR-ih-ah)

This warbler's solid yellow cheeks, bordered by a black eyeline and a black throat, give it its name.

Setophaga — The genus name means "moth eater" from the Greek *setos* (a moth) and *phago* (to eat). The warblers in this genus eat many kinds of insects including moths. Formerly *Dendroica chrysoparia*.

chrysoparia — The specific epithet means "golden cheeked" from the Greek *chrysos* (golden) and Greek *pareia* (the cheek).

French Name: Paruline à Dos Noir
Spanish Names: Chipe de Mejilla Dorada; Chipe Caridorado

Black-throated Green Warbler
Setophaga virens
(see-TOFF-ah-gah VER-enz)

The name is descriptive of the breeding male, black throat and olive-green upperparts. The female is also olive-green, but she has a yellow throat.

Setophaga — The genus name means "moth eater" from the Greek *setos* (a moth) and *phago* (to eat). The warblers in this genus eat many kinds of insects including moths. Formerly *Dendroica virens*.

virens — The specific epithet is Latin for "greenish" for the olive-green plumage in both sexes.

French Name: Paruline Verte à Gorge Noire
Spanish Names: Chipe de Dorso Verde; Chipe Dorsiverde; Reinita Cariamarilla
Other Names: Green Black-throat; Evergreen Warbler; Green Black-throated Flycatcher; Reinita Verdosa

Canada Warbler
Cardellina canadensis
(kar-deh-LINE-ah can-ah-DENS-is)

The Canada Warbler is named for its breeding range, which is mostly in Canada from Nova Scotia west to northeastern British Columbia. It also nests in the northeastern and north-central states south through the Appalachians to Tennessee.

Cardellina — The genus name means "little goldfinch" from the Latin *carduelis* (a goldfinch) plus a diminutive suffix. *Cardellina* was formerly a monotypic genus encompassing only the Red-faced Warbler. It may refer to the European Goldfinch (*Carduelis carduelis*), which also sports a red face. Formerly *Wilsonia canadensis*.

canadensis — The specific epithet is Modern Latin for "of Canada."

French Name: Paruline du Canada
Spanish Names: Chipe de Collar; Chipe Collarejo; Reinita Pechirrayada
Other Names: Canada Necklace; Necklace Warbler; Speckled Canada Warbler; Spotted Canada Warbler; Canadian Warbler; Canadian Flycatching Warbler; Canada Flycatcher; Reinita de Canada

Wilson's Warbler
Cardellina pusilla
(kar-deh-LINE-ah pew-SILL-ah)

Ornithologist Alexander Wilson described this species in volume three of his American Ornithology (1811). He gave it the scientific name *Muscicapa pusilla* (very small flycatcher) and the common name Green Black-capped Flycatcher. Its current common name derives from *Sylvia wilsonii*, the name Charles Bonaparte gave it. Bonaparte also erected the genus *Wilsonia*, which formerly embraced the Hooded Warbler, Canada Warbler, and Wilson's Warbler. But these three species have now been merged into different genera, and *Wilsonia* is no longer a valid taxon.

Cardellina — The genus name means "little goldfinch" from the Latin *carduelis* (a goldfinch) plus a diminutive suffix. *Cardellina* was formerly a monotypic genus encompassing only the Red-faced Warbler. It may refer to the European Goldfinch (*Carduelis*

carduelis), which also sports a red face. Formerly *Wilsonia pusilla*.

pusilla — The specific epithet is Latin for "very small." Wilson's Warbler is among the smallest in the family.

French Name: Paruline à Calotte Noire

Spanish Names: Chipe de Corona Negra; Chipe de Wilson; Reinita Gorrinegra

Other Names: Pileolated Warbler; Wilson's Pileolated Warbler; Golden Pileolated Warbler; Northern Pileolated Warbler; Black-capped Warbler; Green Black-capped Warbler; Black-cap; Wilson's Black-cap; Wilson's Flycatching Warbler; Wilson's Black-capped Flycatching Warbler; Green Black-capped Flycatcher; Wilson's Flycatcher; Yellowhammer

Red-faced Warbler
Cardellina rubrifrons
(kar-deh-LINE-ah RUBE-reh fronz)

This warbler sports a "face aglow like a poppy in bloom," that contrasts with its neutral-colored (gray, white, and black) plumage.

Cardellina — The genus name means "little goldfinch" from the Latin *carduelis* (a goldfinch) plus a diminutive suffix. Of course this is a Wood-Warbler, not a finch, but perhaps it was named after the European Goldfinch (*Carduelis carduelis*), which also sports a red face.

rubrifrons — The specific epithet means "red forehead" from the Latin *ruber* (red) and *frons* (the forehead).

French Name: Paruline à Face Rouge

Spanish Names: Chipe de Cara Roja; Chipe Carirrojo

Painted Redstart
Myioborus pictus
(my-yoh-BORE-us PICK-tus)

Redstart is from the German *rothstert* meaning "red tail." This species comes by its name by association with the American Redstart; it was formerly placed in the same genus *Setophaga*. Actually the two are not closely related. Not only that, but there is no red in the Painted Redstart's tail. Its tail shows white patches instead, so most of the species in this genus go by the more appropriate name Whitestart. So far the AOS hasn't seen fit to change the name to conform to the rest of the genus. It does share similar behavior with the American Redstart, though, in that it fans its tail and spreads its wings to display the white patches. Painted refers to the flashy color pattern of black, white, and red.

Myioborus — The genus name means "fly eater" from the Greek *myia* (a fly) and *borus* (devouring). Like the American Redstart, the Painted Redstart sometimes sally gleans by darting out from a perch to catch flying insects.

pictus — The specific epithet is Latin for "painted."

French Name: Paruline à Ailes Blanches

Spanish Names: Chipe de Ala Blanca; Pavito Aliblanco

Other Name: Painted Whitestart

Red-faced Warbler, by Louis Agassiz Fuertes

> **Sidebar 42**
> **Genus Piranga**
> **Piranga Tanagers**
>
> Tanager is from *tangara*, "a small colorful bird" in the language of the Tupi Indians of Brazil. The five tanagers in the genus *Piranga* were formerly classified in the family Thraupidae, the true tanagers, colorful songbirds of the neotropical rainforests.

Family Cardinalidae
Cardinals, Grosbeaks, and Allies

Hepatic Tanager
Piranga flava
(pie-RANG-ah FLAH-vah)

Hepatic is from the Latin word *hepaticus* (of the liver), referring to the male's dull brick red plumage.
Piranga — The genus name is from the Tupi (Brazilian) Indian word *tijepiranga*, a name they used for some small bird.
flava — The specific epithet is Latin for "yellow" or "golden-yellow" and refers to the color of the female. Apparently the type specimen was a female.
French Name: Piranga Orangé
Spanish Names: Tángara Encinera; Tángara Bermeja

Summer Tanager
Piranga rubra
(pie-RANG-ah RUBE-rah)

English naturalist Mark Catesby called this neo-tropical migrant (it winters from central Mexico to the Brazilian Amazon) the Summer Redbird to distinguish it from the Northern Cardinal, which is a permanent resident.
Piranga — The genus name is from the Tupi (Brazilian) Indian word *tijepiranga*, a name they used for some small bird.
rubra — The specific epithet is from the Latin *ruber* (red) and describes the male's plumage, which is entirely rose red.

French Names: Piranga Vermillon; Tangara Vermillon
Spanish Names: Tángara Roja; Tángara Veranera
Other Names: Western Summer Tanager; Redbird; Smooth-headed Redbird; Cooper's Tanager; Crimson Tanager; Rose Tanager; Calico Warbler; Bee Bird

Scarlet Tanager
Piranga olivacea
(pie-RANG-ah ah-liv-AY-see-ah)

"A cardinal is just red, but a tanager is SCARLET!" — Dan Quinn (1988)

"This splendidly appareled bird — a flash of color from the tropics — invariably causes an exclamation of surprise and delight to burst from the lips of even the most unemotional observer. A sight of him through the opera-glass is an unexpected revelation of vivid scarlet, the like of which is only comparable to one of those brilliant

Scarlet Tanager and Rose-breasted Grosbeak, by Louis Agassiz Fuertes

aniline dyes which fairly makes the eyes swim! The whole plumage of the bird, except wings and tail, is an intense red-scarlet; not a vermilion color, for that lacks life, but a vivid hue such as one can only produce by super-imposing Geranium Lake upon Scarlet Vermilion."
— F. Schuyler Mathews (1904)

Not to disparage the Northern Cardinal, which is a beautiful bird in its own right. But it does seem to pale in comparison with the almost fluorescent red of a male Scarlet Tanager in fresh breeding plumage as described above.

Piranga — The genus name is from the Tupi (Brazilian) Indian word *tijepiranga,* a name they used for some small bird.

olivacea — The specific epithet means "olive-green" from the Latin *oliva* (olive), which describes the female's color. Apparently the type specimen was either a female or a non-breeding male that molts into olive-green plumage, but retains his black wings and tail.

French Names: Piranga Éscarlate; Tangara Éscarlate

Spanish Name: Tángara Escarlata

Other Names: Canada Tanager; Red Bird; Summer Redbird; Black-winged Redbird; Firebird; King Bird; Pocket-bird; Cardinal Bird; Soldier Bird; War Bird; Scarlet Sparrow; Bludfink; Bludfogel; Oiseau Rouge; Escarlatina

Western Tanager
Piranga ludoviciana
(pie-RANG-ah lewd-oh-viss-ih-ANE-ah)

This tanager is named for its breeding range in the western United States and Canada.

Piranga — The genus name is from the Tupi (Brazilian) Indian word *tijepiranga,* a name they used for some small bird.

ludoviciana — The specific epithet is Modern Latin for "of Louisiana." It refers not to the state, but to the Louisiana Territory that includes what is now most of the western United States. The type specimen was collected on the Lewis and Clark Expedition in Idaho.

French Names: Piranga à Tête Rouge; Tangara à Tête Rouge

Spanish Names: Tangara de Capucha Roja; Tángara Occidental; Tángara Carirroja

Other Name: Louisiana Tanager

Flame-colored Tanager
Piranga bidentata
(pie-RANG-ah by-den-TAY-tah)

Flame-colored describes the bright orange plumage of the male.

Piranga — The genus name is from the Tupi (Brazilian) Indian word *tijepiranga,* a name they used for some small bird.

bidentata — The specific epithet means "having two teeth" from the Latin *bi* (two) and *dentatus* (toothed). It refers to the visible notches in the upper mandible.

French Name: Piranga a Dos Rayé

Spanish Names: Tangara de Dorso Rayado; Tángara Dorsirrayada

Western Tanager, by Louis Agassiz Fuertes

Crimson-collared Grosbeak
Rhodothraupsis celaeno
(row-doe-THROP-sis seh-LEE-no)

Grosbeaks are named for their large triangular bills, adapted for cracking open seeds. This species is named for the male's blood-red collar that extends from nape to the shoulders and belly.

Rhodothraupsis — The genus name means "rose tanager" from the Greek *rhodon* (a rose) and *Thraupsis*, a genus of tanager.

celaeno — The specific epithet is from the Greek *kelainos* (dark-colored or black with blood).

French Name: Cardinal à Collier
Spanish Name: Picogrueso Cuellirrojo

Northern Cardinal
Cardinalis cardinalis
(car-din-*AY-lis*)

"A flash of red, vivid against the spring sky, flits across the meadow and comes to rest amid the white blossoms of a dogwood. *Whoit whoit whoit, cheer cheer cheer* sings the fiery bird, and the whistle echoes and re-echoes over the fresh green fields. Such flamboyant good looks and proud voice distinguish the cardinal, or redbird, as he is often called . . . Only the summer tanager rivals the male in full red color, but the tanager lacks the proud crest which the cardinal raises and lowers at will. A black mask, a stout coral-red bill, and dark red feet also mark the cardinal. So vivid is his color that he was named cardinal for the red hat and robes of a prince of the church." — Arthur A. Allen (1964)

The Cardinal is named for the Cardinals in the Roman Catholic Church, whose scarlet robes suggest the color of the male's plumage. Northern distinguishes our species from ones in South America, such as the Vermilion Cardinal (*C. phoeniceus*).

Cardinalis — The genus/species name is Latin for "principal" or "important" derived from *cardo* (a hinge). The Cardinals were the senior bishops of the Roman Catholic Church, the policies of which hinged on their decisions. The reference to the bird is, of course, the red color of the robes the Cardinals wore.

French Name: Cardinal Rouge
Spanish Name: Cardenal Norteño
Other Names: Redbird; Cardinal Redbird; Crested Redbird; Virginia Redbird; Cardinal Bird; Red Cardinal; Common Cardinal; Gray-tailed Cardinal; Arizona Cardinal; Florida Cardinal; Kentucky Cardinal; Virginia Cardinal; Virginia Nightingale; Cardinal Grosbeak; Common Cardinal Grosbeak; Red Grosbeak; Red Bluejay; Cardenal Rojo; Rota Fogel

Pyrrhuloxia
Cardinalis sinuatus
(car-din-AY-lis sin-you-AY-tus)

The common name (pronounced peer-uh-LOCKS-ih-ah) used to be the genus name as well. This species has now been merged into the genus *Cardinalis*. Pyrrhuloxia is derived from the Greek words *pyrrhula* and *loxias*. *Pyrrhula* is a name Aristotle used for the Eurasian Bullfinch (*Pyrrhula pyrrhula*). It stems from *pyrrhos* (flame-colored) and refers to the touches of red the male shows in his crest, face, tail, and wings as well as to the red stripe down the breast. The bullfinch itself has rose red underparts. *Loxias*, which means "crooked," refers to the bird's curved, parrot-like bill.

Cardinalis — The genus name is Latin for "principal" or "important" derived from *cardo* (a hinge). The Cardinals were the senior bishops of the Roman Catholic Church, the policies of which hinged on their decisions. The reference is to the plumage of the Northern Cardinal, the color of the robes the Cardinals wore.

sinuatus — The specific epithet is Latin for "bent" or "bowed" and also refers to the shape of the bill.

French Name: Cardinal Pyrrhuloxia
Spanish Name: Cardenal Desértico
Other Names: Arizona Pyrrhuloxia; Texas Pyrrhuloxia; Gray Cardinal; Texan Cardinal; Texas Cardinal; Bullfinch Cardinal; Bullfinch; Gray Grosbeak; Parrot-bill

Yellow Grosbeak
Pheucticus chrysopeplus
(FEW-tih-kus Kris-oh-PEP-lus)

The Yellow Grosbeak is named for the male's yellow plumage, although his wings and tail are black with white markings.

Pheucticus — The genus name is from the

Greek *pheutikos* (shy, retiring or tending to avoid). It probably pertains to this species' secretive nature during the breeding season. They are heard more often than seen.

chrysopeplus — The specific epithet means "golden-robed" from the Greek *khrusos* "gold" and *peplos* "a robe."

French Name: Cardinal Jaune
Spanish Name: Picogrueso Amarillo

~

Rose-breasted Grosbeak
Pheucticus ludovicianus
(FEW-tih-kus loo-doe-viss-ih-ANE-us)

"Strikingly garbed in black and white, with a showy shield of bright rose red on his breast and a splash of the same color on the underside of each wing, he is a picture of devil-may-care gallantry . . ." — Robert S. Lemmon (1951)

This grosbeak gets its name from the rose red wedge on the breeding male's chest. It is used in courtship display.

Pheucticus — The genus name is from the Greek *pheutikos* (shy, retiring or tending to avoid). It probably pertains to this species' secretive nature during the breeding season. They are heard more often than seen.

ludovicianus — The specific epithet is Modern Latin for "of Louisiana," the state where the type specimen was collected.

French Name: Cardinal à Poitrine Rose
Spanish Names: Picogordo de Pecho Rosa; Picogrueso Pechirrosado
Other Names: Common Grosbeak; Summer Grosbeak; Rose-breast; Potato-bug Bird; Linnet; Throat-cut; Degollado; Piquigrueso Rosado

~

Black-headed Grosbeak
Pheucticus melanocephalus
(FEW-tih-kus meh-lan-oh-SEE-fal-us)

The male of this species has a black head, but so does the Rose-breasted Grosbeak.

Pheucticus — The genus name is from the Greek *pheutikos* (shy, retiring or tending to avoid). It probably pertains to this species' secretive nature during the breeding season. They are heard more often than seen.

melanocephalus — The specific epithet means "black head" from the Greek *melas* (black) and *kephalos* (headed).

French Name: Cardinal à Tête Noire
Spanish Names: Picogordo Tigrillo; Picogrueso Tigrillo; Picogrueso Cabecinegro
Other Names: Common Grosbeak; Western Grosbeak; Rocky Mountain Grosbeak; Black-headed Song Grosbeak; Black-head

~

Blue Bunting
Cyanocompsa parellina
(sigh-an-oh-KOMP-sah parr-eh-LINE-ah)

This visitor from Mexico is named for the male's deep blue plumage, considerably darker than that of the Indigo Bunting.

Cyanocompsa — The genus name means "dark blue pretty one" from the Greek *kuanos* (dark blue) and *kompsos* (pretty or elegant).

parellina — The specific epithet is Modern Latin for "violet-colored" or "litmus violet" and refers to the dark blue color verging on violet.

French Name: Évêque Paré
Spanish Names: Colorín Azul Negro; Colorín Azulinegro

~

Blue Grosbeak
Passerina caerulea
(pass-er-EYE-nah seh-ROO-lee-ah)

The male's deep blue plumage gives this bird its name. The only other color this grosbeak shows is the chestnut of the two wing bars.

Passerina — The genus name is Latin for "sparrow-like."

Rose-breasted Grosbeak and Northern Cardinal, by Louis Agassiz Fuertes

caerulea — The specific epithet is Latin for "blue." It can mean sky blue or, in this case, a rich, deep blue.
French Name: Passerin Bleu
Spanish Names: Picogorgo Azul; Picogrueso Azul
Other Names: Western Blue Grosbeak; California Blue Grosbeak; Blue Song Grosbeak; Big Indigo; Blue Pop; Azulejo

Lazuli Bunting
Passerina amoena
(pass-er-EYE-nah ah-MEE-nah)

"The Lazuli-painted Finch should be called the Blue-headed Finch; for the exquisite blueness of his whole head, including throat, breast, and shoulders, as if he had been dipped so far into blue dye, is his most distinguishing feature. The Bluebird wears heaven's color; so does the Jay and likewise the Indigo Bird; but not one can boast the lovely and indescribable shade, with its silvery reflections, that adorns the Lazuli . . .Altogether he is charming to look upon." — Olive Thorne Miller (1917)

Pronounced LAZZ-you-lye. Lapis lazuli is a deep blue semiprecious stone used in jewelry. The reference is to the male's blue breeding plumage. Bunting is believed to be derived from the German *bunt* meaning "speckled" or "mottled." It was originally applied to small, brown Old World birds in the family Emberizidae. Our colorful buntings in the family Cardinalidae are not closely related. They are sometimes collectively called tropical buntings, because they winter in the American tropics.
Passerina — The genus name is Latin for "sparrow-like."
amoena — The specific epithet is Latin for "lovely," "delightful," "charming," "dressy," or "pleasant," all of which describe this bird.
French Name: Passerin Azuré
Spanish Names: Colorín Lázuli; Colorín Lazulita
Other Names: Lazuli Painted Bunting; Lazuli Painted Finch

Lazuli Bunting, by Louis Agassiz Fuertes

Indigo Bunting
Passerina cyanea
(pass-er-EYE-nah sigh-ANE-ee-ah)

"The male has such a peculiar color; no bird outside of the tropics has such a peculiar blue as the male Indigo Bird. It isn't an indigo color but rather a deep ultramarine blue. Just as you have made up your mind that that is the right name of the color, you get the bird in a different light and behold he is grayish blue or azure-blue, or maybe olive-blue. At least there is no confusing him with any other bluish bird." — *Birds of America* (1917)

Indigo is a blue dye made from plants in the genus *Indigofera*. The word derives from the Latin *indicum* (of India), the country where the dying herbs originated. The reference is to the breeding male's vivid blue plumage. Actually there is no blue pigment in an Indigo Bunting's feathers. The feathers are blackish, which you can see if you dip one in alcohol or view it backlit. The color is structural, caused by the refraction of light. Minute air pockets called vacuoles in the feathers scatter the blue part of the spectrum, while a pigmented layer containing melanin absorbs the other wavelengths in the spectrum. This is called the Tyndall effect, the same phenomenon that makes the sky appear blue. The shade of blue varies with the lighting, as described above.

Passerina — The genus name is Latin for "sparrow-like."

cyanea — The specific epithet is from the Greek *kuanos* (dark blue).

French Name: Passerin Indigo

Spanish Names: Colorín Azul; Azulillo Norteño

Other Names: Indigo Painted Bunting; Indigo Bird; Blue Bird; Indigo Bluebird; Indigo Finch; Blue Finch; Blue Canary; Blue Linnet; Azulejo; Blofogel; Gorrion Azul; Oiseau Bleu; Oiseau de Montreal

Varied Bunting
Passerina versicolor
(pass-er-EYE-nah ver-SICK-uh-lor)

Varied refers to the male's multicolored plumage. Although it appears black in poor light, in sunlight it shows a plum-purple body, a blue head and rump, and a red patch on the nape. Roger Tory Peterson wrote that the Varied Bunting is "colored like an Easter egg."

Passerina — The genus name is Latin for "sparrow-like."

versicolor — The specific epithet is Latin for "variegated," "parti-colored," "of various colors."

French Name: Passerin Varié
Spanish Name: Colorín Morado
Other Names: Beautiful Bunting

Painted Bunting
Passerina ciris
(pass-er EYE-nah SIGH-ris)

"No other North American species is so brightly colored, or wears such a Joseph's coat of startling contrasts. There is no blending of shades whatever, the different hues are as sharply defined as if they were cut by a straight edge. No wonder many people seeing it for the first time can scarcely credit their eyes, because nothing else approaches it. Many other bright birds occur hither and yon about the country, but for flaming, jewel-like radiance, the nonpareil, as we know it in the South, literally fulfills the name; it is "without an equal."" — Alexander Sprunt, Jr. (1968)

Painted refers to the male's bright tropical colors that look as though they were painted on, violet-blue head and nape with red eye ring, lime-green mantle, blood-red rump, parrot green wing coverts, scarlet underparts, and touches of claret-red in the wings and tail. Pete Dunne says the colors "make the bird look like it was painted by a crayon-wielding three-year-old." An Indian legend has it that the Painted Bunting was the last bird to receive its colors. By the time the Great Spirit got to it, the paint pots were nearly empty. So the Painted Bunting got a coat of many colors from the remnants that were left.

Painted Bunting, by John James Audubon

Passerina — The genus name is Latin for "sparrow-like."

ciris — The specific epithet is Latin from the Greek *kiris*, a name Dionysius used for some bird, not further identified. According to a Greek legend, the kiris was formerly a princess, Scylla, the daughter of the King Nisus of Megara. The king sported a lock of purple hair that made him invincible and protected his kingdom. So when Minos, the King of Crete, invaded Megara, Scylla viewing the countryside from the parapet fell madly in love with the enemy. She would do anything to win him over, so she cut off her father's purple lock while he slept and presented it to Minos. But Minos was appalled at Scylla's treachery, that she would betray her father and her people, and he rejected her. Scylla, however, would not give up and dove into the water to swim after Minos' departing ship. Almost immediately a sea eagle attacked her, and Scylla drowned. The gods, taking pity on her, changed her into a bird, the kiris, which was persistently pursued by the eagle. As it turned out, the eagle was her father, whom the gods had also transformed into a bird. In naming the Painted Bunting, Linnaeus apparently took a circuitous route and made a connection between the king's lock of purple hair and the bunting's violet-blue head.

French Name: Passerin Nonpareil

Spanish Names: Colorín de Siete Colores; Colorín Sietecolores; Azulillo Sietecolores

Other Names: Painted Finch; Paradise Finch; Nonpareil; Pope; Red Pop; Mexican Canary; Texas Canary; Mariposa; Mariposa Pintada; Arco-iris; Verderon

Dickcissel
Spiza americana
(SPY-zah ah-mer-ih-CANE-ah)

"While some other birds are equally numerous, there are few that announce their presence as persistently as this species. All day long, in spring and summer, the males, sometimes to the number of a dozen or more for each meadow of considerable extent, perch upon the summits of tall weed-stalks or fence-stakes, at short intervals crying out:

Dickcissel, by John James Audubon

See, see — Dick, Dick-Cissel Cissel," therefore "Dick Cissel" is well known to every farmer's boy as well as to all who visit the country during the season of clover-blooms and wild roses, when-"Dame Nature" is in her most joyous mood." — Robert Ridgway (1895)

The common name is onomatopoetic suggesting the song, as described above. It is sometimes rendered *dik dik siss siss siss*.

Spiza — The genus name is a word Aristotle used for some finch not further identified. Later authors believe it to be the Chaffinch (*Fringilla coelebs*). The Dickcissel was formerly classified in the Finch family Fringillidae.

americana — The specific epithet is Modern Latin for "of America." Gmelin originally placed the Dickcissel in the genus *Emberiza*, to which the European buntings belong. The specific epithet distinguished this species from these Old World birds.

French Name: Dickcissel d'Américique
Spanish Names: Arrocero Americano; Sabanero Americano; Sabanero Arrocero
Other Names: Black-throated Bunting; Little Field Lark; Little Meadowlark; Judas-bird

Family Thraupidae
Tanagers

Bananaquit
Coereba flaveola
(see-REB-ah flay-vee-OH-lah)

This bird does not feed on bananas, but probes flowers with its long, thin bill for nectar and also takes small insects. Some sources say banana refers to the bird's yellow markings. It could also be a Carib (Venezuelan) Indian word for this or some other bird. Quit is also probably of West Indian origin and may be from a call note. Known as Bahama Honeycreeper until 1973.

Coereba — The genus name is from the Tupi (Brazilian) Indian *guira coereba*, their name for some finch-sized blue, black, and yellow nectar-feeding bird.

flaveola — The specific epithet means "little yellow one" from the Latin *flavus* (yellow) and the diminutive suffix *–olus* (small). The Bananaquit is four to five inches long and has a bright yellow rump and breast band.

French Name: Sucrier à Ventre Jaune
Spanish Names: Platanero; Reinita-Mielera
Other Names: Bahama Bananaquit; Bahaman Honeycreeper; Black and Yellow Creeper; Sugar Bird; Yellow See-see; Black See-see; Banana Bird; Banana Yoky; Beany Bird; Beeny Quit; Yellow-breast; Paw-paw Bird; Marley Quit; Bessie Bird; Bessie Coban; John Cropple; Psyche; Honey-sucker; Siguita; Reinita; Reinita Comun; Gusanero; Sucrier; Teasy

Morelet's Seedeater
Sporophila moreleti
(spore-OFF-ih-lah more-LAY-eye)

Seedeater describes this bird's main diet of grass seeds, although it takes some insects, too. Typically it forages while clinging to the stems of tall grasses as it plucks the seeds directly from the seedheads. Less commonly, it forages on the ground.

This species is named for Pierre Marie Arthur Morelet. See specific epithet below. Until 2018, Morelet's Seedeater and the Cinnamon-rumped Seedeater (*S. torqueola*) of western Mexico were considered a single species, the White-collared Seedeater.

Sporophila — The genus name means "seed loving" from the Greek *sporos* (a seed) and *philos* (loving).

moreleti — The specific epithet honors French naturalist and artist Pierre Marie Arthur Morelet (1809–1892), who collected in the Azores, the Canary Islands, and tropical America. Formerly *Sporophila torqueola*.

French Name: Sporophile de Morelet
Spanish Name: Semillero cuelliblanco
Other Names: Sharpe's Seedeater; Morrelet

Extinct Species and Subspecies

Labrador Duck
Camptorhynchus labradorius
(kam-toe-RING-kus lab-rah-DOR-ih-us)

This duck is named for the province in northeastern Canada, where it is supposed to have nested from the south coast northward. There is, however, little evidence to substantiate this. In fact, Audubon found none there when he visited Labrador in 1834. The reasons for its extinction are unknown. Market hunting and sport hunting may have played a role, but the duck was not considered good-eating. Perhaps the decline of mussels and other shellfish due to industrial pollution along the eastern seaboard, where this species wintered, was a factor. The Labrador Duck was said to be more dependent on such food than most sea ducks. The last two individuals recorded were taken by hunters, one off Long Island in 1875, the other at Elmira, New York in 1878.

Camptorhynchus — The genus name means "flexible beak" from the Greek *kamptos* (flexible) and *rhynchos* (the beak) referring to the soft, leathery texture of the upper part of the bill.

labradorius — The specific epithet is Modern Latin for "of Labrador."

French Name: Eider du Labrador
Other Names: Pied Duck; Skunk Duck; Sand Shoal Duck

Heath Hen
Tympanuchus cupido cupido
(tim-pan-YOU-cuss kew-PIE-doe)

The Heath Hen was the eastern subspecies of the Greater Prairie-Chicken, whose main range during Colonial times was the Atlantic seaboard from southern Maine south to northern Virginia. Its name refers to its preferred habitat of heathland barrens, an open plain with a scattering of shrubby vegetation such as scrub oak and stunted pines and an

Labrador Duck, by Louis Agassiz Fuertes

understory of grasses, sedges, forbs, and heaths such as blueberry and bearberry. The Heath Hen was heavily hunted to the extent that it was extirpated from the mainland by 1870 if not before. Now there was only a small population, about 300, on Martha's Vineyard. By the 1890s the population had declined to about seventy individuals. Conservation efforts allowed the population to increase to nearly 2000 birds by 1915. But then a series of unfortunate events, a devastating wildfire in the spring of 1916, an unusual influx of migrating Northern Goshawks during the winter of 1916–1917, an epidemic of blackhead disease introduced with domestic turkeys, and severe winters decimated the population. There was a partial recovery until there were 600 counted in 1920. Then there was another rapid decline down to thirteen in 1927. The last Heath Hen died on March 11, 1932.

Tympanuchus — The genus name means "neck drum" from Greek *tumpanon* (a kettledrum) and Modern Latin *nucha* (the neck). The reference is to the yellow-orange air sacks on either side of the neck, that ar inflated during courtship. They make a booming sound, sort of like blowing across the mouth of a soda bottle.

cupido — The specific epithet is Latin for Cupid, the Roman god of love. Cupid is, of course, familiar to anyone who has ever sent a valentine. In art Cupid is usually depicted as a winged infant carrying a bow and quiver of arrows. The reference is to special neck feathers called pinnae that are raised like rabbit ears when the males are displaying. The pinnae suggest Cupid's wings.

French Names: Bruyère; Cocq de Bois d'Amérique
Spanish Name: Gallina de Brezo
Other Names: Eastern Prairie-Chicken; Eastern Pinnated Grouse; Heathcock; Heathen

Eskimo Curlew
Numenius borealis
(new-MEAN-ih-us bor-eh-AY-lis)

"The story of the Eskimo curlew is just one more pitiful tale of the slaughter of the innocents. It is a sad fact that the countless swarms of this fine bird and the passenger pigeon, which once swept across our land on migrations, are gone forever, sacrificed to insatiable greed of man." — Arthur Cleveland Bent (1929)

The Eskimo Curlew takes its name from its nesting habitat on the Arctic tundra. This bird's population was devastated by market hunting in the late 19th and early 20th centuries. About two million Eskimo Curlews were killed each year toward the end of the 19th century. Hunters called them Dough-birds, because their breasts often split open on impact exposing a layer of fat beneath the skin. The population never recovered, and the last confirmed sightings were on Galveston Island, Texas in 1962 and on Barbados in 1963. More recent but unconfirmed reports come from Texas (1981 and 1987), Canada (1987), Argentina (1990), and Nova Scotia (2006).

Eskimo Curlew, by John James Audubon

Great Auk, no artist credited

Numenius — The genus name is derived from *noumenios*, a name used by Hesychius and associated with the curlew. It means "new moon" from the Greek *neos* (new) and *mene* (the moon) and refers to the long, curved bill, suggesting a new crescent moon.

borealis — The specific epithet is Latin for "northern" or "of the north." The reference is to this species' breeding habitat in the Arctic.

French Name: Couris Esquimau
Spanish Name: Zarapito Esquimal
Other Names: Little Curlew; Small Curlew; Esquimaux Curlew; Small Esquimaux Curlew; Little Sickle-bill; Prairie Pigeon; Dough-bird; Doe-bird; Corbigeau; Fute; Guilbueach; Playero Arctico

Great Auk
Pinguinus impennis
(PIN-gwin-us im-PEN-iss)

Auk stems from the Old Norse *alka*, a name for various seabirds and believed to be imitative. The Great Auk was the largest member of the family. Heavy human exploitation doomed the Great Auk to extinction. Sailors routinely took both adults and young for food. These were clubbed and salted down, or live birds were herded onto ships as a source of fresh meat. Eggs were taken, too. Great Auks were also used for bait, as a source for oil, and their feathers were used to stuff mattresses. The last record of this species in the wild was from Iceland in 1844. The last North American record was from Funk Island off the coast of Newfoundland in 1841.

Pinguinus — The genus name means "white head" from the Welsh words *pen* (the head) and *gwyn* (white) and refers to the large oval white spot between the bird's bill and eye. This is the origin of the common name for the superficially similar but unrelated birds of the Southern Hemisphere we now call penguins.

impennis — The specific epithet means "without feathers" from the Latin *im* (without) and *pennis* (feathers), but here it means "wingless" and refers to the Great Auk's tiny vestigial wings. This was the only member of the family that was flightless.

French Name: Grand Pingouin
Spanish Name: Alca Gigante
Other Names: Penguin; Garefowl; Wobble

Passenger Pigeon
Ectopistes migratorius
(eck-toe-PIS-teez my-grah-TOR-ih-us)

"The passenger pigeon was such a spectacular species in its migratory flights, its roostings, and its nestings, in which such enormous numbers took part, that there are many references to it from the times of the earliest pioneers." — Charles Wendell Townsend (1932)

The Passenger Pigeon may well have been North America's most abundant bird. Migrating flocks were said to be in excess of a billion birds, maybe even two billion. But abundance is no guarantee against extinction. Passenger, meaning "wayfarer" or "traveler," refers to this species seasonal migrations in spectacular flocks that darkened the sky. This species quickly declined from market hunting and destruction of its habitat. The Passenger Pigeon required mature forests for nesting with their crops of mast, beechnuts, acorns, and chestnuts. A bird shot by a boy with a BB gun in Pike County, Ohio in March 22 or 24, 1900 is the last authenticated record of a wild Passenger Pigeon, but there were other reports from 1902, 1905, and 1907. The last Passenger Pigeon, a female named Martha, died in the Cincinnati Zoo on September 1,1914.

Ectopistes — The genus name means "moving about" or "wandering" from the Greek *ektopistikos* (migratory). See common name above.

migratorius — The specific epithet is Latin for "migratory."

French Names: Pigeon Migrateur; Tourte Voyageuse

Passenger Pigeon, by Louis Agassiz Fuertes

Other Names: Wild Pigeon; Wood Pigeon; Migratory Pigeon; Red-breasted Pigeon; Blue Pigeon; Blue-headed Pigeon; Blue Meteor

Ivory-billed Woodpecker
Campephilus principalis
(cam-PEFF-ih-lus prin-sih-PAY-liss)

"The bills of these Birds are much valued by the Canada Indians, who made Coronets of 'em for their Princes and great warriors, by fixing them round a Wreath, with their points outward. The Northern Indians having none of these Birds in their cold country, purchase them of the Southern People at the price of two, and some-times three, Buck-skins a Bill." — Mark Catesby

This woodpecker's ivory-white bill gives it its name. These were traded among the Indians as explained in the above passage. The Ivory-billed Woodpecker was devastated by intense logging of its primeval forest habitat

Ivory-billed Woodpecker, male (left), female (right), by Allan C. Brooks

and by hunting by collectors. It is probably extinct, but there is hope it still exists. Although there are published reports by expeditions to Florida, Louisiana, and Arkansas between 2005 and 2009, there is no conclusive evidence that the Ivory-bill is still in existence.

Campephilus — The genus name means "caterpillar loving" from the Greek *kampe* (a caterpillar) and *philos* (loving). In this case it should be translated "grub loving," since the principal prey of this species was the larvae of wood-boring beetles.

principalis — The specific epithet is Latin for "princely" or "imperial" from *princeps* (a chief) and refers to this species' large size (larger than a crow) and striking appearance.

French Name: Pic à Bec Ivoire
Spanish Names: Carpintero Real; Picomaderos picomarfil
Other Names: Ivory-bill; White-billed Woodpecker; Southern Giant Woodpecker; King of the Woodpeckers; Indian Hen; Woodchuck; King Woodchuck; Woodcock; Elvis in Feathers; Logcock; Log-god; Lord God Bird; Grand Pique-bois; Poule de bois; Kent; Kate; Caip

Carolina Parakeet
Conuropsis carolinensis
(kon-your-OP-sis car-oh-lin-EN-sis)

How cool would it be to go out on a bird walk and discover a flock of colorful parrots with bright green bodies and orange and yellow heads? We associate these birds with tropical rainforests, but there was one species native to eastern North America, that occasionally wandered as far north as the Great Lakes. Unfortunately farmers routinely slaughtered whole flocks of these little parrots, because of their fruit-eating habits. They were also victims of the millinery trade and many were captured to be sold as pets. The last sighting in the wild was in Missouri in 1905, and the last known individual died in the Cincinnati Zoo in 1918.

Conuropsis — In 1891, the Italian ornithologist Adelardo Salvidori raised the genus name which means "having the appearance of cone tail" from the Greek *konos* (a cone) and *oura* (the tail) plus *opsis* (appearance). His intent was to show a similarity between the Carolina Parakeet and tropical parrots in the genus *Conurus* (now *Aratinga*). All of these parakeets have long, pointed tails.

carolinensis — The specific epithet is Modern Latin for "of Carolina."

French Name: Conure de Caroline
Spanish Name: Cotorra de Carolina
Other Names: Carolina paroquet; Caroline Parrot; Wild Parrot; Kelinkey

Dusky Seaside Sparrow
Ammodramus maritima nigrescens
(am-OD-rah-mus mar-IT-ih-mah nih-GRES-enz)

This subspecies of the Seaside Sparrow was formerly considered a full species. It had a very limited range in the saltmarshes within a ten-mile radius around Titusville, Florida. Seaside refers to this species habitat of coastal saltmarshes. Dusky describes the dark blackish

Carolina Parakeet, by Allan C. Brooks

color, compared to the paler nominate subspecies. This species never was common, so human activities were especially detrimental. A scheme of mosquito control around the Kennedy Space Center by flooding Merritt Island devastated the sparrows' nesting grounds. Marshes were drained to facilitate road construction, and pollution and pesticides took their toll. By 1979, only six were left, all males. A captive breeding program was begun, crossing these birds with another subspecies, Scott's Seaside Sparrow (*A. m. peninsulae*). But the program was disbanded in the mid-1980s, and the last Dusky Seaside Sparrow died on June 17, 1987.

Ammodramus — The genus name means "sand runner" from the Greek *ammos* (sand) and *dramein* (to run).

maritima — The specific epithet is Latin for "maritime" or "of the sea."

nigrescens — The subspecific epithet is Latin for "blackish."

Other Name: Merritt Island Sparrow

Bachman's Warbler
Vermivora bachmanii
(ver-MIV-or-ah back-MAN-ih-eye)

Audubon named this warbler in honor his "amiable friend," Dr. John Bachman, a minister who discovered this species near his home in Charleston, South Carolina, in July of 1833. Bachman's Warbler was a habitat specialist, requiring dense stands of natural cane on both its breeding and its wintering grounds. It nested in deep swamp forests in the southeastern states. It never was very common and its population was fragmented. Its forests were cut down for timber and to clear land for

Bachman's Warbler, by John James Audubon

agriculture and its wintering grounds in Cuba were converted to sugarcane fields. The last confirmed sighting of a Bachman's Warbler was in South Carolina in 1962.

Vermivora — The genus name means "worm-eating" from the Latin *vermis* (a worm) and *voro* (to eat). The name refers not to earthworms, but to caterpillars, an important food of these warblers, particularly when they are feeding young.

bachmanii — The specific epithet commemorates the reverend John Bachman (1790–1874). See common name above.

French Name: Paruline de Bachman
Spanish Name: Reinita de Bachman
Other Name: Bachman's Oyster Swamp Warbler

Part III

Appendixes

Appendix I
Collective Nouns for Flocks of Birds

There are a number of terms that refer to groups of birds of a particular species or family. Many are obsolete and most are not in common usage anymore, but they are a part of the history of human interactions with birds. If you start to repeat these terms in the field, you may find your fellow birders distancing themselves from you.

Flock is the common term used for any group of birds whether of one species or several. Many species migrate in flocks (waterfowl) or occur in flocks (waxwings) when not nesting. In Alfred Hitchcock's famous movie *The Birds*, amateur ornithologist Mrs. Bundy said, "I have never known birds of different species to flock together. The very concept is unimaginable." Mrs. Bundy wasn't too observant, for there are many examples of species traveling in mixed flocks, from little bands of chickadees, titmice, nuthatches, creepers, kinglets, and Downy Woodpeckers foraging in a winter woodland to huge mixed flocks of blackbirds, grackles, cowbirds, and starlings.

While you won't generally use these words (with the possible exceptions of raft of ducks, covey of quail, kettle of hawks, and perhaps skein of geese), a knowledge of them may prove helpful if you are a crossword puzzle fan or if you are ever a contestant on *Jeopardy*.

aerie of eagles (also a name for eagles nests)
aigrette — The lacy nuptial plumes of egrets.
ascension of larks
badling of ducks
ballet of swans
band or **band party** of jays
battery of hens
bellowing of bullfinches
bevy of quail
bew of partridge
boil of hawks (two or more circling in the sky)
bouquet of pheasants (when flushed)
brood of penguins or the offspring of gamebirds still under parental care
building of rooks
bunch of ducks

cast of hawks or falcons
cauldron of raptors
chain of bobolinks
charm of finches or hummingbirds
chattering of starlings, goldfinches, or hummingbirds
charm of finches
clamour of rooks
cloud of starlings
cluster of knots.
clutch of chicks
colony of gulls, auks, penguins, or vultures
commotion of coots
company of parrots
congregation of plovers or rooks
congress of ravens
conspiracy of ravens

convocation of eagles
cote of doves
cover/covert of coots
covey of partridges or quail
crèche of penguins
deceit of lapwings
descent of woodpeckers
dissimulation of birds (in general)
dole of doves or turkeys
drift of quail
dropping of pigeons
drove of geese
drum of goldfinches or hummingbirds
drumming of grouse
dule of doves
durante of toucans
exaltation of larks
fall of woodcock

flamboyance of flamingos
flight of birds (any species in the air)
flush of mallards
gaggle of geese
gallon of petrels
game of swans
gang of turkeys
gattling of woodpeckers
gulp of magpies or cormorants
hedge of herons
herd of cranes, swans, or wrens
host of sparrows
hover of hummingbirds
kettle of hawks (riding on thermals) or nighthawks
kit of pigeons
knob of wigeon
leash of plovers
line of geese
loft of pigeons
match of nightingales
mews of hawks or hens
mob of emus
murder of crows or magpies
murmuration of starlings
muster/mustering of storks
nest of pheasants
nide of pheasants or geese
nye of pheasants (on ground)
ostentation of peacocks
pack of grouse or gulls
paddling of ducks (on water)
parade of penguins
parcel of penguins or hens
parliament of owls or ravens
party of jays
passager of falcons
peep of chickens
piteousness/pitying of turtle doves
plump of wildfowl
posse of turkeys
prattle of parrots
pride of peacocks
quarrel of sparrows
raffle of turkeys
raft of ducks
rafter of turkeys
regatta of swans
richness of martins
rookery of penguins
roost of hens
run of poultry
rush of swallows
scold of jays
screw of soaring birds (eg., hawks or storks)
sedge of bitterns or cranes
siege of herons or cranes
skein of waterfowl (in flight)
sord of mallards
spring of teal
stand of flamingos
stare of owls
storytelling of crows, ravens, or rooks
strand of silky flycatchers
swoop of swallows
tank of petrels
team of ducks (in flight)
tiding of magpies
trembling of finches
tribe of sparrows
trimming of finches
trip of dotterel
trittering of magpies
troop of doves
troubling of goldfinches
unkindness of ravens
vein of goldfinches
voler of birds
waddling of ducks
wake of buzzards
walk of snipe
watch of nightingales
wedge of geese (in V formation)
whiteness of swans
wing of plovers
wisp of snipe

Appendix II
Glossary

Alcid — A member of the family Alcidae. Includes auks, auklets, murres, murrelets, guillemots, and puffins.

alpine — Describes the habitat in the mountains above timberline.

American Ornithologists' Union — Abbreviated AOU. Now the American Ornithological Society (AOS). In 2016, the AOU merged with the Cooper Ornithological Society to form the American Ornithological Society.

American Ornithological Society — In 2016, the AOU merged with the Cooper Ornithological Society to form the AOS. It is an international ornithological organization founded in 1883, and based in the United States. Its mission is "to advance the scientific understanding of birds and disseminate ornithological knowledge, enrich ornithology as a profession and mentor young professionals, and promote a rigorous scientific basis for the conservation of birds." It publishes the *AOS Checklist of North American Birds*, the standard authority on the names and taxonomy of North American birds. Its scientific journals are *The Auk* and *The Condor*.

auriculars — The feathers that cover the ear openings.

Aves — The taxonomic class of vertebrates to which all birds belong.

binomial nomenclature — The system of assigning a two-part scientific name to every described organism. Each scientific name consists of a genus and species.

bivalve — A mollusk whose shell consists of two hinged valves. Examples are clams, oysters, mussels, and scallops.

boreal — Pertains to northern coniferous forests of Canada and the northern United States.

brood parasitism — The practice by one species of laying its eggs in the nest of another species.

call — A vocal sound not connected with reproduction (see song). Examples are alarm calls, contact calls, and begging calls.

circumpolar — Occurring in the Northern Hemisphere in both North America and Eurasia.

congener — A member of the same genus.

conifer — A cone-bearing, usually evergreen, tree such as a pine, fir, or spruce.

conspecific — Belonging to the same species. For example, the Oak Titmouse and Juniper Titmouse were formerly considered conspecific as the Plain Titmouse.

Corvid — A member of the family Corvidae. Includes crows, ravens, jays, and magpies.

courtship — Behavior involved in attracting a mate.

coverts — The smaller feathers that cover the bases of the flight feathers and tail feathers.

crepuscular — Active at dawn and dusk.

crissum — The undertail coverts.

crop — A swelling of the esophagus that stores food prior to digestion.

culmen — The ridge on the upper portion of the bill.

dabbler — A surface-feeding duck that often feeds by tipping up — head under water, tail in the air. Examples are mallard, gadwall, and pintail.

diurnal — Active in the daytime.

drake — A male duck of any species.

eclipse plumage — The dull-colored plumage into which some species of male ducks molt into during a flightless period following the breeding season.

endemic — Refers to a species whose range is restricted to a specific region. For example, the Island Scrub-Jay is endemic to Santa Cruz Island off the California coast.

eponym — A name that commemorates a person.

erythrism — Unusual red pigmentation in the plumage of a bird.

exotic — Refers to any species that is not native.

facial disc — The circle of feathers, surrounding the eyes of owls and some other birds, that funnels sound to the ears.

family — A taxonomic category within an order that contains one or more genera.

feral — Refers to a domestic bird or other animal that is living in the wild.

field mark — A distinctive feature of a bird such as an eyering or wingbar that helps to identify it.

finch — A member of several families of seed-eating birds with conical bills. Included are the families Fringillidae (goldfinches, crossbills, purple finches, and redpolls), Phoceidae (weaver finches), and Estrelididae (waxbills). The latter includes such familiar cagebirds as the Strawberry Finch and the Zebra Finch. Loosely, a seed-eating bird in several related families such as Cardinalidae (cardinal grosbeaks) and Embereizidae (New World sparrows). These were formerly classified in the family Fringillidae.

forage — To search for food.

frontal shield — A horny or leathery extension of the bill onto the forehead, seen in some species of birds such as coots and gallinules.

gallinaceous — Refers to chicken-like birds in the order Galliformes. Includes partridges, quail, pheasants, grouse, and turkeys.

genus (plural: **genera**) — A taxonomic category within a family that contains one or more species.

gorget — The brightly colored, iridescent throat patch of a male hummingbird.

gular pouch — A throat pouch as on a pelican or cormorant.

habitat — The area where an organism usually occurs.

hawking — A foraging strategy in which the bird flies out from a perch to catch an insect in midair and returns to the same or nearby perch. Also called flycatching.

holotype — The single specimen (usually a museum study skin) designated as the type for describing and naming a species. See type specimen.

hover gleaning — Hovering while searching for insects on leaves, limbs, or tree trunks.

immature — A young bird that has not acquired its adult plumage, but may be capable of breeding.

incertae sedis — Latin for "of uncertain placement," this a term for a taxonomic group whose broader relationships are unknown or undefined.

irruption — The periodic movement of a species in large numbers into an area outside its normal range.

juvenile — A young bird that has not reached sexual maturity.

kleptoparasitism — The harassment of one bird by another in order to force it to relinquish its catch. Also called piracy.

lek — A staging area where males of certain species such as grouse display to attract a mate.

malar — Refers to the cheekbone or the side of the head.

mandible — Either part, upper or lower, of a bird's bill.

mantle — The back and upper sides of the wings.

mast — Bulky, fibrous food such as nuts, acorns, and conifer seeds.

migration — The seasonal movement of birds to and from their breeding grounds.

mimicry — The imitation of the call or song of other species.

mnemonic (or **mnemonic device**) — Putting a bird's song or call into words as an aid to remembering. A mnemonic for the Eastern Towhee's song is *Drink you tea*.

mobbing — The massing together of small birds, often mixed species, and their attack on a common enemy, such as an owl or house cat.

molt — The process of shedding and renewing worn feathers.

monotypic — A genus or family that contains only one species.

morph — One of several color forms that occurs

Glossary

within a species, such as the white morph and blue morph of the Snow Goose.

naricorns — The sheaths that enclose the nostrils of albatrosses and petrels.

neotropical migrant — A species that breeds in the United States and/or Canada and winters in the American tropics — Mexico, the West Indies, and Central and South America. Examples include hummingbirds, vireos, thrushes, wood warblers, tanagers, and orioles.

New World — The western hemisphere — North and South America.

nocturnal — Active at night.

nuptial plumes — The ornamental feathers displayed by herons and egrets during the breeding season.

Old World — The eastern hemisphere — Eurasia, Africa, and Australia.

order — A taxonomic category that contains one or more families.

ornithology — The branch of biology that deals with the study of birds.

passerine — A member of the order Passeriformes — the perching birds or songbirds. Examples include flycatchers, swallows, wrens, thrushes, wood-warblers, sparrows, blackbirds, and finches.

peep — A colloquial name for the smaller sandpipers in the genus *Calidris*, such as the Least and Western Sandpipers.

pelagic — Refers to an organism that occurs in or over the open ocean far offshore.

perch gleaning — A foraging strategy in which the bird searches foliage and other surfaces for prey without flying from the searching position.

plumage — All the feathers that cover a bird as a whole.

primaries — The largest and outermost flight feathers, attached to the manus which corresponds to the human hand.

raptor — A bird of prey such as a hawk, falcon, or owl.

retrices — The tail feathers.

rictal bristles — Hair-like feathers at the base of bill in certain species such as flycatchers and nightjars that presumably aid the birds in catching insects.

sally gleaning — A foraging strategy in which the bird searches for prey while perched, then darting out to snatch an insect off a distant surface.

scapulars — The feathers of the shoulder.

secondaries — The flight feathers on the trailing edge of the wing, attached to the ulna.

shaft — The midrib of a feather.

shorebird — A name for a member of several families in the order Charadriiformes that tend to frequent seashores and lakeshores. Includes plovers, sandpipers, oystercatchers, stilts, and avocets. Called waders in Great Britain.

song — Often musical vocalizations used to identify a territory and to attract a mate. See call.

species — A population of interbreeding individuals, possessing common characteristics distinguishing it from other similar populations.

speculum — A patch of contrasting, often metallic, color on a dabbling duck's wing.

staging area — A place where large numbers of migrating birds stop to rest and feed before continuing their journey.

stoop — The nearly vertical dive of a falcon onto its prey.

subspecies — A race or variety within a species.

supercilium — The eyebrow.

taiga — An evergreen forest of northern regions.

talon — The claw of a bird of prey.

tautonym — A scientific name whose genus and species are identical.

taxon (plural taxa) — A category of scientific classification such as an order, family, or genus.

taxonomic order — A list of species in presumed evolutionary sequence, beginning with the most primitive and ending with the most advanced species. Also called checklist order.

taxonomy — The science concerning the classification of organisms.

tertials — The innermost feathers on the upper surface of the wing.

toponym — A name that refers to a region. Example: Mississippi Kite (*Ictinia mississippiensis*).

transient — An individual or species that crosses a region to and from its breeding and wintering grounds, but does not otherwise occur in that area.

tundra — The treeless plain of arctic regions. It is an important breeding ground for waterfowl and shorebirds.

type locality — The place where the type specimen was collected.

type specimen — The first specimen of a new species from which it is described and named. Also called holotype. The type specimen is preserved as a study skin, stored on its back in a drawer with a label tied on with a thread to one leg as a permanent museum record.

upland — Refers to an area far from floodplains, wetlands, and coastlines.

vagrant — A bird that strays outside of its normal range.

zygodactyl — A foot with the toes arranged 2 pointing forward and 2 backward as in cuckoos and woodpeckers.

Appendix III
An Introduction to the Naturalists Mentioned in the Book

Abert, James William (1820–1897) — Abert was a naturalist, artist, and topographical engineer with the Army Corps of Engineers. He described the flora, fauna, and geology of the Canadian River Valley in eastern New Mexico and the Texas Panhandle, and collected specimens for Baird at the Smithsonian. He took part in the Shenandoah Valley campaign during the Civil War. After retiring from the military in 1864, Abert held a number of civilian jobs: a merchant in Cincinnati, an examiner of patents in Washington, D.C., and a professor of English literature at Missouri State University. Abert's Towhee (*Melozone aberti*) is named in his honor. Abert's (Tassel-eared) Squirrel (*Sciurus aberti*) is named for James' father Colonel John James Abert (1788–1863), who was the head of the Topographical Engineers for many years.

Adams, Edward (1824–1856)) — Edward Adams was a British naval surgeon and naturalist. He made two exploratory expeditions to the American Arctic, collecting birds, insects, plants, and geological specimens. He also drew sketches of Arctic scenes. In 1848, he joined James Clark Ross's expedition to search for Sir John Franklin. But after eighteen months, they were unsuccessful. In 1850, Adams was assigned assistant surgeon on the *Enterprise* under Captain Richard Collinson. This voyage discovered the Northwest Passage across the northern coast of North America. In 1856, Adams sailed to the west coast of Africa, where he contracted typhus and died at age thirty-two. He is buried in Sierra Leone. The Yellow-billed Loon (*Gavia adamsii*) is named in his honor.

Alexandre, Dr. M. M. (fl. 1846)) — Dr. Alexandre was a French physician, who collected zoological specimens in Mexico and sent them back to France.

Allen, Arthur Augustus (1885–1964) — Arthur A. Allen was professor of ornithology at Cornell University from 1916 to 1953. He was also a lecturer and photographer. Allen received his PhD in 1911; his doctoral thesis was *The Red-winged Blackbird: A Study in the Ecology of a Cattail Marsh*. Frank Chapman praised this work calling it "the best, most significant biography which has thus far been prepared of any American bird." In 1919, Allen began to teach the first wildlife conservation course in the United States. He received the Outdoor Life Medal in 1924 for his research on the diseases of the Ruffed Grouse. He published papers in scientific journals and also wrote articles for popular magazines such as *National Geographic*. Allen was a co-founder of the Cornell Laboratory of Ornithology in 1957. In 1929, Allen and his colleague Peter Paul Kellogg began to record bird sounds. It started as an assignment for a motion picture corporation to record the singing of birds synchronized with motion pictures. After the project, Allen and Kellogg continued to record bird songs to produce phonograph records. Three of these — *Song Birds of America, Bird Songs in Your Garden*, and *Dawn in a Duckblind* — came in spirally bound books with color illustrations and text. The Laboratory's Macaulay Library now houses the world's largest collection of natural sounds in their archives, more than 165,000 recordings of birds, whales, bats, frogs, insects, and other animals. Among

Allen's other published works are *Laboratory Notebook* (1927), *The Book of Bird Life* (1930), *American Bird Biographies* (1934), *The Golden Plover and Other Birds* (1939), and *Stalking Birds with Color Camera* (1951).

Allen, Charles Andrew (1841–1930) — Charles Allen was an amateur collector of birds in California. He moved from his home state of Massachusetts to the edge of the redwood forest north of San Francisco, where dust from the planing mill where he worked took a toll on his health. He had learned taxidermy from James Gatly of Boston. When the Civil War broke out, Allen served with the First Massachusetts Regiment for two years. Before moving to California, he had an opportunity to learn about seabirds by taking a job as a fisherman on the Grand Banks of Newfoundland. Allen's Hummingbird (*Selasphorus sasin*) is named for him.

Anderson, Mary Virginia Childs (1833–1912) — Mary Virginia Childs was born into a military family. Her father was General Thomas Childs of Pittsfield, Massachusetts. She married U.S. Army surgeon Dr. William Wallace Anderson at Wilmington, North Carolina in 1855. Virginia was an accomplished singer and musician, so when her husband was sent west to Fort Burgwyn, New Mexico, they took her piano along by covered wagon. It arrived banged up and out of tune, but Dr. Anderson was able to restore it almost as good as new. While stationed in New Mexico, Dr. Anderson collected birds for Baird at the Smithsonian. When South Carolina seceded from the Union in 1861, Dr. Anderson resigned from the U.S. Army and moved his family back east. He joined the Confederacy, initially as a surgeon but soon was promoted to Medical Inspector and Superintendent of Vaccination of the Armies, Hospitals and Camps of Instruction of the Confederate States. After the war, the Andersons resided at his parents' home Borough House in Stateburg, South Carolina. There Virginia and her husband were instrumental in founding the Stateburg Literary and Musical Society. The monthly events included plays, musicals, poetry readings, dances, and banquets. Virginia's Warbler (*Oreothlypis virginiae*) is named in her honor.

Anna, Duchess of Rivoli (1806–1896) — Anna was the wife of Prince Francois Victor Massena, Duc de Rivoli. Audubon met her in Paris in 1828, and commented on her charm and beauty. Her husband owned a collection of 12,000 specimens of hummingbirds, one of which was the type specimen of Anna's Hummingbird (*Calypte anna*) which was named in her honor. The collection was later sold to the Academy of Natural Science of Philadelphia.

Audubon, John James (1785–1851) — John James Audubon is so well known, even by the general public, that he is usually referred to only by his last name. He is known as the Artistic Father of American Ornithology. Audubon was born on the island of Santo Domingo (now Haiti), the illegitimate son of Jean Audubon, a French sea captain, and his mistress Jeanne Rabine, a French Creole chambermaid from Nantes. She died six months after Audubon's birth and he was raised in Paris by his stepmother. When Audubon was eighteen, his father sent him to manage his farm in Mill Grove, Pennsylvania. Audubon, however, had no penchant for farming or any of the other jobs he attempted.

Audubon's talent was, instead, in painting. His best known work is *Birds of America*, a collection of life-size portraits of North American birds in natural settings, consisting of 435 full-color paintings of 489 species. The first edition of his book was the Double Elephant Folio which refers to its size (39½ inches x 29½ inches). Audubon's assistant Joseph Mason painted the backgrounds, but is uncredited in the book. Audubon went to Philadelphia and New York in 1823 to find subscribers to finance his project. Having no luck there, he sailed to Britain in 1826. He exhibited his work in Liverpool and Manchester. Audubon travelled to Edinburgh to find an engraver who did the first few plates until a strike prevented them to continue. Audubon found another engraver in London who completed the work. Audubon was able to fund his project by gaining subscribers through his lectures on ornithology and life on the American frontier. Audubon was a colorful character who, sporting flowing locks and wearing a fur cap, hunting shirt, and wolf skin jacket presented himself as an American woodsman. He also wrote an *Ornithological Biography* in five volumes, a 3000-page series of life histories of all the birds he had illustrated in *Birds of America*. Audubon collaborated with his friend John Bachman in writing and illustrating a three-volume work on mammals, *The Viviparous Quadrupeds of North America* (1846–1854). In 1841, he bought twenty-four wooded acres on Manhatten Island and built a wooden house overlooking the Hudson River. He called his place Minnie's Land, and it was the family home for the rest of his life. Audubon went on several expeditions to collect and paint birds, places including the Florida Keys, Labrador, the Gulf States, and finally up the Missouri River to Fort Union, North Dakota, near the Montana border. Of the 160 copies originally printed, 120 copies of *Birds of America* are known to still exist; thirteen of these are in private collections. *The Economist* magazine estimates, that when adjusted for inflation, five out of the ten highest prices ever paid for printed books were for *Birds of America*. In 2000, a sheikh from Qatar purchased a copy at Christie's auction for $8.8 million. That same year the Fox-Bute copy was also auctioned at Christie's for $8,802,500. In 2005 an unbound copy sold for $5.6 million. In 2010, a complete copy of the first edition was sold at Sotheby's in London for £7,321,250 (about $11.5 million). In 2012, another first edition was auctioned at Christie's for $7.9 million. Audubon's Shearwater (*Puffinus lherminieri*) and Audubon's Oriole (*Icterus graduacauda*) honor his name. The western subspecies of the Yellow-rumped Warbler (*Setophaga coronata audubuni*) was formerly considered a full species, Audubon's Warbler. The Crested Caracara (*Caracara cheriway*) was formerly known as Audubon's Caracara.

Bachman, Dr. John (1790–1874) — The Reverend John Bachman was a Lutheran pastor and naturalist, who resided in Charleston, South Carolina. He was the first to describe many North American mammals. Bachman collaborated with his friend John James Audubon on several natural history projects, including writing the text for *Viviparous Quadrupeds of North America*. Audubon's two sons married Bachman's two daughters. The Black Oystercatcher (*Haematopus bachmani*), Bachman's Sparrow (*Peucaea aestivalis*), and the extinct Bachman's Warbler (*Vermivora bachmanii*) are named in his honor.

Bailey, Florence Merriam (1863–1948) — Florence Augusta Merriam was an early proponent of observing birds in the field with optics, as opposed to collecting them with a shotgun. She was also the first female member of the AOU, elected in 1885. She published her first book *Birds Through an Opera Glass* in 1889, considered to be the first field guide. When she contracted tuberculosis, she traveled extensively in the West, primarily California, Arizona, and Utah, seeking an open-air cure in the drier climate. Her books *My Summer in a Mormon Village* (1894) and *A-birding on a Bronco* (1896) were based on her experiences on these travels. In 1895, her chronic illness cured, she moved in with her older brother and his family in Washington, D.C. Her brother Clinton Hart Merriam was the first chief of the Bureau of Biological Survey and one of the country's leading biologists. He was also one of the founding members of the AOU. Dr. Merriam employed a young naturalist, Vernon Bailey, who was also a family friend. In 1899, following the publication of her fourth book, *Birds of Village and Field*, Florence and Vernon were married. For the next three decades the Baileys traveled throughout the West, conducting biological surveys for the federal government. Vernon collected mammals, reptiles, and plants; Florence wrote about the birds she observed. In 1902, she published *Handbook of Birds of the Western United States* as a companion to Frank Chapman's *Handbook of Birds of Eastern North America*. Through several revisions, it remained a standard manual for almost fifty years. When Florence took over an ornithological study, after its researcher died unexpectedly, the result was *Birds of New Mexico* (1928). For this work she was made the first woman fellow of the AOU in 1929 and received the Brewster Medal in 1931. Her final book, *Among Birds in the Grand Canyon National Park*, was published by the

National Park Service in 1939. A subspecies of the Mountain Chickadee (*Poecile gambeli baileyae*) is named in her honor. It is also called the Bailey Mountain Chickadee or simply Bailey's Chickadee.

Baird, Lucy Hunter (1848–1913) — Lucy Hunter Baird was the only child of Spencer Fullerton Baird and Mary H. C. Baird. Her father encouraged her to play with snakes so she would not have an irrational fear of them and other creeping things. When Lucy was fifteen, she spent a summer with her family at Woods Hole, Massachusetts. From 1877–1887, she assisted in secretarial work at the Smithsonian Institution and U.S. Fish Commission. After her father died, Lucy intended to write his biography in collaboration with Baird's successor, Professor G. Brown Goode. But with Goode's untimely death and Lucy's frail health, their biography didn't come to pass. The task was taken up by William H. Dall, who had known Baird for more than twenty years and was greatly influenced by him. His book *Spencer Fullerton Baird, A Biography* was published in 1915. Dall dedicated his book to Lucy, "To the memory of a devoted daughter Lucy Hunter Baird." Lucy's Warbler (*Oreothlypis luciae*) is named in her honor.

Baird, Spencer Fullerton (1823–1887) — Known as the "Nestor of American Ornithology," Baird brought the knowledge of North American avifauna from the pioneer stage to the modern era. He served as secretary of the Smithsonian Institution (1878–1887) and persuaded congress to build the National Museum of Natural History. He commissioned Army surgeons, including Charles Bendire and Elliott Coues, to collect zoological specimens on the western frontier. These and his own field work became the basis for a report (part of a survey for the railroad route to the Pacific) on birds of the United States, later reissued as *Birds of North America* (1859). Baird also created and headed the U.S. Commission of Fish and Fisheries and founded the Marine Biological Laboratory at Woods Hole, Massachusetts. He published extensively not only on birds, but also on mammals, reptiles, and fish. Baird described fourteen species of American birds including Aleutian Tern, Gila Woodpecker, Yellow-bellied Flycatcher, Couch's Kingbird, Northwestern Crow, and Kirtland's Warbler. T. S. Palmer wrote: "Baird did more than any other man of his time to advance the study of ornithology and other branches of zoology." Baird was highly regarded by his peers, as illustrated in the following passage:

"Prof. Baird lived on a higher plane of life and breathed a purer atmosphere than most men. Quiet and unassuming, with a nature as gentle as a child's, his natural superiority never failed to show itself when he was with other men; not even when among the distinguished men who gathered in the winter at the national capital . . . Prof. Baird had the enviable gift not only of endearing everyone to him who came in contact with him, but of inspiring them with his own enthusiasm and energy." — Livingstone Stone (1898)

Baird's Sandpiper (*Calidris bairdii*) and Baird's Sparrow (*Centronyx bairdii*) honor his name, as also do a Hawaiian bird, the Akikiki or Kauai Creeper (*Oreomystis bairdi*), and a number of other tropical birds, Baird's Trogon (*Trogon bairdii*), Baird's Flycatcher (*Myiodynastes bairdii*), Cozumel Vireo (*Vireo bairdi*), Banded Prinia (*Prinia bairdii*), Peg-billed Finch (*Acanthidops bairdi*), and the Cuban subspecies of the extinct Ivory-billed Woodpecker (*Campephilus principalis bairdii*). The names of animals in several other classes also honor Baird. Mammals include Baird's Shrew (*Sorex bairdii*), Baird's Pocket Gopher (*Geomus breviceps*), Baird's Tapir (*Tapirus bairdii*), and Baird's Beaked Whale (*Berardius bairdii*). Reptiles include Baird's Rat Snake (*Pantherophis bairdi*) and Baird's Patch-nosed Snake (*Salvadora bairdi*). Several species of fish are named for him, the genus *Bairdiella* in the Drum and Croaker family Sciaenidae, Baird's Slickhead (*Alepocephalus bairdii*), Lancer Dragonet (*Callionymus bairdi*), Mottled Sculpin (*Coltus bairdii*), Bumphead Damselfish (*Microspathodon bairdii*), Marlin-spike Grenadier (*Nezumia bairdii*), and Red River Shiner (*Notropis bairdi*). Invertebrates include crustaceans Tanner Crab (*Chionoecetes bairdi*) and Red Lobster (*Eunephrops bairdii*), and finally the butterfly

An Introduction to the Naturalists Mentioned in the Book

Baird's Swallowtail (*Papilio machaon bairdii*), a subspecies of the Old World Swallowtail.

Barrow, Sir John (1764–1848) — Sir John Barrow was second Secretary of the Admiralty for more than forty years. He was responsible for the civil administration of the Royal Navy. His influence was largely responsible for many Arctic expeditions led by such explorers as James Clark Ross, John Franklin, Edward Sabine, and John Richardson. The existence and discovery of the Northwest Passage was a matter of conviction and national pride with Barrow. He wrote *Voyages of Discovery and Research within the Arctic Regions* (1846). Barrow was one of the main founders of the Royal Geographical Society and served as chairman at its first public meeting in 1830. Barrow's Goldeneye (*Bucephela islandica*) is named for him. Point Barrow, Barrow Straights, and Barrow Sound in the Arctic and Cape Barrow in the Antarctic are also named in his honor.

Bartram, William (1739–1823) — William Bartram was the son of eminent botanist John Bartram, and was a learned botanist himself as well as an artist-naturalist. Elliot Coues dubbed him the "Godfather of American Ornithology" because he was a mentor to Alexander Wilson. Several English patrons commissioned his paintings. Bartram also sent seeds to correspondents abroad, thus introducing American plants to European gardens. In 1773, Bartram began a four-year trip to the Southeast, where he collected plants and seeds for British physician and botanist Dr. John Fothergill. He published the story of his expedition in 1791 with the impressive title *Travels Through North and South Carolina, Georgia, East and West Florida, the Cherokee Country, the Extensive Territories of the Muscogulges, or Creek Confederacy, and the Country of Choctaws, Containing an Account of the Soil and Natural Productions of Those Regions, Together with Observations on the Manners of the Indians*. Bartram maintained five acres of gardens on his 200+ acre estate on the west bank of the Schuykill River near Philadelphia. His gardens attracted visitors from near and far. Bartram received such notable guests as Thomas Jefferson, Benjamin Franklin, John Madison, George Washington, Alexander Wilson, and Thomas Nuttall. The Upland Sandpiper (*Bartramia longicauda*) is named in his honor.

Bell, John Graham (1812–1889) — For fifty years, John Graham Bell was the best known taxidermist in New York. His shop was a meeting place for naturalists including Spencer F. Baird, John L. LeConte, and George N. Lawrence. He also taught an eleven-year old Theodore Roosevelt how to mount mammals and prepare study skins. John Bachman suggested Audubon employ Bell as his taxidermist on the Missouri River expedition. Later Bell made a collecting trip to California. Bell's Vireo (*Vireo bellii*) and Bell's Sparrow (*Artemisiospiza belli*) are named in his honor.

Bendire, Charles Emil (1836–1897) — Major Bendire was a U.S. Army officer, oologist, and one of the founding members of the AOU. Born Karl Emil Bender in Konig im Odenwald in the Grand Duchy of Hesse-Darmstadt, Bendire emigrated to New York with his brother Wilhelm. He changed his name upon enlisting in the military at age eighteen. He was stationed at various posts in the West from Arizona and New Mexico to Washington and Montana. During his military career, Bendire collected for Baird, kept meticulous notes on his observations, and collected 8000 birds' eggs. When he donated his egg collection to the National Museum of Natural History, he was made honorary curator of oology in 1883. Bendire compiled two volumes of *Life Histories of North American Birds*, which was completed by A. C. Bent. Bendire's Thrasher (*Toxostoma bendirei*) is named for him. Also the species name of the Marsh Shrew (*Sorex bendirii*) commemorates Charles Bendire.

Bent, Arthur Cleveland (1866–1954) — Arthur Cleveland Bent was an amateur ornithologist, best known for his monumental *Life Histories of North American Birds* (1919–1968). After graduating from Harvard, he went into business, becoming a manufacturing and public utility tycoon. But he also had a lifelong interest in birds, submitting articles to ornithological journals. In his mid-forties with the financial means from his business ventures, Bent traveled across North

America. He amassed a collection of 30,000 eggs, now housed in the Smithsonian. Although an amateur, Bent served as president of the AOU. In 1910, the Smithsonian requested Bent to finish the life history series begun by Charles Bendire. For the next forty-four years until his death at age eighty-eight, Bent produced nineteen volumes, with two more in preparation that were published posthumously. Independently wealthy from his success in business, Bent took no payment for this venture. He compiled an incredible amount of information from the scientific literature, his own observations, and from input of more than 800 correspondents, scattered from the arctic to the tropics. Of this accomplishment, Scott Weidensaul wrote, "Comprising 9,500 pages of text, the *Life Histories* were at once enormously informative and immensely readable, and they remain incredibly relevant today; no other single resource contains as much sheer information on the continent's birds, and Bent's series is still one of the most-cited works of ornithological literature."

Bewick, Thomas (1754–1828) — Thomas Bewick — with a last name pronounced Buick, like the car — was an English artist and engraver. He apprenticed seven years to Ralph Beilby who owned an engraving business. Bewick learned to engrave silver, copper, and wood, and he produced trade cards, labels, and billheads. He went into partnership with Beilby, a relationship that lasted twenty years. Bewick is best known for his woodcut illustrations in *General History of Quadrupeds* (1790) and volume two of *The History of British Birds* (1797–1804). The latter sold thousands of copies and did more to arouse an interest in birds among the general public than any previous work. Bewick's Wren (*Thryomanes bewickii*) is named in his honor.

Bicknell, Eugene Pintard (1859–1925) — Bicknell was a New York banker, amateur ornithologist, and the youngest of the founding members of the AOU. His *Review of the Summer Birds of a Part of the Catskill Mountains* was an important ornithological study of that region. He also studied botany and concentrated on that subject from 1895 to 1917. At the time when ornithology was accomplished with a shotgun, Bicknell much preferred to observe birds in the field rather than shoot them. Bicknell's Thrush (*Catharus bicknellii*) is named in his honor.

Blackburn, Anna (1740–1793) — An English botanist and patron of ornithology, Anna Blackburn curated a private museum of natural history specimens at Fairfield, her residence in Lancashire. Her fine collection consisted of bird skins, birds' eggs, insects, fish, seashells, fossils, and dried plant material. Her brother Ashton collected birds for her in New York, New Jersey, and Connecticut at the time of the American Revolution. She corresponded with Linnaeus, offering to send him specimens of birds and insects she believed were not in his *Systema Naturae*. Since he was ill at the time, it is not known if he described any species from her collection. She also corresponded with German zoologist Peter Simon Pallas and exchanged pressed plants and mineral specimens for birds, plants, and seeds he had collected in Siberia. Anna's museum was an important source of reference specimens used by many eminent naturalists of her time. She received such notable guests as Johann Reinhold Forster, Thomas Pennant, Johan Christian Fabricius, and possibly John Latham. Anna Blackburn never married, but it is said she used the title Mrs., because she felt it gave her more status. Although Mrs. Blackburn never published any scientific papers, she was highly regarded by the scientific community. Linnaeus wrote, "She is a true naturalist whose esteem I covet." The Blackburnian Warbler (*Setophaga fusca*) is named in her honor.

Blanchan, Neltje (1865–1918) — Neltje Blanchan De Graff was a nature writer who helped to popularize the new conservation movement of the late 19th and early 20th centuries. Her titles include *Bird Neighbors* (1897), *Birds that Hunt and Are Hunted* (1898), *Wild Flowers: An Aid to Knowledge of our Wild Flowers and their Insect Visitors* (1901), *Birds Every Child Should Know* (1907), *The American Flower Garden* (1909), and *Birds Worth Knowing* (1917). While her writing lacked depth scientifically, it did have a lyrical style.

John Burroughs called her work reliable and said it was "written in a vivacious strain by a real bird lover." Sometimes it veered to the sentimental and moralistic, dividing the avian world into "good" birds and "bad" birds. But in her defense, that was the general mindset of her day. Blanchan was married to publishing giant Frank Nelson Doubleday.

Bonaparte, Charles Lucien Jules Laurent (1803–1857) — Known as the Father of Systematic Ornithology, Charles Lucien Bonaparte was a nephew of Emperor Napoleon. Born in Paris, he spent four and a half years (1823–1828) in the United States where he resided in Bordentown, New Jersey, and Philadelphia. There he began to update Alexander Wilson's *American Ornithology*, which became *American Ornithology; or, The Natural History of Birds Inhabiting the United States Not Given by Wilson*. This was published in four volumes from 1825–1833. Bonaparte also published short papers in the journals of the Academy of Natural Sciences of Philadelphia, describing new species and revising the nomenclature of known species. From 1827–1828, he published a comparative list of the birds of Rome and Philadelphia, his *Catalogue of the Birds of the United States* in the Lyceum of the Arts and Sciences, and *The Genera of North American Birds* in *Annals of the Lyceum of Natural History of New York*. Early in 1828, Bonaparte moved to Rome. There he turned his attention to the classification of Italian birds and animals. His last volume dealing with North American birds was *A Geographical and Comparative List of the Birds of Europe and North America* in 1838. After moving to Paris, Bonaparte began his most ambitious project, the *Conspectus Generum Avium*, which was to catalog every known species of bird in the world. He published the first volume before the end of 1850. Bonaparte died while working on the second volume. The *Conspectus* was never finished, but the second volume was published late in 1857. Bonaparte was a well-respected ornithologist in both the United States and Europe. Bonaparte's Gull (*Chroicocephalus philadelphia*) is named in his honor.

Bonaparte, Zénaïde Laetitia Julie (1801–1854) — Princess Zénaïde Bonaparte was the eldest daughter of Joseph Bonaparte, the King of Spain, the niece of the Emperor Napoleon, and cousin and wife of ornithologist Charles Lucien Bonaparte. They were married in Brussels in 1822. After spending a few months in Italy, the couple moved to her father's estate at Point Breeze near Bordentown, New Jersey, where they resided from 1823 to 1828, before returning to Europe. Zénaïde enjoyed the company of her father and sister Charlotte, while her husband tended to his work in nearby Philadelphia. She loved poetry and drama and enjoyed the arts in that cultural center. After 1849, the couple lived apart, and they were legally separated in 1854. Some sources give her name as Zénaïde Charlotte Julie Bonaparte. The genus *Zedaida*, which encompasses seven species including the Zenaida Dove, Mourning Dove, and White-winged Dove, commemorates her name.

Bond, James (1900–1989) — "Bond. James Bond." Birders and movie goers alike may be amazed to learn there really was a James Bond, an American ornithologist, not a British secret agent with a license to kill. There is, however, a connection between the ornithologist and 007. Ian Fleming, author of the Bond novels, was a birder himself who regularly referred to his copy of *Birds of the West Indies* by James Bond. In choosing a name for his protagonist, Fleming explained, "I wanted the simplest, dullest, plainest-sounding name I could find, 'James Bond' was much better than something more interesting, like 'Peregrine Carruthers' . . . It struck me that this brief, unromantic, Anglo-Saxon and yet very masculine name was just what I needed, and so a second James Bond was born."

Ornithologist James Bond was born in Philadelphia, but after his mother died, he moved to England with his father in 1914. After graduating from Trinity College, Cambridge, in 1922, he returned to Philadelphia where he worked for a banking firm for three years. Bond's interest in natural history prompted him to leave the banking business and accept a position with an expedition to the Amazon sponsored by the Academy of Natural Sciences, where he later served as Curator of Birds. James Bond became a world authority on West Indian birds, ultimately visiting more than eighty islands of the Caribbean and the Bahamas and collecting 294 species of birds. This resulted in his publishing the definitive book on the subject, *Birds of the West Indies* (1937), and more than 100 scientific papers. He was a fellow of the AOU and a member of the British Ornithologists' Union. Bond was awarded the Musgrave Medal from the Institute of Jamaica in 1952 and the Brewster Medal from the AOU in 1954 for his work on West Indian birds. In 1975, he received the Leidy Medal from the Academy of Natural Sciences. In 1964, James Bond and his wife Mary paid a visit to Ian Fleming at his estate in Jamaica. Fleming presented him with a first edition copy of *You Only Live Twice* inscribed, "To the real James Bond, from the thief of his identity." In 2008, the book was sold at auction for $84,000. *Birds of the West Indies* was reprinted in the Peterson Field Guide series in 1993.

Botteri, Matteo (1808–1877) — Botteri was born on the Dalmatian island Lesina (now Hvar, Croatia). He collected in Greece and Turkey as well as his homeland. In 1853, the Royal Horticultural Society of London sent him to Mexico to collect plants. He also sent material to the Academy of Sciences of Paris. Botteri settled into the Mexican state of Orizaba, 4000 feet above sea level, where he spent the rest of his life, returning to Europe briefly only once (1863–1864). He founded a small museum there, and in 1864, he became Professor of Languages and Natural History at Orizaba College. Botteri mastered a dozen languages including classical Greek, modern Greek, Latin, Italian, French, Spanish, German, and English. He had a broad interest and knowledge in the sciences as well, including botany, conchology, ichthyology, entomology, geology, mineralogy, astronomy, ethnology, and etymology. He sent some material to the Smithsonian Institution and in 1866, became a corresponding member of the Entomological Society of Philadelphia. Botteri's Sparrow (*Peucaea botterii*) is named in his honor.

Brandt, Johaan Friedrich (1802–1879) — Johaan Brandt was an eminent German zoologist. He worked as a doctor's assistant for nine months, but became so discouraged that he never practiced medicine again after age twenty-nine. He lectured on the topics of botany and pharmacology. Brandt became director of the Zoological Museum at the Academy of Sciences in Saint Petersburg and described some of the natural history specimens (mammals and birds) brought back from the Russian American possessions. Brandt wrote 300 scientific papers, two thirds of which were on ornithology. Brandt's Cormorant (*Phalacrocorax penicillatus*) is named for him.

Brelay, Aglae (fl. 1839) — Little is known about Aglae Brelay, except that she was enthusiastic about ornithology and helped her husband M. Charles Brelay curate his collection of several thousand specimens. The author Frederick de Lafresnaye gave the Rose-throated Becard the specific epithet *aglaiae* in honor of Aglae Brelay, even though he did not ordinarily approve of naming birds for "women, who are often strangers to the love of ornithology." Lafresnaye apparently was impressed with Madame Brelay's passion for birds and made an exception. He described eleven birds from Monsieur Brelay's collection, but only four proved to be new species.

Brewer, Thomas Mayo (1814–1880) — Dr. Brewer was a physician, newspaper editor, and ornithologist. He published only the first volume of *North American Oology* in 1857 and co-wrote *History of North American Birds* with Baird and Ridgway. He practiced medicine only briefly. His advocacy of the House Sparrow put him at odds with many of his peers, particularly Elliot Coues. Brewer contributed scientific papers to the Boston Society of Natural History for forty years. He corresponded with collectors in America and Europe with whom he bought or exchanged bird skins and eggs. He is said to have amassed the finest private collection of eggs in North America at the time. Brewer's Sparrow (*Spizella breweri*) and Brewer's Blackbird (*Euphagus cyanocephalus*) commemorate his name. The Hairy-tailed Mole (*Parascalops breweri*) and the Beach Vole

An Introduction to the Naturalists Mentioned in the Book

(*Microtus breweri*) are also named for him.

Brewster, William (1851–1919) — Brewster has been called "one of the greatest and most naturally gifted field ornithologists that America has ever produced." He was a founder member of the AOU, and its president from 1895–1898. He organized the Massachusetts Audubon Society and was principle founder and first president of the Nuttall Ornithological Club. Brewster published *The Birds of the Cambridge Region of Massachusetts* (1906) and *Birds of Lake Umbagog* (1924). His specialties were the birds of New England and the American Southwest. Brewster's extensive collection of bird skins is now housed in the Cambridge Museum of Comparative Zoology. Brewster's Warbler, a hybrid, not a true species, is named for him.

Buller, Sir Walter Lawry (1838–1906) — The son of a Cornish missionary, Buller was a lawyer and New Zealand's first notable ornithologist. He was appointed government interpreter at Wellington at age seventeen and was made Native Commissioner for the Southern Provinces in 1859. In 1871, he went to England as secretary to the Agent-General. He spent three years in England, where he became a friend of William Swainson. Buller then returned to Wellington where he practiced law for the next twenty-four years. Buller published more than seventy scientific papers on birds and wrote *History of Birds of New Zealand* (1872–1873). He received many honors for his zoological work, and Queen Victoria knighted him for his services as a Commissioner. Following his death, Buller's bird collection went to Canterbury, New Zealand. Three of Buller's earlier collections had already been disposed of by the time of his death. One went to the Dominion Museum in Wellington. The second went to Lord Walter Rothschild's private collection. The Carnegie Museum of Natural History in Pittsburgh purchased the third for £1000. Buller's Shearwater (*Ardenna bulleri*) is named in his honor.

Bullock, William (1775–1840) — A jack of many trades, William Bullock described himself as a "Silversmith, Jeweller [*sic*], Toyman, and Statue Figure Manufacturer." He was also an antiquarian, a showman, and an amateur naturalist. He started a museum in Sheffield, which he moved to Liverpool and ultimately to London's Piccadilly Square. The museum displayed 32,000 curiosities (many brought back by Cook's voyage) and more than 3000 bird specimens. In 1819, he decided to get rid of the museum by auctioning off its contents. The sale went on for twenty-five days. Among the bidders were Sir Walter Scott, William Leach, and William Swainson. Bullock made two trips to Mexico, where he invested in silver mines and collected bird specimens, some of which were new to science. Bullock's Oriole (*Icterus bullockii*) is named in his honor.

Bulwer, James (1794–1879) — Bulwer was an English clergyman, artist, and amateur naturalist. His specialty was conchology. He became a Fellow of the Linnaean Society on the strength of his knowledge of mollusks. He was ordained a deacon in 1818 and in 1822, a priest. In 1823, Bulwer was appointed curate of Booterstown, Dublin. From 1833–1838, he was curate of Saint James Chapel, Piccadilly, where he was present at Queen Victoria's coronation. Sometime in between, Bulwer travelled through Spain, Portugal, and Madeira. His companion Alfred Lyall wrote an account of their experiences in *Rambles in Madera and Portugal* (1826). Bulwer contributed the appendix. In 1839, he returned to his birthplace of Norfolk, where he spent the rest of his life. Bulwer wrote only one scientific paper (the topic was the mollusks of the Irish Sea), but contributed eleven papers to *Norfolk Archaeology* from 1847 to 1879. Bulwer's Petrel (*Bulweria bulwerii*) is named for him.

Burroughs, John (1837–1921) — Known as the Father of the American Nature Essay, John Burroughs ranked second only to Thoreau as an author in that genre. Affectionately known as the Hudson River naturalist and the Grand Old Man of Nature, he was one of the most popular and respected authors of his time. In 1864, Burroughs accepted a position as a clerk with the Treasury Department in Washington, D.C. and eventually became a federal bank examiner. During his free time, he wrote about the outdoors, which resulted in his first published collection of nature essays *Wake Robin*. In 1874, Burroughs bought a nine-acre farm near West Park, New York, which became his Riverby estate. There he continued to write, grow crops, and to work as a federal bank examiner. In 1895, Burroughs bought additional land near Riverby and built an Adirondack-style cabin, which he called Slabsides. There he received such distinguished guests as Theodore Roosevelt, Walt Whitman, John Muir, Thomas Edison, Harvey Firestone, and Henry Ford. In 1911, Burroughs refurbished an old farmhouse, which he named Woodchuck Lodge. This became his summer home. Burroughs was a prolific writer and published regularly throughout his life. His last two volumes *Under the Maples* (1921) and *The Last Harvest* (1922) were published posthumously. The John Burroughs Medal is awarded to excellence in nature writing.

Cabot, Samuel (1815–1885) — Dr. Cabot was a physician and Curator of the Department of Ornithology at the Boston Society of Natural History. In 1841, he went on an important collecting trip to the Yucatan Peninsula, where he discovered several new species. He published a number of papers on his discoveries there. Dr. Cabot's collection of 3000 mounted birds is now housed at the Museum of Comparative Zoology, Harvard. The Sandwich Tern (*Thalasseus sandvicensis*) was formerly known as Cabot's Tern.

Carson, Rachel L. (1907–1964) — Rachel Carson was a biologist and later Editor in Chief of publications with the U.S. Fish and Wildlife Service. A gifted nature writer, she is noted for her lyrical prose and ability to interpret science for the general reader. She wrote a trilogy of books about the sea, *Under the Sea Wind* (1941), *The Sea Around Us* (1951), and *The Edge of the Sea* (1955), but she is best known for her classic *Silent Spring* (1962), in which she warned of the threats to wildlife and human health from the unregulated use of pesticides. *Silent Spring* is credited in launching the modern environmental movement. Her last book *The Sense of Wonder* was published posthumously in 1965.

Cassin, John (1813–1869) — Cassin was one of the leading taxonomists of the 19th century and described 198 species of birds. He served as official ornithologist on Admiral Perry's voyage to Japan. He was the first American ornithologist to become an authority on birds of the world. For more than twenty-five years, Cassin was Curator of Ornithology at the Academy of Natural Sciences of Philadelphia. He took no salary for this position. Birds named in his honor include Cassin's Auklet (*Ptychoramphus aleuticus*), Cassin's Kingbird (*Tyrannus vociferans*), Cassin's Vireo (*Vireo cassinii*), Cassin's Sparrow (*Peucaea cassinii*), and Cassin's Finch (*Haemorhous cassinii*).

Catesby, Mark (1682–1749?) — Before Audubon and Wilson, there was Mark Catesby, an English naturalist and illustrator, whom historians credit as "the founder of American ornithology." He wrote and illustrated a two-volume work, *Natural History of Carolina, Florida, and Bahama Islands* (1731–1743), the first comprehensive, illustrated work on the natural history of North America. In addition to birds (109 species), it includes mammals, reptiles, fish, insects, and plants. Species whose names commemorate Mark Catesby include the American Bullfrog (*Lithobates catesbeianus*) and two wildflowers, Catesby's Trillium aka Bashful Wakerobin (*Trillium catesbaei*) and the Southern Red Lily (*Lilium catesbaei*).

Chapman, Frank Michler (1864–1945) — Frank Chapman was curator of ornithology at the American Museum of Natural History in New York from 1908 to 1942. He was a field naturalist, photographing and recording data on North American birds for more than fifty years and popularizing birding in the United States. In 1899, he launched *Bird-Lore Magazine*, which he would edit for the next thirty-six years. Nearly from its beginning such eminent writers as John Burroughs, Bradford Torrey, Florence Merriam, William Brewster, Robert Ridgway, Ernest Seton Thompson, William Beebe, and Mabel Osgood Wright contributed articles to the magazine. Through the magazine and his other published work such as *Handbook of Birds of Eastern North America* (1895) and *Color Key to North American Birds* (1903), Chapman became a great popularizer of birding. *Bird-Lore* eventually became *Audubon Magazine*. In 1900, Chapman began the first

Christmas Bird Count in protest to the "side hunt" or "match hunt" in which teams of gunners went out in the field on Christmas Day and shot every creature they encountered. The Christmas Bird Count has now expanded to include more than 2000 counts across the Americas from Prudhoe Bay to Tierra del Fuego.

Clark, John Henry (ca.1830–1885) — John H. Clark was a mathematician and surveyor. He served with the U.S. and Mexican Boundary Survey from 1851 to 1855. During this time, he collected specimens for Baird, who considered Clark a member of his family. Clark also helped prepare the various Boundary Survey publications. John Cassin included some of Clark's notes in his *Illustrations of the Birds of California, Texas, Oregon, British and Russian America* (1853–1856). Clark served as a U.S. Commissioner of the Mexican Boundary Commission from 1858 to 1862 and was astronomical observer on the Wheeler Expedition in 1874. Clark's Grebe (*Aechmophorus clarkii*) is named for him.

Clark, William (1770–1838) — Meriwether Lewis chose his army buddy Captain William Clark as the co-leader of their celebrated expedition (1804–1806) that explored the newly acquired Louisiana Territory. Clark was an experienced surveyor and took the role of cartographer on the expedition. In 1807, five months after their return, Clark resigned from the army and was made Superintendent of Indian Affairs for the Louisiana Territory. He was much respected by the Indians, and this role as mediator between the natives and the whites was considered as important as Clark's role as explorer. In 1813, Clark was appointed governor of the Missouri Territory. Clark's Nutcracker (*Nucifraga columbiana*) is named in his honor as also is a genus of more than forty species of wildflowers of the western United States including Farewell-to-Spring (*Clarkia amoena*), often grown as a garden ornamental, Ragged Robin or Deerhorn Clarkia (*C. pulchella*), the first member of the genus described, and Lewis's Clarkia (*C. lewisi*) that honors both explorers. The specific epithet of the Cutthroat Trout (*Oncorhynchus clarki*) also commemorates Captain Clark.

Cook, James (1728–1779) — Captain Cook was a British naval officer and explorer. He made three expeditions to the Pacific. He commanded the *Endeavor*, and from 1768 to 1771, he explored much of the South Pacific and charted the coastlines of New Zealand and eastern Australia. His second voyage went from 1772 to 1775. He returned to New Zealand and circumnavigated Antarctica. German naturalist Johann Reinhold Forster and his son George accompanied Cook on this voyage. In 1778, he made a third voyage, this time with the *Resolution* and the *Discovery*. He sailed again to New Zealand, then to the Hawaiian Islands, then to the west coast of North America, anchoring off the coast of Vancouver Island. From there they followed the coast northward to the Bering Strait. At least 120 species of birds were collected on this voyage including endemic species from Hawaii. Surgeon-naturalists William Anderson and William Ellis along with artist John Webber collected most of the birds in the Pacific Northwest. These included species new to science that were subsequently described by British naturalist John Latham or German naturalist Johann Friedrich Gmelin. Among them were Fork-tailed Storm-Petrel, Surfbird, Marbled Murrelet, Ancient Murrelet, Whiskered Auklet, Rufous Hummingbird, Steller's Jay, Varied Thrush, Savannah Sparrow, and Golden-crowned Sparrow. On their return to Hawaii, Cook was killed when his crew got into a skirmish with the Hawaiian natives. Cook's Petrel (*Pterodroma cookii*) was named in his honor.

Cooper, William C. (1798–1864) — Independently wealthy, William Cooper was a well-rounded naturalist well-versed in ornithology, herpetology, botany, malacology, and paleontology. He also began a systematic study of conchology. He had studied zoology in Europe. He made his specimens accessible to fellow naturalists including Audubon, Bonaparte, Nuttall, and DeKay. Cooper edited the last two volumes of Bonaparte's *American Ornithology*. He was one of the founders and first recording secretary of the Lyceum of Natural History (now the New York Academy of Sciences).

His son James was one of the army-surgeons who collected for Baird. The Cooper's Hawk (*Accipiter cooperii*) and Olive-sided Flycatcher (*Contopus cooperi*) are named in his honor.

Cory, Charles Barney (1857–1921) — Cory was born into a wealthy Boston family. He devoted himself to a life of pleasure, travelling and pursuing sporting and literary interests. He excelled at pistol shooting, billiards, and golf, winning several championships. He was a life member of the Nuttall Club and one of the founding members of the AOU. Cory became an authority on the birds of the West Indies. He wrote *Birds of the Bahama Islands* (1880), *The Birds of Haiti and San Domingo* (1885), and *The Birds of the West Indies* (1889). In 1893, he donated his collection of 19,000 bird skins to the Field Museum in Chicago, where he was made an honorary curator. Cory was definitely of the shotgun school of ornithology. When he was shown a flyer on the details of an upcoming Audubon Society meeting, Cory replied, "I am not interested. I do not protect birds. I kill them." But to his credit, Cory maintained one of the first bird sanctuaries in the United States at his 1000-acre estate at Hyannis, Massachusetts. In 1906, when he lost the family fortune through bad investments, Cory had to give up his independent lifestyle to take a salaried position as Curator of Zoology at the Field Museum.

Costa, Louis Marie Pantaleon, Marquis de Beau-Regard (1806–1864) — Costa had been interested in ornithology and mineralogy since age fifteen. and was an avid collector of hummingbirds. Costa was a soldier in the Royal Sardinian Piedmontese Army. He began his career at fifteen as equerry to Prince Charles Albert. He rose to become Captain of the Cavalry and Head Equerry to Charles Albert, who succeeded to the throne in 1832. Costa left the army to serve as a senator for Savoy in the Sardinian Parliament. In 1860, Costa turned down a seat in the French Senate. Instead he became chairman of the Savoy Academy. In 1878, Adolphe Boucard, a dealer in natural history specimens, purchased Costa's hummingbird collection. Costa's Hummingbird (*Calypte costae*) honors his name.

Couch, General Darius Nash (1822–1897) — Couch was a U.S. Army officer and Union General. He entered West Point in 1842 and graduated with such Civil War luminaries as George B. McClellen, Stonewall Jackson, Ulysses S. Grant, Ambrose E. Burnside, and William B. Franklin. He fought in the Mexican War and later was stationed in Pennsylvania and North Carolina. In 1853, he took a leave of absence to make a zoological expedition to northern Mexico. There he collected specimens for Baird at the Smithsonian. On his return, he married and eight months later resigned from the military. He took a job with the Taunton Copper Company that was run by his wife's family in Massachusetts. When the Civil War broke out, Couch volunteered for the Union Army. He fought at Antietam, Fredericksburg, Chancellorsville, and Gettysburg. After the war he ran an unsuccessful campaign for the governorship of Massachusetts, worked as a customs official in Boston, and served as president of a Virginia mining and manufacturing company. Couch's Kingbird (*Tyrannus couchii*) is named for him.

Coues, Elliot (1842–1899) — Dr. Elliot Coues, his surname pronounced cows, was one of the most colorful of the later 19th century ornithologists and is said to be second in importance at that time only to Spencer Fullerton Baird. As a young man, he became acquainted with Baird, who in 1860 sent him on an expedition to Labrador to collect seabirds. Upon his return, he published *Notes on the Ornithology of Labrador* (1860). From 1862 to 1864, Coues served as a medical cadet in the Union Army during the Civil War. As a surgeon-naturalist, he collected for the National Museum while stationed at Fort Whipple near Prescott, Arizona. While serving in the southwest, Coues had some horrendous encounters with hostile Indians. Nevertheless, he developed a respect and sympathy for them. Coues was also an early advocate for women's rights on one hand, yet he disparaged early birders, particularly the females, as "opera-glass fiends." From 1873 to 1876, Coues was surgeon-naturalist with the U.S. Northern Boundary Commission. Then he was secretary and naturalist for the U.S.

Geological and Geographical Survey of the Territories from 1876 to 1880. Coues accepted a professorship in 1882 at Columbian College (now George Washington University) where he taught anatomy. He was one of the founders of the AOU and edited its journal, *The Auk*. His published work includes *A Field Ornithology* (1874), *Birds of the Northwest* (1874), *Fur-Bearing Animals* (1877), *Birds of the Colorado Valley* (1878), *A Bibliography of Ornithology* (1878–1880), and *New England Bird Life* (1881). His most influential publication is *Key to North American Birds* (1872). It had been called "one of the best if not the best bird book ever written." Frank Chapman wrote that it was "an inexhaustible store of information, its technicalities so humanized by its author that they were made attractive and intelligible even to the novice . . . The work of a great ornithologist and a master of the art of exposition." The *Key to North American Birds* went through five editions in three decades. Coues' friend, bird artist Louis Agassiz Fuertes, illustrated the final two editions. Coues was highly opinionated and could be quite caustic. He got into feuds with several of his fellow naturalists, most notably with Thomas Brewer over the introduction of the House Sparrow to North America. To the chagrin of his scientific colleagues, Coues got involved with spiritualism and Theosophy later in life. The Greater Pewee (*Contopus pertinax*) was formerly known as Coues' Flycatcher.

Coues, Grace Darlington (1847–1939) — Grace Coues was the sister of ornithologist Elliot Coues. She lived in Zurich, then in London with her husband Charles Albert Page, whom she married in 1867. When he died, she returned to Washington with the children to live with her mother. In 1884, she married Dana Estes, director of Estes and Lauriat Publishing House. Estes studied archeology, and he and Grace travelled to London, Italy, and Egypt. Estes is considered to have been the first American to travel up the Nile to Uganda and the Congo. Grace's Warbler (*Setophaga graciae*) is named for Grace.

Craveri, Frederico (1815–1890) — Craveri was an Italian chemist and naturalist. Born in Turino, he moved to Mexico City at age twenty-five. There he earned a degree in chemistry and pharmacology at the university. He worked in Mexico for twenty years teaching chemistry and collecting natural history specimens for the Academy of Sciences in Turino. His work took him to many of the mining districts of Mexico including the silver mines around the city of Guanajuato. At the request of the Mexican government, he took samples of guano for chemical analysis from seabird colonies along the Sea of Cortez to assess its potential for an organic fertilizer industry. Craveri's Murrelet (*Synthliboramphus craveri*) is named in his honor.

Dawson, William Leon (1873–1928) — William Leon Dawson was an ornithologist who began as a Seventh-day Adventist minister. He took his Bachelor of Divinity degree from Oberlin Theological Seminary, but by the early 1900s he chose ornithology as his profession. Dawson photographed birds and displayed his collection of photos and his egg collection at his studio at Los Colibris in Mission Canyon, California. In 1916, he founded the Museum of Comparative Oology (now the Santa Barbara Museum of Natural History) and served as the museum's first director. He also founded The Birds of California Publishing Company. Dawson lectured widely on birds and wrote many articles and books on the subject. His works include *Birds of Ohio: A Complete Scientific and Popular Description of the 320 Species of Birds Found in the State* (1903), *Birds of Washington: A Complete Scientific and Popular Description of the 372 Species of Birds Found in the State* (1909), and *Birds of California: A Complete Scientific and Popular Description of the 580 Species of Birds Found in the State* (1923).

Degland, Côme Damien (1787–1856) Dr. Degland was a French naturalist and chief physician at the Hôspital Saint-Saveur in Lille, France. He was a founder and also director of the Lille Natural History Museum, where his collection of 1800 European bird specimens is housed. In 1821, he published a catalog of the museum's beetles and a two-volume catalog of the birds of Europe in 1849. The White-winged Scoter (*Melanitta deglandi*) is named for him.

Fischer von Waldheim, Johann Gotthelf (1771–1853) — Fischer was a German naturalist with expertise in anatomy, geology, paleontology, and entomology. He was also an authority on the history of printing. In 1804, he became Professor of Natural History at Moscow University and also served as Director of the Natural History Museum. The Spectacled Eider (*Somateria fischeri*) is named in his honor.

Forbush, Edward Howe (1858–1929) — Edward Forbush was a notable ornithologist and author from Massachusetts. At age sixteen, he was appointed Curator of Ornithology of the Worcester Natural History Society's museum. In 1893, he was appointed Ornithologist to the Massachusetts State Board of Agriculture, and in 1908, he became the Massachusetts State Ornithologist. He was founder of the Massachusetts Audubon Society and first president of the Northeastern Bird-banding Association (now the Association of Field Ornithologists). He did research in an attempt to save the last remaining Heath Hens of Martha's Vineyard. Forbush is best known for his three-volume *Birds of Massachusetts and Other New England States* (1925–1929).

Forster, Johann Reinhold (1729–1798) — Johann Forster was a German naturalist and translator. He studied for the ministry and served as pastor in a country parish for twelve years. But in 1765, he left the church for an assignment under Catharine the Great to inspect new colonies being established along the Volga River. After a falling out with the Russian government, Forster emigrated to England where he taught natural history and modern languages for three years at Warrington Academy. Then in 1772, he and his son George served as naturalists on Captain Cook's second voyage to the South Pacific. In the southern ocean, he discovered five new species of penguins and studied albatrosses and petrels. After returning from Cook's expedition, Forster became professor of minerology at Halle University where he taught for eighteen years. Forster was the first naturalist to attempt to catalog fauna of the New World in his *A Catalogue of the Animals of North America* (1771). It listed 302 species of birds. Forster's Tern (*Sterna forsteri*) is named in his honor.

Franklin, John (1786–1847) — Sir John Franklin was an officer in the Royal Navy, best known for his Arctic expeditions. He enlisted in the navy in 1800, six weeks before his fourteenth birthday. He accompanied his uncle on an exploratory voyage to Australia (1801-1803). Franklin saw action during the Napoleonic Wars and the War of 1812, and he served as governor of Van Diemen's Land (Tasmania), a British penal colony, from 1836 to 1843. Franklin made four expeditions to the Arctic. His first voyage was in 1818, in an unsuccessful attempt to reach the North Pole. He made three excursions to the Canadian Arctic in search of the Northwest Passage. Franklin never returned from his final one in 1845. After two years had passed and no communication from the expedition, his wife Lady Jane Franklin urged the Admiralty to send a search party. Some thirty expeditions searched for the lost ships between 1847 and 1859. In 1850, several ships found relics of Franklin's expedition of Beachy Island in Wellington Channel. In the 1980s, a team found the remains of three crewmen on Beachy Island. The cause of death seemed to be lead poisoning, although the source of the lead could not be determined. Franklin's Gull (*Leucophaeus pipixcan*) and Franklin's Grouse (*Falcipennis canadensis franklini*), a subspecies of the Spruce Grouse, are named for him. Franklin is also honored by several place names including a street in Adelaide, South Australia; a neighborhood in Winnipeg, Manitoba; a high school in Yellowknife, Canada; an island off Antarctica and another off Greenland; Franklin Sound north of Tasmania; and Franklin Straight in Arctic Canada. A research vessel and a shrub rose cultivar are also named for him.

Gambel, William (1823–1849) — William Gambel was a collector and a protégé of Thomas Nuttall. As a teenager, he had accompanied Nuttall on field trips to the Carolinas and to New England. Gambel was the first naturalist to collect extensively in California. Back in Philadelphia, he became friends with some of the leading naturalists of the time including John Cassin, Spencer

Fullerton Baird, Adolphus Heerman, and Edward Harris, and he had met Audubon. Gambel published a series of scientific papers and established himself as an authority on West Coast birds. Cassin incorporated much of this information in his book on birds of the Pacific Coast. Gambel drew three plates for Nuttall's book on trees. Gambel had hoped to become curator at the Philadelphia Academy of Sciences, but John Cassin quashed his chances by supporting Joseph Leidy instead. Gambel completed medical training, but found it impossible to become established as a physician in Philadelphia, so he decided to move back to California. He left Philadelphia with Isaac J. Wistar in April, 1849. They traveled to Independence, Missouri, where Wistar had a rendezvous with thirteen young men who he was to lead to the gold fields of California. Gambel joined a party who crossed the Sierra Nevadas on foot in winter. He contracted typhoid while tending sick gold miners and died on December 13th at the age of twenty-six. Gambel's Quail (*Callipepla gambelii*), the Mountain Chickadee (*Poecile gambeli*), and Gambel Oak (*Quercus gambelii*) are named in his honor. Also the genus *Gambelia*, which encompasses two species of Leopard Lizards, is named for him.

Gould, John (1804–1881) — John Gould was a British ornithologist. He was probably the most prolific publisher and author of ornithological works in the world with forty-one works on birds and 2999 illustrations by various artists including his wife Elizabeth. He established a taxidermy business, and later used this skill when he obtained the position of first curator of the Zoological Society of London. Gould traveled widely throughout Europe and Asia. His first work was *A Century of Birds of the Himalaya Mountains* (1831). He and his wife spent nineteen months in Australia, studying its fauna from 1838 to 1840. This resulted in Gould publishing *The Birds of Australia* (1840–1848) in seven volumes with 600 illustrations and descriptions of 300 new species of birds. He became known as the Father of Australian Ornithology. Gould also published *The Birds of Europe* (1832–1837), *The Mammals of Australia* (1845–1863), *A Monograph of the Trochilidae or Family of Hummingbirds* (1849–1861), *The Birds of Asia* (1850–1883), *The Birds of Great Britain* (1862–1873), *Handbook of the Birds of Australia* (1865), and *The Birds of New Guinea and the Adjacent Papuan Islands* (1875–1888).

Gundlach, Johannes Christopher (1810–1896) — Dr. Gundlach was Cuba's greatest naturalist. He was born in Marburg, Germany, and received his Ph.D. in Zoology from the University of Marburg in 1838. He arrived in Cuba in January of 1839, where he resided for the rest of his life except for occasional visits to Europe. Gundlach prepared a reference collection of bird skins and began to publish his observations. He corresponded with American ornithologists, including Baird, Brewer, and Lawrence, and published scientific papers in Spanish, German, and English. Gundlach could prepare skeletons of decaying specimens with no discomfort because he had lost his sense of smell from a gun accident. During the winter of 1891–1892, Boston ornithologist Charles B. Cory, who had a special interest in Caribbean birds, visited Gundlach. Dr. Gundlach took his guest on field trips around Havana and gave him access to his collection. In 1892, he sold his zoological collection to the Havana Institute Museum for $8000.00 in Spanish gold and was appointed its lifelong curator. His most comprehensive work was *Ornitologia Cubana* (1893). Gundlach's Hawk (*Accipiter gundlachii*), the Antillean Nighthawk (*Chordeiles gundlachii*), Cuban Vireo (*Vireo gundlachii*), and Bahama Mockingbird (*Mimus gundlachii*) are named for him.

Hammond, William Alexander (1828–1900) — Dr. Hammond was an army surgeon who collected specimens for Baird and encouraged John Xantus to do the same when they were both based at Fort Riley, Kansas. He served as Assistant Surgeon with the Medical Department of the Army and was stationed at nine different posts in three years. After leaving the military, he accepted the Chair of Anatomy and Physiology at the University of Maryland. He edited medical journals, published scientific papers, and wrote a text book on diseases of the nervous system. He even wrote novels and plays. When the Civil War broke out, Hammond re-entered the army as head of the Medical Department. As Surgeon General (1862–1864), he organized the Army Medical Museum, initiated the construction of new military hospitals, and founded an army medical school and lab. He was court-martialed and dismissed from the service after clashing with the Secretary of War, but was fully exonerated fourteen years later.

Harris, Edward (1799–1863) — Harris was a gentleman farmer of Moorestown, New Jersey, and an amateur ornithologist. He became a patron of Audubon, buying several of his paintings. Harris accompanied Audubon to the Gulf of Mexico (1837) and on the Missouri River expedition (1843), where he kept a journal for seven months. After visiting Normandy, he introduced Percheron draft horses to the United States in 1839. Percheron Park in Harris's hometown commemorates the event. In 1845, he relinquished his farming interests and turned to civil and cultural affairs in Moorestown. Harris' farm house, now known as the Smith-Cadbury Mansion, houses The Historical Society of Moorestown. Harris's Hawk (*Parabuteo unicinctus*) and Harris's Sparrow (*Zonotrichia querula*) are named for him. Harris's Antelope Squirrel (*Ammospermophilus harrisii*) also commemorates his name.

Heermann, Adolphus Lewis (1818–1865) — Dr. Heermann was an army surgeon and naturalist, who served with the Pacific Railroad Survey. He collected specimens in California, Arizona, and New Mexico for the Philadelphia Academy of Natural Sciences. He was particularly interested in birds' eggs and is credited with coining the term "oology." His "Notes on the Birds of California," published in the *Journal of the Academy of Natural Sciences of Philadelphia* (1853), is considered one of the best early accounts of the avifauna of that state. In his later years, Heermann suffered from lameness due to a condition known as *tabes dorsalis*, brought about by advanced syphilis. He died in a hunting accident, when he stumbled and his gun discharged. Heerman's Gull (*Larus heermanni*) and Heermann's Kangaroo Rat (*Dipodomys heermanni*) are named in his honor.

Henslow, John Stevens (1796–1861) — Henslow was a British clergyman and professor of botany at Cambridge University. He became a friend of Audubon and advised him on the booksellers of England when he was seeking subscribers for his *Birds of America*. It was Henslow who recommended his student Charles Darwin to serve as naturalist aboard the *Beagle* on her round-the-world expedition. Darwin had all the specimens he collected shipped to Henslow. Henslow compiled the *Catalogue of British Plants and Dictionary of Botanical Terms*. Henslow's Sparrow (*Centronyx henslowii*) is named for him.

Holboell, Carl Peter (1795–1856) — A captain in the Royal Danish Navy, Holboell undertook an expedition along the west coast of Greenland in 1818 to study whaling. During this time, he also collected specimens for the Royal Natural History Museum of Copenhagen. In 1824, he resigned from the navy and and returned to Greenland where he worked as Royal Inspector for Trade and Whale Fishery. His most important written work was *Ornithological Contributions to the Fauna of Greenland* published in *Naturhistorisk Tidsskrift* (1842–1843). Holboell was lost at sea when his ship went down en route to Greenland. The Red-necked Grebe (*Podiceps grisegena*) was formerly known as Holboell's Grebe. A plant in the mustard family, Holboell's Rock Cress (*Arabis holboelli*), is also named for him.

Hornemann, Jens Wilken (1770–1841) — Hornemann was Professor of Botany at the University of Copenhagen. He was the main author among eight Danish naturalists who wrote the fourteen-volume *Flora Danica* (1806). The Hoary Redpoll (*Acanthis hornemanni*) is named in his honor.

Hutchins, Thomas (1730–1790) — Dr. Hutchins was a British physician, employed as Hudson's Bay Company's surgeon at York Factory, Manitoba. He also found time for research, including the study of edible wild plants that might prevent scurvy. When Andrew Graham came on board as acting chief, he encouraged Hutchins to record observations on wildlife, including species new to science. The two collaborated in keeping detailed meteorological and natural history observations. Graham was the more experienced partner in describing natural history specimens. The specimens collected were sent to the Royal Society of London. After retiring from active service, Hutchins spent the last years of his life in England, working as corresponding secretary for Hudson's Bay Company. During this time, he came into contact with the eminent naturalists Thomas Pennant and John Latham. Hutchins provided both with information on Canadian wildlife. Pennant and Latham acknowledged their gratitude to Hutchins in their writings. But much of the material Hutchins provided was taken from Graham's manuscript *Observations on Hudson's Bay*. Therefore Hutchins won an undeserved reputation as the leading authority on Hudson Bay's flora and fauna. The Cackling Goose (*Branta hutchinsii*) is named for him.

Hutton, William (fl. 1851) — There is very little information on William Hutton. From the notes that accompany his specimens, we know he collected in California and around Washington, D.C. He sent these to Baird at the National Museum. He apparently resided, at least for a time, in San Diego. The last specimens he collected were from the vicinity of Washington, D.C., and were dated May, 1857. He was never heard from after that.

Kennicott, Robert (1835–1866) — Kennicott was a naturalist who collected for the Smithsonian, and was a founder of the Chicago Academy of Sciences. At age sixteen, he spent the winter of 1852–1853, with Dr. Jared Kirtland, who taught him about birds, reptiles, fish, and insects. He began sending specimens to the Smithsonian as a teenager, and when Baird became its Assistant Secretary, he trained Kennicott as a naturalist and collector. Kennicott spent several winters cataloging specimens at the Smithsonian. He and several other young naturalists formed a group called the Megatherium Club. In 1856, Baird commissioned Kennicott to publish "The Quadrupeds of Illinois, Injurious and Beneficial to the Farmer" for the *Agricultural Report of the Patent Office*. Baird also sent him on a three-year expedition (1857–1859) to western Canada, Great Slave Lake, and the Yukon and Mackenzie River valleys. His main goal was to find the breeding grounds of familiar birds that were only known as migrants back home. Travelling on foot and by canoe and dogsled, Kennicott collected 282 birds and 230 mammals as well as snakes, fish, and plants. He also collected Indian clothing and weapons and compiled one of the first dictionaries of the native tribal languages. In 1865, Kennicott led an expedition to the Yukon for the Western Union Telegraph, which planned to lay a cable connecting North America with Eurasia via the Bering Strait. Kennicott was to chart a route through the wilderness from Fort Nulato to Norton Sound. He had hoped to collect natural history specimens, as well. In May of 1866, Kennicott's companions found him dead on the banks of the Yukon River. He had died from heart failure at age thirty. Kennicott had suffered from ill health for most of his life. The Western Screech-Owl (*Megascops kennicottii*), also known as Kennicott's Screech-Owl, is named for him.

Kirtland, Jared Potter (1793–1877) — Born in Connecticut, Dr. Kirtland resided for most of his adult life in Ohio. He moved to Poland, Ohio, near Youngstown in 1823, where he practiced medicine for the next fourteen years. While residing there, he served as representative in the Ohio Legislature for three terms (1829–1835). A staunch abolitionist, Kirtland is said to have made his house a station on the Underground Railroad. During 1837 and 1838, Kirtland participated in the Ohio Geological Survey and was responsible for the zoological section. His checklist of the birds of Ohio, published in the *Second Annual Report of the Geological Survey of Ohio* (1838), listed 222 species. An early environmentalist, Kirtland was deeply concerned about the destruction of wildlife habitat through the clearing of forests and of the pollution of streams by industry and agriculture. Kirtland corresponded with such luminaries as Spencer Fullerton Baird, John Bachman, and Robert Kennicott. Dr. Kirtland later taught medicine at the Cincinnati Medical College until 1842, then transferred to the Willoughby Medical School near Cleveland. He became a founder of the Cleveland Medical College (now the Case Western Reserve College of Medicine), where he taught until he retired in 1864. Kirtland founded the Cleveland Academy of Natural Sciences (later the Kirtland Society of Natural Sciences) and served as its first and only president from 1845 to 1875. Eventually the society merged with the Cleveland Museum of Natural History that now houses Kirtland's bird collection. In 1840, Kirtland bought land just west of Cleveland in Rockport Township (now Lakewood), where he created a show place he named Whippoorwill Farm. There he built a stone cottage, and he maintained fruit orchards, greenhouses, apiaries, flower gardens, and an arboretum. The farm also had a large plantation of white mulberry trees for the rearing of silkworms. Kirtland developed more than thirty cultivars of cherries, and was known to his friends as the "Cherry King." His neighbors knew him as the "Sage of Rockport." Jared Kirtland is commemorated by Kirtland's Warbler (*Setophaga kirtlandii*) and Kirtland's Snake (*Clonophis kirtlandii*).

Kittlitz, Friedrich Heinrich (1779–1874) — Kittlitz was a German soldier, naturalist, and artist. He joined the military at age fourteen and left the army at age twenty-six, having achieved rank of captain, to pursue a career in natural history. In August of 1826, he departed on the corvette *Senjawin* on a round-the-world voyage. As part of the scientific staff, Kittlitz collected specimens in Alaska, the Aleutians, the Pribilof Islands, and Kamchatka. The *Senjawin* then sailed to the South Pacific, where he collected on the Carolines and the Marianas. Kittlitz produced several books based on the voyage: *On Some Birds from Chile* (1830), *On Some Undescribed Birds from the Islands of Luzon, the Carolines, and the Marianas* (1831), *Engravings Illustrating the Natural History of Birds* (1832–1833), and *Twenty-four Views of the Vegetation of the Coasts and Islands of the Pacific* (1844). Kittlitz'a Murrelet (*Brachyramphus brevirostris*) is named for him.

Krutch, Joseph Wood (1893–1970) — Krutch was a naturalist, writer, and critic. He became theater critic for *The Nation* from 1924 to 1952 and taught English at Columbia University from 1937 to 1952. He wrote biographies of Edgar Allan Poe, Samuel Johnson, and Henry David Thoreau, but he is best known for his nature books. He published his first nature book, *The Twelve Seasons*, in 1949. In 1955, Krutch received the National Book Award for *The Measure of Man*. He wrote most of his nature books after he moved to Tucson in 1952, partly for health reasons. These include *The Voice of the Desert* (1954), *The Great Chain of Life* (1956), and *The Grand Canyon: Today and All Its Yesterdays* (1957).

La Sagra, Ramón de (1801–1871) — Ramón de La Sagra was an economist and botanist. Born in Spain, he emigrated to Cuba in 1821. The following year, he was appointed Director of the Havana Botanical Gardens and served in that capacity until 1834. During this time, he collected specimens and established a model farm. In 1835, he returned to Europe, settling in Paris. La Sagra wrote *Principios de Botanica Agricola* (1833) and thirteen volumes of *Historia, Fisica, Politica y Natural de la Isla de Cuba* (1839–1861).

Lawrence, George Newbold (1806–1895) — George N. Lawrence was a New York businessman and ornithologist, and a founding member of the AOU. Lawrence, along with Cassin and Baird, who wrote most of the 1000 page text, contributed to volume nine of the Pacific Railroad Reports in 1858, a volume reissued two years later as *Birds of America* (1860). Following the publication of this work, Lawrence specialized in neotropical birds, describing more than seventy species collected in the West Indies and Central and South America. He sold his collection of 8000 specimens to the American Museum of Natural History. Lawrence's Goldfinch (*Spinus lawrencei*) is named for him. Lawrence's Warbler, a hybrid and not a true species, is named for George N. Lawrence's nephew Newbold Trotter Lawrence.

Lawrence, Louise de Kiriline (1894–1992) — Louise de Kiriline Lawrence was a nurse, naturalist, and author. She was born Louise Flach in Sweden. Her lineage included royalty and aristocracy on both parents' sides.

She became a nurse and during the Russian Revolution, she was stationed at a camp in Denmark, where she treated soldiers wounded by the Bolsheviks. There she met her first husband Lieutenant Greb de Kiriline, a Russian officer. He was later killed in Siberia, but his fate was unknown to Louise, who searched for him for several years thereafter while continuing to work as a nurse. In 1927, Louise emigrated to Canada, settling in Bonfield, near North Bay, Ontario, where she worked as a Red Cross nurse. Dr. A. R. Dafoe, who was the physician for the Dionne quintuplets (born 1936), chose Louise to assist him during the quints' critical first year. She wrote a book about her experience, *The Quintuplets First Year* in 1936. In 1939, Louise married her second husband, Len Lawrence, who would be her companion and mentor for the next fifty years. About this time, Louise began a second career as a naturalist and author. She wrote more than 500 reviews, seventeen scientific papers, and five books on natural history, including *Loghouse Nest* (1945), *A Comparative Life History Study of Four Species of Woodpeckers* (1967), *The Lovely and the Wild* (1968), *Mar: A Glimpse into the Natural Life of a Bird* (1976), and *To Whom the Wilderness Speaks* (1980). She received the John Burroughs Medal in 1969 for *The Lovely and the Wild*. Louise was also a prolific contributor to *Audubon Magazine*. She published her autobiography, *Another Winter, Another Spring: A Love Remembered*, in 1977.

Leach, William Elford (1790–1836) — William Leach was a British zoologist and a world authority on crustaceans, but he also studied birds, mammals, and insects. He took an M.D. from Saint Andrews University, but apparently never practiced medicine, preferring to pursue zoological interests instead. He became assistant librarian in the Zoological Department with the British Museum, then assistant keeper of the Natural History Department. He set about reorganizing the classification and exhibits in the conchological and entomological departments. While with the museum, Leach wrote *Zoological Miscellany* (1814–1817), a *Monograph of the British Crabs, Lobsters, Prawns, and other Crustacea with predunculated eyes* (1815–1817), a *Systematic catalogue of the Specimens of the Indigenous Mammalia and Birds that are preserved at the British Museum* (1816), and a *Synopsis of the Mollusca of Great Britain* (1820). He also wrote zoological appendices for several Arctic and African expeditions and contributed articles for the *Encyclopedia Britannica*. Leach's Storm-Petrel (*Oceanodroma leucorhoa*) is named for him.

LeConte, John Lawrence (1825–1883) — Dr. LeConte was the preeminent entomologist of the 19th century. He was a member of a prominent Huguenot family who fled to America circa 1700. His father, Major John Eatton LeConte, also a naturalist, had a great influence on him. Trained as a physician, LeConte never practiced medicine, except during the Civil War, when he served as medical officer with the Medical Corps of the Union Army, within which he achieved the rank of Lieutenant Colonel. Over a forty-year period he published scientific papers on such subjects as geology, ethnology, paleomammlogy, as well as entomology. Like the Creator, LeConte had "an inordinate fondness for beetles." He described more than 5000 species, and many were named in his honor. His beetle collection of 6000 type specimens was left to the Museum of Comparative Zoology at Harvard. LeConte gathered the scattered publications of pioneering entomologist Thomas Say in two volumes, *The Complete Writings of Thomas Say on the Entomology of North America* (1859). LeConte's Thrasher (*Toxostoma lecontei*) and LeConte's Sparrow (*Ammospiza leconteii*) were named for him.

Leopold, Aldo (1887–1948) — Aldo Leopold was an ecologist, nature writer, educator, and founder of the science of wildlife management. He developed the modern environmental ethic that emphasizes wilderness preservation and biodiversity. His teachings had a profound influence on the environmental movement. He began his career with the U.S. Forest Service in 1909, initially stationed in the Arizona Territory, then in New Mexico from 1911 to 1924. During this time he developed the first comprehensive management plan for the Grand Canyon and wrote the first game and fish handbook for the Forest Service. One of his duties as forester was killing bears, mountain lions, and wolves for the federal predator control program. Leopold eventually challenged this policy, when he came to realize predators were vital to a healthy natural ecosystem. In 1933, he was appointed professor in the Agricultural Economics Department at the University of Wisconsin, Madison, where he taught the first course ever on wildlife management. In 1935, he helped to found the Wilderness Society. Leopold's classic book,

A Sand County Almanac, was published posthumously in 1949. In 1982, Leopold's five children started a nonprofit conservation organization, the Aldo Leopold Foundation of Baraboo, Wisconsin, whose mission is "to foster the land ethic through the legacy of Aldo Leopold."

Lesson, Marie Clémence (1796–1834) — Marie Clémence was a French artist who specialized in natural history subjects, particularly plants and birds. She trained in Paris under Gerard van Spaendonck, a Dutch master of botanical illustrations, at the Jardin du Roi. Marie married French naturalist René P. Lesson in 1827, becoming his second wife. She helped to illustrate at least two of her husband's ornithological works. In 1832, the Lessons moved to the coast at Rochefort hoping the sea air would cure Marie's consumption, but she died of cholera two years later at age thirty-eight. The Blue-throated Mountain-gem (*Lampornis clemenciae*) is named in her honor.

Lesson, René Primavère (1794–1849) — René Lesson was a French physician and naturalist. From 1822–1825, he served as surgeon and naturalist aboard *La Coquille* on a round-the-world voyage to South America, the South Pacific, Australia, and Asia. On their return, Lesson was sent to Paris to study the expedition's collections which were placed with the Museum d'Histoire Naturelle. For his part, Lesson was promoted to Pharmacist First Class and received the Legion of Honour. Lesson published many books and papers on ornithology and other natural history topics.

Lewis, Meriwether (1774–1809) — Captain Meriwether Lewis is best known as co-leader of the Lewis and Clark Expedition, also known as the Corps of Discovery. He was private secretary to Thomas Jefferson, who chose him to lead the expedition. Jefferson wrote, "It was impossible to find a character who, to a complete science in botany, natural history, mineralogy, & astronomy, joined the firmness of constitution & character, prudence, habits adapted to the woods, & familiarity with the Indian manners & character, requisite for this undertaking. All the latter qualifications Capt. Lewis has." Lewis in turn chose William Clark, a friend from their military days, to accompany him. The journey took a year and a half and covered more than 4000 miles to and from the Pacific coast. Lewis recorded in his journal information on American Indians, plants, animals, fossils, geological formations, and the topography of the land. The expedition also collected specimens to take back to Washington. Upon his return, Lewis was appointed to the governorship of the Louisiana Territory. While travelling through Tennessee, Lewis was found shot to death at Grinder's Stand, an inn on the Natchez Trace. It has never been determined whether his death was murder or suicide. Lewis's Woodpecker (*Melanerpes lewis*) commemorates his name. He is also honored by *Lewisia*, a genus of Rocky Mountain wildflowers known as Bitterroot.

L'Herminier, Felix Louis (1779–1833) and **Dr. Ferdinand Joseph L'Herminier** (1802–1866) — Felix L. L'Herminier was a French naturalist commissioned as second class chemist at Guadaloupe. Later he became chief chemist at the military hospital on Marie-Colante and master of the mint at Guadaloupe. He collected specimens of mammals, birds, reptiles, insects, live plants, and seeds on various West Indian islands and in French Guyana. In 1815, L'Herminier was exiled when the island was taken over by the British. He settled in Charleston, South Carolina, and sold his collections to the Charleston Museum, where he was made its first director (1816–1819). In 1819, he returned to Guadaloupe, where his titles of King's Naturalist and Director of the Botanic Gardens were restored. Felix's son

Ferdinand practiced medicine on Guadaloupe for forty years. He served as chief medical officer at the civil hospital at Point a Pitre and hospice of Saint Elizabeth. He received the Legion of Honor for his work following an earthquake in 1843. Dr. L'Herminier gained international recognition for his classification of birds based on their bone structure. The species name of Audubon's Shearwater (*Puffinus lherminieri*) honors either the father or the son; we don't know which. It has been suggested that perhaps the shearwater was named for both. But in that case, the species name would end with the plural masculine genitive suffix —*orum*.

Lichtenstein, Martin Henrich Carl (1780–1857) — Dr. Lichtenstein was a German physician and naturalist. He explored and collected extensively in South Africa (1802–1806) and while there became the personal physician to the Dutch Governor of the Cape of Good Hope. He was professor of Zoology at Berlin University, and he founded the Berlin Zoo in 1815. It was said to be one of the finest in Europe. The Altamira Oriole (*Icterus gularis*) was formerly known as Lichtenstein's Oriole, and Lichtenstein's Kingbird is an alternate name for the Tropical Kingbird (*Tyrannus melancholicus*).

Lincoln, Thomas (1812–1883) — At age twenty-one, Thomas Lincoln accompanied Audubon on his Labrador expedition, but he never traveled extensively after that. Lincoln returned to the family homestead near Dennysville, Maine, to help his brother Edmund manage their 10,000-acre farm. It produced hay, grain, apples, vegetables, and timber, which were shipped out of Eastport from the family's own wharves. Lincoln became a staunch abolitionist and was an accomplished artist of watercolor paintings. His subjects were birds and seashells. The clapboard house, where Lincoln resided all his life, is said to be one of the best examples of colonial architecture in New England. It is now the Lincoln House Country Inn. Lincoln's Sparrow (*Melospiza lincolnii*) is named in his honor.

McDougall, Peter (1777–1814) — His surname is variously spelled McDougall, MacDougall, or M'Dougall. From 1804 to 1809, Dr. McDougall practiced medicine with another physician in Glasgow, Scotland. Then he took a position as surgeon at the Glasgow Royal Infirmary. He was not appointed the following year because of a disagreement over his license to practice surgery. He returned to general practice without his partner. He fell ill, possibly from typhus, and died in April of 1814 at age thirty-seven. Dr. McDougall's epitaph reads, "His talents were but beginning to be known — his worth was known to many." Two weeks later the entire contents of his house were offered for sale. Two months after that, McDougall's extensive collection of birds from all over the world was sold at auction at Mr. Angus's Academy on Ingram Street. The collection included 101 foreign birds in twelve glass cases, mostly colorful species from the American tropics such as parrots, hummingbirds, and toucans. Some were also from North America and India. Twenty-seven glass cases housed 150 British birds including a case of the Roseate Terns (*Sterna dougallii*) that commemorate his name. Additionally there were seventy-five uncased birds plus other natural history specimens, three snake skins, two swordfish bills, an armadillo, an alligator, a bat, and a chest of drawers full of seashells from the Caribbean and the East Indies. One item that was not sold, but apparently stolen, was the "horn of a sea unicorn" (actually a narwhal tusk). There were also thirty-two numbers of George Grave's *British Ornithology* and five volumes of John Latham's *General History of Birds*. William Bullock may have been one of the dealers who attended the sale.

MacGillivray, William (1796–1852) — MacGillivray was a Scottish ornithologist from Aberdeen. In the fall of 1819, MacGillivray hiked from Aberdeen to London, a distance of more than 830 miles. He spent the week mostly at the British Museum studying the collection of British birds, then took a steamboat back to Aberdeen. In 1823, he and his family moved to Edinburgh where he became secretary and assistant to Professor Jameson and keeper of the Edinburgh University Museum. In 1831, he was appointed Conservator of the Museum of Edinburgh College of Surgeons, where he worked for ten years. It was during this time that he edited Audubon's *Ornithological Biography*, completing it in 1839. He also published his own books including *Descriptions of the Rapacious Birds of Great Britain* and the five-volume *A History of British Birds* (1837–1852). In 1841, he returned to Aberdeen University where he became Professor of Natural History at Marischal College, teaching zoology in the winter and botany in the summer. MacGillivray's Warbler (*Geothlypis tolmie*) is named for him.

McCown, John Porter (1815–1879) — A West Point graduate, McCown was an army officer who collected in Texas and sent specimens to George N. Lawrence of the Philadelphia Academy of Natural Sciences. He published several papers on the birds of Texas. After Texas, McCown was stationed at army posts around the country, including locations in North Carolina, New York, Kansas, Nebraska, and South Dakota. When the Civil War broke out, he resigned from the Union Army to fight for the Confederacy as a Lieutenant Colonel with the Tennessee Artillery Corps. He was promoted to Brigadier General, then to Major General. He also served in the Seminole War in Florida. After the war, he taught school near Knoxville, Tennessee, and finally retired to Magnolia, Arkansas, to be with his brother who served there as a judge. McCown's Longspur (*Rhynchophanes mccownii*) is named for him.

McKay, Charles Leslie (1855–1883) — McKay was a soldier with the U.S. Army Signal Service, stationed at Fort Alexander (now Nushagak), Alaska, on Bristol Bay. There he manned the weather station and collected natural history specimens for Baird at the National Museum. He amassed more than 400 specimens, 340 bird specimens, twenty-three species of mammals, 123 species of plants, as well as fishes, minerals, and native artifacts. McKay drowned when his canoe capsized on a collecting trip. His body was never found. There was a rumor of foul play, but that was never proved. McKay died just 2 days shy of his 28th birthday. McKay's Bunting (*Plectrophenax hyperboreus*) is named in his honor.

Masséna, François Victor, 2nd Duke of Rivoli and 3rd Prince of Essling (1799–1863) — The Duke of Rivoli was the son of André Masséna, one of Napoleon's marshals and an amateur ornithologist. He owned a collection of 12,500 bird specimens from all over the world, including many hummingbirds. The collection is now with the Philadelphia Academy of Natural Sciences. Rivoli's Hummingbird (*Eugenes fulgens*) is named for him. Masséna Partridge is an older name for the Montezuma Quail (*Cyrtonyx montezumae*).

Mathews, F. Schuyler (1854–1938) — Mathews was a naturalist who wrote down the songs of birds he heard in the woods and fields around his home in Campton, New Hampshire. He was also a composer, and he translated the songs into musical notes. Mathews then published his *Field Guide of Wild Birds and Their Music* (1904), which documented the songs of 82 species. Other books by Mathews include *Field Book of American Wildflowers* (1909), *Field Book of American Trees and Shrubs* (1898), and *The Book of Birds For Young People* (1921).

Mauri, Ernesto (1791–1836) — Mauri was a professor of practical botany and director of the Rome Botanical Gardens. He also published several papers on paleobotany. A good friend of Charles Lucien Bonaparte, he assisted Bonaparte when he was writing his *Iconografia della Fauna Italica* (1832–1841). The Western Sandpiper (*Calidris mauri*) is named for him.

Mearns, Edgar Alexander (1856–1916) — Mearns was a U.S. Army surgeon and one of the founding members of the AOU. He was stationed in Mexico from 1892–1894, and served with the U.S. and Mexican Boundary Commission. Mearns collected 30,000 natural history specimens (birds, mammals, reptiles, fish, and insects) between El Paso and the Pacific coast. He also collected in the Philippines (1903–1907) and East Africa (1909–1912). He published more than 100 descriptions of African birds. In 1909, he accompanied his friend Teddy Roosevelt on a hunting trip to East Africa. The Montezuma Quail (*Cyrtonyx montezumae*) was formerly known as Mearns's Quail.

Michahelles, Georg Christian Karl Wilhelm (1807–1834) — Karl Michahelles was a German physician and zoologist. He studied medicine at the University of Munich, receiving his doctorate in 1831 with the thesis *Das Malo Di Scarlievo in Historischer und Pathologischer Hinsicht*. While studying in Munich, Michahelles made the acquaintance of naturalist Lorenz Oken, who encouraged his interest in natural history. Dr. Michahelles collected extensively in Dalmatia and Croatia and became well known for his study of birds. He moved to Greece where he intended to practice medicine and study wildlife, but he died of dysentery at age twenty-seven. The Yellow-legged Gull (*Larus michahellis*) is named in his honor.

Miller, Olive Thorne (1831–1918) — Olive Thorne Miller was the pen name of Harriet Mann Miller. She is best known as an author of children's books, particularly on nature. She published her first bird book, *Bird Ways*, in 1885. Among her other books are *Little Folks in Feathers and Fur, and Others in Neither* (1875), *In Nesting Time* (1888), *A Bird-Lover in the West* (1894), *The First Book of Birds* (1899), *The Second Book of Birds: Bird Families* (1901), *With the Birds in Maine* (1904), and *The Children's Book of Birds* (1915). She published 375 articles in religious weeklies and other publications including *Harper's Weekly* and *St. Nicholas Magazine*. Sara A. Hubbard, director of the Illinois Audubon Society introduced Miller to birding. She studied birds in a series of field trips she took across the United States from 1883 to 1903. She joined the Audubon Societies in their goal of stopping the slaughter of birds for the millenary trade. In 1901, she was one of three women elected to membership in the AOU. Through her career, she published 780 articles, one booklet on birds, and twenty-four books. Professional biologists praised her work for its accuracy.

Morelet, Pierre Marie Arthur (1809–1892) — Arthur Morelet was a French naturalist and a member of the Commission to Algeria. He was an artist of natural history subjects and had a particular interest in molluscs, especially African species. He published several scientific papers on molluscs. Morelet's Seedeater (*Sorophila moreleti*) is named for him. Also a treefrog, a crocodile, a millipede, and several gastropods honor his name.

Murphy, Robert Cushman (1897–1973) — Robert Cushman Murphy was one of the most important ornithologists of the 20th century and a world authority on oceanic birds. He was Chairman of the Department of Birds with the National Museum of Natural History from 1921 to 1955, first working under Frank Chapman. He served as President of the AOU from 1948 to1950. In 1912, he set sail on the *Daisy*, a New Bedford whaling ship, for subantarctic islands. As naturalist, he collected specimens of birds, marine mammals, and plants for the American Museum of Natural History. In 1947, he published an account (from his diary and letters to his wife) of his whaling voyage as *Logbook for Grace*. His first book was *Bird Islands of Peru* (1925), but his best known work is the scholarly *Oceanic Birds of South America* (two volumes, 1936) for which he received the John Burroughs Medal and the Brewster Medal of the AOU. Murphy published nearly 600 articles in scientific journals and popular magazines, such as *National Geographic* and *Natural History*. In 1957, Murphy and other Long Island residents filed an unsuccessful lawsuit against the USDA and state agencies to stop the aerial spraying of DDT. Rachel Carson wrote an account of this in *Silent Spring*. Besides Murphy's Petrel (*Pterodroma ultima*), a louse, spider, fish, plant, lizard, an Antarctic inlet, two mountains, a county park, and a middle school are named in his honor. Murphy once said, "As a scientist, I'd as soon have a louse named for me as a mountain."

Neboux, Dr. Adolphe Simon (fl. 1840) — Dr. Neboux was a French physician who studied medicine at the naval hospital at Cherbourg. He served as physician on several voyages, including a thirty-one-month around-the-world trip aboard *La Venus*. He collected specimens and wrote a paper describing eight new species, but only one of these is considered valid today. Dr. Neboux published a book in which he outlined recommendations for providing health care for the poor of Paris. His final assignment was a voyage aboard the frigate *La Gloire* for a three-year stay in Brazil. This took a toll on his health, from which he never fully recovered. The Blue-footed Booby (*Sula nebouxii*) is named in his honor.

Nelson, Edward William (1855–1934) — Edward W. Nelson was a naturalist who was sent to Alaska at Baird's suggestion. There he was appointed by the Army Signal Corps to study weather and collect natural history specimens — plants, mammals, birds, fish, and insects — for the National Museum. His interest in the art and everyday items of the indigenous people earned him the nickname *The Man Who Collected Good-For-Nothing Things*. He spent four years (1877–1881) in Alaska. When he contracted tuberculosis, his mother moved him to Arizona where he could collect in a drier climate. He also collected in California and Mexico. He recovered from the tuberculosis, but he had a heart ailment for the rest of his life. In 1890 and 1891, Nelson accompanied Clinton Hart Merriam, A. K. Fisher, and Vernon Bailey on the Death Valley Expedition for the U.S. Biological Survey. Nelson served as president of the AOU (1908–1910) and the third Chief of the U.S. Biological Survey (1916–1927). In that capacity, he was instrumental in negotiating the Migratory Bird Conservation Act, Migratory Bird Hunting Stamp Act, and the Alaska Game Law. Nelson's Sparrow (*Ammodramus nelsoni*) is named for him, as well as seven subspecies of American birds and some 120 species and subspecies of mammals including Nelson's Antelope Squirrel (*Ammospermophilus nelsoni*) and Nelson's Pocket Mouse (*Chaetodipus nelsoni*), two species of reptiles, five species of fish, and two species of butterflies. Nelson's Island on the Alaska coast is also named in his honor.

Nice, Margaret Morse (1883–1974) — Affectionately known as the "Song Sparrow Lady," Margaret Morse Nice was America's most important female ornithologist. She and her husband Leonard Blaine Nice met at Clark University when they were both graduate students there. He first taught at Harvard, then took a faculty position at the University of Oklahoma. Margaret and Blaine birded throughout the state from 1913–1927. From this experience, they co-authored *Birds of Oklahoma*, published as a University of Oklahoma bulletin in 1931. When ornithologist George Miksch Sutton published his definitive *Oklahoma Birds* in 1967, he gave full credit to the Nices' work, writing in the introduction that it was of "inestimable value" for the information it provided. In 1928, the Nices moved to Columbus, Ohio, where Blaine accepted a professorship at Ohio State University Medical School. Here at Interpont, the Nices' sixty-acre property along the Olentangy River, Margaret began her landmark eight-year field study of the Song Sparrow. In 1943, she published *Studies in the Life History of the Song Sparrow* in two volumes. Ethologist Konrad Lorenz wrote, "Her paper on the song sparrow was, to the best of my knowledge, the first long term field investigation of the individual life of any free living wild animal." Margaret received numerous honors for her research including the AOU's Brewster Medal in 1942. In addition to her Song Sparrow study, she wrote nearly 250 scientific papers on birds, more than 3000 book reviews, and seven books including *The Watcher at the Nest* (1939) and her autobiography *Research Is a Passion with Me*, published posthumously in 1979. Behaviorist Nikolaas Tinbergen said of Margaret Morse Nice, "An American housewife was the greatest scholar of them all."

Nuttall, Thomas (1786–1859) — Thomas Nuttall was an English botanist and ornithologist. He apprenticed as a printer, but came to Philadelphia in 1808, where he came under the influence of botanists Benjamin Smith Barton and William Bartram. Nuttall went on several collecting trips in the South and West between 1809 and 1819. From these experiences he published his two-volume *Genera of North American Plants* (1818), *A Journal of Travels into the Arkansas Territory* (1821), and *A Manual of the Ornithology of the United States and Canada* (1832–1834). The latter was the first compact, inexpensive field guide. In 1822, Nuttall was appointed Curator of the Botanic Garden at Cambridge and lecturer of natural history at Harvard University. He held these positions until 1834, when he and John Kirk Townsend joined the Wyeth Expedition to the Oregon coast. In 1842, Nuttall returned to England, where he had inherited his uncle's estate. He resided there for the remainder of his life. The Common (formerly Nuttall's) Poorwill (*Phalaenoptilus nuttallii*), Nuttall's Woodpecker (*Picoides nuttallii*), and the Yellow-billed Magpie (*Pica nuttalli*) are named in his honor. The Mountain Cottontail (*Sylvilagus nuttallii*), Golden Mouse (*Ochrotomys nuttallii*), Pacific Dogwood (*Cornus nuttallii*), Daguo Dujuan Rhododendron (*Rhododendron nuttallii*), Nuttall's Sunflower (*Helianthus nuttallii*), Nuttall's Violet (*Viola nuttallii*), and Nuttall's Blister Beetle (*Lytta nuttalli*) are also named for him. The Olive-sided Flycatcher (*Contopus cooperi*) was formerly placed in the genus *Nuttallornis*.

Oberholser, Harry Church (1870–1963) — In 1895, Dr. Oberholser began a forty-six-year career as biologist with the U.S. Biological Survey (now the U.S. Fish and Wildlife Service). One of his first assignments was to collate data on the distribution and migration of birds. From 1900–1902, Oberholser conducted a field study of the birds of Texas. His senior colleague Vernon Bailey and wildlife artist Louis Agassiz Fuertes accompanied him the second year. The data he collected resulted in his two-volume *The Bird Life of Texas*, published eleven years after his death in 1974. Oberholser also wrote *Birds of Mt. Kilimanjaro* (1905), *Birds of the Anamba Islands* (1917), and *The Bird Life of Louisiana* (1938). He also published nearly 900 scientific papers in ornithological journals. During his years in government service, Oberholser lectured on wildlife conservation, organized a national waterfowl census, developed bird banding, and identified bird remains in court cases. His colleagues nicknamed him H2O, because he was a staunch prohibitionist. After retiring from the Fish and Wildlife Service in 1941, Oberholser served seven years as Curator of Ornithology with the Cleveland Museum of Natural History. Oberholser was an avid baseball fan, following the Washington Senators. He also collected coins and stamps, and sang in a choir. The Dusky Flycatcher (*Empidomax oberholseri*) is named for him.

Pallas, Peter Simon (1741–1811) — Pallas was a German zoologist and geographer, considered one of the greatest naturalists of the 18th century. He received his doctorate when he was just nineteen years old. He was a member of the Saint Petersburg Academy of Science and led an academy expedition in which he studied many regions in Russia and part of Mongolia. He wrote *A Journey Through Various Provinces of the Russian State* (1771) and *A History of the Mongolian People and Asian-Russian Fauna* (1811). Pallas described many species of birds, mammals, fish, and insects and several species of birds are named for him. Also a volcano on the Kurile Islands and a reef off New Guinea commemorate his name.

Paris brothers (fl. 1837) — They were obscure French businessmen who collected in Mexico and sent zoological specimens back to Paris. Scott's Oriole (*Icterus parisorum*) is named for them.

Parkes, Kenneth Carroll (1922–2007) — Kenneth Parkes was the Curator of Birds with the Carnegie Museum of Natural History for forty-four years and was one of America's leading avian taxonomists. He completed his undergraduate and graduate work at Cornell University under Arthur A. Allen. His doctoral thesis dealt with the taxonomy of North American birds. Parkes described new subspecies of birds from a dozen Latin American countries and wrote more than 500 scientific papers. He was interested in bird art and judged several art shows. He also helped select front pieces for the *Wilson Bulletin*. Parkes served as President of the Wilson Ornithological Society (1974–1975) and Vice-president of the AOU (1975–1976). He was a life member of the Cornell Laboratory of Ornithology and served on its administrative board. Parkes donated his professional library to the Cornell Lab. The Northern and Louisiana Waterthrushes (formerly in the genus *Seiurus*) have been merged into the newly erected genus *Parkesia*, which commemorates Kenneth Parkes.

Pennant, Thomas (1726–1798) — Pennant was a Welsh naturalist who studied mammals as well as birds. He was much influenced by Willughby's *Ornithologiae*, which he received when he was twelve years old. Pennant corresponded with such luminaries as Linnaeus, Gilbert White, Brünnich, Otto Müller, and Fabricius. He also counted Buffon and Voltaire as his friends. Pennant became a popular author, writing on his travels throughout Europe. His *Tour in Scotland* (1771) encouraged tourism in the Scottish Highlands. He once met German naturalist Peter Simon Pallas in the Netherlands, and the two discussed natural history topics at length. On his travels through Europe, Pennant kept detailed notes on the birds he saw. His works in natural history include *British Zoology* (1761–1766), *Indian Zoology* (1769), *Synopsis of Quadrupeds* (1771), and *Genera of Birds* (1777). Pennant's *Arctic Zoology* (1785) is considered his most important work and one in which he described many new species. A North American mammal, the Fisher (*Martes pennanti*), is named for him. It is also known as Pennant's Marten.

Peterson, Roger Tory (1908–1996) — Ornithologist and artist Roger Tory Peterson is best known as the inventor of the modern field guide. His was not the first, but it was innovative, simplifying the identification of birds in the field. Peterson's seventh-grade teacher, who encouraged her class to join a Junior Audubon Club, had a great influence on him. Peterson trained as an artist at the Art Student League (1927–1928) and the National Academy of Design (1929–1931). When Peterson was seeking a publisher for his book in the early 1930s, the country was deep into the Great Depression. After several rejections, Houghton-Mifflin agreed to publish his book. But they were cautious, the initial printing would be only 2000 copies and Peterson would relinquish royalties on the first 1000. When the book was on the shelves in 1934, it sold out the first week. *A Field Guide to the Birds* has since gone through five editions, and despite competition by newer titles it is still one of the most widely used by amateurs and professionals alike. Peterson also edited the growing number of titles in the Peterson Field Guide series, covering everything from mammals, birds' nests, reptiles, fish, and moths to wildflowers, trees and shrubs, coral reefs, the atmosphere, and stars and planets. There are more than forty titles in the series. Peterson was honored with more than thirty awards during his lifetime. He was even nominated for the Nobel Peace Prize twice. His most notable honors include William Brewster Memorial Award, AOU (1944); John Burroughs Medal (1950); Gold Medal, New York Zoological Society (1961); Arthur A. Allen Award, Cornell Laboratory of Ornithology (1967); Audubon Conservation Medal, National Audubon Society (1971); Gold Medal, World Wildlife Fund (1972); Joseph Wood Krutch Medal, Humane Society of the United States (1973); Conservation Achievement Award, National Wildlife Federation (1975); Horatio Alger Award (1977); Master Artist Award, Leigh Yawkey Museum (1978); Gold Medal, Philadelphia Academy of Natural Sciences (1980); Ludlow Griscom Medal, American Birding Association (1980); Presidential Medal of Freedom (1980); James Smithson Bicentennial Medal, Smithsonian Institution (1984); and the Eisenmann Medal, Linnaean Society (1986). The Roger Tory Peterson Institute of Natural History was founded in Peterson's hometown of Jamestown, New York, in 1984. It is charged with preserving Peterson's lifetime body of work and making it available for educational purposes. Paul Erhrlich (1988) wrote, "In this century no one has done more to promote an interest in living creatures than Roger Tory Peterson."

Pettingill, Jr., Olin Sewall (1907–2001) — Pettingill was an author and cinematographer of nature subjects. As an undergraduate at Bowdoin College, he studied the last three Heath Hens on Martha's Vineyard in 1927. Later as a graduate student at Cornell University, he conducted his Ph.D. dissertation on the American Woodcock. Between 1939 and 1992, Pettingill published ten books on birds, including *A Guide to Finding Birds East of the Mississippi* (1951) and *A Guide to Finding Birds West of the Mississippi* (1953). Pettingill made several ornithological films, which often aired as part of the Audubon Screen Tours. He also provided footage for four of Walt Disney's *True-Life Adventures* films including the Academy Award-winning *The Vanishing Prairie* (1954). He held several distinguishing positions during his lifetime, President of the Wilson Ornithological Society (1948–1950), member of the Board of Directors of the National Audubon Society (1955–1974), and a Life Fellow of the AOU. He received three awards: the Arthur A. Allen Medal in 1974 from Cornell, the Ludlow Griscom Award in 1982, and the Eisenmann Medal in 1985. He made two TV appearances, one on *The Today Show*, the other on the popular game show *To Tell the Truth*.

Richardson, Sir John (1787–1865) — Richardson was a Scottish naval officer and Arctic explorer. He accompanied Franklin on his first two expeditions and later searched for the lost Franklin expedition. Richardson wrote volumes on quadrupeds and fishes for *Fauna-Borealis Americana* and contributed appendices of several Arctic expeditions. The Cackling Goose (*Branta hutchinsii*), formerly considered a subspecies of the Canada Goose, was also known as Richardson's Goose. The Boreal Owl (*Aegolius funereus*) was formerly known as Richardson's Owl. Richardson's Ground Squirrel (*Spemophilus richardsonii*), Richardson's Collared Lemming (*Dictrostonyx richardsoni*), and the Water Vole (*Microtus richardsoni*) are also named for him.

Ridgway, Robert (1850–1929) — Robert Ridgway was Curator of Ornithology at the National Museum (1880–1929) and one of the founding members of the AOU. As a teenager he collected and sketched the birds around his home in Richland County, Illinois. At age fourteen, he began to correspond with Baird at the Smithsonian. Baird appointed Ridgway zoologist on the Geological Survey to the 40th parallel when he was only seventeen. On the survey, he did field work in Utah, Nevada, and Wyoming. In the late 1890s and early 1900s, he made collecting trips to Florida, Alaska, and Costa Rica. Ridgway co-wrote *A History of North American Birds* with Baird and Brewer and *The Birds of Middle and North America* (1901–1950), this latter work completed by Herbert Friedmann. Ridgway proposed a color system in which the hues of a bird's plumage were described and given precise names, 1115 in all. These were published in *Color Standards and Nomenclature* (1912). After retiring, Ridgway bought eighteen acres of farmland for a bird sanctuary, Bird Haven. Only a remnant remains today, where there is a memorial to this important naturalist. The Buff-colored Nightjar (*Antrostomus ridgwayi*) is named for him. It was formerly known as Ridgway's Whip-poor-will. A Mexican bird, the Aztec Thrush (*Ridgwayia pinicola*), also commemorates his name.

Ripley, Sidney Dillon (1913–2001) — S. Dillon Ripley was a wildlife conservationist and ornithologist, and a world authority on the birds of Southeast Asia. During WWII, he served in the Office of Strategic Services in Southeast Asia. His position as an intelligence officer allowed him to bird in sensitive areas. He was a member of the AOU, becoming an elective member in 1942 and a fellow in 1951. After the war, he taught at Yale, and in 1954, became a full professor and director of the Peabody Museum of Natural History. He served on the board of the World Wildlife Fund for a number of years, and from 1964 to 1984, he was Secretary of the Smithsonian Institution. In 1970, he helped to found *Smithsonian* magazine. He successfully defended the National Museum of Natural History against a lawsuit that objected to the *Dynamics of Evolution* exhibit. In 1985, Ripley was awarded the Presidential Medal of Freedom. Fifteen colleges and universities, including Brown, Cambridge, Harvard, Johns Hopkins, and Yale awarded him honorary degrees.

Ross, Bernard Rogan (1827–1874) — Bernard Ross was born in Londonderry, Ireland, but resided in Canada for most of his life. He was Chief Trader with the Hudson's Bay Company and a naturalist who studied the fauna of the Canadian boreal forest. He collected mammals, birds, eggs, fish, and insects, as well as Indian clothing and artifacts. These were sent off to the Smithsonian, the British Museum of Natural History, and the Royal Scottish Museum.

Ross is considered one of the most outstanding contributors to a second resurgence of the Hudson's Bay Company's natural history investigation. In 1863, Ross was a foundation fellow of the Anthropological Society. He became a fellow of the Royal Geographical Society in 1864. He was also a corresponding member of the New York Historical Society, and a correspondent of the Academy of Natural Sciences of Philadelphia and of the Natural History Society of Montreal. Ross's Goose (*Anser rossii*) is named in his honor.

Ross, James Clark (1800–1862) — James Ross was a navy officer and explorer. He joined the Royal Navy at age twelve and accompanied his uncle Sir John Ross on his first Arctic voyage in 1818. From 1819 to 1827, he went on four more Arctic expeditions in search of the Northwest Passage, this time under Sir William Parry. From 1829 to 1833, he made another voyage to the Arctic with his uncle. On this trip they discovered the position of the Magnetic North Pole at Cape Adelaide on Boothia Peninsula in northern Canada on June 1, 1831. Ross commanded the HMS *Erebus* and HMS *Terror* on an Antarctic expedition from 1839 to 1843. His final trip to the Arctic was in 1848, to search for the lost Franklin Expedition. Ross's Gull (*Rhodostethia rosea*) is named for him, as is the Ross Seal (*Ommatophoca rossii*). Also the Ross Sea, Ross Ice Shelf, and Ross Island are named in his honor.

Sabine, Sir Edward (1788–1883) — Edward Sabine was an English explorer and scientist. He was an authority on Earth's magnetic field and its use in navigation. He served as astronomer on two voyages to the Arctic in search of the Northwest Passage. The first in 1818 was with John Clark Ross; the second in 1819–1820 was with William Parry. He also made a voyage to the West Indies, Ascension Island, and Sierra Leone in 1821–1823. He was elected Fellow of the Royal Society in 1818 and served as its president from 1862 to 1871. Sabine also had a 70+-year career with the Royal Artillery, retiring in 1877 with the rank of general. In 1835, Sabine began the first systematic magnetic survey ever made in the British Isles, probably his most important scientific achievement. He published his finding in *Contributions to Terrestrial Magnetism*, which he began in 1840. Sabine's Gull (*Xema sabini*) is named in his honor.

Say, Thomas (1787–1843) — Thomas Say is known as the Father of American Entomology. He was William Bartram's grandnephew. Say described 1155 species of beetles, 225 species of flies, 100 species of true bugs, and more than 400 species of insects in other orders. He served as chief zoologist with Major S. H. Long's expedition to the Rockies. Say was the editor of Charles Bonaparte's *American Ornithology*. The Phoebe genus *Sayornis* (Say's bird) was erected in his honor. The common, genus, and species names of Say's Phoebe (*Sayornis say*) all refer to Thomas Say.

Sclater, Dr. Philip Lutley (1829–1913) — Dr. Sclater was a British ornithologist and a world authority on the birds of Central and South America. He was founder and first editor of *The Ibis*, the journal of the British Ornithologists' Union. Sclater practiced law for a number of years, but gave that up to devote his life to ornithology. He became Secretary of the London Zoological Society. He devised a classification of six biogeographical regions of bird distribution. He wrote several books including *Exotic Ornithology* (1866), *Birds of the Challenger Expedition* (1881), and *Argentine Ornithology* (1888). Dr. Sclater donated his collection of 9000 specimens of more than 3000 species in installments to the British Museum of Natural History. The Mexican Chickadee (*Poecile sclateri*) is named for him. A number of foreign birds are also named for Dr. Sclater or his son William Lutley Sclater.

Scott, Winfield (1786–1866) — Winfield Scott was General in Chief of the U.S. Army for twenty years. He was nicknamed "Old Fuss and Feathers" for his meticulousness in dress and conduct. Scott was a commander in the Mexican War. In 1852, he ran for president under the Whig party, but was soundly defeated by Franklin Pierce. Scott's Oriole (*Icterus parisorum*) is named for him.

Skutch, Alexander (1904–2004) — Although he took his doctorate in botany, Alexander Skutch was considered one of the world's greatest ornithologists. After arriving in Panama on a research fellowship to study banana diseases, he came under the spell of tropical birds. He spent more than forty years studying the habits of little-known species in Panama, Honduras, Guatemala, Ecuador, Venezuela, but mostly in Costa Rica, where he bought a farm in 1941. Skutch wrote more than forty books on birds and nature topics and more than 200 scientific papers on ornithology. Among his books are *Life Histories of Central American Highland Birds* (1967), *A Naturalist in Costa Rica* (1971), *Studies of Tropical American Birds* (1972), *The Life of the Hummingbird* (1973), *A Naturalist on a Tropical Farm* (1980), *Birds of Tropical America* (1983), and *Nature Through Tropical Windows* (1984).

Smith, Gideon B. (1793–1867) — Dr. Gideon Smith was a Baltimore physician who received his MD at age forty-seven. He was an early proponent of sericulture, an industry that proved too labor intensive to be profitable in the United States. He sold millions of silkworm eggs and planted a fast-growing strain of mulberry as forage for the silkworms. Dr. Smith also edited the earliest volumes of *Journal of the American Silk Society*. He acted as Audubon's agent in Baltimore in the sale of the octavo edition of *Birds of America*. In 1848, he was expelled from the Baltimore Medical Society for unprofessional conduct, the particulars of which are not known. Smith's Longspur (*Calcarius pictus*) is named in his honor.

Sprague, Isaac (1811–1895) — Isaac Sprague was America's leading botanical artist. He illustrated Asa Gray's *The Botanical Textbook* (1845). While Gray appreciated the high quality of Sprague's work, he was frequently frustrated with his slowness. Later Sprague produced less technical but more decorative illustrations for popular works. He accompanied Audubon on his Missouri River expedition in 1843. Sprague's Pipit (*Anthus spragueii*) is named for him.

Stejneger, Leonhard Hess (1851–1943) — Dr. Stejneger was a Norwegian ornithologist and herpetologist. In 1881, he moved to Washington, D.C. and became a U.S. citizen in 1887. He was hired by the Smithsonian Institution in 1884 and worked under the supervision of Spencer Fullerton Baird. Beginning as Assistant Curator of Birds, Stejneger was promoted to Curator of Reptiles in 1889, then to Curator of Reptiles and Amphibians in 1899. From 1911 until his death in 1943, Stejneger held the position of Head Curator of Biology. He participated in several expeditions to the northern portions of North America and published more than 400 scientific papers on birds, reptiles, fur seals, and other topics. Stejneger became fascinated with the life of German explorer George Wilhem Steller, resulting in his publishing an authoritative biography on Steller in 1936. Stejneger is commemorated in the names of Stejneger's Scoter (*Melanitta stejnegeri*), Stejneger's Petrel (*Pterodroma longirostris*), Stejneger's Stonechat (*Saxicola stejnegeri*), and Stejneger's Beaked Whale (*Mesoplodon stejnegeri*).

Steller, George Wilhelm (1709–1746) — Dr. Steller was a German naturalist and explorer, and was a physician in the Russian service. He studied medicine at Halle University. He was an assistant at the Academy of Sciences in Saint Petersburg. Dr. Steller was listed as ship's surgeon and mineralogist on Vitus Bering's Kamchatka Expedition (1740–1742) to Alaska. On the return trip, violent gales blew the ship far off course. In late November, they landed on Bering Island, mistaking it for the mainland. Vitus Bering and a few of his crew, some suffering from scurvy, died there. When a storm cast the ship up on the beach, Steller and the remaining survivors were stranded for the next nine months (1741–1742). During his time on Bering Island, Steller chronicled the flora and fauna. This included dissecting a beached marine mammal that bears his name, Steller's Sea Cow (now extinct). Eventually Steller and his companions were able to get off the island by building a smaller vessel from the remains of the old one in the spring of 1742. They embarked in August and arrived in Kamchatka thirteen days later. Steller spent the next two years exploring the Kamchatka peninsula south to the Kuril Islands. Birds named for Steller are Steller's Eider (*Polysticta stelleri*), Steller's Sea-Eagle (*Haliaeetus* *pelagicus*), and Steller's Jay (*Cyanocitta stelleri*). Mammals bearing his name are the aforementioned Steller's Sea Cow (*Hydrodamalis gigas*) and the Northern Sea Lion (*Eumetopias jubatus*), also known as Steller's Sea Lion.

Sutton, George Miksch (1898–1982) — George Miksch Sutton was an American ornithologist and artist. When he was a teenager, he began to correspond with nature artist Louis Agassiz Fuertes, who invited Sutton to spend a summer with him and his family. In 1918, Sutton worked at the Carnegie Museum of Natural History in Pittsburgh. He was put in charge of the museum's egg collection. Sutton also travelled with the museum staff on field expeditions to Labrador and other northern regions. He was expelled from Bethany College in 1919 for leading a student protest against the mandatory ROTC training, but in 1923, the college granted him his bachelor degree. Sutton served as Pennsylvania State Ornithologist from 1925 to 1929. He published his first book in 1928, *An Introduction to the Birds of Pennsylvania*. In 1931, Sutton and four other birders arrived on the western shore of Hudson Bay. On June 16, he became the first person to discover a nest of Harris' Sparrow. He received his Ph.D. from Cornell University in 1938, then worked at Cornell as curator of the Louis Agassiz Fuertes Memorial collection of birds. Sutton taught zoology at the University of Oklahoma from 1952 to 1968 and published *Oklahoma Birds: Their Ecology and Distribution with Comments of the Avifauna of the Southern Great Plains* in 1967. Ultimately, he wrote thirteen books and illustrated at least eighteen others. After retiring, Sutton stayed on at the university as Professor Emeritus and curator of birds at the Stovall Museum of Science and History. Sutton received the John Burroughs Medal in 1962 for conservation writing, and in 1967 was named to the Oklahoma Hall of Fame. In 1972, The government of Iceland awarded him the Knight Cross of the Order of the Falcon for his study of Icelandic birds. Iceland also issued a postage stamp with Sutton's painting of a Gyrfalcon. Sutton's Warbler, a hybrid, not a true species, is named for him.

Swainson, William (1789–1855) — William Swainson was a British naturalist and illustrator. He practiced lithography so he could illustrate his own books, and he illustrated a great number of scientific and popular works by other authors as well. He served with the army commissariat in Malta and Sicily from 1807–1815. Swainson was elected a Fellow of the Linnaean Society in 1816 and the Royal Society in 1820. From 1816–1818, he collected in eastern Brazil, returning to England with a large collection of zoological specimens including 20,000 insects and 760 bird skins. Swainson was a very prolific writer; his works include *Instructions for Collecting and Preserving Subjects of Natural History* (produced in 1808 for the Liverpool Museum), *Zoological Illustrations* (1820–1823), *Naturalists' Guide* (1822), *Exotic Conchology, or Coloured Lithographic Drawings of Shells* (1822), and *Birds of Brazil* (1834–1835). He also wrote the section on birds for Sir John Richardson's *Fauna Boreali-Americana* and contributed to Lardner's Cabinet Encyclopaedia (1834–1840) and Jardine's Naturalist's Library (1834–1846). Swainson described and named more than twenty species of North American birds. In 1840, he moved his family to New Zealand, where he resided for the rest of his life. Swainson's Hawk (*Buteo swainsoni*), Swainson's Thrush (*Catharus ustulatus*), and Swainson's Warbler (*Limnothlypis swainsonii*) are named for him.

Thayer, John Eliot (1862–1933) — John Thayer was a wealthy patron of ornithology, who sent collectors to the more remote regions on North and Central America. He founded the Thayer Museum in Lancaster, Massachusetts. It was said to be the largest private collection of birds in the United States. The collection, consisting of 28,000 skins, 3500 mounted birds, and 15,000 nests and eggs, was donated to Harvard University's Museum of Comparative Anatomy. Thayer's Gull (*Larus argentatus thayeri*), now considered a subspecies of the Herring Gull, is named for him.

Todd, Walter Edmond Clyde (1874–1969) — W. E. Clyde Todd began his career working for the U.S. Department of Agriculture. In 1891, he left his government job and contracted with the Carnegie Museum of Natural History in Pittsburgh to collect birds in western Pennsylvania. Soon after, he joined the museum where he was employed for the rest of his professional life. He did field work in Pennsylvania and also in northeast Canada. In fact, he made more than twenty expeditions to northern regions, and Arctic birds became his specialty. He was a long-time member of the AOU and was elected Fellow Emeritus in 1968. Todd was concerned with environmental issues such as urban sprawl and habitat fragmentation. He was also critical of public museums who collected multiple specimens of birds and their eggs as wasteful and not contributing to the science of ornithology. In 1942, he bought seventy-one acres on the site of his grandfather's farm to save it from logging. He donated the property to the Audubon Society of Western Pennsylvania (ASWP) which maintains it as the Todd Nature Reserve in Butler County. Todd donated an additional sixty-one acres in 1956. The ASWP has continued to acquire property, and the reserve now encompasses 224 acres. The Society annually bestows the W. E. Clyde Todd Award in recognition of "an individual who has made an outstanding contribution to conservation in western Pennsylvania." Todd's published work includes *The Birds of the Santa Marta Region of Colombia: A Study in Altitudinal Distribution* (1922) for which he was awarded the Brewster Prize, *Birds of Western Pennsylvania* (1940), and *Birds of the Labrador Peninsula and Adjacent Areas* (1963).

Tolmie, William Fraser (1818–1886) — Dr. Tolmie was a Scottish physician and one of the most esteemed pioneers of the Pacific Northwest. In 1833, the Hudson's Bay Company assigned him to Fort Vancouver. For twenty-five years, he was involved as medical officer, Indian trader, and superintendent of agricultural operations in the Puget Sound area. Tolmie collected plants and bird skins, most of which were sent to Scotland. But some, by way of his friend John Kirk Townsend, found their way to the Philadelphia Academy of Science and the Smithsonian. William Hooker named several plants in Tolmie's honor. Tolmie studied the native languages and sent Indian clothing and artifacts to museums in Scotland. Tolmie was the first white man to ascend the highest slopes of Mount Ranier. He was appointed Chief Factor of the Hudson's Bay Company in 1855 and served in that capacity until his retirement in 1859. The specific epithet of MacGillivray's Warbler (*Geothlypis tolmiei*) honors Dr. Tolmie.

Torrey, Bradford (1843–1912) — Bradford Torrey was a New England outdoor writer. He published thirteen nature books, many of which were compilations of essays he had written for the *Atlantic Monthly*. He also contributed field observations for such scientific journals as *The Auk, The Condor*, and *Bird-Lore*. From 1886 to 1901, he was an editor with the popular magazine *Youth's Companion*. In the 1890s, Torrey edited a deluxe edition of *Walden*. He also edited the first version of *Thoreau's Journal* in fourteen volumes as part of a twenty-volume Manuscript Edition of *Thoreau's Complete Works* (Houghton-Mifflin Company, 1906). Torrey's books found an enthusiastic audience of readers, who delighted in his keen observations of the natural world.

Townsend, John Kirk (1809–1851) — John K. Townsend was a Philadelphia naturalist, born into a prominent Quaker family. He was elected a member of the Academy of Natural Sciences of Philadelphia in 1833 and made curator in 1842. In 1834, he accompanied English botanist Thomas Nuttall on Nathaniel Wyeth's second geographical and commercial expedition across the Rockies to the Pacific coast. The American Philosophical Society and the Academy of Natural Sciences each gave him $100.00 in advance for a share of the specimens he would collect. Townsend described many new species of birds and sent specimens to Audubon. While stationed at Fort Vancouver, Washington, Townsend and Nuttall got the opportunity to visit the Hawaiian Islands, where they collected for nearly three months. In 1837, Townsend returned to Philadelphia by boat, sailing around Cape Horn. He wrote an account of the trip, *A Narrative of a Journey across the Rocky Mountains to the Columbia River and a*

Visit to the Sandwich Islands, Chile, &c. (1839), now considered an important historical document on the Wyeth Expedition during the pioneer days of the country. From 1842–1845, Townsend worked for the National Institute of Washington, D.C. (a forerunner of the Smithsonian), obtaining and mounting birds for their exhibits. Townsend died at age forty-one from chronic arsenic poisoning from exposure to the chemicals he used to prepare zoological specimens. Townsend's Solitaire (*Myadestes townsendi*) and Townsend's Warbler (*Setophaga townsendi*) are named in his honor. A number of small mammals, Townsend's Mole (*Scapanus townsendii*), Townsend's Big-eared Bat (*Corynorhinus towsendii*), Townsend's Chipmunk (*Tamias townsendii*), Townsend's Ground Squirrel (*Spermophilus townsendii*), Townsend's Vole (*Microtus townsendii*), Townsend's Pocket Gopher (*Thomomys townsendii*), and the White-tailed Jackrabbit (*Lepus townsendii*), also commemorate his name.

Traill, Dr. Thomas Stewart (1781–1862) — Thomas Traill was a Scottish physician and professor of medical jurisprudence at the University of Edinburgh. He was a founder of the Royal Institution of Liverpool and was instrumental in establishing a museum of natural history in South Kensington. Traill also edited the eighth edition of the *Encyclopedia Britannica*. He became a friend of Audubon and assisted him in getting subscribers to *The Birds of America*. The Willow Flycatcher (*Empidonax traillii*) is named for him. The Willow and Alder Flycatchers were formerly considered a single species, Traill's Flycatcher.

Vaux, William Sansom (1811–1882) — William Vaux was an eminent mineralogist and patron of the Academy of Natural Sciences of Philadelphia, where, for nearly fifty years, he served it in various capacities as auditor, curator, and vice-president. He also served as president of the Zoological Society of Philadelphia and was one of the original members of the American Association for the Advancement of Science. He amassed an impressive collection of mineral specimens, said to be the finest in the United States. After the Civil War he made several collecting trips to Europe. Vaux bequeathed his mineral collection, library, and archaeological materials to the Academy, along with a generous endowment for their maintenance. Vaux's Swift (*Chaetura vauxi*) is named in his honor.

Verreaux, Jules Pierre (1807–1873) and **Jean Baptiste Edouard** (1810–1868) — These brothers were collectors and dealers in natural history specimens. Many of their bird skins are now in the collections of American museums. Both brothers explored and collected in South Africa, China, Indochina, and the Philippines. In 1842, the Musée d'Histoire Naturelle in Paris sent Jules to Australia as an ornithologist and plant collector. Five years later he returned to France with a collection reported to total 115,000 specimens. The family business, the *Maison Verreaux* in Paris, was both a private museum and a distributor of exotic specimens to collectors worldwide. It was said to be "one of the greatest, if not the greatest emporium of natural history that the world has ever seen." The White-tipped Dove (*Leptotila verreauxi*) is named for the Verreaux brothers.

Wetmore, Frank Alexander (1886–1978) — Alexander Wetmore was an American ornithologist and avian paleontologist. He began his career as taxidermist at the Denver Museum of Natural History in 1909. He is best known for his extensive field work in Latin American countries. In 1911, he studied the birds of Puerto Rico. He travelled throughout South America for two years while working for the U.S. Bureau of Biological Survey, studying bird migration between the two continents. He was appointed Assistant Secretary of the Smithsonian Institution in 1925 and became its 6th Secretary from 1945 to 1952. He served as president of the AOU from 1926 to 1929. Wetmore also studied birds in Haiti, the Dominican Republic, Guatemala, Costa Rica, Mexico, Panama, and Colombia. His published works include *A Systematic Classification for the Birds of the World* (1930), *Birds of Haiti and the Dominican Republic* (1931), and *The Birds of the Republic of Panamá*

(1965). Numerous species and subspecies of birds (both living and fossil), mammals, amphibians, insects, molluscs, and plants commemorate his name.

Whitney, Josiah Dwight (1819–1896) — Whitney was the preeminent geologist of the 19th century. He had intended to study law, but switched to geology. He wrote *The Metallic Wealth of the United States* (1854) that remained a standard reference for sixteen years. From 1855 to 1858, he was involved in geological surveys in Iowa, Illinois, and Wisconsin. He was the State Geologist of California from 1860 to 1874. Later he was appointed Professor of Geology and Director of the School of Mining and Practical Geology at Harvard. His last great work was *Climatic Changes of Later Geological Times* (1882). The Elf Owl (*Micrathene whitneyi*) is named for him. Also Mount Whitney, the highest peak in the forty-eight contiguous states, commemorates him.

Williamson, Robert Stockton (1824–1882) — Lieutenant Williamson was a topographical engineer who led several surveying expeditions on the West Coast. His first assignment was in 1849, in northern California, where the goal was to find a railroad route from the Mississippi River to the Pacific Ocean. The surveying team identified a number of possibilities. In 1855, he was assigned to find a line to connect Los Angeles and San Francisco with Oregon and the Washington Territory. Williamson wrote volume five of the Pacific Railroad Reports, *Report of Explorations in California for Railroad Routes to Connect with the Routes near the 35th and 32nd Parallels of North Latitudes* (1857). Williamson served on General Burnside's staff during the Civil War and attained the rank of Lieutenant Colonel. Following the war, Williamson returned to California, where he worked as an engineer with the lighthouse service. Williamson's Sapsucker (*Sphyrapicus thyroideus*) is named for him.

Wilson, Alexander (1766–1813) — Pioneer naturalist Alexander Wilson is known as the Father of American Ornithology. He was born in Paisley, Scotland, where he apprenticed as a weaver and was an itinerate poet. Inspired by Robert Burns, Wilson wrote pastoral pieces, ballads, and satirical verses about the conditions of the weavers in the mills. The latter got him into trouble, when he lampooned a mill owner during a labor dispute. He was charged with libel, fined, and imprisoned for several months. Upon his release, he emigrated to America where he taught school for seven years in the Philadelphia area. Wilson became friends with William Bartram, who became his mentor encouraging his interest in ornithology. Wilson travelled throughout the eastern states from New England to the Southeast, collecting specimens and painting them. This resulted in his nine-volume *American Ornithology* (1808–1814), which illustrated 268 species of birds. Wilson died while the ninth volume was in preparation. His friend and patron George Ord completed and published it. Wilson's hometown of Paisley did not forget him. There on the banks of the River Cart, is a memorial with the inscription, "Remember Alexander Wilson 1766–1813. Here was his boyhood playground." There is also a statue of Wilson on the grounds of Paisley Abbey. Species that commemorate Alexander Wilson are Wilson's Storm-Petrel (*Oceanites oceanicus*), Wilson's Plover (*Charadrius wilsonia*), Wilson's Phalarope (*Phalaropus tricolor*), Wilson's Snipe (*Gallinago delicata*), and Wilson's Warbler (*Cardellina pusilla*). The Veery (*Catharus fuscescens*) is sometimes called Wilson's Thrush. The Hooded Warbler (*Setophaga citrina*), Wilson's Warbler, and the Canada Warbler (*Cardellina canadensis*) were formerly classified in the genus *Wilsonia* (erected by Charles Bonaparte in honor of Wilson in 1838), but it is no longer considered a valid taxon. The Wilson Ornithological Society also commemorates Wilson's name. Wilson's Warbler is the logo for its quarterly scientific journal *The Wilson Bulletin*.

Wollweber (fl. 1840) — Wollweber was an obscure (we don't even know his first name) German collector who sent specimens from Mexico back to Germany. The Mexican Jay (*Aphelocoma wollweberi*) and Bridled Titmouse (*Baeolophus wollweberi*) are named for him.

Woodhouse, Samuel Washington (1821–1904) — Dr. Samuel Woodhouse was a Philadelphia physician whose interest in natural history was influenced by John Cassin, Thomas Nuttall, William Gambel and others with the Philadelphia Academy of Natural Sciences. Woodhouse served as surgeon-naturalist on several expeditions to the western frontier including one under Lieutenant Lorenzo Sitgreaves to the Zuni and Little Colorado rivers in 1852. This expedition was the first to encounter the Petrified Forest. He experienced two mishaps on this adventure: a bite on the index finger by a rattlesnake he was trying to subdue and a Yavapai arrow in the leg while he was sitting by a campfire. Woodhouse kept extensive field notes on the birds and mammals he encountered and described several new species, including White-throated Swift, Black-capped Vireo, Cassin's Sparrow, Abert's Squirrel, Ord's Kangaroo Rat, and Desert Pocket Mouse. He later went on expeditions to Central America and during the Civil War he was a surgeon at Eastern Penitentiary in Philadelphia. He was also a corresponding member of the AOU. Woodhouse published *A Naturalist in Indian Territory: The Journal of S. W. Woodhouse, 1849–50*. Woodhouse's Scrub-Jay (*Aphelocoma woodhouseii*), Woodhouse's Toad (*Anaxyrus woodhousii*), and a wildflower Woodhouse's Bahia (*Picradeniopsis woodhousei*) commemorate his name.

Wright, Charles (1811–1855) — Charles Wright was a plant collector whose forays were funded by Harvard Professor of Botany Asa Gray. Gray also supplied Wright with books and plant presses. Wright collected mainly in the desert southwest, Texas, New Mexico, and Arizona, as well as in Cuba. Wright served as botanist and surveyor for the U.S. and Mexico Boundary survey. His collections from two trips to Texas form the basis for Asa Gray's two-part *Plantae Wrightianae* for the Smithsonian Contributions to Knowledge (1852–1853). The Gray Flycatcher (*Empidonax wrightii*) is named for him.

Wright, Mabel Osgood (1859–1934) — Mabel Osgood Wright was a naturalist, photographer, and author of books and articles on nature topics. *A New England May Day* (1893), which appeared in the *Evening Post*, was her first published work. She believed all living things had their natural rights. In that vein, she collaborated with Elliot Coues in writing *Citizen Bird: Scenes from Bird-life in Plain English for Beginners* (1897). She was contributing editor to *Bird-Lore* and founded the Connecticut Audubon Society in 1896 serving as its president for twenty-six years. Mrs. Wright designed and constructed Birdcraft Sanctuary, the first bird preserve of its kind, on the grounds of the Connecticut Audubon Society. She named it for one of her most successful books. Mrs. Wright was also one of the first of three women elected to membership to the AOU. Her other works include *The Friendship of Nature, a New England Chronicle of Birds and Flowers* (1894), *Birdcraft: A Field Book of Two Hundred Song, Game, and Water Birds* (1895), *Four-footed Americans* (1898), *Flowers and Ferns in Their Haunts* (1901), *The Heart of Nature* (1906), *Gray Lady and the Birds: Stories of the Bird Year for Home and School* (1907), *The Making of Birdcraft Sanctuary* (1922), and her autobiography, *My New York* (1926).

Xantus, John (1825–1894) — Probably the most colorful and eccentric of the 19th century naturalists, John Xantus was a collector for the Smithsonian. Much of what we know about him, we don't really know about him. This is because the writings of his exploits, published in his native Hungary, were prone to embellishments, plagiarisms, or pure fabrications. He apparently had delusions of grandeur, and in fact, has been called "a kind of 19th-century Walter Mitty." Xantus once posed for a portrait wearing a U.S. Navy Captain's uniform, even though he never served in the navy. He was born in Hungary where he studied law, passing the bar in 1847. He is said to have become an exile, following his participation in a failed revolt against the Austrian Empire (1848–1849). He fled to England, then to America in 1851. He claimed to have held a succession of jobs including newspaper boy, sailor, store clerk, bookseller, pharmacist, bordello piano player, piano teacher, canal digger, engineer, railroad cartographer, and university professor. We do know he enlisted in the U.S. Army under the alias Louis de Vesey in October, 1855.

Xantus was stationed at Fort Riley in the Kansas Territory. There he became friends with Dr. William Hammond, the assistant surgeon, and one of the medical officers who was collecting natural history specimens for Baird at the Smithsonian. Dr. Hammond showed him how to collect and prepare specimens. Xantus sent his first collections to the Academy of Natural Sciences of Philadelphia, to which he was elected a life member in December, 1856. At Hammond's urging, Xantus began to send specimens to the Smithsonian. He also corresponded with Baird, who arranged to have him transferred to Fort Tejon in California, where he also collected. After he had served three years in the military, Xantus transferred to Cape San Lucas at the southern tip of Baja California. There, also with Baird's influence, he was employed as tidal observer with the Coast Survey and continued to collect for the Smithsonian. Eventually Xantus returned to his homeland where he became a founder of the Zoological and Botanical Gardens in Budapest and became its first director. From 1869–1871, he went on a collecting trip to eastern Asia and Indonesia and sent specimens back to the National Museum of Hungary. Upon his return, he was appointed Curator of Ethnology at the museum. The Guadalupe Murrelet (*Synthliboramphus hypoleucus*) was formerly known as Xantus's Murrelet. Xantus's Hummingbird (*Hylocharis xantusii*) is also named for him, as are *Xantusia*, a genus of night lizards, and several species of plants. In all, nearly fifty species of organisms bear the specific epithet *xantusi*, *xantusii*, *xantii*, *xantisiana*, or *veseyi*.

Bibliography

American Heritage Dictionary, The, fourth edition, Houghton Mifflin Company, Boston, MA, 2006.

American Ornithological Society *Checklist of North and Middle American Birds*, 7th Edition (60th Supplement), 2019.

Attenborough, David, *The Life of Birds*, BBC Books, London, UK, 1998.

Atwater, Sally, and Judith Schnell, *Ruffed Grouse*, Stackpole Books, Harrisburg, PA, 1989.

Austin, Jr., Oliver L., *Birds of the World*, Golden Press, Inc., New York, NY, 1961.

Backhouse, Frances, *Woodpeckers of North America*, Firefly Books, Buffalo, NY, 2005.

Bent, Arthur Cleveland, *Life Histories of North American Diving Birds* (U.S. National Museum Bulletin 107), Washington, D.C., 1919.

_____, *Life Histories of North American Gulls and Terns* (U.S. National Museum Bulletin 113), Washington, D.C., 1921.

_____, *Life Histories of North American Petrels and Pelicans and Their Allies* (U.S. National Museum Bulletin 121), Washington, D.C., 1922.

_____, *Life Histories of North American Wild Fowl* (part 1) (U.S. National Museum Bulletin 126), Washington, D.C., 1923.

_____, *Life Histories of North American Wild Fowl* (part 2) (U.S. National Museum Bulletin 130), Washington, D.C. 1925.

_____, *Life Histories of North American Marsh Birds* (U.S. National Museum Bulletin 135), Washington, D.C., 1927.

_____, *Life Histories of North American Shore Birds* (part 1) (U.S. National Museum Bulletin 142), Washington, D.C., 1927.

_____, *Life Histories of North American Shore Birds* (part 2) (U.S. National Museum Bulletin 146), Washington, D.C., 1929.

_____, *Life Histories of North American Gallinaceous Birds* (U.S. National Museum Bulletin 162), Washington, D.C., 1932.

_____, *Life Histories of North American Birds of Prey* (part 1) (U.S. National Museum Bulletin 167), Washington, D.C., 1937.

_____, *Life Histories of North American Birds of Prey* (part 2) (U.S. National Museum Bulletin 170), Washington, D.C., 1938.

_____, *Life Histories of North American Woodpeckers* (U.S. National Museum Bulletin 174), Washington, D.C., 1939.

_____, *Life Histories of North American Cuckoos, Goatsuckers, Hummingbirds, and Their Allies* (U.S. National Museum Bulletin 176), Washington, D.C., 1940

_____, *Life Histories of North American Flycatchers, Larks, Swallows, and Their Allies* (U.S. National Museum Bulletin 179), Washington, D.C., 1942.

_____, *Life Histories of North American Jays, Crows, and Titmice* (U.S. National Museum Bulletin 191), Washington, D.C., 1947.

_____, *Life Histories of North American Nuthatches, Wrens, Thrashers, and Their Allies* (U.S. National Museum Bulletin 195), Washington, D.C., 1948.

_____, *Life Histories of North American Thrushes, Kinglets, and Their Allies* (U.S. National Museum Bulletin 196), Washington, D.C., 1949.

_____, *Life Histories of North American Wagtails, Shrikes, Vireos, and Their Allies* (U.S. National Museum Bulletin 197), Washington, D.C., 1950.

_____, *Life Histories of North American Wood Warblers* (U.S. National Museum Bulletin 203), Washington, D.C., 1953.

_____, *Life Histories of North American Blackbirds, Orioles, Tanagers, and Allies* (U.S. National Museum Bulletin 211), Washington, D.C., 1958.

Bent, Arthur Cleveland, and Collaborators, compiled and edited by Oliver L. Austin, Jr,

Life Histories of North American Cardinals, Grosbeaks, Buntings, Towhees, Finches, Sparrows, and Allies (parts 1-3) (U.S. National Museum Bulletin 237), Washington, D.C., 1968.

Berger, Cynthia, *Owls (Wild Guide)*, Stackpole Books, Mechanicsburg, PA, 2005.

Birkland, Tim R., *The Magpies*, T & AD Poyser, Ltd., London, UK, 1991.

Blanchan, Neltje, *Bird Neighbors*, Garden City Publishing Co., Inc., New York, NY, 1897.

_____, *Birds Every Child Should Know*, Doubleday, Page & Company, New York, NY, 1907.

_____, *The New Nature Library: Game Birds. Life Histories of One Hundred and Seventy Birds of Prey, Game Birds and Water-Fowls*, Doubleday, Page & Company, New York, NY, 1916.

_____, *The Nature Library Birds*, Wm. H. Wise & Co., New York, NY, 1930.

Bond, James, *Birds of the West Indies* (Peterson Field Guides), Houghton Mifflin Company, Boston, MA, 1993.

Borman, Susan, Robert Korth, and Jo Temte, *Through the Looking Glass . . . A Field Guide to Aquatic Plants*, Wisconsin Lakes Partnership, Stevens Point, WI, 1997.

British Ornithologists' Union, *The British List*, 9th edition, December, 2017.

Brynildson, Inga, and Woody Hagge, *Birds in Art, The Masters*, Konecky & Konecky, New York, NY, 1990.

Carson, Rachel, *Silent Spring*, Houghton Mifflin Company, Boston, MA, 1962.

Chapman, Frank M., *Birds of Eastern North America*, D. Appleton-Century Company, New York, NY, 1923.

Choate, Ernest A., *The Dictionary of American Bird Names*, The Harvard Common Press, Boston, MA, 1985.

Clark, William S., and Brian K. Wheeler, *A Field Guide to Hawks of North America*, Houghton Mifflin Company, Boston, MA, 2001.

Collins, Jr., Henry H., and Ned R. Boyajian, *Familiar Garden Birds of America*, Harper & Row, Publishers, New York, NY, 1963.

Conder, Peter, *The Wheatear*, Christopher Helm, London, UK, 1989.

Cox, Randall T., *Birder's Dictionary*, Falcon Publishing, Inc., Helena, MT, 1996.

Dalton, David A., *The Natural World of Lewis and Clark*, University of Missouri Press, Columbia, MO, 2008.

Daniel, Thomas M., *Jared Potter Kirtlan: Naturalist, Physician, Sage of the Western Reserve*, Sigel Press, Medina, OH, 2015.

Dawson, William Leon, and Lynds Jones, *The Birds of Ohio, A Complete Scientific and Popular Description of the 320 Species of Birds Found in the State*, The Wheaton Publishing Company, Columbus, OH, 1902.

Donald, Paul F., *The Skylark*, T & A D Poyser, London, UK, 2004.

Dunn, Erica H., and Diane L. Tessaglia-Hymes, *Birds at Your Feeder*, W. W. Norton & Company, Inc., New York, NY, 1999.

Dunn, Jon L., and Kimball L. Garrett, *A Field Guide to Warblers of North America*, Houghton Mifflin Company, Boston, MA, 1997.

Dunne, Pete, *Pete Dunne's Essential Field Guide Companion*, Houghton Mifflin Company, Boston, MA, 2006.

Dunne, Pete, David Sibley, and Clay Sutton, *Hawks in Flight*, Houghton Mifflin Company, Boston, MA, 1988.

Earley, Chris G., *Warblers of Ontario*, Friends of Point Pelee & Lithosphere Press, Leamington, Ontario, Canada, 2001.

Eastman, John, *Birds of Field and Shore*, Stackpole Books, Mechanicsburg, PA, 1997.

Eastman, John, *Birds of Forest, Yard, & Thicket*, Stackpole Books, Mechanicsburg, PA, 1997.

Eastman, John, *Birds of Lake, Pond, and Marsh — Water and Wetland Birds of Eastern North America*, Stackpole Books, Mechanicsburg, PA, 1999.

Eckert, Allan W., *The Owls of North America*, Weathervane Books, New York, NY, 1973.

Ehrlich, Paul R. et al., *The Birder's Handbook: A Field Guide to the Natural History of North American Birds*, Simon and Schuster, Inc., New York, NY, 1988.

Ehrlich, Paul R., et al., *The Birdwatcher's Handbook: A Guide to the Natural History of the Birds of Britain and Europe*, Oxford University Press, Oxford, UK OX2 6DP, 1994.

Eiserer, Len, *The American Robin — A Backyard Institution*, Nelson-Hall, Inc. Publishers, Chicago, IL, 1976.

Elliott, Lang, *The Songs of Wild Birds*, Houghton Mifflin Company, Boston, MA, 2006.

Evans, Howard Ensign, *Pioneer Naturalists: The Discovery and Naming of North American Plants and Animals*, Henry Holt and Company, New

York, NY, 1993.
Forbush, Edward Howe, *A History of the Game Birds, Wild-Fowl and Shore Birds of Massachusetts and Adjacent States*, Massachusetts State Board of Agriculture, 1916.
Forbush, Edward Howe, and John Richard May, *A Natural History of American Birds of Eastern and Central North America*, Bramhall House, New York, NY, 1925.
Fogden, Michael, Marianne Taylor, and Sheri L. Williamson, *Hummingbirds: A Life-size Guide to Every Species*, HarperCollins Publishers, New York, NY, 2014.
Gabrielson, Ira N., and Frederick C. Lincoln, *The Birds of Alaska*, The Stackpole Company, Harrisburg, Pennsylvania, and The Wildlife Management Institute, Washington, D.C., 1959.
Gallagher, Tim, *The Grailbird: Tthe Rediscovery of the Ivory-billed Woodpecker*, Houghton Mifflin Company, Boston, MA 2005.
Gayley, Charles Mills, *The Classic Myths in English Literature and in Art*, John Wiley & Sons, NY, 1939.
Godfrey, W. Earl, *The Birds of Canada*, National Museums of Canada, Ottawa, ON, Canada 1986..
Gotch, A. F., *Birds: Their Latin Names Explained*, Blandford Press, Poole, Dorset, UK, 1981.
Greenoak, Francesca, *All the Birds of the Air, the Names, Lore, and Literature of British Birds*, Andre Deutsch Limited, London, UK, 1979.
Gruson, Edward S., *Words for Birds, A Lexicon of North American Birds with Biographical Notes*, Quadrangle Books, Inc., New York, NY, 1972.
Harrison, Peter, *Seabirds, An Identification Guide*, Houghton Mifflin Company, Boston, MA 1983.
Hayman, Peter, and Philip Burton, *The Birdlife of Britain & Europe*, Mitchell Beazley Publishers, London, UK, 1976 and 1986.
Henshaw, Henry W., et al, *The Book of Birds*, The National Geographic Society, Washington, D.C., 1925.
Holloway, Joel Ellis, *Dictionary of Birds of the United States*, Timber Press, Inc., Portland, OR, 2003.
Howell, Steve N. G., *Hummingbirds of North America*, Academic Press, San Diego, CA, 2002.
Hutchins, Ross E., *Grasshoppers and Their Kin*, Dodd, Mead & Company, New York, NY, 1972.
Jobling, James A., *A Dictionary of Scientific Bird Names*, Oxford University Press, New York, NY, 1991.
Johnsgard, Paul A., *North American Owls: Biology and Natural History*, Smithsonian Institution Press, Washington DC and London, UK, 2002.
Kaufman, Kenn, *Lives of North American Birds*, Houghton Mifflin Company, Boston, MA, 1996.
Kaufman, Kenn, *Kaufman Guide to Birds of North America*, Houghton Mifflin Company, New York, NY, 2000.
Kaufman, Kenn, and Patricia Manzano Fischer, *Guía de Campo a las Aves de Norteamérica*, Hillstar Editions LS, 2005.
Kress, Stephen W., *National Audubon Society Birder's Handbook*, Dorling Kindersley Limited, London, UK, 2000.
Kennedy, Des, *Living Things We Love to Hate — Facts, Fantasies & Fallacies*, Whitecap Books, Vancouver BC and Toronto ON, Canada, 1992.
Kress, Stephen W., *The Audubon Society Handbook for Birders*, Charles Scribner's Sons, New York, NY, 1981.
Kroodsma, Donald, *The Singing Life of Birds: The Art and Science of Listening to Birdsong*, Houghton-Mifflin, Boston, MA, 2005.
Krutch, Joseph Wood, and Paul S. Erikson, *A Treasury of Birdlore*, Paul S. Erikson, Inc., New York, NY, 1962.
Leahy, Christopher, *The Birdwatcher's Companion, An Encyclopedic Handbook of North American Birdlife*, Hill and Wang, New York, NY, 1982.
Lederer, Roger, and Carol Burr, *Latin for Bird Lovers*, Timber Press, Portland, OR, 2014.
Lembke, Janet, *Dangerous Birds: A Naturalist's Aviary*, Lyons & Burford, Publishers, New York, NY, 1992.
Lemmon, Robert S., *Our Amazing Birds*, The American Garden Guild and Doubleday & Company, Inc., New York, NY, 1951.
Leopold, Aldo, *A Sand County Almanac*, Oxford University Press, New York, NY, 1949.
Limburg, Peter, *What's-in-the-Names of Birds*, Coward, McCann & Geoghegan, Inc. New York, NY, 1975.

Lockwood, William Burley, *The Oxford Book of British Bird Names*, Oxford University Press, Oxford, UK, 1984.

Madge, Steve, and Hilary Burn, *Waterfowl: An Identification Guide to the Ducks, Geese and Swans of the World*, Houghton Mifflin Company, Boston, MA, 1988.

Mathews, F. Schuyler, *Field Guide of Wild Birds and Their Music*, G. P. Putnam's Sons, NY and London, UK, 1904.

Mathews, F. Schuyler, *The Book of Birds for Young People*, G. P. Putnam's Sons, NY and London, UK, 1921.

McCormac, James S., and Gregory Kennedy, *Birds of Ohio*, Lone Pine Publishing International Inc., Edmonton, AB, Canada, 2004.

Mearns, Barbara, and Richard Mearns, *Audubon to Xantus: The Lives of Those Commemorated in North American Bird Names*, Academic Press Limited, London, UK, 1992.

Moss, Stephen, *Remarkable Birds*, Harper-Collins Publishers, New York, NY, 2008.

New Oxford American Dictionary, Second Edition, Oxford University Press, 2005.

O'Brien, Michael, Richard Crossley, and Kevin Karlson, *The Shorebird Guide*, Houghton Mifflin Company, Boston, MA, 2006.

Orkin, Mark M., *Speaking Canadian English, An Informal Account of the English Language in Canada*, General Publishing Company Limited, Toronto, ON, Canada, 1970.

Pearson, T. Gilbert, et al., *Birds of America*, Garden City Publishing Company, Inc., Garden City, NY, 1936.

Peterjohn, Bruce G., *The Birds of Ohio*, Indiana University Press, Bloomington and Indianapolis, IN, 1989.

Peterson, Roger Tory, *A Field Guide to the Birds*, Houghton Mifflin Company, Boston, MA, 1980.

Peterson, Roger Tory, *A Field Guide to Western Birds*, Houghton Mifflin Company, Boston, MA, 1990.

Pough, Richard H., *Audubon Land Bird Guide*, Doubleday & Company, Inc., Garden City, NY, 1946.

Pough, Richard H., *Audubon Water Bird Guide*, Doubleday & Company, Inc., Garden City, NY, 1951.

Rapai, William, *The Kirtland's Warbler: The Story of a Bird's Fight against Extinction and the People Who Saved It*, The University of Michigan Press, Ann Arbor, MI, 2012.

Reader's Digest, Book of British Birds, Drive Publications Limited, Berkeley Square House, London, UK, 1985.

Reader's Digest, Book of North American Birds, The Reader's Digest Association, Inc., Pleasantville, NY, 1990.

Rue, III, Leonard Lee, *Game Birds of North America*, Harper & Row, New York, NY, 1973.

Sandrock, James, and Jean C. Prior, *The Scientific Nomenclature of Birds of the Upper Midwest*, University of Iowa Press, Iowa City, IA, 2014.

Sayre, James Kedzie, *North American Bird Folknames and Names*, Bottlebrush Press, Foster City, CA, 1996.

Sibley, David Allen, *The Sibley Guide to Birds*, Alfred A. Knopf, New York, NY, 2000.

Sibley, David Allen, *The Sibley Guide to Bird Life & Behavior*, Alfred A. Knopf, New York, NY, 2001.

Skutch, Alexander F., *The Life of the Hummingbird*, Crown Publishers, Inc., New York, NY, 1973.

Soothill, Eric, and Peter Whitehead, *Wildfowl of the World*, Blandford Press, Ltd., London, UK, 1978.

Sprunt, Alexander, Jr., and E. Burnham Chamberlain, *South Carolina Bird Life*, University of South Carolina Press, Columbia, SC, 1949.

Stanwell-Fletcher, Theodora C., *The Tundra World*, Little Brown and Company, Boston, MA, 1952.

Stephenson, Tom, and Scott Whittle, *The Warbler Guide*, Princeton University Press, Princeton, NJ, 2013.

Stickney, Eleanor H., *The "Whys" of Bird Names*, Vantage Press, New York, NY, 2009.

Strickland, Dan, *Birds of Algonquin Provincial Park*, The Friends of Algonquin Park in cooperation with Ontario Ministry of Natural Resources, Whitney, ON, Canada, 1995.

Sutton, George Miksch, *High Arctic — An Expedition to the Unspoiled North*, Paul S. Eriksson, Inc., New York, NY, 1971.

Terres, John K., *The Audubon Society Encyclopedia of North American Birds*, Alfred A. Knopf, Inc., New York, NY, 1991.

Thompson, A. Landsborough (editor), *A New Dictionary of Birds*, McGraw-Hill Book Company, New York, NY, 1964.

Todd, W. E. Clyde, *Birds of Western Pennsylvania*. University of Pittsburgh Press, Pittsburgh, PA, 1940.

Trumbull, Gurdon, *Names and Portraits of Birds Which Interest Gunners With Descriptions in Language Understanded of the People*, Harper & Brothers, Franklin Square, New York, NY, 1888.

Turner, Angela K., *Hamlyn Species Guides: The Swallow*, Hamlyn Limited, London, UK, 1994.

Van Perlo, Ber, *Birds of Mexico and Central America*, Princeton University Press, Princeton, NJ, 2006.

Welker, Robert Henry, *Birds & Men, American Birds in Science, Art, Literature, and Conservation, 1800–1900*, Harvard University Press, Cambridge, MA, 1955.

Wells, Diana, *100 Birds and How They Got Their Names*, Algonquin Books of Chapel Hill, Chapel Hill, NC, 2002.

Wetmore, Alexander, et al., *Song and Garden Birds of North America*, R. R. Donnelley and Sons Co., Chicago, IL, 1964.

Wetmore, Alexander, et al., *Water, Prey, and Game Birds of North America*, R. R. Donnelley and Sons, Chicago, IL, 1965.

Williamson, Sheri L., *A Field Guide to the Hummingbirds of North America*, Houghton Mifflin Company, Boston, MA, 2001.

Woods, Robert S., (compiler), *The Naturalist's Lexicon — A List of Classical Greek and Latin Words Used or Suitable for Use in Biological Nomenclature*, Abbey Garden Press, Pasadena, CA, 1944.

Index I
Common Names

Albatross, Black-footed 158
   Laysan 157
   Short-tailed 158
Anhinga..................... 176
Ani, Groove-billed 75
   Smooth-billed 75
Auk, Great 370
Auklet, Cassin's 132
   Crested 133
   Least 133
   Parakeet 132
   Rhinoceros................ 134
   Whiskered 133
Avocet, American............ 102

Bananaquit 367
Beardless-Tyrannulet,
   Northern 231
Becard, Rose-throated 231
Bittern, American 178
   Least 179
Black-Hawk, Common 196
Blackbird, Brewer's 338
   Red-winged.............. 336
   Rusty 338
   Tricolored 337
   Yellow-headed 327
Bluebird, Eastern 276
   Mountain................ 277
   Western 277
Bluethroat 275
Bobolink.................... 329
Bobwhite, Northern.......... 50
Booby, Blue-footed.......... 172
   Brown................... 173
   Masked 172
   Red-footed.............. 173
Brant....................... 21
Budgerigar.................. 230
Bufflehead 42
Bulbul, Red-whiskered 272
Bunting, Blue 363
   Indigo................... 364
   Lark 311
   Lazuli................... 364
   McKay's................. 308
   Painted 365
   Snow.................... 307
   Varied 365
Bushtit 264

Canvasback 32
Carcara, Crested............ 225
Cardinal, Northern 362
Catbird, Gray 284
Chachalaca, Plain 49
Chat, Yellow-breasted 326
Chickadee, Black-capped 261
   Boreal................... 262
   Carolina................. 260
   Chestnut-backed 262
   Gray-headed............. 262
   Mexican 261
   Mountain................ 261
Chuck-will's-widow 79
Chukar 53
Collared-Dove, Eurasian...... 68
Condor, California 188
Coot, American.............. 98
Cormorant, Brandt's 174
   Double-crested 174
   Great.................... 175
   Neotropic................ 174
   Pelagic.................. 175
   Red-faced............... 175
Cowbird, Bronzed 337
   Brown-headed 337
   Shiny 337
Crane, Sandhill.............. 99
   Whooping 100
Creeper, Brown 266
Crossbill, Cassia 302
   Red 301
   White-winged........... 302
Crow, American 254
   Fish..................... 255
   Northwestern 254
   Tamaulipas 254
Cuckoo, Black-billed 74
   Mangrove 73
   Yellow-billed............ 73
Curlew, Bristle-thighed...... 110
   Eskimo 370
   Long-billed 111

Dickcissel................... 366
Dipper, American........... 272
Dotterel, Eurasian........... 108
Dove, Inca 69
   Mourning 69
   Spotted.................. 69

   White-tipped............. 70
   White-winged........... 69
Dovekie 129
Dowitcher, Long-billed...... 120
   Short-billed 120
Duck, American Black........ 30
   Falcated 28
   Harlequin 39
   Labrador 369
   Long-tailed 42
   Masked 46
   Mottled.................. 31
   Muscovy 25
   Ring-necked 36
   Ruddy 47
   Tufted................... 36
   Wood.................... 25
Dunlin 116

Eagle, Bald................. 194
   Golden 191
   White-tailed 195
Egret, Cattle................ 183
   Great.................... 180
   Reddish 183
   Snowy 181
Eider, Common 39
   King 38
   Spectacled 38
   Steller's.................. 37

Falcon, Aplomado 226
   Peregrine 227
   Prairie................... 228
Fieldfare.................... 281
Finch, Cassin's 300
   House................... 299
   Purple................... 300
Flamingo, American 63
Flicker, Gilded 222
   Northern 221
Flycatcher, Acadian 237
   Alder 238
   Ash-throated 232
   Brown-crested 232
   Buff-breasted 240
   Cordilleran 240
   Dusky................... 239
   Dusky-capped........... 232
   Fork-tailed.............. 236

Gray 239
Great-crested. 232
Hammond's 239
LaSagra's 232
Least 238
Olive-sided 236
Pacific-slope 239
Scissor-tailed 235
Sulphur-bellied 233
Vermilion 241
Willow 238
Yellow-bellied 237
Frigatebird, Magnificent 171
Fulmar, Northern 161

Gadwall 28
Gallinule, Common 98
Purple 97
Gannet, Northern 173
Garganey 26
Gnatcatcher, Black-capped . . . 272
Black-tailed 271
Blue-gray 271
California 271
Godwit, Bar-tailed 111
Black-tailed 112
Hudsonian 112
Marbled 112
Goldeneye, Barrow's 44
Common 44
Golden-Plover, American 105
European 105
Pacific 105
Goldfinch, American 304
Lawrence's 304
Lesser 303
Goose, Barnacle 21
Cackling 22
Canada 22
Emperor 20
Greater White-fronted 21
Ross's 21
Snow 20
Goshawk, Northern 193
Grackle, Boat-tailed 339
Common 339
Great-tailed 339
Grebe, Clark's 65
Eared 64
Horned 64
Least 63
Pied-billed 63
Red-necked 64
Western 65
Grosbeak, Black-headed 363
Blue 363
Evening 297
Pine 298
Rose-breasted 363
Yellow 362

Ground-Dove, Common 70
Ruddy 70
Grouse, Dusky 58
Ruffed 54
Sharp-tailed 58
Sooty 58
Spruce 56
Guillemot, Black 130
Pigeon 130
Gull, Black-headed 137
Black-tailed 139
Bonaparte's 137
California 140
Franklin's 138
Glaucous 142
Glaucous-winged 142
Great Black-backed 142
Heerman's 139
Herring 141
Iceland 141
Ivory 136
Kelp 143
Laughing 138
Lesser Black-backed 141
Little 138
Mew 139
Ring-billed 140
Ross's 138
Sabine's 136
Slaty-backed 141
Western 140
Yellow-footed 140
Yellow-legged 141
Gyrfalcon 226

Harrier, Northern 192
Hawk, Broad-winged 198
Cooper's 192
Harris's 196
Ferruginous 200
Gray 197
Red-shouldered 198
Red-tailed 199
Rough-legged 200
Sharp-shinned 192
Short-tailed 198
Swainson's 198
White-tailed 197
Zone-tailed 199
Hen, Heath 369
Heron, Great Blue 180
Green 183
Little Blue 181
Tricolored 181
Hummingbird, Allen's 91
Anna's 89
Berylline 92
Black-chinned 89
Blue-throated 87
Broad-billed 92

Broad-tailed 90
Buff-bellied 93
Calliope 91
Costa's 90
Lucifer 87
Rivoli's 86
Ruby-throated 87
Rufous 91
Violet-crowned 93
White-eared 93

Ibis, Glossy 185
White 185
White-faced 185

Jacana, Northern 109
Jaeger, Long-tailed 128
Parasitic 127
Pomarine 127
Jay, Blue 251
Brown 249
Canada 247
Green 250
Mexican 253
Pinyon 250
Steller's 250
Junco, Dark-eyed 314
Yellow-eyed 315

Kestrel, American 225
Killdeer 107
Kingbird, Cassin's 234
Couch's 233
Eastern 234
Gray 235
Thick-billed 234
Tropical 233
Western 234
Kingfisher, Belted 211
Green 212
Ringed 211
Kinglet, Golden-crowned 272
Ruby-crowned 273
Kiskadee, Great 233
Kite, Hook-billed 190
Mississippi 196
Snail 196
Swallow-tailed 190
White-tailed 190
Kittiwake, Black-legged 135
Red-legged 136
Knot, Red 113

Lapwing, Northern 104
Lark, Horned 256
Limpkin 99
Longspur, Chestnut-collared . 306
Lapland 305
McCown's 306
Smith's 306

Common Names

Loon, Arctic 153
   Common 154
   Pacific 153
   Red-throated 153
   Yellow-billed 155

Magpie, Black-billed 253
   Yellow-billed 254
Mallard 29
Mango, Green-breasted 86
Martin, Purple 259
Meadowlark, Eastern 330
   Western 331
Merganser, Common 46
   Hooded 45
   Red-breasted 46
Merlin 226
Mockingbird, Bahama 287
   Northern 287
Mountain-gem, Blue-throated . 87
Murre, Common 129
   Thick-billed 129
Murrelet, Ancient 132
   Craveri's 132
   Guadalupe 131
   Kittlitz's 131
   Long-billed 130
   Marbled 131
   Scripps's 131
Myna, Common 290

Nighthawk, Antillean 78
   Common 77
   Lesser 77
Night-Heron, Black-crowned . 184
   Yellow-crowned 184
Nightjar, Buff-collared 80
Noddy, Black 143
   Brown 143
Nutcracker, Clark's 253
Nuthatch, Brown-headed 266
   Pygmy 266
   Red-breasted 265
   White-breasted 265

Oriole, Altamira 333
   Audubon's 333
   Baltimore 333
   Bullock's 333
   Hooded 332
   Orchard 332
   Scott's 335
   Spot-breasted 333
   Streak-backed 332
Osprey 189
Ovenbird 340
Owl, Barn 201
   Barred 206
   Boreal 207
   Burrowing 205

   Elf 205
   Flammulated 201
   Great Gray 206
   Great Horned 203
   Long-eared 207
   Northern Hawk 204
   Northern Saw-whet 207
   Short-eared 207
   Snowy 203
   Spotted 206
Oystercatcher, American 102
   Black 103

Parakeet, Carolina 372
   Green 229
   Monk 229
   White-winged 229
Parrot, Red-crowned 230
Partridge, Gray 53
Parula, Northern 352
   Tropical 353
Pauraque, Common 78
Pelican, American White 177
   Brown 177
Petrel, Bermuda 163
   Black-capped 163
   Bulwer's 164
   Cook's 163
   Fea's 163
   Herald 162
   Mottled 163
   Murphy's 162
Pewee, Greater 236
Phainopepla 291
Phalarope, Red 126
   Red-necked 126
   Wilson's 125
Pheasant, Ring-necked 53
Phoebe, Black 240
   Eastern 240
   Say's 241
Pigeon, Band-tailed 68
   Passenger 371
   Red-billed 68
   Rock 67
   White-crowned 68
Pintail, Northern 31
   White-cheeked 31
Pipit, American 296
   Red-throated 295
   Sprague's 296
Plover, Black-bellied 104
   Common Ringed 106
   Mountain 108
   Piping 107
   Semipalmated 107
   Snowy 106
   Wilson's 106
Poorwill, Common 79
Prairie-Chicken, Greater 59

   Lesser 59
Ptarmigan, Rock 57
   White-tailed 58
   Willow 56
Puffin, Atlantic 134
   Horned 134
   Tufted 135
Pygmy-Owl, Ferruginous 205
   Northern 204
Pyrrhuloxia 362

Quail, California 50
   Gambel's 51
   Montezuma 52
   Mountain 49
   Scaled 50
Quail-Dove, Key West 71
Quetzal, Eared 209

Rail, Black 95
   Clapper 95
   King 96
   Virginia 96
   Yellow 95
Raven, Chihuahuan 255
   Common 256
Razorbill 129
Redhead 36
Redpoll, Common 301
   Hoary 301
Redshank, Spotted 124
Redstart, American 349
   Painted 359
Redwing 282
Roadrunner, Greater 74
Robin, American 282
   Rufous-backed 282
Rosy-Finch, Black 299
   Brown-capped 299
   Gray-crowned 298
Rubythroat, Siberian 275
Ruff 114

Sage-Grouse, Greater 55
   Gunnison's 56
Sanderling 116
Sandpiper, Baird's 117
   Buff-breasted 118
   Curlew 115
   Least 118
   Pectoral 119
   Purple 117
   Rock 117
   Semipalmated 119
   Sharp-tailed 115
   Solitary 123
   Spotted 123
   Stilt 115
   Upland 109
   Western 119

White-rumped 118	Fox 313	Western 361
Sand-Plover, Lesser 106	Golden-crowned. 315	Tattler, Wandering 123
Sapsucker, Red-breasted. 217	Grasshopper 309	Teal, Baikal 26
Red-naped. 217	Harris's 315	Blue-winged 26
Williamson's 216	Henslow's 320	Cinnamon 27
Yellow-bellied. 217	House. 294	Green-winged. 32
Scaup, Greater 36	Lark 310	Tern, Aleutian 144
Lesser 37	LeConte's. 318	Arctic 147
Scoter, Black 41	Lincoln's 322	Black. 145
Stejneger's. 41	Nelson's 319	Bridled 143
Surf 39	Olive. 310	Caspian 145
Velvet 40	Rufous-crowned. 324	Common 146
White-winged 40	Rufous-winged. 308	Elegant. 149
Screech-Owl, Eastern. 202	Sagebrush 317	Forster's 148
Western 202	Saltmarsh. 319	Gull-billed 144
Whiskered 203	Savannah 320	Least. 144
Scrub-Jay, California 252	Seaside. 319	Roseate. 146
Florida 251	Song 322	Royal 148
Island 252	Swamp 323	Sandwich 148
Woodhouse's 252	Vesper 317	Sooty. 143
Sea-Eagle, Steller's 195	White-crowned. 315	White-winged 145
Seedeater, Morelet's. 367	White-throated 316	Thrasher, Bendire's 286
Shearwater, Audubon's. 166	Spindalis, Western 326	Brown. 285
Black-vented 166	Spoonbill, Roseate 186	California. 286
Buller's 164	Starling, European 289	Crissal 287
Cory's. 164	Starthroat, Plain-capped 87	Curve-billed 284
Flesh-footed 166	Stilt, Black-necked 101	LeConte's. 282
Great. 165	Stint, Little 118	Long-billed 285
Manx 166	Stint, Red-necked 115	Sage 287
Pink-footed 166	Stork, Wood 169	Thrush, Aztec 283
Short-tailed 165	Storm-Petrel, Ashy 160	Bicknell's 279
Sooty. 165	Band-rumped 161	Clay-colored 282
Shoveler, Northern. 27	Black. 161	Dusky. 281
Shrike, Loggerhead 242	Fork-tailed 160	Eyebrowed 281
Northern 242	Leach's 160	Gray-cheeked 279
Siskin, Pine 303	Least. 161	Hermit 280
Skimmer, Black. 149	White-faced 159	Swainson's. 280
Skua, Great 126	Wilson's 158	Varied. 283
South Polar 127	Surfbird 114	Wood 281
Skylark, Eurasian 256	Swallow, Bahama. 258	Titmouse, Black-crested 263
Smew 45	Bank 257	Bridled 262
Snipe, Wilson's 120	Barn 259	Juniper 263
Snowcock, Himalayan. 53	Cave 260	Oak. 263
Solitaire, Townsend's 278	Cliff. 259	Tufted. 263
Sora. 96	Northern Rough-winged . . 258	Towhee, Abert's 323
Sparrow, American Tree 313	Tree. 257	California. 324
Bachman's 309	Violet-green. 258	Canyon. 323
Baird's 320	Swamphen, Purple. 97	Eastern. 325
Black-chinned 312	Swan, Mute 23	Green-tailed 325
Black-throated. 310	Trumpeter 23	Spotted. 325
Bell's 317	Tundra 25	Trogon, Elegant 209
Botteri's 308	Swift, Black 83	Tropicbird, Red-billed. 152
Brewer's. 313	Chimney 83	Red-tailed 152
Cassin's 309	Vaux's. 85	White-tailed 151
Chipping 311	White-throated 85	Turkey, Wild 60
Clay-colored 312		Turnstone, Black. 113
Dusky Seaside. 372	Tanager, Flame-colored. 361	Ruddy 112
Eurasian Tree 294	Hepatic. 360	
Field 312	Scarlet. 360	Veery 278
Five-striped 310	Summer 360	Verdin 263

Common Names

Violet-Ear, Mexican 86
Vireo, Bell's 243
    Black-capped. 243
    Black-whiskered 247
    Blue-headed 245
    Cassin's 245
    Gray 244
    Hutton's. 244
    Philadelphia 246
    Plumbeous. 245
    Red-eyed 247
    Warbling 246
    White-eyed 243
    Yellow-green. 247
    Yellow-throated 244
Vulture, Black 187
    Turkey 187

Wagtail, Eastern Yellow. 295
    White. 295
Warbler, Arctic 274
    Bachman's 373
    Bay-breasted 353
    Black-and-white 343
    Blackburnian. 353
    Blackpoll 355
    Black-throated Blue 355
    Black-throated Gray. 357
    Black-throated Green. 358
    Blue-winged 343
    Canada. 358
    Cape May 350
    Cerulean 352
    Chestnut-sided 354
    Colima 345
    Connecticut. 346
    Golden-cheeked 358
    Golden-winged. 343

    Grace's 357
    Hermit 357
    Hooded 349
    Kentucky 348
    Kirtland's 350
    Lucy's. 345
    MacGillivray's 347
    Magnolia 353
    Mourning 347
    Nashville 346
    Olive. 292
    Orange-crowned 345
    Palm 355
    Pine. 355
    Prairie. 356
    Prothonotary. 343
    Red-faced. 359
    Swainson's. 344
    Tennessee. 344
    Townsend's 357
    Virginia's 346
    Wilson's 358
    Worm-eating. 341
    Yellow 354
    Yellow-rumped. 356
    Yellow-throated 356
Waterthrush, Louisiana. 341
    Northern 341
Waxwing, Bohemian 290
    Cedar 291
Wheatear, Northern. 275
Whimbrel. 111
Whip-poor-will, Eastern 80
    Mexican 81
Whistling-Duck, Black-bellied . 19
    Fulvous 19
Wigeon, American 29
    Eurasian. 28

Willet 124
Woodcock, American 122
Woodpecker, Acorn. 214
    American Three-toed. 218
    Arizona 220
    Black-backed. 218
    Downy 218
    Gila. 215
    Golden-fronted. 215
    Hairy 219
    Ivory-billed 371
    Ladder-backed 219
    Lewis's. 213
    Nuttall's. 219
    Pileated 222
    Red-bellied 215
    Red-cockaded 219
    Red-headed 213
    White-headed 220
Wood-Pewee, Eastern 237
    Western 236
Wren, Bewick's. 270
    Cactus 270
    Canyon. 267
    Carolina 270
    House. 267
    Marsh. 269
    Pacific. 268
    Rock 267
    Sedge 269
    Winter 268
Wrentit. 274

Yellowlegs, Greater 124
    Lesser. 125
Yellowthroat, Common. 348

Index II
Scientific Names

Accipiter
  cooperii 192
  gentilis .193
  striatus .192
Acridotheres
  tristis. 290
Actitis
  Macularia 123
Aechmophorus
  clarkii 65
  occidentalis 65
Aegolius
  acadicus 207
  funereus 207
Aeronautes
  saxatalis .85
Aethia
  cristatella 133
  psittacula 132
  pusilla 133
  pygmaea 133
Agelaius
  phoeniceus 336
  tricolor .337
Aimophila
  ruficeps .324
Aix
  sponsa 25
Alauda
  arvensis. 256
Alca
  torda 129
Alectoris
  chukar 53
Alle
  alle. 129
Amazillia
  beryllina .92
  violiceps .93
  yucatenansis 93
Amazona
  viridigenalis 230
Ammodramus
  savannarum 309

Ammospiza
  caudacuta 319
  leconteii. 318
  maritimus 319
  nelsoni. 319
Amphispiza
  bilineata 310
Anas
  Acuta 31
  Bahamensis 31
  crecca 32
  fulvigula 31
  platyrhynchos 29
  rubripes. 30
Anhinga
  anhinga 176
Anous
  minutus 143
  stolidus 143
Anser
  albifrons 21
  caerulescens 20
  canagicus 20
  rossii 21
Anthus
  cervinus 295
  rubescens 296
  spragueii 296
Antigone
  canadensis. 99
Antrostomus
  arizonae. 81
  carolinensis. 79
  ridgwayi 79
  vociferous 80
Aphelocoma
  californica 252
  caerulescens 251
  insularis 252
  wollweberi. 253
  woodhouseii 252
Aquila
  chrysaetos 191
Aratinga
  holochlora 229

Archilochus
  alexandri. 89
  colubris .87
Ardea
  alba 180
  herodias. 180
Ardenna
  bulleri .164
  carneipes 166
  creatopus. 166
  gravis .165
  grisea. .165
  tenuirostris 165
Arenaria
  interpres 112
  melanocephala. 113
Arremonops
  rufivirgatus. 310
Artemesiospiza
  belli 317
  nevadensis. 317
Asio
  flammeus. 207
  otus 207
Athene
  cunicularia 205
Auriparus
  flaviceps 263
Aythya
  affinis 37
  americana 36
  collaris .36
  fuligula .36
  marila .36
  valisineria 32

Baeolophus
  bicolor .263
  inornatus 263
  ridgwayi 263
  wollweberi. 262
Bartramia
  longicauda 109
Bombycilla
  cedrorum. 291

Bird is the Word

  garrulous 290
Bonasa
  umbellus 54
Botaurus
  lentiginosus 178
Botogeris
  versicolurus 229
Brachyramphus
  Brevirostris 131
  Marmoratus 131
  perdix 130
Branta
  bernicla 21
  canadensis 22
  hutchinsii 22
  leucopsis 21
Bubo
  scandiacus 203
  virginianus 203
Bubulcus
  ibis .183
Bucephala
  albeola 42
  clangula 44
  islandica 44
Buteo
  albicaudatus 197
  albonotatus 199
  brachyurus 198
  jamaicensis 199
  lagopus 200
  lineatus 198
  nitidus 197
  platypterus 198
  regalis 200
  swainsoni 198
Buteogallus
  anthracinus 196
Butorides
  virescens 183

Cairina
  moschata 25
Calamospiza
  melanocorys 311
Calcarius
  lapponicus 305
  ornatus 306
  pictus 306
Calidris
  acuminate 115
  alba .116
  alpina 116
  bairdii 117

  canutus 113
  ferruginea 115
  fuscicollis 118
  himantopus 115
  maritima 117
  mauri 119
  melanotos 119
  minuta 118
  minutilla 118
  ptilocnemis 117
  pugnax 114
  pusilla 119
  ruficollis 115
  virgata 114
Calliope
  calliope 275
Callipepla
  californica 50
  gambelii 51
  squamata 50
Calonectris
  diomedea 164
Calothorax
  lucifer 87
Calypte
  anna 89
  costae 90
Camptostoma
  imberbe 231
Campylorhynchus
  brunneicapillus 270
Caracara
  cheriway 225
Cardellina
  canadensis 258
  pusilla 358
  rubrifrons 359
Cardinalis
  cardinalis 362
  sinuatus 362
Cathartes
  aura 187
Catharus
  bicknelli 279
  fuscescens 278
  guttatus 280
  minimus 279
  ustulatus 280
Catherpes
  mexicanus 267
Centrocercus
  minimus 56
  urophasianus 55

Centronyx
  bairdii 320
  henslowii 320
Cepphus
  columba 130
  grylle 130
Cerorhinca
  monocerata 134
Certhia
  americana 266
Ceryle
  alcyon 211
  torquata 211
Chaetura
  pelagica 83
  vauxi 85
Chamaea
  fasciata 274
Charadrius
  alexandrines 106
  hiaticula 106
  melodus 107
  mongolus 106
  montanus 108
  morinellus 108
  semipalmatus 107
  vociferous 107
  wilsonia 106
Chlidonias
  Leucopterus 145
  niger 145
Chloroceryle
  americana 212
Chondestes
  grammacus 310
Chondrohierax
  uncinatus 190
Chordeiles
  acutipennis 77
  gundlachii 78
  minor 77
Chroicocephalus
  philadelphia 137
  ridibundus 137
Cinclus
  mexicanus 272
Circus
  hudsonius 192
Cistothorus
  palustris 269
  platensis 269
Clangula
  hyemalis 42

Scientific Names

Coccothraustes
   vespertinus 297
Coccyzus
   americanus 74
   erythrophthalmus 73
   minor 73
Coereba
   flaveola 367
Colaptes
   auratus 221
   chrysoides 222
Colibri
   Thalassinus 86
Colinus
   virginianus 50
Columba
   livia 67
Columbina
   inca 69
   passerina 70
   talpacoti 70
Contopus
   cooperi 236
   pertinax 236
   sordidulus 236
   virens 237
Coragyps
   atratus 187
Corvus
   brachyrhynchos 254
   caurinus 254
   corax 256
   cryptoleucus 255
   imparatus 254
   ossifragus 255
Coturnicops
   noveboracensis 95
Crotophaga
   ani 75
   sulcirostris 75
Cyanecula
   svecica 275
Cyanocitta
   cristata 251
   stelleri 250
Cyanocompsa
   parellina 363
Cyanocorax
   yncas 250
Cygnus
   buccinator 23
   columbianus 25
   olor 23

Cynanthus
   latirostris 92
Cypseloides
   niger 83
Cyrtonyx
   montezumae 52

Dendragapus
   fuliginosus 58
   obscurus 58
Dendrocygna
   autumnalis 19
   bicolor 19
Dolichonyx
   oryzivorus 329
Dryobates
   albolarvatus 220
   arizonae 220
   borealis 219
   nuttallii 219
   pubescens 218
   scalaris 219
   villosus 219
Dryocopus
   pileatus 222
Dumetella
   carolinensis 284

Egretta
   caerulea 181
   rufescens 183
   thula 181
   tricolor 181
Elanoides
   forficatus 190
Elanus
   leucurus 190
Empidonax
   Alnorum 238
   difficilis 239
   flaviventris 237
   fulvifrons 240
   hammondii 239
   minimus 238
   oberholseri 239
   occidentalis 240
   traillii 238
   virescens 237
   wrightii 239
Eremophila
   alpestris 256
Eudocimus
   albus 185

Eugenes
   fulgens 86
Euphagus
   carolinus 338
   cyanocephalus 338
Euptilotis
   neoxenus 209

Falcipennis
   canadensis 56
Falco
   columbarius 226
   femoralis 226
   mexicanus 228
   peregrinus 227
   rusticolis 226
   sparverius 225
Fratercula
   arctica 134
   cirrhata 135
   corniculata 134
Fregata
   magnificens 171
Fulica
   americana 98
Fulmarus
   glacialus 161

Galliinago
   delicata 120
Gallinula
   galeata 98
Gavia
   adamsii 155
   arctica 153
   immer 154
   pacifica 153
   stellate 153
Geococcyx
   californianus 74
Geothlypis
   formosa 348
   philadelphia 347
   tolmiei 347
   trichas 348
Geotrygon
   chrysia 71
Glaucidium
   brasilianum 205
   gnoma 204
Grus
   americana 100
Gymnogyps
   californianus 188

Gymnorhinus
   cyanocephalus..............250
Haematopus
   bachmani..................103
   palliatus..................102
Haliaeetus
   albicilla...................195
   leucocephalus.............194
   pelagicus..................195
Heliomaster
   constantii..................87
Helmitheros
   vermivora.................341
Heteroscelus
   incanus...................123
Himantopus
   mexicanus................101
Hirundo
   rustica....................259
Histrionicus
   histrionicus................39
Hydrocoloeus
   minutus...................138
Hylocharis
   leucotis....................93
Hylocichla
   mustelina.................281

Icteria
   virens.....................326
Icterus
   bullockii..................333
   cucullatus.................332
   galbula...................333
   graduacauda..............333
   gularis....................333
   parisorum.................335
   pectoralis.................333
   pustulatus................332
   spurius...................332
Ictinia
   mississippiensis...........196
Ixobrychus
   exilis.....................179
Ixoreus
   naevius...................283

Jacana
   spinosa...................109
Junco
   hyemalis..................314
   phaeonotus................315

Lagopus
   lagopus....................56
   leucurus...................58
   mutus.....................57
Lampornis
   clemenciae.................87
Lanius
   excubitor..................242
   ludovicianus..............242
Larus
   argentatus................141
   cachinnans...............141
   californicus...............140
   canus....................139
   crassirostris..............139
   delawarensis.............140
   dominicanus.............143
   fuscus...................141
   glaucescens..............142
   glaucoides...............141
   heermanni...............139
   hyperboreus.............142
   livens....................140
   marinus..................142
   occidentalis..............140
   schistisagus..............141
Laterallus
   jamaicensis................95
Leptotila
   verreauxi..................70
Leiothlypis
   celata....................345
   crissalis..................345
   luciae....................345
   peregrina.................344
   ruficapilla................346
   virginiae.................346
Leucosticte
   atrata....................299
   australis..................299
   tephrocotis...............298
Leucophaeus
   atricilla..................138
   pipixcan..................138
Limnodromus
   griseus...................120
   scolopaceus...............120
Limnothlypis
   swainsonii................344
Limosa
   fedoa....................112
   haemastica...............112
   lapponica.................111
   limosa...................112

Lophodytes
   cucullatus..................45
Loxia
   curvirosta................301
   leucoptera................302
   sinesciuris................302

Mareca
   americana.................29
   falcata....................28
   penelope..................28
   strepera...................28
Megascops
   asio......................202
   kennicottii................202
   trichopsis.................203
Melanerpes
   aurifrons.................215
   carolinus.................215
   erythrocephalus..........213
   formicivorus.............214
   lewis.....................213
   uropygialis...............215
Melanitta
   deglandi...................40
   fusca.....................40
   nigra.....................41
   perspicillata...............39
   stejnegeri..................41
Meleagris
   gallopavo..................60
Melopsittacus
   undulatus................230
Melospiza
   georgiana................323
   lincolnii..................322
   melodia..................322
Melozone
   alberti...................323
   crissalis..................324
   fuscus...................323
Mergus
   merganser.................45
   serrator...................46
Micrathene
   whitneyi.................205
Mimus
   gundlachii................287
   polyglottos...............287
Mniotilta
   varia.....................343
Molothrus
   aeneus...................337
   ater......................337

bonariensis 337
Morus
   bassanus 173
Motacilla
   alba 295
   tsutchensis 295
Myadestes
   townsendi 278
Mycteria
   americana 169
Myiarchus
   cinerascens 232
   crinitus 232
   sagrae 232
   tuberculifer 232
   tyrannulus 232
Myioborus
   pictus 359
Myiodynastes
   luteiventris 233
Myiopsitta
   monachus 229

Nomonyx
   dominicus 46
Nucifraga
   columbiana 253
Numenius
   americanus 111
   borealis 370
   phaeopus 111
   tahitiensis 110
Nyctanassa
   violacea 184
Nycticorax
   nycticorax 184
Nyctidromus
   albicollis 78
Oceanites
   oceanicus 58
Oceanodroma
   castro 161
   furcata 160
   homochroa 160
   leucorhoa 160
   melania 161
   microsoma 160
Oenanthe
   oenanthe 275
Oporornis
   agilis 346
Oreotyx
   pictus 49

Oreoscoptes
   montanus 287
Ortalis
   vetula 49
Oxyura
   jamaicensis 47

Pachyramphus
   aglaiae 231
Pagophila
   eburnean 136
Pandion
   haliaetus 189
Parabuteo
   unicinctus 196
Parkesia
   motacilla 341
   noveboracensis 341
Passer
   domestica 294
   montanus 294
Passerculus
   Sandwichensis 320
Passerella
   Iliaca 313
Passerina
   amoena 364
   ciris 365
   cyanea 364
   versicolor 365
Pelagodroma
   Marina 159
Pelecanus
   erythrorhynchos 177
   occidentalis 177
Perdix
   perdix 53
Perisoreus
   canadensis 247
Petrochelidon
   fulva 260
   pyrrhonota 259
Peucaea
   aestivalis 309
Peucedramus
   taeniatus 292
Phaethon
   aethereus 152
   lepturus 151
   rubricauda 152
Phainopepla
   nitens 291
Phalacrocorax
   auritus 174

brasilianus 174
carbo 175
pelagicus 175
penicillatus 174
urile 175
Phalaenoptilus
   nuttallii
Phalaropus
   fulicaria 126
   lobatus 126
   tricolor 125
Phasianus
   colchicus 53
Pheucticus
   chrysopeplus 362
   ludovicianus 363
   melanocephalus 363
Phoebastria
   albatrus 158
   Immutabilis 157
   nigripes 158
Phoenicopterus
   ruber 63
Phylloscopus
   borealis 274
Pica
   hudsonia 253
   nuttalli 254
Picoides
   arcticus 218
   tridactylus 218
Pinicola
   enucleator 298
Pipilo
   chlorurus 325
   erythropthalmus 325
   maculatus 325
Piranga
   bidentata 361
   flava 360
   ludoviciana 361
   olivacea 360
   rubra 360
Pitangus
   sulphuratus 233
Plectrophenax
   hyperboreus 307
   nivalis 308
Plegadis
   chihi 185
   falcinellus 185
Pluvialis
   apricaria 105
   dominica 105

fulva 105
squatarola 104
Podiceps
auritus .64
grisegena 64
nigricollis 64
Podilymbus
Podiceps 63
Poecile
atricapillus 261
carolinensis 260
cinctus 262
gambeli 261
hudsonicus 262
rufescens 262
sclateri 261
Polioptila
caerulea 271
californica 271
melanura 271
nigriceps 272
Polysticta
stelleri .37
Pooecetes
gramineus 317
Porphyrula
martinica 97
porphyrula 97
Porzana
carolina 96
Progne
subis .159
Protonotaria
citrea .343
Psaltriparus
minimus 264
Pterodroma
arminjoniana 162
cahow 163
cookii .163
feae 163
hasitata 163
inexpectata 163
ultima 162
Ptychoramphus
aleuticus 132
Puffinus
lherminieri 166
opisthomelas 166
puffinus 166
Pycnonotus
jacosus 272
Pyrocephalus
rubinus 241

Quiscalus
major 339
mexicanus 339
quiscula 339
Rallus
elegans 96
limicola 96
longirostris 95
Recurvirostra
americana 102
Regulus
calendula 273
satrapa 272
Rhodostethia
rosea .138
Ridgwayia
pinicola 283
Riparia
riparia 257
Rissa
brevirostris 136
tridactyla 135
Rostrhamus
Rynchops
niger .149
Salpinctes
obsoletus 267
Sayornis
phoebe 240
nigricans 240
saya 241
Scolopax
minor 122
Seiurus
aurocapillus 340
Selasphorus
calliope 91
platycercus 90
rufus 91
sasin 91
Setophaga
americana 352
caerulescens 355
castanea 353
cerulean 352
chrysoparia 358
citrina 349
coronate 356
discolor 356
dominica 356
fusca .353
graciae 357

kirtlandii 350
magnolia 353
nigrescens 357
occidentalis 357
palmarum 355
pensylvanica 354
petechial 354
pinus .355
pitiayumi 353
ruticilla 349
striata 355
tigrina 350
townsendi 357
virens 358
Sialia
currucoides 277
mexicana 277
sialis .276
Sibirionetta
formosa 26
Sitta
canadensis 265
carolinensis 265
pusilla 266
pygmaea 266
Somateria
fischeri 38
mollissima 39
spectabilis 38
Spatula
clypeata 27
cyanoptera 27
discors 26
querquedula 26
Sphyrapicus
nuchalis 217
ruber .217
thyroideus 216
varius 217
Spindalis
zena 326
Spinus
flammea 301
hornemanni 301
lawrencei 304
pinus .303
psaltria 303
tristis .304
Spiza
americana 366
Spizella
atrogularis 312
breweri 313
pallida 312

Scientific Names

passerina 311
pusilla 312
Spizelloides
   arborea 313
Sporophila
   moreleti 367
Stelgidopteryx
   serripennis 258
Stercorarius
   longicaudus 128
   maccormicki 127
   parasiticus 127
   pomarinus 127
   skua .126
Sterna
   dougallii 146
   forsteri 148
   hirundo 146
   paradisaea 147
Sternula
   antillarum 144
Streptopelia
   chinensis 69
   decaocto 68
Strix
   nebulosus 296
   occidentalis 206
   varia .206
Sturnella
   magna 330
   neglecta 331
Sturnus
   vulgaris 289
Sula
   dactylatra 173
   leucogaster 173
   nebouxii 172
   sula 173
Synthliboramphus
   antiquus 132
   hypoleucus 131
   craveri 132
   scrippsi 131

Tachybaptus
   dominicus 63

Tachycineta
   bicolor 257
   cyaneoviridis 258
   thalassina 258
Tetraogallus
   himalayensis 53
Thryomanes
   bewickii 270
Thryothorus
   ludovicianus 270
Toxostoma
   bendirei 286
   crissale 287
   curvirostre 284
   lecontei 282
   longirostre 285
   redivivum 286
   rufum 285
Tringa
   flavipes 125
   melanoleuca 124
   semipalmatus 124
   solitaria 123
Troglodytes
   aedon .267
   hiemalis 268
   pacificus 268
Trogon
   elegans 209
Turdus
   grayi .282
   iliacus 282
   migratorius 282
   pilaris 281
   rufopalliatus 282
Tympanuchus
   cupido cupido 369
   cupido pinnatus 59
   pallidicinctus 59
   phasianellus 58
Tyrannus
   couchii 233
   crassirostris 234
   dominicensis 235
   forficatus 235
   melancholicus 233

   savanna 236
   tyrannus 234
   verticalis 234
   vociferans 234
Tyto
   alba 201

Uria
   aalge .129
   lomvia 129

Vanellus
   vanellus 104
Vermivora
   bachmanii 373
   cyanoptera 343
   chrysoptera 343
Vireo
   altiloquus 247
   atricapillus 243
   bellii .243
   cassinii 245
   flavifrons 244
   flavoviridis 247
   gilvus 246
   griseus 243
   huttoni 244
   olivaceus 247
   philadelphicus 246
   plumbeus 245
   solitaries 245
   vicinior 244

Xanthocephalus
   xanthocephalus 327
Xema
   sabini 136

Zenaida
   asiatica 69
   macroura 69
Zonotrichia
   albicollis 316
   atricapilla 315
   leucophrys 315
   qureula 315